YOUNG SOEHARTO

YOUNG SOEHARTO

The Making of a Soldier, 1921–1945

DAVID JENKINS

MELBOURNE UNIVERSITY PRESS

"For if we are to understand changes in human history, human philosophy, we must always remember the importance of single generations. One generation of men may be bound together by common experiences from which its fathers and sons are exempt; and if those experiences have been signal, terrible, inspiring, they will give to that generation a character distinctive to itself, incommunicable to other men. How can we who lived through the 1930s, whose minds and attitudes were formed by the terrible events of those days, understand or be understood by men to whom those events are mere history, reduced to the anodyne prose of textbooks? Of course not every generation has common experiences sufficient to mark it out in this way; the experiences, if they are to have this effect, must be powerful, formidable, inspiring. But if they are inspiring, then there are such generations. Spaniards, in their history, talk of 'the generation of '98' as an enormous, significant fact which alone gives meaning to a part of its course. In Europe the generation of the 1930s may well prove similar. And in seventeenth-century Europe, and particularly Protestant Europe, the generation of the 1620s was the same."

Hugh Trevor-Roper, *The Crisis of the Seventeenth Century: Religion, The Reformation, and Social Change* (New York: Harper & Row, 1967)

"I returned, and saw under the sun, that the race is not to the swift, nor the battle to the strong, neither yet bread to the wise, nor yet riches to men of understanding, nor yet favour to men of skill; but time and chance happeneth to them all."

Ecclesiastes 9:11

"According to Mr Wöller, the Dutch are the most humane of the imperialist powers. If so, God knows what the others can be like."

George Orwell, in a review of *Zest for Life*, a novel by Johann Wöller, *Time and Tide*, 17 October 1936

In memory of

PAMELA WINIFRED ANN JENKINS, 1943–1998

and

JAMIE ANDREW JENKINS, 1970–1996

MELBOURNE UNIVERSITY PRESS
An imprint of Melbourne University Publishing Limited
Level 1, 715 Swanston Street, Carlton, Victoria 3053, Australia
mup-contact@unimelb.edu.au
www.mup.com.au

First published in Singapore by ISEAS Publishing, 2021
This edition published 2021

Cover design by Philip Campbell Design
Cover image of Lt. Col. Soeharto, Yogyakarta, 1949
(Indonesia Press Photo Service, IPPHOS)
Typeset by Superskill Graphics Pte Ltd
Printed in Australia by McPherson's Printing Group

NATIONAL LIBRARY OF AUSTRALIA
A catalogue record for this book is available from the National Library of Australia

9780522878844 (paperback)

Contents

Foreword

David Jenkins' biography of the late dictator of Indonesia, General Suharto, is truly extraordinary. The only other grand biographies of famous Indonesians—Rudolf Mrázek's on the country's first Prime Minister, Sutan Sjahrir, and Harry Poeze's on the legendary communist Tan Malaka—were written long after their heroes were dead, and depended mainly on archival sources.

Jenkins became very well known for his book *Suharto and His Generals*, published in 1984 when the dictator was at the peak of his power. This work relied substantially on the author's astonishing store of intimate interviews with senior and high-ranking generals of Suharto's generation. The biography still relies on Jenkins' unique access to the military elite right up to the present, which one can only explain by his calm, tact, patience, and friendly sobriety. But it also relies on Jenkins' searches in all kinds of newly-opened archives, not only in Indonesia, but in the UK, Japan, the Netherlands, the US and Australia.

Rather than spending a lot of time and paper denouncing the brutal and secretive dictator of 30+ years (in the manner of most academic work on Suharto), Jenkins does a great job of locating him within the turbulent framework of Indonesia's society and politics from the last years of firm Dutch colonial rule, the violent Japanese Occupation, the revolutionary war 1945–49 which ended with worldwide recognition of the country's independence, the creation and downfall of constitutional democracy, the deepening of the Cold War, the overthrow of Sukarno's populist-authoritarian Guided Democracy, the vast massacres of the left in 1965–66, and Suharto's own coming to power.

The most fascinating part of the book is what Jenkins discovered about Suharto's parents, his childhood and (minimal) education, his training in the colonial military, his experiences in the Japanese-formed Peta military, and his activities during the Revolution. He had to ease his way through a vast amount of lies, propaganda, secretiveness, and prejudices. As a much-respected long-time journalist, Jenkins' prose is excellent, without any academic gobbledygook, his analysis is almost always astute and balanced, and his attitude is based on the big questions of how and why a man like Suharto could not only come to power but could also maintain it so long.

*Ben Anderson**

* The late Benedict R. O'G. Anderson was the Aaron L. Binenkorp Professor of International Studies Emeritus at Cornell University. He was a founding editor of the journal *Indonesia* and the author of *Java in a Time of Revolution: Occupation and Resistance, 1944–46* and *Imagined Communities: Reflections on the Origin and Spread of Nationalism.*

A Note on Spelling and Names

It is difficult to be systematic when spelling Indonesian names. During the colonial era, Indonesian words and names were rendered in Roman script using Dutch spelling conventions, with the system being formalized early in the twentieth century. The use of these conventions (*dj* for the English *j*, *j* for *y*, *sj* for *sh*, *tj* for *ch* and *oe* for *u*) lent, at least for English-speakers, an air of grace and elegance, not to say romance and exoticism, to place names such as Tjilatjap and Soerabaja as well as a certain heaviness to some of the longer personal names, especially the more elaborate Javanese ones. Between 1947 and 1972 the Indonesian government reformed the spelling system. Some Dutch vowel and consonant forms were discarded and the spelling adapted to the form used in Malaysia, although not consistently. In this book I use the modern spelling for most place names: Jakarta, not Djakarta; Cianjur, not Tjiandjur; Surabaya, not Soerabaja, Yogyakarta, not Jogjakarta. For convenience, however, I refer to Java and Sumatra, not Jawa and Sumatera. Throughout the book the place names employed are those in use today, not those of the colonial period, thus Jakarta for Batavia and Bogor for Buitenzorg, except where these places are referred to in contemporary documents. The island of Sulawesi is referred to as such, not as Celebes. There is a minor convention which uses "Borneo" for the whole of that island (in recognition of the Malaysian presence there) and "Kalimantan" for the Indonesian regions (irrespective of administrative division).

Personal names present more of a problem. The 1947–72 reforms were intended to apply to personal names, which would have seen Soemitro

Djojohadikoesoemo stripped back to Sumitro Joyohadikusumo, Soetjipto become Sucipto, Roem become Rum and Tjan become Can. But many Indonesians, having a sentimental attachment to the old spelling and/or an aversion to the new forms, did not change their names. (Some Indonesians appear to have adopted the older spellings in order to suggest they have a colonial-era pedigree.) This has led to some confusion.

President Soeharto stuck to the "old" Dutch spelling of his name, rather than switch to "Suharto". In November 1965, as he was consolidating his power following a strike by the leftwing September 30th Movement, the army newspaper *Berita Yudha* ran an article under the heading, "The name of the Minister/Army Commander", advising that the correct spelling was "Soeharto". From some time in the mid-sixties, when he altered his signature quite radically, Soeharto deftly avoided the issue of the *oe* or *u* by signing himself "S/Harto". Falling into step, his wife, Siti Hartinah Soeharto, signed herself "T. S. Harto," the "T" coming from "Tien", an abbreviation of "Hartinah." Indonesia's first president had taken quite the opposite tack. While giving instructions that his name was to be written as "Sukarno", he went on signing himself, by force of habit and sentiment, "Soekarno".

Sukarno and Soeharto were each given only one name at birth, a common practice in Java. In a surprising number of books, Indonesia's first Head of State is referred to as Achmad Sukarno or Achmed Sukarno. In his 1966 autobiography, Sukarno explained how that error came about: "Some stupid newspaperman once wrote my first name was Achmed. Ridiculous. I am just Sukarno. Having only one name is not unusual in our society."* In 1991, after making the pilgrimage to Mecca, Soeharto took the title "Haji" and added the name "Mohammad" to his existing Javanese name.

This book makes one or two compromises of its own on spelling. I have sought, wherever possible, to spell personal names according to individual preferences. This is done not solely out of respect but because it looks more than a little odd to have a caption on a photograph identifying someone as, say, "Murdani" when the individual in question is wearing a plastic name tag saying "Moerdani". It is often difficult to know how one should refer to an individual Indonesian when his or her name is mentioned for a second or subsequent time, or is listed in a bibliography.

---

* *Sukarno: An Autobiography, As Told to Cindy Adams* (Hong Kong: Gunung Agung, 1966), p. 26.

This is especially true when two Muslim names come together or when a Muslim name is paired for example with a Sundanese or Javanese name. While it seems clear that Abdul Gafur cannot sensibly be called Abdul on second reference, Kemal Idris could be either Kemal or Idris. Although Javanese who happen to have more than one name often prefer to be known by their first name (for example, Sumitro, Roeslan, Prabowo), for the purpose of this book I sometimes use their last name, especially in the bibliography. Chinese names are a problem too. Most Indonesians identified as being of Chinese descent trace their origins to the Hokkien, Hakka and Teochew-speaking communities of southern China whose pronunciation of Chinese names is significantly different from "standard" Mandarin Chinese. When spelled using European language conventions, Indonesian Chinese personal names can take many forms. Most Southeast Asian Chinese have resisted adopting the pinyin transcription, and so their names are presented here, as far as possible, according to their known preferences.

The titles of newspapers, periodicals, books and other contemporary written sources are given in their original spellings, as are quotations from such sources. Foreign language terms are italicized throughout the text and footnotes except where these have come into common English usage. Names of organizations are not italicized, even when they include foreign terms. Koran is spelled Qur'an.

The spelling of Dutch has also undergone reform since World War II. In this book I have adopted the modern spelling whenever appropriate. Thus the Dutch colonial army, or KNIL, which returned to Indonesia in 1945, is spelled Koninklijk Nederlands-Indisch Leger, as it was in the late 1940s, rather than Koninklijk Nederlandsch Indisch Leger, its pre-war name. The names of organizations that had ceased to exist by the time the new spelling system was adopted retain the old spelling. Dutch family names are listed in both the Bibliography and the Index without regard to words such as "van" and "de". When mentioning Japanese names, I follow the Japanese custom and put the family name before the given name. The only exception to this is when a Japanese author, writing in a language other than Japanese, reverses his or her customary name order. In such cases, I list the name in the way it has been given (and recorded in other works), except in the Bibliography and the Index, where the family name precedes the given name, with no comma between the two. Diacritical marks have been omitted.

A Glossary of words and abbreviations used in the text can be found at the back of the book.

A Note on Military Organization

LATE DUTCH COLONIAL PERIOD

In 1940, the Royal Netherlands Indies Army (KNIL) had a strength of about 40,000 men, built around a ground combat force of nineteen "field [infantry] battalions", each of about 875 men, eighteen "garrison battalions", which were not in fact battalions at all, and a rapidly expanding air wing. Seventeen of the infantry battalions were based on Java, with fourteen earmarked solely for defence against an external enemy and two (or by one account three) engaged in *maréchaussée* (internal security) duties. The other two battalions were stationed in the East Kalimantan "oil ports" of Balikpapan and Tarakan, where they too were expected to provide defence against external attack. In Palembang, South Sumatra, the most lucrative of the oil-producing regions in the Netherlands East Indies, the Dutch would establish a small "mobile battalion".

Elsewhere in the Outer Islands, the KNIL was responsible essentially for the maintenance of law and order in support of the civil power, although in 1939 it had taken on some external defence responsibilities. Officers were rotated on an individual basis between Java and widely dispersed garrisons and stockades beyond the Java Sea; units, right down to nineteen-man *brigades*, were rotated as units. By December 1941, KNIL numbers had swollen to just over 113,000, with 94,000 men on Java and some 19,000 in the Outer Islands.[1] In early 1942, the colonial army stood at 121,200. But this included 19,000 Indonesians and 8,500 Dutchmen serving as part of a Dad's Army on plantations and in the cities, and 4,700 elderly soldiers who had been recalled to duty. Also included were 11,400 Dutchmen serving as part of the Home Guard.[2] This force was not, by any stretch of the imagination, a plausible deterrent to a nation like Japan, which was increasingly intent on seizing the great East Indies oilfields. In an appraisal written at the time, the 1940–42 Australian Chief of the General Staff, Lieutenant General V.A.H. Sturdee, advised that the KNIL "should be regarded more as well-equipped Home Guards than an Army capable of undertaking active operations in the field."[3]

JAPANESE OCCUPATION

In March 1942, having gained control of the Outer Islands, the Japanese put 55,000 seasoned troops ashore on Java. In nine days they overwhelmed the Dutch and a small Allied contingent. Five months later most of the Japanese combat forces had been shipped out, to Burma, to the eastern region of the archipelago and to Guadalcanal. To make up for the units that had been redeployed, the commander of the Japanese Sixteenth Army was sent "ten battalions of aged soldiers", or roughly 10,000 men in all. Short of manpower, the Sixteenth Army established, trained and armed a decentralized Java Volunteer Defence Force, which was known to them as the Giyugun and to the Indonesians as Peta. By late 1944, Peta consisted of sixty-nine Indonesian battalions (*daidan*), with a total strength of about 37,500 men. Sixty-six of these battalions were on Java, the other three on Bali. Each *daidan* had about 500 men and was commanded by an Indonesian *daidancho*, whose rank was roughly equivalent to major. Below the *daidan* there were four companies (*chudan*), each commanded by a *chudancho*, whose rank was equivalent to captain. Each *chudan* consisted of four infantry platoons (*shodan*), each commanded by a *shodancho*, who was the equivalent of a first lieutenant. On Sumatra, the Japanese set up a separate 20,000-strong Giyugun, with 150-man *chudan* as the largest fighting units.

FRENCH INDOCHINA
ANDAMAN SEA
THAILAND
SOUTH CHINA SEA
Banda Aceh
Penang
Strait of Malacca
MALAYA
BRUNEI
Medan
Pematang Siantar
Kuala Lumpur
Malacca
SARAWAK
SINGAPORE
SUMATRA
Pekanbaru
Pontianak
Bukittinggi
Padang
KALIMANTAN
Jambi
Muntok
BANGKA
Palembang
Banjarmasin
Bengkulu
Batavia (Jakarta)
JAVA SEA
MADURA
Bogor
Semarang
INDIAN OCEAN
Bandung
JAVA
Solo
Surabaya
Yogyakarta
Denpasa
Netherlands East Indies
0
500 miles
0
500 km

PHILIPPINES
SULU SEA
Davao
PHILIPPINE SEA
PALAU
N
W
E
S
NORTH BORNEO
PACIFIC OCEAN
CELEBES SEA
Tarakan
MOROTAI
Menado
Ternate
Gulf of Tomini
MOLUCCA SEA
NUMFOOR
BIAK
Balikpapan
Sorong
SULAWESI
Hollandia
Kendari
BURU
Ambon
WEST NEW GUINEA
Makassar
BANDA ISLANDS
BANDA SEA
Boven Digul
FLORES
Dili
Endeh
PORTUGUESE TIMOR
ARAFURA SEA
Merauke
Kupang
TIMOR SEA
Darwin
AUSTRALIA
Gulf Of Carpentaria

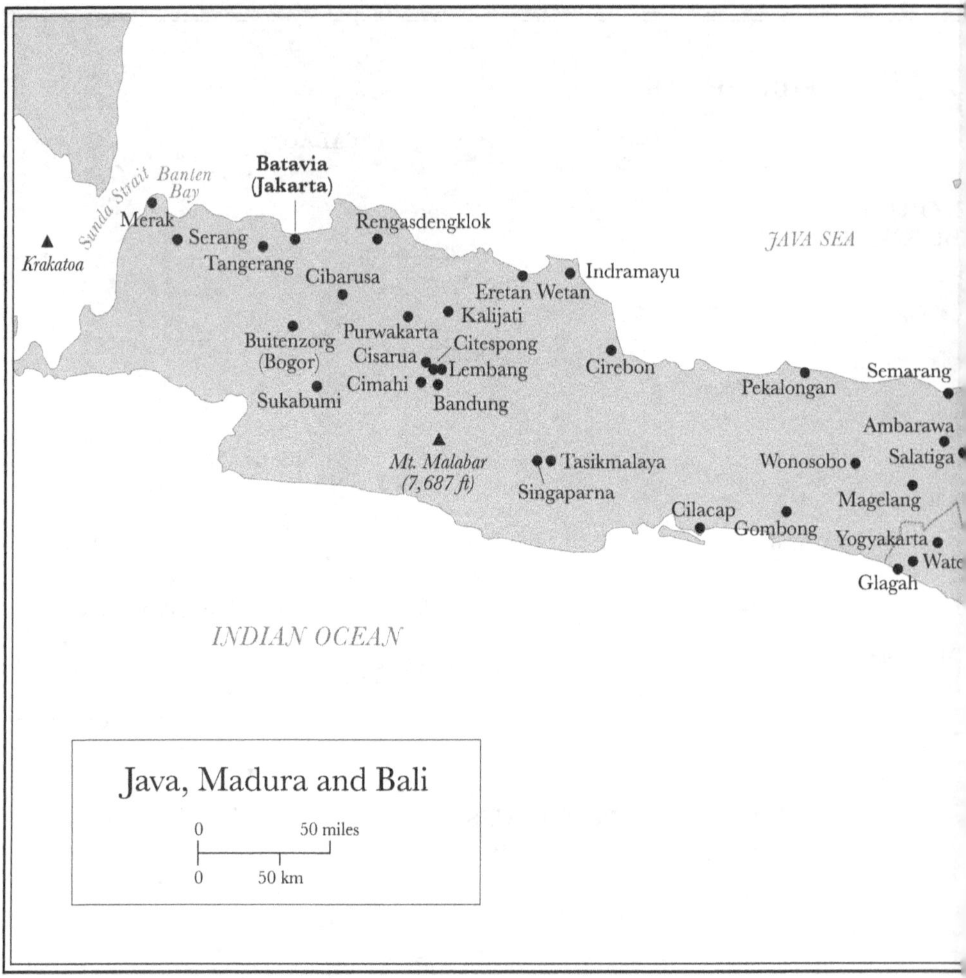
Java, Madura and Bali
0
50 miles
0
50 km
Batavia
(Jakarta)
Sunda Strait
Banten
Bay
Merak
Serang
Tangerang
Krakatoa
Rengasdengklok
JAVA SEA
Cibarusa
Eretan Wetan
Indramayu
Kalijati
Purwakarta
Buitenzorg
(Bogor)
Citespong
Cisarua
Lembang
Cimahi
Bandung
Sukabumi
Cirebon
Pekalongan
Semarang
Ambarawa
Salatiga
Mt. Malabar
(7,687 ft)
Tasikmalaya
Singaparna
Wonosobo
Magelang
Cilacap
Gombong
Yogyakarta
Glagah
INDIAN OCEAN

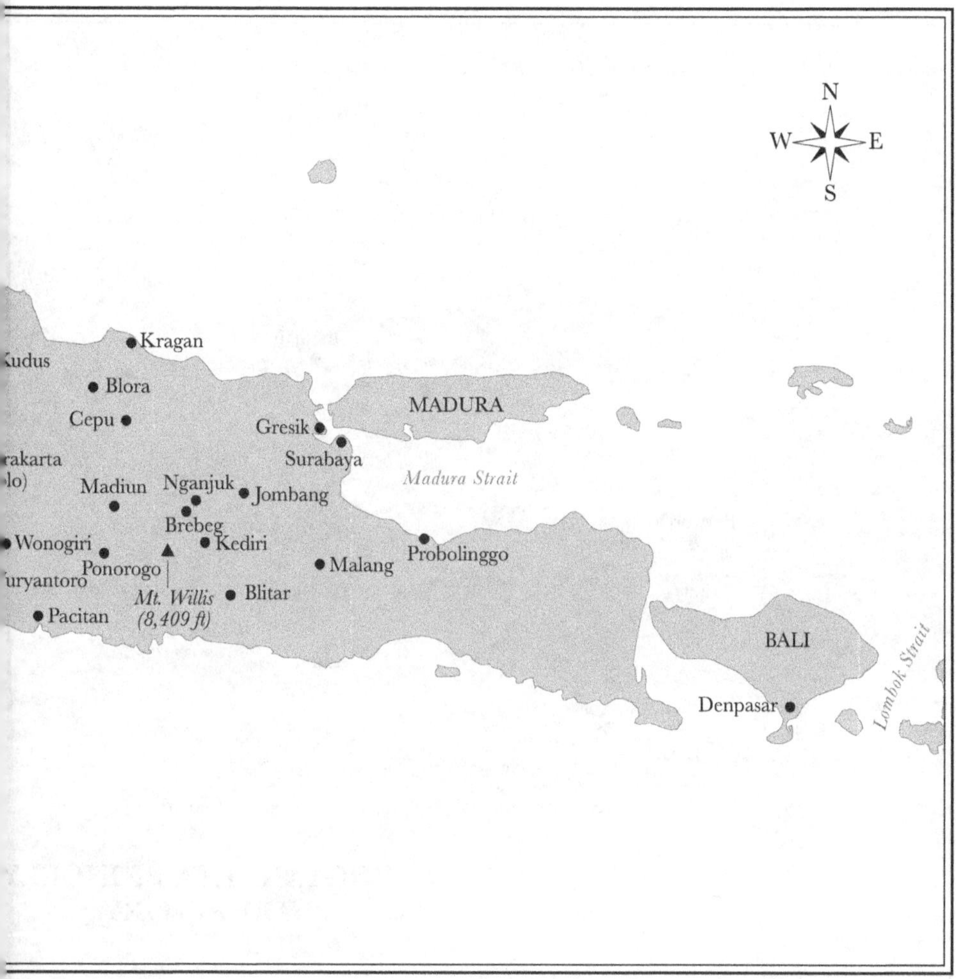
N
W
E
S
Kragan
Blora
Cepu
MADURA
Gresik
Surabaya
Madura Strait
Madiun
Nganjuk
Jombang
Brebeg
Wonogiri
Kediri
Ponorogo
Probolinggo
Malang
Mt. Willis
(8,409 ft)
Blitar
Pacitan
BALI
Lombok Strait
Denpasar

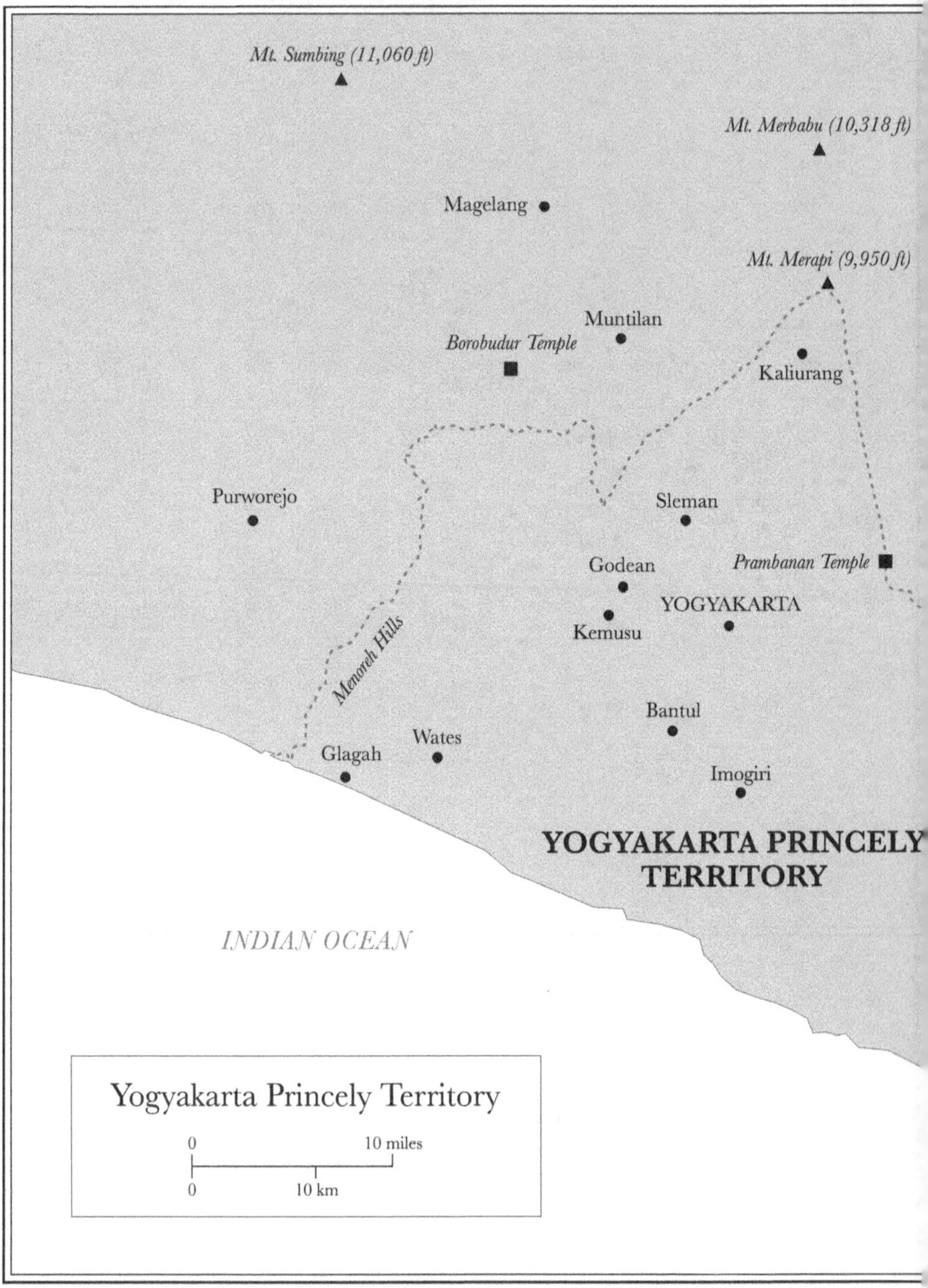
Mt. Sumbing (11,060 ft)
Mt. Merbabu (10,318 ft)
Magelang
Mt. Merapi (9,950 ft)
Muntilan
Borobudur Temple
Kaliurang
Purworejo
Sleman
Godean
Prambanan Temple
YOGYAKARTA
Kemusu
Menoreh Hills
Bantul
Wates
Glagah
Imogiri
YOGYAKARTA PRINCELY TERRITORY
INDIAN OCEAN
Yogyakarta Princely Territory
0
10 miles
0
10 km

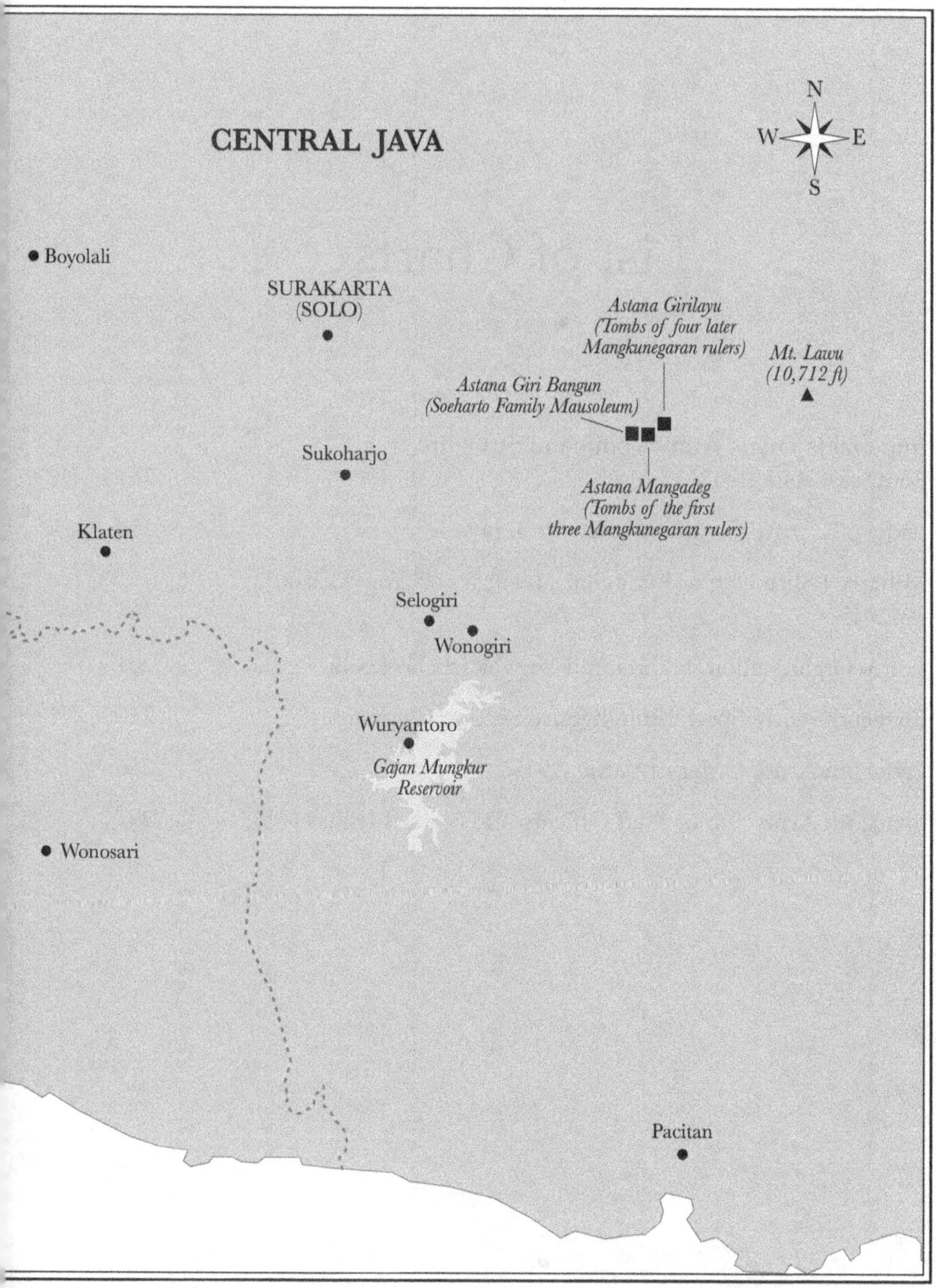
CENTRAL JAVA
N
W
E
S
Boyolali
SURAKARTA
(SOLO)
Astana Girilayu
(Tombs of four later
Mangkunegaran rulers)
Mt. Lawu
(10,712 ft)
Astana Giri Bangun
(Soeharto Family Mausoleum)
Sukoharjo
Astana Mangadeg
(Tombs of the first
three Mangkunegaran rulers)
Klaten
Selogiri
Wonogiri
Wuryantoro
Gajan Mungkur
Reservoir
Wonosari
Pacitan

List of Charts

Preface

At around 7:15 a.m. on Friday, 1 October 1965, Lieutenant Colonel Untung, a battalion commander in President Sukarno's Tjakrabirawa palace guard, issued a startling proclamation over Radio Republik Indonesia. A hitherto unknown "September 30th Movement", he declared, had saved the head of state from a CIA-backed "Council of Generals" which was plotting to overthrow the government. What Untung did not disclose was that three or four hours earlier Tjakrabirawa troops had murdered the Army Commander, Lieutenant General Achmad Yani, and two other prominent generals in their homes and had kidnapped and murdered, or were about to murder, three more generals. The Defence Minister, General A.H. Nasution, had narrowly escaped assassination; his five-year-old daughter had been mortally wounded, a young lieutenant seized and murdered. By late that afternoon, Major General Soeharto, the commander of the Army Strategic Reserve (Kostrad), had marshalled a counter force, won over a battalion of September 30th troops guarding key locations in central Jakarta and put a second battalion to flight. A botched and brutal strike against army leaders known for their hostility to the large Indonesian Communist Party (Partai Komunis Indonesia, PKI) had failed. And although there remained a dangerous standoff in Central Java, where many units had come out in favour of the September 30th Movement, the power balance in Jakarta had changed irrevocably.

On the following Monday, a day of strong emotion and high drama in Indonesia, the army recovered the bodies of the six generals and the lieutenant from a disused well known as the Crocodile Hole. The corpses were bloated and blackened, in most cases barely recognizable. Eleven days later, Soeharto gave a report on recent developments to leaders of the National Front, a left-leaning body Sukarno had established to mobilize political parties and other groups behind government policies.[1] "We have found the bodies of the generals," he said at one point, in what appears to have been an informal exchange with front members. "But I am also a general and many of you don't know me." He then gestured towards K.P.H. Haryasudirja Sasraningrat, a thirty-nine-year-old Javanese aristocrat who was Minister for Water Resources in Sukarno's cabinet. "If you have any questions about me," he continued, "well, Mr Haryasudirja can answer you." Haryasudirja "knows me very well." This was unexpected. Haryasudirdja was taken aback. "He appointed me!" the former cabinet minister recalled many years later.[2]

Unexpected or not, it was a shrewd gambit by Soeharto. Haryasudirja, a senior prince of the Pakualaman, the minor court in Yogyakarta, *did* know Soeharto.[3] They went back twenty years. A sociable, well-educated man, fluent in Dutch, English and German as well as Javanese, Indonesian and Sundanese, Haryasudirja had been associated with a group of young democratic socialists (and some others more to the left) who met regularly at a house in the densely-settled Pathok quarter of Yogyakarta during the 1942–45 Japanese occupation—a house where Soeharto had, at the age of twenty-four, come calling immediately after the war, seeking to learn something about politics. Their paths had crossed again during the bitterly fought 1945–49 Indonesian National Revolution against the Dutch, who were seeking to regain control of their lucrative Southeast Asian colony. In 1947–48, the prince, by then a first lieutenant in the Indonesian National Army, and several other junior army officers had lived in the same small but elegant Dutch-era housing complex as Lieutenant Colonel Soeharto, sharing with him their rice and *lauk pauk*, the various side dishes that accompany the rice: vegetables and perhaps a bit of meat or fermented soy bean cake (*tempé*). He had, following Soeharto's marriage in nearby Solo in December 1947, helped arrange a wedding party in Yogyakarta, allowing Soeharto to introduce his wife to his friends and acquaintances, most of them army colleagues who had not been able to attend the wedding.

Haryasudirja's older brother, Captain Frans Hariadi, had been one of Soeharto's battalion commanders until he was killed in a clash with Dutch troops in January 1949. On Soeharto's orders, neatly typewritten at a guerrilla village south of Yogyakarta and carried twenty miles by a courier who made his way on foot across open country, skirting Dutch outposts and patrols, Haryasudirja had become the acting commander of his brother's battalion. He had led the battalion, one of Soeharto's best, for the rest of the year, participating in heavy fighting against the Dutch. In March 1949, when Soeharto commanded a two thousand-man attack on Dutch-occupied Yogyakarta, Haryasudirja, then aged twenty-three, had led two hundred men into the heart of the city, where they opened fire on a Dutch post in front of the two-storey Merdeka Hotel. At one stage, some of his men were only twenty yards from the Dutch, who returned fire with Bren guns, killing several guerrillas. Haryasudirja and his subordinates survived a heavy Dutch counter-attack by dropping down into storm water drains and scrambling five or six hundred yards to the shallow Winongo River. He found Soeharto, who had left the city thirty minutes earlier, at a forward command post on the opposite bank. As Indonesian troops hurriedly withdrew from the city, Soeharto calmly finished a bowl of *soto babat* (tripe soup).

When, at the end of the year, the Dutch cut their losses, recognized Indonesia's independence and pulled out (while retaining control of mountainous West New Guinea, over which negotiations were to continue), Haryasudirja returned to civilian life and studied engineering. Now, in the complex world of post-coup Jakarta, with tension high and many cross-currents running, this Roman Catholic engineer from Central Java was well qualified for the role that Soeharto had just assigned him. He not only knew the general well; he had six other useful attributes: he was a nationalist, a cabinet minister and a moderate; he was non-Communist, non-party and non-Islamic.

The morning after Soeharto's speech to the National Front, President Sukarno, believing that the dead generals may indeed have been plotting against him, was still downplaying the significance of their deaths. This kind of killing, he had said, was "something ordinary and normal in a revolution", "a ripple in the ocean." But senior army officers remained incensed. They were convinced that the Indonesian Communist Party was behind the Untung "coup." A ruthless purge of the party was already underway. And at the Presidential Palace that day a reluctant Sukarno found himself obliged to formally install Soeharto as the new Army Minister concurrently Army Commander. The atmosphere was icy. Before the ceremony, Soeharto stood with his adjutant in one corner of the marble-floored reception hall, rather reserved, almost shy, not wanting to push himself forward in a gathering such as this, even as he was moving so decisively on the political stage, drawing enormous power into his own hands. None of the members of Sukarno's hundred-strong cabinet approached him, and the three Communist ministers were noticeably absent. None of the ministers except Haryasudirja really knew him. Haryasudirja was standing that morning with several of his ministerial colleagues. He did not notice Soeharto enter. When someone said to him, "We know that you were with Soeharto during the Revolution. Where is he?", Haryasudirja scanned the room. Spotting Soeharto in the corner, he went over to speak to him, thinking, as he said later, that Soeharto looked "lonely."[4]

As it happened, President Sukarno also knew Soeharto well, had known him in fact almost as long as Haryasudirja had. Unlike his Minister for Water Resources, Sukarno did not particularly like Soeharto: he considered him stubborn, as indeed he was. In 1946, when a group of left-leaning army officers kidnapped Prime Minister Sutan Sjahrir, Sukarno had put Soeharto in an invidious position by insisting that he detain his own divisional commander, an order Soeharto had chosen not to obey. Soeharto had proven hard-headed once again—Sukarno always used the Dutch word: *koppig*—in 1958. While serving as the regional commander in Central Java, he had incurred Sukarno's displeasure by working closely with the staunchly anti-Communist provincial governor and by complaining to the President about the growing influence of the Communist Party. As Soeharto told the story, Sukarno became "rather angry" at his "respectful" expressions of concern and was adamant that the PKI had a legitimate role to play. "And this is my business," the President is said to have declared. "You, Soeharto, you are a soldier. Politics is my business. Leave these matters to me."[5]

Now, seven years later, politics was increasingly Soeharto's business.[6] And now, it was clear, he had no intention of leaving those matters solely to Sukarno. On the contrary, he was moving to sideline the charismatic President, who had been the towering figure on the Indonesian political stage for the best part of forty years and Head of State for twenty. This would, it is true, be a long and drawn-out process—death by a thousand cuts. Sukarno still commanded great support, not least in parts of the armed forces. Cautious by nature, Soeharto had no wish to plunge the nation into civil war, although he was willing to countenance a swift and murderous purge of the left. He took for his motto an old Javanese adage: *alon-alon asal kelakon* (slow but sure).[7] This caution was to serve him well in the months ahead. "If Yani had lived through that coup attempt in '65," claimed Colonel George Benson, a former US defence attaché who had known the late Army Commander well and who had coached and encouraged him when he spent a year at the prestigious US Army Command and General Staff College at Fort Leavenworth, Kansas, "there would have been a civil war right on the spot. He never would have had the patience to deal with the President the way Soeharto did.... He just wouldn't have had the patience to do it."[8]

At this time most Indonesians were like the National Front delegates whom Soeharto had addressed on 15 October and the cabinet ministers who gathered at the palace the following day. All they really knew about Soeharto was that he had held a number of centrally important army commands, that he had taken charge of the nation in a time of crisis and that he was now directing a terrifying house-to-house *razzia* against known or suspected Communists—a *razzia* in which perhaps half a million people would be slaughtered, mainly in Java and Bali but also in North Sumatra, with another million consigned to a nationwide chain of concentration camps in what was to become, both literally and figuratively, the Gulag Archipelago.[9]

"In terms of the numbers killed," the US Central Intelligence Agency would observe in 1968, "the anti-PKI massacres in Indonesia rank as one of the worst mass murders of the 20th century, along with the Soviet purges of the 1930s, the Nazi mass murders of the Second World War, and the Maoist bloodbath of the early 1950s."[10] At no time, either in public or private, would Soeharto be heard to express a word of regret or remorse for the wave of killing which accompanied his ascent to power.[11] These murders were to cast a dark shadow over the nation he ruled. No one could ever forget who had sent the army out to train, coordinate and incite the anti-Communist civilian death squads, although it is true that many of the vigilantes, especially those in conservative rural Muslim communities, needed little encouragement to hunt down and kill Communists. Nor would the killing end in 1965–66. Ten years later Soeharto would systematically destabilize, and then invade, Portuguese East Timor, creating conditions which lead to the unnatural death of perhaps 100,000–150,000 of the territory's 700,000 people.

When Soeharto successfully demanded in March 1966 that Sukarno give him full executive authority, Indonesia was a deeply divided nation, fractured along ideological, class, religious and ethnic lines. The state was barely functioning. The economy was in disarray, wrecked by war, rebellion, agitational politics and mismanagement. Inflation was running at over 600 per cent. Soeharto took over a nation in chaos, the largest in Southeast Asia, almost three times more populous than Vietnam, where the United States was beginning to commit regular army units to fight communism, and transformed it into one of the "Asian miracle" economies—only to leave it back on the brink of ruin when he was forced from office thirty-two years later. As the World Bank noted soon after his fall in 1998, "A country that achieved decades of rapid growth, stability and poverty reduction, is now near economic collapse .... No country in recent history, let alone one the size of Indonesia, has ever suffered such a dramatic reversal of fortune."[12] In August the following year, Professor Subroto, a dapper, bow-tie wearing economist who had served as a cabinet minister under Soeharto for seventeen years, observed, "The work of the past 30 years has been evaporating before our eyes ... the country could descend into chaos and even break up."[13]

II

Young Soeharto, although complete in itself, is the first volume in a three-volume series that will chart the rise to power of one of Asia's most brutal, most durable, most avaricious and most successful dictators—if, in speaking of success, we focus on the relative stability of his time in office and the achievement of 8 per cent per annum GDP growth over twenty years, and ignore the fact that Soeharto left the economy back in chaos when he departed; that East Timor, the only territory he annexed, voted overwhelmingly for independence only fifteen months after his fall; and that he created no political or state institutions but instead undermined the institutions he found, rickety though they were, and kept society suppressed for more than three decades.[14] In tracing the eventful arc of former President Soeharto's early decades, these volumes will seek to provide not only a fuller, richer, more nuanced portrait of the man himself, but also bring to life the story of Indonesia's birth as an independent nation. The man who was to become Indonesia's second Head of State emerges as an outsider who overcompensated for the difficult hand that life had dealt him, who trusted only his family and his closest colleagues, who was obsessive in his attention to detail, ruthless in his pursuit of objectives and indifferent to considerations of propriety.

Astute and watchful, quick to strike down potential challengers, Soeharto remained in power longer than any other major Third World leader apart from Kim Il Sung, Fidel Castro, Muamar Gaddafi and Lee Kuan Yew. During this time, no fewer than seven US presidents occupied the White House. A man of resourcefulness and guile, an enigma even to his closest associates, obsessed with stability, order and economic development, finding relaxation in farming, golf and deep-sea fishing, he was one of the most complex and important Third World leaders of the post-World War II era.

Soeharto was cut from very different cloth, emotionally and ideologically, from an earlier generation of charismatic post-colonial figures such as Sukarno, Ho Chi Minh, Jawaharlal Nehru and Colonel Gamal Abdel Nasser, men who were in varying degrees on the left of the political spectrum, just as Soeharto was on the right of that spectrum. Yet he achieved far more for his nation in material terms that any of those men despite economic upheavals late in his presidency: in 1993 the World Bank began to refer to Indonesia as one of the eight "miracle" economies of Asia.[15] Soeharto's successful combination of authoritarian rule and firm economic management gave Indonesia, a mendicant among nations when he came to office, a foothold in the global economy. It was an approach taken by a number of other conservative—albeit highly dissimilar—Third World leaders, including Lee in Singapore, Augusto Pinochet in Chile and Park Chung Hee in South Korea. It was an approach taken also by Deng Xiaoping, once the antithesis of a conservative, as he steered China towards a booming market economy.

Under Soeharto, Indonesia achieved impressive economic advances, attracting investment from the United States, Japan and Western Europe. As well as being a goldmine (sometimes literally) for major US resource companies (Caltex, Exxon, Freeport), it caught the eye of AT&T and Nike, amongst others. With the economic wheels beginning to turn and with money flowing at last into the nation's coffers, Soeharto was able to preside over a Green Revolution, a Family Planning Revolution and a major expansion of the education system. Had Indonesia maintained the fertility rates of the 1950s over the half century to 2020, the population would not stand at about 280 million, as it does today. Instead, there would be an additional 50 to 65 million mouths to feed, children to educate and workers to employ. As the demographer Terence Hull notes, "That is a burden no government would have welcomed."[16] But

Indonesia also suffered far more than any of its neighbours at the time of the 1997–98 Asian Financial Crisis. In the period after that it became the focus of controversial International Monetary Fund and World Bank rescue packages. Twenty-two years after Soeharto was driven from office Indonesia is growing again and seen by many as one of the most important developing nations in the world, along with countries such as Brazil and India.

Because of its size and location, Indonesia has been courted since independence by most of the major powers: by the Soviet Union, which in the early 1960s provided it with warships and modern, long-range bombers; by the United States, which trained so many of its economists and army officers and which invested heavily in its oil industry, and by China, which courted its first President and Communist Party, only to be locked out for nearly two-and-a-half decades after the turmoil of 1965. A nation born amid violent upheaval, Indonesia has resorted to military force three times to advance its domestic and foreign policy goals—against the Dutch in West New Guinea, against the Malaysians, British and Australians in Malaysia and against the left-leaning Fretilin independence movement in Portuguese East Timor. It has been seen by its neighbours, not least Australia, as restless, volatile and expansionist. It is the only nation to have withdrawn from the United Nations. Sukarno took it out (or at least announced that he was taking it out) at the end of 1964; Soeharto is sometimes said to have taken it back in nearly two years later, although in point of fact Indonesia had remained a member—albeit non-participating—during that time.[17]

III

This volume traces the story of how Soeharto began his rise to power, an ascent which would be capped by those thirty-two years (1966–98) in office, first as Army Commander, then as Acting President and finally, in 1968, as the President of Indonesia, which was to become, with the collapse of the Soviet Union, the fourth most populous nation on earth.

But this, it is important to stress, is not simply a book about one man.

In recounting how Soeharto rose from poverty to power it seeks to provide an accessible introduction to the complex, but dramatic and often utterly absorbing, social, political, religious, economic and military factors that have shaped, and which continue to shape, Indonesia, a nation which was proclaimed on 17 August 1945, two days after the Japanese surrender, and which was to weather many intense storms in the years thereafter. This is the story of how a new nation came into being, how it fought for its independence and how it made its way in the world. Indonesia's experiences were replicated, in one form or another, in many other former colonies in the mid-twentieth century. In this book, the focus is not just on individuals and events and great historical forces, vital as they are, but also on institutions—not least educational institutions, including military and para-military training centres—and the role they played in the period of late Dutch colonial rule and of Japanese occupation.

Soeharto did not create modern Indonesia, of course. That honour belongs to leaders such as Sukarno, Mohammad Hatta and the many other nationalists who had been active in the pre-war independence movement and who had in some cases endured long periods in Dutch prisons or in mind-numbing internal exile in remote corners of the Netherlands East Indies. But Soeharto played an increasingly important role as a military commander during the 1945–49 war of independence. Through a fortuitous combination of birth, geography, training and circumstance, he was present at many of the most significant stages of modern Indonesian history, both before and after independence, and not always on the sidelines. That can be said about few other people, civilian or military. For that reason, an account of Soeharto's career serves as a strong connecting thread, linking the events that make up Indonesia's often turbulent and violent history. This volume takes the story from Soeharto's birth in a hamlet in Central Java to his service in the Royal Netherlands Indies Army, his time as a policeman under the Japanese and then as a soldier in the Japanese-created Java Volunteer Defence Force, which was known to the Indonesians as Peta. Subsequent volumes will trace his role as a military commander and guerrilla leader in the late 1940s, his emergence as an important mid-level officer in the Indonesian National Army and his merciless suppression of the Communist Party in 1965–66.

Unlike many of those who rose to prominence during the Indonesian Revolution, Soeharto was "not propp'd by ancestry"; he came from a humble rural background. Unlike others who would go on to hold the high ground in the Indonesian Army, he had not enjoyed a first-rate Dutch high school education. Nor had he attended a prestigious overseas staff college or gained experience abroad as a military attaché. However, Soeharto possessed what Joseph Conrad called "ability in the Abstract." This ability was recognized in succession by the Dutch, by the Japanese, by his fellow Indonesians (albeit in the latter case with some reluctance), by the Americans, by fellow Southeast Asian leaders and by many others as well.

Although Soeharto ruled Indonesia for so long, little has been written about his early life, his actions during the Revolution, his role as an important army officer under Martial Law in the late 1950s, his central role as the commander of a large, multi-service military operation designed to seize West New Guinea from the Dutch and his subsequent role during Sukarno's 1963–66 "Confrontation" with Malaysia, which saw Indonesian air, sea and land operations against British, Australian and Malaysian forces on the Malay Peninsula and in the British North Borneo territories. Nor has there yet been a full account of his actions during the convulsive political events of 1965. This work will trace the significant events of that life and career. How did Soeharto, a man of such modest social origins and limited education, rise to such a pinnacle of power, supplanting so many better-educated and more sophisticated army officers, to say nothing of highly skilled civilians? How far was his character shaped by the unique cultural, political and religious traditions that govern the life of the Javanese, the dominant ethnic group in Indonesia? Why was his rise to the presidency accompanied by such widespread, centrally directed violence? What part did chance play in his career? What part did money, status, family, authority and friends—if indeed there were many friends—play in his thinking? How, if at all, did his thinking about personal enrichment differ from that of his fellow army officers? And where can the line be drawn in Indonesia between what is excessive and what is acceptable?

To adapt a phrase—and indeed a format—used by Paul Preston in the introduction to his magisterial biography of General Franco, a similar leader in some respects, not least in his willingness to promote the use of exemplary terror, these are important questions with a crucial bearing on Indonesian and Southeast Asia history and they can be answered only by close observation of the man.[18] It is a central thesis of this study that a better understanding of Soeharto's early life and of the kind of man he was is essential if we are to comprehend his later actions, both for good and ill. These volumes seek to recreate the various worlds in which Soeharto lived and worked; worlds which often succeeded one another in quick succession, like sets on a revolving stage, as when the era of Dutch colonialism gave way suddenly to the period of Japanese occupation and when that, in turn, was replaced by an independent Indonesian Republic, the creation of which brought a whole series of quite separate, rapidly changing and often highly complex environments of its own.

These volumes will place Soeharto within those worlds; they will examine in detail the circumstances of his childhood and his career as an army officer; they will establish where he was at key moments, what experiences he underwent, who he was working with, what orders he issued and how he was regarded by his friends, family, colleagues and opponents, as well as by outside observers. Only by doing this can one hope to understand the factors that shaped the man who was to have such a profound and prolonged impact on Indonesia. Trifles, as Dickens has observed, make the sum of life.

As part of this undertaking the present book will examine the various cultures—Javanese, Dutch colonial, military and Japanese modern—which were, in Ruth McVey's apt phrase, "jostling for influence" in this period, changing and transforming the thinking of Soeharto and his cohorts.[19] One of the main benefits of examining both the milieu and the actions of Soeharto is that it affords us an enhanced understanding of the turbulence of the times and of the cultures that were in play.

In the early years of Soeharto's army-backed "New Order" administration, some political analysts argued that the system of government in Indonesia appeared to be strongly influenced by traditional Javanese political culture. They maintained that Soeharto had recreated the atmosphere of a Javanese *kraton* (royal palace), in which politics was frequently a matter of court intrigue and in which one powerful "prince" was played off against another to the benefit of the ruler. The idea took root that New Order Indonesia was influenced to a disproportionate degree by traditional political culture. It cannot be denied that the rich cultural traditions of Java left an indelible mark on Soeharto. Nor can it be denied that he presided over a latter-day "court", just as Sukarno had done before him. But arguments about the importance of "culture" need to be treated with great care, especially when they impinge on politics. This book argues that we should not place too much reliance on cultural analysis when looking at Soeharto, a leader who, for all his putative "Javaneseness", does not fit comfortably into some of those traditions but who, often enough, deviates from them.[20] The skills that Soeharto brought to the Presidency were not uniquely Javanese or Indonesian political skills. Rather, they were skills that transcended cultural and national boundaries and which are found in any number of other countries. In Soeharto's Indonesia, Harold Crouch has observed, aspects of traditional culture were applied in a modern setting.[21] The mixture is what counted. Culture reinforced and legitimated behaviour that was not derived exclusively from that particular environment.

It is quite possible, as critics sometimes suggested, that Soeharto's political style had something in common with that of the sultans of Mataram, who dominated East and Central Java between 1582 and 1755. But judging the former Indonesian leader solely by those standards does him a great disservice. As a President seeking to advance his policy goals, and to bring others along with him, Soeharto had far more in common with a number of European and Latin American military officers who assumed high political office—one thinks of Napoleon, Franco and Pinochet—and with a civilian ruler such as Bismarck, although it needs to be added at once that Soeharto, unlike Napoleon and Bismarck, was not a man who had a high regard for workable political institutions or who saw himself as a lawgiver. On the contrary, he was a man who stacked representative bodies with toadies and time-servers and who made a mockery of the notion of judicial independence.[22]

He also had something in common with President Lyndon Baines Johnson, who, although operating in a world of strong institutions, used money and the force of his personality to secure his political goals. There was, as well, one other thing these two men had in common. Johnson, inheriting John F. Kennedy's cabinet, "would remind people again and again that in the chamber where these great decisions were made, there sat the head of the Ford Motor Company, a Rhodes scholar, the dean of Harvard University, and one graduate of San Marcos State Teachers College."[23] Soeharto was not a man given to that sort of boasting, but it was clear to his colleagues that he derived a similar satisfaction from the fact that his cabinets, which were packed at any one time with half a dozen ministers with PhDs in economics or demography or law from prestigious US and Canadian universities, took their marching orders from someone who had never gone beyond the Muhammadiyah *schakelschool* (link school), which was part of the elementary school system for "native" Indonesians, which he attended wearing a *kain* (sarong) and going barefoot. Nor did it displease him that for five years he had as his Vice President, Sultan Hamengku Buwono IX of Yogyakarta, a descendant of the great rulers of Mataram, a man who had lived in Holland for nine years and had attended the University of Leiden, where he majored in economics.

This book will also examine the place of religion in Indonesia, a country which, although it is neither an Islamic nor a secular state, but something deliberately ill-defined between those two poles, has more Muslims than any other nation. Islam has played a vital—and frequently divisive—role in Indonesian politics since the Proclamation of Independence in 1945, and is central to an understanding of both the nation in general and Soeharto in particular. Soeharto came to the Presidency with a deep scepticism, if not hostility, towards political Islam, although in later years, even before his command over his natural power base in the army slackened, he was to make overtures to the Islamic community. This initial scepticism was shaped partly by his early religious upbringing. While nominally Islamic, this upbringing owed more to Javanese religion (*agama Jawa*), also known as *kebatinan*, a varying mix of Hindu, Buddhist, Islamic and animist elements, than it did to purely Islamic rituals and beliefs. As one scholar notes, many nominally Islamic Javanese refer to themselves as *kejawen* ("Javanist"), practitioners of *Islam Jawa* (Javanese Islam), "with the understanding that they place more emphasis on the mystical than the legal or ritualistic dimensions of Islam."[24]

But his views were shaped, too, by his experiences as a soldier who had taken part in a frequently bitter post-independence struggle against Islamic extremists. A subsequent volume will look at the role Soeharto played in pursuing and eliminating members of a Central Java battalion which, in the early fifties, threw its weight behind the Darul Islam (Abode of Islam) movement, which sought to create an Islamic state. The intolerance and ferocity of this movement, which was active in West Java, Aceh, South Kalimantan and South Sulawesi, claiming an estimated 25,000 lives, left an abiding aversion to fundamentalism in Indonesia, a nation which had rejected arguments for an Islamic State when the Constitution was drawn up in 1945.[25]

And while the battle against the Darul Islam seemed to have been won by the early sixties, the spore of Islamic radicalism can lie dormant in Indonesian soil for many years. As President, Soeharto would use the army to deal with periodic incidents of Islamic terrorism, almost certainly aware that some of those actions had been secretly funded and encouraged by Major (later Lieutenant) General Ali Moertopo, one of his key intelligence aides, in an attempt to discredit mainstream Islam ahead of a general election in 1977. Islamic fundamentalism resurfaced with devastating effect in the years immediately after Soeharto's fall in the guise of Jemaah Islamiyah (Islamic Community), a terrorist organization founded by two radical preachers who felt persecuted by Soeharto. Jemaah Islamiyah, which had fraternal relations with al-Qaeda but which was not a subordinate organization, was responsible for a series of deadly terrorist bomb attacks. In the largest of these attacks, in Bali in October 2002, Islamic extremists killed more than two hundred people, including eighty-eight Australians and thirty-eight Indonesians; more than two hundred others were injured. In tracing the origins of the push for an Islamic state these volumes seek to provide a backdrop to an issue that continues to divide Indonesians.

At the same time, this study will focus on the emergence of the army as an increasingly powerful political actor in Indonesia, especially after December 1948, when the civilian leaders surrendered to the Dutch, leaving the army to go on fighting. They will show how the army was created out of many disparate armed groups and how army officers came to believe that the army was entitled to play a central role in Indonesian politics, a belief that ran contrary to those of the nation's early civilian rulers, who accepted as a given the notion of civilian supremacy. These volumes will show how the army officer corps, and in particular General Nasution, played a central role in overthrowing Indonesia's system of parliamentary democracy (1950–57) and was able to gain support for the fundamental principles of Guided Democracy (1959–65).[26] Guided Democracy was a form of authoritarian rule in which the army shared extensive power with Sukarno, even as it sought to curb the influence of a resurrected Communist Party, on which Sukarno, seeking to counterbalance the army, would come to depend. Guided Democracy was to provide, in time, the highly convenient underpinnings for Soeharto's New Order government.

Woven into a subsequent volume will be an account of Soeharto's growing involvement in fund-raising and corruption. In 1949 Soeharto and a freewheeling captain from the Diponegoro Division motor pool established a private vehicle repair shop and a bus and trucking company using four requisitioned military vehicles. This was one of Soeharto's first ventures into the world of business. And although the company was small and set up ostensibly to provide jobs for demobilized soldiers, it would pave the way for a slew of similar, and much larger, ventures in the fifties—ventures with ambitions so broad and accountability standards so opaque that fellow officers in Central Java were soon expressing concern at what they saw as entirely unacceptable behaviour. The same volume will describe the opium smuggling which military officers engaged in during the Revolution—at the behest, it is true, of Indonesia's civilian government. As he nurtured the Indonesian economy after 1965, drawing in billions of dollars in foreign investment, spinning wealth out of oil and gas, timber and rubber, presiding over a world of monopolies and kickbacks, Soeharto and his family saw their fortunes rise in lock-step. No one knows for sure how much wealth the Soeharto clan accumulated over the years—and much of that wealth was lost during the Asian Financial Crisis of 1997–98—but pre-crash estimates ranged from US$3 billion to a scarcely credible US$32 billion.[27]

More broadly, this is a study about the Generation of '45, the generation of Indonesians who fought for their nation's independence, a generation which truly was "bound together by common experiences" from which its fathers and sons were exempt, experiences sufficiently "signal, terrible, inspiring" that they give to that generation a character distinctive to itself.[28]

IV

Anyone undertaking a study of Soeharto faces a problem which Paul Preston identifies in his biography of General Franco. "The Caudillo," he wrote, "remains an enigma. Because of the distance that Franco so assiduously built around himself through deliberate obfuscations and silences, we can be sure only of his actions, and, provided they are judiciously evaluated, of the opinions and accounts of those who worked with him. This book is an attempt to observe him more accurately and in more detail than ever before .... [it is] a close study of the man."[29] This life-and-times study of Soeharto's early years draws partly on the rich veins of archival material that are to be found in the Netherlands, the United Kingdom, Japan, Australia, the United States and Indonesia itself. But even more importantly it draws on the "opinions and accounts" of the former president's military and civilian contemporaries, a large number of whom I had an opportunity to interview and whose evidence, it is hoped, has here been judiciously evaluated. That interviewing began during my two postings as a foreign correspondent in Jakarta, first in 1969–70, then in 1976–80. It gathered pace in 1981–82 when I was researching the book *Suharto and His Generals: Indonesian Military Politics 1975–1983*.[30] It slowed considerably but did not cease in the decade from 1983–93, when the Indonesian Government banned my entry into the country following the publication of that book (which was also banned) and a subsequent article I wrote in the *Sydney Morning Herald* about the financial affairs of the Soeharto family.[31] The bulk of the interviewing, however, was conducted between 1993–2019, when I was allowed back.

If Soeharto emerges from these pages not simply as the corrupt dictator of later popular shorthand but also as a polite, clever and capable young man who carries with him the baggage of a troubled childhood, who is quick to find his way in the world and quick to seize opportunities for self-advancement, who is hardened by parental neglect as well as by war and revolution, and plagued by corrosive greed, then it will be due in large part to this combination of oral history and archival research. Over the past five decades scores of people who knew Soeharto well or who worked with him have shared their recollections and observations of the man.[32] In multiple ways, they have thrown light on important events in Soeharto's life, for which, too often, written records are inadequate or simply non-existent.

Soeharto himself gave few interviews. Although I was to observe him up close many times—at his home, at the Merdeka Palace in Jakarta, on the golf course, in parliament, at military parades, at his ranch in the hills behind Bogor, at ceremonies in Bandung, Jatiluhur, Yogyakarta and Blitar—an interview had seemed quite out of reach when the editor of the Melbourne *Herald* demanded, on a Thursday morning in early November 1969, that I snare just such an on-the-record meeting in a matter of days to "round out" the package of feature-length profiles I had sent him after calling on five prominent Indonesians. As luck would have it, I managed to obtain the required Soeharto interview the following Sunday morning, after politely badgering several presidential aides. We sat under a giant *beringin* (banyan) tree in the lushly expansive grounds of the Bogor Palace, where the President had come to promote a humanitarian project and open a display of artifacts—grass skirts, penis gourds, spears, wooden shields—from West New Guinea, which he, as the military commander charged with preparing a massed assault on the territory, had done as much as anyone, save Sukarno, to wrest from the Dutch. During the interview he was affable but preternaturally cautious. On foreign policy, he expressed views of moderation and restraint, although he clearly retained a deep and abiding distrust of China, which, in his view, had encouraged a Communist lunge for power in 1965. He stressed the importance of regional harmony; he called for closer relations with

Australia. I have always suspected that Siti Hartinah Soeharto, whom I had interviewed at their home a few weeks earlier and who was with him at Bogor that day, helped persuade her husband to give the interview. At our initial meeting, the First Lady had asked how old I was and whether I was married; she had nodded approvingly when I said that I was about to get married. She had gone on to speak at some length about their own married life and their aspirations for their children, aspirations which were all quite conventional.

A month or two later I had another opportunity to observe Soeharto at close quarters, this time at the Rawamangun Golf Course in Jakarta. This was thanks to the late Burt Glinn, an American member of the Paris-based Magnum photo agency, whom I had met at the bull races on Madura, the island off the north coast of East Java. Burt had made his name ten years earlier with an arresting portfolio of black-and-white images of Fidel Castro's triumphant entry into Havana. Now, he had been retained to take a number of formal and informal shots of this ideologically very different Third World leader ahead of his call later that year on President Nixon at the White House. Soeharto, arriving in the front seat of an army jeep, had no objections to my coming along; and for the next couple of hours we accompanied the President and his golfing partner around the course. Security seemed minimal: a couple of slightly-built men with white shirts worn outside their trousers.

Afterwards, the President invited us back for afternoon tea at his house at No. 8 Jalan Cendana, a narrow, tree-lined street in Menteng, only 300 yards from my own house at Jalan Rasamala 4. Madam Soeharto greeted me warmly, reassured to learn that I was now married. Then, quite unexpectedly, the First Lady said she had something for me. An aide disappeared into a side room and reappeared with a bulky, gift-wrapped box. This, it turned out, was a wedding present. A photographer was summoned to record, there in the Soeharto family sitting room, an impromptu presentation ceremony. Later, I walked back to our house, my view of the broken concrete path and open manholes impeded by the package. Inside the box was a twenty-one-piece set of Yogyakarta silverware. There was, I was keenly aware, an ethical dilemma here: a journalist should not accept a gift from a foreign Head of State. But I could not see then, and cannot see now, how it would have been possible to refuse without causing acute embarrassment to the Indonesian President and his wife. There had been no forewarning, no chance to say quietly, via intermediaries, that while I was deeply touched by the kind thought, this might be a bit awkward. In the years since then, I have comforted myself with that and one other reflection. This, it appeared, was a personal initiative of Ibu Tien Soeharto. It was not as though the President of the Republic of Indonesia was seeking to suborn some stripling from the last major newspaper this side of the South Pole.

As I walked home, carrying this package, I passed, on the corner of Jalan Cendana and Jalan Jusuf Adiwinata, a small, graceful but slightly run-down Dutch villa. This was the home of Raden Darsono Notosudirdjo, a seventy-three-year-old Javanese *priyayi*, or member of the traditional bureaucratic class of Java. In 1917, Darsono had been an enthusiastic supporter of the Bolshevik Revolution. Three years later—and more than twelve months before Soeharto was born—he had co-founded, with Semaun, a railway union activist, the PKI, the first Communist Party in Asia, beating Mao Zedong and his Chinese Communist colleagues by a year and Ho Chi Minh and the Vietnamese (later the Indochinese) Communist Party by ten years. At the time that Soeharto, the Army he commanded and civilian vigilantes destroyed it, "down to the roots", in the blood-spattered months of late 1965 and early 1966, the PKI was the largest Communist Party in the world outside the Soviet Union and China.

Darsono, who had gone into political exile in January 1926 (he made his way to Moscow), who had resigned from the party in the late 1920s and who had long since abandoned his early Marxist beliefs, was a warm, wise, courtly and reflective man. My predecessor had taken me to meet him within days of my arrival in Indonesia and I had come to know him quite well. Every week or two I would drop in at his house, bringing a pile of foreign newspapers and magazines, which were not widely available then and which he read avidly. Sitting out on his marble-floored verandah in the late afternoon, drinking thick Javanese *kopi tubruk*, listening to his accounts of the great political struggles of the twenties—the railway strike and the pawnbroker's strike; the time he and others spent in Dutch jails; the internal party squabbles; listening to his recollections of Trotsky's strong attack on Stalin at a Comintern meeting in Moscow; listening to what he himself had said to Stalin and why he became disenchanted with the Soviet leader; listening to his reminiscences about former revolutionaries and colleagues, whose names, like his, had long been bywords in modern Indonesian history (Tan Malaka and Alimin, Musso and D.N. Aidit), listening to him speak about his years abroad

("I have never seen Sumatra, Bali, Kalimantan but I have seen Vladivostok, Moscow, Berlin, The Hague")—it was impossible not to catch something of the spirit and excitement, the sense of hope and expectation, that had fired the imagination of young Communists and revolutionary socialists during the early years of Indonesia's fight for independence.

And how extraordinary, I always thought as I passed this house or when I caught up with Darsono, on one occasion in the company of Semaun, who had also returned from Moscow, how bizarre, that the man who had co-founded this party and the man who had destroyed it, should be living here only two or three doors from one another, behind the barbed wire street barricades that were dragged into place at dusk each day by heavily-armed members of the presidential guard. At the end of my first posting in Indonesia, Darsono gave me a small farewell present—a glazed plate with a traditional Chinese painting of peony flowers and a small bird, accompanied by a flourish of Chinese calligraphy conveying wishes for good luck and long life. The plate, which was mounted on a wire frame, stands to this day on a shelf in my sitting room. When Darsono died in 1976, the Indonesian Government—Soeharto's Government—offered his family the honour of burial in a heroes cemetery.[33] Needless to say, there had been no such honours in 1965–66 for those who had continued to believe in the party. Their bodies had been dumped in unmarked graves or cast into rivers and left to float downstream.

By the time I began this project I was not well placed to seek further interviews with Soeharto or indeed members of his family. They had taken exception to the 1986 *Sydney Morning Herald* article. This was understandable but unfortunate. I like to think that, had things been different, Soeharto would have enjoyed revisiting many of the matters canvassed in this book and would have been prepared to give his own version of them, a version which, I suspect, would have thrown additional light on subjects not adequately addressed in his rather self-serving "autobiography." That said, he might not have welcomed some of the judgments reached in this book.

The interview material gathered in the course of this project allows us, I believe, to get closer to the inner man than has hitherto been possible. It allows us to see how Soeharto came to be as he was. Unlike the flamboyant and charismatic Sukarno, who lived his life so publicly, captivating mass audiences with his speeches, lingering over breakfast each morning on a terrace at the back of the palace, with cabinet ministers, army officers,

Communist Party leaders, diplomats, hangers-on and assorted young women drifting in and out, Soeharto was a socially reticent man who cloaked his feelings behind a deceptively serene smile, although he, too, had endless meetings with political, religious, military and social leaders, seeking to bend them to his will, as had Sukarno before him. In the words of Roeslan Abdulgani, a close political associate of Indonesia's first president and who, being infinitely adaptable, went on to serve the man who banished Sukarno to soul-destroying house arrest where a Military Police general denied him the medicines he urgently needed, Sukarno was an open book, Soeharto a closed book. And yet it is precisely this inner man which is so important and which needs to be unearthed.

These volumes show how Soeharto's personality and character developed and changed over the years; they show how he thought and acted. In the process, a darker picture emerges. We see a man who, even in his earlier years, was not only more ruthless and more calculating than hitherto imagined but greedier too, caring deeply about the welfare of his family and his subordinates and willing to place great trust in his close associates, but watchful, resentful and vindictive, sensitive to slights and always nursing grudges.

In his three-volume work *The Age of Roosevelt, Volume I: The Crisis of the Old Order, 1919–1933,* Arthur M. Schlesinger, Jr. makes the point that the reputation of a commanding figure is often at its lowest in the period ten to twenty years after death. "We are always," he writes, "in a zone of imperfect visibility so far as the history just over our shoulder is concerned [....] There are, however, compensating advantages in writing so soon—in particular, the opportunity to consult those who took part in great events and thus to rescue information which might otherwise elude the written record."[34] This reminder is especially apt in the case of Indonesia where, it often seems, too little is written down and too many "rescue missions" need to be mounted. Indeed, the problem is so great that the author who comes late to a study of the Indonesian independence struggle can often feel as if he or she is engaged in a race against time, hoping to meet as many people as possible while they, and the author, are still on deck. I count myself extremely fortunate that so many of those who played a part, large or small, in the momentous events leading up to Indonesia's Proclamation of Independence and its emergence as an independent Republic have been available, and willing, to spend valuable time giving their accounts of those events. An historian studying the

American Revolution cannot hope, of course, to meet George Washington or Thomas Jefferson. In Indonesia it was possible, when I first lived in Jakarta, and for many years thereafter, to call on any number of men and women who had played a role in the birth of that nation.

While researching this book I had an opportunity to visit many of the places in Java and the Outer Islands where Soeharto lived, studied, worked or fought—Kemusu, Yogyakarta, Solo, Magelang, Malang, Bogor, Glagah, Jakarta, Ambarawa, Banyubiru, Semarang, Makassar and Ambon—as well as the Soeharto family mausoleum, the Astana Giri Bangun, which the President built on a sacred hillside set aside for the tombs of the Mangkunegaran royal family, the smaller of the two Solonese courts. In doing so, it was possible to retrace his footsteps, sometimes literally as well as figuratively.

"If you would like to understand this power structure now," the late Lieutenant General G.P.H. Djatikusumo, a prince of the dominant royal court of Solo, liked to say when people asked him about Indonesian politics in the early 1980s, "you cannot afford not to study the anatomy of the Peta," the Japanese-sponsored Indonesian defence force.[35] If you would like to understand something about modern Indonesia more broadly, one might add, it is necessary to study Soeharto.

Soeharto Family Tree

(Simplified)

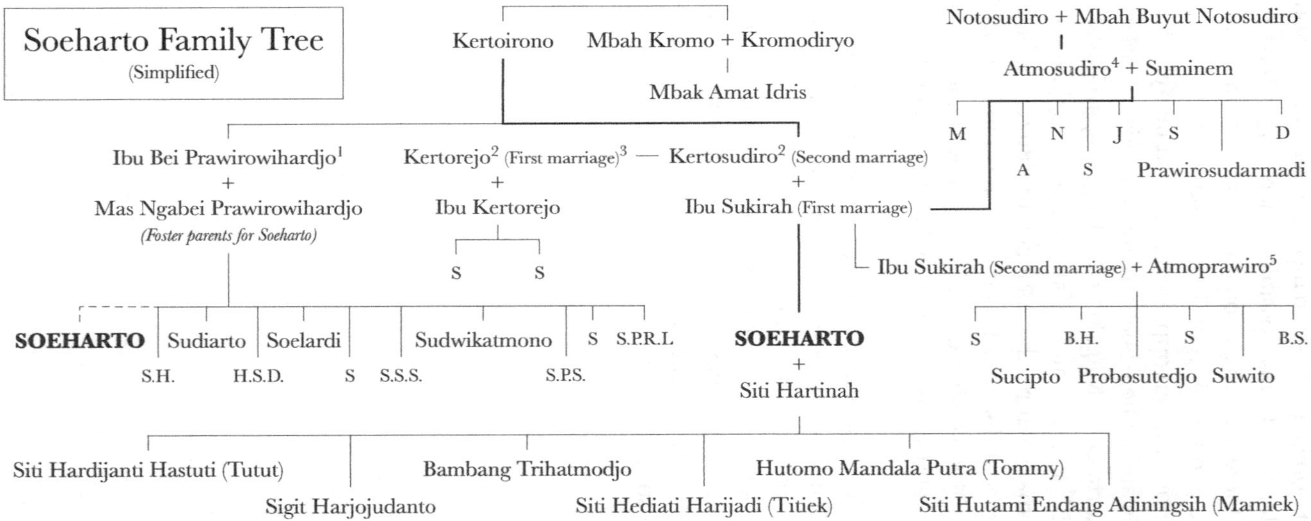

Source: Soeharto, *Otobiografi*; Probosutedjo, *Saya dan Mas Harto*; *Silsilah Presiden Soeharto* (Sekneg); Angus McIntyre, *The Indonesian Presidency* and O. G. Roeder, *Anak Desa*.

1. Ibu Prawirowihardjo and Prawirowihardjo cared for Soeharto for several years. Their own children's full names were Ny. Sukatinah Hardjoso, Sudiarto, Ny. H. Suliatun Dwidjokartono, Soelardi, Sudarsono, Ny. Sri Sudarni Sarbini, Sudwikatmono, Ny. Sri Peni Sukarno, Sujono and Ny. Sri Purwaningsih Rusman Laman.

2. Soeharto's father changed his name several times. He was known as Panjang aka Kertorejo/Kertosudiro/Notokarijo. Notokarijo is the name he took for his third marriage. Soeharto listed his half-siblings from this union as Ny. Moersiati Harsono, Santoso, Ny. Sutinah Djoehron Sutiwibowo and Ny. Martini Tubagus Sulaeman.

3. Soeharto's half-siblings from his father's first marriage were Ny. Sastroharyono and Sumowiyatmo.

4. Soeharto's mother's siblings were, according to Soeharto, Mangkusudiro, Ny. Atmowiharjo, Notosuparto, Ny. Suwarso, Ny. Jayengsudiro, Sumadi, Prawirosudarmadi and Ny. Dipodiwarno. According to his half-brother Probosutedjo, the siblings were Dasuki (Mangkusudiro), Supilah (Sastroharjo), Supardi (Notosuparto), Sukarno (Jayengsudiro), Sumadi, Sutimah (Warsosudiro), Sudarmadi (Prawiro Sudarmadi) and Sukinah (Dipodiwarno).

5. Soeharto's half-siblings from his mother's second marriage were, according to Soeharto, Sukiyem, Sucipto, Ny. Basirah Harjowijatmo, Probosutedjo, Ny. Suminah, Suwito and Ny. Bries Suhardjo. According to Probosutedjo, the siblings were: Sukiyem, Sucipto, Basirah, Suprobo (Probosutedjo), Ny. Suminah, Suwito and Ny. Noek Bresinah.

1

"The Sultan came to me and asked about that family tree"

In later life, when he ruled so watchfully over Indonesia, President Soeharto was wont to make two observations about his early childhood. The first was that he was an authentic product of rural Java and that the nine years he spent in the impoverished hamlet of Kemusu, six miles west of the court city of Yogyakarta, had left him with an abiding interest in agriculture. The second was that his childhood had been a time of acute deprivation, both material and emotional, owing to the fact that his mother abandoned him when he was less than six weeks old and that he was shunted thereafter from one family to another, feeling for much of the time neglected and rejected. As a child, he wrote many years later, "I had to endure such suffering which perhaps others could not imagine."[1] As a soldier and national leader, Soeharto was frequently devious and duplicitous, given to falsehoods and mendacity, as leaders so often are. But there has never been any reason to doubt the veracity of the two claims he made about his early life in rural Java. Those years were to shape him in profound ways. They left an indelible imprint not just on the man but also on his presidency, which was to stretch over three remarkable decades.

II

Kemusu stood on a low plateau of land six feet above the surrounding rice fields, an island in a flat and watery realm, one of several thousand such islands scattered across the fertile plains of Central Java, a region of such abundance that it had sustained a succession of powerful kingdoms, first Hindu-Buddhist, then Islamic, before the Dutch gained full control of Java in the early nineteenth century.[2] It was a world of simple houses and markets, redolent of humid, red-brown earth. The rice fields, which were divided into a patchwork of holdings, some no larger than a tennis court, were watered by an irrigation system of such complexity and ingenuity that the fertile soil brought forth two crops a year.

In December, when the West Monsoon arrived, sweeping down from the Asian land mass and bolstered by winds from the Indian Ocean, immense clouds gathered over Java, colliding violently in the afternoon sky, bringing darkness and driving rain, tearing at the palm trees and the banana fronds, a reminder of how, in Indonesia, the forces of nature manifest themselves in sometimes destructive ways. The deluge would last for an hour or so, punctuated by the reverberations of tropical thunder and by flashes of lightning, after which there was an extraordinary clarity in the air and a welcome respite from the enervating heat. This season of rain continued until February, the wettest month, filling the dams and flooding the rice fields.

During the planting season, the fields were the scene of unremitting industry, the men ploughing behind water buffalos, or weeding or levelling saturated mud with hoes and bamboo poles, preparing the soil for the new crop, the women working ankle-deep in adjoining plots, bent double, transplanting rice seedlings into the flooded fields, the seedlings all in perfect rows, so that the entire rice plain was soon cloaked in green. Later, when the crop was ready for harvest, the fields teemed once more with humanity, the women working under a sweltering sun, cutting, carrying and threshing the rice, by now ripened to a vibrant gold. After a short break, they would plant the next crop. In June, when the East Monsoon arrived, carrying air heated over the baking deserts of Central Australia and moisture sucked up from the Arafura Sea, there was another season of rain, albeit a much weaker one, which continued until August, when the winds began to weaken. In the dry season, the soil would be so parched and deeply cracked that it took an effort of will to believe that the fields would become, with the return of the drenching West Monsoon, once more flooded and succulently green.*

The hamlet was a place of darker greens, the houses standing in perpetual shade, sheltered under a dense canopy of coconut palms and surrounded by banana fronds, mango trees and ripening jackfruit. In the midst of this greenery there was a small brick Muslim prayer house (*langgar*) but not, as yet, a mosque of any kind, quite unlike the situation today, when mosques have appeared in most of the larger hamlets, each surmounted by a dazzling silver dome and a crescent moon of hammered tin. The prayer house ministered to the needs of a small minority of villagers—and Soeharto's father was not among them—who were pious rather than simply nominal Muslims. During the day the village was quiet, almost soporific, save for the rustling of birds high up in the mango trees and the occasional crowing of a rooster.

The house in which Soeharto was born was on the southern side of the village, close to a small private graveyard. Unlike the graveyard, which is still there, walled and damp, the house is gone. Soeharto pulled it down when he came into money and put up a large brick building with parking for a fleet of cars.† The original house, which would have been enlarged and improved when his father became a hamlet official, with villagers under an obligation to help, is likely to have been a rectangular structure of about four by five metres, with a frame of wooden pillars and crossbeams, and walls made from *gedék* (panels of woven or plaited bamboo).[3] Although such houses traditionally have no windows, light is able to enter through gaps in the upper part of the sidewalls. The house—and most of the others in the hamlet—had a thatch roof made from overlapping layers of coconut leaves, although by the early twenties some houses were tiled.[4] The substitution of tiles for thatch was promoted by a Dutch campaign to eradicate bubonic plague, which had been introduced to Java in 1910 by rats in a shipment of Burmese rice. The tiles, made locally from light red soils and delivered by ox-cart, had a shiny patina if wood had been used to fire the kiln, but were often black if rice husks had been used as

* In recent years the regularity of the rainy season has become less evident.

† This was on a par with—but not as regrettable as—President Sukarno's decision to demolish the Jakarta villa in which he was living in 1945 and from the verandah of which he proclaimed Indonesia's independence. The historic house was replaced by a large and unlovely office block.

fuel. If there was foliage above a house, pale tiles quickly became black as well. The floor is likely to have been of packed earth, dry and well swept. The furniture would have been basic: a table, some chairs, one or two simple beds. There was a well at the side and a small garden planted with corn, onions, chilli and cooking spices. No grass or shrubs grew in the area around the house, the Javanese having an abiding fear of snakes.

From the house you could hear the sound of unseen water, rushing along an irrigation ditch at the edge of the village. You could also hear, twice a day, the express trains which sped by on a narrow-gauge track about five hundred yards away, travelling back and forth along the length of Java, linking Batavia (later renamed Jakarta), the thriving commercial centre on the northwest coast, with Surabaya, the great port city 530 miles away at the eastern end of the island. The train, with its powerful Hartmann-Chemnitz coal-burning steam locomotive and its wailing siren, was a reminder, here among the volcanoes and the palm trees of Central Java, of the forces that were transforming the Netherlands East Indies, shaking an old society loose from its moorings.[5] It provided one of the fastest narrow-gauge services in the world.

The child was born, the official histories record, on 8 June 1921, during the early part of the East Monsoon, when the wind was blowing from Australia, although no one in the family seems to have been quite sure of the day or even the month.[6] His father decided to call him Soeharto, a name created from the Sanskrit-derived prefix *soe*, which means good, much, right or very, and *harto*, which means money, property, riches or treasure. In later years, Soeharto's colleagues and critics, some of them four-star generals, were to cover their mouths with one hand and observe with sly disapprobation that the child had been aptly named: Soeharto was to have a remarkable fixation on wealth and, when eventually he became President, he and his family were to accumulate riches on a prodigious scale, disregarding all proprieties.

Names were important to Soeharto's father. He had started out in life, some sources contend, as Wagiyo, although the villagers often called him Panjang, the respectful high Javanese (*kromo*) version of the everyday *dowo*, meaning long, perhaps because he was long-legged, but changed his name each time he married, a common practice in Java, where a change in circumstances is often accompanied by a change in name. And, as he was to marry three times, he was to have no fewer than four names in all, not counting his nickname. At the time of his first marriage, he adopted the name Kertorejo, which he created by taking the first part of his father's name and the second part of his father-in-law's name.[7] Soeharto has given more than one version of what happened to that marriage. According to an account published in 1976 and based on material Soeharto himself supplied, it did not last long because after the birth of two children, a son and a daughter, Kertorejo separated from his wife. Then, finding that he could not stand living alone without a wife, he remarried.[8] By 1989, when Soeharto's autobiography appeared, the story had changed somewhat. Kertorejo had only remarried, he now claimed, after his first wife died. Whatever the truth of the matter, Kertorejo took as his second wife a village girl called Sukirah, changing his name to Kertosudiro, which is how he will be referred to in these pages. This marriage, which was brief and tempestuous, leaving a residue of bitterness on both sides, resulted in the birth of the child he named Soeharto. It was followed by a third marriage, and yet another name change.[9] The third marriage produced four more children, which meant that Soeharto was to have six half-brothers and sisters on his father's side.[10]

Kertosudiro was an *ulu-ulu*, an official responsible for the equitable distribution of irrigation water in the hamlet. Marine sediment, topped up with frequent deposits of volcanic ash, has made much of lowland Java extraordinarily fertile. But water has always been the great productivity multiplier, and as early as the seventh century AD the astute management of Java's water resources was bringing forth abundant rice surpluses. Over the centuries, the Javanese developed an intensive irrigation system on this land, a world of ditches and sluices, dams and aqueducts, dykes and flooded rice terraces, with water being channelled, in precisely determined quantities, to a succession of fields, descending, almost imperceptibly in most cases, from one terrace to another but sometimes actually carried to higher fields by means of scoops and waterwheels and ingenious bamboo pipes that harnessed the flow of fast-running streams and sent them "uphill." Water was carried across ravines in aqueducts supported on bamboo posts. The Dutch, no strangers themselves to hydraulic preoccupations and with access to cement, augmented all this by damming rivers and building a major network of secondary and tertiary canals, complete with aqueducts, siphons and sluices. The result is an extraordinarily effective ecosystem, one in which water brings nutrients onto the irrigated rice terrace (*sawah*), replacing those drawn from the soil.

The supply and control of water, the American anthropologist Clifford Geertz has observed, is the key factor in wet-rice cultivation, more important than the type of soil, and the regulation of water in a terrace is a matter "of some delicacy".[11] It requires skill in knowing how much water to allocate (excessive flooding can be as great a threat as insufficient inundation), careful attention to drainage and astute timing. Ideally, rice seedlings are planted in a well-soaked field with little standing water, after which the depth of the water is increased gradually up to six to twelve inches as the plant grows and flowers, at which time the water is gradually drawn off, until the field is dry for harvest. The water should not be allowed to stagnate, but kept moving gently over the terrace to aerate the soil. Periodic draining is necessary for weeding and fertilization. When many small plots are drawing water from one source and when double cropping exists, the distribution of water becomes even more complex. Although Kertosudiro was probably illiterate (as were 96 per cent of the people in rural Yogyakarta at that time), that was no drawback.[12] Regulating water did not depend upon written records; it was done by common agreement and discussion.

Neither the Kemusu headman nor his various assistants, of whom there might have been a dozen or more, received a salary as such. However, each was allotted some of the best and most productive village "office land" (*tanah bengkok*) for the term of his appointment. According to Soeharto, Kertosudiro owned no land himself but was allocated about one hectare of village land, which he worked with a hoe, not having enough money for a water buffalo.[13] The implication is that the family was not at all well off. Here, as is often the case, Soeharto is being disingenuous. He does not explain how it was that Kertosudiro, ostensibly a landless peasant, was appointed *ulu-ulu*. As a rule, a man would not be considered for such a position unless he had some standing in the village; and by village tradition you did not have standing unless you owned some land; if you were landless, you were a nobody and your chances of being chosen as *ulu-ulu* very remote. Be that as it may, as *ulu-ulu* Kertosudiro would have been a man of some prestige in the hamlet, with a voice in village affairs; villagers would have needed to stay on good terms with him.[14]

It is unlikely that Kertosudiro ploughed or planted or harvested himself. After the dry season, the land would have been impossibly hard and not amenable to hoeing. It may be true that he did not own a water buffalo. But on Java there were—and still are—professional ploughmen who undertake such work, using their own oxen or water buffalo, and he is likely to have hired such a team. For the other work, he is likely to have drawn on reciprocal village labour that was due to him by virtue of his position as *ulu-ulu*. He would have benefited, too, from the other traditional duties and services owed to him by the villagers, who had to pay village officials a fixed amount of rice per year, offer them food at celebrations and work in their households for a certain amount of time.[15]

Nor would a man with one hectare of irrigated land (which probably consisted of three or four separate parcels, rather than a single holding) have been seen in the village as poor. On the contrary, that hectare would have put him in the top economic group in Kemusu, probably the top 10 per cent in terms of income.[16] In the 1920s, many farmers did not own much land at all, apart from small house gardens. A survey taken in Java in 1903 showed that 16 per cent of holdings were under 0.18 ha, 33 per cent under 0.35 ha and 47 per cent under 0.53 ha. Fifty-five years later, when the population of Java had doubled, some 70 per cent of farmers cultivated less than half a hectare.* Under the pressure of increasing numbers and limited resources, Geertz argued in 1963, Javanese village society did not bifurcate into a group of large landlords and a group of oppressed near-serfs but divided the economic pie into ever more minute pieces in what he dubbed "shared poverty". "Rather than haves and have-nots, there were, in the delicately muted vernacular of peasant life, only *tjukupans* and *kekurangans*—"just enoughs" and "not quite enoughs."[17] Later scholars have questioned the assertion that economic differences were muted. Anne Booth, an economic historian who has studied social stratification in late colonial Indonesia, believes that Geertz was rather inclined to downplay the economic and social differences in rural Java when he wrote his 1963 study, although she allows that he worked in East Java where things may have been different.[18]

In the twenties, one hectare might have yielded 2.5 tons of rice from the first wet season crop and two tons from the second.† That was enough

* By regional standards, these were postage-stamp plots.

† Today, that same hectare might produce ten tons of rice a year, or more than twice the yield in the inter-war years. The increase stems partly from the Soeharto government's decision in the late sixties to improve the irrigation and transport systems, and allow the price of rice to increase to something approaching its market value, and partly to the introduction of high-yielding varieties of "miracle" rice (which allow farmers to plant up to three crops a year), chemical fertilisers and pesticides, all of which, by a stroke of great providence, became available during Soeharto's presidency, allowing him to promote the goal of rice self-sufficiency. That said, much still depends of the inherent fertility of the soil, which in the Kemusu area is good. These days, a man with one hectare of irrigated land would be considered extremely well off by village standards.

to feed a family for a year with a small surplus left over for sale, allowing for the purchase of salt and other necessities.[19] It may be wrong to make too much of plot size distinctions, however. At that time, virtually all Javanese in rural areas were miserably poor. And because Kertosudiro's hectare was something he enjoyed by virtue of his office, not something he owned, he could not pass it on to his children; Soeharto and his siblings would have no inheritance.

The problem for many peasant farmers in a wide crescent of land on the western flank of the city of Yogyakarta—although not necessarily in Kemusu—was that the Dutch colonial authorities were not content to let well enough alone.[20] They were in the East Indies for commercial gain and they needed access to much of this fertile, well-flooded tract of land—and similar tracts in East Java—to plant sugar, a commodity which brought them immense profits in the years before the Great Depression of 1929, when the market collapsed.[21] Javanese villagers were obliged to plant sugar on their land as and when it suited the Dutch, who had the sugar industry under tight control, their agents moving from one village to another, always demanding the best land, always knowing exactly how far they could promote their interests without quite driving the landowners beyond the point of despair.

For many years Soeharto was remarkably unforthcoming about his father. All he ever said in his published recollections was that his father had taken his official duties seriously, had married three times, had changed his name three times, had had seven children, had dressed in the traditional Javanese manner, wearing a folded *batik* headdress (*blangkon*), a long-sleeve, embroidered jacket (*surjan*) and a tubular skirt (*kain*), and that he had dropped out of Soeharto's life for long periods of time, all but abandoning the boy, only to reappear, with Dickensian unpredictability, at critical moments, steering him towards relatives who could give him a better chance in life.

In 1974, while outlining his family history, Soeharto went out of his way to stress that his father, who died in 1951, enjoyed seeing his first grandchild, Tutut, who was born in 1949. In a caption in his autobiography, he referred to his "beloved father", Kertosudiro. There is no suggestion anywhere else in the book, however, that there was any particular warmth in the relationship between father and son and little reason in the circumstances why there should have been. Indeed, Soeharto seems to have become quite critical of his father as he grew older. At the age of eighty-six, he would remember Kertosudiro not as the wise and dutiful father of earlier accounts but as a man who spent his free time gambling and smoking.[22] Kertosudiro needed so much money to support these habits, it was now alleged, that Sukirah was forced to sell her jewellery, becoming increasingly frustrated and eventually returning to live with her parents.

For many years Soeharto was almost equally unforthcoming about his mother, who is said to have been sixteen and "known for her beauty" when she met Kertosudiro.[23] (Sukirah may, in fact, have been younger than that. Village girls in Java usually married between the ages of twelve and fifteen.[24]) There was almost nothing about her in the semi-authorized 1969 biography of the President, in which the German author refers to her not as Sukirah but as Fatimah.[25] Later, it is true, Soeharto did provide a few titbits of information about his mother. He offered no fond recollections of the time he spent in her company, however, and the reader of his autobiography is left with a sense that he felt no more attachment to her than he did to his father. Indeed, he seems to have been only too happy to be away from her. In one place in the book he recalls how, as a child, he was distressed at having been sent back to live with his mother. That said, there were occasional intimations of filial piety. In 1975, the Armed Forces newspaper reported that Soeharto made a point of returning to Central Java every year in the month of Ruah in the Javanese/Islamic calendar to scatter flowers on his parents' graves.[26] In 2007, a sympathetic biographer painted a more positive picture of the relationship between mother and son. This was based not on anything Soeharto said, however, but on a reading of his notoriously enigmatic smile, bolstered by supposition and speculation. "There was always a twinkle of joy and a radiance in Pak Harto's face whenever I referred to Ibu Sukirah," she wrote.* "Pak Harto must have been proud of her and must have loved her dearly."[27]

Sukirah was the second of nine children of a man named Atmosudiro, a relatively well-off farmer in the northern part of the hamlet, and it is unlikely that her material circumstances changed greatly at the time of her marriage to Soeharto's father, which appears to have taken place in the second half of 1920. Brief as it was to be, their time together would

* *Pak*, an abbreviation of *bapak* (father), can be used as a form of address to an older man or as a title conveying respect. *Ibu* (mother) is used as a form of address to an older woman or one of high standing.

have been marked by a number of traditional village ceremonies. In 1920, with Java riding the wave of the post-war economic boom, it is quite likely that the wedding of the irrigation official of Kemusu and the daughter of a reasonably well-to-do farmer was celebrated by an elaborate *slametan*, a ceremony marked by feasting and entertainment, at which benign spirits are invoked and harmful spirits propitiated.[28]

We can also safely assume that another kind of *slametan*, this one known as a *tingkepan*, would have been held to mark the seventh month of Sukirah's pregnancy. If so, it is likely to have followed a fairly well-established format. A dish of rice would have been made available to each guest, with white rice on top and yellow underneath, the white rice symbolizing purity, the yellow love. There would also have been rice mixed with grated coconut and a whole stuffed chicken, to honour the Prophet Mohammad and bring well-being to the guests and the unborn baby. Usually too, as Geertz has noted, an offering would be made to *Dewi Pertimah*, or "The Hindu Goddess, Fatimah—i.e., Mohammad's daughter with a Hindu title!"[29] Nine round balls of rice would symbolize the so-called Nine Saints (*Wali Sanga*), religious teachers who were among the earliest proselytizers of Islam in Java in the 1400s and 1500s. As Geertz writes, what is immediately striking about such ceremonies is "the rich mixture of Islamic, Hindu-Buddhist, and native spirits, deities, and culture heroes into one grand syncretism. Hindu goddesses rub elbows with Islamic prophets and both of these with local *danyangs* [guardian spirits]; and there is little sign that any of them are surprised at the others' presence."[30] At the *tingkepan*, Sukirah would have put on a *kain* made of a special type of heavy cotton which would not fade and which symbolized "the lasting relationship between the mother and the child throughout life, their life-long inseparability."

Later, when the child was born, a village midwife, or *dukun bayi*, who was in this case the baby's great-aunt, would have cut the umbilical cord with a bamboo knife, rubbed turmeric into the wound and tied the cord. The baby, and then the mother, would have been washed as the midwife chanted spells to ensure their well-being. Finally, the *dukun* would have placed the baby on a low table and slapped the table three times "to startle the baby so that he will be accustomed to such surprises and less likely to be severely startled later in life."[31]

This, then, was the world into which Soeharto was born, a world which was on the surface Islamic, and in which indeed most villages and towns had strong pockets of devout Muslims, who were known as *santri*, but a world still profoundly influenced by traditions and beliefs dating from Java's pre-Islamic past. It was, in short, a world with many religious and cultural cross currents. Soeharto, like most Javanese, was to have little difficulty adjusting to these sometimes contradictory elements.

But for all the care taken to appease the spirits, it was not, for Soeharto's parents, an especially happy world. Their married life, as Soeharto himself admitted, "was not harmonious and they were divorced after I was born."[32] Divorce was not uncommon in Java; at around this time, the ratio of divorces to marriages was over 50 per cent.[33] Not long after she gave birth, Sukirah began to behave in a manner which suggested that she was either emotionally disturbed or suffering from postnatal depression, perhaps even postnatal psychosis. At a press conference he called in 1974 to reject a claim that he was of aristocratic descent, Soeharto said that before he was forty days old his mother wandered off, perhaps because of a family quarrel.[34] No one knew where she had gone. The Javanese term for this was *ngebleng*. Probosutedjo, one of seven children from Sukirah's second marriage, "confirmed" the story. Sukirah had hidden herself away in a room within the upper roof of a local house and had remained there for a week.[35] When eventually found, she was close to exhaustion. She had had nothing to eat or drink for a long time and was unable to breastfeed her child.[36]

At the *tingkepan*, Sukirah had taken part in a ceremony symbolizing the life-long inseparability between mother and child. In the event, mother and child were separated soon after Soeharto's birth. At what appears to have been a time of grave concern for his mother's mental equilibrium, the baby was placed in the care of his great-aunt, Mbah Kromodiryo, the midwife who had delivered him. She was a younger sister of his paternal grandfather.[37] It was the beginning of what was to be a deeply disrupted childhood.[38] Soeharto was to remain with Mbah Kromo, as she was commonly known, for the next four years, at which time his mother, who had by then remarried, came and took him back. Mother and son would spend only five of his first fourteen years living under the same roof, however.

Soeharto never supplied any explanation for the alleged quarrel that sent his mother into hiding. But according to a note on his family tree, when Soeharto was forty days old his father divorced his mother.[39] If that is true it would indicate that the divorce took place at about the time Sukirah went into seclusion and a week before Soeharto was handed over to his great-aunt. Others have claimed less plausibly that Kertosudiro divorced his wife before the child was born.[40] What had happened? Some prominent Javanese, a number of whom had a long and close association with Soeharto, were of the view that the marriage had become increasingly unstable in the months before Soeharto's birth, and had descended into acrimony and recrimination. While that was broadly in accord with Soeharto's own observation that his parents' married life was not harmonious, they claimed there was more to the story than this. The reason for this disharmony, they maintained, was that Soeharto's "real" father was a senior member of the Yogyakarta court, perhaps even the Sultan himself. This man had had a dalliance with the young woman before her marriage and, on discovering she was pregnant, had passed her on to someone else, a common practice in the courts of Central Java.[41] Angry and humiliated when he discovered the truth, Kertosudiro is said to have turned against his wife, their final quarrel driving her into hiding.[42]

Soeharto was not illegitimate—a child born in wedlock is not illegitimate, at least in a modern legal sense. What is more, the claim that he had royal blood flowing through his veins may be entirely spurious. Many members of the Indonesian elite have an insatiable appetite for rumour and gossip, the more elaborate and implausible the better. Stories of this kind are always in circulation, linked in some cases to extraordinary conspiracy theories. President Sukarno had not been exempt from such claims. He was variously said to have been the illegitimate son of a Dutch coffee planter who farmed him out to a lowly schoolteacher and his wife; the illegitimate son of a Eurasian plantation overseer, or, more grandly, the son of the flamboyant Sunan Pakubuwono X (r. 1893–1939), head of the principal royal house in Surakarta (Solo).[43] In the case of Sukarno, as in the case of Soeharto, it was said that the child's ostensible father could not have paid for his education and that he must therefore have been supported by a well-to-do patron.

There are, it is true, aspects of Soeharto's claim to humble beginnings that invite scepticism. As the Australian historian R.E. Elson notes in his political biography of Soeharto, "the picture of shadowy parents, an obviously distraught mother, a father who disappears almost immediately after Soeharto's birth but who nonetheless keeps a watching brief on his progress, is certainly in accord with the notion that Soeharto was an illegitimate child."[44] Elson concludes that Soeharto was probably the illegitimate son of a well-placed villager or someone of means who might have come in continuing contact with villagers. It is very unlikely, in his view, that Soeharto was related to anyone with royal blood.

It is all but impossible, a century later, to establish the veracity of any claim about Soeharto's parentage, still less that he was of royal descent, a claim that he was to reject, angrily and publicly, in 1974. But the claims were to be made, on and off, over many decades and while they may be without foundation, they cannot be dismissed out of hand. In his autobiography, Soeharto includes the tantalizing observation that his mother and her grandfather, Notosudiro, had a "working relationship" with an official of the court of Yogyakarta.[45] The alleged connection is intriguing. By his own account, other village children taunted him with suggestions there was something improper in his family's relationship with the palace. In his autobiography, Soeharto wrote, "I have a vivid recollection of an ugly-looking buck-toothed boy who used to ridicule me.... Although we played marbles together, he was much older. He would incite other friends to call me *Den bagus tahi mabul (tahi kering)*."[46] In the English-language version of the autobiography, this is described as "rude and scornful phrase meaning 'a dirty son of the nobility.'" A more direct translation might be "a useless shit son of the nobility." *Den bagus* is short for *Raden Bagus*, a Javanese nobility title for men, slightly higher than Raden. The term can be used, in the sense of "sir", for a person in a village who has some money or education. *Tahi kering* is dried excrement. The passage seems to say that he was called "*Den*" because there was a family-like relationship with someone in the Kraton (Royal Palace). *Den* or *Gus* can be used to mean something like "young master."[47] Notosudiro and Ibu Sukirah were called *Den*, Soeharto writes, because of their working relationship with a *sentono* [family member of the sultan, of a low rank] who worked as a supervisor in the Kraton.* "That was why I was often called *Den*, to which I always objected. That annoyed me. I wondered what their real idea was of calling me *Den*. Was it to insult me or were they just teasing? At the time I was only eight. I thought the boy might be jealous. Perhaps he thought I was really only

* *Sentono*, or more correctly *sentana*, can be used to describe a child adopted by parents of higher status. In this context it may mean servant.

the son of a poor family, so why should I be called *Den*? I felt troubled. Coming from a poor home, I still had to endure such taunts. But I never told anyone about this."

This kind of taunting seems to be an insult directed against someone for whom some other person assigns status. It is as if the older boy were saying, "Some people think you are a *den bagus*, but actually you are a jumped-up kid and a bundle of shit!" One should not make too much of the insult; boys everywhere enjoy teasing and tormenting each other.

III

The suggestion that Soeharto was a son of the nobility was made not only by children in pre-war Kemusu. It was to surface in the early years of Soeharto's presidency and would be given a certain amount of credence, not least in court circles in Yogyakarta.* Several versions of the story were in circulation. According to the most frequently cited account, Soeharto was the illegitimate son of Raden Rio Padmodipuro, a young Javanese aristocrat.[48] Raden Rio was descended from Sultan Hamengku Buwono II, the ill-fated son of one of the most powerful and successful Central Java monarchs since the great days of the Mataram dynasty, which dominated central and eastern Java between 1582 and 1755 and which was eclipsed by the Dutch only in 1830.[49] In 1920, Raden Rio was serving as an apprentice at the Kraton in Yogyakarta, drawing a nominal salary but supporting himself by running a business in which women produced stamp-*batik* (*batik cap*) decorated with traditional motifs, applying wax to the cloth with metal stamps and dipping the material into vats of aniline dye.[50] Before her marriage, it has been claimed, Soeharto's mother worked in Klaten, twenty miles northeast of Yogyakarta, for an ethnic Chinese businessman who supplied textiles and wax to Raden Rio, who was then in his early twenties. According to court gossip, Sukirah caught Raden Rio's eye while she was employed in his *batik* enterprise—an attractive girl of fifteen or sixteen, dressed in a tightly-wrapped breast cloth (*kemben*) and bending

* It is not uncommon for a parvenu to lay claim to royal antecedents in an attempt to boost his or her legitimacy, only to have those claims dismissed out of hand by the aristocracy. In this case, more than a few members of the Javanese nobility were willing to acknowledge Soeharto as their own—or at least partly their own. It was Soeharto who emphatically rejected any such link.

over a vat of dye.[51] Not long afterwards, it is claimed, Sukirah became pregnant.

In later years, it would become a staple of court gossip that one of four men—the young but well-born Raden Rio; the ethnic Chinese merchant in Klaten; the elderly Sultan Hamengku Buwono VII (r. 1877–1921), to whom she may have been presented by Raden Rio, or the Crown Prince who became Hamengku Buwono VIII (r. 1921–1939)—was the real father of her child.[52] Was Soeharto the illegitimate son of Raden Rio? Some prominent Indonesians professed to believe that he was. One of them was Haryasudirja, the prince from the Pakualaman court. As we have seen, Haryasudirja had enjoyed a long and mostly close association with Soeharto. He was the man Soeharto would nominate in 1965 as someone who could answer "any questions about me", although he may not have had this particular question in mind when he did so. By the late 1990s, Harysudirja, like many others from the inner circle, had become disenchanted with Soeharto, however. Haryasudirja was also close to Sultan Hamengku Buwono IX. According to Haryasudirja, the Sultan, who served for five years (1973–78) as Soeharto's Vice President, was convinced that Soeharto was indeed a son of Raden Rio, who, by the late 1930s, had come to hold high office in the palace under Hamengku Buwono VIII. If true, that would have made Soeharto and the Sultan distant relatives.

On one occasion, the Sultan was talking at his Jakarta home with Haryasudirja, who claimed to have acted routinely as go-between when Soeharto was President and the Sultan his Vice President, Soeharto having been preternaturally reluctant to deal directly with the Sultan.[53] "Har," the Sultan is said to have remarked, using his friend's nickname, "do you know who the father of Harto is?" When Haryasudirja replied that he did not, the Sultan reportedly pointed to a small photograph that had been taken in 1939 during the funeral of his own father, the eighth sultan. The photograph showed Raden Rio, by that time adjutant to the late ruler, holding the sacred yellow *payung* (parasol) over the coffin. "Look!" the Sultan is quoted as saying. "He is the father, the man who held the *payung* when my father died."[54] Haryasudirja said that this exchange strengthened his own belief that Soeharto was of royal descent. What is more, he was convinced that Soeharto believed it too. Soeharto, he said, felt that he had some aristocratic blood, "although not officially."[55] Soeharto's reluctance to deal directly with the Sultan was seen as proof that the President was of part-royal blood. As Haryasudirja put it, "if he is alone with Hamengku Buwono, he doesn't know what attitude he should have."[56] The list of people of royal or part-royal descent who believed—or who were said to believe—that Soeharto had some royal blood included not only Sultan Hamengku Buwono IX and Prince Haryasudirja, but also Brigadier General R.M. Jono Hatmodjo. Jono was a grandson of Mangkunegoro VI, a former ruler of the subsidiary court in Solo.[57] He was also an uncle of the First Lady, Siti Hartinah Soeharto, who was widely known as Ibu Tien.[58]

Mohammad Roem, a respected modernist Muslim politician who had served as Interior Minister twice between 1946 and 1948, as Foreign Minister and Interior Minister in the early 1950s and as Deputy Prime Minister in 1956–57, was another who said he believed the story about Soeharto being a member of the Yogyakarta royal family. When an article making this claim appeared in the Indonesian press, Roem maintained, the Sultan said to Soeharto, "Now I should call you uncle!" Soeharto was not amused and said, "I am the President. You are the Vice President."[59] In 1974, Soeharto confirmed that the Sultan had indeed raised the matter with him. Hamengku Buwono IX, he told the press, "came to me and asked about that family tree; I answered that it was not true."[60] Soeharto cannot have been too upset with the Sultan, however. Although the Sultan had brought the matter up not long after he became Vice President in 1973, Soeharto would urge him to accept a second five-year term (1978–83). As it happened, the Sultan would be irritated by then that Soeharto had not bothered to consult him on important issues; he made his excuses and declined.[61] As will be seen, two other court-related figures were to give public backing to the Raden Rio story, only to recant when Soeharto expressed his anger.

Could Soeharto have been of part-Chinese descent? The claim found backing in some quarters. Mashuri Saleh, who was Soeharto's neighbour in the mid-sixties and who went on to serve as his Education Minister and Information Minister (1968–78), later expressed the view that Soeharto's father was "a peripatetic village trader of Chinese descent."[62] The problem with that claim is that Mashuri had a habit of making odd and unsubstantiated remarks. For example, he once insisted improbably that a Soeharto-owned palace in Solo had footings of pure gold. One of Mashuri's friends, a senior figure in a prominent Jakarta think-tank, conceded that the minister was loose-lipped. "I used to tease him.

'You are not Menteri Penerangan [Minister for Information] but Menteri Pengelapan [Minister for Darkening].... You don't make things clearer but darker.' "[63] Haryasudirja also thought it possible that Soeharto's father was Chinese but conceded there was no way of knowing. Asked once if there was anything about Soeharto that supported the claim that he may have been of part-Chinese descent, he replied, "Only his eyes!", adding, after the briefest of pauses, "And also his character about money!"[64] Asked whether he thought Soeharto had any royal blood or not, he said, "I think according to his eyes he has some Chinese blood. According to his face he has some royal blood."[65]

As later events were to show, Soeharto resented deeply any suggestion that his mother became pregnant outside marriage. But he seemed to take it in his stride when there were suggestions that he looked a little Chinese. In 1994, the Governor of Bank Indonesia, Adrianus Mooy, anxious to have his term extended, came up with the idea of a new Rp50,000 plastic bank note, which would be manufactured in Australia and which would bear Soeharto's likeness. Mooy was apprehensive when he went to the Presidential Palace to submit the design, having observed that on the specimen note Soeharto looked both cross-eyed and Chinese. As it happened, Soeharto did not mind that his eyes appeared narrow. "I look," he said with a smile, "like a Chinaman!" (*"Saya seperti orang Cina!"*)[66] But he wanted the designers to fix the cross-eyes. In short, there is no convincing evidence in support of the second of the four claims about Soeharto's "true" father.

The third claim, that Soeharto was an illegitimate son of the seventh Sultan, is even less persuasive. Hamengku Buwono VII was eighty-one years old and had been on the throne for forty-three years when, in January 1921, he abdicated, "feeling the weight of his great age."[67] According to a Dutch doctor who was the personal physician of his two successors, the Sultan's abdication was instigated by the Dutch because he was senile.[68] It was at just this time that Soeharto was conceived. The claim that Soeharto was the illegitimate offspring of the eighth Sultan, and thus a half brother of the ninth, is still less credible. The Crown Prince had sailed for the Netherlands in September 1919 on an extended "study tour" and did not return to Yogyakarta until February 1921. Although the man who was to become the eighth Sultan was deemed to have all the usual magical attributes of Javanese royalty—one of which was the power to have intercourse with a woman from afar (*kemet*)—and is said to have fathered some seventy-five children, only four fewer than the number attributed to his philoprogenitive father, it is unlikely that he could impregnate a woman on the other side of the world.[69]

Nor, for that matter, is there any necessary association between noble birth and fine features. Over the years, some Indonesians were to claim that Soeharto had neither the complexion nor the appearance of a Javanese peasant. As a young man, they noted, he had been widely admired for his good looks. His appearance was refined (*halus*); this pointed to elevated ancestry. That argument is not persuasive. "Soeharto," the Indonesian historian Onghokham once observed, "has a classical Yogya rural face. I wonder sometimes how these people could produce such handsome people. It's not unusual." Nor, added Ong, pointing to Sultan Hamengku Buwono IX with his "protruding chin", does aristocratic birth guarantee elegant features.[70] Soeharto's half-brother, Probosutedjo, had the same pale complexion and smooth features as Soeharto.

If some prominent Indonesians found it diverting to speculate on such matters, others ruled out any association between the nation's second president and the royal house of Yogyakarta. Selo Soemardjan, who spent four decades as private secretary to the ninth Sultan, rejected out of hand any suggestion that Soeharto was of royal descent. "Let them talk!" he declared in 2000, two years after Soeharto was forced from office. "I know! It doesn't mean that I do not respect his parents as farmers or as village people. I do respect them. But if you say that he has aristocratic blood in his veins, I say, 'No!'"[71] Selo was, however, of non-aristocratic background. And as Haryasudirja saw it, the Sultan, as a close friend and a fellow prince, was able to confide in Haryasudirja in ways he could not have done with his private secretary, however highly the latter was regarded.

IV

Soeharto's claim that he was the son of a low-level village official was challenged in dramatic fashion in October 1974 when *POP* magazine, a fortnightly specializing in sport, entertainment and film, published an article, "Puzzle in Soeharto's Line of Descent", picking up the allegation that he was the illegitimate child of Raden Rio.[72] According to the magazine, which based its account on interviews with Raden Rio's younger brother, Raden Mas Purbo Waseso (Romo Gayeng), and brother-in-law, Sastroatmodjo, Raden Rio had been obliged to entrust his wife and six or seven-year-old (*sic*) son, Raden Soeharto, to a villager named Kertorejo "in order to fulfill an obligation to marry the daughter of an influential *wedana* (district chief)."[73] Neither side had attempted to make contact with the other and the father had died in 1962 without seeing his son again. At the end of his life, *POP* alleged, Raden Rio "suffered anxiety which could not be resolved because he very much yearned for his child, Raden Soeharto." It added, in what looks for all the world like a gratuitous and inexplicable twist of the knife, that Raden Rio's grave "seems neglected now, a fact which cannot be reconciled with his son's position as President of the Republic of Indonesia." According to *POP*, Soeharto's grandfather was the older brother of the grandfather of the then Vice President, Sultan Hamengku Buwono IX, meaning that the latter could by rights refer to the head of state as "uncle."[74]

The article seemed to suggest that it was because Soeharto was of royal blood that he was fit to hold office as President.[75] In Java, there was a belief in former times that if a commoner came to hold a great office of state, it was because a superior seed (*bibit unggul*) had been implanted in the womb of his or her mother through the intervention of the gods. This, it was thought, conferred special powers on the child: it gave him a mystical legitimacy; it entitled him to be where he was. By 1974 such beliefs were not held so widely. But their existence lent resonance to the story. The *POP* article, with its claims that Sukirah had been impregnated by a young aristocrat, seemed to have been penned by someone who was anxious to associate Soeharto with the Javanese nobility and who appeared to think it could do no harm to "explain" the presidential ascendancy in cultural terms.

Who was responsible for the *POP* article? One of those who backed its publication was Lieutenant General Ali Moertopo, a freewheeling army intelligence officer. Moertopo had served under Soeharto in Central Java in the late 1950s and had gone on to become one of his close confidants. He was the head of Opsus, a contraction of Operasi Khusus (Special Operations), an independent intelligence organization which Soeharto set up in the early sixties. Opsus played an important role in ending Indonesia's 1963–66 armed "Confrontation" of Malaysia. It soon earned an unsavoury reputation at home, however, employing strong-arm tactics to shape the outcome of political party leadership contests and carrying out other black bag operations for Soeharto. In effect, Moertopo was an Indonesian equivalent of René Savary, Napoleon's Minister of Police, "the hero of so many unpleasant or sinister jobs."[76] Since 1966 Moertopo had been a key "political" general on the President's personal staff, a core member of his kitchen cabinet. In late 1974 Moertopo remained influential. However, his stocks had slipped somewhat during the anti-government, anti-Japanese Malari riots that had rocked Jakarta in January that year.[77] He was seeking at this time to get back into Soeharto's good graces.

The general manager of *POP* was a Moertopo subordinate, Lieutenant Colonel Aloysius Soegianto, a man aptly described by Hamish McDonald as "an elegant, mustachioed former Special Forces ... officer who held side-interests in publishing and film-making."[78] Soegianto was from a Central Java *priyayi* family. His wife was related to the Mangkunegaran, the minor court in Solo.[79] Moertopo evidently decided that Soeharto would be pleased if people were to learn that their President was of royal descent. To this end, he either suggested that Soegianto publish an article to that effect or supported the idea when it was made by someone else.[80] According to Major General Sukotjo Tjokroatmodjo, who was at that time the Deputy Provost Marshal General of the Military Police Corps (Corps Polisi Militer, CPM) and, as such, the arresting officer in the court case that followed publication of the *POP* article, Moertopo did this without consulting anyone. "Everybody was investigated by my office," Sukotjo recalled, "so I read all the records."[81] Sukotjo took the view that this was "the beginning of the downfall of Ali Moertopo."

If Moertopo was seeking to please Soeharto, his plan misfired badly. "They wanted to curry favour with [*menjilat*] Soeharto actually, to please Soeharto," one of Moertopo's former advisers recalled. "[They wanted to say] 'You are a king! Not only by physical acceptance, legal acceptance, but also divine acceptance!"[82] While Moertopo may not have known exactly what was going into the magazine, he had supported the idea in general. "He thought this was also good, to praise," the adviser recalled. But Moertopo and Soegianto had strayed into a deeply sensitive part of the President's past. "You try to lick but it is a wound in there! So you lick the wound [and] it's painful to Soeharto. His intention was licking, actually." The aim had been to get closer to Soeharto, by praising him and suggesting that he was not just a common man. "But Soeharto felt that it was an insult ... because it was insulting his mother."[83] Moertopo was one of several high-level officials who attended the press conference at which Soeharto denounced the article.[84] At that gathering Soeharto took a swipe at Moertopo's organization, saying, "I know that one of the promoters is someone from Opsus."[85]

In pre-war Java few rural families would have objected if a daughter became pregnant to a prince or minor royal. Being a child, legitimate or not, of royal blood was regarded as an honour. This was a far from uncommon occurrence and one that brought considerable standing both to the young woman in question and to her parents. In the courts of Java, a woman who became the concubine (*selir*) of a prince took an even bigger step up, because the status of children was determined by the position of their father. If she became the wife, even the second or third wife, of a sultan or the *sunan* (ruler of Surakarta), her sons would become princes, her daughters princesses. This would be a source of intense pride to her parents. What is more, her parents and other relatives could expect to see various material advantages coming their way.

Soeharto, however, took grave exception to the suggestion that anything like this had happened, and he did not confine himself to the business of "clearing" his name. *POP* was closed down and the Military Police brought in to arrest those responsible for publishing the article. The editor-in-chief was sentenced to a term of imprisonment. The author of the article recanted.[86] One of the magazine's two sources, Sastroatmodjo, said that he and Raden Rio's brother had based their account on stories they had heard from *kampung* (village) people, so "it's just empty talk."[87] The day after the article appeared, Probosutedjo held a press conference to refute the suggestion that his half-brother was of royal descent. This, he said, slandered his parents and ancestors.[88]

A few days later, Soeharto called a press conference of his own at Bina Graha, the office block he had had built inside the grounds of the Presidential Palace, to reject the claim that he was descended from the nobility. In the course of doing so, he produced "some elderly people, living witnesses who knew for certain of my actual background."[89] In the press conference, which lasted for almost two hours and during which his eyes "at times ... filled with tears" as he spoke of his late parents, Soeharto insisted that he was the son of a low-level village official who had not owned even a small portion of land, and recalled the suffering he had undergone as a child.[90] As he wrote later, "I pointed out that the wrong story circulated about my family descent could not only affect my personal reputation and that of my family but also have a negative influence on our country and people."[91] If the story had gone on unchecked, he said, giving expression to his characteristic obsession with order and harmony, "people would question from where the President was actually descended. If this kind of talk ensued, people would take sides, for and against the issue. Each would defend his own standpoint and conflict might very well follow." This would create a situation ripe for subversion and political intimidation that could eventually jeopardize national stability. If the story were true, it would suggest that his mother had been a woman of questionable morals. "How was it possible to dispose of a wife and a six-year-old [*sic*] child so easily? Was the marriage illegal? If so, the child must be illegitimate. Well, wouldn't this affect the honour of the country and the people?" The article in *POP*, he said, "hurts my feelings." Soeharto told the press that he had been hearing about this matter for a long time. Someone had sent him a letter setting it out; he had replied saying that it was not true. Later, as we have seen, he had told the Sultan the same thing.[92]

Three things are striking about Soeharto's response to the *POP* article, quite apart from the fact that he was abandoned by his mother not at six years but at six weeks. The first is the depth of his anger at the claims that had been made. The suggestion that Sukirah might have been a woman of loose morals cut deeply. This was partly because the President saw this, with good reason, as a slur on his mother's reputation. But it may have been partly too because of the Islamic theory of illegitimacy and partly because he felt that the "revelations" undermined his claim to be of modest origins.

Soeharto, it is clear, held Ali Moertopo and his Opsus subordinates responsible for the *POP* article, as indeed they were. Ever suspicious, he is said to have wondered what plots his long-time intelligence aide might be hatching. Instead of seeing this for the ham-fisted attempt at ingratiation it was, some well-placed Indonesians claim, Soeharto gave every sign that he suspected Moertopo coveted the presidency himself.[93] This, it appears, lay behind his odd warnings about the national security implications of such an article. By nature and upbringing, Soeharto was a man who kept his emotions on a tight rein, achieving a degree of composure that made him all but impenetrable, even to those in his inner circle. During his thirty-two years in power, he sought to project an image of dignified, unruffled calm. He gave public vent to his feelings only half a dozen times—and almost invariably in reaction to what he saw as attacks on himself or his family.* This was one such occasion and it was accompanied by a barely

* In private, too, he generally kept a tight rein on his emotions. When angry, however, he could be cold, arrogant, dismissive and intimidating.

veiled threat. There was, Soeharto noted, a Javanese proverb: *Sadumuk bathuk, sanyari bumi*. In his autobiography the President translates this, somewhat blandly, as, "Don't encroach upon the rights of others or you'll be in serious trouble." But, as Soeharto pointed out in an appendix to that book, there is a darker threat implicit in the saying, a sense that one is entitled to risk one's life and even spill blood in defence of one's property or family honour.

Moertopo's career never regained its high trajectory. It is true that he would go on to play a key role in covert operations in Portuguese East Timor ahead of Indonesia's brutal 1975 invasion. But in 1978 he would be shunted sideways into the powerless position of Minister for Information.* The *POP* affair was a blow as well to Soegianto's already chequered military career, although he would be involved in Moertopo's attempt to destabilize East Timor.[94] It was sometimes claimed that Soegianto's eclipse stemmed in part from the fact that he was a man from the Yogyakarta-Solo heartland who, unlike Moertopo, a man of part-Arab descent from Pekalongan, on the north coast of Java, should have known better than to engage in speculation about Soeharto's ancestry.

The second striking thing about Soeharto's response to the article is the sense of self-pity and resentment that runs through his accounts of his childhood. This trait, which was never far from the surface, suggests that the President never quite got over the hurt and rejection he felt in his early years. Finally, it is impossible not to be struck by the way in which the President, who had come to office in 1967 with a certain degree of hesitancy and humility had, by 1974, taken on the some of the trappings of kingship, and now was only too ready to assert that an attack on him as an individual was an attack on the entire nation. That said, he was not the only Indonesian president to feel that he or she had an obligation to protect the institution of the presidency.

V

If, as he insisted, Soeharto was not connected in any way to the nobility, it may be thought he had an odd way of showing it. As President, he was to

* It was, some thought, ironic that Soeharto chose Moertopo, a master of misinformation, as his Minister of Information.

display a keen interest in royal tombs, royal palaces and royal traditions. What lay behind this fixation? The most plausible explanation is that Soeharto was ministering to the aspirations of his wife. The First Lady was a descendant, albeit some grades down, of the Mangkunegaran court in Solo, and thus one of the Mangkunegaran kin (*kerabat*).[95] As some people saw it, she was seeking a higher social status—as if being the wife of the President was not elevated enough. Others believed she was anxious to rehabilitate her family's name. According to one version of events, her father, R.M. Soemoharjomo, a pre-war *wedana*, first in Wonogiri, a rural town to the south of Solo, and then in nearby Wuryantoro, had fallen into disfavour with the Mangkunegaran court because of some alleged wrongdoing. Pensioned in 1941, he had taken his family back to Solo.[96] No one seemed to know, or been willing to say, what Soemoharjomo was alleged to have done or whether he had been judged harshly or not. But according to Haryasudirja, he was "more or less in disgrace" in Mangkunegaran circles. "Well," Haryasudirja added, "maybe he is right; we don't know yet. But as far as we know it was not on account of patriotism or something like *perjuangan* [lit., struggle; the fight for national independence.]"[97] One of Ali Moertopo's former advisers supports the "rehabilitation" claim. Soeharto, he argues, wanted to help his wife put matters right. He decided to act "because the wife is from that line and the father was a bit in disgrace … I think he did it for her."[98]

What kind of "rehabilitation" was Ibu Tien seeking for her late father? That is not clear. All we know is that matters quickly developed a life of their own. Brigadier General Jono Hatmodjo, who was, as noted earlier, a grandson of Mangkunegoro VI and an uncle of the First Lady, had once been close to Ibu Tien and her mother, K.R.A.Y. Soemoharjomo: the First Lady's father was buried in the same graveyard as Jono's grandfather.* In the late 1960s, however, Jono's branch of the family and Ibu Tien fell out. The problem arose, Jono maintained, when the First Lady asked Jono's eldest brother, Major General K.R.M.H. Jonosewojo Handayaningrat, to erect a roof over her father's grave.[99] He declined. According to Javanese custom, only a ruler, his wife and his sons are entitled to have a structure over their graves. She continued to insist; he continued to refuse. Relations

---

* K.R.A.Y. stands for Kanjeng Ratu Ayu, a title for female members of the aristocracy.

soured. Unable to get the roof she wanted, Jono claimed, the First Lady decided to construct a lavish family mausoleum, the Astana Giri Bangun, on a hillside set aside for the tombs of Mangkunegoro I (r. 1757–95) and his successors.[100] Jono believed that, in backing his wife on this matter, Soeharto was "violating completely the custom of the kings."[101] The royal family had been upset, but there was nothing they could do: it was a fait accompli.[102] After that, Jono said, there was no further contact between the two sides.[103]

The decision to build the Astana Giri Bangun was made by the Mangadeg Foundation, a "cultural body" which ostensibly brought together the Soeharto family and the Mangkunegaran Palace in Solo. President Soeharto was chairman of the foundation. According to one of Ali Moertopo's key advisors from that time, Mangkunegoro VIII, the vice-chairman of the foundation, was "a bit afraid to resist directly" when the President expressed interest in the mausoleum project.[104] According to another account, Ibu Tien set up the foundation to support various projects in Solo, particularly the rebuilding of the tomb of Mangkunegoro I. In return, the wife of Mangkunegoro VIII, who was said to be quite unscrupulous about the sale of Mangkunegaran titles and privileges to Jakarta patrons willing to put up money for rebuilding works, awarded her the title of Bendara Raden Ayu, which is "usually reserved for female children of senior princes of the Central Java courts by official wives."[105] On 8 June 1971, the President and First Lady presided at the dedication ceremony of the Mangadeg Foundation.[106] As their car prepared to make its way slowly back from the royal graves, a palace chronicle recorded in courtly Javanese verse,

> Coins were tossed out as tinkling token gifts
> for those behind seeing off
> the departing Guests.
> Most happy were the People,
> receiving so many coins as alms,
> freed from misfortune.[107]

The royal custom of distributing coins as alms tossed from His Majesty's automobile's window, the anthropologist John Pemberton notes, "was one of Pakubuwono X's best known and most popular gestures of kingly beneficence" and a gesture which had not, it appears, been performed by

Javanese rulers since 1939.[108] The 1971 chronicle was remarkable, Pemberton argues, for its disclosure of just how lofty the Soehartos' aspirations were at that relatively early point in the New Order rule. It is written "in precisely the fashion that a longing for royal origins calls for."[109] One might add that the choice of that particular date for the dedication ceremony—8 June 1971, was the President's fiftieth birthday—could suggest that Soeharto family interests were as much to the fore as those of the Mangkunegaran court. Nor was that the only explicit link to Soeharto. Construction of the mausoleum complex began on 27 November 1974, "a Kliwon Wednesday, the same as Soeharto's day of birth."[110] (Kliwon is the fifth day of the Javanese five-day week.) The Astana Giri Bangun was completed in 1976.

The contrast between the Astana Mangadeg, final resting place of the first three Mangkunegoro rulers, and the Soeharto family mausoleum could not have been greater. Until then, the Mangkunegaran tombs had stood in solitary and respectful isolation. Nestled on a ridgeline in the western foothills of Mt Lawu (10,712 feet), they were twenty-two miles southeast of Solo and exactly 666 meters (2,185 feet) above sea level. The royal tombs were modest and discreet, even a little down-at-heel, a cluster of courtyards and antechambers behind mildewed walls; each small structure had a roof of common house tiles. Although high on the ridgeline, the buildings could not be seen until you were almost upon them, buried as they were in a grove of bamboo and saplings.

The Soeharto mausoleum stands, in all its gleaming newness, a little further down the ridgeline, a symphony of marble, glass and polished teak. Designed on traditional Javanese lines, with a tapered roof, it is larger and grander than the royal tombs.* A paved road runs all the way up to the main building, with fifteen-ft high stone embankments in places to prevent mudslides. Built by the Mangadeg Foundation, which would later renovate the tombs of the first three rulers of that dynasty, it cost a significant sum but sought to absorb through proximity some of the magical aura of the royal tombs.† What is more, the name of the

---

* Soeharto was buried there on January 29, 2008, alongside his wife, who had died in 1996. As president, he had ordered that a similar, but perhaps slightly smaller, mausoleum be built at Blitar in East Java over the grave of his predecessor, President Sukarno, never mind the fact that Sukarno had made it clear that he wanted to be buried under a tree in West Java.

† The Soeharto mausoleum cost "only" US$1.5 million, the government insisted, not US$10 million, as some critics claimed.

Soeharto mausoleum, Giri Bangun, is a composite of the names of two Mangkunegaran burial sites. "The Soeharto tomb," James Siegel has noted, "is intended to link itself in the series of Mangkunegaran tombs and thus to participate in the sacredness, the tomb of Mangkunegoro I in particular being thought to be a repository of sacred power."[111] Soeharto, who had officiated at the dedication of the Mangadeg Foundation in 1971, returned five years later to preside over the inauguration of the mausoleum itself. Some time afterwards, the remains of Ibu Tien's father were removed from his previous burial ground and re-interned in the new complex, which has a very grand roof. In 1988, her mother was buried there as well.[112]

If the Soeharto family had dealings with the Mangkunegaran court, with which there was a certain filial connection, it was to establish as well a link with the family of the Sunan, the ruler of the principal court in Solo. At some stage, the President and First Lady came into possession of a small but elegant Javanese palace, the Ndalem Kalitan (1789), in the heart of Solo.* The palace had belonged to Gusti Kanjeng Ratu Alit, a daughter of Pakubuwono X. How and when did it change hands? Divergent accounts circulated. According to one version of events, by the early 1970s Ratu Alit had fallen into debt. Soeharto "rescued" her, ending up with the palace.[113] In an account given by Soeharto's authorized biographer, Ibu Tien bought Ndalem Kalitan "from a princess who needed money."[114] In still another account, Soemoharjomo's family bought the palace.[115] Then, not long afterwards, the First Lady bought it from her family. This story may account for claims that the palace was somehow "an inheritance of the Ibu line."[116] Mashuri, the sometimes erratic former Information Minister, questioned that argument. "Soeharto said it was an inheritance of the Ibu line," Mashuri told a friend. But that, Mashuri declared, was not the case. Mashuri is alleged to have told the President, "You bought that! Because you have money."[117] It is not clear that Soeharto ever did make the inheritance claim. It is even less likely that Mashuri levelled his charge directly at the President, although he did make the claim to friends.

* The palace, with its high-walled compound, its neatly-tended garden and its airy, open-sided *pendopo* (pavillion), complete with white marble floors and portraits of the President and the First Lady, provided a comfortable retreat when members of the Soeharto family were in Solo.

By and large, it is true, the primary Solonese court remained indifferent to feelers from Jakarta. From 1968 on, New Order officials reportedly sought, without success, to convert the palace into a national monument. At one point, "the Soeharto group" apparently offered to buy outright the Langenharja pleasure retreat, which had been built in the 1870s on the outskirts of Solo by Pakubuwono IX.[118] In time, however, the court was to prove less stand-offish. In 1991, Pakubuwono XII, anxious to fund the Kraton's spiritual and cultural life but always strapped for cash, came up with a plan to build a luxury hotel in his decaying palace compound.[119] Before long, Soeharto had approved a scheme under which his second son, Bambang Trihatmodjo, a prominent businessman, would invest in a five-star, 150-room hotel. The Sunan was delighted. In the event, he ran into opposition from one of his daughters and from a growing number of Solonese. The idea withered on the vine.

Nor was Soeharto interested only in palaces and royal burial sites in and around Solo. At one time, it has been claimed, he instructed his half-brother, Probosutedjo, "to buy all the palaces of the princes in Yogyakarta."[120] That may overstate the case. It would appear that Probosutedjo bought only one palace in the city. This was the Ndalem Ngabean, once the residence of Prince Hangabei, a title awarded to the eldest son of the Sultan; this lovingly restored complex is now the Ndalem Ngabean Hotel Yogyakarta.[121] To critics, all this presumption, all this impertinence, all this self-promotion, the acquisition of palaces, the construction of a tomb on a sacred royal hillside, did not reflect Javanese values; rather, it was a contradiction of *satria* (noble, or knightly) values. Soeharto's behaviour, some thought, was Pharaonic rather than Sultanic.

If, as seems likely, Soeharto was doing no more than attend to the concerns of his wife, that did not stop some people arguing that he felt he was indeed of part-royal descent and that he derived some comfort and inner strength from that thought—while being unwilling to say as much publicly because it would besmirch his mother's reputation.* Others

* Rosihan Anwar, a prominent newspaper editor from West Sumatra, had attended the prestigious pre-war Dutch-language AMS-A senior high school in Yogyakarta and had come to know Soeharto when he was a military commander in Central Java in the late 1940s. He believed that the President would have seen nothing odd about subscribing to the *priyayi*

argued that Soeharto—or at least some members of his family—had come to see themselves, in a remarkably short time, in neo-royalist terms. Yet another explanation, one favoured by Haryasudirja, who had by the year 2000 known Soeharto for more than half a century but who was by then openly critical of the former president, is that Soeharto wanted to show people that he had more power than the feudal rulers. "So it means," Haryasudirja argued, "it is more overcompensation."[122]

Equally interesting is the way in which Soeharto is portrayed in two hagiographic films—*Janur Kuning* (Yellow Coconut Leaf) and *Serangan Fajar* (The Dawn Attack)—made when the President was at the height of his power. In both these films, the scholar Krishna Sen writes, Soeharto appears as the central revolutionary figure, owing his aura as a protective leader of the people "not merely to his immediate revolutionary activity but (particularly in *Serangan Fajar*) by some inexplicable genealogy through which he inherits the historic and mythical mantle of royal heroes of the past."[123]

Intimations of some inexplicable genealogy are to be found, too, in the Museum Purna Bhakti Pertiwi, a garish architectural confection which Soeharto and his wife built on the outskirts of Jakarta. The museum houses five monumental, elaborately-carved teakwood depictions of Soeharto's achievements as well as family mementoes, uniforms, medals, *wayang* puppets, big game trophies and gifts from local and foreign leaders. Rich in Javanese symbolism, the museum features uplifting tales from the Ramayana and the Mahabharata about princes who prepared themselves for, and subsequently attained, power. Two carved tree trunks in the entrance lobby tell the *wayang* story of Raden Parikesit, "born when the kingdom was in ruins." He was "the anchor of hope for the rebuilding of Hastinapura"; a man who would "bring the kingdom back to its glory." When he grew up, the visitor is

---

outlook while seeking to stress his peasant origins. "It's very natural with a man of Soeharto's origins," he claimed. "It depends. One day he says, 'I'm *wong cilik*, I'm an ordinary man', as proven in the *POP* case. On other occasions, 'I am *priyayi*.' He doesn't see any contradiction. It's quite natural. He moves from one to the other. In this case, because his wife is from the low nobility of Mangkunegaran, he feels his humble birth should have some compensation.... Actually, he's not from humble birth.... People are saying that he's an offshoot of the Sultan there in Yogya. But you can't prove [it]." Interview, Rosihan Anwar, Jakarta, July 21, 1995.

informed, "Parikesit was crowned as King."[124] This seems to foreshadow, not very subtly, the message of the five teakwood panels. The first of these depicts the period from "the birth of Bapak Soeharto" until the formation of the Java Volunteer Defence Force. The second covers the period from the "Proclamation [of Independence] until the Wedding of Bapak Soeharto". And so on until one comes to the struggle against the September 30th Movement, which launched its murderous strike against the army's top brass in 1965; Soeharto's installation as Acting President in 1967; the general election of 1971, and the "awarding of the 'United Nations Population Award'" in 1989.[125]

Traditional Javanese rulers, whether legitimate successors or usurpers, had not been above inventing illustrious lineages for themselves and claiming that their ascent to power had been due in part to supernatural intervention. President Sukarno, too, had laced his life with a number of spurious or exaggerated claims, starting with one about his birth in Surabaya being marked by a cosmologically significant event. At that time, he liked to say, Mt Kelud, a nearby volcano, erupted; superstitious people had prophesied that this was a greeting to baby Sukarno. He also claimed to be a descendant of the Sultan of Kediri, although no one took that seriously, perhaps because there had never been a Sultan of Kediri.[126] Soeharto, referring pointedly to those claims, insisted, as we have seen, that there was nothing special about his own origins: he was just a village boy. His attack on those associated with the *POP* magazine allegations was in keeping with that claim. That, however, did not stop some of his aides and acolytes linking him in some ill-defined way with royal heroes from the past—a linkage he did little, if anything, to dispel.

VI

Whatever the truth of the various claims, the six-week-old Soeharto was placed in a good home after being taken from his mother. His great-aunt, Mbah Kromo, seems to have been a devoted mother-substitute. Sometimes, she carried the child with her as she made her rounds of the villages, delivering babies and attending to new mothers, many of whom felt sorry for the "motherless" child in their midst and nursed him along with their own new arrivals. "It seems," Soeharto recalled, "that I was breastfed by those mothers who had given birth to their own children with Mbah Kromo's help."[127] From time to time, the infant Soeharto, "separated from his parents, was sometimes pitied, but consoled with the words, 'How lucky you are, *tholé*.* It seems your [great-aunt] loves you more than your own mother could.' "[128]

On the face of it, Soeharto was fortunate that his separation from his mother came at six weeks rather than during the period between about six months and six years of age. As the British child psychiatrist and psychoanalyst John Bowlby has noted, it is unlikely that a child develops any significant attachment to a preferred figure before about six weeks and it may be some weeks later.[129] By six months, the situation has changed dramatically. The responses of protest, despair and detachment that typically occur when a child aged over six months is separated from his or her mother and placed in the care of strangers are due mainly to "loss of maternal care at this highly dependent, highly vulnerable stage of development."[130] The young child's "hunger for his mother's love and presence is as great as his hunger for food" and in consequence her absence inevitably generates "a powerful sense of loss and anger."

According to Bowlby, the loss of a mother figure, either by itself or in combination with other variables, is capable of generating responses and processes of the kind "known to be active in older individuals who are still disturbed by separations that they suffered in early life. Amongst these responses and processes and amongst forms of disturbance are, on the one hand, a tendency to make excessive demands on others and to be anxious and angry when they are not met, such as is present in dependent and hysterical personalities; and, on the other, a blockage in the capacity to make deep relationships, such as is present in affectionless and psychopathic personalities."[131] The other side of this coin is that Soeharto may have been subject to just these kinds of responses when he was taken, at the age of four, from his great aunt, a much-loved mother-figure, and sent back to his mother, a woman who, it seems, might as well have been a stranger to him. In other words, paradoxical as it sounds, his return to his mother may have generated feelings of maternal deprivation that were to have a profound influence on his personality.

* *Tholé* is a Javanese term of address for a small boy, abbreviated from *konthol*, which can probably best be translated as "(male) genitalia", although the rather clinical word "genitalia" does not capture the earthy character of *konthol*. I am grateful to George Quinn for his observations on this point.

In his autobiography, Soeharto paints a fond picture of the time he spent with his great-aunt's family during his first four years, although it is unlikely he remembered much from that period. At times, when Mbah Kromo was called away on her duties as a midwife and was unable to take him with her, she would leave him in the care of her adult daughter, Mbak Amat Idris, who appears to have quickly become one of several subsidiary attachment figures in his early life.* At other times, he would accompany his great-uncle, Mbah Kromodiryo, to the rice fields.

> Sometimes he carried me on his back while working the land and, when I grew up, let me ride the plough. It was great fun, moments that I will always treasure, when I would sit on the plough and spur the buffalo on, steering [it] left or right. I would leap into the rice field, playing in the water, getting covered in mud. When I became tired, I was told to wait at the ditch by the roadside. My days in the field with Mbah Kromo also gave me the chance to catch eels, which were turned into a dish that I continue to like very much to this day.[132]

In writing about his great-uncle, a man who was presumably well into middle age, Soeharto adopts a tone that contrasts sharply with the detachment that marks his observations about his parents. Recounting an incident in which a sickle slipped from his hand and fell onto his bare foot, he writes, "At first the cut didn't seem serious but after a while it turned into a nasty wound. Mbah Kromo cared for me with such tender love that I can still feel it today."[133]

VII

Looking back over Soeharto's life, one is forced to conclude that it was parental abandonment which had the deepest impact on him. In the opinion of a number of those who knew him well, Soeharto believed that he had been rejected by his parents and never forgave them for this. He had, during a profoundly disrupted childhood, been farmed out to a succession of relatives and foster parents; and while some were to show him warmth and consideration, others treated him with indifference or disdain, working

* In a family relationship, the Javanese word *mbak* can be "older sister" or a term of address to a younger woman who is nevertheless older than the speaker.

him hard, offering him little. He was shaped, too, by poverty and by a realization that his prospects were not especially bright. It is hard to think of any way that knowing he may have been of aristocratic origin helps us understand Soeharto, unless one considers that the thought of such linkages left him with a sense of particularity or entitlement.

We cannot leave the matter there, however. As noted earlier, Soeharto vehemently rejected any suggestion that he was of royal descent. He may have been entirely justified in doing so. But even if we accept that, we are left with the fact that, on becoming President, he wasted little time in taking on some of the trappings of kingship: tossing coins from his limousine to grateful commoners; buying up palaces and royal retreats, and building a family mausoleum on a remote mountain ridge set aside for Javanese kings. The initiative for some, perhaps all, of these actions may have come from his wife, but Soeharto seems to have embraced them readily enough. And if he was angered when sycophantic army officers and editors sought to promote what he saw as a spurious claim of aristocratic ancestry, he seems to have had few, if any, objections when equally sycophantic museum directors and film makers portrayed him in quasi-royal terms. Sukarno may have retailed a threadbare story about his descent from a non-existent Sultan of Kediri. But neither he nor any of the five presidents who came immediately after Soeharto were to act in quite such a brazenly "royal" manner.

In his 2015 biography of Hamengku Buwono IX, John Monfries writes that some time in the 1970s the Sultan "confirmed to his associates his belief that Soeharto was illegitimate."[134] As Monfries rightly observes, "Few of these issues are the stuff of statesmanship, but personal tensions can arise from objectively minor irritations between political actors and can then have political effects." While there is no reason to believe that Soeharto harboured a lasting grudge against the Sultan for raising this issue with him, the *POP* affair had political repercussions. It deepened Soeharto's suspicions of Ali Moertopo, a key member of his inner ruling circle. Nor can Soeharto have been unaware that other members of the political elite were speaking of such matters behind cupped hands. It was proof, if proof were needed, that one could never be too vigilant.

2

"The cork on which the Netherlands floats"

By virtue of his birth, the infant Soeharto was simultaneously the subject of two very different sovereigns. One was Queen Wilhelmina of Orange-Nassau, a forty-year-old Caucasian Christian, heir to an unbending Calvinist tradition, who lived half a world away, presiding over her flat and prosperous North Sea kingdom and its distant dominions, most notably the East Indies, where Dutch fortunes were thought by some to be at the high meridian of their glory. The other was Sultan Hamengku Buwono VIII, a forty-one-year-old Javanese Muslim who was not long back from the Netherlands, which, as we have seen, he had visited during his latter years as Crown Prince. The product of a distinctly non-Calvinist tradition, the Sultan was eventually to acquire not only a *permaisuri* (principal consort, or sultana) but seven minor wives, numerous concubines and those seventy-five children.[1]

The Sultan lived behind the walls of the Kraton, a sprawling complex of buildings, at the centre of which stood the Golden Pavilion, where the rulers were enthroned. The Kraton was a world unto itself, somnolent and enclosed, the atmosphere languorous, the sound of gamelan music washing, gentle and percussive, over the great courtyards and walled tropical gardens. Although it had been all but powerless for ninety years, the Sultanate, and its attendant minor court, the Pakualaman, stood at the very centre of Java, both culturally and geographically. And Java was, in turn, the most populous and most important island in the Netherlands East Indies. Therein lay the seeds of so many of the problems that were to bedevil independent Indonesia. If we are to understand the world in which Soeharto came to power it is necessary to say something about the complex factors which shaped that world.

II

The motto of the nation that Soeharto was to rule for so long is "Unity in Diversity". But forging a unified nation out of such extraordinary geographic, ethnic, linguistic, cultural, religious and political diversity was never going to be easy. An archipelago of more than 17,000 islands, Indonesia extends across more than one-eighth of the world's circumference at the equator, a distance of 3,400 miles from east to west and 1,200 miles from north to south. It lies between two continents, Asia and Australia, and between two great oceans, the Indian and the Pacific. As such, it straddles the vital sea lanes between Europe and the Middle East on the one hand and the industrialized economies of East Asia on the other. Hour by hour, an endless succession of supertankers pass, with their forbidding bulk and bulbous domes, down the shallow Straits of Malacca and on through the South China Sea, carrying oil and liquified natural gas (LNG) from the Middle East to the industrial powerhouses of China, Taiwan, Japan and South Korea. Equally large vessels make their way through the Lombok Strait, carrying iron ore and LNG from Western Australia to Northeast Asia. The products of those manufacturing states and territories pass westward along the same trade routes, and, of course, across the Pacific. The nuclear submarines of several nations pass, silent and submerged, through some of the main Indonesian straits, which offer the quickest passage between the Indian and Pacific Oceans.

There are five major Indonesian island groupings, with striking disparities in land area and population densities. On Java and Bali, which are home to more than thirty volcanoes, some of them active, a combination of rich soil and abundant rainfall proved ideal for intensive wet rice cultivation, paving the way for rapid population growth. In the so-called Outer Islands, where the soils were often poor and the forest cover extensive, shifting cultivation was more common and population densities lower. These differences are clearly evident in the ratio of population to land area. Java, which is about the size of England and Wales combined, or a little larger than New York State, is home to 156 million people. It has 56.2 per cent of Indonesia's population shoehorned into 7 per cent of the nation's land area. Sumatra, which is almost the size of Spain, has a quarter of Indonesia's land and 16 per cent of its people. Kalimantan (Indonesian Borneo), which is somewhat larger than Spain, has 28 per cent of the land and only 5 per cent of the population. The remote, resource-rich provinces of western New Guinea have 22 per cent of the land and 1 per cent of the population.

The people who inhabit this archipelago are basically of Malay stock, descendants of Austronesians who came by sea from Taiwan in about 4000 BC, bringing with them "the technology of pottery, bows and arrows and outrigger canoes."[2] The easternmost islands remain largely Melanesian, although there is no clear line dividing these two groups, more a blurring of the two, as in Timor. However, these two worlds tend to rub up against one other, like shifting tectonic plates, generating considerable friction, not least because the eastward expansion of the dominant Malay world has tended to resume in recent decades. The Malay world is, in turn, subdivided into at least fourteen major ethnic groups, each with its own region, cultural identity and language. Roughly forty per cent of the indigenous population identify themselves as Javanese, a people who originate in densely-settled East and Central Java but who are also now found in significant numbers in several parts of the Outer Islands. The second largest ethnic group (15 per cent) are the Sundanese, whose homeland is West Java.

As has often been noted, ecology and ethnicity help to explain some of the dominant themes of Indonesia's history. "One of these," writes the Australian historian John Legge, "is the interplay between land and sea—between agricultural societies and commercial societies, between kings and merchants, between Java and the Outer Islands."[3] From about the fourth century AD, small Hindu and Buddhist courts began to appear in what is now Indonesia, some of them in the trading centres that had emerged at the mouths of great rivers in the Outer Islands, others in the heartland of Central and East Java. The biggest of the early kingdoms was Srivijaya (seventh to eleventh centuries), a maritime empire centred on southern Sumatra and ruled by a line of Mahayana Buddhists. By the end of the seventh century, Srivijaya was "a prosperous entrepôt where ships going to and coming from China and India gathered while waiting for the winds to change."[4] Rice was imported from Java and there was a lucrative trade in camphor, pepper, sandalwood, cloves, nutmeg and mace.

Before long, major Hindu-Buddhist kingdoms were to emerge in the fertile plains of east and central Java, in the shadow of imposing volcanoes. The first of these, the Hindu state of Mataram, flourished in central Java in the early part of the eighth century. It gave way to a line of Buddhist kings, known as Sailendra, who held sway over the same area from about AD 760–860, only to be replaced by a new Hindu-Buddhist kingdom. These states were not, like Srivijaya, mercantile and maritime, flavoured with a dash of piracy and plunder, drawing their lifeblood from the seaborne commerce that passed their front door. They were instead inland empires, based on intensive wet rice cultivation and on the elaborate social and economic order necessary to sustain it, hierarchical in nature, drawing heavily and enthusiastically on Indian tradition, not least in religion and architecture.

Unlike Srivijaya, which has disappeared almost without trace, the rulers in Central Java have left behind some of the most splendid monuments in Southeast Asia, architectural wonders that rank alongside Angkor Wat in Cambodia and Pagan in Burma (Myanmar). One of these is the symbolic temple mountain of Borobudur, a squat but imposing structure built in about AD 800 during the Sailendra Dynasty, its lower terraces decorated with splendid bas-reliefs, its upper galleries housing distinctive bell-shaped stupas, each of which originally encased a statue of a seated Buddha. Another is the darkly imposing ninth century Hindu temple complex of Prambanan, dedicated to Durga, the consort of Shiva, god of destruction and fertility. Soeharto was born in the rich cultural heart of this region. Borobudur is fourteen miles northwest of the hamlet in which he spent his early childhood; Prambanan is fourteen miles to the east.

By the early tenth century, the centre of political gravity had moved to East Java, an area blessed not only with equally abundant rice surpluses but also with better access to the sea, providing the basis for an empire that was to influence much of the archipelago. Situated half way between the eastern Spice Islands and the trading artery of the Straits of Malacca, East Java became a thriving port, cornering the trade in rice, cloves, nutmeg and mace. Merchants arrived from the Arabian Peninsula, India, China, Thailand, Cambodia, Vietnam and the Spice Islands. In the fourteenth century, new and important trade links were forged with Western Europe, where an insatiable appetite developed for Asian spices, which were used as a preservative for meat. Buoyed by commerce, East Java was soon "one of the world's richest lands, as bullion, gold and silver vessels, silk and the world's best porcelain, lacquerware, chemicals and manufactures poured in."[5] The glory that was East Java reached its zenith in the later fourteenth century, during the era of Majapahit (1293–c.1527), the last and the greatest of the pre-Islamic Southeast Asian island empires.

For nearly a thousand years, Indian influences—political and religious, architectural and cultural—had had a profound impact on what was to become the modern state of Indonesia. "The ancient Hindu-Buddhist city-states," Clifford Geertz has noted, "were headed by a king who was also a God, a divine monarch enthroned at the very peak of spiritual refinement upon a symbolically divine mountain set at the exact centre of his squared-off capital.... Spiritual power flowed outward and downward from its royal fountainhead, attenuating as it sank through each layer in the bureaucracy, draining weakly at last into the peasant masses."[6] Those influences, which overlay an earlier core of animism, remain important to this day. But they were to be overlaid, in turn, by the coming of Islam.

During the course of the thirteenth century Islam began to percolate slowly through archipelagic Southeast Asia, starting in North Sumatra but soon spreading to Brunei on the north coast of Borneo, to Trengganu on the Malay Peninsula and to East Java. The new religion seems to have been carried initially by the Muslim merchants who had long dominated the maritime trade routes. But it has been plausibly argued that learned Muslim mystical teachers, perhaps claiming supernatural powers, also played an important role, and that it was in fact Sufi holy men who converted some important members of the Majapahit court.[7]

The slow but steady Islamization of the archipelago was given a significant boost in the early 1400s when the ruler of Malacca, on the west coast of the Malay Peninsula, converted to Islam, "assuming new and imposing Persian-style titles" and proclaiming himself both sultan and syah "thus raising himself above all other princes in the area who ...bore the simpler title raja."[8] Islamization accelerated in the sixteenth and seventeenth century. From Malacca, increasingly the commercial hub of island Southeast Asia, Islam established or expanded its beachheads, in the eastern Spice Islands of Tidore and Ternate, in Brunei, in Demak on the north coast of Java, in Banten in West Java and in southern Borneo, southern Sumatra, Lombok, Makassar and Sumbawa. In the Islamic schools that sprang up in one trading port after another, converts and their children became familiar with the fundamental precepts of Islam—the need to perform the ritual prayers five times daily, to recite the Qur'an, to pay alms, to fast during Ramadan, to make the pilgrimage to Mecca if possible and to respond to any call to join a *jihad*, or holy war.[9]

The coming of Islam, the historian Merle Ricklefs has noted, is often thought of as peaceful, since there is no evidence of foreign military expeditions imposing Islam by conquest. "But once an Indonesian Islamic state was founded, Islam was sometimes spread from there to other areas by warfare.... This does not necessarily mean that such wars were fought primarily in order to spread Islam; the roots of these struggles were perhaps more commonly dynastic, strategic and economic. But Islamization often followed upon conquest. Islam was spread in Indonesia not only by persuasion and commercial pressures, but by the sword as well."[10] Goa (Gowa) in south Sulawesi is a case in point. Following his conversion to Islam in the early 1600s, the Raja of Goa called on neighbouring kingdoms to accept the Islamic faith. When only minor states responded as desired, he declared a Holy War. The kingdoms of Soppeng, Wajo and Bone were defeated "and declared converted to Islam."[11]

As Islam seeped through the archipelago during the fifteenth century, the Hindu-Buddhist kingdom of Majapahit found itself in decline, facing competition from a number of rival ports, especially Malacca. In 1528, Majapahit was occupied by a coalition of Javanese Muslim rulers. The royal family fled to Bali, which remains predominantly Hindu to this day. With the fall of Majapahit the centre of political gravity returned in time to central Java, where a new inland state appeared, claiming for itself the name Mataram and centred on the present-day city of Yogyakarta. Unlike the earlier Hindu kingdom of that name, which had held sway over central Java six centuries earlier, the new Mataram was ruled by men who had converted to Islam, although the religion they followed was somewhat cut off from the Islamic influences that had helped shape the now-eclipsed states on the north coast of Java.[12] By the mid-1600s, Mataram controlled the huge rice granaries of both central and east Java.

Mataram, historians note, had the misfortune to blossom at a time when Dutch commercial impulses, supported by the careful accumulation of capital and backed by an initial advantage in military technology, were posing a major threat, especially in the thinly populated areas of the north coast, which were accessible by sea and vulnerable to naval gunfire. In 1602 the United East India Company (Vereenigde Oost-Indische Compagnie, or VOC) was set up with an official monopoly on all Dutch trade east of the Cape of Good Hope and the right to exercise sovereignty in that region on behalf of the Dutch state.[13] The company expanded rapidly, acquiring forts and ports and making extraordinary profits from the trade in cloves and nutmeg. But VOC fortunes declined over the next two centuries and the company was wound up, bankrupt, in 1799, its debts and possessions taken over by the Dutch government. In 1811, after France had occupied the Netherlands, the British East India Company sent a force to seize Java and other Dutch possessions in the archipelago. During this campaign, British forces captured and sacked the Kraton of the Sultan of Yogyakarta. The company set up an interim administration and appointed Thomas Stamford Raffles, a gifted, reform-minded thirty-year-old, as lieutenant-governor. The colony was handed back to the Dutch in 1816.

After the bloody Java War (1825–30), in which Central Java aristocrats struggled in vain to fend off the predations of the restored colonial power, and in which at least 200,000 Javanese died, the Dutch turned to the business of making profits.[14] Their chosen instrument was the Cultivation System, introduced in 1830 and requiring each village to produce export crops, especially coffee, sugar, tobacco and indigo for the colonial government.[15] The results of this policy were dramatic. At long last, Ricklefs has noted, "steady and immense profitability was achieved."[16] For Holland, ruled by the prodigal King Willem I and close to bankruptcy following the 1830 secession of Belgium, the massive surplus generated in the East Indies was providential in timing and indispensable in impact. The Cultivation System, a penny-pinching Minister of Colonies, Jean Chretien Baud, reminded Governor-General Pieter Merkus in 1842, was "the only system by which Java can remain 'the cork on which the Netherlands floats.'"[17] And so it remained. Between 1851 and 1866, remittances from Java were responsible for about one third of Dutch state revenues. These revenues "kept the domestic Dutch economy afloat: debts were redeemed, taxes reduced, fortifications, waterways and the Dutch state railway built, all on the profits forced out of the villages of Java."[18]

To administer this island, with its bountiful supplies of rice and its lucrative commercial crops, the Dutch recruited junior members (in age and rank) of the Javanese royalty and high aristocracy. These "younger brothers" (*para yayi*, or *priyayi*, as they were later known) were members of an essentially feudal elite, there being at that time no real bureaucracy in the Western sense, in contrast with China and Vietnam.[19] As the Dutch moved to establish more modern forms of administration, and as the functions of the government proliferated in the nineteenth century, the members of the ruler's extended family, joined by a growing intake of talented, well-off commoners (the so-called new *priyayi*), became a colonial native bureaucracy in the full sense. With that, the term *priyayi* came to refer to the salaried officialdom on Java. In the twentieth century, "the new *priyayi* were destined to play a crucial role. Those who remained in the bureaucracy joined the older *priyayi* to become the backbone of first Dutch, then Japanese, then Indonesian administrations. Those who turned their backs on government service led the anti-colonial movement and created the independent state."[20] By the end of the nineteenth century, the Cultivation System had produced mass suffering on Java, especially in the 1850s and early 1860s, and led to scattered local revolts.

By around this time there was a small but important ethnic Chinese community in the Netherlands East Indies. Chinese traders had begun arriving sometime around the tenth century. They lived in separate communities in the coastal ports; many married local women; a few became ministers in local courts. As the years passed, resident Chinese "continued to adopt local ways at the expense of their Chinese customs and a distinct local Chinese culture, called Baba or *peranakan*, emerged, mainly on Java."[21] By 1860 there were an estimated 222,000 Chinese in the Netherlands East Indies. Two great migratory waves would bring more Chinese to the East Indies in the sixty years to about 1930. The newcomers, who retained many of their Chinese ways and who did not mix so readily, were known as *totoks*, a term meaning full-blooded or newcomer and usually referring to Chinese or Dutchmen.

Although the Dutch had had a firm grip on Java since 1830 they were slow to expand their presence in the Outer Islands. Late in the nineteenth century they began to address that oversight, drawing into the fold as many as 300 self-governing principalities, some of them large, some of them minuscule. In many cases, the Dutch found it easy enough to persuade a traditional ruler to pledge allegiance. In other cases they met fierce resistance and were obliged to fight long and bitter campaigns, unleashing the full force of their East Indies Army (Oost-Indische leger), which would become known after 1933 as the Royal Netherlands Indies Army (Koninklijk Nederlands-Indisch Leger, KNIL). The Aceh War, which lasted for thirty years (1873–1903) by some counts and about forty years (1873–1913) by others, making it the longest war in colonial history anywhere, was a case in point. During that time, the Acehnese, led mainly by the *ulamas* (Islamic leaders, scholars), not the feudal rulers, who were quick to collaborate with the Dutch, lost 100,000 dead.[22] The colonial army death toll was 12,500—2,000 killed in action and another 10,500 dying of cholera and epidemics. Another 20,000 were wounded.[23] Elsewhere in the archipelago the army was bludgeoning other opponents into submission. In the final battles on Bali in 1906 and 1908, the royal families of Badung and Klungkung committed collective suicide, men, women and children advancing slowly into the fire of the Dutch guns, to fall in piles of blood-soaked corpses.[24]

By about 1910, the boundaries of the present state of Indonesia had been roughly drawn by this colonial army "at a great cost in lives, money, devastation, social cohesion and human dignity and freedom."[25] Traditional rulers remained, "often with vastly increased wealth and splendour", but for the most part it was the *controleur*, a lower level Dutch official, who was in command.[26] As a result of these changes, many Indonesians had been forced into a more modern age.[27] What is more, the peoples of Indonesia had been given "a potential common enemy." For the time being, it is true, there was no sense of common Indonesian identity. But that was to come in the early decades of the twentieth century.

The Dutch were now in a position to exploit the Outer Islands in the same way they had exploited Java. And exploit them they did, carving out plantations of rubber and palm oil, dredging the rivers for rich alluvial tin, sinking one new oil well after another. This was now mainly a matter of private capitalism, rather than state enterprises, and much more international, not just Dutch. Royal Dutch Shell was the great symbol of that internationalization; founded in 1907, it was the first of the oil multinationals.[28] By 1930, Royal Dutch Shell was producing about 85 per cent of Indonesia's oil, with two major US producers, Caltex and Stanvac, also taking up concessions.

At the same time, the Dutch had begun to feel the first twinges of guilt over their rapaciousness in the East Indies. In 1899 a Dutch lawyer who had spent seventeen years in the East Indies argued that the Netherlands owed its colonial subjects a "debt of honour" for the prodigious wealth it had drained from the Indies under the Cultivation System and a corresponding obligation to raise living standards and promote economic development.[29] In 1901, the government introduced the so-called Ethical Policy, aimed at making some restitution for that exploitation. Under the new policy, there was to be greater government involvement in economic and social affairs. There was to be new funding for health, education, communications, irrigation and other infrastructure projects. All the same, there were limits to what the Dutch were willing or able to do.

Nor were conditions at all static. Irresistible political, demographic, economic, religious, racial and social forces were building in the East Indies, brought on by decades of rapid change. An expansion of the education system, though limited, had produced rising literacy levels, even if adult literacy was still derisory (7.4 per cent in 1930). Newspaper circulation was growing. The construction of the railway system had made it easier for people to move about, broadening their horizons. The rapid decline in infant mortality and the introduction of anti-epidemic measures in the 1880s and 1890s had augmented a surge in population which had been gathering pace since early in the nineteenth century. In the two years after World War I, the East Indies enjoyed an economic boom. But this fuelled a huge increase in the cost of living, especially in the towns and cities of Java, leading to widespread poverty and malnutrition. In the middle of 1921, the world economy went into recession, greatly exacerbating the hardship in the East Indies, especially on Java.

It was at just this time that Soeharto was born.

3

"They regard Holland as a very weak power"

If Yogyakarta was the domain of the eighth sultan in the Hamengku Buwono line, it was home, too, of the Pakualaman, the minor court, which had been established with the blessing of the British after they captured Java during the Napoleonic Wars. In Surakarta (Solo), which lay forty miles to the northeast, was the Sunanate, which, like Yogyakarta, the Dutch administered separately from the rest of Java and which also had an attendant minor court, the principality of the Mangkunegaran. These four small courts were all that remained of the once powerful state of Mataram, which had in effect been drawn and quartered during years of palace intrigue and colonial intervention.

II

The Princely Territory of Yogyakarta—as distinct from the small city of the same name—was a compact and overwhelmingly rural kingdom with a sixty-mile-wide base on the Indian Ocean and, in the north, a triangle of territory extending up to the summit of Mount Merapi (9,550 feet), one of the most destructive of Indonesia's active volcanoes, of which there are 129 by one estimate. Almost perfectly conical, Merapi rises, blue and immense, out of the plains of Central Java twenty miles north of the city of Yogyakarta, a plume of volcanic gasses, ash and steam drifting from its peak. It is a striking reminder of both the beneficial and destructive forces of nature. In 1930, when Soeharto was nine, Merapi would erupt, killing more than 1,300 people.

In the city of Yogyakarta, which had a population of 136,000 in 1930, three quite distinct communities lived side by side, one European, one Javanese, the other Chinese.[1] The Europeans, of whom there were around 5,600, exercised all political power and had their hands on the main economic levers, while going to some lengths to maintain the fiction that authority resided in the Sultan who, like his predecessors, concealed lack of power beneath a façade of court ceremony and by a cultivation of the traditional arts. Both the Dutch and the Javanese were much concerned with status, hierarchy, appearance, order and discipline. At the apex of the European social pyramid in Yogyakarta sat the Dutch Resident and his senior civil service officials, including a Dutch Assistant Resident.* The Resident had his offices in a small neoclassical palace in the heart of the town, across the road from the ramparts of Fort Vredeburg and a short carriage ride from the Kraton. One tier below the Resident came the director of the local branch of the semi-governmental Javasche Bank (Bank of Java) and the commander of the garrison. Still further down were the managers of the big sugar mills, the managers of the private banks, the teachers, the engineers and the more junior army officers, some of them Dutch, some of them Eurasian.

This social stratification was mirrored precisely in the seating arrangements in the dining room of the Sociëteit "De Vereeniging", or "*soos*", the Dutch club, which had been founded in 1822. This was the social heart of the local Dutch community and it stood alongside the Resident's palace. At the club, which was open for lunch and dinner, and which organized dances and an occasional film, civilians and army officers, most of them in the distinctive *jas toetoep*, a jacket of white drill with a stiff high collar and no lapels, dined and sipped their *kopi tubruk*, smoked their cigars and drank their whisky or *jeneva* (a strong Dutch gin), read the newspapers and spoke perhaps of the bleak economic outlook

* The office of Resident was upgraded to that of Governor in 1934.

or the news from Europe or about murmurings of native unrest. In the evening, men wore a smoking jacket, or tuxedo, always white, and with a stiff white detachable collar on their shirt. (Their wives, waging an endless battle against tropical heat and perspiration, often brought spare detachable collars.) Almost all the Europeans and most of the well-to-do Eurasians were members of the club. It was not open, at least in the early years, to Indonesians. It was also off limits to colonial army non-commissioned officers (NCOs) and privates, even those who were fully European.

At the apex of the Javanese social pyramid sat the Sultan, presiding over elaborately delineated sub-tiers, which included the princes, the *patih* (grand vizier), the regents and the other high officials. The Resident, who had "graciously consented" to the Sultan's ascension only four months before Soeharto's birth and on whose arm the Sultan went forth on official occasions, rather in the manner of a bride going to the altar, was responsible for ministering to the ruler's self-esteem and ensuring that he supported Dutch policy. A half squadron of KNIL horse cavalry was kept in Yogyakarta as an honour guard for the Sultan, providing an escort of pomp and circumstance when he went out in his state carriage.[2] Powerless though he was, the Sultan presided over a world in which the ruler was seen as an instrument of the cosmic order, preserving harmony, discipline and equilibrium within his realm.[3] This was an arrangement which suited the Dutch admirably and to which the Javanese nobility had resigned themselves, although there was growing resentment at the Dutch presence among the younger princes.

In 1930 there were 8,900 Chinese in Yogyakarta. Most were Hokkien, members of a dialect group from southern Fujian on the China coast opposite Taiwan. Most were *peranakan*: many had some Indonesian ancestry; many had adopted some local customs. Those at the lower end of the social scale spoke Javanese, those in the middle "Chinese Malay".[4] The children of the more prosperous Chinese attended Dutch schools and spoke Dutch, but they were few in number. The Chinese were merchants, shopkeepers and petty traders. Some of the wealthier ones were prominent in the *batik* industry or had shops on Jalan Malioboro, the main street. The Chinese were also *tukangs* (skilled labourers or craftsmen); they worked as tailors, tinsmiths, furniture makers and so on. As in other cities and towns in the East Indies, a Dutch-appointed Chinese mayor, or captain, served as an intermediary between the colonial state and the Chinese community, keeping a register of names and looking out for Chinese interests.

For the most part, Dutch officials confined themselves to the main towns, a world of government offices and police stations, of big banks and trading houses, of schools and hospitals, of clubs and cinemas. The officials responsible for everyday affairs at the lower levels of the administrative structure were Javanese, retainers of the Sultan. This had consequences in hamlets such as Kemusu. "Nowadays," Soeharto was to observe in the final months of his presidency, "they teach school children how hard Dutch repression was. But to tell you the truth, I never saw a Dutchman [when I was small.] The Dutch all lived in splendid houses in the towns and controlled the Javanese community through *pribumi* [indigenous] officials who were employed by the government and through Chinese merchants and so on. Kemusu, where I was born, was a farming village with no running water and no electricity, having nothing to do with the Dutch."[5]

That did not mean that Kemusu and other rural villages around Yogyakarta had been unaffected by Dutch colonialism. On the contrary, the influence of the Dutch, for good and ill, lay all around. It could be seen in the fields of sugar cane and tobacco that stretched for mile after mile, generating such great profits for European commercial interests while imposing an onerous burden on traditional farmers. It could be seen in the narrow-gauge and often moveable rail lines that snaked across the plains, enabling cane to be brought in to the Dutch-owned sugar mills. It could be seen in the heavier gauge railway line which linked Yogyakarta to Jakarta and Surabaya. It could be seen in the road and rail bridges that had been thrown across the nearby Progo River, anchored solidly on concrete pilings and with box-like iron girder spans. It could be seen in the tarred roads that were beginning to link the major towns of Java and in the broad new canals that had been constructed, with their weirs and heavy sluice gates, to meet the needs of the sugar industry, which had an insatiable thirst for water.

Most of this infrastructure had been put in place to advance Dutch commercial interests. But as a result of the Ethical Policy, benefits were beginning to flow, albeit slowly, to ordinary Javanese. By the time Soeharto was born, Kemusu had a primary school, where the children of small land owners could get three years of rudimentary education, assuming of course that their parents could afford the fees, the Dutch colonial government being all too aware that there were practical limits to the amount of funding that could be made available in the name of ethics. The impact of the

Ethical Policy could be seen, too, in something as mundane as the tiled roofs that were beginning to appear on some of the village houses. Until the early twentieth century, houses had been built with roofs of thatch. As recounted earlier, these harboured rats and other vermin and the Dutch had decreed that houses were now to have tiled roofs.[6] This had helped to contain the rats. But it had given the houses a rather creaking, crooked look. The roofs sat too heavily on lightly-framed structures, in much the same way that Dutch colonial rule sat too heavily on Java, creating the sagging "saddle-roof" effect that one still sees on some older buildings, even in the heart of Yogyakarta.

III

Although Soeharto's first four years seem to have been passed in some contentment, even happiness, he had been born into an unsettled and uncertain world, with Java in the grip of profound social and economic change. Many Europeans, it is true, were complacent in the early twenties about the Dutch position in the Netherlands East Indies. The Dutch colonial authorities, however, had ample grounds for concern. There were threats from both within and without. Japan, which had astonished the world when it decisively defeated Imperial Russia's Baltic Fleet at the 1905 Battle of the Tsushima Strait and which had succeeded in gaining control of Korea and Taiwan, was casting a covetous eye on the Netherlands East Indies, with its abundant oil, tin, rubber and rice. The Dutch, a senior British official noted in 1921, had been "in terror of Japan" during World War I, fearing that Tokyo would ignore Dutch neutrality and make a lunge for their lucrative and lightly defended tropical possession.[7] And although that had not occurred and the Dutch now welcomed the influx of Japanese capital, if only to balance British and American interests, the fear of Japan remained. Nor, it seemed, were those fears unfounded. The Japanese were "obsessed by the idea that their country is one day destined to be the mistress of the Pacific and of its islands. They regard Holland as a very weak Power, and her colonial empire as doomed to disruption. Japan must have a say in the disposal of this rich empire. So she is steadily increasing her knowledge of the country, her vested interests therein, and the numbers of her merchants and colonists."[8]

There was a threat, too, from new ideas that were abroad in the world. In 1916, Lenin had put forward the thesis that revolutions in overseas colonial possessions were both possible and desirable and might serve to hasten revolution in Europe, thus advancing world revolution.[9] This doctrine was approved when communists from around the world gathered in Moscow in July 1920 for the second Congress of the Communist International (Comintern). "Following the dimming of hopes for an early revolution in Europe," one historian has noted, "all eyes were fixed on Asia."[10]

The ideas of Marx and Lenin were to fire the imagination of many young Asian revolutionaries, not least in the East Indies, China and Vietnam.[11] In 1914, Hendricus Josephus Franciscus Marie Sneevliet, a dapper, haughty, thirty-one-year-old son of a Jewish cigar maker in Rotterdam and a man whose commitment to revolutionary socialism was to have a significant impact in both Indonesia and China, established a small Marxist-oriented Indies Social Democratic Association (Indische Sociaal-Democratische Vereeniging, ISDV). The left wing of this association was to provide the core of the later Indonesian Communist movement. That process took off when, in Semarang in May 1920, two young Javanese activists, Semaun and Darsono, changed the name of the ISDV to the Communist Association in the Indies (Perserikatan Kommunist di India, PKI), the first such party in Asia.

Known after 1924 as the Indonesian Communist Party (Partai Komunis Indonesia), the PKI would become, in time, the third largest Communist party in the world. When the Comintern delegates gathered in Moscow in July 1920, the Communist Association in the Indies was two months old. In July 1921—the month in which Soeharto was abandoned by his mother—Mao Zedong was one of thirteen Chinese and two foreigners who assembled at a house in the French concession of Shanghai for the founding congress of the Chinese Communist Party. One of the foreigners was Sneevliet.[12] That same year, Ho Chi Minh joined the French Communist Party and began to work with the Comintern. Early in 1930, ten years after the Indonesians founded the PKI, he was to establish the Vietnamese Communist Party, which, later that year, changed its name to the Indochinese Communist Party on instructions from Moscow.

The PKI would be crushed three times in the next four decades—by the Dutch when it staged an ill-prepared rebellion in 1926–27, by the three-year-old Republican government when the party backed an equally ill-prepared rebellion at Madiun in 1948, and finally in 1965, when Soeharto launched a merciless purge of party supporters following the murder of six key generals. Those who had planned the first of these actions envisioned an Indies-wide uprising against the Dutch, but rebellions broke out only in Banten, West Java, (November 1926) and West Sumatra (January 1927).

The revolt cost the party dearly. The Dutch arrested 13,000 people, shot some who had taken part in killings, and sentenced 4,500 to prison terms. More than 1,300 were sent into internal exile at Boven Digul, a camp on the remote and inhospitable upper reaches of the Digul River in West New Guinea.[13] The Communist Party was banned. Many prominent non-Communist leaders were also detained or sent into internal or external exile. This put an end to Communist activity in the Indies until after World War II.

Nor was it only revolutionary Marxism which posed a threat to an established order in Asia in 1921. In India, Gandhi's non-cooperation movement was making dramatic gains, with the British facing a continent-wide campaign against their rule.[14] In the Dutch Indies, a similarly restless spirit was emerging. The first stirrings had come in 1908 with the founding of a society called Budi Utomo (Noble Endeavour), which sought to promote the study of Javanese culture and to achieve improved access to Western education.[15] In the event, Budi Utomo was to remain a vehicle for the Javanese aristocratic class, with no mass base, and was soon overshadowed by three other organizations, all of them explicitly nationalist.

The most important of these was the Sarekat Islam (Islamic Union), which was established in 1912 out of an organization set up to defend the interests of Javanese *batik* merchants against the inroads of ethnic Chinese traders. After a successful boycott of Chinese *batik* dealers and a related upsurge in Chinese-Indonesian violence across Java, Sarekat Islam developed, at a speed that alarmed many Europeans, into the first mass political movement in Indonesia, attracting perhaps as many as half a million members, first in the cities, then in the countryside.[16] Sarekat Islam proclaimed its loyalty to the Dutch but it was soon giving vent to dislike not only of the Chinese but also of *priyayi* officials and the Dutch. Central to the group's success was the widespread belief that Haji Oemar Said Tjokroaminoto, the charismatic Sarekat Islam leader, might be the long-awaited *Ratu Adil*, or "Just Prince", the messianic figure who, according to traditional texts, would liberate Java from foreign domination.[17] Before long, Tjokroaminoto would be overshadowed by his more charismatic protégé, a young, well-educated man named Sukarno, who, in 1945, was to become Indonesia's first President. By early 1921, the year of Soeharto's birth, the nineteen-year-old Sukarno had begun his political career.

The second organization that came to prominence at this time was Muhammadiyah ("Followers of Muhammad"), a Muslim educational and social welfare association that sought a purified Islam stripped of local accretions. Founded in 1912 by a mosque official in Yogyakarta and drawing much of its support from Muslim traders in the city, Muhammadiyah steered clear of direct involvement in politics. However, it was to declare in 1924 that Islam and Communism were incompatible and was to advocate in 1945 that Indonesia become an Islamic state. By 1938 Muhammadiyah was claiming a membership of 250,000 and had spread throughout the main islands of Indonesia.[18] It ran more than 800 mosques and prayer houses and nearly 1,800 schools, at one of which Soeharto was by then a student. The third of these organizations, the PKI, gave expression to radical socialist ideas.

By the early 1920s the foundations had been laid for what was to become a powerful and multi-faceted Indonesian nationalist movement. This was divided, it has often been argued, into three main streams, respectively Islamic, Marxist and secular nationalist, although the appropriateness of those distinctions is now challenged by some historians. Sukarno would later seek to unite these very different elements, or at least paper over the gap between them, in the name of anti-Dutch unity. As it happened, the attempt to unite Islam and Marxism in Indonesia was doomed to failure.

None of this, it is true, was to have much impact in the small world of Soeharto's village, at least for now. But Soeharto had been born at a time when a new sense of Indonesian identity was emerging. As the American scholar Ruth McVey has noted, the word "Indonesia" had begun to replace the colonial "Indies" in political discussions; in intellectual circles people began to talk seriously about an Indonesian state, and Indies Malay—the future Bahasa Indonesia—began to be spoken instead of Dutch by Indonesian delegates to the Volksraad, an advisory People's Council established by the Dutch in 1916.[19] In October 1928 delegates to a Youth Congress in Jakarta would declare their support for three ideals: one homeland, Indonesia; one nation, Indonesia, and one language, Bahasa Indonesia. They would also formally adopt a flag of red over white. The song *Indonesia Raya* ("Great Indonesia"), later to become the national anthem, was performed for the first time in public at the congress, to great applause.

IV

For the time being, however, it was poverty, rather than politics, that was of pressing concern in villages such as Kemusu. This was a time of acute hardship. For all its fertile soil, natural beauty and rich historical associations, Central Java was a deficit area, a region of want and malnutrition. One reason for this was that the population had been growing at what appeared to be an unsustainable rate. No one knows what the population of Java was in 1800. The best estimates put the figure at between seven and ten million in 1815.[20] By 1920, it had risen to almost 35 million, due in part to Dutch public health measures, including a rise in smallpox vaccinations and an expansion of paramedical services in the last half of the nineteenth century.[21] By 1940, it was close to 50 million. That is a five-fold increase in 125 years even if one accepts the higher figure of ten million in 1815. By one estimate, Asia as a whole only doubled its population in the 150 years to 1950.[22] This made Java one of the most densely populated regions in the world. When a census was taken in 1930 it found that the largely rural territory of Yogyakarta had the second highest population density on Java, after Surabaya, at that time the largest city in the East Indies. This was putting extreme pressure on agricultural land and resulting in low rice production per capita.[23]

In Central Java, rice was the staple food only of the relatively well off; poorer people were forced to eat maize and cassava for many months of the year.[24] Men took up secondary jobs during the slack season, many producing roof tiles. Women sought menial work, which, however poorly paid, helped supplement their family incomes. In 1930, Yogyakarta had the highest rates of female labour force participation in the colony, with 60 per cent of women engaged in some kind of work, mostly as agricultural labourers, handicraft workers or petty traders.

The problems created by rapid population growth had been exacerbated by Dutch commercial greed. In April 1921, the government-subsidized *Neratja* newspaper reported, there was so much land in the Yogyakarta region under contract to the sugar factories that farmers could no longer adequately look after the needs of their wives and children.[25] This had resulted in a large number of poor women seeking work in the city and environs of Yogyakarta. "They are cloth traders," the paper wrote, "and outside the town they even work as labourers, hauling water, dragging sand and stones etc, all of which they do not because they like it but from poverty."[26] Many other women were engaged in the production of *batik tulis* (handmade batik), either in *batik* workshops or at home. Still others worked in agricultural processing, making *tahu* (soybean curd) or *tempé*, or found work in tobacco processing.

The onset of an international recession was compounding these problems, especially in the cities and towns of Java. For two years after World War I, the East Indies had ridden on the back of an economic boom, with profits high and most employers granting large wage increases.[27] This helped feed huge increases in the cost of living, with the rice index jumping from 140 in 1919 to nearly 230 the following year. The boom ended abruptly in the middle of 1921. As the world went into recession, exports—and government revenues—fell. In an attempt to balance the East Indies budget, the incoming Dutch Governor-General slashed public expenditure and increased taxes. The weight of the new taxes was placed on an already overtaxed Indonesian population.[28] The union movement, which had grown both in strength and militancy during the boom years, challenged these moves.[29] In August 1921, a strike closed down Surabaya harbour, the hub for all seaborne commerce in the eastern islands of the archipelago. In 1922 and 1923, the situation grew even worse, with Java hit by two great strikes, the largest of their kind during the colonial period. The first was organized by pawnshop workers, the second by railway workers. Both were crushed, the latter "swiftly and ruthlessly."[30]

V

When Soeharto was four, his mother reappeared and took him to live with her and her new husband, Atmoprawiro. Given the affectionate nature of the relationship between the small boy and his great-aunt, this must have been an upsetting separation, the more so in that there is nothing to indicate that Sukirah had kept in close touch with her son in the years since his birth. Soeharto gives no hint, however, of any distress he might have felt, simply noting that his mother soon gave birth to her second child, a daughter who died shortly afterwards. Then came six other children, all of whom survived. Soeharto eventually had twelve half-brothers and sisters. There is nothing to indicate that he felt especially close to any members of this ever expanding body of half-siblings. Of the twelve, the only one who features prominently in his later life is Probosutedjo; he was to become a privileged and prosperous businessman under the New Order government, the beneficiary of various credits and concessions.*

Sukirah seems to have found herself in reduced circumstances following her second marriage and was obliged to take on some of the menial work that was the common lot of village women in this part of Java. Sometimes, according to Soeharto, she "worked as a street vendor to help boost our modest income."[31] During his presidency, Soeharto seldom missed an opportunity to emphasize the acute poverty he had experienced in his stepfather's house. The household economy was "tight" and he was not given any trousers until he was five, something he found deeply embarrassing. "It was only after I became five years old that I got to wear knee-length black trousers for the first time in my life. I remember I was often teased by kids in the village with nasty words. Even as a little boy I felt how poor I was more often than just once or twice."[32] This remembrance of poverty, the Indonesian newspaper editor and ambassador Sabam Siagian felt, explained a great deal. "He is ... very conscious of the fact that he comes from a fairly humble background in Java and had a Javanese king, the Sultan, as his deputy. After the Sultan was sworn in as Vice President, Soeharto was unable to conceal a mood of almost gleeful satisfaction. With his hand cupped in front of his mouth in a gesture of confidentiality and a little smugness, he said to a friend, 'I have a Javanese king working for me now!'—or words to that effect."[33]

Significantly, it is, once again, an older male relative, in this case his mother's father, Atmosudiro, for whom Soeharto feels a special affection. One morning, he relates, his grandfather gave him the task of taking a water buffalo to the rice fields. On the way, the buffalo slipped into an irrigation ditch and was carried along with the stream. Frightened, Soeharto jumped in and followed him, eventually finding himself stuck, unable to move forward or backward. He knew he was expected in the rice field by 7:00 a.m. but here he was stuck in the river, crying and feeling sorry for the buffalo. To his relief, his grandfather sent someone to look for him "and all turned out well".[34] On another occasion his grandfather gave him a goat, which filled him with delight. "The animal became a friend I would never forget."

---

* In 2005 Probosutedjo was sentenced to four years' jail for corruption. He admitted giving his lawyer US$1.6 million to bribe prosecutors and judges dealing with his appeal.

In his memoirs, Soeharto recounts only one story from this time about his mother and it concerns a drama that seems to have played itself out largely in her absence. "I recall the day when Ibu Sukirah was about to leave for the market," Soeharto writes, speaking of his mother with an air of detached formality. "She gave me a *bil*, a coin worth half a cent, but I accidentally swallowed it. I cried and cried, scared to death, and, worse still, other kids told me the coin would stay inside me forever." His fears were eventually assuaged by "the advice of my elders, who assured me that I was all right."

Soeharto's recollections of Buyut Notosudiro, his maternal great-grandmother, are more powerfully charged, a study in resentments nurtured for more than sixty years. On one occasion Soeharto was playing with a boy named Darsono, who, though described as a brother, seems to have been a cousin of some sort. Soeharto's great-grandmother "had just made a shirt and asked me to try it on, and I felt so happy. Suddenly, though, she took a closer look at me and exclaimed, 'Oh, you're Harto! Get your brother, Darsono!' Mbah Buyut told me to let Darsono try on the shirt and then told him it was his; it wasn't meant for me. I was devastated. My heart cried, 'Mbah Buyut loves Darsono more than me.'" Darsono, it appears, was the son of a well-to-do family. "His parents were much better off than mine. So why did my great grandmother give the shirt to a boy who already had enough? I felt humiliated, hurt, very forlorn and sad. I wondered why life was like this. I thought, we were both her great-grandchildren. Why were we treated differently? Mas Darsono already had enough shirts. I didn't. Why did great grandmother make one for him and not for me?"

Soeharto seems to have been close to neither of his parents, feeling apparently that they had rejected him. Instead, he sought out love and acceptance in the homes of other relatives. The picture that emerges is of a child who felt, with some reason, that he had been hard done by, brought up as he was amid considerable poverty. As a boy, Soeharto seems to have been quite insecure, grateful for small acts of kindness yet brimming with resentment towards those who had slighted him, always conscious of scores that needed to be settled.

When did Soeharto start school? The evidence is contradictory. In the late 1960s, he seems to have told O.G. Roeder, a West German journalist who produced a semi-authorized biography, that he began school at the age of eight, which would probably mean the latter half of 1929.[35] He also seems to have told a Japanese correspondent that he was eight when he entered elementary school.[36] That may be correct. But, as will be seen, it does not tie in with what Soeharto said about his subsequent move to a school in Wonogiri. Whatever the truth of the matter, he was enrolled in the village school in Puluhan (Buluan), Pedes, a hamlet not far from his stepfather's house, having shown that he could reach over the top of his head with his right hand and touch his left ear.[37] The Dutch used this simple but effective method as a way of determining how old a child was in places where there were seldom any reliable birth records. Later, after his mother and stepfather moved to the southern part of Kemusu, he attended the village school in Pedes. In each case, Soeharto and other village children walked to school, barefoot and wearing a red Javanese *kain* (*bebet*) and belt.

As a newly-enrolled student in one of the local village schools (*desascholen*), also known as people's schools (*volksscholen*), Soeharto was a direct beneficiary of the Ethical Policy. In 1900, there had been only 266,000 Indonesian pupils in private or government schools in the whole of the Netherlands East Indies.[38] Almost all were children of upper class or well-to-do Indonesian and Chinese families and even they found there were clear limits to what they might expect from the education system. Mass education for lower-class Indonesians did not begin until village schools were introduced in 1907. These schools, which were funded mainly by the fees they levied but with government subsidies, offered a three-year course in the vernacular language and focused on basic literacy, numeracy and practical skills. The number of village schools grew rapidly.[39] By 1930–31, when Soeharto was in his second year, about 1.6 million Indonesians were in the vernacular primary schools, obtaining at least a modicum of education. Another 85,000 were in the infinitely more prestigious European school system, where the language of instruction was Dutch.

Soeharto was in a class of twenty-five at the village school and sat on a bench at the back. The curriculum covered five subjects: reading, writing, counting, drawing and singing. Students were taught to read and write in both the Javanese Palawa script, which is adopted from a form of Sanskrit used in the coastal regions of south India in the fourth century AD, and the Roman script. Although he was not the best in the class, his teacher Sastrodihardjo recalled, "Soeharto liked reading and counting very much. In these two lessons he always got good marks."[40] School fees ranged from two and a half cents to 10 cents a month, depending on the ability of the parents to pay. In Soeharto's case, the fee was five cents. This suggests that his stepfather was not quite as poor as Soeharto was later to make out or that he received help from some other quarter. According to Roeder, this school was at Tiwir, about four miles from the village.

In the Dutch East Indies, as in other European colonies of the time, children received an education shaped to a disproportionate degree by a colonial view of the world. The standard atlas used in the more prestigious elementary schools was a case in point. Although Holland is only a third the size of Java, a full page was devoted to each of the twelve Dutch provinces. The 3,400 mile-wide Netherlands East Indies appeared on a single page. As Indonesians were not slow to note, this meant that the great rivers of Borneo or Sumatra looked much the same as the short canals of a Dutch province. When it came to history, the emphasis was on "the history of the fatherland." Students learned about the accomplishments of Dutch national heroes, including men such as Van Heutsz, who had subjugated the East Indies, sometimes with extreme brutality. There was no mention of Indonesian resistance leaders, who were seen by the Dutch as wrong-headed or self-seeking. There was no mention of what Indonesians saw as the National Awakening of 1908 or the Youth Pledge of 1928.

Soeharto entered primary school at a time when Java was beginning to feel the impact of the Great Depression. Overnight, the sugar market collapsed, producing massive unemployment. It is true that rice farmers now had more land for rice, but they had lost almost all of the income from sugar industry payments for wages, rents and compensation. Since the price of rice collapsed, too, having extra rice production did nothing to replace the income lost from sugar. For landless labourers, the situation was bleaker still.

VI

In 1930 or 1931, when Soeharto was nine and in his second year in the *desascholen*, his life was subjected to further disruption.[41] Without warning, his father appeared and announced that he was disappointed with the way his son was being brought up in Kemusu and not satisfied that he was getting an adequate education at the village school.[42] As Soeharto recalled, "Seeing a poverty-stricken household, he said, 'This child cannot grow into an upright man if left here. He needs [a proper] education.'"[43] Soeharto, he felt, "could expect a better home and upbringing" if he were living with a family that was better off.[44] On an earlier occasion Soeharto had painted a more graphic picture of his plight. In 1971 he is said to have told a friend that he was at that time "a dirty, ragged, unlettered urchin" who spent his days tending his stepfather's sheep [*sic*; goats]. "I was very dirty and I wore only a ragged pair of dirty shorts," he said. "My father 'kidnapped' me and took me to Yogya and bought me trousers and a shirt in a Japanese shop."[45] The story had a ring of authenticity, but some of the details look wrong and there may have been some misquoting or exaggeration.

As it happened, Kertosudiro's younger sister was married to a *priyayi* agricultural officer, Mas Ngabei Prawirowihardjo, who was "more prosperous than any farmer."[46] The couple lived in Wuryantoro, a town more than forty miles to the southeast and twenty-four miles south of Solo. Kertosudiro had arranged that henceforth Soeharto would live with them.[47] As Soeharto later recounted, his father came to the point rather abruptly. "Harto," he said, "I know a better place for you. You had better go to Solo [sic], to your aunt. I've already talked to her. She agrees."[48]

It is quite common in Java for children to be sent to live with more prosperous relatives.[49] This custom, which the Javanese call *ngéngér*, can confer obvious material and educational benefits on a child. He or she is taken into the household of an uncle or aunt and treated as a member of the family, dining with them and attending a better school than might otherwise be possible, acquiring in the process a moral debt (*utang budi*) which can never be repaid. But there are benefits, too, for the foster parents, some of whom may be childless, others of whom may not as be quite as altruistic as they would like people to believe. One such benefit is that the foster child is obliged to do various household chores in return for food and board. Another is that the practice "greatly enhances the social prestige of the foster parents", some of whom, driven by ambition, have been known "to take in as many impoverished nephews and nieces as possible", often exploiting them and treating them worse than servants, who are at least paid.[50]

In Soeharto's case, there were two highly unusual aspects of the *ngéngér* arrangement. The first is that his father made the decision to send the boy away without consulting Sukirah, who had now had care of their son for five years. Knowing that she was bound to object, thus making the child "an object of struggle and dispute", he simply turned up and spirited the boy out of the village, in effect kidnapping him. Soeharto was not permitted to say goodbye to his mother or to any of his half-brothers and sisters.[51] He was told instead that he could say farewell to only two people, his great-aunt and his schoolteacher. The second unusual aspect of the *ngéngér* arrangement is that Soeharto was to be left in a distant and unfamiliar town, without any of the customary back-up arrangements. There were to be no routine visits by either or both parents, arriving with some fanfare from the village, dressed in their best clothes, bringing roasted corn and other small treats. There were to be few visits back to a home base during school holidays. At nine, Soeharto was to be cut off almost entirely from his immediate family and friends, sent to live first with an aunt and uncle, then with a succession of foster families, some of whom, it has been claimed, were to treat him harshly.[52]

There were three people who might have been upset, if not traumatized, by Soeharto's sudden disappearance from the village. One was his mother, who, it would appear, had become quite attached to him, even if he was less attached to her. Soeharto made it clear in 1974 that she would have refused to let him go. But in the various accounts he gave of his early life, he does not give any hint that he felt his mother had been harshly done by or that he sympathized with her plight. In these accounts, the emphasis is always and almost exclusively on his own suffering. Soeharto's only hint at the grief his mother may have felt comes when he indicates, almost in passing, that she was still "longing for me" nearly a year later.[53]

Another person who might have been upset was Soeharto's great-aunt, who had served as an effective mother-substitute during the boy's early years and who still seemed to see a great deal of him. Soeharto does seem to allow that his departure from the village in such charged circumstances left his great-aunt deeply upset, although her feelings were presumably kept in check by the knowledge that her nephew was seeking to give his son a better chance in life. As one biographer wrote, "Tears came into the eyes of the old woman who once had helped to deliver him and who had taken care of him for many years. She embraced the child and told him: 'Be a good boy. Be helpful and never forget other people.'"[54]

The third person who would have been upset was Soeharto himself. In his autobiography Soeharto was to dismiss this extraordinary episode in one bland sentence. But his sense of loss and dislocation is evident in an account he provided in 1969. According to his biographer, "The boy was shocked for the moment. He did not want to leave the small joys of his life in the village. He did not argue as he had never opposed his father, but it was bitter not to be allowed to say goodbye to his closest friends.

His father took him quietly from the village without informing the other families."[55] There is nothing here, or in any of the other accounts that he gave, to indicate that he felt any regret at not being able to say goodbye to his mother. He did find it difficult—"a sad affair"—to leave his goat, however. He fondled the animal and called it pet names and "remembered all the adventures they had experienced together." Once that was done, the goat was sold at the village market. Soeharto's schoolmaster said goodbye and left his pupil with a homily. "Be honest," he told the boy. "Wherever you go, work and learn."[56]

With these exchanges out of the way, Kertosudiro and his son climbed into a *dokar*, a two-wheeled pony trap, and left the village for the nearby Rewulu railway station, the father relieved presumably that the operation had been carried out without his former wife learning of his intentions. From Rewulu, father and son took a train to the Tugu Station in the heart of Yogyakarta. Here, the proceeds from the sale of the goat were used to buy Soeharto a pair of trousers, a shirt and a hat at the Japanese-run Fuji store in Jalan Malioboro. He changed into the clothes at once, leaving his old ones behind, a symbolic as well as a practical break with the past. Later that day, father and son went on by bus to Solo.[57]

4

"An invisible motivating force"

In 1930, Surakarta (Solo) was a small and neatly laid out court city where two very different worlds, one Javanese and ostensibly Islamic, the other Dutch and stoutly Christian, had coexisted for a century, since the end of the Java War, just as they had in Yogyakarta. At the heart of the town stood the Kraton of the seriously overweight Susuhunan (Sunan) Pakubuwono X, a monarch of intemperate habits and eccentric pursuits who had been on the throne for thirty-six years, in the course of which he acquired a consort, forty secondary wives, forty-five children and seventy grandchildren.* Pakubuwono X, who was sixty-three in 1930 and who is remembered today "as the last Surakarta king endowed with a truly regal aura", was held in awe by many Javanese.[1] It was said that his mystical eye could see events which occurred anywhere in his kingdom and he was known "to converse with all animals in their respective languages".[2] He

* The Sunan's principal consort was a younger sister of the Sultan of Yogyakarta, Hamengku Buwono VIII. From time to time the royal couple would visit her relatives in Yogyakarta. On these occasions, the Sunan and his consort travelled in an expensive, late-model limousine, followed by a string of other vehicles bearing relatives and senior court officials. The Sunan's secondary wives, all forty of them, came along at the end of the procession, travelling together in a bus. Upper-class boys would come out to watch and nudge one another as the bus went by.

Pakubuwono means the Axis of the Cosmos, in much the same way that Delphi was known, in the sixth century BC, as the *omphalos*, the Navel of the World.

was best known, however, for his capacity to harness the power of magic and for his exceptional skill at prophecy, gifts which he was said to have inherited from his forebears.

Like his nine predecessors and his distant relatives in Yogyakarta, Pakubuwono X had no political or military power, this being firmly in the hands of the Dutch governor, a man who towered over him when the two appeared together on high occasions of state, the former dressed in great finery, his blue velvet jacket bedecked with honorary medals the size of small plates and worn over a batik *kain*, his left hand clutching the elbow of the governor in the approved manner. But the Sunan was "tremendously popular and nettled the Dutch through a series of royal progresses in which he was lionised by his people as if he were in fact the island's true ruler."[3] On these journeys, His Royal Highness was in the habit of tossing coins as alms to his appreciative subjects from the window of his automobile, a monarchical prerogative which, as we have seen, Soeharto was to revive when he dedicated the refurbished gravesite of Mangkunegoro I and others from that court in 1971, only three years into his presidency.[4]

A little to the north of the Kraton stood the palace of Prince Mangkunegoro VII, the head of the smaller of the two Solonese courts. To the east of the two palaces lay the modern heart of the city, with its Dutch banks and commercial houses, its churches and schools, its government offices and clubs, its telegraph offices and hotels, its hospitals and clinics, most of them imposing buildings, whitewashed and stolid, many with neoclassical façades. Here, too, were Chinese shops and pharmacies and restaurants, some with traditional North Sea step gables or cornices. Many of the streets had names—Beatrixlaan, Heerenstraat, Gouverneurslaan, Van Limburg Stirumlaan—more suited to Amsterdam or The Hague than they were to a city in Central Java. They were lined with casuarina (*cemara*) trees and well swept. During the morning the town was busy and crowded. Later, in the heat of the day, the mood was unhurried, almost soporific, and the streets were quite often empty, except for a few cars, which had running boards and canvas hoods, and four-wheeled pony traps. A tram ran along the main street.

II

O.G. Roeder claimed in his 1969 biography that Kertosudiro and his son travelled by train from Yogyakarta to Solo. From Solo's Balapan railway station, he wrote, they made their way to the home of Kertosudiro's younger sister, Ibu Bei Prawirowihardjo, or Bu Bei as she was widely known, and her husband, Ngabei Rawit Prawirowihardjo, or Prawiro for short. Where exactly did this couple live? According to Roeder and to a Japanese journalist who interviewed Soeharto three decades later, Ibu Bei and her husband were living in Solo, although they were to move later that year to Wuryantoro.[5] Soeharto does not seem to have distanced himself from Roeder's claim when it was made (and it is possible that he did not see the later Japanese-language account). But in 1974, at the press conference called to refute the *POP* magazine allegations, and later, in his 1989 autobiography, the President gave a different account.[6] His aunt and uncle, he said, were living in Wuryantoro at the time. He and his father had arrived in Solo by bus and had continued, on another bus, to Wonogiri, a market town twenty miles to the southeast. From there, they had taken a taxi to Wuryantoro, a further eight miles to the southwest. They arrived at Kertosudiro's brother-in-law's house at around 9:00 p.m.[7] On arrival, according to Soeharto, who recalled the conversation many years later in somewhat stilted language, his father told the couple, "I leave Soeharto with you. Please take care of him. I am afraid of what will become of him if he stays in Kemusu. Therefore, I will be most grateful if my son can receive the education and upbringing he deserves."

If it is true that Ibu Bei and her husband were living at that time in Solo, Soeharto would have found himself in an unfamiliar city, where life, though unhurried by the standards of Jakarta or Surabaya, was faster and more complex than it had been in the village. According to Roeder's account, Soeharto was somewhat awestruck by Solo, bewildered during his first weeks by the crowds and the traffic.[8] Even if, as seems more likely, Soeharto was taken directly to the less hurried world of Wuryantoro, he was now living in a sizable town.

Solo, with its twin courts, its spendthrift and squabbling rulers (both destined to be swept aside in 1946 in a wave of revolutionary anti-feudalism) and its languid self-belief that it, not Yogyakarta, was the true centre of Javanese culture and tradition, was to occupy an important place in Soeharto's life in the years ahead, almost as important as Yogyakarta itself. Soeharto was to live within the domain of the Solonese rulers for the next four or five years and would return to the city of Solo in 1944, as a trusted junior officer under the Japanese. As a young regimental commander in Yogyakarta in 1946–48, he would witness—and for a time be swept along in—the sometimes deadly social and political surges emanating from Solo, by that time a crucible of violent revolutionary change, renowned for its unruly politics and its "Wild West" atmosphere. In 1948 he was to marry a young woman from the outer fringes of the Mangkunegaran royal family. The marriage would reinforce his identification with the city and would lead in time to his decision to build his family mausoleum on a hillside reserved for the tombs of the Mangkunegaran rulers.

Soeharto's move to Wuryantoro, which was part of the Mangkunegaran domain, meant that he now found himself in the home of unfamiliar relatives—his third family in five years. He would soon begin at a new *desascholen*, his third in two years. His childhood remained unstable. But if he had been uprooted from his village, there were three factors that helped compensate for the profoundly disruptive changes in his circumstances.

First, his aunt and uncle seem to have taken him into their home without reservation, treating him as one of their own children, of whom there were eventually ten in all. Soeharto became close to his cousin Soelardi, a boy some two years his junior who was the couple's fourth child. (The couple's seventh child, a boy named Sudwikatmono, was to become a prominent businessman under Soeharto's New Order government, doing well from government favours.) Speaking many years later about his aunt, a woman who is said to have combined "uncommon force and honesty" with her affection for Soeharto, and about his uncle, Soeharto said, "I was regarded as their eldest son and given the same treatment as their own sons, such as Soelardi."[9] On another occasion he said, "I came to look on her and her husband as my parents. I could feel the love they had for me."[10]

Over the years, Soeharto made numerous efforts to repay his aunt and uncle for all they had done for him. He put money into his aunt's bank account (which, it is said, she never touched); arranged for the couple to have a television set (she resisted this on the grounds that everyone in the neighborhood would want to watch and "My house won't be my own"), and urged her to have a telephone installed (she fretted that she would have to put money aside to pay for incoming calls). Bu Bei would not allow Soeharto to change the thatched shack at the back of the house where she cooked for the family. And although Soeharto would send his own doctor frequently to see her, it is said she would take medicine only if Soeharto himself spelled out the details. "There were lovely scenes as he opened the bottles and explained patiently when and how she must take the medicines," a friend was quoted as saying. "And she would take them."[11] When Bu Bei died in September 1971, Soeharto made a point of flying to Central Java with his wife in the presidential Jetstar to sit by her coffin all night receiving mourners and attend her funeral the following day. He had not been able to attend his own mother's funeral in 1946, caught up as he was in the armed struggle against the Dutch.

Second, Soeharto's surroundings were, as Hamish McDonald wrote after a visit in 1977, "of a distinctly higher social level than in his mother's home."[12] It is true that Wuryantoro does not lie in a rich agricultural region, one blessed, like Kemusu, with fertile soil and abundant water. As McDonald noted, "the houses are small and shabby, and the people poor. The surrounding hills are deforested and eroded, the farming yields poor, and the dry season long and severe." Prawiro and his wife lived in a low, wooden-walled and windowless house which "looks mean by present Indonesian city standards, but by the measure of the time and place ... was quite substantial." Socially and materially, Soeharto had come up in the world.

Finally, Soeharto was probably getting a better education than he would have received in Kemusu. He was enrolled in the third grade at a local *desascholen* and seems to have done well. "I studied each subject diligently," he wrote in his autobiography, "especially maths, which I liked so much and excelled in [so much] that I won special praise from the teacher."[13] While at this school, Soeharto "was asked by the head teacher to manage a small library, where a two cent fee was charged for every book borrowed".[14] That revelation may have no significance beyond the fact that it seems to have been the first time that Soeharto was entrusted with any special responsibilities, a sign presumably that he was considered honest and reliable.

There was, however, only so much that could be done at this late stage to make up for the deficiencies in Soeharto's education. His uncle, an agricultural official working on experimental farms, would almost certainly have had a good command of Dutch. His children attended a local Dutch-Native School where they were receiving a good primary education with Dutch as the medium of instruction.[15] Soeharto, on the other hand, had come up through the village school system. That meant that when he went off each morning to a Javanese-language people's school, Soelardi was at the HIS, being carried inexorably forward in a Dutch-language stream. At his school Soelardi became acquainted with Siti Hartinah, the future First Lady. She was the second of eleven sons and daughters of R.M. Soemoharjomo, the *wedana* in Wonogiri. Hartinah's mother was the daughter of R.M. Panji Hatmohudojo, an artillery lieutenant in the Mangkunegara Legion, a small, Dutch-sanctioned royal army.[16] As noted earlier, Hartinah was a fourth or fifth grade descendant of one of the ruling princes.

In Wuryantoro, Soeharto's life appears to have followed the normal patterns of boyhood. At one time, according to his teacher, a man named Djojosujitno, Soeharto got into a serious fight with the son of the chief police officer of the district, the two boys surrounded by a crowd of other schoolchildren.[17] In his memoirs, Soeharto is at pains to deny the story, insisting that he engaged in only one fistfight, a clash in Kemusu that ended in tears. In his spare time, Soeharto liked to roam the fields with a home-made catapult (*plintheng*), apparently killing birds and small animals. His uncle thought this cruel and the boy was often scolded. According to Roeder, he "made good by carefully cultivating the small garden at the back of his uncle's house, planting and tending vegetables for the family kitchen."[18]

Soeharto writes in his memoirs that his life among the farmers in Kemusu during difficult times in the twenties "had aroused in me a distinct feeling of sympathy for them". These feelings had been nourished by the knowledge and experience he gained from his uncle in Wuryantoro. Often, he recorded, he accompanied his uncle on his inspection rounds, learning from him not only the theory of agriculture but also about the practical aspects of farming. "I remember that at three experimental farms where he worked … Pak Prawirowihardjo let me till the land, which I really began to love. I learned even more from listening to his conversations with farmers." On one occasion, his uncle received an award from the *bupati* (regent) in recognition of his success in introducing *orok-orok,* a shrub that could be used to fertilize barren land. "Pak Prawiro's tireless work and creativity inspired me. I became more energetic and even won a contest in growing crops, coming in ahead of his sons in the categories of onions and garlic, which were rated the best."[19] This was to be the first of many claims by Soeharto that he was the best at some exam or test. Some of those claims are demonstrably untrue.

When Soeharto had been living with his aunt and uncle for a little over a year, his stepfather, Atmoprawiro, turned up in Wuryantoro with two other male relatives to say that his mother was longing for her son and wanted him back. Soeharto conveys the impression that he had no wish to stay for any length of time in Kemusu, where he would be in a house with his mother's growing number of children by her second husband. He was in no position to argue, however. His stepfather took him back there, presumably with the consent of his aunt and uncle, promising he would return him to Wuryantoro after Lebaran, the holiday at the end of the fasting month, when school would resume. "But," Soeharto writes, unable to conceal his bitterness after nearly sixty years, "that promise was broken. I had to stay much longer at Kemusu and went to school in the village of Tiwir."[20] Speaking of this event on another occasion, Soeharto said, "I was again taken away to my mother's place ... Looking back, I realise I suffered greatly in my childhood as a result of my parents' ill-feeling towards one another."[21]

There is nothing to indicate that Sukirah's longing for her son manifested itself in any special treatment towards him. If it did, Soeharto thought it not worthy of mention. As far as one can tell, he couldn't wait to leave her house. A year was to pass, however, before his aunt and uncle came to take him back to Wuryantoro to continue his education there. His tally now was three families, three major moves and spells at four separate primary schools. He was eleven or twelve. Nor was that the end to all the moving. There would soon be new relatives with whom he would be obliged to live. There would soon be new schools that he would be obliged to attend, although none of them of any great educational repute and none in which the principal language of instruction was Dutch, the mastery of which was the key to advancement in the world beyond the school gate.

III

In the pre-war East Indies there was a daunting—but not impermeable—barrier between two main educational systems.[22] On one side of that barrier was a prestigious Dutch-medium system, both public and private, which catered to students from primary school through to university entrance. On the other side was a government-run primary school system where teaching was in the vernacular languages. There were as well private schools of one kind or another, some of them providing both primary and secondary education.

Children of higher-status and/or well-to-do Indonesians and those from wealthy Chinese families were able to enter the Dutch-language system if they could establish that they spoke Dutch as their first language at home or had at least a good command of Dutch and if their parents could meet the minimum income requirements. The most privileged of these children were those who spent seven years at a European Lower School (Europese Lagere School, ELS) and another five at a Higher Civil School (Hogere Burger Scholen, HBS), of which there only a dozen in the entire East Indies.[23] The HBS offered a rigorous secondary education that followed the Dutch metropolitan curriculum and qualified graduates for admission to university in the Netherlands or allowed them to enter one of the faculties (*hoge scholen*) for law, medicine and technology that had been established in Jakarta or Bandung.[24] Sukarno, Indonesia's first president, graduated from the HBS system.[25] So, too, did a significant number of other Indonesians who were to hold high office in post-war governments, in the bureaucracy or in the Indonesian army.[26] For most Indonesians, however, a HBS education was out of the question. In the late thirties the monthly tuition fee was *f*12.50, equal to about 600 kg of rice. That meant a child's father had to be at the salary level of a *wedana* or above. In a typical HBS class there might have been one or two *pribumi* students and four or five Chinese; the rest would have been Dutch or Eurasian.[27]

Other well-off Indonesian children were able to get a good education by spending seven years in a Dutch-Native School (Hollandsch-Inlandsche Scholen, HIS) and three—or, in many cases, four—years at a More Extensive Lower Education (Meer Uitgebreid Lager Onderwijs, MULO) school, which was a sort of junior high. The MULO system had a so-called Preparatory Class (Voor-Klas) for students who were not fluent in Dutch or not otherwise ready to proceed directly to the first class, adding a fourth year to their time in the MULO system.[28] Apart from the extra study, they were taught, quite literally, how to hold a knife and fork, and other (Western) social niceties. When a student was sixteen or seventeen and had graduated from MULO, he or she might spend three years at a prestigious General Intermediate School (Algemene Middelbare School, AMS), of which there were only eight in the colony. Like the HBS, the AMS was designed to carry promising students through to university entrance level.[29] Sutan Sjahrir, who would become Indonesia's first prime minister in late 1945, had graduated from an AMS high school and gone on to study law in Leiden. A number of the young men who were to become senior army officers during the first twenty to thirty years of independence had also graduated from the AMS. Many others had found their AMS education cut short by the arrival of the Japanese.[30] An even larger cohort of officers had reached the MULO stage.

Whichever of these two Dutch-medium streams a student entered, he or she received a thorough education. In the early years of school, students took about a dozen subjects. Dutch, English, French and German were compulsory, although German would be dropped when Germany invaded Holland in May 1940. They also studied Latin, Greek, mathematics, science, history, geography, biology and possibly another science.[31] Indonesian high school students were required to read European literature—Dutch, English, French and German—in the respective languages. In short, young Indonesians in this system found themselves immersed in a predominantly European world: European languages, European literature, European philosophy, European history, European geography. Those who came up through these schools were part of an exceptionally favoured—and exceptionally small—minority. In 1930, there were fewer than 85,000 Indonesian students in the European school system, or 0.14 per cent of the total population of the Dutch East Indies.[32]

Alongside this Dutch-medium system there existed 9,600 government village schools of the kind Soeharto had attended in Kemusu and elsewhere and a smaller number of vocational schools. There were, as well, a large number of good private schools run by bodies such as Muhammadiyah and Taman Siswa (Garden of Pupils), a pre-war nationalist school system influenced by the principles of Montessori and Rabindranath Tagore, and a large number of rural *pesantren*, or Islamic boarding schools, some of which provided a decidedly indifferent education. It was impossible for a student to go directly to university from any of these schools.

These distinctions were to be of key importance when it came to the selection and promotion of officers in the post-war Indonesian army. By and large, men who had come up through the non-European stream were to find themselves excluded from the upper echelons of the army. Soeharto was to prove one of the few exceptions to the rule. The deficiencies in his education would nearly—but never quite—stymie his chances of preferment. There would be a price to pay, however. Many officers who had received a Dutch-language education would come to feel superior to those who had not, as Soeharto was to discover and resent. In later years, some army colleagues and prominent civilians were to argue that Soeharto suffered from a strong inferiority complex. He was, they suggested, envious (*iri hati, sirik*) of those who came from more privileged backgrounds, jealous of their attainments and status.

Though complex, this system had provided education, often of the highest standard, to children of those of means. It had also offered a rudimentary education to those whose parents could afford to send them to a village or urban primary school. The problem was that the less prestigious primary school system did not tie in with the secondary school system. As a result, it was not possible for a village child to proceed to the secondary level, which existed only in the European system.[33] That was precisely the situation in which Soeharto would have found himself had he been born a decade or so earlier. As it happens, in 1921, the year of his birth, the colonial government had sought to address that deficiency by setting up the first *schakelschool* (link school), one of a number that were to follow. These were designed to connect the village school system, where the vernacular language was used and the education was rudimentary, to the parallel and more prestigious Dutch-language stream. Under this system, a village child who had completed three years of education could spend five years at a *schakelschool*, where the instruction would be given, at least in part, in Dutch. At that stage, he or she would, in theory, be at the same level as a child who had completed seven years of primary education in a Dutch-Native school. From there, it would be possible to go on to a MULO junior high or to a vocational school.

In the event, the Link School system was of little significance in the wider educational context. (In 1938, when there were nearly two million children in indigenous schools, most of them in village schools, there were only 5,023 students in Link Schools.[34]) But it turned out to be providential for Soeharto, who had been moving like a pinball between three rural and urban *volksscholen*—in Puluhan, in Wuryantoro, in Tiwir and once again in Wuryantoro—with two of those schools in and around the village of Kemusu and the other one in a town more than forty miles to the east, a significant distance at that time, particularly for someone from a poor family.

In about 1934, when he had spent four years in various *volksscholen*, a year more than was customary for a village child, Soeharto enrolled in the *schakelschool* in Wonogiri.[35] By this time, he would have been twelve or thirteen. This was an enormously important step in his life. He now jumped out of the Javanese-language education stream, with all its limitations (only 40 per cent of primary school students remained long enough to become literate), into a system designed to prepare students for higher, Western education. In Wonogiri, Soeharto was to make his first painful acquaintance with the Dutch language, with its difficult grammar and, for those taking it up late, equally difficult pronunciation.[36] Soeharto's grasp of Dutch would never be good, which was to make it hard for him to compete with his better-educated army contemporaries. But he had at least a smattering of the language. When he was President and B.J. Habibie, a favoured subordinate and his eventual successor, was Minister for Research, Soeharto would sometimes react to something that upset him by expressing himself in Dutch. "Rudy!" he would say, "*Dat mag je niet doen. Dat is fout.*" ["Rudy, you can't do that! It's wrong!"][37]

There were limits, however, to what the *schakelschool* could offer. It was part of the elementary school system for "native" Indonesians, a poor cousin of the elite primary schools which offered students seven years of instruction, all of it in Dutch. Given all this, there was never much prospect that Soeharto, who had always been far outside the elite stream, would ever reach, let alone complete, junior high school. The chances of him gaining a senior high school education were still more remote, even assuming that his parents could afford the fees, which were quite beyond them. He was not just in the wrong educational stream; he had never really had a chance to make the change. Soeharto had started at the village school when he was eight and stayed on in that system for four years. That meant he would have been seventeen by the time he finished *schakelschool* and was ready to begin junior high, while most of the new pupils would have been be thirteen. He would have been twenty by the time he completed junior high and twenty-one if he were required to do an additional MULO "prep" year. He would have been twenty-four before he completed senior high school.

In short, a good secondary education was out of the question. Soeharto may have had a more favoured education than most Indonesians. But he was never going to catch up educationally with the Dutch-speaking sons of the Javanese, Sundanese and Outer Island urban elite, young men who were about to make the transition from privileged primary school to privileged secondary school. From this group would come virtually every senior officer with whom Soeharto would be competing for promotion and overseas staff college courses in the fifties and early sixties. To most of them, he would always be something of an outsider, someone from a very different and relatively humble background, competent enough and pleasant enough but taciturn and distant, not a man one got close to. To most of these officers, the Dutch language came easily. When Soeharto began at the *schakelschool* the most that he could hope for was that he might in time qualify for enrolment in one of the Dutch-run *vakscholen*, which were low-level vocational schools. He might perhaps become a mechanic or an electrician or a carpenter.

If political leaders such as Sukarno, Hatta and Sjahrir had digested Western thinking, Slamet Bratanata, a bright, outgoing and sometimes acerbic former cabinet minister, once reflected, then so too had a "second wave" of army officers. Below that, however, was a third group "who have no notion at all."[38] Soeharto, Bratanata thought, was in the third group: he had gained his view of the world from the rigid moral certitudes of the *wayang* (Javanese shadow plays) he so much enjoyed; a world where, for example, a prince might be obliged to murder the father-in-law for whom he has great respect because the latter is from an inappropriate background. "Soeharto is just the *dalang* (puppeteer) type, the *wayang*-educated type. Here you have the *wayang*-educated type. Here you have the Fabian House or the Marxist-educated type. What is the *wayang* type? .... [T]hey derive their wisdom about how to behave from the *wayang* stories. If you read the *wayang* stories, 'That's how a king should behave, how a soldier should behave.'" Raden Arjuna, the great and graceful warrior of the Mahabharata, had hesitated to kill his uncle, who was also his teacher. But Prabu Kresna, who was descended partly from the gods, had told him, "No, it is the duty of a fighting prince to kill for a purpose and to have no remorse about it; it is just something one has to do in the course of one's duty, without sentiment; nothing personal." On hearing this, Bratanata liked to point out, Arjuna had killed his uncle.

Major General Achmad Sukendro, a robust, outgoing anti-Communist officer from Central Java, made his career in the West Java Siliwangi military region and served in the late 1950s as head of army intelligence under General Nasution, earning a reputation as an astute and ruthlessly practical operator. He expressed a similar view to Bratanata. Speaking of Soeharto, he said, "He is a traditional Javanese, so this patrimonial system he gets it from his birth, his education in Solo (sic). This patrimonial system is not unknown to him. The whole education of Soeharto is this. And modernised by his military training and background. Even the military system is patrimonial—*sistem bapak*."[39]

IV

In the short term, Soeharto faced other, more pressing problems. He had to contend not just with another new school (with a very different regime) and another new town but with another new foster family. In an arrangement that seems to have been made by his father, Soeharto, together with his cousin Soelardi, went to live in Selogiri, a small town about four miles northwest of Wonogiri. They boarded there with one of Soelardi's older sisters, who, like Soeharto's aunt, was married to an agricultural officer.

Although there is no indication that either of Soeharto's parents bothered to visit him in Wuryantoro or Selogiri, he is said to have made an effort to keep in contact with his father. Soelardi's older brother, who also lived in Selogiri, had bought Soelardi a bicycle, a prized possession in those days. About once a month—or so Soeharto later claimed—he and Soelardi rode to his father's house in Kemusu, generally staying overnight.[40] During school holidays, Soeharto would stay for several days, renewing acquaintances with former friends. The claim that such journeys took place is important because it would suggest that Soeharto made a determined effort to keep in contact with his father, who, though he went to some trouble to foster his son out, is generally presented as someone who otherwise had little or no contact with him. The story is implausible, however. Soeharto was only thirteen when he lived in Selogiri and Soelardi only eleven or twelve. The return journey to Kemusu was 110 miles. This would have been a dauntingly long round-trip for two boys on an adult bicycle. Nor can there have been as many trips as Soeharto suggests, unless they continued after he moved on from Selogiri.[41]

As it happened, the marriage of Soelardi's sister broke down and Soeharto had to move yet again, this time to Wonogiri, where he lived with another of his father's relatives, Hardjowidjono, a retired railway employee. Hardjowidjono and his wife had no children and Soeharto, by now well versed in the obligations of the *ngéngér* system, under which children are sent to live with more prosperous relatives, helped them around the house in return for his board. In some Javanese families, a foster child may find himself or herself treated quite harshly, even cruelly, by his or her relatives, worked as hard as any servant but given no payment for the work done. There are grounds for believing that Soeharto now found himself in just such a position. Because money was short, he got work assisting in the contract-sewing of brassieres. "I managed to finish 20 pieces a day," he said.[42] He seems to have given most, if not all, of the money he earned to his foster parents. In an account he gave in 1998, Soeharto said he was treated at this time "as a live-in student and houseboy."[43] He cleaned the house before leaving for school. He bought food from the market. He went to the well for water. He helped sell Ibu Hardjo's handicrafts.

"Sometimes," he wrote, "I even had to cook in the afternoon or when I didn't go to school. But I never complained."

There were, it is true, some benefits from the arrangement. "I learned many useful things at Pak Hardjo's home," Soeharto recalled. "I became a worker, someone who could stand on his own feet if necessary. And I knew I could learn many things quickly."[44] On another occasion Soeharto said, "My friends often came to help me because they needed me to play soccer. I did well both academically and in sports. For soccer, we used a handmade ball made of ragged cloth and stuffed with fruit peel. Proper soccer balls were too expensive."[45] One of his friends from those days, Warikin, recalled that Soeharto played in defence but often scored goals; "he could run fast, his muscles were as strong as rattan, his body tough. He attacked the ball and played hard."[46]

But none of that could assuage his sense that life had dealt him a bad hand. Already deeply scarred by the experiences of his early childhood, Soeharto seems to have found life in Wonogiri much harder than he ever publicly acknowledged. When he was a servant, said Mashuri, the one-time neighbour who spent ten years in his cabinet, he was determined to get rich. This determination was shaped by a powerful need for revenge. He wanted revenge because the rich family of his master had not treated him kindly. Soeharto had not been paid a wage and he ate his master's leftovers.[47]

Another former friend and cabinet minister, the aristocratic Haryasudirja, went further than this. He claimed that Soeharto was someone who bore a grudge not only against his father's relatives in Wonogiri but against his father and mother as well. Soeharto, he said, had gone out of his way to repay them in kind. "He would like to take some revenge," Haryasudirja said, "because his parents didn't take care of him."[48] Soeharto had blamed his parents for the fact that he had been adopted out to other families; he had not made a practice of visiting his mother's grave and may not even have known where his father was buried.[49] This alleged neglect of his mother's grave had created a serious strain in his relations with his half-brother, Probosutedjo, in the mid-sixties, not long before Soeharto rose to power.[50] Haryasudirja may have overstated the case. As we have seen, there are reports from at least 1975 that Soeharto was visiting his parents' graves each year.

Be that as it may, Soeharto was certainly capable of bearing a grudge. He seemed to recall clearly every slight or wrong committed against him, however trivial, storing each incident away in his prodigious memory, waiting for the time when he could settle each score, deriving a deep and obvious satisfaction once that had been accomplished. "This fellow," said Nono Makarim, a former editor of the newspaper *Harian Kami* and by the 1980s a prominent corporate lawyer, "has a very long political memory. He is a vengeful man, just as he remembers good services rendered and rewards them, sometimes too generously."[51]

In the opinion of Habibie, who became an *anak mas* (favoured child) of the future President, Soeharto's "bad childhood" might have been "an invisible motivating force" in his subsequent life.[52] Because he had not lived with his real father as he grew up and because he had been treated as second-best when living with various foster families, Habibie speculated, Soeharto had sought to compensate: he had sought to control himself, had sought to avoid making mistakes, had striven to do everything perfectly. "Maybe that's the reason why he's modest and quiet. Maybe that is a kind of invisible inferiority complex." But, Habibie added, Soeharto had never insulted anyone or played dirty games. "I never heard him ... make an embarrassing remark or insulting remark about whoever. Never! Never! Maybe because of his experience of childhood."

An Indonesian politician who saw a good deal of the President in the early years of his New Order government endorsed the view that the years of childhood neglect took a heavy psychological toll on the young Soeharto and that he never forgave his parents for treating him badly. Soeharto, he thought, was "a very lonely man."[53] He had been a rejected child, and the hardships and hurts of his childhood had made him asocial and egocentric, although not necessarily antisocial. He had withdrawn into himself, had become self-centred and inconsiderate of others. He had come to believe that he had to be careful at all times, suspicious of enemies who lay in wait. "And that is the drive behind him, according to me. That 'never again will I undergo this kind of experience of being rejected or neglected or belittled, humiliated' and so on and so on. 'Never again!'" Believing that the world was unforgiving and that he could not depend on others, Soeharto had set out to make himself strong and impervious to attack. He had been determined, too, that his own family would never suffer the economic privations he had endured. In this way, it was claimed, parental neglect created fertile soil for the corruption that was to become such a feature of Soeharto's adult life. Determined that his children would never suffer as he had suffered, Soeharto decided to store up capital for them. "And when it started, there was no stopping him." At the same time, the ex-politician suggested, Soeharto was a victim of his farmer's mentality. Soeharto lived a fairly spartan life, even when he was President: he ate simple food; he lived in an unremarkable house. But like a farmer who provides against an uncertain future by hoarding stock in his *lumbung* (rice barn), he went on acquiring wealth because it brought him peace of mind.

Some Western scholars have argued that Soeharto's troubled childhood left him not only self-sufficient and inward-looking to a high degree but straining for self-control. Soeharto, the Australian political scientist Angus McIntyre suggests, was a man "taxing his mind to maintain his composure. By thinking ahead, trying to anticipate events (especially disruptive ones), and thereby avoiding shocks, he tried to create the inner calm that more predictable parental behaviour than he enjoyed bestows naturally on its beneficiaries."[54] This, McIntyre maintains, goes some way towards explaining Soeharto's cautious, realistic and ultimately successful approach to politics. There was, however, a downside. This personal disposition "manifested itself in solipsism (other people did not loom large on Soeharto's mental screen) and coldness (he likened his mind to a computer)." Drawing on the works of writers who have depicted composure as a form of self-holding undertaken when the mother's care becomes tantalizingly unpredictable, McIntyre asks whether this is what happened in Soeharto's case. It is, he acknowledges, a drastic form of adaptation to substitute mind for mother, "but the circumstances here were themselves drastic, causing Soeharto, one imagines, much confusion, bitterness and despair."[55] The historian R.E. Elson has suggested that the emotional and material trials of Soeharto's childhood and youth "shaped an introspective and exceedingly self-reliant turn of mind."[56]

It does seem clear that the hardships and deprivations of childhood influenced Soeharto's character in profound ways. In his youth, the evidence suggests, he was polite and well-mannered but silent, self-contained and ruminative, intensely conscious of the inequities of life and harbouring a deep resentment towards those who had treated him unkindly. He came to value stability and predictability. He came to value security, both material and emotional. He went to great lengths to maintain his composure and sought, wherever possible, to anticipate events that might prove disruptive. He developed a certain inner coldness and vindictiveness, although these aspects of his personality were not immediately apparent, being disguised by an outwardly warm and pleasant manner.

It would be wrong, however, to make too much of the argument that Soeharto's style and behaviour as President can be explained by his disrupted childhood. That is part of the explanation, but only part. Several other factors were at work. First, as McIntyre himself notes, there is a consonance between Soeharto's carefully erected composure and Javanese cultural norms, which encourage just such a mastery of the emotions.[57] That said, it would be equally wrong to put too much emphasis on "culture" when seeking to explain Soeharto's behaviour as President. Many Javanese are not shaped by culture in this way; Sukarno is an obvious example. Second, Soeharto's military training under the Dutch and the Japanese and his experience of the revolutionary impulses let loose during the struggle for independence left him, as they left so many of his military colleagues and contemporaries, with a deep desire for order, stability and predictability. In short, Soeharto's behaviour as President was a product not simply of childhood trauma but also of cultural conditioning, military training and first-hand experience as an army officer serving in unstable and unpredictable times, a product of lessons learned and digested, of experiences filed away in a highly retentive mind.

5

"What kind of Islam is this?"

If Soeharto had spent his first eight or nine years in a hamlet west of Yogyakarta, he was to spend most of the four or five years that followed in the three small or medium-sized towns—Wuryantoro, Selogiri and Wonogiri—southeast of Solo. His character, already shaped by a sense of grievance, rejection and humiliation, by an awareness of the intrinsic inequalities of life and by a powerful desire to better himself, was now to be influenced in three additional ways. First, as an adolescent he was to develop an abiding interest in Javanese religion, or Javanese mystical beliefs as it is also known, rather than in Islamic rituals and beliefs, about which he had in any case only a rudimentary knowledge. In the course of that process, he was to learn more about the distinctive Javanese philosophy of life. Second, he was to absorb many of the values of the *priyayi*, the Javanese official class. Finally, he was to develop a deep interest in the subject of agriculture. These values and these interests were to remain with him for life and were to have a profound influence on his presidency. This chapter will focus on his interest in Javanese religion, which, for many years, perhaps always, appeared to loom larger in his life and his thinking than any strict adherence to Islam.

II

As noted earlier, Islam has played a vital—and frequently divisive—role in modern Indonesian politics, and during his presidency Soeharto was to promote his own surprisingly rigid views on the subject, drawing on beliefs he began to acquire during his early years in Central Java. Although nine out of every ten Indonesians identify themselves as Muslims, on Java, Clifford Geertz argued in his 1960 book *The Religion of Java*, it is necessary to distinguish between three broad cultural-religious communities, or *aliran* (streams).[1] One community (*abangan*) is made up of those who, while nominally Muslim, follow a syncretic Javanese religion that often incorporates elements of animism, Hinduism, Buddhism and Sufism, the mystical tradition of Islam, with an emphasis on ascetic practice, meditation and mysticism.

While acknowledging the Qur'an as "the ultimate source of all religious wisdom and knowledge", the Indonesian anthropologist Koentjaraningrat wrote in 1989, the average Javanese syncretic Muslim has practically no knowledge of this sacred book; even intellectual followers of Javanese religion show a striking lack of interest in the Qur'an and other sacred Muslim texts.[2] For nominal Muslims, the scholar Merle Ricklefs writes in his three-volume study of political and religious change on Java, Islam was largely a source of ritual practice at certain stages of life. An *abangan* rarely or never prayed, could not recite the Confession of Faith (*Syahadat*) or the Qur'an, rarely or never fasted during Ramadan and would almost certainly not contemplate the pilgrimage to Mecca. "But at birth and burial, *abangan* would expect Islamic rituals to be carried out. And some version might be wanted at a circumcision or wedding."[3] In 1930, Ricklefs observes, the Javanese were predominantly rural dwellers, impoverished, ill-educated and mostly *abangan*. At that time, of course, Soeharto was nine years old and living in rural Java. These days, *abangan* are "more likely to call themselves *kejawen* (Javanese, or Javanist, implying truly authentic Javanese identity); probably because of the implication that those called *abangan* were people without religion, whereas *kejawen* claim to have a coherent, but truly Javanese, set of beliefs." For pious Muslims, *abangan* or *kejawen* "is sometimes taken to mean just followers of *kebatinan* [mysticism, spiritualism] sects rather than a broader social category." The term *kepercayaan* is also used in place of *kebatinan*.

A second community (*priyayi*) consists of bureaucrats and functionaries, a number of them shaped by or aspiring to the values of a pre-Islamic worldview. The third community (*santri*) is made up of pious or orthodox Muslims. It is divided, in turn into two quite distinct—and rival—groups, one of them rural-based and traditionalist, the other urban-based and modernist. The orthodox groups differ, essentially, over two things: sources of law and cultural accommodation. The traditionalist community, which draws its support from a network of Islamic boarding schools (*pesantren*), especially in East and Central Java, and many of its leaders from a small circle of prestigious East Java religious families, stresses the importance of the four medieval schools of Islamic law and has been influenced by many local customs and ideas. The modernist community, which had its origins late in the nineteenth century when Javanese studying in Cairo came under the influence of the Islamic reform movement and the teachings of Mohammad Abduh (1849–1905), stands for a return to what it calls the fundamental truths of the Qur'an, stripped of all medieval accretions, while at the same time making use of modern scientific advances. Modernists tend to be scriptural and puritanical. They largely bypass the medieval law schools which the traditionalists regard as essential. They tend to reject cultural practices not set out in the Qur'an; traditionalists will accept them as long as they are not prohibited in the Qur'an.

Geertz's formulation was extremely influential for many years. Modern scholars continue to accept his broad categorization of three cultural-religious communities on Java, but they distance themselves from certain aspects of his analysis. His approach, they say, does not adequately encompass certain aspects of Javanese life. Writing in 1973, Benedict Anderson noted that Geertz's seminal work on the *aliran* had had an enormous impact on virtually all Indonesian specialists. But, he continued, political scientists had treated the three *aliran* as parallel vertical pyramids, frequently overlooking or underestimating the power relationships between them. Anderson argued persuasively that the *priyayi*, the "literate upper tiers of Javanese society", are, in fact, the power-holders within the *abangan* community.[4] A failure to make this distinction, he believed, had allowed some analysts to underplay "the real class conflict within the Indonesian (here particularly the Javanese) social system. The *abangan* were always conceived more as *abangan* than peasants, the *santri* more as *santri* than as businessmen and rural landowners, the *priyayi* more as *priyayi* than as aristocrats and officials."*

* Class distinctions had, of course, been emphasized by the PKI, before the party was destroyed in late 1965 by forces loyal to Soeharto.

Furthermore, political scientists had been inclined to treat *aliran* cleavages "as constant givens within Indonesian society, rather than as changing products of the historical process."

Other scholars were to elaborate on the second of those points. They faulted Geertz for characterizing *abangan* culture as deeply Hindu-Buddhist, when he should, they thought, have recognized its significant Islamic content.[5] In his 2012 book, Ricklefs takes issue with Geertz's belief that the *abangan* community is something fixed and immutable, impervious to Islamic penetration. That, he argues, is not the case. Rather, there has been, over hundreds of years, a sometimes glacial, but nevertheless remorseless, and now accelerating, process of Islamization on Java.[6] These days, too, Geertz's modernist-traditionalist paradigm is less and less used.

Although he makes no explicit mention of the fact in his memoirs, Soeharto came from a decidedly *abangan* background. He was part of a community which distanced itself not only from the Islamic modernists of the cities and large towns but also from Java's conservative rural Muslims, even though the religious practices of the latter take account of many traditional Javanese beliefs widely accepted in the *abangan* community. It is unlikely that Soeharto received much, if any, rudimentary instruction in the tenets and practices of Islam, unlike the children of the pious Muslim minority, who would have attended lessons given by the village religious functionary (*modin*) at the prayer house (*langgar*). It is unlikely that he was taught to recite the Islamic Confession of Faith—"There is no God but Allah and Muhammad is His Prophet". It is unlikely that he learnt the prayers that are supposed to be performed five times a day, at dawn, at noon, in the mid-afternoon, after sunset and in the early evening. He would have been aware, however, that some in Kemusu were devout Muslims. He would have grown up with the call of the *modin* summoning the faithful to prayer, the sonorous cry of "*Allahu Akbar*" ("God is Great") resonating through the palm fronds. He would have seen *santri* villagers making their way to the *langgar* for the noon prayers each Friday, washing their feet and hands before entering and then chanting the prescribed Arabic phrases and making the prostrations towards Mecca. He would have been familiar with the Fast, which is observed by all devout Muslims between dawn and dusk during the month of Ramadan. Indeed, it is possible that he and the other *abangan* children would have been present at the *langgar* for the prayers that were held on the morning of Idul Fitri, the end-of-Fast holiday, perhaps drinking from a young coconut in a symbolic breaking of the Fast. From time to time he would have seen a *haji*, a man, much respected, who had made the pilgrimage to Mecca, a rare event in those days when the practice was still, for most people, prohibitively expensive.

In the later years of his presidency, when it had become politically expedient for him to court the Islamic modernists whom he had once viewed with such suspicion and hostility, Soeharto was to play up the extent and depth of his early exposure to Islam, painting a picture of a pious boy who took his religious instruction seriously and who carried his Islamic beliefs with him into adulthood.[7] Few were persuaded by the case he made. Indeed, many of those who knew him well as a young man reacted with derision, portraying this as an example of Soeharto's dishonesty and hypocrisy. The evidence suggests that they were right to be sceptical. For Soeharto, as for so many others of an *abangan* orientation, Islam does not seem to have been more than a veneer at that time, an encrustation on a set of earlier beliefs, including a veneration of local spirits. None of his army colleagues could recall a time during the 1945–49 Revolution or during the early years of independence when he routinely performed the prayers and made the prostrations towards Mecca. None could remember him attending the mosque on Friday or fasting during Ramadan. Indeed, the very suggestion that he might have done these things had them shaking their heads and smiling in disbelief or competing with one another to reject the notion as unthinkable. What they did remember was that Soeharto was an adherent of Javanese religion. Some, particularly those who looked down on him, went even further and claimed that he was associated with *ilmu klenik*, a contemptuous term used by educated and upper-class people for a combination of "superstition, mumbo-jumbo and muddled peasant error."[8]

On Thursday, 24 February 1966, when he was consolidating his grip on power, having presided over a purge which had claimed the lives of many hundreds of thousands of Communists and alleged Communists, Soeharto held a meeting at Army Headquarters with a delegation from the anti-Communist Front Pancasila.[9] Members of the delegation, which was led by Harry Tjan, the secretary of the front, included Kiai Dahlan, a leader of the traditionalist, rural-based Nahdlatul Ulama (NU), or Revival of the Islamic Scholars' Party, and Lukman Harun, the chairman of the Muhammadiyah Youth Association.[10] Flanked by five fellow generals,

Soeharto made no secret of the fact that he was an *abangan* Muslim, as most insiders were well aware. He also made it clear that he was strongly opposed to any suggestion that Islamic law be applied in all its rigour to those who were only nominally Muslim. A month earlier, NU supporters had held an anti-Communist "show of force" in Jakarta, waving banners calling for a return to the Jakarta Charter, a discarded draft preamble to the 1945 Constitution that would have required all Muslims to follow Islamic law, which is known in Indonesian as *Syariat* (or *Syariah*) *Islam* and in Javanese as *Saréngat Islam*.

During the meeting, Soeharto questioned Dahlan about these calls. "I saw," he said, "that at the recent parade the NU was flying banners in support of the Jakarta Charter. What does it mean?" When Dahlan said a return to the Jakarta Charter would ensure "that the Muslims will follow the religious life and not be easily influenced by Communist atheistic teaching," Soeharto responded with a further question. "What," he asked, "is *Saréngat Islam*?" When Dahlan answered that question, Soeharto asked, "And what about people like me who are *abangan* and others who are Islam *abangan*? Are you going to force us to take part in [Islamic] prayers and observe all the other obligations?"[11] When Dahlan replied that such matters were up to the conscience of the individual, Soeharto brought him up short. "If it is so," he said, "then don't discuss this anymore. There's no need!" Afterwards, Lukman Harun told friends that Soeharto "seems to have an allergy to things that smell of Islam" [*"betapa alerginya Soeharto terhadap hal-hal yang berbau Islam"*].

Some time later, Soeharto received Subchan Z.E., a prominent NU activist who was chairman of the Front Pancasila, and several others at the Army Strategic Reserve (Kostrad) headquarters. When Subchan said at one stage that "with God's blessing" (*"Ridlo* [*Ridho, Réla*] *Allah"*) something or other would happen, Tjan recalled, Soeharto was "very much disturbed." He "interrogated" Subchan. "Why must you use *'Ridlo Allah?'* " he asked "dejectedly". Soeharto's reaction came as a surprise. "We knew he was *abangan,*" Tjan said. "But this was the first time he revealed himself as *abangan*, saying to Muslim leaders, 'Why do you mingle this with *syariah.*' It was the first indication, the flash of fire, that he meant what he said, even though it was expressed in a soft way. His manner was always soft." Those present grasped immediately where Soeharto was coming from. After the meeting, Subchan, who was from a *santri* family in Kudus, thirty-two miles northeast of Semarang, told the others, "Wah, this Soeharto is indeed a genuine *abangan*!"[12] At around the same time, Soeharto invited former Prime Minister Ali Sastroamidjojo, the general chairman of the large Indonesian Nationalist Party (PNI), to his home. He told his guest he was worried about a split in the PNI, as that party "could be a counter-balance to the Muslims."[13]

A close reading of the accounts Soeharto has provided of his early life reinforces the impression that his religious outlook was shaped more by Javanese religion than by Islam. In his 1969 biography, Roeder claimed that Soeharto's religious education "was not neglected" in Wuryantoro since the Prawirowihardjo's were "true believers".[14] That could mean almost anything. What we know is that in the late 1980s, when Soeharto was beginning to reach out to the Islamic community, he was keen to rework the story of his early life, placing a greater emphasis on Islam. In his 1988 autobiography the President wrote that he "underwent serious religious training because my uncle and his family were firmly steeped in the spiritual way of life."[15] In the evenings, he said, he learned to read the Qur'an at the *langgar*, often staying there all night with friends. He also joined Hizbul Wathon, the boy scout movement of Muhammadiyah. The reader of these passages is invited to conclude that Pak Prawiro was a deeply religious man who took Islam seriously. But the religious training seems not to have been solely Islamic. Indeed, the autobiography contains a passage that hints at something else. "In addition," Soeharto writes, with a rare trace of drollery, "I also received spiritual training from my foster father, such as fasting every Monday and Thursday and sleeping on the verandah of the house.* I followed all his advice consistently and faithfully. But there was one suggestion I didn't take up—sleeping on a *pawuhan*, a burnt-rubbish dump." Practices of that kind are more associated with Javanese mysticism than they are with conventional Islam.

It does not follow from this ambivalence, however, that Soeharto or his parents or his various foster families rejected Islam completely.

* In Java, there are two kinds of fasting, one associated with Islam, the other dating from pre-Islamic times. Orthodox Muslims are required by the Qur'an to fast only during the month of Ramadan and only in daylight hours. The Javanese call this duty either *puwoso* or *poso* (i.e., *puasa*). Another kind of fasting, Benedict Anderson observes, is called *mutih*, from *putih* (white), meaning you only eat white-coloured food, plain rice, the white of eggs and so on.

As noted above, many of those who follow Javanese religion have no difficulty absorbing elements of Islamic practice into lives shaped by pre-existing animist, Buddhist and Hindu beliefs. Circumcision is a case in point. This practice has been adopted by many people who could not be seen as devoutly Islamic. On Java, most Muslim boys are circumcised sometime between the ages of ten and fourteen, with a *slametan* held the evening before the operation.[16] More often than not, this is an occasion for conspicuous spending, with hired gamelan orchestras and shadow plays and as many as 200 invited guests attending a secular reception after the *slametan*. Soeharto, at fourteen, was at the upper end of the usual age bracket when the operation was held, the procedure having been delayed owing to a lack of funds. On the morning of the operation he would have sat in a tub of water for an hour or so and then dressed, wearing a new white muslin cloth under his sarong. He would have read the Islamic Confession of Faith and been circumcised by a specialist called a *calak* "who was often also either a barber, a butcher or a curer" and who would have used a knife called a *wesi tawa* (literally "scrap iron"†), probably with no antiseptic on hand.[17] Soeharto does not say where he was when the circumcision took place or whether either or both of his parents were present, although it would have been remarkable had they not been there. His mother, in particular, would have had an important role to play.

If the boy faints during the circumcision operation, Clifford Geertz has noted, his mother rubs his face with her sarong. When the operation

---

> This has nothing to do with Islam, but is bodily self-mortification, for a time set by the faster or by a spiritual adviser, and is continuous for 24 hours. It is believed to lower physical desires of all kinds, keep one watchful, and of heightened spirituality. It is usually done either as a spiritual exercise or to gain the power to achieve certain objectives, for example, passing an exam. This is much older than *puwoso*, and certainly comes from pre-Islamic culture.... One has to keep these two types of fasting distinct, since the Muslim fast is subjection to Allah's command, is non-continuous, is practiced socially in a group, and is not power-oriented, while the other is self-chosen, continuous, practiced individually, and highly power-oriented.

Benedict Anderson, personal communication. Soeharto is said to have adopted pre-Islamic fasting practices on a number of occasions before and after he became President.

† Geertz translates *wesi tawa*, less alarmingly, as "iron you can't feel."

is over, he is laid on a low bed and his mother steps across him three times, "demonstrating that she, too, is free of any hidden feelings toward the boy which might hamper the necessary process of his growing emotionally away from her toward manhood. This state of weakened emotional investment in one's immediate environment, or self-induced distance and disciplined aloofness from all events in the transient world of men—they call it having a 'flaccid heart'—is among the most valued of Javanese feeling patterns: *iklas*."[18] In view of the fact that Soeharto assigns his mother no more than a cameo role in his life story and that he recalls with such intensity the dismay he felt at being sent back to live with her when he was eleven, it seems reasonable to assume there was little danger that Sukirah might have hampered the process of him growing emotionally away from her. Soeharto, thanks to his disturbed and disrupted childhood, was well on the way to cultivating a disciplined aloofness and a suitably flaccid heart. After the ceremony, Soeharto felt "so happy and I was truly grateful."

Although he had been circumcised—the Indonesian word is *mengislamkan*, meaning to become Islamized—and claims to have been truly grateful, Soeharto's spiritual development was shaped increasingly at this time by Javanese religion, not by the tenets of Islam. When living in Wonogiri, he made the acquaintance of Romo Daryatmo, a noted mystic and faith healer, then in his mid-thirties. Daryatmo was to have a profound influence on Soeharto's life.* Tall and somewhat gaunt, with liquid brown eyes and immensely thick eyebrows, he combined a calm and quiet manner with a commanding presence. He was, like Soeharto's father, an irrigation official, and he seems to have spent much of his time trying to introduce aspects of the elaborate Balinese irrigation system into Java; that, in itself, would have been of interest to Soeharto, who was to have a lifelong preoccupation with anything touching on agriculture.

In his autobiography Soeharto refers to Daryatmo as a *kiai*, an old Javanese word which has two different meanings, depending on whether

---

* *Romo* is a high Javanese term for *bapak*, or father. In his official biography of Siti Hartinah Soeharto, Abdul Gafur refers to this man as Ki Daryatmo, Ki being a title of respect for men of religious learning.

the speaker is *abangan* or *santri*.[19] In its original meaning, which survives, this is a respectful form of address for something full of magical or spiritual power, either a human being or an inanimate magically powerful object such as a *gamelan* instrument or a royal carriage. The word later came to be applied to learned, respected *ulamas*, or teachers of Islam, especially as a form of address. Daryatmo was a Muslim and he knew the Qur'an. Indeed, Soeharto describes him as a *muballigh*, which is an Islamic term for a preacher.[20] But if he was a religious scholar, it was more in a Javanese *abangan* sense than in a conventional Islamic sense. He was a practitioner of Javanese religion, an adherent of *kebatinan*, a kind of "mystic father", a *kiai kebatinan* as it were, a man who used some Islamic words and sayings but who would have done so in a Javanese fashion. He was also a *dukun*, or traditional healer.

Soeharto was introduced to Daryatmo by his new foster-father, Hardjowidjono, who was both a follower and a near neighbour of the religious scholar-cum-healer. Before long, Soeharto had himself become a follower, finding in Daryatmo an approachable and learned man, a missing father figure who seemed to be in communion with the mysterious cosmological forces that govern the world. In his view, and in the view of many others in that area, Daryatmo had mastered the arcane disciplines through which a man can establish a harmonious relationship with God and could draw on his spiritual powers to cure the sick. "Whenever Pak Hardjo went to see him," Soeharto recalled, "he took me along and I was allowed to listen to their talks on religion and philosophy. I listened carefully to his dissertations on the Holy Qur'an. I learned about *samadi*, or meditation, and what *kebatinan*, or mysticism, was. He had many devotees, the devout and honest *kiai*, who was against any form of injustice."[21] In his memoirs, Soeharto devotes an entire page to this man, the obvious warmth of his account standing in stark contrast to the picture he conveys—or rather does not convey—of his parents. "I remember very well how kind he was," Soeharto wrote. "*Kiai* Daryatmo's way of giving explanations and teachings was really interesting to me. I was very keen to listen to his talks on the philosophy of life. Apparently, he, too, took a liking to me."[22]

What exactly are the Javanese mystic beliefs that were to feature so prominently in Soeharto's life? Followers of *kebatinan* seek to gain a deeper understanding of the meaning of existence, searching for the truth of the inner self, or *batin*.[23] Their aim is to establish a mystical union with God, either alone or through a school, of which there are hundreds. On Java, it is widely believed that a knowledge of the ultimate *rasa*, "which is at once the individual's true self (*aku*) and a manifestation of God (*Gusti*, Allah) within the individual" can be achieved through "a purity of will" and "a concentration of inner effort".[24] An individual can reach that state by "a disciplined withdrawal from mundane concerns for more or less extended periods of time and concentration upon inward things." The most important disciplines if one is to achieve this state are fasting and staying awake, although sexual abstinence can also help. Once this state has been achieved, an increased spiritual strength "allows one to pursue one's aims in this world with a fixed and unchanging will instead of being pulled here and there by distracting elements."[25] By making regular contact with God through meditation, it is said, or by going to places—a certain mountain, an ancient temple—that have been indicated by God, an individual can receive direct guidance from the Almighty. In view of this possibility of direct guidance from above, some Javanese believe that organized religion is almost superfluous.

Many Javanese are drawn to *kebatinan* because they are not satisfied with the way religion is taught and because the rituals of the organized religions are seen as foreign to Javanese culture.[26] They draw comfort from the fact that the science of Javanese traditional belief is expressed in their own language and is thus more accessible than ideas expressed in Arabic, a language which many Javanese find difficult and remote. Javanese who follow this path may say they profess Islam and they may find some use for Qur'anic verses, but they only take what they want from Islam. In the words of Mohammad Said Reksohadiprodjo, an expert on Javanese mystic belief, "a follower believes his *kepercayaan* goes much deeper than religion. He feels superior. He feels people who follow religion are only following outer things, not the essential things."[27]

In its purest form, *kebatinan* may not appear to be all that different from organized religion, save for the absence of prophets, holy books and widely accepted places of worship and save for the fact that some of the many hundreds of schools have set codes and formulas to govern the practice of meditation. However, *kebatinan* is closely intertwined with the practices of Javanese magic and sorcery, which involve an attempt to shape the forces of the supernatural order, both for good and ill. Some practitioners seek to achieve not only oneness with God and a certain degree of perfection; they seek power over their circumstances and over other people. Many schools are said to be intimately involved with various forms of white or black magic.*

There is no evidence that Daryatmo engaged in black magic, although one can never be sure of these things, if only because it is rare to find a *dukun* who will admit that he practices sorcery. But it is clear that he did engage in white magic, using his spiritual powers to diagnose ailments through numerology, through meditation or through a simple analysis of the symptoms. According to Major General Sudjono Humardani, a spry and slightly-built Javanese officer whom Soeharto befriended in the late fifties and who shared with him an interest in *kebatinan*, Daryatmo could heal seriously ill people simply by offering them a glass of tap water or even, if God so directed, a flower or stone.[28] Once his diagnosis had been made, he would prescribe the appropriate herbal remedy and place a spell upon it. Geertz has drawn attention to the inherent ambiguity of the *dukun's* power, "trafficking as he does both with God and with devils, able to sicken people as well as to cure them, and engaging both in devout supplications to a high God and in dubious contracts with less elevated spirits—*ndukuni* ('to *dukun* someone') means both to cure a person of a disease and to sorcerise a person into having one."[29]

* On Java, Professor Koentjaraningrat has noted, a *dukun* may seek to harness his unique spiritual powers to achieve any one or more of four major objectives. He may, for example, employ "white magic" to achieve a beneficial outcome for society in general, reciting magical spells and incantations to produce rain or a more bountiful harvest. Alternatively, he may employ white magic to ward off a natural disaster or to cure a sick person, healing being one of the strongest suits of the *dukun*. More negatively, a *dukun* may engage in "black magic", using his powers of sorcery in a vengeful and destructive manner on behalf of a client who wants to cause harm to an enemy or rival, killing him, perhaps, or making him vomit blood. In some cases, it is believed, a *dukun* can kill someone from a distance; the body of a victim may be found many miles away with needles in his stomach. It is this kind of magic, which is known as *guna-guna*, which tends to give *kebatinan* a bad name. Finally, a *dukun* may be consulted for his expertise in divination and numerology, which can be invaluable to someone wishing to know the most auspicious day to hold a certain event or to locate the place where thieves have hidden stolen goods. White magic amounts to little more than faith healing, as it is practised in some Christian sects. Black magic is an obscure art in which a mystic consciously misuses his spiritual power to the detriment of someone else. For details, see Koentjaraningrat, *Javanese Culture*, pp. 398–426.

Soeharto, introduced at about fourteen into this world of abstruse and profound knowledge, marvelled at its blend of magic, sorcery and spiritual power. Before long, he moved into Daryatmo's house, where he worked as a part-time assistant, rising early to prepare the master's coffee, joining him in reciting the dawn prayer, accompanying him on his rounds as an irrigation official, listening attentively as he discoursed on spiritual matters and dispensed advice, helping him as he prepared Javanese herbal remedies.[30] All of this had two consequences. First, it gave Soeharto a rare and valuable insight into Javanese religion, Javanese mysticism, Javanese medicine and Javanese philosophy, laced where appropriate with a dash of Islam; it also deepened his knowledge of agriculture. In Wonogiri, as in Wuryantoro, Angus McIntyre writes, we see Soeharto standing with his elders "listening and learning, thinking hard and, above all, being curious."[31] This, McIntyre argues, was one of the strongly positive aspects of his childhood and early youth and it helped compensate for some of the negative ones. Second, and perhaps more important, was the emotional significance of the bond that developed between Daryatmo and Soeharto. Coming as he did from an unsettled and unstable childhood, Soeharto found a sense of personal meaningfulness in the learning and orientation he acquired at this time. Daryatmo was not only teaching him things. In a way, "this man was perhaps pulling the threads of his life together and giving him a sense of direction [and] this was helping him to consolidate a kind of adolescent identity." Soeharto had not been flattened by his childhood. He had been able to turn negatives into positives.

Intelligent and impressionable, seeking to make sense of his place in the world, Soeharto found much in *kebatinan* that was congenial and he became in time an ardent believer in such practices, which seem to have become of far greater importance to him than the precepts of Islam, although he was still acknowledging the importance of Islam in January 1998, four months before his fall from power. "I am a Muslim," he said at that time, adding carefully but perhaps not quite truthfully, "I never failed to perform my prayers every day from my childhood." But, he went on, "it was only after I entered elementary junior high (sic) that I got to learn the Islamic creed. I had an opportunity to visit Kiai Daryatmo, the famous religious teacher.... Kiai Daryatmo emphasized that a man should have a sound spirit, with Islamic philosophy in harmony with mysticism. He had a strong influence on my spiritual development. Even now, it is to his teachings that I turn when I don't know what to do in politics."[32]

Daryatmo's supplicants came from all walks of life. Some wanted help with ailments such as skin disease or persistent fever. Others sought counsel on marriage or business problems or on difficulties they were having in dealing with the authorities. Some felt they were possessed by spirits or other entities. Some were being blackmailed. Soeharto looked on admiringly as Daryatmo ministered to their needs. "And I knew," he wrote, "that many of those who had sought his help and followed his advice recovered from their illnesses or were able to solve their problems."[33] At the prayer house in Daryatmo's home, Soeharto learned "a great deal ... about religion and belief in God. I heard first-hand the advice he gave to people who asked. They were educated people, traders, employees, as well as farmers and vendors."[34] Soeharto was to keep in touch with Daryatmo for decades to come. "He was the respected elder I would visit when I was regimental commander at Salatiga."

Daryatmo was politely evasive when asked in late 1969 about his relationship with the President. He acknowledged that Soeharto still came to see him but said the visits were infrequent. In five years, Soeharto would call on him "perhaps twice". When asked when the President had made his last visit, he replied brightly, "Oh, in August!"[35] At that time Daryatmo was living in a rambling wooden house in the hills outside Wonogiri together with his wife and nine of his thirteen children. Now seventy, he sat on the front verandah each day receiving visitors and dispensing advice. He relied, he said, on his spiritual power to "draw out" the problems and sicknesses of those who sought his help. He said he could not explain his mystic powers; he just had them in his head. According to Mashuri, the former cabinet minister, Soeharto called on Daryatmo at least once a month and sought his guidance.[36]

In his autobiography, Soeharto was to recall with pleasure the time he spent with Daryatmo. "I was allowed to help him write prescriptions for traditional medicine he gave to the sick—strange-sounding medicine made of rare herbs as well as the kind that grew in abundance in the village. Sometimes I stayed until late at night jotting down the advice he gave to those who were ill. That was how I became familiar with all types of leaves, roots, shrubs and herbs."[37] In different circumstances, it seems not impossible that Soeharto might have become a *dukun* himself. As Koentjaraningrat has pointed out, prospective *dukuns* learn their skills by serving as apprentices to established practitioners. Quite often, an established *dukun* will take his son or daughter as an apprentice "and in this way the profession is 'inherited'".[38] But if that possibility was ever canvassed, nothing came of it. What is clear is that Soeharto felt more than a sharp pang of regret when he was forced to leave Wonogiri. "To all good things an end must come," he wrote many years later, "and this was true of my relationship with Pak Daryatmo."

For a time in the 1960s and 1970s it was widely believed in Jakarta that Sudjono Humardani, by then a member of Soeharto's kitchen cabinet, was several rungs further up the spiritual ladder than Soeharto and dispensed guidance to him on *kebatinan*. In his memoirs, Soeharto was at pains to reject the idea. "One hears people talk about Sudjono Humardani as if he knew more about Javanese mysticism than me," he wrote, managing to sound churlish, conceited, mean-spirited, graceless and insecure all at once. "In point of fact, Djono himself used to do the *sungkem* [show respect by kneeling and pressing one's face to another's knees] to me. He considered me his senior and more knowledgeable about mysticism.... I just listened to make him feel good, but did not take in everything he said.... So those who thought that Djono was my guru in mysticism had it wrong.... He would ask me about it, not the other way around. He himself once said, 'I am a student of Pak Harto.'"[39]

In private, Soeharto was even more critical of his late colleague. People had said that Sudjono was his superior, he told Colonel Dwipa, a trusted associate who had dinner with Soeharto and his family at least once a week and who oversaw the production of the President's autobiography, "but he actually kissed my feet."[40] As Sabam Siagian observed in 1989, "It's that boy from Kemusu village who has outlived, physically and politically, all his rivals and challengers. He triumphed over [General] Yani, who won the prize as the top foreign student at Fort Leavenworth. He, Soeharto, has triumphed over all these clever people.... People like [General] Nasution and [Lieutenant General] Kemal Idris only gave him six months in 1966. He has triumphed. He has been there twenty-three years. He has outlived ... all those who were once so important."[41]

Despite Soeharto's written insistence that he knew more about mysticism than Sudjono, one prominent officer was inclined to play down the President's interest in, and knowledge, of *kebatinan*. General L.B. (Benny) Moerdani, a Eurasian Christian special forces officer and intelligence czar in whom Soeharto would repose enormous trust and power in the 1970s and 1980s, only to cut him loose abruptly when Moerdani tried to warn him of a growing popular backlash against the business dealings of the

Soeharto children, took issue with the view that Soeharto was a follower of *kebatinan*. In an interview in 1998, well after he had been pushed aside, Moerdani drew a distinction between *kejawen* and *kebatinan* and rejected the suggestion that Soeharto was a *kebatinan* man. "No, no," he said. "Pak Harto is not a *kebatinan* [man]. Pak Harto is a square realist. He's not *kebatinan*. That's what people think .... People think that Pak Harto is *kebatinan* because Pak Djono is around. And Pak Djono is a man who, whether you like it or not, he is a *kebatinan* fellow. Finish!" Pressed on this matter, Moerdani said, "Pak Harto is a *kejawen*. *Kejawen* is nothing to do with *kebatinan*. He is 100 per cent Javanese. And that's not to imply that he is a *kebatinan* fellow also."[42]

Soeharto's association with Javanese religion was to be of fundamental importance during the early years of his presidency. For much of his time in office he was thought to be hostile to political organizations based on Islam and willing to go out of his way to curb their influence. Concerns of this kind were to form the backdrop to two of the great political crises of the seventies. In 1973, the New Order government introduced a unified national Marriage Bill which would, inter alia, have outlawed polygamy. This provoked intense anger among Muslim groups, which saw it, correctly, as a modern and secular law applicable to all Indonesians and, as such, in their eyes an attack on fundamental precepts of Islam. The bill was eventually withdrawn, a decisive parliamentary victory for the Muslim side of politics. At the same time, however, Muslim MPs felt constrained to endorse the Broad Outlines of State Policy (GBHN), a palace-inspired document which spoke in several places of the responsibility of citizens to practise their *agama dan kepercayaan* (religion and [Javanese] mystical beliefs). Five years later, the government sought to toughen up the language about *kepercayaan* in the GBHN. That move angered both traditionalist and modernist Muslims. They feared that the Soeharto group was trying, step by step, to raise Javanese mystical beliefs to the same level as the five religions officially recognized by the Indonesian state. That would have had profound political consequences, robbing Muslims of their claim to represent nearly 90 per cent of the population, with a concomitant reduction in government funding for mosques and Islamic schools. Muslim leaders were not slow to condemn the move. In an interview in March 1978, Mohammad Natsir, a modernist Muslim leader and former prime minister, made it clear that he saw followers of *kepercayaan* as Muslims, of a certain kind, and that he would oppose any attempt to have them separated from the Islamic faith. In his view,

> *Kepercayaan* is something like syncretism—a hotchpotch of all creeds; you find Buddhist and animist and Islamic [elements]—and it is flourishing mainly in Central Java, especially around Yogya and Solo.... Other Indonesians know what it is, but up to now we haven't paid much attention because they call themselves Muslims.... The people of Central Java still regard themselves as [followers of] Islam—though not pure Islam, of course. My analysis is there is a certain elite [group] of people, intellectuals, [who] are practising *kepercayaan* and *kebatinan* [and] who want to unite all these people into one group and upgrade [them] into a political group and create a group with special rights in the political field. It is not a question of religion; it is a question of politics.... Step by step they are trying to raise it to the level of other religions. The direct consequence is that people who regard themselves now as Muslims, practising Islam and having marriages according to Islamic law, will ... proclaim themselves separate and have their own ceremonies and their own graveyards and will have their own group. If these people are really convinced [about] what is going on, we don't object. But the grass roots people don't understand. Up to now, the Muslims regard themselves as Muslims and behave ... as Muslims, even though they don't do everything as Muslims. [Muslims] can tolerate there being some differences of opinion. But now there will be a split between the Muslims and [the followers of] *kepercayaan*.... [If the government succeeds it] could create a lot of trouble.... So it's not just religion but politics—an attempt to create a new political precept hostile to Islam. The Secretariat Kepercayaan is in Bina Graha [the presidential office building].[43]

In 1978, Soeharto appointed Roeslan Abdulgani, a gregarious and loquacious former cabinet minister who had been a devoted follower of President Sukarno, as the head of his advisory council on Pancasila, the Five Principles (belief in one supreme God, nationalism, humanitarianism, popular sovereignty and social justice) drawn up by Sukarno and later adopted as the state "ideology" or doctrine.[44] It did not take Roeslan long to discover there were significant differences in the way these two men saw Pancasila, differences which Roeslan might have guessed at beforehand. Soeharto's pre-eminent fear, Roeslan maintained, was Islam; this fear arose from the president's deep-seated attachment to *kebatinan*. Sukarno's primary fear had been imperialism; he had seen imperialism as a threat not only to the state but a threat to himself because in the late 1950s, as he saw it, members of Masyumi, a modernist Muslim political party, with Natsir prominent among them, had conspired with Western-oriented army officers linked to the Indonesian Socialist Party (PSI). As Roeslan put it,

> The Pancasila of Sukarno is an anti-colonial Pancasila and it is Pancasila which is based on the unity of the nation. And if there are Communists, then as long as they accept the Pancasila and Muslims accept the Pancasila they can go ahead. But the behaviour of this group—the Masyumi plus the PSI—is a threat to him personally and also a threat to the state. For Soeharto, the perception of the threat to him is coming from the whole of Islam. It's not just Masyumi but all [Islam]. It stems from his *kebatinan*. Well, you can say it stems from his *abangan*, or *priyayi*, [outlook] but I don't use that word.... So he would like to give the Pancasila a kind of moral value, ethical values. But what kind of ethical values? Ethical values coming from the Javanese way of life.... Sukarno's only obsession was anti-colonialism. "If the Islam wing is anti-colonial, agree! Go with me! Whether you are mystical or not, whether you are moderate or not..." Soeharto is different. He sees in the Pancasila something that is according to *kebatinan*. So why should Islam come with new ethical values? For example, [he thinks] the Javanese alphabet is actually a source of wisdom.[45]

Roeslan Abdulgani was not the only person to draw attention to Soeharto's abiding distrust of Islam. At the time of the 1977 general elections, the President had received Ignatius Joseph Kasimo, Frans Seda and several others from the old Catholic Party. Before they were seated, he reportedly said, "Our common enemy is Islam."[46]

If Soeharto and his *abangan* and Catholic advisers seemed determined in the 1970s to curb the power of political Islam, it was not just Muslim leaders such as Natsir who were dismayed. Many other Indonesians believed that this approach was misguided and, indeed, likely to prove counter-productive. One of them was Soedjatmoko, a prominent intellectual whom Soeharto had sent as his ambassador to the United States in 1968, only to place him under house arrest for months and subject him to interrogation at the time of the anti-government Malari riots in 1974. Soedjatmoko believed that the fear of Islam was a greatly exaggerated fear. Major General Ali Moertopo and his advisers had, he thought, done the country a very great disservice because the fears they had, and had engendered in others, of Islam had become self-fulfilling; fearing Islam, they had promoted policies that only made their fears come true. They had ignored the great changes that were taking place amongst Muslims. Many of the younger Muslim intellectuals had left the idea of a Muslim state behind them. There was still a fundamentalist fringe, but it was no more than that. At the same time, there was enough combustible material in Indonesian society to keep alive the fear of Islam.

> What has kept Sukarno in power so long? It's the fact that the *abangan*, the Catholics and the Protestants were more afraid of Islam than of the Communists. The same groups supported the army, and I think that fear is being manipulated for power reasons. Many seriously fear it [Islam]. But a leadership that would know how to handle the Muslims and had closer cooperation with them would be able to reduce the fear to more manageable proportions.[47]

There was no question, Soedjatmoko believed, that Islam was in crisis. Islam had just begun to come to grips with the modern world; and Islam would be a problem for a long time to come. "But one doesn't deal with the problem by throwing all the Muslims onto one heap and dealing with them. There is a fundamental identification with Islam in Indonesia, even with the *abangan*." Soeharto had made a tactical blunder in pushing all the Muslims into one political grouping. His advisers had been carried away by intellectual constructs and had failed to understand the nature of Islam. Sukarno had had the sense to see that one cannot govern Indonesia unless all or most of the Muslims participate. Many in the army harboured a fear of Islam because they had had to fight both the 1948–62 Darul Islam movement, which sought not only independence from the Dutch but also the establishment of an Islamic state, and the 1956–58 PRRI/Permesta regional rebellion. But not all Muslims, Soedjatmoko noted, had sided with those causes. That was true, of course. One might add that the initiative for the regional rebellion had come not from the leaders of the Muslim parties, although some of them, including Natsir, were to flee later to rebel-held areas; rather, it had come from elements within the army itself and from civilians associated with the Indonesian Socialist Party. Soedjatmoko, who had himself been a member of the PSI, did not believe in 1978 that there was a desire to establish a "Wahhabite Saudi Arabian" form of Islam in Indonesia.

> At the same time, there is a very interesting backlash against the greed and materialism associated with development. It is a moral backlash which, given the transitional nature of the society, becomes a religious thing: Muslims become more Muslim. It is essentially the yearning for moral rectitude in the face of morally reprehensible behaviour.... So we are really involved in great historical processes which we very rarely see, let alone understand, but which are of great importance in the Third World. In a way it might make Indonesia more difficult to govern.... This only heightens the government's fear of Islam.[48]

General Nasution, a devout Muslim who had been Army Chief of Staff, and then Defence Minister, for all but a few of the fifteen turbulent years to 1965, felt much the same way as Soedjatmoko. The so-called "Islam phobia" which people spoke of stemmed in his view from "the character of the present power base, where non-Muslim groups are dominating and defending this base."[49]

Soeharto's distrust of Islam was no less apparent five years after the 1977 elections. In a chapter he contributed to a book published in 2010, Ken Ward, an Australian political analyst, zeroed in on a transcript of a talk, never published in Indonesia, that Soeharto gave to a delegation from the pro-government National Indonesian Youth Committee (Komite Nasional Pemuda Indonesia, KNPI) in July 1982.[50] In this talk, Ward wrote, Soeharto "combines the role of political leader outlining ... the concrete tasks ahead with one akin to that of the *guru* of a Javanese mystical sect explaining the meaning of life to a group of initiates." Soeharto's objective seemed to be to establish the ancient origins of Pancasila, which, in his view was a heritage of the ancestors of modern Indonesians.[51] And apart from one or two nods in the direction of non-Javanese, Ward notes, "Soeharto clearly saw those ancestors as being Javanese." Those ancient Indonesians were beyond praise; the Javanese alphabet—which, as we have seen, is derived from a form of Sanskrit, although Soeharto did not remind his visitors of that—contained the essence of Javanese philosophy. Javanese wisdom, Soeharto told his visitors, centres on submission to Almighty God. Why then, he asked rhetorically, was religion revealed (*diturunkan*) not in Indonesia but "over there". The answer was clear. "God indeed loves humankind and it was over there (*disitulah*) that God's position was not understood, wasn't it? Therefore God had to send his Prophet with all his revelations to lead the people who lived there to the right path." As Ward observes, "Soeharto's implication was that the ancient Javanese were ahead of the Arabs in understanding God and did not need a prophet to be sent among them. Moreover, the teaching that the Prophet was to impart had already been discovered by the Javanese." Soeharto's remarks, Ward argues, should be seen as another chapter in Hinduized Java's centuries-old debate with Islam, rather than a consistent defence of imagined ancient Javanese beliefs against all foreign religions. His talk that night was a high-water mark of his advocacy of a view of Indonesia inspired by Javanese concepts. It was "one of the most uncompromising statements of a Javanist outlook issued by an Indonesian power holder."

If this was the high-water mark, within five or six years the tide appeared to be going out. Soeharto may have gone head-to-head with Muslim groups in the 1970s, but he began to show more interest in Islam—and take a more accommodating approach to it—in the late 1980s.[52] For example, he invited Kyai Haji Kosim Nurseha, an Islamic scholar associated with the army's Islamic Spiritual Centre (Pusat Rohani Islam, or Pusrohis), to give his family private instruction in Islamic devotion.[53] When he published his autobiography in 1989, the final paragraph consisted of just two words: "*Insya Allah!*" ("God willing!"). This was, it is true, twenty-three years after he had chastised Subchan, the NU chairman, for using "*Ridlo Allah*", a broadly similar phrase. Still, it showed just how much his rhetoric had changed. At the same time, he gave new political opportunities to devout Muslims. In 1990 he sponsored the establishment of the All-Indonesia Union of Muslim Intellectuals (Ikatan Cendekiawan Muslim se-Indonesia, ICMI), under his protégé, Bacharuddin Jusuf Habibie, a German-trained aeronautical engineer who was Minister for Research (1978–98). The following year he made the pilgrimage to Mecca with his family, after which he was formally known as Haji Mohammad Soeharto. He began to tolerate more overt expressions of Islamic piety in daily life.[54] He began using the Islamic term *bismillah* ("In the name of God") when making speeches, something he had not done in the past.[55] At the same time, it was reported that he had begun praying five times a day.

What lay behind this apparent change in tack? One possibility is that Soeharto was simply covering his religious bets as he aged. If that were so, his move in the direction of Islam happened to coincide with changing patterns of religious identity on Java, where the *abangan* world itself was now seen as less of a bastion against Islam than had earlier been supposed. A more common—and not necessarily contradictory—view had it that Soeharto was covering his political bets; that he was courting the Islamic community to compensate for an erosion of support in the army, his erstwhile power base. His behaviour, critics said, was opportunistic, hypocritical; his late-flowering interest in Islam was done for political or personal advantage. Soeharto had been an adherent of Javanese religion as a child and as a younger man; it was unlikely he had changed his outlook this late in life. In this view, the transcript of the KNPI talk captured Soeharto at his most sincere; what came through was his devotion to Javanese beliefs. To followers of Javanese religion, the pilgrimages that mattered were not the ones you made to Mecca but the ones you made to the graves of your parents or to the graves of the *Wali Sanga*, the first nine apostles of Islam in Java. Strict Muslims did not visit graves; that was ancestor worship.

One of those taken aback by the establishment of ICMI was Moerdani, a Roman Catholic who harboured deep reservations about political Islam. Moerdani loathed Habibie and was keen to see the army maintain a strong influence on government policy. When he asked Soeharto, "Why ICMI? You can always rely on the army," the President reportedly sought to reassure him by implying this was just a tactical manoeuvre. "The chairman is Habibie," Soeharto is alleged to have said, "and I can always tell him what to do."[56] Habibie was an *anak buah*, a younger associate, a follower. The message was, "He is my boy!" Moerdani may or may not have believed those assurances. But he would claim some years later that he did not read much into the president's newfound interest in Islam. Soeharto, he observed, had begun to pray regularly after making the *haj* in 1991. "He has become religious, because now he prays five times a day. In the past he didn't know how to pray [*sic*]."[57] But none of that, Moerdani argued, was significant: a person might pray five times a day but that did not necessarily mean that he or she was a good Muslim.

Merle Ricklefs, reaching back into the Javanese past, argues persuasively that Soeharto was probably replicating what Sultan Agung (r. 1613–46), the greatest king of post-Majapahit Java, had done 350 years earlier, namely "mobilising the supernatural powers of Islam so that they supported, rather than threatened, the regime. Neither Soeharto, nor Sultan Agung, thought it was necessary to abandon the occult powers of Java to do that."[58]

Whether or not Soeharto would have drawn a parallel himself with the actions of Sultan Agung, we can be confident that he had not turned his back entirely on Javanese religious precepts and practices. When he and his wife celebrated their fortieth wedding anniversary in December 1987, their eldest daughter, Hardiyanti Rukmana (Tutut), published *Butir-Butir Budaya Jawa* (Seeds of Javanese Culture), a 205-page compendium of Javanese moral guidance (*pituduh*) and prohibitions (*wewaler*) which the President had complied and passed on to his children since their childhood.* This work, which is written in the Javanese script, with accompanying translations into Indonesian and English, is thought to have been compiled by Empu Romo Diyat (R.P. Soediyat Prawirokoesoemo), a mystical leader

---

* The full title is *Butir-Butir Budaya Jawa: Hanggayuh Kasampurnaning Hurip Berbudi Bawaleksana Ngudi Sejatining Becik* [Seeds of Javanese Culture: Striving for the Perfection of a Life that is Generous and Set Upon the Right Path, Striving for the Essence of the Good]. I am indebted to Roeslan Abdulgani for my copy of part of this document, to Arief Djati for clarification on the five points set out below and to Merle Ricklefs for this translation of the full title of *Butir-Butir Budaya Jawa*. According to Tutut, the Soeharto children found the guidance in *Butir-Butir Budaya Jawa* "extremely precious and useful".

Item No. 143 of the *Butir-Butir Budaya Jawa* reads as follows:

Dora sing ora kena paukuman ana limang werna:

1) *Manawa pinuju among suka ana jagongan.*
2) *Naliko dadi penganten bakda ketemu sepisanan.*
3) *Menawa perlu kanggo ngreksa bandha.*
4) *Yen perlu kanggo ngreksa umur.*
5) *Yen perlu kanggo ngreksa tentreming kulawarga.*

Dora limang werna iku diarani dora sembada (goroh wenang). Dora liyane kena paukuman.

[There are five categories of lies which are not punishable:

1) The kind of tall stories men and boys tell each other [not expecting to be believed] to entertain each other while doing *jagongan* [that is, sitting together in a covered open hut when it gets dark, smoking and chatting to stave off night time boredom].
2) The lies you tell your bride on your wedding day. [This comes from the era when young people were married without previously knowing each other. The key word is *sapisanan*, which means "first time only." Getting acquainted on the wedding day they should break the ice by telling friendly lies to each other ("How handsome you are", "How beautiful you are" and so on). But once they are really husband and wife, they should not lie to each other ever again.]
3) The lies you tell to preserve your assets or property.
4) The lies you tell to preserve your life.
5) The lies you tell to preserve the peacefulness and harmony of your family.

These five categories of lies are called white lies (legitimate lies). Other lies are punishable.

from Semarang and one of Soeharto's spiritual gurus.* The aphorisms in the book were based mainly on eighteenth and nineteenth century works from Surakarta which uphold what Ricklefs calls the Mystic Synthesis, a reconciliation of Javanese identity and spiritual forces and Islamic identity and observation.[59] "The maxims chosen by Soeharto as 'a guide in life' for his children," Ricklefs observes, "included ideas entirely unacceptable to orthodox Muslims."[60]

When Ibu Tien Soeharto died on 28 April 1996, the President did not observe all the Muslim rites. The body of the First Lady, it is widely believed, was not wrapped in white muslin in the usual Muslim fashion. And before the coffin was lowered into the grave, and while the nation watched in fascination on television, the President opened the lid and put something in: a written wish or cherished quotation perhaps, or maybe a photograph or her favourite piece of jewellery. There was no *imam* (Islamic leader) reciting the Muslim Confession of Faith a number of times into the ear of the deceased and delivering a funeral speech to her, first in Arabic and then in Javanese. Habibie was at the Soeharto family mausoleum that day with his wife and two sons. At one stage, Habibie's thirty-two-year-old elder son, Ilham Akbar Habibie, remarked, just a little too loudly, so that his voice carried and was heard by others, "What kind of Islam is this?"[61]

Ilham Habibie was not alone in wondering about the form of the ceremony. As a retired three-star general put it, "It proves that they are not normal Muslims, but Muslims with a strong *kepercayaan* aspect. It happened quite often that people did not consider Ibu Tien as Muslim. But that religious attitude can be found among other people from Solo. The *kejawen* factor is strong. That happened quite often among the *priyayi* of Java. However it is now gradually disappearing because of the strengthening of Islam. In the past, many of my friends did not make the *shalat* [ritual prayers performed five times a day] although they said they were Muslims. Nowadays that attitude has changed. Almost every

* Soediyat is said to have predicted many years earlier that the *wahyu* (divine radiance) would fall on Colonel Sadikin, an up-and-coming army officer, after President Sukarno, only to revise that prophecy when his wife went off with Sadikin.

Muslim is now making the *shalat*, although perhaps not fully five times a day."[62]

Three days after the funeral there was a *slametan*, in which offerings of small rice-flour pancakes and cones of rice were made, as is customary in Java. This was followed by other, similar ceremonies, after seven days, forty days, 100 days and 1,000 days. "In Saudi Arabia you don't do that!" Moerdani observed, with customary bluntness. "You keep your rice and eat it yourself, not throw it away to the ghosts or something... This is not a Muslim [practice]."[63] That did not necessarily mean, Moerdani maintained, that Soeharto was involved in *kepercayaan*. "He is not. Or he might not be. But he comes from that area and he is trying to prove that, 'I listen to you. Your non-Islamic practices [are] something that you cannot just throw away. And so I push it.' It doesn't mean that he is doing the same thing."

Looking back on these events some years later, Lieutenant General Sayidiman Suryohadiprojo, who had long been seen as a leading army intellectual, gathered the various religious, political and social strands together in an artfully—and tactfully—oblique formulation which managed to suggest nonetheless that Soeharto had not forsaken his *abangan* roots, merely played up the Islamic element to serve his immediate political ends. The implementation of Islamic rituals in Javanese society, Sayidiman observed, was not free from Javanese traditions. But while it was true that followers of the Nahdlatul Ulama, the conservative, rural-based Muslim political party, were generally more influenced by local traditions than supporters of the modernist Muhammadiyah, both considered themselves as part of Islam. "So I think that was the case [with] Ibu Tien Soeharto's funeral ceremony. I cannot guarantee that my opinion about Pak Soeharto's interest in Islam is right. But I think that he was also influenced by his problems of governance. Therefore I might say that ... Sultan Agung as a model or example might not be far from the truth. Yes Islam has now many faces. But the essence is still *tauhid*, or the belief that there is only One Almighty God ruling Nature. Therefore I am convinced that Pak Soeharto was sincere when he started to adhere to Islam next to his *abangan* or traditional Javanese way of communicating with Nature."[64]

6

"Soeharto is a closed book"

During his time in Wuryantoro and Wonogiri, Soeharto was exposed more fully to a Javanese philosophy of life. Many of the principles of that philosophy have been distilled into a set of aphorisms; and in later life, Soeharto was to make much of these sayings, which, in his view, embodied eternal truths, although some of the less central points in the canon might be thought so nebulous and so generalized as to be all but meaningless.

One favourite Soeharto aphorism provides guidance on how a person should behave as a member of society. It can be summarized as the "three don'ts", all of them close in meaning: don't be easily surprised or shocked by anything, but remain calm; don't be overwhelmed by anything or any person; don't act haphazardly (*ojo kagelan, ojo gumunan, ojo gugupan*). A fourth "don't" that commended itself to him, and which is a moral command, not behavioural advice, is *ojo dumeh*, which means "be aware of yourself, who you are." For example, "Don't, just because you get promoted, start being arrogant" and "Don't, just because you are handsome, exploit women."[1] As Soeharto saw it, these four points made it clear that if one wanted to be successful in society, it was necessary to develop self-awareness and self-confidence. By knowing oneself and being self-assured, one would not be thrown by unexpected developments, nor would one become overbearing and arrogant. These prescriptions, he wrote, "became the guiding principles of life which gave me strength to face problems which otherwise might have shaken me."[2] The value of this guidance lay, he believed, in its emphasis on instilling the attitudes of patience, fortitude and acceptance of fate, based on self-confidence.[3]

As an army officer and as President, Soeharto seemed to personify a number of these attributes, achieving a state of measured calm and disciplined self-control. But as he got older, and more convinced that he was indispensable, he seemed less able and less willing to cloak a fundamentally arrogant and overbearing nature. In the late eighties, Soeharto invited a large group of people, including all his cabinet ministers and fourteen former student leaders, to the Merdeka Palace to see the film *Jakarta '66*, which focused on the tumultuous events surrounding his rise to power. Afterwards he addressed those present. "The message of the speech," recalled Nono Makarim, the former newspaper editor, "was, 'Look guys, I did it! Nobody else. It's me. Don't get any ideas. I could do it again."[4]

A second, not dissimilar, saying that stayed with him expresses the view that one can feel indomitable in life, not because one has supernatural powers or authority but because of one's ability "to protect the tranquility and peace of the soul" and because one possesses "the joy and spirit of life to face any situation or event."[5] A third, *alon-alon asal kelakon* (slow but sure), expresses the idea that one should take one's time before undertaking any task, weighing up all the factors in advance, the important thing being to ensure that things are done well. Soeharto was to live up to this maxim throughout his adult life. He was methodical in his preparations, calculating his own moves, anticipating the expected counter moves of any opponent, not wanting any surprises in life, not wanting any failure or the humiliation which comes with failure. He had in fact a strong urge to control events, one that can perhaps be traced back to his childhood. As President, Soeharto sometimes planned his moves five years in advance, not least when it involved his own re-election.[6]

A fourth Javanese aphorism which commended itself to the future President was *tut wuri handayani*. This describes the actions of an adult who is teaching a child to walk, standing immediately behind, perhaps holding the child's hands, ready to prevent him or her from falling. In his autobiography the President suggests that the essence of this saying is that a teacher or a leader should set a good example to his pupils or followers. "When in their midst," he advised, "be their driving or motivating force. At the rear, observe their progress." Under Soeharto's New Order government, this phrase came to be associated with paternalism and authoritarianism. As one author has noted, the formulation was used by the army leaders to describe their relationship with non-military organizations and the people in general.[7]

Soeharto was proud of his understanding of things Javanese and he included in his autobiography an appendix with an Indonesian translation of about twenty Javanese aphorisms. This annoyed a number of non-Javanese. "It makes me feel like a foreigner," complained Sabam Siagian, a Christian Batak who had grown up in Jakarta and who went on to edit the respected Protestant-backed *Sinar Harapan* newspaper. "He keeps falling back on old Javanese adages. It shows the poverty of his intellectual thought."[8] Some Muslims might have felt equally offended. As noted earlier, some of Soeharto's adages included ideas quite unacceptable to orthodox Muslims.

Soeharto's behaviour also mystified and annoyed some high-status Javanese, who felt that he had a less than perfect understanding of Javanese culture. In 1978, at the time he became a member of the Supreme Advisory Council (Dewan Pertimbangan Agung, DPA), Lieutenant General Djatikusumo, a prince from the dominant royal court of Solo, told Harry Tjan Silalahi he did not understand Soeharto's utterances on *kejawen*. "And I'm a Javanese," he declared.[9] In September 1998, less than four months after Soeharto's resignation, three retired Javanese generals spoke privately and with sometimes breathtaking frankness about what they saw as Soeharto's failure to uphold the Javanese values he claimed to so greatly admire. Before the President had stepped down, one of these generals recalled, "A very good friend from Solo, a very cultured man, respected, told me, '*Mas*, I'm a Javanese.* But if I see Pak Harto I become *malu*. I become ashamed.... he claims that he is Javanese but he doesn't [act] like a Javanese. His behaviour is not Javanese. Not cultured.'" Citing a Dutch proverb he considered apposite, the retired general continued, "The Dutch are very realistic. You may dress yourself like a sultan or you may dress yourself in a general's uniform, but if you are basically *dasar*, basically not well equipped..."[10] He allowed the sentence to trail away and then said, still effortlessly patronizing, "We can understand! Because his environment was not that way."

* *Mas* means elder brother and is most commonly used to address a slightly older male.

This was the authentic voice of *priyayi* condescension, the dismissive sniff of a man who had grown up in a Westernized, Dutch-speaking world and who looked down on Soeharto from a higher social plane. It was made by someone who now felt secure enough to vent his long-suppressed feelings about the perceived shortcomings of a former colleague, a comment made by a man who had, incidentally, been rewarded for his earlier, unquestioning loyalty to Soeharto with a succession of plum assignments. It was, at the same time, the authentic voice of the old Dutch-educated military elite, a group of officers against whom Soeharto had had to battle for so long. A number of these men had looked on him, when he was on the way up, with something akin to the "cascades of disdain" which Napoleon had experienced when he was in the company of his fellow cadets at the École Militaire.

II

As well as this grounding in religion and Javanese mystical beliefs, and in the opaque mysteries of Javanese philosophy, Soeharto found himself exposed to the values of the *priyayi*, the Javanese official class. In his early childhood, Soeharto had become familiar with what Geertz calls "the values that animate traditional Javanese peasant culture: the mutual adjustment of interdependent wills, the self-restraint of emotional expression, and the careful regulation of outward behaviour."[11] Now, plucked from his village and living in quick succession with four urban families, he came into contact with people on the lower rungs of the *priyayi* ladder. From about this time, his identity began to crystallize around a *priyayi* world view.

Although the *priyayi* and the *abangan* have a broadly similar world view and share much in the way of religious belief and practice, Geertz notes, the *priyayi* world is concerned above all with etiquette, art and mystical practice.[12] Two concepts are central to this world view. One is *halus*, which means "pure, refined, polished, polite, exquisite, ethereal, subtle, civilized, smooth." The other, *kasar*, "is merely the opposite: impolite, rough, uncivilized." Between these two poles, writes Geertz, the *priyayi* arranges everyone from peasant to king.[13] Geertz draws attention to the long history of the *priyayi* ethic "with its intense sense of status differences, its calm assertion of spiritual superiority and its dual emphasis on the inner life of refined feeling and the external life of polite form."[14] The spiritually enlightened Javanese, he notes, aims for emotional quiescence, "for passion is *kasar* feeling, fit only for children, animals, peasants and foreigners.... Emotional equanimity, a certain flatness of affect, is, then, the prized psychological state, the mark of the truly *alus* character."[15]

There are three main values involved in this calming process. One is *ikhlas*, which means pure-hearted, disinterested, doing things because they ought to be done; it is the opposite of *pamrih*, which involves doing something with a concealed ambition or interest.[16] Another is *sabar*, which is close to *ikhlas*, and which means patient, not getting into a huff, not displaying unseemly eagerness and passion and not being obsessed with one's own self-interest. A *sabar* man, it has been said, advances carefully through experience, stepping tentatively. His aim is to "go gingerly through life as a caterpillar inches over water." The third of these values is *trima*, or *nrimo*, which involves accepting the inevitable with grace and which is close to fatalism.[17] As Anderson notes, these were understood to be aristocratic values, but they seeped down into the lower orders.*

It is impossible, reading through a list of *priyayi* values, not to be struck by the extent to which these values were cultivated by Soeharto, who came into contact with them from the age of nine and who was later to be schooled in them by his wife, who was from a *priyayi* family. Soeharto may not have been born into the *priyayi* world, but he exemplified many of its values. In the words of Selo Soemardjan, a prominent Javanese social scientist, a cultured Javanese "has learned through his culture to control his feelings and in no way reveal his emotions when in communication with others."[18] That makes it "extremely difficult" for foreigners, and even for non-Javanese Indonesians, to know whether a Javanese is delighted, sad, hurt, approving, disapproving, filled with hate or filled with joy. "After a lengthy discussion about state affairs with President Soeharto ... ministers and other high-ranking officers very often have to seriously contemplate the hidden, but real, meanings of what the President has said or indicated by his words or smiles." Few would have argued with that assessment.

* These attributes are on display in the *wayang* iconography. People who have these values are given faces painted black (*sabar*) or gold (*ikhlas*). People without these qualities usually have red faces, denoting anger and pride, and are usually the bad guys. The modern *priyayi* mentality, Benedict Anderson has argued is "an ugly combination of pseudofeudal and Dutch-derived petit bourgeois elements." Anderson, personal communication.

Soeharto was a man of extraordinary composure. He seemed not just imperturbable but impenetrable. This may have been due in part to his nature and to the fact that he was a product of a disrupted childhood: he lacked emotional warmth. But it was also due to the fact that he had steeped himself in Javanese disciplines that elevate composure to an art form, blanketing any outward manifestation of feeling an emotion. "Sukarno," said Roeslan Abdulgani, "was an open book. Soeharto is a closed book."[19] This was, in some respects, the secret of his power. As Napoleon advised Eugene de Beauharnais, his stepson and the viceroy of Italy, in 1805, "the strength of a silent prince cannot be measured."

How much did Soeharto's Javanese beliefs shape his political outlook? That, the political analyst Ken Ward writes, remained debatable. The president's usually controlled behaviour "was certainly heavily influenced by Javanese precepts of inner calm reflected in external passiveness." Moreover, Soeharto "often" indulged in practices aimed at placating supernatural forces. At the same time, Soeharto's desire to rule over a de-politicized realm was in harmony not only with authoritarian Javanese tradition but also with the practices of the Dutch colonial state, the practices of the Imperial Japanese Army and with the effects of military officer training. "None of the major influences in Soeharto's early life," Ward observes, "prepared him to tolerate open conflict or to foster political freedom."[20]

III

The other important strand that runs through the pattern of Soeharto's adolescence is his prolonged exposure to, and developing interest in, agriculture. Soeharto spent his first nine years in a village in Central Java and returned there in his mid-teens. His father was an irrigation official. His great-uncle, with whom he lived until he was four, was a farmer. His stepfather, with whom he then lived until he was nine, was also a farmer. And although much of his adolescence was spent in towns, three of the four foster families with whom he lived in the thirties were associated with agriculture. Two of his foster-fathers were agriculture officers. A third was an irrigation official. An attachment to the land, to the rhythms of planting and harvesting, to the care of animals and the upkeep of complex irrigation systems, was deeply ingrained in Soeharto during his years in Kemusu, and he acquired a keen and increasingly informed knowledge of agriculture during his time in Wuryantoro and Wonogiri.

It has been argued that rural Java did not leave a deep imprint on Soeharto, if only because he spent most of his time in an urban environment after the age of nine. As one scholar sees it, "his romantic remembrances of village life—eating eels, tending cattle—have the strained quality of one trying one's best to be what one is not."[21] This view seems untenable. The sights, smells and sensations of rural life affected Soeharto profoundly and remained with him all his life. And when eventually he had both power and money (and the possession of the one led inexorably to the acquisition of the other), he carved out a 750-hectare mini-ranch, the Tri-S (*sari silang* stud), at Tapos in the foothills south of Bogor, finding solace and contentment among his cattle, his model dairy, his chaff cutters and his *lamtoro* trees. ("The leaves are good fodder," he liked to explain, "the wood makes the very finest charcoal, it can be pulped for paper and the young seeds taste delicious in a *botok* [a dish made of coconut and meat or fish.])"[22] If George III was the farmer king, Soeharto was the farmer President, even if his keenness to project an image of simplicity and benevolence was undermined somewhat by the fact that he had acquired the land through duress, his strong-arm men having forced smallholders to sell up against their will. At the same time, Soeharto was not above polishing his credentials as a farmer-president much concerned with the welfare of the peasantry.

One of Soeharto's first decisions as Acting President in 1967 was to reverse the long-standing neglect of the agriculture sector. He had a great hunger for facts of every kind, not least about agriculture, showing an interest in everything from new fertilizers and pesticides to new rice varieties. He also had a prodigious memory, as Major General Sutjipto, the ill-starred Minister of Agriculture in the 1966–68 Ampera cabinet, was to discover to his cost. During an agriculture crisis in 1967, Sutjipto gave Soeharto an unjustifiably optimistic account of the situation, bolstering his case with a mass of statistics. Three weeks later, Soeharto summoned Sutjipto to his office and quoted back to him, in astonishing detail, what Sutjipto had told him. Sutjipto had thought he could bluff his way through his encounter with the President, losing him in the minutiae of the agriculture portfolio. But as Soeharto recalled their earlier conversation in forbidding detail, his anger concealed beneath a mask of equanimity and calm, Sutjipto realized the enormity of his mistake, the blood draining from his face. "Saudara [Brother] Minister," Soeharto said, using a term of address that is common in official situations, "three weeks ago you told me this, this, this." "He repeated everything," recalled Jusuf Wanandi (Liem Bian Kie), who at around that time became an aide to Major General Ali Moertopo, one of Soeharto's key political generals, and who was still in awe, twenty-five years later, of Soeharto's grasp of the agricultural issues. "Sutjipto was white! He thought he could bullshit this man with figures, right! Could not! … And after that Sutjipto was finished! One year [in the job]! Incredible! …. Everything by heart, man! Sutjipto! Poor chap!"[23] Nor was Soeharto any more forgiving when lower level officials sought to pull the wool over Jakarta's eyes. On one occasion he used an unusually harsh word, *ngecap* (which means bullshitting, making things, especially the speaker, sound better than they are), when describing reports by local officials about village development.[24]

During his presidency, Soeharto loved nothing more than talking to groups of peasants about animals and crops, often with the television cameras present so that the whole nation could sit in. On such occasions he was in his element, relaxed and confident, holding forth about all kinds of agricultural developments, in the manner of an aristocratic landowner addressing his workers, but formidably well informed all the same. At the weekends he liked to spend time at Tapos. Sometimes he would invite large groups of visitors—thirty or forty ethnic Chinese tycoons, perhaps, or all twenty-seven provincial governors or a visiting prime minister and his entourage—to join him. They would listen dutifully as he showed off his pure-bred Santa Getrudis and his cross-bred local cattle, spoke expertly about producing methane gas from cattle manure and held forth on the finer points of artificial insemination. ("To be sure of ovulation," he would say, "place the back of your hand, never the palm, lightly against the cow's membrane there where it swells and reddens. With practice you can detect small temperature changes.")[25] In 1976 Soeharto invited a group of provincial governors to Tapos. He wanted them to raise the protein level of village diets by upgrading local livestock, and he promised a pure-bred bull from the ranch to each province. The mood was jocular, informal. "When should a cow get married?", one of the governors asked. "Don't worry," Soeharto replied, "the bull knows when and where."[26]

In the mid-eighties, as complaints about corruption grew stronger, Soeharto scoffed at allegations that he had built a palatial mansion, a swimming pool and a helipad at his ranch. "What is conspicuous at Tapos," he said, truthfully enough, "is the smell of cow dung", adding that the "smell makes me feel relaxed."[27] In 1976, the Australian Prime Minister, Malcolm Fraser, a wealthy grazier from Victoria's Western District, visited Indonesia. Knowing of Soeharto's interests, he presented him with a Murray Grey stud bull, a gift that was much appreciated, even if, as the Australian ambassador, Richard Woolcott, later ruefully admitted, "it failed to perform."[28]

In farming, as in politics, Soeharto could, it is true, be too clever by half. In 1988 he told a group of Indonesian newspaper editors he had invited to Tapos how he had recently bought a number of Australian cows. Putting one hand over his mouth in a gesture of greed, he confided that most of the cows had been in calf, which meant that he had got two for the price of one. "There is a peasant cunning about it," one of the editors complained later. "It wasn't done to project a common man touch but because he obviously thought he had been clever."[29] One evening, when Soeharto was relaxing at home in his sarong, a sign that things were informal, Colonel Dwipa asked him what he was thinking about. Was it affairs of state? "No," he replied. "I have found that being President is not as difficult as people may imagine. I was thinking of my cows at Tapos."[30] In short, Soeharto's interest in agriculture was deep and abiding.

IV

It is not clear how long Soeharto stayed in Wonogiri, attending the *schakelschool* and helping Daryatmo with his curing practices, although he seems to have been in the town for several years. All he says is that he was "forced to leave Wonogiri and Pak Daryatmo's house just because of a school regulation that students must wear short pants and shoes, which my parents could not afford."[31] What is clear is that this was an unsettling experience, both educationally and emotionally, not least because he had grown so fond of Daryatmo. His education in Wonogiri abruptly terminated, Soeharto returned to Kemusu. He does not say whether he went to live at his mother's house or his father's, although it was presumably the latter, given that his father continued to fund his education. But he notes that a substitute plan was devised for him. From now on, it was decided, he would attend a school in Yogyakarta run by Muhammadiyah, which was not averse to helping those from an *abangan* background.[32] Here, he could wear a *kain* (sarong, tubular skirt) and go barefoot. "I didn't feel uneasy because I wasn't the only one dressed like that," he recalled many years later. "There were many others like me."[33]

There were at that time a number of different Muhammadiyah schools in Yogyakarta, including a *schakelschool* of the kind Soeharto had been attending in Wonogiri. The future president attended this institution, not, as has been suggested, a Muhammadiyah junior high school, or MULO, which was further up the educational ladder.[34] He stayed at the school for several years. "In the context of the times and the fate of his fellows," Elson has written, "this was an extraordinarily privileged level of educational achievement, even though formally he had not reached a high standard of schooling."[35] That is true. But there is an important caveat that must be added. There was only so much benefit a *schakelschool* education—especially a Muhammadiyah *schakelschool* education—could confer. Soeharto had been given a chance to make the jump from the village school system, where pupils were taught in the vernacular language, into a system designed to carry people over to the Dutch-language stream. But he could never hope to catch up educationally with the middle-class Javanese children who were attending Dutch-language junior and senior high schools in the cities and towns of Java.

Yogyakarta was a "student town." In the late 1930s it boasted seven senior high schools—the government-run HBS, AMS-A, AMS-B and HIK schools, the privately-operated Taman Madya and two privately-run HIK teachers' training schools, namely the Taman Guru and one run by Muhammadiyah—not to mention half a dozen junior high schools, all of them offering students a far better education than that afforded Soeharto.[36] Although he was to spend nine or ten years in the school system, Soeharto did not begin, let alone complete, junior high school, even if, as a student at the *schakelschool*, he was in a half-way house of sorts. This was to put him at a distinct disadvantage when it came to finding a job. It was to put him at an even greater disadvantage when, in later years, he was making his way up the army ladder, competing with officers who had completed, or almost completed, senior high school at the time the Japanese arrived in the East Indies. Soeharto was nothing if not diligent, however. In 1948, after his marriage to Hartinah, a primary school teacher, he is said to have begun evening classes at a Senior High School (Sekolah Menengah Atas, SMA) in Yogyakarta. This study was interrupted by his pressing military responsibilities in the late 1940s but he reportedly completed the course in the early 1950s.[37] Hartinah encouraged and helped him.

Soeharto claimed in his memoirs that he rode a bicycle every day from Kemusu to Yogyakarta to finish his studies at the Muhammadiyah school.[38] Whenever the bicycle was "out of order", he said, he would get up at 4:00 a.m. and walk more than six miles to school; all of this, he said, "was just a kind of test to me."[39] Soeharto's claim that he had a bicycle is curious. Bicycles were expensive and much-valued possessions at that time, owned only by the well-to-do and not lightly handed over to young people. Not many Javanese villagers had bicycles. And if a man could afford a bicycle he could presumably afford short pants and shoes for his children. "I don't believe that he owned a bicycle," said a former Indonesian politician who grew up in Yogyakarta in the thirties and forties and who came to know Soeharto well. "It's just make-believe!"[40]

Soeharto says he finished school in 1939, which means that he would have been almost eighteen. He was clearly too old to be thinking about enrolling at a MULO junior high, where the incoming students would have been thirteen or fourteen. Nor is it at all certain that his five years at a *schakelschool* would have brought him to the necessary standard, either in language skills or familiarity with "the Dutch social way of life." He would, however, have been quite well placed to undertake a vocational course. That was not to be. Although Soeharto wanted "very much" to continue his studies, "my father and relatives could not afford my school fees and expenses any more." As Soeharto told the story, his father said, "Son, this is as much as I can give you to continue your schooling. From now on you had better look for a job. And when you're working, then, God willing, you can carry on with your studies at your own expense."[41]

After leaving school, Soeharto made numerous attempts to find work, meeting with no success. Eventually he returned to Wuryantoro "where I knew many people who might be able to help me." There, after further unsuccessful attempts to find a job, he landed a position as a probationary clerical assistant with the local branch of the General People's Credit Bank (Algemeene Volkskredietbank, or AVB), which provided cheap credit to the indigenous community.[42] It was his job to accompany a bank clerk as he went from village to village on his bicycle, collecting credit applications from farmers and petty traders, who would gather at the office of the village head. The job required that Soeharto wear full Javanese dress, with a *batik* headdress (*blangkon*), traditional jacket (*béskat*) and *kain*. Soeharto did not find the work interesting, but thought that it was better than having no job at all. During his time with various foster families, he wrote later, he had learned "a great deal about the needs of ordinary villagers." But in these meetings with farmers in the presence of a more senior bank clerk and the village heads, he remained characteristically silent. It seemed, he thought, more appropriate for him to listen and learn.

Despite the routine nature of the work, Soeharto was now receiving a regular, modest, salary. There were other benefits as well. His superiors put him in charge of the circulation of magazines and newspapers at the office in Wuryantoro and he began to read various publications before passing them on. At night, hungry for knowledge and keen to better himself, he studied bookkeeping, urging Kamin, a friend, to join him. "The village chief said he thought I was bright," Soeharto told a Japanese journalist many years later, "and it seemed that I was quick to learn. In fact, in less than two months I was able to do book keeping."[43]

The job at the bank ended abruptly. Soeharto was to claim in later life that he had borrowed a *kain* from his aunt because his own was becoming threadbare and no longer fit to wear in his position as an assistant to the village bank clerk. He then had an unfortunate accident. When he was getting off his bicycle, the *kain* became caught by a spring under the saddle and tore. "My aunt was furious and snapped at me. It was the only good *kain* she had." That, Soeharto said, ended his work at the bank.[44] The claim strains credulity; it is reasonable to assume that someone on his salary would have had enough income to buy a new sarong. Whatever the truth of the matter, Soeharto was not sorry to leave the bank. He could not, however, bring himself to look at Kamin when they shook hands. "I was sad to leave him as he had been a good friend."[45] This, it is worth noting, is one of the few times when Soeharto refers to a friend. In a long and very full life he was to have many acquaintances and subordinates but remarkably few friends.[46]

Decades later, when Soeharto was heading a notoriously corrupt government, rumours circulated that he had lost his job at the credit bank not because of a torn *kain*, a story which struck many as inherently implausible, but because he had misappropriated money from the bank. According to one version of the story, Soeharto embezzled twelve guilders and fled to Solo. There, it is said, he was able to obtain a letter from the *mantri polisi*, a low-level government employee, declaring that he had a clean record.[47] According to another version, he stole money from the bank and evaded the justice system by joining the Royal Netherlands Indies Army (KNIL).[48] There is no evidence to support the allegation of theft, however, and it may well be a latter invention. It is true that, not long after he left the bank, Soeharto applied to join the KNIL. But the Dutch were particular about those they recruited for the KNIL and would have checked Soeharto's character and background.[49] Had there been any whiff of impropriety, he would not have been accepted into the colonial army.

V

In 1939, as Soeharto began to make his way in the world, the Dutch appeared to have the nationalist movement well under control. The most prominent of the nationalist leaders was Sukarno, the man Soeharto would eventually succeed as president. Sukarno was born in Surabaya on 6 June ("Double Six") 1901.[50] His father, a primary school teacher, was a Javanese *priyayi* of theosophical leanings. His mother, he claimed, was a Balinese of the Brahmin class, a niece of the last King of Singaradja, who had been "cheated out of his kingdom, fortune, home, lands and all his possessions by the Dutch." That may or may not be true; some have suggested that Sukarno's mother may have been of lower class origin.[51] Be that as it may, Sukarno said his mother passed on to him her hatred of the Dutch. Sukarno's parents met when his father was teaching at the government elementary school in Singaraja. Her parents, Balinese Hindus, refused to allow their daughter to marry Sukarno's father, who was Javanese and nominally Muslim. The couple eloped.

When Sukarno was in his early teens his father, who had coached him rigorously, wangled a place for him in the Dutch-language HBS in Surabaya. And because the family was living six hours away at the time, he arranged for his son to board at the *kampung* house of his friend Tjokroaminoto, the Sarekat Islam leader. One of the other boarders was Alimin Prawirodirdjo, who would go on to lead the Indonesian Communist Party. Another was Musso, who would also lead the party. "Tjok was my idol," Sukarno wrote in his autobiography. "I was his student. Consciously and unconsciously he moulded me. I sat at his feet and he gave me his books, he gave me his values." Sukarno accompanied Tjokroaminoto to speaking engagements, watching, learning. One thing he noticed was that his mentor never raised or lowered his voice: his speeches were flat and boring. Sukarno, who was to become such a gifted and engaging speaker, capable of holding an audience's attention for hours on end, took note. Once, when Tjokroaminoto could not make a speech, Sukarno filled in for him. It was the beginning of his long political career. Sukarno graduated from the HBS in 1921, a few days after his twentieth birthday. He had hoped to go on university in the Netherlands. His mother would not hear of it, however. Instead, he enrolled in the Technische Hogeschool, or Technical Faculty, in Bandung.

Sukarno, who founded the Indonesian National Party in 1927, became increasingly prominent and outspoken. He was arrested and jailed in 1929 and then arrested again in 1933. Fearing further trouble, the Dutch decided to send him to the isolated Boven Digul camp in West New Guinea. Sukarno, whose courage was to falter at several key moments in the nationalist struggle, "wept and begged for mercy" and the Dutch sent him instead to Endeh in Flores, before transferring him to Bengkulu, in southwest Sumatra.[52] Two other prominent nationalists, Mohammad Hatta, who would go on to become Indonesia's first Vice President, and Sutan Sjahrir, who was to become the nation's first Prime Minister, were not so fortunate.* Arrested in 1934, they joined scores of fellow nationalists in Boven Digul, before being transferred in 1936 to a more comfortable life in Banda Neira in the Moluccas.

As the thirties progressed Dutch repression became increasingly severe. Indonesians, especially those who had to deal with the Dutch, grew wary, even fearful. Sabam Siagian, the son of the Rev. Isac Siagian, a Lutheran minister, recalled an incident in the late 1930s involving a copy of Sukarno's rambling but rousing Dutch-language defence speech, "*Indonesia Klaagt Aan!*" ("Indonesia Accuses!"), delivered at his 1930 trial in Bandung. The speech was secretly circulated among high school students. Siagian's cousins often came to stay at his house in Kwitang in central Jakarta and their friends would drop in to visit. "One day," he said, "I discovered a brochure covered with a newspaper, owned by one of them. Out of curiosity I opened it and still remember vividly that it was Sukarno's '*Indonesia Klaagt Aan!*' My mother immediately reprimanded me. I was not supposed to touch it."[53]

Sukotjo Tjokroatmodjo, who was five years older than Sabam Siagian and who would go on to become the Deputy Director of the Military Police Corps, had a similar experience. His father worked for the Dutch

* The former is often wrongly described as "Dr Hatta". The man who became the nation's first Vice President studied economics at Rotterdam (1923–32) and got an MA, which means he was actually Drs, not Dr.

state railway and was not permitted to mingle with nationalists. In the late 1930s, when Sukotjo was nine or ten, he heard people in Surabaya singing *Indonesia Raya,* the nationalists' anthem. When he arrived home, humming the tune, his father was alarmed and angry. "Don't do that!" he told his son. "The police will come here." In 1941, Sukotjo returned home from junior high school with a flag on his bicycle with the words, "Indonesia *berparlemen*" ("A parliament for Indonesia"), a slogan of the day. Once again, his father was angry. "Put that away," he warned.

In Yogyakarta in the late 1930s life proceeded at a calm, unhurried pace. Selo Soemardjan, who would go on to spend forty years as private secretary to Sultan Hamengku Buwono IX, was serving at that time as an apprentice in the civil service of the sultanate, attached to the *bupati* of Gunung Kidul (Southern Mountains), a "minus" area southeast of Yogyakarta. Looking back sixty years later, Selo observed that people in Yogyakarta had had nothing in particular against the Dutch; there was nothing, he said, that would stir the Indonesians into action against the colonial power.[54]

That may have been true in one sense. But Bruce Lockhart, who had served in Russia as Britain's first envoy to the "provisional" Lenin government and who visited Java in the mid-thirties, was one of those who came away with a sense of forces stirring beneath the surface.[55] In Jakarta, Lockhart called on the Dutch Governor General, Bonifacius Cornelis de Jonge, a tall aristocratic-looking man. "My predecessor made too many promises," De Jonge told his visitor. "I always preface my remarks to the nationalists with one sentence: 'We Dutch have been here for three hundred years; we shall remain here for another three hundred. After that we can talk.'"[56] A week or so later, on his last night in Yogyakarta, Lockhart had a late-night meeting at the Kraton with a Javanese prince who had studied in the Netherlands. Asked if the sultans still had any power, the prince smiled "rather sourly" and replied, "Only the shadow. Look at my relative, the Sultan of Djokja. He is a songless canary in a golden cage." The prince was convinced, however, that the prestige of the white man in the East had gone forever. Nationalist feeling was strong, even among the poorest Javanese; they had come to realize that the Dutch gave them enough to eat and no more. Dutch Java was a hundred years behind British India in the move towards self-government, but since the war progress in Java had been more rapid. As the prince saw it, Dutch imperialism was doomed.

Nor was conflict restricted to Dutch-Indonesian relations. Social pressures were bubbling to the surface. Despite Dutch repression, the historian Anthony Reid notes, the tensions that were to give rise to the bloody "social revolutions" of 1945–46 were clearly evident at the local level.[57]

As a schoolboy in Yogyakarta, Soeharto had become aware of the nationalist movement. But unlike some other students, he had no nationalist aspirations of any kind. Indeed, the activities of those who were anti-Dutch left him unmoved. "There were stories about political leaders organising public meetings," he recalled. "Even at school, students talked about the issues that were raised at public meetings. However, I was not impressed by all that talk. I concentrated on my studies."[58] Later, as an employee of the bank, he remained circumspect, having no wish to alienate the colonial authorities and put his job at risk. In a long account of his life which he gave the *Nihon Keizai Shimbun* in 1998, Soeharto claimed that the nationalist movement "was led by intellectuals who had returned from studying in Holland and by Communist activists who had gradually been gaining power."[59] While there was some truth in the observation about students who had come back from Holland, there was no truth in the observation about Communists. The Dutch had come down hard on local Communists in the wake of the rebellion in 1926–27. The party was to remain dormant for the best part of twenty years.

In the same account, Soeharto succeeded in conveying, albeit inadvertently, some sense of how he felt about the nationalist cause in the late thirties. Conjuring up images of racist signs allegedly put up by the Dutch, he implied that he was becoming just a little put out by colonial rule. At the same time, he hinted at a preference for the peace and order of the status quo, and readily admitted that he put his own interests above those of some future Indonesian state. "Many meetings were held in Yogyakarta, where it used to be quiet," he recalled. "The world was getting restless. I had been feeling annoyed whenever I saw a sign at the entrance of a Dutch facility saying 'Dogs and Natives not admitted'. But my mind was preoccupied with the search for a job and I was also aware that I would just end up being arrested by the Dutch police if I attended the gatherings so I let them pass by."[60]

Soeharto was not alone in claiming that the Dutch erected signs saying "*Verboden voor honden en Inlanders.*" Lieutenant General Sayidiman, a leading army intellectual, was convinced that just such a sign had been placed in front of the pre-war Cikini swimming club in Jakarta, although he did not see it himself.[61] Claims of this nature appear to be unfounded. There is no convincing evidence that the Dutch, whatever feelings of racial superiority they may have had, were crass enough to behave this way, still less that they did it as a matter of course. Soeharto—or perhaps his Japanese scribe—seems to have recycled an untrue, or at least badly garbled, claim that Western colonialists placed a "Dogs and Chinese Not Admitted" sign at the entrance to the Public Garden at the northern end of the Bund in pre-World War II Shanghai and transferred the story to Java.[62] Historians have questioned the claim that there were racist signs of this nature in the East Indies, as have Dutch men and women who lived in pre-war Java.

In 1995, the Dutch novelist Hella Haasse remarked that as a young girl in the 1930s she often went to the Cikini swimming club but never saw such a sign. Asked about Soeharto's assertion that such signs existed, Colonel Heshusius, who grew up in pre-war Yogyakarta, said the claim "was a joke." It was possible, he thought, that some individuals had spoken that way in a Dutch club while drinking whisky or *jenever*, "but it was never stated … at the swimming pool."[63] What seems most likely is that Indonesians, aware that they were not allowed at certain swimming pools and tennis clubs, were receptive to suggestions that such signs must have been found at such places. The supposed word order—first dogs and then natives—was also offensive, as indeed was the alleged use of the word *inlander*, which Indonesians deeply disliked.[64]

Be that as it may, Soeharto's words are revealing. Indonesian nationalists had been campaigning for years against the colonial authorities, with some paying a heavy price for their activism. Soeharto's nationalist credentials were non-existent at this time. Indeed, as events were to show, he was willing to sign up as a foot soldier of a colonial army that had been set up to keep Indonesians silent and subservient if that would improve his prospects.

Soeharto's application to join the KNIL produced no immediate reply and he continued his search for work, this time in Solo. At one stage, a friend suggested that he enlist in the Royal Netherlands Navy, which maintained a flotilla in the East Indies. The only vacancy they had was for a cook, he recalled, "so I decided to leave this option until the last." Still without a job, he returned to Wuryantoro, occupying himself by participating in various community self-help projects, building a prayer house, digging ditches, repairing a rice barn. As he said later, his future looked bleak. Then, when he was least expecting it, a letter came from the KNIL, inviting him to sit for an entrance exam at Magelang, a garrison town in the foothills twenty-seven miles northwest of Yogyakarta. Soeharto, who was eighteen, travelled to Magelang, sat the exam and was accepted for the KNIL. It was to be the beginning of a military career that would carry him, in little more than twenty-five years, to a position where he wielded immeasurably greater power and influence than any Javanese sultan or Dutch governor general had ever enjoyed.

As President, Soeharto was to give two very differing accounts of his decision to join the colonial army. In the late sixties, he made no attempt to pretend that his application had been motivated by nationalism. He had not been interested in a military career before he enlisted in the KNIL, he told O.G. Roeder. Rather, it had been "the desire to see other parts of the country which made him join the army.... Like other young men of his age, he was fond of adventure and he hoped the army would give him a life of adventure, which would contrast sharply with the poor conditions of his boyhood."[65] In other words, Soeharto was looking for two things, adventure and a secure, well-paid job, with the emphasis likely to have been very much on the latter. There was nothing unusual in this; most of the Javanese who joined the KNIL were driven by financial considerations. Roeder has suggested, tentatively, a third factor may have shaped his thinking: "Perhaps, too, he was longing for a shelter in the community after the years of being pushed from place to place, without a parental home and a satisfying profession."[66] There could be an element of truth in that, although it is more probable that Soeharto only became aware of that satisfying sense of being part of an organization after he had joined up. There is little to indicate that he was expecting anything special when he enlisted. As he wrote in his memoirs, "It did not occur to me that my application would be the beginning of a career I would enjoy."[67]

When Soeharto published his autobiography in 1989, he made no attempt to revise that picture he had painted twenty years earlier. By 1998, it was another matter altogether. "I think realistically," he now declared. "I thought that if I joined the army I would have a chance to acquire advanced knowledge and [an understanding of] the technology of developed countries. I would then be able to make myself useful in the struggle for our country's independence."[68] It is difficult to take this claim seriously. There is no reason to believe that in 1940 Soeharto gave a moment's thought to the idea of an independent Indonesian state or that he envisaged a role for himself in helping secure that independence. The idea of using the resources of a foreign power to achieve that goal only arose in the years after 1943 when young Indonesians were offered military training in the Peta, the auxiliary defence force set up on Java by the Japanese Sixteenth Army. In 1940, Soeharto was not using the Dutch (except insofar as he needed their money): he was allowing them to use him. He was not thinking of some future independent Indonesia but of himself. In 1940, as in later years, Soeharto was very much the safe player, a man who looked first to his own interests. At the same time, he should not be judged too harshly for his lack of nationalist spirit at this time. The future president was still in his teens and had yet to be touched in any significant way by the idea of independence, which tended to be stronger among those who were better educated.

VI

By any yardstick, Soeharto had an exceptionally difficult childhood, one that left scars that were to remain with him for life. He was an unwanted child, abandoned at birth by his mother and of little interest to his father, at least initially. By the time he was seventeen he had been shunted between no fewer than eight families, treated with kindness by some but as little more than a servant by others. He had attended six schools. The blame for this, he seems to have thought, not without justification, could be laid at the feet of his parents. And if they had been guilty of largely pushing him out of their lives, he was to do much the same to them. It is impossible, reading through the various accounts that Soeharto gave of his childhood, not to be struck by the way in which he wrote his parents out of his life. He recalls with great affection the "tender love" of his great-aunt, who cared for him in Kemusu during his first four years. He remembers with gratitude that his aunt and uncle in Wuryantoro took him in and treated him as their own child. He recalls the kindness of Romo Daryatmo. There is nothing in this vein about either his mother or his father. In his autobiography, it is true, he claims to have realized in his adolescent years "how much I loved my parents and how much I was loved by them", but there is something hollow and unconvincing about this observation. It is strikingly at odds with Soeharto's later observation that the ill will between his parents had created an environment in which he suffered abuse.

The picture, however, is not unreservedly bleak. Soeharto may have had a poor and dislocated childhood. But as Angus McIntyre has shown, he was not flattened by his childhood.[69] On the contrary, he was able to make something of it. He was able to compensate for a lack of parental love and attention. He was able to draw strength from adversity. Hardship served as a spur to his ambition, breeding an intense desire for self-improvement. This ability to turn negatives into positives was to serve him well in the years ahead. He emerged from his childhood not only as inward-looking and detached, potentially ruthless and vindictive, but also as intelligent, thoughtful, cautious and realistic—useful attributes in an army officer and head of state. These virtues, when coupled with his high ability, his determination to succeed and his remarkable run of good fortune, helped him overcome his humble origins and mediocre education. They help to explain his success in becoming and staying president. They help to explain the successes of his presidency.

Soeharto's prospects, when he left school, were not promising. But he did have three things in his favour. First, he was endowed, as we have seen, with natural ability and a steely determination. Second, his father had, for all his other parental shortcomings, given him a rare and precious chance in life by sending out as an *orang ngéngér*, to be reared by better-off relatives; this took Soeharto into the wider world of late colonial urban Java. Finally, he was a beneficiary of educational reforms only recently introduced by the Dutch. The establishment of both the village school system in 1907 and the *schakelschool* system in 1921 were of inestimable value to Soeharto, who throughout his life was to draw no end of benefit from changes introduced by the dominant authority on Java, be it the Dutch colonial government, the Japanese occupation force or the subsequent Republic of Indonesia. In his youth and indeed for much of his life, Soeharto was like a body surfer, capable and strong in his own right but having the waves form up most fortuitously just as he needed them, carrying him forward in sustained and powerful surges, compensating to some extent for the emotional and financial deprivation of his early life.

That said, Soeharto would never receive the kind of education many of his contemporaries and future army rivals were to have, a missed opportunity of which he would always be acutely conscious. Worse still, he was to feel in later years the disdain of better-educated brother officers, men who had acquired, seemingly so easily, the skills and social graces which he had had to work so hard to attain. That would lead, in time, to new resentments, many of them carefully nurtured against the day when the scores could be settled. There would be other kinds of resentment, too: resentment against officers who had, as he saw it, thwarted or betrayed him; resentments against those whom he suspected of harbouring radical plans to overturn a social system which he had come to accept and value. Vengeance always rated highly among the Soeharto attributes.

ABOVE: Lt. Col. Soeharto, white shirt, stands alongside an ailing Gen. Sudirman, the Supreme Commander of the Indonesian Army, at a military parade in Yogyakarta in 1949. The earliest known photographs of Soeharto date from 1947. (*Ipphos*)

RIGHT: President Sukarno reviews Soeharto's troops in Yogyakarta in 1948. Soeharto, who would replace Sukarno as head of state in 1968, walks behind him and to the right. (*Ipphos*)

ABOVE: Two girls ride past an entrance marker at Kemusu, the Central Java hamlet where Soeharto was born in 1921. (*David Jenkins*)

MIDDLE: Many traditional houses in Kemusu have been replaced by more modern structures. (*David Jenkins*)

BELOW: Boys riding water buffaloes, Java, *c*. 1930. Soeharto spoke fondly of similar experiences during his childhood. (*Nationaal Museum van Wereldculturen TM-60002540*)

RIGHT: Central Java farmer gathers stubble in a parched rice field during the dry season. (*David Jenkins*)

BELOW: Women transplanting rice seedlings in Central Java. (*David Jenkins*)

ABOVE: The Astana Giri Bangun, a family mausoleum President Soeharto and his wife, Ibu Tien Soeharto, built on a sacred royal hillside southeast of Solo, seen here in 1979. (*David Jenkins*)

BELOW LEFT: The mausoleum outshines the nearby Astana Mangadeg, burial place of the early rulers of the Mangkunegaran line, as it was in 1979. The royal graves have since been refurbished. (*David Jenkins*)

BELOW RIGHT: Brig. Gen. Jono Hatmodjo, a grandson of Mangkunegoro VI and an uncle of Ibu Tien. In building the mausoleum, he said, Soeharto was "violating completely the custom of the kings." (*David Jenkins*)

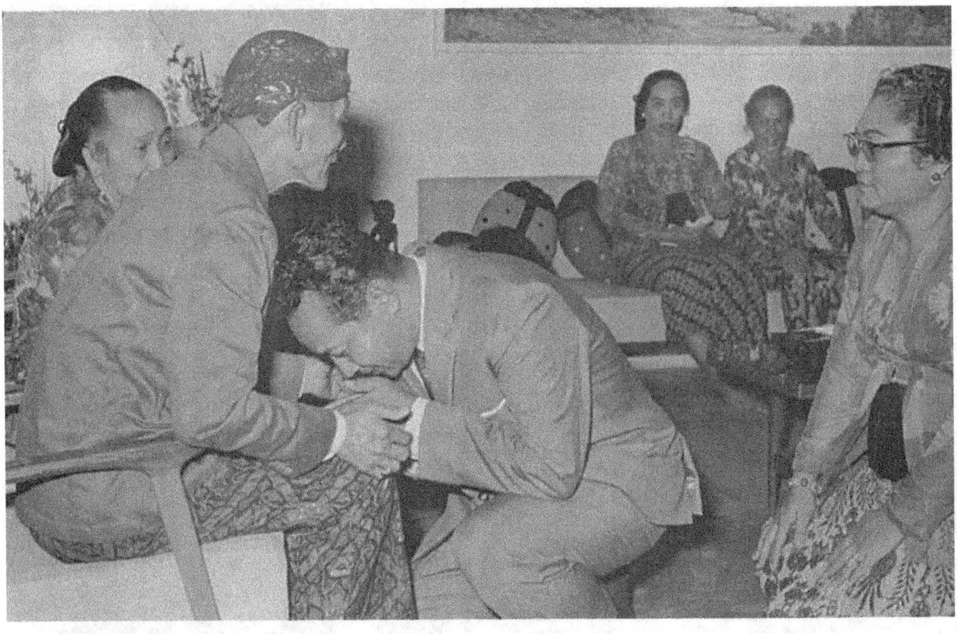

TOP LEFT: A painting of Soeharto's father, Kertosudiro, a village irrigation official. There are no photographs of Soeharto's mother, Sukirah, who died in 1946. (*Soeharto: Pikiran, Ucapan, dan Tindakan Saya*)

TOP RIGHT: Ibu Bei Prawirowihardjo, Kertosudiro's younger sister. She became in effect Soeharto's foster mother when he was eight or nine. (*Soeharto: Pikiran, Ucapan, dan Tindakan Saya*)

ABOVE: Soeharto pays his respects to his father-in-law K. R. M. T. Soemoharjomo, a member of the Mangkunegaran court. Ibu Tien is on the right. (*Deppen*)

LEFT: "Everybody was investigated by my office." Maj. Gen. Sukotjo Tjokroatmodjo, centre, the Military Police arresting officer in the *Pop* magazine case, seen here in 2013 with two Japanese-trained friends, Maj. Gen. Soetarto Sigit, left, and Lt. Gen. Purbo Suwondo. (*David Jenkins*)

LEFT: Lt. Gen. Ali Moertopo, right, head of Opsus, a freewheeling intelligence body set up by Soeharto, pictured in 1979 with Dr Widjojo Nitisastro, the nation's leading technocrat. In 1974, Moertopo knew in advance that a subordinate, Col. Aloysius Soegianto, was planning to publish an article alleging that Soeharto was of aristocratic descent. (*David Jenkins*)

LEFT: Col. Soegianto, centre, who published the article which so angered Soeharto, seen here in 1997 with two of Moertopo's former civilian advisers, Harry Tjan Silalahi, left, and Jusuf Wanandi (Liem Bian Kie). (*David Jenkins*)

ABOVE LEFT: Sultan Hamengku Buwono VII of Yogyakarta (r. 1877-1921), who is said to have fathered seventy-nine children. He abdicated at eighty-two, "feeling the weight of his great age." (*Royal Netherlands Institute of Southeast Asian and Caribbean Studies (KITLV) and Leiden University Library/Wikimedia Commons TM-60001464*)

ABOVE RIGHT: Sultan Hamengku Buwono VIII (r. 1921-39), in full Western uniform. (*Public domain/Nationaal Museum van Wereldculturen TM-60035934*)

RIGHT: Governor Lucien Adam and Sultan Hamengku Buwono IX on the day of the latter's installation in March 1940. In 1974 Soeharto told the Sultan, who was by then his Vice President, that the family tree published in *Pop* magazine "was not true." (*Nationaal Museum van Wereldculturen TM-60036088*)

ABOVE: The Ndalem Kalitan (1789), a palace in the heart of Solo. Soeharto's family bought this retreat from a daughter of Sunan Pakubuwono X, a former ruler of the preeminent Surakarta court. The two Surakarta courts were formally abolished in 1946 but retain an informal status. (*David Jenkins*)

ABOVE: The *pendopo*, or open-sided reception hall, of the Ndalem Kalitan, pictured in 2008. (*David Jenkins*)

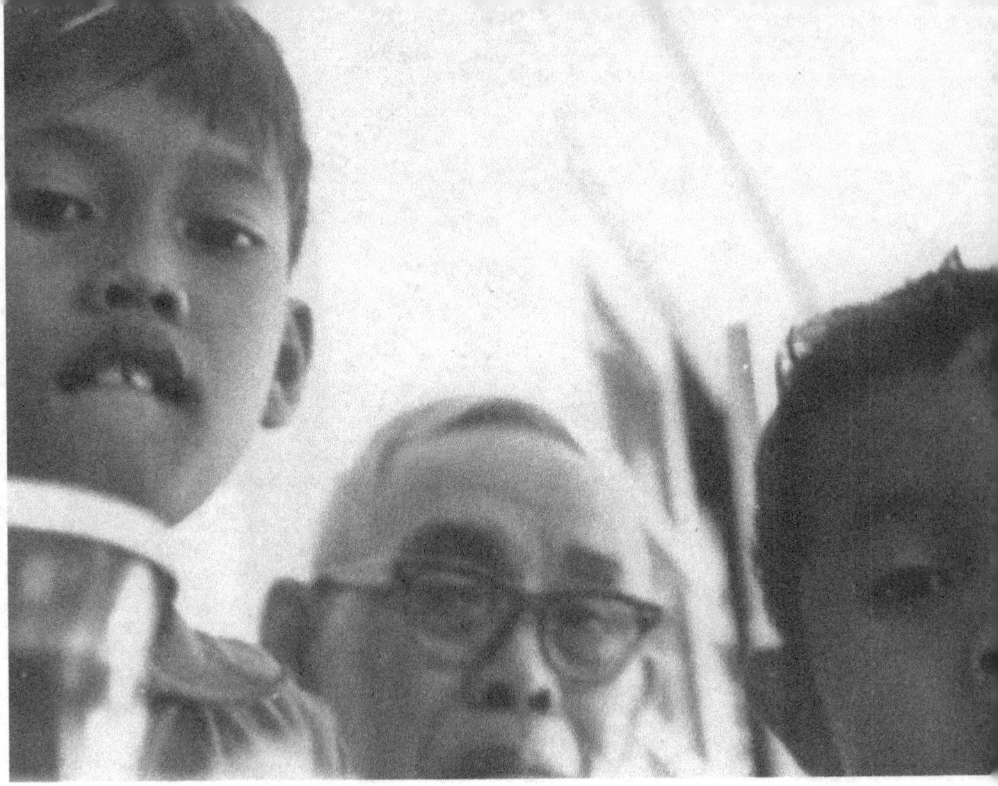

ABOVE: "I was very keen to listen to his talks on the philosophy of life. Apparently, he, too, took a liking to me." Romo Daryatmo, a noted mystic and faith healer who had a profound influence on Soeharto's life, at his home in Wonogiri, Central Java, in 1969.

RIGHT: Maj. Gen. Sudjono Humardani, right, seen here with Jusuf Wanandi in 1979. Sudjono and Soeharto, who met in the 1950s, had a shared interest in Javanese religion and were deeply wary of political Islam. (*David Jenkins*)

ABOVE: A pre-war *volksschool* in West Java. Soeharto attended a series of village schools. These offered a basic education in the vernacular language, in his case Javanese. (*Wikimedia Commons TM-10002284*)

LEFT: Children in the first year of a pre-war *schakelschool* (link school) in Purworejo, Central Java. These schools, of which there were few, connected the village school system to the parallel and infinitely more prestigious Dutch-language stream. Soeharto spent about five years in a *schakelschool*. (*Wikimedia Commons TM-10002279*)

LEFT: First-year students at a HBS senior high school in Buitenzorg (Bogor) in 1937. Most senior officers in the post-war Indonesian Army had attended a good Dutch high school. Soeharto had not. On paper, this put him at a major disadvantage. (*Nationaal Museum van Wereldculturen TM-33000428*)

ABOVE: Aerial view of the Batavia (Jakarta) railway station, upper left, c. 1933-35. In the foreground are the offices of the Javasche Bank (left) and the Netherlands Trading Society (NHM). (*NMVW TM-10014030*)

ABOVE: A busy shopping street in Jakarta, *c*. 1940. (*Nationaal Museum van Wereldculturen TM-60037888*)

ABOVE: A train passes over a rail bridge in the mountains of West Java, *c.* 1925. The Dutch invested heavily in infrastructure, driven by a desire to maximize profits. (*Nationaal Museum van Wereldculturen TM-10007531*)

ABOVE: Sugar mill, Candi Sewu, Java, *c.* 1905. Planters made huge returns from the cultivation of sugar on Java in the period before the Great Depression. (*Nationaal Museum van Wereldculturen TM-10011760*)

ABOVE: H. J. F. M. (Henk) Sneevliet, a dapper Dutch Communist whose commitment to revolutionary socialism was to have a significant impact both in Indonesia and China.

RIGHT: Darsono and Semaun in Jakarta in 1970, fifty years after they founded the Indonesian Communist Party (PKI) and five years after Soeharto destroyed it. Darsono lived a few doors from Soeharto. (*David Jenkins*)

ABOVE: Tan Malaka, once Moscow's chief agent of revolutionary change in Southeast Asia, would later distance himself from both the Soviet Union and the PKI. (*Spaarnestad SFA 003006269*)

LEFT: Sukarno and Mohammad Hatta, Indonesia's two most prominent nationalist leaders. Sent by the Dutch into internal exile in the early 1930s, they would agree to cooperate with the Japanese in 1942. They used this opportunity, distasteful as it was, to advance the nationalist cause. (Netherlands Institute for Sound and Vision/NIOD, still from the Nippon Eigasha Djawa film *Bezoek Generaal Tojo en instelling van de Centrale Raad van Advies*, 1943)

ABOVE LEFT: Sutan Sjahrir, a social democratic leader imprisoned by the Dutch, was to remain aloof from the Japanese. He became Indonesia's first prime minister (1945-47). (*Imperial War Museum* SE 6717)

ABOVE RIGHT: Governor General B. C. de Jonge, right, and his successor, A. W. L. Tjarda van Starkenborgh, Jakarta, 1936. De Jonge told a British visitor: "I always preface my remarks to the nationalists with one sentence: 'We Dutch have been here for three hundred years; we shall remain here for another three hundred. After that we can talk.'" Van Starkenborgh spent the years 1942-45 in Japanese detention. (*Wikimedia Commons TM-10018818*)

ABOVE: Soldiers of the Dutch colonial army close in a tight circle around their officer, a formation they adopted when attacked by indigenous enemies. By 1940, the year Soeharto joined the KNIL, more than 300,000 people of the archipelago had died in the struggle against the Dutch. (*NMVW TM-60036641*)

ABOVE: In Bali in 1906, the Raja of Badung and several hundred followers, attired in white, advanced into the Dutch guns in a *puputan* (collective mass suicide). Dutch colonial troops, upper left, survey the dead. (*Hendrik Maurits van Weede. NMVW TM-60015988*)

MIDDLE: Balinese dead lie on the ground during the Dutch drive to suppress Balinese forces in Badung. (*H. M. van Weede, NMVW/Wikimedia Commons TM-60050659*)

BELOW: The former KNIL barracks in Malang, East Java. In 1941 Corporal Soeharto commanded a fifteen-man *brigade* in the colonial army's 13th Battalion at Malang. (*David Jenkins*)

ABOVE: Members of the KNIL air wing (KNIL-ML) pose in front of an advanced US-made Martin B-10 bomber. In the late 1930s, the KNIL was scrambling to turn itself into a modern defence force capable of seeing off a Japanese lunge for the Dutch East Indies. (*Nationaal Museum van Wereldculturen TM-60044204*)

BELOW LEFT: Dutch policeman and Indonesian assistant. "The Dutch police force in the countryside was very much feared…" (*Nationaal Museum van Wereldculturen TM-60025380*)

BELOW RIGHT: Pumping petrol across the street from the offices of the Yamato Shokai, a Japanese trading company, Java, c. 1923-25. In the 12 years to 1936, the number of Japanese in the East Indies rose from 4,000 to 7,000. (*Nationaal Museum van Wereldculturen TM-30008822*)

7

"I was suited to the disciplined life of the military"

On 10 May 1940, Hitler reneged on his promise to respect Dutch neutrality and unleashed a devastating blitzkrieg against the Low Countries. After five days of fighting, the Dutch commander-in-chief surrendered, unable to hold out against the German onslaught and unwilling to accept further destruction of Dutch cities. On the same day, Queen Wilhelmina, who now headed a Dutch Government-in-exile in London, having vetoed a cabinet decision to move to Jakarta because she "could not stand the tropical climate", announced that the Dutch people in the colonies would fight alongside the Allies, by which she meant they would continue in the struggle against Hitler.[1] What was less clear, at least to the British, was whether the Dutch would be prepared to resist a Japanese invasion of the Netherlands East Indies.[2] While it seemed increasingly likely that the Dutch would resist, they were still playing for time, hoping to forestall an attack with their pledge, which they would give Tokyo on 6 June, to go on selling the Japanese strategic raw materials, including tin, rubber, oil and bauxite, from the East Indies so long as these did not fall into German hands.[3]

The Dutch felt that if the Japanese could not obtain these commodities through negotiation they would be increasingly tempted to take them by force.[4] They knew they could not hope to defend the East Indies on their own. Nor did they have any guarantee that the British or the Americans would come to their aid if the NEI were attacked. Those concerns were not misplaced. "We cannot foresee the time," the British Chiefs of Staff had concluded in 1937, "when our defence forces will be strong enough to safeguard our territory, trade and vital interests against Germany, Italy and Japan simultaneously."[5] Nothing had changed since those words were written. On the contrary, the scenario the defence chiefs had considered was now unfolding. On 10 June 1940, less than a week after the mass evacuation of British and French troops from Dunkirk, Italy declared war on Britain and France. With their backs to the wall in Europe and the Middle East, the British would be able to provide few additional resources in the Far East should Japan strike south. The United States was to remain at peace for another eighteen months, until the Japanese strike at Pearl Harbor. Southeast Asia was living on borrowed time.

As these dramatic events unfolded, Soeharto began his military career. On 1 June, two weeks after the Dutch surrender in Holland and five days before his nineteenth birthday, he joined a six-month basic infantry training course at the KNIL's 3rd Depot Battalion in Gombong, a garrison town seventy-five miles west of Yogyakarta. Housed within the brick and stone ramparts of an old fortress, the depot battalion was a world of order and discipline, of parades and drill, of classroom training and field exercises, humming with a sense of purpose, officers and NCOs conducting training sessions, recruits cleaning their weapons or lining up for meals in the companies' kitchen, bugles sounding reveille, men of the barrack guard turning out smartly at dawn and dusk for the raising and lowering of the *driekleur*, the red, white and blue Dutch national flag. It all made a deep impression on Soeharto. "I was nineteen years old," he recalled. "The school had been built in the nineteenth century in the Western style and it looked like a palace in comparison with the surrounding farm houses. It is still there, lying in ruins now. Here, for the first time, I got to know what a modern organization was like."[6] Some recruits take an instant dislike to service life. Soeharto relished it. "We were drilled from morning to night. It was an entirely different experience from what I'd had at school and when I worked as a clerical assistant in the village bank. But I liked it and was beginning to see that I could live on my service earnings."[7] Recalling these events nearly six decades later, he said, "I realised I was suited to the disciplined life of the military."[8]

For the Dutch in the East Indies, this was a time of immense anxiety and uncertainty. Nor can Soeharto, who had signed up for three years' service in the KNIL, with a further twelve years in the reserves, have been immune from concerns about the future. Since the fall of Poland in October 1939, the local newspapers had been full of warnings of war and chaos. Now, Holland too had fallen. In Southeast Asia, the threat of a Japanese invasion loomed large. Soeharto would have read something of these developments and reflected on their implications. It is difficult to imagine that he was thinking at that time of a secure, permanent job in the KNIL. In the short term, however, there were certain benefits. At the age of eighteen, he had landed a job that would provide a regular income and new challenges. And while he may not have realized it initially, the colonial army would provide him with an environment which met many of his deeper emotional needs. Since birth, he had been shunted from one family to another, feeling unloved and unwanted for much of that time. He had been searching for "a more ordered and stable life".[9] He found this order and stability in the army. He enjoyed the routine and the predictability of peacetime military life. He enjoyed the discipline, the security, the companionship and the sense of purpose. He liked the recognition that came when he displayed ability and initiative. He liked the fact that the army offered an escape from what threatened to be a life of relentless poverty. In time, Soeharto would elevate his own personal search for order and stability into an effort to bring order and stability to an entire nation.

II

In joining the KNIL, Soeharto was joining a singular kind of army, one in a state of belated and hasty transition at the eleventh hour. After years of neglect, the force was expanding rapidly to meet the threat posed by an expansionist Japan. This was to provide unique opportunities for Soeharto. Although he would spend only twenty-one months in the Dutch colonial army, it would be a crucial stage in his life.

In 1940, the KNIL was a deeply flawed institution, both morally and structurally.[10] One problem was that it had a distinctly unsavoury reputation. Another was that it was hopelessly overstretched. The KNIL was a force with a history written in blood, most of it Indonesian blood. Formed in 1830 at the end of the Java War, it had seen continuous action during the nineteenth century, when the Dutch were bringing the remainder of the archipelago under their sway, often at a great cost in Indonesian lives. During this time, KNIL units were routinely sent on campaigns (*expedities*) to the Outer Islands, sometimes for years at a time, to put down local resistance. In the official and unofficial histories of the KNIL, five words appear repeatedly as shorthand explanations for the despatch of these troops: *onlusten* (unrest), *opstand* (uprising), *verzet* (resistance), *ongeregeldheden* (disturbances) and *moeilijkheden* (problems). In many cases, the words used fall well short of the mark. For much of the nineteenth century the KNIL was not simply suppressing unrest but engaged in open warfare against those sultans, rajas and minor princes (and their people) who refused to accept Dutch sovereignty. The KNIL had faced its greatest challenge in Aceh, where the Dutch were at war, on and off, for forty years, from 1873 to 1913. But the fighting—and the slaughter—had been heavy and continuous in many other parts of the archipelago, especially in Bone, the Buginese state in southern Sulawesi, and in Bali. In the period from 1825 to 1940, the year Soeharto joined the colonial army, more than 300,000 people of the archipelago had died in the struggle against the Dutch.[11]

In 1940 the Dutch colonial army remained deeply unpopular in some parts of the Outer Islands, where the memories of brutal subjugation were still fresh. But on Java, which had been at peace for 110 years, since the end of the Java War, the army was an accepted part of everyday life, not especially popular perhaps but disciplined up to a point and quite well trained. The tramp of soldiers marching through garrison towns such as Magelang or Malang would have elicited no more than a curious glance, if that. It was the Dutch colonial police force, not the KNIL, which was treated warily, the police having the power to arrest people.* In the words of a retired Indonesian general who grew up in the late 1930s across the road from the KNIL garrison in Malang, the soldiers of the colonial army

* In the case of an emergency, as for example during the PKI rebellion of 1926–27, the KNIL was sent in to provide "military assistance". In extraordinary circumstances such as this, the colonial army had permission to open fire as and when necessary.

were "very well accepted, especially on Java.... On Java, they were just part of the life here."[12] There was, however, one important exception to that rule. In nationalist circles the KNIL was seen as an institution red in tooth and claw, on which Dutch power ultimately rested. Indonesians such as Soeharto, who had volunteered for service in the army, were looked on with a mixture of scorn and pity. They were seen by many in the nationalist movement as men who had sold out to Dutch colonial power, putting their own interests above those of their compatriots.

Nor, for much of its existence, had the Indies Army been held in high esteem in Dutch society. The dominant figures in the Netherlands East Indies were the senior colonial officials, the big planters, the big bankers and the businessmen who ran the five great Dutch trading and shipping companies. The KNIL Commander-in-Chief was, of course, part of that world. He was the head of the War Department in the colony under the Governor General, who was in turn under the Minister of Colonies in the Netherlands. As such, the KNIL chief was on the same level as the heads of the departments of internal affairs, economic affairs, finance, transport, justice, religion and so on. He and his senior staff officers and regimental commanders were fully accepted in polite society, as were more junior officers. In Dutch colonial society as a whole, however, the KNIL was seen as a mercenary, low-class, low-status organization. This disdain stemmed partly from the fact that the KNIL was such a crude instrument of Dutch power. But there was more to it than that. In the complex social order of the Netherlands East Indies, the KNIL was itself a complex social organism, riddled with class, status and racial distinctions. Like most armies, the KNIL distinguished between officers, NCOs and soldiers. But it had overlapping racial distinctions that were important as well.

During the first three centuries (1600–1900) of the Dutch presence in the East Indies, but especially during the military pacification campaigns of 1875–1905, liaisons between European men and local women produced a large mixed-race community. "The Dutch," a British Admiralty *Manual of Netherlands India* sniffed not long after World War I, "used to regard the natives and their women as instruments to be used for their convenience, and it was usual and conventional for each man to have a native mistress or wife."[13] In 1854, spurred by the need to draw a distinction between new Western civil and criminal codes on the one hand and the various forms of Indonesian customary law (*adat*) on the other, the Dutch had divided the population of the East Indies into two legal categories, Europeans and

Inlanders ("Natives"), with each group having its own courts.* So-called Foreign Orientals, mainly Chinese, Arabs, Indians and a small number of Japanese, were equated with natives. However in 1899, bowing to pressure from an increasingly assertive Japan, the Dutch agreed to legally "equate" Japanese with Europeans.† In 1925 the Dutch created a third legal category for (non-Japanese) Foreign Orientals.[14]

The rules governing just who was European were interpreted with some flexibility. If a European man married a non-European woman, his wife was incorporated into the European population group. If a European man had a child with a native woman (*nyai*) to whom he was not married, the child acquired European status if his or her father "recognized" that child as his own; if he did not, the child would be native. In 1942, the overall population with European status was around 280,000, of whom about one-third were full-blood European (*totoks*). The other 186,000 or so were the wives or acknowledged children, or descendants, of a European father and an indigenous mother. Beyond that, of course, lay a large "unrecognized" community of people with "native" status but some European ancestry.

These legal provisions notwithstanding, social, economic, class and racial factors worked to the disadvantage of those of mixed-race background, who were known as Eurasians or Indo-Europeans (with the pejorative abbreviation *Indo*, although they also used this term themselves.)[15] In the late 1800s, many of the Europeans in the NEI had in fact been Eurasian. From 1900 onwards, they were gradually marginalized as more women entered the colony from the Netherlands, making the European elite increasingly white. At the same time, the emergence of a large, cheap, educated "native" workforce pushed Eurasians out of many white-collar jobs. The "true Dutch" of the wider European community tended to

---

* In 1940, when Soeharto joined the KNIL, the word *inlander* was still used, both officially and unofficially, to describe "native" people. However, many Indonesians considered the term offensive. In Dutch circles, the "better" word for Indonesians was *inheems* (native people). It was used officially to describe those who were neither European nor Eurasian. In private conversation, Dutchmen frequently used *inlander* when referring to those of non-European or non-Eurasian background.

† In 1905 there were fewer than 1,000 Japanese in the NEI, of whom 80 per cent were women, many of them hairdressers and prostitutes.

look down on impoverished but legally European people of mixed-race origin, often portraying them as lazy, stupid, oversexed and unable to speak proper Dutch. "The *Indos*," it has been said, "overcompensated by disdaining the natives."[16]

No distinction, legal or otherwise, was drawn in either the colonial civil service or the KNIL between full-blood Europeans—whether they were Indies-born or "imported" from Holland—and Eurasians recognized as Europeans, some of whom, despite their often imposingly long Dutch, German or perhaps Hungarian names, were of predominantly non-European background and appearance. The sole exception, a symbolically important one, was that only a Dutchman could be appointed Governor General. In the KNIL, *totoks* and "acknowledged" Europeans served together, played football together, went to church together. All were referred to as Europeans: the word Eurasian was never used.[17] Nor did the KNIL have any invisible barriers to advancement that favoured full-blood Europeans. When Soeharto joined the colonial army, a Eurasian, Lieutenant General Gerardus Johannes Berenschot, was commander-in-chief. By way of contrast, a clear distinction between full-blood Europeans and those of mixed race was often made in the banks, trading houses and shipping companies of the Netherlands East Indies, where *Indos* were often found in menial or middle-ranking positions and made to feel inferior to both "imported" and locally-born Europeans.

Once one got past the legal provision that treated "acknowledged" Eurasians as Europeans, the KNIL was absolutely obsessed with race. Some of the racial distinctions were horizontal. The officer corps was almost exclusively "European" in the broad local definition of the term (about half of the officers were "true Dutch", the other half Eurasian), the non-commissioned officers drawn from either a "European" or "native" background, with a preponderance of the latter, and the soldiers for the most part native.[18] But most of the segregation was vertical, the Dutch having built watertight bulkheads between soldiers of different ethnic backgrounds, at least on Java, where most of the infantry battalions were based. Similar vertical divisions existed within the horse cavalry, which had totally separate European, Menadonese and Javanese platoons. This may have been done in part because it fitted the needs of a policy of divide-and-rule, under which the suspicions and aspirations of one ethnic group were used to counterbalance the suspicions and ambitions of other ethnic groups, a common practice in Western colonies. But there were also practical considerations, and these may have been more important. The policy ministered to ethnic self-esteem and allowed soldiers to speak their own languages. It reduced the potential for inter-ethnic and inter-religious conflict. For example, the Christians ate pork and prayed in church, practices which set them apart from Muslims.

If the KNIL was viewed with some disdain in 1940 this was due not so much to the behaviour of the "true Dutch" officers, the most senior of whom always sat at the high table in colonial society. Nor was it due to any deep aversion to the "native" NCOs or foot soldiers. Rather, the problem lay with the European and Eurasian NCOs and foot soldiers, the men who provided the tough inner core of the KNIL infantry battalions, most of which had one European company. The Dutch had always had a fear, not unreasonable in the circumstances, that it could be unwise to train and arm large numbers of Indonesians lest they turn on their colonial masters. In the period from 1855 to about 1900 European and Eurasian soldiers made up no more than one-third of the army.[19] At the end of the nineteenth century the Dutch sought to ensure that at least 50 percent of KNIL soldiers were European, in the narrow definition of that term. They tried to meet that target during the latter stages of the Aceh War by recruiting large numbers of mercenaries, "mostly of the worst sort."[20] Indeed, at that time, the Dutch Indies Army had many characteristics of the French Foreign Legion; many of the mercenaries came from Germany and Belgium. It soon became obvious, however, that the 1:1 target could not be achieved. On the eve of World War I only one in four KNIL soldiers was European or Eurasian. By 1920, it was one in five, and foreigners were no longer being recruited.

European soldiers were highly valued by their battalion commanders because they were politically reliable, better educated and thought to be more dependable in a crisis. They were seen as better able to provide leadership to indigenous troops. But they were a rough-and-ready lot, notorious in respectable society for their dissolute and disreputable ways, for their drinking, their brawling and their whoring. Before 1890 recruits in Holland who wanted to join the colonial army were given elementary training at the Colonial Recruiting Centre (Koloniaal Werfdepot) in Harderwijk, a small provincial garrison town which was known, for the quality of the men it turned out, as "the sink-hole of Europe" (*gootgat van Europa*).[21] By 1909, all such recruit training had been transferred to the Koloniale Reserve in the old fortress town of Nijmegen.

In the late nineteenth century, the European soldier in the Indies Army was, by virtue of being a military man, on the fringe of colonial society. "While his bravery was rewarded with the highest honours," write two Dutch historians of the KNIL, "he was socially a pariah, rejected by the Europeans in the colony and treated as a leper. Only officers were received in society."[22] The lower ranks "were seen as the dregs of society, as social irredeemables of low birth and trifling value, fit only to serve as cannon fodder."[23] Until the early years of the twentieth century, many of these soldiers offended upper-class civilian sensibilities by living openly in the barracks with a *nyai*, or concubine, usually a woman of lowly Javanese origin. The mixed race children of these unions added to a growing number of Indo-Europeans, many of whom went on, in turn, to serve in the army.[24] In the opinion of many Dutchmen, the main problem with the KNIL was that it was full of unreliable and incompetent Eurasians.[25]

By 1940 the quality of men from the Koloniale Reserve had risen: most of the soldiers who had trained in Nijmegen were seen as potential NCOs. Nevertheless, the ordinary Dutch soldier still found himself shunned by respectable society. "He had," observed Colonel Joop Nortier, who commanded a post-World War II KNIL battalion, "only his soldier friends, the *tangsi* [barracks] and the *kampung*. One had to be at least an NCO to be accepted."[26] And even then there were restrictions. European NCOs were not permitted to join the *sociëteit*, or Dutch club, the social centre of the European/Eurasian community in each main town.

When it came to recruiting Indonesians for the KNIL, the Dutch made no secret of the fact that they preferred Menadonese, Ambonese and Timorese. Men from those regions were thought to make good soldiers and, as Christians, were considered to be "closer" to the Dutch. This gave rise to the myth, accepted at face value by many historians and widely propagated by Javanese, Soeharto included, that the KNIL was made up largely of Menadonese and Ambonese.[27] That was never the case. At no stage were the Dutch able to draw more than a limited number of KNIL soldiers from those relatively small ethnic pockets. Nor were there ever more than a small number of Sundanese, Madurese, Buginese, Acehnese, Malay and Batak recruits. There were, on the other hand, any number of willing Javanese and the colonial army recruited them in significant numbers. In 1929 Javanese accounted for 40 per cent of the manpower of the KNIL.[28] In 1937 there were more Javanese (12,700) in the KNIL than all other indigenous troops (12,400) combined; the Menadonese came a poor second, with 5,100 soldiers, the Ambonese third, with 4,000.[29] As the Dutch saw it, the Javanese were good and malleable soldiers. They did what was asked of them. They did not complain. But the Javanese recruits were driven, as the Dutch were well aware, by a different calculus. In Menado and Ambon, where there was a strong attachment to the Dutch, it was considered an honour to serve in the KNIL. On Java, men tended to enlist out of necessity, not out of any commitment to the Dutch cause. Soeharto was of this ilk. He needed a job. He needed an income. Nor did he have any deeply-held political views which would trouble his conscience. Indonesian nationalism meant little to him.

If the indigenous foot soldiers of the KNIL came of necessity from a number of different ethnic groups, that fitted in very well with Dutch plans. As noted above, the Dutch worked on the principle of divide-and-rule, relying not only on physical force, embodied in the form of the KNIL and the colonial police force, but also on psychological force. As Roeslan Abdulgani put it, the Dutch "imprint in you the idea that you are nothing, that you are not a nation, that you are just *suku-suku* [individual ethnic groups], meaning natives who are fighting against each other, so you cannot be united."[30] There is no doubt that the Dutch did indeed make that argument.

III

The other major problem facing Dutch officers was that the KNIL was overstretched. The colonial army of 1940 was not only surprisingly small given the vastness of the archipelago and the size of the population (seventy million, with nearly fifty million of them on Java); it was an institution with a split personality, with two distinct and in some ways irreconcilable functions, a defect which left it dangerously weakened.[31] For more than one hundred years, the KNIL had been, first and foremost, a force held in reserve to deal with any outbreaks of unrest, available if necessary to back up the civil service, the various police forces and the secret police. (By the 1930s, it is true, those civilian institutions had little difficulty maintaining law and order across Holland's vast and immensely profitable tropical possession.) But the KNIL was also responsible, together with the modest Far Eastern squadron of the Dutch Navy, for defending the Netherlands East Indies against external attack.[32] That meant, in 1940, that it was scrambling to prepare for an expected onslaught from the forces of Imperial Japan, a nation in an aggressively expansionist mood, hungering after the oil, rubber and tin of the NEI. These twin responsibilities imposed intolerable strains on the KNIL, which had been allowed to run down both before and during the Depression and which was now making a belated effort to modernize and expand.[33]

In 1940 the KNIL had a strength of about 40,000 men, built around a ground combat force of nineteen "field battalions", each of about 875 men; eighteen "garrison battalions" and a rapidly expanding air wing, the creation of which was imposing severe strains on the "old" KNIL, with many of the most promising infantry officers being drawn off to train as pilots and navigators. All but two of the field [infantry] battalions were stationed on Java, with fourteen earmarked for defence against an external enemy and two (or by one account three) set aside for *maréchaussée* (internal security) duties.[34] The other two battalions had been stationed since 1936 in the East Kalimantan "oil ports" of Balikpapan and Tarakan, where they too were expected to provide defence against external attack. In Palembang, the most bountiful of the oil-producing regions, the Dutch would establish a small "mobile battalion".[35]

Elsewhere in the Outer Islands, the KNIL was responsible, almost exclusively, for the maintenance of law and order in support of the civilian police, although it had taken on some external defence responsibilities in 1939. The Dutch maintained a dozen main garrisons in the islands beyond Java, with some of their soldiers quartered in two venerable seventeenth century fortresses—Fort Rotterdam (1673) in Makassar and Fort Victoria (1605) in Ambon.[36] Beyond these centres, KNIL units were small and lightly armed, scattered in more than a hundred penny packets, each consisting of an officer and up to thirty to forty enlisted men, set down in remote jungle stockades, in outposts at the mouths of great river systems or on small islands, often with their own army patrol boats. These outposts—or "detachments" as the Dutch called them—appeared on the headquarters wall charts as fly spots stretching in a vast arc from Aceh in the northwest to West New Guinea in the southeast. Detachments were grouped together for administrative purposes in twelve misleadingly-named "garrison battalions" (*garnizoenbataljons*), which were not in fact battalions at all. Even in Aceh, where the KNIL was still obliged to maintain a large number of troops for internal security, the army operated in small units. In the Outer Islands, units might find themselves involved in the suppression of banditry or rebellion or lending assistance to the civil power.[37] Officers were rotated on an individual basis between Java and these outposts; units, right down to the smallest of them, were rotated as units.

This strict division of functions between internal security and external defence influenced the tactics, organization and mentality of the pre-war KNIL.[38] In the Outer Islands the standard patrolling unit was a nineteen-man section, or *brigade*, as it was somewhat confusingly known.[39] These *brigades* were lightly armed, each man issued with a carbine and *klewang* (a sabre or machete with a broad, curved blade). Indeed, the Dutch called this force "a carbine and *klewang*" army. The use of even light machine guns was exceptional in the Outer Islands. That meant, as Colonel Alex Kawilarang a Dutch-trained Indonesian officer, noted dryly (and with only slight exaggeration) many years later, that "if the Japanese are invading Sumatra, there are no light machine guns!"[40] Each *brigade* was assigned three civilian convicts as porters; many of the porters had received long sentences for murder, mostly for crimes of passion. In any given year there was a constant coming and going, with men setting off on three or four-year postings or returning to Java, the married ones accompanied by their wives and children, embarking on one of the Royal Mail Steam Packet Company (Koninklijke Paketvaart Maatschappij, KPM) ships that tracked between the great ports of the archipelago, sometimes travelling further afield on smaller government cargo ships or local trading vessels, the capillaries of a thriving archipelagic transportation network.

On Java, which was under firm Dutch control, except for occasional outbreaks of banditry or an unmanageable bout of labour unrest, perhaps at a sugar factory, the routine was very different, with battalions training continuously for modern warfare. Infantry sergeants and enlisted men returning from law and order postings in the Outer Islands had to be reintegrated into an army designed to operate not in nineteen-man sections but in platoons, companies and battalions that were to be ready to fight against a foreign enemy equipped with tanks, mortars and artillery and supported by modern aircraft.[41]

Had he enlisted a few years earlier, Soeharto would have found himself slotted effortlessly into this bifurcated colonial army, training on Java for conventional warfare, serving routine four-year tours in the Outer Islands, a soldier in the pay of a European power, upholding the authority and profitability of Queen Wilhelmina's colonial empire, advancing slowly up the military ladder, hampered by his modest social origins and educational attainments. These were anything but normal times, however. Though he may not have known it, Soeharto had entered a system which was carrying men of ability forward at an extraordinary rate in an army desperately trying to rebuild and refashion itself. As it happened, he had many of the necessary attributes for a successful military career: courage, fitness, ability, quickness of mind, a capacity to remain cool under pressure and an unusual blend of caution and decisiveness.

IV

At Gombong, Soeharto was thrown together with scores of other young men, all of them grateful to have landed a job with a regular income, all of them no doubt a little bewildered by the world in which they now found themselves. What sort of men were they? The KNIL, like any other military organization, was looking for certain basic qualities in its recruits. Physique was obviously important. A man had to be able to march and to live in the field, often for extended periods and in considerable discomfort. He needed a good heart, good lungs, good eyesight, good feet. He needed to be resourceful and adaptable. Recruits for short-term service in the KNIL generally were selected from those with at least a minimum of primary education, although Soeharto was to claim, somewhat improbably, that among those signing on for long-term service were "boys who'd never been to school".[42] An unquestioning loyalty to Dutch colonial rule was also considered essential, although the Dutch were realistic enough to recognize that one "could not look into a man's heart" to see where his loyalties lay—one reason why they had always preferred where possible to recruit European and Eurasian soldiers.

At the quartermaster store Soeharto was issued with clothing, bedding and personal equipment. This included four sets of uniform, all in the distinctive dark green cotton drill of the KNIL, and three pairs of leather boots, an unimaginable luxury for a young man who, only a short time before had gone about Yogyakarta in bare feet.[43] Dressed in his new uniform, Soeharto was no longer just another anonymous subject of a European colonial power but a soldier in the service of a foreign sovereign, subject to strict military discipline. There was, however, no requirement that he take an oath of loyalty to his exiled Queen: only officers swore such an oath, on obtaining their commissions.[44]

Apart from all the marching, which he was to recall so clearly half a century later, Soeharto was given a thorough grounding in the skills he would need as an infantry private, whether serving in a conventional battalion on Java or in a nineteen-man patrol unit in the Outer Islands. In the years immediately after 1899, most KNIL soldiers were issued with the 6.5mm Mannlicher M-95 bolt-action repeating rifle, which had a five-round magazine and a bayonet. This was an 1895 Austrian weapon which the Dutch manufactured under licence at the Hembrug ordnance factory in the Netherlands. By 1940, however, all non-European KNIL units had long since switched to the M-95 carbine, which was better suited to the shorter stature of the indigenous troops and which came with a *klewang* in place of a bayonet.[45] Soeharto was taught to strip and assemble the Mannlicher carbine. He was instructed in marksmanship, which involved firing a variety of weapons on the rifle range, sometimes with his gas mask fitted, the Dutch being concerned that the Japanese might employ gas in any attack. He was taught to strip and assemble the 6.5mm Danish-made Madsen light machine gun, an effective but complicated weapon. He was put through road and field work, in which men were taught the basics of patrolling, of advancing over open terrain and through jungle. He went on endurance marches and night exercises. He learned to bivouac and to cross rivers and ditches.

Back at the barracks, the pressure was maintained, with class work, weapons drill, marching drill, guard duty and sports events. As part of his training for operations in the Outer Islands, Soeharto was taught how to cut down those colonial subjects who took up arms against the Dutch, using his well-weighted KNIL *klewang*, which was heavier at the end so the blow would be more efficient. He practised these skills by slashing at the flank of a banana-tree trunk, which was thought to give the "feel" of a human body. He practised, too, by engaging in hand-to-hand combat drills with fellow students, wearing a mask and body protector. He was taught how to hold his carbine in his left hand as a shield and bring his blunt training *klewang* down on an opponent's body or head. He was taught how a nineteen-man KNIL patrol had to close in a tight circle (*alarmpositie*, or *sikap awas*) when under attack from an indigenous enemy, the officer or NCO in the centre giving commands.

The instructors at Gombong were lieutenants, sergeants and sergeant-majors, hand-picked men with many years' experience in the colonial army, the officers among them European or Eurasian, the NCOs drawn in equal numbers from either European, Eurasian or indigenous backgrounds. These instructors presided over what was in many ways an excellent training regime. But there was a limit to what could be taught. For one thing, the time devoted to training had been cut back drastically, to allow more men to be pushed through. For another, it was impossible to prepare soldiers adequately for both internal security duties and modern warfare against an external enemy. As a retired Dutch colonel observed, "You would learn both. That was the weakness of the KNIL, the two systems. That was the extreme weakness."[46]

Although Soeharto and most of his fellow recruits had only a rudimentary, and generally passive, knowledge of Dutch, that presented no immediate difficulty. Unlike the French, the Spaniards and the Portuguese, the Dutch had never sought to impose their language on most of their colonial subjects, although fluency in Dutch was of course essential if a man were to hold any office of importance in the Netherlands East Indies. There were two official languages in the KNIL: Dutch and Malay. Malay, which was the lingua franca at the lower levels, was the language of instruction at Gombong, where recruits were drawn from across the archipelago. In the barracks Dutch and half a dozen vernacular languages were spoken, including Malay, Javanese, Sundanese, Menadonese and Ambonese. In the KNIL, orders on parade were given in Dutch or Malay. But many day-to-day conversations were conducted in a mix of languages, punctuated with military slang and swearwords.

Those undertaking basic training at Gombong, the Javanese in particular, tended to be reserved, respectful, and well-behaved, pleased to have been accepted for service in what seemed such a powerful institution, eager to learn and to do well, a bit wide-eyed and innocent, holding their officers and NCOs in considerable awe. As recruits, they were worked hard, with parades and training conducted six days a week, including Saturdays. The one day off was Sunday, when many of the Christians would attend church. Muslims were encouraged to visit the mosque on Fridays but few Javanese recruits did so.[47] Soeharto, as we have seen, appears to have had no strong interest in religion, at least of the institutionalized kind, at this time.

As a recruit, Soeharto was not especially well paid. In 1940, a Javanese private earned only three guilders a month, about the same as a low-level bank clerk.[48] But he was well looked after. He was eating some meat and half an egg each day, which would have been unusual in Kemusu, and the accommodation was incalculably better than he had enjoyed in the village. Besides, with all his food and accommodation costs met, he was able to save most of his pay.

Gombong was a prosperous town, drawing its wealth from the surrounding countryside, much of which was given over to rice and sugar, the Java sugar industry having made a big comeback after 1937. But it benefited, too, from its status as a garrison town, home to several hundred KNIL soldiers. For those with money, which basically meant Europeans, some Eurasians, some Chinese and a few Javanese, the town offered all the usual diversions of East Indies urban life: clubs, tennis courts, swimming pools, cinemas, small restaurants, ice cream parlours, tailor shops and photo shops. On his days off, Soeharto was free to go into Gombong. He was obliged, as was every KNIL soldier below the rank of sergeant, to wear his uniform on such occasions. But this was no problem; on the contrary, most KNIL soldiers were only too pleased to be seen in uniform, this being a sign that they counted for something, however lowly their position.

In 1940, soldiers were a familiar sight in the streets and night-markets of Gombong, buying small items under the hiss of kerosene lamps, stopping for *sate* or heavily sugared tea at a roadside stall, or attending perhaps to some of the other, more urgent requirements of military life. Prostitution was rife in the Netherlands East Indies, not least in the garrison towns, each of which had a well-defined red light area. For an ordinary soldier, bars and brothels were too costly. But street prostitution was common and many young men had their first sexual encounter in some anonymous room in a side street or alley.[49] Back at the barracks, those who had reason to fear they might have contracted VD would disinfect themselves with the tubes of salvarsan, which were kept in a room in the bathroom block. The KNIL went through a great deal of salvarsan but army doctors were never quite sure why that was, given that salvarsan was also popular with those seeking to remove stains from their military uniforms. There is no evidence that Soeharto showed any interest in such distractions. However, he was no prude and in later years he would tease fellow officers who were renowned womanizers.

As Soeharto was beginning his basic training at Gombong the German army was carrying all before it in Western Europe, its mechanized divisions plunging deep into France. On 14 June 1940, the Wehrmacht entered Paris. A week later, the collaborationist regime in Vichy signed a humiliating armistice. The fall of Holland and France had an immediate impact in Asia. On 25 June the Japanese General Staff and War Ministry drafted plans to attack Western colonies in Asia.[50] A surprise attack on the great British naval base at Singapore would be followed by the invasion of the Netherlands East Indies. (Japanese intelligence operatives prided themselves that they had been able to get hold of NEI military maps, which they smuggled out in sugarcane stalks.)[51] On 3 July the Imperial Japanese Army decided that Tokyo should not hesitate to go to war with Britain and said that the resources of the East Indies should be brought under Japanese control so that Japan might become economically independent of Britain and the United States. A month later, the Imperial Japanese Navy adopted this position too. The Navy Minister chose to ignore the results of tabletop war games which showed, correctly as it turned out, that the Navy would not be able to protect the sea lanes from the Netherlands East Indies to Japan, calling the whole strategy into question.[52]

On 1 August 1940, the new Japanese government called for "the construction of a New Order* in greater East Asia."[53] In a position paper submitted to the Army and Foreign Ministries the same day, the Navy recommended the stationing of troops in French Indochina as a first step to gain control over Thailand, Burma and Malaya. This, as it was well aware, was a high-risk strategy. "If … Japan occupies all of French Indochina," the paper argued, "there is a strong possibility that the United States will tighten its embargo. An American embargo on scrap iron and oil would

* The phrase "New Order" is of interest. As Benedict Anderson has noted, the two endlessly repeated slogans of the late colonial regime were *rust en orde* (peace and order) and *opbouw* (development). "Characteristically," he writes, "the Suharto regime simply Indonesianized these slogans in the Orde Baru (New Order) and *pembangunan* (development)." See Benedict Anderson, "Indonesian Nationalism Today and in the Future", *New Left Review* 235 (1999): 14. It might be argued that the terminology was derivative in other ways as well. In 1940–41 there had been much talk about a New Order (*Neues Ordnung*) in Europe, with plans for a Reichsmark currency bloc. What was afoot, the historian Michael Burleigh writes, "was an old-fashioned economic imperialism, with an industrially developed core surrounded by a periphery producing food and raw material." See Michael Burleigh, *The Third Reich: A New History* (London: Pan Books, 2001), p. 424. It is arguable too that the tainted terminology of German fascism and Japanese militarism became doubly derivative when Soeharto picked up the phrase "New Order" and applied it to his political system in 1966.

be a matter of life and death to the Empire. In that event the Empire will be obliged to attack the Dutch East Indies to secure oil."[54] The logic of the argument was inescapable. In 1940, Japan's annual rate of oil consumption was five million tons, 80 per cent of it supplied by the United States. In the Dutch East Indies, the annual rate of oil production was eight million tons.[55] If the Imperial Japanese Navy, by now a formidable force, indeed the third largest Navy in the world, could find a way to neutralize the US Pacific Fleet at Pearl Harbor and the nucleus of Britain's small Far Eastern Fleet, the prize was there for the taking.

V

The prize had never looked more defenceless. For one thing, the task of safeguarding the East Indies was so dauntingly large. Holland was a small nation—the population in 1940 was only nine million—with a mercantile rather than a military tradition, in the homeland at least, not in the colonies, responsible for the defence of a possession on the other side of the world, vast in area, rich in natural resources, home to seventy million people, coveted by the Japanese and stirred by a small but troublingly persistent independence movement. Holland had neither the manpower nor, in the immediate post-Depression period, the money to meet the potential challenges it faced in defending the Indies. In 1940 the colonial army was in no position to defend Java and the three Outer Island oil ports, let alone the rest of the archipelago, against a determined and well-equipped enemy. Nor was the Navy's Far Eastern squadron in any position to turn back a major naval attack. Denied the funds it needed and slow in its response to the threat posed by the large and modern Japanese Navy, it consisted essentially of only four light cruisers, seven destroyers and fifteen submarines.[56] That was nothing to the massive naval forces the Japanese would throw at the East Indies.

For another thing, old certitudes had been called into question. It had been British naval policy since the Napoleonic Wars, if not earlier, to "protect" weak states located at the key gates into Continental Europe, mainly Portugal at the mouth of the Mediterranean (against the Spanish and the French) and the Low Countries, especially Holland at the mouth of the Rhine and the Scheldt and controlling river access into the heart of the Continent (against Prussia-Germany and France).[57] Portugal and Holland relied on the hegemon to protect them, even if at times their pride was hurt. British protection extended to the Dutch possessions in Southeast

Asia. Shielded by Britain's Royal Navy, the Dutch were able to use their colonial army mainly for internal purposes. The rise of Japan after 1899 to the position of major naval power alarmed the Dutch, who were less sure of British support and concerned about Anglo-Japanese deals. But there was little they could do. Holland was insignificant in Europe, with no military power and only beginning to industrialize. In Europe, UK-German rivalry also alarmed them.

For a hundred years, Holland had maintained its policy of strict neutrality in Europe and the Far East, an approach which had helped save the nation, but only just, from the devastation that befell much of neighbouring France and Belgium during World War I. And, although in 1940 the Dutch harboured the deepest misgivings about Japanese intentions, there was a hope, amounting at times to self-delusion, that Japan would respect Dutch neutrality and make no attempt to seize the East Indies. That hope was coupled with a belief that, in the event of war, the British, and perhaps the Americans, would use their naval forces to block any Japanese southward drive, although even in late 1940, after the Germans had overrun Holland, the Dutch could not bring themselves to say this openly, or even confide it privately, to their British allies, feeling it would compromise their neutrality, which they clung to in the Far East.

The Dutch would not even discuss with the British their arrangements to continue selling critical war materials, including oil and rubber, to Tokyo, a policy they pursued in the hope that this would keep the Japanese tiger at bay. In July 1940, six weeks after the evacuation of British and French troops from Dunkirk, a senior British diplomat, Sir Nevile Bland, invited the Dutch Foreign Minister, E.N. van Kleffens, to dinner in London. Bland was seeking information on economic relations between the Netherlands and Japan. He got nothing out of his guest "in spite of sherry, hock, claret and port." This "oyster-like attitude", a British official noted somewhat sourly, was "not very satisfactory considering that the NEI will be entirely dependent on us for any protection they may wish against Japanese aggression."[58] As it turned out, the dangerously overstretched British were unwilling to make a commitment to defend the Netherlands East Indies without a guarantee of American support, which the Americans were reluctant to provide.[59]

To make matters worse, the Dutch had been guilty of extraordinary complacency. For many years the KNIL had been operating on the basis of unrealistic strategic assumptions. When, in 1927, the Netherlands

Government had drawn up a Defence Foundation policy paper (De Defensiegrondslagen), it had clung to the principle of strict neutrality while privately believing, or at least hoping, that the British and Americans would never allow the East Indies to fall under enemy (by which it meant Japanese) control. The 1927 document decreed that the KNIL's first task was internal security; its second task was maintaining neutrality and resisting any sudden surprise attack. The authors of the defence paper underestimated Japanese capacities. A large-scale attack was nearly impossible, they believed, because any hostile Japanese force would have to pass French, American and British possessions. Britain ruled the waves; Singapore was invincible.[60] The most likely threat to the Netherlands Indies was, they felt, a *coup de main*, a swift but essentially limited surprise attack aimed at seizing critical points (*kwetsbare punten*) in the Outer Islands, the oilfields at Tarakan or Balikpapan, perhaps, or the air and naval base at Ambon.[61] This, the Dutch planners persuaded themselves, just a little too conveniently, would involve a force of no more than 4,000 men, put ashore from a fast cruiser squadron with no accompanying troop carriers.[62]

Only in the mid-1930s had the Dutch modified their plans. It was, they now agreed, absurd to discount the threat of a large-scale Japanese attack, especially as a solution to their defence dilemma now seemed so obvious. Rapid advances in air power had made it possible for land-based bombers to attack an enemy fleet far out to sea. Once that had become clear, the Dutch set about transforming the tiny KNIL air wing, known after 1940 as the KNIL-Militaire Luchtvaart, or KNIL-ML, into a de facto air force that would be equipped with the latest bomber aircraft. At the same time, they began to reorganize and modernize the colonial army.

Modernization was long overdue. For many years, the Dutch had allowed the KNIL to atrophy. The Dutch colonial army that entered the thirties had changed little since the days of the Aceh War. It was run-down, underfunded and undermanned, with obsolete equipment and obsolete doctrines, crippled by years of neglect and penny-pinching. In response to the world economic crisis, which had had such a catastrophic impact on exports from the East Indies, especially sugar, The Hague had slashed the budgets of all ministries, including the Ministry of Colonies, which was responsible for the KNIL. The appropriation for colonial defence, which was 140 million guilders in 1929 (with 76 million guilders for the army), had been reduced to about 50 million guilders in 1933.[63] The impact was devastating. There was virtually no spending on weapons or vehicles. Promotions came slowly. Morale plummeted.[64] Harriet Ponder has left a record of her impressions of the KNIL in 1934. "I am afraid that by no possible stretch of the imagination can either the European or native 'rankers' of the army in Java be called smart or soldierly in appearance," she wrote. "But then neither can their officers. The men are unshaven; their uniforms are baggy and shapeless; harness and equipment are dirty and uncared for; and the 'army,' as it straggles past on its morning exercise, the native ranks shuffling painfully in huge, unaccustomed boots, is anything but an impressive sight, except, perhaps, by virtue of numbers."[65]

In early 1940 KNIL infantry battalions had few trucks, jeeps or motorcycles and almost no staff cars. Away from the limited rail network a KNIL battalion moved by foot. Supplies of food, water and ammunition were brought along behind in two-wheeled carts, drawn by small Indonesian ponies. Ponies were also used to transport the heavy machine guns and the 81mm mortars of the heavy weapons company. They were used to haul the mobile kitchens and the mobile hot water and tea carriages, the Dutch having no wish to have soldiers fill their water bottles in kampungs or muddy streams and perhaps succumb to dysentery, typhus and cholera. In an 875-strong battalion, there were no fewer than 110 ponies and 45 carts. Only three men—the battalion commander, his adjutant and the commander of the heavy weapons company—accompanied their units on horseback, each mounted on a "Waler", the redoubtable Australian stock horse widely regarded as "the best all-round war horse in the world."

Seen from afar, a KNIL battalion on the move was not unlike something which might have been encountered in Europe during the Napoleonic wars, advancing at three miles an hour, the speed at which a man could march, the supply trains following behind, accompanied by the jingle of bridles and the creaking of axles.[66] The KNIL cavalry units were equally outdated. When Soeharto joined in 1940, the seven cavalry squadrons on Java still used horses. Each squadron consisted of 160 men, each horseman (*cavalier*) mounted on a "Waler" and armed with a carbine and long sabre. Trumpets were used to marshal units for the forming up or the charge, just as they had been in Napoleonic Europe.[67] The mountain artillery battalions were no more modern.[68]

Change was on the way, however. As the world economy began to recover, there was more money for defence spending. Defence outlays for the Dutch empire tripled in the four years to 1937, from *f* 120 million to *f* 360 million, with more than half that sum earmarked for the East Indies, where the NEI government had to support both the KNIL, including its new and costly air wing, and underwrite the locally deployed Royal Navy squadron.[69] In 1937 the Dutch spent *f* 98 million in the Netherlands and *f* 235 million in the NEI. There was new thinking too. By mid-1940, when Soeharto began his basic training at Gombong, the Dutch were working feverishly to implement a plan that called for an entirely revamped KNIL.

The most striking feature of the plan was the emphasis on air power. The Dutch had begun to build, almost from scratch, a large and modern air force in the East Indies.[70] Starting in 1936, they ordered 120 US-made Glenn Martin B-10 bombers, a revolutionary aircraft which had entered service in the US Army Air Corps in 1934. The first modern all-metal bomber, the Glenn Martin was capable of carrying a 2,200lb bomb load and was faster than any contemporary fighter. This was a promising start. But as the world rearmed the Dutch found themselves competing against other nations, especially Britain and France, in the race to buy US military aircraft. In October 1939 they got permission to order 24 Curtiss Hawk 75A fighters, but by then these planes were rapidly becoming obsolescent. A year later, they were able to order 72 sturdy but obsolete US-made Brewster Buffalo fighters. Later still, they ordered 162 B-25 Mitchell medium bombers, a far more promising aircraft, to replace the by now obsolete Glenn Martins. As it happened, the Mitchells would not arrive in time to be of any use.[71]

By the time of Pearl Harbor, the KNIL-ML would have 100 bombers, 108 fighters, 36 reconnaissance planes, 106 training planes and 19 transport planes, or 369 aircraft in all, with 300 more on order.[72] The Royal Netherlands Naval Air Service (MLD) had 68 modern long-range flying boats (33 Dornier Do-24s and 35 Consolidated Catalinas) and 6 Fokker float planes. This combined air force was the largest, but not necessarily the most powerful, Western air force in Southeast Asia, eclipsing the US Army Air Force in the Philippines (which had 277 planes when the Japanese attacked on 8 December 1941) or the British Royal Air Force detachment in Malaya.[73] As well, the Royal Netherlands Indies Airline (KNILM) had twenty transport aircraft. That was an impressive number of aircraft, but it was never going to be enough to stem the tide. The Japanese had twice as many planes, a better fighter in the Mitsubishi Zero and pilots who had gained invaluable combat experience in China.[74]

As the orders were placed for military aircraft, the Dutch began training thousands of pilots, navigators, wireless operators, bombardiers and ground technicians. It was a formidable undertaking. In the five years to 1942, the KNIL air wing was to grow from 400 to 5,000 men. Many of the Dutch and Indonesian pilots came straight out of secondary school; some lied about their age, claiming to be 18 when they were only 16 or 17. Unfortunately for the Dutch, the KNIL-ML pilots had received far too little training in air combat and air-to-air gunnery by the time war broke out.[75] They would be swept brutally aside by the light, long-range Zeros. The Dutch also embarked on a major programme of airfield construction. In the late 1930s there had been only half a dozen significant airfields on Java. In 1941, after Pearl Harbor, the Dutch would decide they needed no fewer than 100 rudimentary airfields on the island, enough to handle not only their own growing air force but also the hundreds of British, American and Australian aircraft which were expected to arrive to help defend the so-called "Malay Barrier", the string of naval and air bases running from Singapore to Darwin.

At the same time, the Dutch had embarked on a gradual rearmament of the KNIL land forces, with heavy emphasis on mobility and firepower. Under new plans, there were to be new trucks, new jeeps and new weapons for the infantry battalions; there were to be new tanks and new tracked vehicles for the armoured corps. Henceforth, it had been decided, Java would be defended by six mechanized, independent brigades, each of about 5,000 men; these were to be modelled on the German Panzer regiments which had torn so successfully across Poland in 1939 and Western Europe in 1940.[76] This, it was plain, was no longer the KNIL of popular imagination. The anaemic colonial army of 1936, one largely preoccupied with police duties in the Outer Islands, soldiers going out on patrol with carbines and *klewangs*, junior officers dreaming of attacks on remote palisades, was on its way to becoming a very different beast, one in which considerations of external defence came first.

There was a compelling logic behind the new Dutch strategy. A powerful KNIL air wing could deploy reconnaissance and bomber aircraft hundreds of miles out to sea, menacing any Japanese naval force well before it could put troops ashore. A mechanized KNIL land force, backed by an armoured corps of more than 600 tanks, could close on any force that did manage to land, on Java at least. But the KNIL high command faced two insurmountable problems. First, the officers and men of the

KNIL land forces were still expected to fulfill two very different functions, shuttling back and forth between units training on Java for conventional warfare and others assigned to internal security tasks in the Outer Islands. Second, there was simply too much catching up to be done and too little time in which to do it. There were formidable organizational, equipment, financial and personnel problems. The capitulation of the Netherlands greatly exacerbated those difficulties.

The establishment of an air wing was creating immense disruption at a time when the KNIL was hard put simply to modernize its land forces. The fact that this fledgling air service took many of its pilots and mechanics from the infantry units created problems which were compounded by the loss of other experienced infantry personnel to the rapidly expanding armour and artillery units. Until the late thirties, 85 per cent of all KNIL soldiers and NCOs had been attached to infantry units. Now, hundreds of the most experienced men were lost, a blow from which the infantry never fully recovered. Nor would the modernization of the air wing be completed in time.

On the weapons and equipment front, too, the Dutch had left their run too late. In the early 1930s, when there had been any number of weapons available on the international arms market, the Dutch had had no money to buy them. Now, as the world rearmed, the Dutch had the money but found it difficult to find suppliers, given that every other nation seemed to be rearming too. Even when suppliers were found, equipment often arrived too late to be of use. The United States was unwilling to sell the Dutch any of the better American tanks, which were reserved for the US Army and for Britain and the Soviet Union. One of the few makes available was the Marmon-Herrington light tank, which had been judged inadequate by the US Army. In 1940, having no other option, the Dutch placed an order for 500 Marmon-Herringtons, planning to deploy all 500 in Java. In the event, only seven would arrive by the time the Japanese landed in Java in March 1942 and only five of those seven would be active during the eight-day campaign preceding the Dutch surrender on Java.[77]

There were problems, too, obtaining ammunition, much of which was of the wrong calibre. All KNIL carbines, rifles, light machine guns and medium machine guns used 6.5mm ammunition, which was manufactured at Hembrug and available nowhere else in the world. When the Germans occupied Holland in 1940 there was dreadful panic in the

KNIL. The only ammunition the Dutch could get was British (7.7mm) and American (7.62mm). That meant the KNIL had to rebore the barrels of all its small arms.

The problems on the personnel front were every bit as serious. As noted above, the Dutch had always been wary about training and arming too many Indonesian soldiers. They had been especially wary about having too many Indonesian officers and NCOs in the KNIL. "In an independence movement," Governor General Willem Rooseboom, a retired lieutenant general, had warned in 1903, "native officers will be ... the obvious leaders of the rebels."[78] During World War I, the Dutch decided to admit one—and only one—Indonesian cadet each year at the Royal Military Academy (Koninklijke Militaire Academie, KMA) at Breda, in the south of the Netherlands.[79] Nor, it must be said, did Indonesians show much interest in an officers' commission in the KNIL during the interwar years. In 1935 only 2 per cent of the 1,300 regular officers in the KNIL were of Indonesian descent.[80] In 1940, after the German occupation of the Netherlands and with the growing concerns about Japan, the Dutch put some of their concerns to one side. They admitted the first non-European cadets at the Reserve Officers Training Corps (Corps Opleiding Reserve-Officieren, CORO) in Bandung and set up an "Indische" KMA in Bandung, with no limits on the admission of non-Europeans.[81] In 1941 more than 10 per cent of the KMA cadet corps at Bandung was Indonesian.[82] The conventional military doctrine they studied owed much to German thinking.[83]

As we have seen, the Dutch had also preferred to have a significant number of European NCOs and soldiers in the KNIL (even though they had to pay them more than "native" troops). By 1929, however, the number of Europeans was down to 18 per cent. To maintain the KNIL at desired levels and to ensure the preferred ethnic mix, the Dutch needed an annual intake of 2,000 Dutch and Eurasian volunteers, many of whom were to be trained as NCOs. They never came close to achieving that, although in 1941, it is true, the KNIL would be boosted by the intake of European conscripts. In these circumstances, the only way to boost KNIL numbers was to recruit as many Indonesians as possible and to greatly increase the number of Indonesian NCOs.

VI

All this was to prove an extraordinary boon to Soeharto.

In 1940 the Dutch were looking down the barrel of military defeat in the Netherlands East Indies. They needed to build a force capable of defending their colony against attack by an experienced and well-equipped Japanese force and they needed to do it quickly. Pre-war concerns about the dubious loyalty of Indonesian officers and NCOs were suddenly of less importance. Put bluntly, the KNIL could no longer be so particular about whom it chose to recruit. In an attempt to attract more Indonesian recruits, the KNIL had reduced the period of enlistment from six years to one. The one-year period of basic training had been halved.

The Dutch had also begun to take short cuts in NCO training. Until 1936, the KNIL had been thorough to the point of fastidiousness when it came to training corporals and sergeants. It had taken at least five years, and often a great deal longer, for an Indonesian enlisted man, however able, to reach the rank of sergeant 2nd class. By the time Soeharto enlisted in mid-1940, the KNIL could no longer hope to train NCOs to the old standards. Courses had been shortened, sometimes drastically, and many of the old promotion rules cast aside. It was now possible for an Indonesian to go from civilian to sergeant 2nd class in just seventeen months. All was rush. More than a thousand men were being pushed through the NCO courses each year.[84] Despite the changes, there were never enough NCOs.

To make matters worse, the best of the new sergeants qualified without having spent any time attached to an infantry battalion on Java or on duty in the Outer Islands, an essential requirement if a man were to have a solid understanding of how the army worked in the field. The other side of this coin was that if an able young Indonesian were to join the KNIL in 1940, he would be gaining not just a job and a secure income but would be putting himself in position for possible rapid promotion to corporal or sergeant. It was at precisely this time that Soeharto sent off his application to join the KNIL.

Soeharto was to claim later that he topped his class in recruit training. "I achieved the highest score in this six-month basic course," he wrote in 1998, "and was admitted to the cadre school for non-commissioned officers along with several colleagues. Usually, one needed six or seven years' service as a soldier before one qualified for the school."[85] Such remarks invite the reader to conclude that Soeharto rose at an exceptional rate by dint of ability and sheer hard work. That is not the case. While there can be no doubt that Soeharto was a man of ability, his progress was due mainly to the fact that the Dutch had opted for quantity rather than quality. They were now producing NCOs as fast as they could. It was no longer unusual for a man to be sent straight from recruit training to the KNIL corporals course. By 1940, 30 per cent of the Indonesians who completed recruit training—and 50 per cent of the Europeans and Eurasians—were sent directly to the KNIL corporals school.[86] It is possible, however, that Soeharto was not seeking to exaggerate his achievement. In his autobiography he makes the point that had he joined the KNIL on an old-style "long contract" he would not have been able to progress at this rate for many years.

Where did the NCO training take place? According to Soeharto, the NCO course was also held at Gombong.[87] This is a curious claim. Dutch and Indonesian officers who served in the KNIL insist that Gombong was only used for basic training. All courses for infantry NCOs, they maintain, were held at the garrison town of Magelang or at the cadre school for candidate corporals which had been set up in Yogyakarta to handle the overflow. That said, one retired Dutch officer believes "it might be possible" that in 1940–41 some NCO training was conducted at Gombong. "There were," he said, "many changes as the Pacific War came nearer and nearer."[88]

If Soeharto did in fact transfer to Magelang it would have been the first of many such moves he was to make around the military installations on Java—and sometimes beyond—in a long military career. Magelang stands on a broad and fertile plateau 1,500 feet above sea level. The Merapi and Merbabu volcanoes, joined at the waist, are about fifteen miles to the east; the even higher Sumbing volcano is eleven miles to the northwest. Unlike Merapi, Sumbing is not majestically conical; its top was blown off in some monstrous eruption, giving it the look of a boiled egg partly excavated by a teaspoon. But it has its own joined-at-the-waist partner volcano, the perfectly shaped Sundoro. Magelang had been an important Dutch garrison town since the start of the Java War in 1825. In 1940, it was one of five garrison towns on Java, clean and well-swept, with whole suburbs set aside for the KNIL, each with quiet, tree-lined avenues and well-maintained barracks and houses.[89]

On 2 December 1940, Private 2nd Class Soeharto joined a new intake at the corporals' course. Some of those in his intake were Dutch or Eurasian, but most were Indonesian. Over the next six months Soeharto received advanced training and was taught for the first time to lead and instruct a group of privates. Once again, he found the experience stimulating. He was instructed in the techniques of riot control, this being a core responsibility of the KNIL, which was always ready to deploy infantry in times of unrest, backed up as necessary by mounted cavalry, if the police needed support. He was taught about sanitation and about the regulations governing discipline within the barracks, which were home to Indonesian families from many different ethnic and religious backgrounds. He was taught how to get the best out of the men under his command. Throughout the course, officers and instructors were looking to see if soldiers had leadership potential. A KNIL corporal on Java was the second-in-command in a fifteen-man group (and in the Outer Islands the third in command of a nineteen-man *brigade*) and had to be ready at any moment to stand in for the sergeant. He was, at the same time, the second instructor in his unit, after the sergeant. He had to be, in some respects, a father figure to his men, as did all those above him.

If Soeharto had come first in his recruit training intake he appears to have fared less well on the corporals course. As we have seen, by 1940 the Dutch were sending 30 per cent of the most promising Indonesian recruits and 50 per cent of the best Dutch-Eurasian recruits straight to the corporals course. They were doing the same sort of thing—and using the same ratios—when it came to selecting the most promising corporals for the sergeants course. If Soeharto had done especially well on the corporals course it is likely that he would have been put on the list of those going straight into the next training course for KNIL sergeants. In other words, he would have become, in KNIL slang, a *doorstomer,* or "continuous steamer", a man who was considered to be of such promise that the Dutch were willing to take him to the next level without him having to prove himself first as a corporal in a battalion. Instead, Soeharto was assigned to the 13th Battalion in Malang, East Java, as a deputy squad commander (*sebagai wakil komandan regu*).[90]

Soeharto's claim that he became a deputy squad commander is not in any way surprising if, as seems logical, the word *regu* is translated as "squad", meaning in this context a fifteen-man *brigade,* or one-third of a platoon. Some confusion has arisen, however, because *regu* is mistranslated in both the official English-language and Dutch-language versions of Soeharto's memoirs. In the English version, Soeharto is left claiming that he was appointed a "deputy company commander". This invites derision. No Indonesian corporal, and certainly not a probationary corporal, ever became deputy commander of a 160-man KNIL company, a unit usually headed by a Dutch captain and boasting at least nine sergeants and up to eighteen corporals, most of whom had many years' experience. In the Dutch language version, Soeharto is left claiming that he became the deputy commander of a platoon, a unit of fifty men. This too is impossible.[91] It seems clear, however, that in this case at least Soeharto was not boasting. Rather, he was ill-served by his English and Dutch translators.

In May 1940, the Japanese had asked the Dutch for a firm commitment that they would sell them oil, rubber and other raw materials. The Dutch were wary. In French Indochina, the Japanese were soon pushing for major concessions from the hapless Vichy regime—concessions which, before long, would pose an unmistakable threat to the Americans in the Philippines, the British in Burma, Malaya, Singapore and North Borneo and the Dutch in the East Indies. In late August and early September 1940, the Vichy government, having no real say in the matter, allowed Japan to station up to 25,000 troops in Tonkin in northern Vietnam and use three airbases in Indochina. Japan had secured a key stepping stone on the path to Singapore and the Netherlands East Indies.[92] In October, the Dutch agreed to sell the Japanese 1,800,000 tons of oil, much less than Tokyo was seeking.

In late April 1941, as Soeharto continued his training, Rear Admiral Maeda Minoru, the head of the European section of the Third Bureau (*joho kyoku*) of the Japanese Naval General Staff and elder brother of Captain (later Rear Admiral) Maeda Tadashi, who would go on to play an important role in the run-up to Indonesia's 1945 Proclamation of Independence, reconnoitered Thailand and French Indochina to assess the consequences of a Japanese occupation of southern Indochina.[93] On 5 June he advised Prime Minister Konoe Fumimaro that it would be "quite safe" to make such a move. On 14 July 1941, Tokyo demanded that the Vichy French allow it access to eight air bases in southern Vietnam and Cambodia and three naval bases, including Cam Ranh Bay.[94] Due to "extremely strong insistence" on the part of the Japanese, the French agreed.[95] This put the Japanese within striking distance of the British naval base at Singapore, which was crucial for the Dutch. Forty thousand Japanese troops moved into southern Indochina. On 25 July, Washington froze all Japanese assets in the United States, imposed a total embargo on Japanese trade and ended the export of petroleum to Japan. The Dutch government-in-exile followed suit. This was the de facto end of Dutch neutrality. The Dutch now coupled their fate to that of the United States and Britain. Tokyo was "presented with the stark choice between war and surrender as the American terms for a resumption of trade was the liquidation of all Japanese mainland gains since 1931."[96]

Everything pointed to war. And, if war were to break out, the Japanese were bound to make a sudden lunge for the oil and other resources of the Netherlands East Indies, where the KNIL was not in any position to resist a major assault.

8

A reassuringly familiar world

Soeharto, now wearing the coveted collar patch of a KNIL corporal, left Central Java in July 1941 to join the 13th Battalion (Inf XIII), one of two infantry battalions garrisoned in the hill town of Malang in East Java. Built up over the previous fifty years to serve Dutch commercial interests, Malang stood on a saddle between two groups of mountains: the Kawi and Butak volcanoes were to the west; the impressive Tengger Caldera, which includes the Bromo and Semeru volcanoes, to the east and southeast. The majestic Arjuna volcano lay almost due north. More than 1,300 feet above sea level, Malang was pleasantly cool for most of the year, even cold at times. In 1941 it had a population of 200,000, including 11,000 Europeans. Malang owed its prosperity to the surrounding sugar, tobacco and rubber plantations. But it was also an important garrison town, home to the KNIL 6th Infantry Regiment (6 RI), which was responsible for East Java, with a force of three infantry battalions, two in Malang, the other in Surabaya. The 13th Battalion barracks were in the military quarter of Rampal, immediately east of the railway station in an area that looked more like a spacious colonial suburb than a military base, with the houses of senior officers and NCOs set down in large gardens, with shaded lawns and cascading bougainvillea.

Visitors arriving on foot made their way up Stationweg, a narrow road lined with tamarind trees, and turned right at the main gate. The barracks complex was built according to a standard KNIL formula, with a long, single-storey administrative block facing the road, a heavy enclosed wooden gate in the centre and a guardroom off to the right. Behind the gate and the office of the duty sergeant, with its typewriters, desks and rows of enormous keys (many of the original keys are still there today and still in use), lay the parade ground, which doubled as a soccer field. On each side and to the rear stood any number of neat, single-storey brick buildings, housing offices, classrooms, armouries, storehouses, kitchens, washing areas and row upon row of barracks. The buildings, which have not changed in nearly eight decades, are now home to Infantry Battalion 502, part of the Indonesian Army's Strategic Reserve (Kostrad), the unit Soeharto would command when he came to power in 1965.[1] Elsewhere in the complex were repair depots, garages, blacksmiths shops, a hospital and stables for the cavalry horses and for the pack horses that carried the various parts of the mountain guns. A short distance to the west, on the other side of the station and in one of the more exclusive European quarters of Malang, was Rampal Square. Just off the square, in Idenburgstraat, stood the headquarters of 6 RI, a modern two-storey building with a steep roof and art deco tower, painted white with green trim. The commanding officer of the regiment was Colonel W. van Kuilenburg. Although the KNIL was an accepted part of everyday life on Java at that time, people tended to give the Rampal military quarter a wide berth. In the words of Major General Sukotjo Tjokroatmodjo, who grew up in Malang and who went on to become the deputy chief of the Indonesian Military Police Corps, "No one from the centre of town will walk around there because they see only 'the greens', the KNIL people. And they have a small society in itself, and mostly dominated by Ambonese, and these are not very well liked."[2]

For Europeans, be they civilians or army officers, social life in Malang revolved around the club, which was known as the *sociëteit* "Concordia". It stood on the southeastern corner of the *alun-alun*, a small park, pristine and shady in those days, now grubby and polluted, the air heavy with exhaust fumes. All around were churches, banks, offices, shops and restaurants, many of the more recent ones built in the art deco style of the times. For Soeharto, life centred on the 13th Battalion and the reassuring rhythms and certitudes of military life. Here, for the first time, he found himself not just part of an operational military unit training for conventional warfare but part of a world in which units were segregated for the most part on strict racial lines and in which as many as 900 women and children lived in the barracks along with the 875 men of the battalion.

The policy of racial separation was immediately apparent in the KNIL infantry battalions, which were made up in most cases of three rifle companies and a heavy weapons company, each of about 180 men.[3] In almost every case, the men of the rifle companies were drawn solely from one ethnic group.[4] In a typical battalion, one rifle company would be exclusively European (though there were never enough of these companies to go around), another exclusively Javanese and the third either Menadonese or Ambonese (or, in rare cases, Timorese or Sundanese).[5] As it happened, Soeharto was assigned to a battalion with no European rifle company. One of the 13th Battalion's rifle companies was exclusively Menadonese, another exclusively Ambonese, the third exclusively Javanese. Which ethnic group made the better soldiers? There was a long-running debate about this in the KNIL but in general it was thought by the Dutch that the Menadonese and Ambonese were better than the Javanese. It was agreed, however, that the discipline of the Javanese was far better.

For Soeharto, who had just turned twenty and who was away from Central Java for the first time, this ethnic segregation had certain advantages. As a Javanese, he could only be attached to the Javanese company, which had its own living and cooking areas, situated well apart from those of the other companies in the battalion. To a young man of his background, this would have been a small, self-contained and reassuringly familiar world, almost a village in some respects, with some 200 Javanese women and children living in the barracks with the 180 Javanese soldiers of the company. The language spoken was, for the most part, Javanese. The air would have been heavy with the pungent, warmly evocative aromas of Java, especially *tempé* and clove-filled *kretek* cigarettes. In the afternoon, when the work of the day had finished, off-duty soldiers went about the barracks in sarongs, not military fatigues.

The presence of so many women and children gave this, and indeed every other KNIL compound, an atmosphere quite unlike that to be found in military compounds in most other Western colonial armies, save perhaps those of the Spanish and the Portuguese. Here was a teeming, Bruegel-like canvas of humanity, women tending babies or crouching over smoking charcoal braziers, batik sarongs drying in the sun, children playing games and calling to one another in Javanese, or coming home from school. As one former KNIL officer put it, "During the afternoon and during the night it was quite an Indonesian village. There were hundreds of wives and children. And the privates and corporals didn't wear their uniforms. It was a phenomena. It was a complete native quarter, or *kampung*."[6] Equally reassuring was the fact that Soelardi, Soeharto's cousin, was studying at the agricultural college in Malang. Whenever they had free time, the two young men would catch up, sometimes seeing a movie together.

As an unmarried corporal, Soeharto would have been taken on arrival to one of the corporals' rooms, which were situated at the end of dormitories housing about fifty or sixty unmarried Javanese privates. He slept, as did almost all the other Javanese in the KNIL, on a *tikar*, or plaited bedding mat, which he spread out on the planks of his wooden bunk bed, a Javanese soldier having no interest in a mattress, an item which most Menadonese and Ambonese considered essential. On his bed was a long bolster (*guling*), or "Dutch wife", with a white pillowcase, which he could loosely clasp, allowing air to circulate more easily on hot tropical nights. Married Indonesian corporals and privates lived, with their families, in long dormitories, with one family group to a "room", shut off from the corridor by a green curtain. Their children slept in the space beneath (*kolong*) the raised bed and were known as *anak kolong*, a term used to this day to refer to the children of Indonesian military men.[7] In his memoirs, Soeharto claims implausibly that he was glad that his closest friend, Amat Sudono, had the upper bunk "because this arrangement made it easier for me to get up when I wanted to do my prayers."[8]

At Malang, Soeharto's day was punctuated by the sounds of military life: the measured tramp of boots on asphalt, the ringing of the blacksmiths hammer, the whinnying of horses, the smack of magazines being slammed into machine-guns during training drills, the bark of orders shouted in Dutch or Malay.[9] It would have been punctuated, too, by bugle calls. In an era before radio communications had become widely available, the KNIL conducted all its major activities to the sound of the bugle or, in the case of the cavalry and the mounted artillery, the trumpet. Apart from reveille and lights out, there were tunes, each one quite distinct, to sound various alarms, especially the fire alarm; to announce a general parade; to notify a rifle company of the arrival of the doctor (each company had its own tune); to notify the grooms that the vet was on his way or to tell them it was time to put out the oats for the horses. In the field, there were tunes to signal a company attack or retreat. The sound of a bugle, carried hauntingly on the evening air, could be heard far beyond the barracks as soldiers and their families relaxed in the afternoon or early evening. These tunes were known to everyone, soldier and civilian alike, including the owners of the small food stalls and of course the roving street prostitutes.

Although the men of the rifle companies were worked hard when they were out on field exercises, life in the barracks was not especially demanding. After reveille, at 6:00 a.m., Soeharto attended roll call, bathed and had breakfast, which usually consisted of cold *nasi goreng*. His working day began at 8:00 a.m. and lasted for five hours. With as many as 300 or 400 women, and perhaps 500 children, living in the battalion barracks area, strict rules had to be enforced. Women and children were not permitted under any circumstances to remain in the dormitories between breakfast and lunchtime. At 7:00 a.m. the women and children of each company left the sleeping area for the company "wives' hangar" (*vrouwenloods*). This was a large, open-sided building about the size of a tennis court, with numerous taps, concrete sinks and individual cupboards that could be locked. On most days they remained there until 1:00 p.m., washing, ironing, cooking, chatting, looking after the babies and smaller children. The older children went to school. The wives of married Indonesian corporals and privates visited the local market regularly to buy meat, chicken, fish, spices and vegetables, coming and going through a special gate. They cooked for their husbands and children on small charcoal braziers. Every ten days the company *foerier*, or logistics sergeant, distributed an allowance of rice and salt, and sometimes also tinned food, to the wives of the Indonesian corporals and privates. This was a form of payment in kind, based on the number of people in each family.

At 1:00 p.m. Soeharto and the other bachelors were provided with a hot meal at the company kitchen. He received a mess tin filled with rice, meat, eggs, vegetables and *sambal* (spicy condiments) and took it back to the dormitory to eat. This done, the bugler played the *afslag*, a prescribed tune, unique to the KNIL and indicating that the wives were now permitted to return to the sleeping quarters. On this signal, more than 100 Javanese women, accompanied by an even greater number of children, set out in a mini-stampede from the company wives' hangar to the sleeping quarters, running fast, sarongs snapping, so that they could join their husbands for lunch while the food was still hot, laughing as they ran but finding nothing odd about this practice, which was part of barracks routine. The women and children were free to stay in and around the sleeping quarters from that time until an hour after reveille the next day. Many of the married men and their wives chose to leave the barracks in the late afternoon, the men always in full uniform. But they did not go far and were almost always within earshot of any bugle call that was sounded in the barracks. In the afternoon there was generally a siesta for one-and-a-half to two hours, sometimes followed by sport. There was a second hot meal at night.

The KNIL battalions at Malang had four main tasks. First, they served, as did the other Java battalions, as a manpower "reservoir", providing men for the units in the Outer Islands, receiving back and retraining those who had completed their tours outside Java. Second, they trained in the normal fashion for conventional war, holding a series of exercises, each one larger than the last, culminating in a battalion-strength exercise in November. Third, they were on hand to assist in police duties outside the main towns, where the police presence was often minimal. Finally, they had special militia companies which gave six months' training to eighteen and nineteen-year-old Dutch and Eurasian civilians under the 1918 conscription law.

When Soeharto arrived in Malang, his battalion was engaged in company-size manoeuvres. This would have meant that he spent a good deal of time in the field, looking after his small subsection of the company, mastering the techniques of attack and defence, digging slit trenches, occasionally donning a gas mask. The weapons company would likewise have spent much of its time in the field, its mortars, medium machine-guns and ammunition carried on dozens of Indonesian ponies. There was one break from this routine, however. During his posting Soeharto spent about two weeks on night guard duty in Gresik, a small town northwest of Surabaya. The Dutch had built concrete forts there to protect the entrance to the Surabaya naval base and KNIL infantry units were sent on rotation to defend the gun emplacements. While stationed at Gresik Soeharto contracted malaria. In Malang he had a recurrence of the disease and had to be hospitalized for about two weeks.

As they presided over their ethnically diverse army, the Dutch not only kept one group separate from another in the core infantry companies and horse cavalry platoons but played favourites in matters of pay and conditions. As might be expected, European soldiers and NCOs were paid more than their "native" equivalents. In 1938, for example, a European private received 5.25 guilders a week, as against a Javanese private's 3 guilders. Europeans also received a larger food allowance. But the Dutch also discriminated between different Indonesian ethnic groups, with Menadonese and Ambonese receiving more money and larger food allowances than the Javanese, Sundanese and Timorese. The main reason for this is that the Dutch, locked into a pattern of divide-and-rule, were always looking to recruit Ambonese and Menadonese. They were thought to be "closer" to the Dutch and hence more loyal. But it was partly, too, because men from those regions were not slow to complain about any perceived injustice. The Bataks were seen by the Dutch as even more outspoken and difficult to manage, always arguing the point, one reason why there was only one Batak rifle company in the KNIL, and even then not for very long.

Javanese, on the other hand, tended to suppress any feelings of resentment they may have had. In earlier times, the Dutch had not been above exploiting that characteristic. Prior to 1910, European, Menadonese and Ambonese soldiers were issued with strong leather boots. The Javanese, Sundanese and Timorese were left to go barefoot, even in combat. This stemmed partly, it seems, from inbuilt favouritism. A second factor, however, is that a parsimonious colonial power wanted to keep its costs down. During the Aceh War, the normally reticent Javanese objected to this practice, pointing out that the Acehnese often defended their palisades with sharpened spikes. This was not a problem for the European, Menadonese or Ambonese soldiers. It was a problem for the Javanese and others, who were, quite literally, stopped in their tracks. They complained that all the medals for bravery had gone to others.[10]

Soeharto seems to have accepted this discrimination in pay and conditions with equanimity, as did the other Javanese, who were grateful enough to have a job and not culturally disposed to openly question the wisdom of those set in authority above them. Besides, his Javanese corporal's salary would have been more than adequate for his needs. What is more, he was advancing rapidly up the lower rungs of the military ladder. Despite his limited education and "native" origin, Soeharto was one of about 8,200 NCOs in the KNIL. He had reached the same level as many Dutchmen and Eurasians, who accounted for roughly 15 per cent of all KNIL corporals. What is more, he was on the fast track to the rank of sergeant, where the breakdown was roughly equal between those who were European or Eurasian and those who were Indonesian. These were no small attainments for a young man who had just turned twenty and whose prospects had looked so unpromising only twelve months earlier.

During his Malang posting, Soeharto would have seen just how slowly the planned upgrade of the KNIL was proceeding at the battalion level, notwithstanding the frantic efforts being made to modernize and expand both the army's land force and air wing. He would have seen just how unprepared the army was to fight a conventional battle against a well-trained and well-equipped external enemy. In mid-1941, the KNIL infantry battalions on Java were beginning to receive the first of their US-made staff cars and jeeps, but they still had no trucks for troop transport. And while the cavalry squadrons were beginning to receive the first of their armoured cars, the first Marmon-Herrington tanks were not due until January 1942. All the squadrons had at this time were their 24 Vickers Carden tanks.

In his autobiography Soeharto recalls the names of several Indonesian friends who served with him in Malang. He also mentions three Dutch officers. One of these was his company commander, "Captain Dryber", a misspelling of Drijber.[11] According to Soeharto, Dryber once wrote to him from Holland asking if the President of Indonesia was the same Soeharto who was in his company. Soeharto told his staff to reply that this was indeed the case. To his evident disappointment, he never heard "whether or not he received my letter." The two other Dutchmen who stood out in his memory, but not enough, it seems, for him to give his readers any indication of their character or appearance, were his *sectie* (platoon) commander, "Lieutenant Hyneman", which seems to be a misspelling of Heineman, and his squad leader, whose name is given as "Jansen".[12]

Soeharto did not stay long in East Java. In late 1941 he found himself in Magelang, where he had been accepted for the sergeant's course, which appears to have lasted five months. Twenty years earlier it had been no easy matter for an Indonesian to reach the rank of sergeant, although some had done so. At the very least a man needed exceptional ability, an unblemished record, unquestioned loyalty and at least six to eight years' service before he might aspire to this rank. Now, as we have seen, it was very much easier.[13] The Dutch were taking in a great many more potential NCOs and pushing them through the system, cutting corners and lowering standards.

At Magelang, Soeharto had to apply himself, yet again, to two very different kinds of warfare, one focused on external defence, the other on internal security. As a sergeant in a KNIL infantry battalion he needed a thorough grasp of basic tenets and organization. That meant familiarizing himself with several KNIL manuals on defence against an external enemy. As a sergeant engaged in operations in the Outer Islands, he would need to have a thorough grasp of KNIL law and order duties. The KNIL "Bible" for operations in the Outer Islands and for "police duties" on Java was a small, dark grey manual entitled "Regulations for Exercising the Political and Police Task of the Army" (*Voorschrift voor de Uitoefening van de Politiek-Politioneele Taak van het Leger*, or VPTL) and issued to all officers and NCOs.[14] Available in both Dutch and Malay, the VPTL ran to 152 pages and contained half the tactics of the infantry and the horse cavalry. It was, in effect, a distillation of the lessons the Dutch had learned during the last fifteen years of the Aceh War, setting out all the do's and don'ts for operations against those who might be inclined to take up arms against the colonial power.[15]

The VPTL explained how KNIL patrols were to be conducted, the procedures that were to be followed during operations against defended stockades, the procedures to be adopted when travelling by river, or when arresting people or interrogating prisoners. It also gave sergeants useful advice on what to do when, on jungle operations, they encountered elephants or tigers, which were protected species; it made it clear that on no account was anyone to shoot a bird of paradise. As a sergeant, Soeharto was expected to have the VPTL with him at all times and was expected to know it almost by heart. At the same time he was issued with a weighty 444-page "Annex to the VPTL", which gave a detailed historical account of significant operations, with clear examples of the way in which sergeants, lieutenants and captains had acted, successfully or unsuccessfully, when confronted with challenges during past operations. Most of the Annex dealt with operations in Aceh. But there were also examples drawn from incidents that had occurred in Jambi, Palembang, Kalimantan, Bali, Sumba, Sumbawa, Maluku and West New Guinea. The most recent additions dealt with the 1926–27 Dutch operations against Communists in Banten, West Java, and West Sumatra. At this stage, it did not matter greatly that Soeharto still had no particular proficiency in Dutch. Only later, if he were to advance further up the promotion ladder, would he need greater fluency in Dutch.[16]

II

Not long after Soeharto arrived in Magelang the pressures that had been building in the Far East exploded with extraordinary ferocity. Two hours before the surprise Japanese attack at Pearl Harbor on Sunday, 7 December 1941, Imperial Army troops landed on the Malay Peninsula. They also attacked British forces in Hong Kong. Eighteen days later, on Christmas morning, men of the Hong Kong Volunteer Defence Force were overrun on the Stanley Peninsula at the southern end of Hong Kong Island. Here, "uncontrolled groups of Japanese began butchering the wounded and raping Chinese and British nurses."[17] The outnumbered British surrendered later that day. Three days earlier, Lieutenant General Homma Masaharu's Fourteenth Army had landed on Luzon in the Philippines and marched on Manila. General Douglas MacArthur's American and Filipino forces held out on the rugged Bataan Peninsula until April and on Corregidor Island in Manila Bay until 6 May, costing Homma his reputation and his command. But the overall Japanese campaign in the Philippines went well. As a result, Tokyo brought forward by a month its planned invasion of the Netherlands East Indies.

At midnight on 10–11 January 1942, five weeks after Pearl Harbor, Major General Sakaguchi Shizuo's 5,200-man 56th Infantry Group, known as the Sakaguchi Task Force, landed at the East Kalimantan oil port of Tarakan, which was defended by an 800-man KNIL battalion and 470 gunners and engineers. Four hours later, a Japanese naval landing force went ashore at Menado and Kema in North Sulawesi.[18] Later that morning, twenty-seven Japanese transport planes, flying out of Davao in the southern Philippines and escorted by twice that number of Navy fighters, dropped more than 300 naval paratroopers of the First Yokosuka Special Landing Party at the Langoan airfield, near Menado. Tarakan and Menado were captured that first day.[19] One Japanese force went on to seize all of eastern Kalimantan. A second swept down through Sulawesi, while subsidiary units captured Ambon and Kupang. A third was standing by to take the NEI's most productive oilfields in south Sumatra.

The Japanese occupation of the East Indies was marked from the start by exceptional savagery. At Tarakan, a unit from the Sakaguchi Task Force captured three KNIL officers and twenty-nine infantrymen. Disoriented in scrubby country that all looked much the same, the Japanese asked their prisoners for directions. The POWs refused to help. The next day, after the local Dutch commander had surrendered, the prisoners were blindfolded and their hands tied behind their backs. "We were slaughtered with bayonet thrusts by about 15 Japanese soldiers," recalled Sergeant Major J.M.J. Muller, who somehow survived and whose evidence was tendered at the Tokyo War Crimes tribunal. "We were bayoneted until we gave no more sign of life. These beasts in human shape practiced in this manner [for] man-to-man fighting."[20] The Sakaguchi detachment went on to capture Balikpapan, the oil port 310 miles south of Tarakan, on 25 January. A month later, Japanese troops executed eighty Dutch men and women in Balikpapan in reprisal for the pre-surrender destruction of oilfield installations and storage tanks.[21] On 22 February, the men of the Sakaguchi Task Force boarded troop transports bound for Java, where there were more horrors to come. After the surrender on Ambon, a Japanese admiral ordered the summary execution of more than 300 Australian and Dutch prisoners of war. On Bangka Island, off southeastern Sumatra, the Japanese shot and bayoneted about fifty European men. They then raped more than twenty Australian Army nurses. Afterwards, they ordered the women to form a line and walk into the sea. When the nurses were waist-deep, the soldiers machine-gunned them from behind. Only one, who was at the end of the line, survived.

In the face of relentless Japanese attack, outlying KNIL detachments wilted. Singapore fell on 15 February, attacked from the rear by Japanese troops who had bicycled down the Malay Peninsula, backed by light tanks and by overwhelming air superiority, against which retreating British and Australian forces had no adequate defence. Two days before the city surrendered, Japanese troops entered the Alexandra Barracks Hospital, bayoneting more than 300 hospital personnel and patients. For six weeks, Allied fighter and bomber pilots made a valiant attempt to stem the Japanese advance. But they were swept aside by swarms of Japanese Zeros. At times, Dutch pilots found themselves outnumbered in dogfights by about ten to one. They eventually lost 90 per cent of their aircraft, either in the air or on the ground. As news leaked out that a company of Ambonese had deserted during the Japanese attack at Tarakan, KNIL morale plummeted. It sank even lower when news was received that Singapore had fallen.

By late February the Japanese had seized every major island in the Dutch East Indies except Java. The noose had tightened. Java was isolated. In Magelang, Soeharto was nearing the end of the sergeants' course, expecting to be assigned to a front line unit.

The Dutch had no hope of holding Java. On paper, it is true, they had 50,000 combat troops on Java and 43,000 auxiliary troops.[22] These figures are deceptive, however. The regular colonial army on the island consisted of about 25,000 men, made up of fourteen infantry battalions earmarked for defence against an external enemy, with artillery, ancillary troops and garrison units.[23] This force was untried in battle and did not much impress Allied military commanders.[24] As we have seen, the Dutch had very few tanks and armoured cars. The Home Guard consisted of about 40,000 men but this was "of doubtful value."[25] The government of Australian Prime Minister John Curtin had, unwisely and with many misgivings, allowed 3,400 battle-hardened Australian troops, known as Blackforce, to disembark at Jakarta on 18 February, three days after the fall of Singapore and when the fate of the East Indies was already sealed.[26] The only effective mobile striking forces on Java were the two Australian battalions in Blackforce, two dozen British light tanks and a battalion of American field artillery.[27]

Anticipating correctly that the Japanese would land at either end of the island, the Dutch had deployed their forces accordingly. Their largest force was to the west of Jakarta, supported by various Allied units. A second force, the so-called Bandung Group, was deployed in the eastern part of West Java. Consisting of 5,900 mobile troops and supported by 24 tanks, it was to fall back on the Bandung plateau area with its "great concentration" of military installations: barracks, warehouses, workshops and ammunition factory, as well as an air base of the Royal Netherlands Indies Army air wing.[28] Needless to say, these installations and the city itself were vulnerable to bombing.[29] In East Java the Dutch planned to concentrate their forces, which consisted of little more than the 6th Regiment, in the defence of the naval base at Surabaya. The Dutch intended largely to abandon Central Java: most of their forces there would be used for the defence of West Java.

The Japanese had organized two powerful forces for the capture of Java. A Western Force, which had formed up in Cam Ranh Bay, in Indochina, which was governed by the Vichy French, included fifty-six transport vessels escorted by a light aircraft carrier, six cruisers and nineteen destroyers. It was to put the Japanese 2nd Division ashore at Banten Bay and Merak, at the northwestern corner of Java. The division would drive east to capture Jakarta and Bogor. Subsidiary units would go ashore at Eretan Wetan, about ninety miles east of Jakarta, and strike south in a bid to secure the vital Kalijati airfield, twenty-six miles north of Bandung, where the Dutch planned to make a final stand. An Eastern Force, which had assembled at Jolo in the southern Philippines, consisted of forty-one transports carrying the Japanese 48th Division, a crack unit which had seized Manila on 2 January 1942. It was escorted by four cruisers and nine destroyers and was to arrive off Kragan, about 100 miles west of Surabaya in East Java. Once the Kragan beachhead was secure, a powerful force would strike east towards Surabaya. The Sakaguchi Task Force, which had captured Tarakan and Balikpapan, was assigned responsibility for Central Java.[30] It would race southwest to capture Solo and Yogyakarta before leapfrogging still further ahead to seize the port of Cilacap, on the south coast of the island. This would prevent Allied forces in West Java falling back on Cilacap, the last significant link in the evacuation route between Java and Australia.

The commander of the Java operation, Lieutenant General Imamura Hitoshi, had at his disposal almost 98,000 ground troops, of whom 55,000 were to go ashore in Java. This was more than ten times the number the Dutch had for many years been working on as a basis for their war planning.[31] The infantry were supported by more than sixty medium and light tanks, which had proved their mettle in China, and forty "tankettes". The landings in Java took place on 1 March, delayed only briefly by the Battle of the Java Sea, in which ships of the Imperial Japanese Navy all but eliminated an Allied naval presence in the NEI, sinking five cruisers and six destroyers and losing no ships themselves. Dutch army engineers had done a good job felling trees and destroying bridges ahead of the landings; this slowed the Japanese advance. The colonial army did not do at all well when it came to fighting. Some units made an effort; many put up little, if any, resistance. KNIL ground units, demoralized and immobilized, lacking modern communications and badly led, could do nothing to stem the Japanese tide. The few Australian, British and American units were too small to make a significant difference. Meanwhile, the so-called Shoji Detachment had landed at Eretan Wetan, supported by ten light tanks. Racing south, it had captured the Kalijati airfield by about noon; the airfield was to remain in Japanese hands despite desperate Allied counter-attacks.

The Japanese landing at Kragan was under Lieutenant General Tsuchihashi Yuitsu, commander of the 12,900-strong 48th Division, which, after occupying Manila, had pursued MacArthur's forces as they withdrew to the Bataan Peninsula. The division, already motorized, had commandeered additional vehicles in Manila and brought them to Java. At Kragan, the night was ideal for a landing, with a light offshore wind and the moon one day past full. One Japanese force, the Kaneuji Echelon, led by Major Kaneuji Kenichi and consisting of about three companies, landed at 7:00 a.m. on 1 March, followed later by two other echelons. These units, part of the Sakaguchi Task Force, quickly overcame Dutch opposition.[32]

Once ashore, Tsuchihashi sent his main force eastwards towards Surabaya, which he reached on 8 March. At 10:00 a.m. that day forward units reported a white flag flying on the Wonokromo bridge on the southern approaches to the city. At 1:30 p.m., after some hesitation, Tsuchihashi called off a planned 2:00 p.m. artillery bombardment of Surabaya. For the howitzer battery of the 17th Field Heavy Artillery Regiment, "which had come in high spirits from Manchuria", the Java operation ended with them not having fired a single shot. Owing to the loss of radio sets at Banten Bay, there was no communication between Imamura's headquarters in the west and Tsuchihashi's division in the east until a Japanese plane dropped a communications cylinder at Surabaya nine days after the landings, advising that the Dutch had surrendered.

In the meantime, Sakaguchi's motorized columns had sped southwards and westwards, as had two Japanese battalions from Taiwan, which captured the burning oil fields at Cepu the day after the landing. In Cepu and in nearby Blora, the Japanese raped a large number of women, particularly Dutch and Eurasian women. A witness told the Tokyo War Crimes tribunal in 1946 that in Cepu "women were repeatedly raped" with the approval of a senior officer. The rapes began on Thursday, 5 March 1942, the day that General Tsuchihashi left the town after spending two days there. "The Japanese then appeared, mad and wild," one woman recalled. A Dutch couple and their two daughters, who were aged about fifteen and sixteen, were taken away and "fearfully maltreated." That night the two girls were raped. Two days later, Japanese troops entered a hospital in Cepu where women and children were seated together. Eight married Dutch or Eurasian women were taken away and raped. In the words of one of the victims, "It was a mass, continuous merciless rape." The rapes in Cepu continued for twelve days.[33] In Blora, fifteen mothers and daughters were raped several times a day for three weeks by passing Japanese troops.

Although headed by a two-star general, the Sakaguchi detachment was a force of barely two battalions. To disguise this fact, it divided up into three echelons, each with a strength of less than three companies, hoping to convince the Dutch they faced an entire division. This ploy, and Sakaguchi's bold and rapid charge across Central Java, succeeded. Unnerved, the KNIL was soon in disarray. At dawn on 5 March, Sakaguchi's men stormed into

Solo. At dusk that day, the Kaneuji echelon appeared without warning at Yogyakarta, surprising the Dutch commander and taking 700 prisoners. Barely pausing for breath, Kaneuji raced on towards Cilacap, leaving the prisoners in the hands of three Japanese soldiers—a captain, an NCO and a private. By the time it seized Cilacap, in the early hours of 8 March, the Kaneuji Echelon had averaged an advance of sixty-two miles a day for six days. Other Japanese columns were converging on Bandung from the west and the north. The end was near.

III

At about the time of the Japanese landings, when there was no hope of the Dutch holding Java for more than a week, Soeharto graduated as a sergeant 2nd class and was sent immediately to Bandung. "It was when I was attending the cadre school that the Second World War [sic] broke out," he wrote, clearly referring to the Pacific War. "So when I finished the course at Gombong and was made sergeant, I was transferred immediately to Bandung to join the Reserves at Army Headquarters. I was posted to Cisarua."[34] Cisarua is a small West Java hill resort, about ten miles northwest of Bandung. It was an unimportant location, used by the KNIL as a pasture where horses coming from Australia could be acclimatized.

The commander of the KNIL's 9th Infantry Battalion, Major J.W.G.A. Hoedt, moved through Cisarua on the night of 6–7 March, before setting up a command post at Citespong, some three miles to the southeast and not far west of Lembang.[35] His reinforced battalion, which included an anti-aircraft battery, an extra infantry section, several machine gun and mortar sections and an anti-armour section, had orders to prepare for a counter-attack on the west flank of a Japanese force bearing down on Bandung. That night Soeharto would have heard the guns of two batteries of artillery reverberating through the mountains. At 5:00 p.m. the next day, Hoedt's patrols had fire contact with advance Japanese patrols. But an hour later, in darkness and driving rain, Hoedt was ordered to cease firing.[36] He withdrew, under cover of darkness, to Lembang and continued on to Cimahi. Soeharto remained in Cisarua.

In his memoirs, Soeharto invites the reader to assume that he was attached to a reserve combat unit in Cisarua, by which he almost certainly means what was known at Dutch headquarters as the "Hoedt Group". One other theory has been canvassed, however. According to Colonel Carel Heshusius, a KNIL cavalry officer who carried out reconnaissance patrols for Major Hoedt at that time and who later wrote extensively about the Dutch colonial army, it is possible that Soeharto was serving not as an NCO in a fighting unit but as a *foerier*, or quartermaster-sergeant. This, if true, would put Soeharto's pre-war military career in a rather different light. A *foerier* was in charge of the reserve weapons and ammunition, the horse-drawn mobile cookers and hot water carriages, the stored emergency rations, the spare uniforms and boots, the beds and mattresses, the cupboards and chairs. He had regular contact not just with the men of his company but, when the company was back in the barracks, with their wives as well, being in charge of the distribution of rice and salt.[37]

"As far as I can establish," Heshusius said, "Soeharto was more in charge of stores. In each company of 180 men there was a *foerier*—the Dutch used the French word—or logistical sergeant. He was not in command of fifteen or twenty men, as were most sergeants, but in charge of logistical matters and supplies. The *foerier* was a man clever at writing and bookkeeping."[38] Based on some of his capabilities, Soeharto would no doubt have made an admirable quartermaster-sergeant. But it is highly unlikely that he ever served in such a capacity. For one thing, he did not have more than a rudimentary grasp of spoken or written Dutch, which was essential in a *foerier*. For another, he would have needed a very different kind of military training. Finally, there is no supporting evidence to back such a claim. On the contrary, a number of retired Dutch and Indonesian generals, some of them with no special fondness for Soeharto, are inclined to doubt that he was anything other than a sergeant in a KNIL infantry company.

As it turned out, Soeharto spent barely a week as a sergeant in the KNIL. It was a week of hopelessness and despair for the Dutch, not only because their panicked preparations for war had come too late but because they had no chance of holding off the Japanese once Singapore had fallen. And Singapore, like the Philippines, had been doomed from the start, owing to the British and American inability to project naval power into Southeast Asia and the western Pacific.[39] The fact that the Japanese landed on Java in overwhelming force merely sealed the island's fate. During that first terrible week of March 1942 the impossibility of the Dutch position became obvious. Morale was at rock-bottom.[40] Many infantry units were in disarray. In some places "native troops 'melted away' after first fire contact, leaving behind them bewildered European officers and non-commissioned officers."[41]

In the period before the modernization and organizational upheavals of the late 1930s, the Indonesian soldier had had a close bond with his commander, whether the latter was of high or low rank. A trusted, well-known commander was seen as a *bapak*, or father figure. The old saying was, "*Waar oom voorgaat volgen wij*" ("Where our commander goes, we will follow"), with the word *oom* (uncle) referring to any experienced soldier. During the late 1930s and early 1940s many of those bonds had been severed as officers were sent to join the expanding air wing or reassigned to mechanized armour and cavalry units. When war broke out, some KNIL units had a large number of unknown NCOs and officers. "The newcomers," Colonel Nortier recalled, "were no *bapaks*. The soldiers did not give what they could have given to a well-known and trusted commander. The army was too small to weed out less able commanders. The fighting lasted too short a time to correct combat failures. The constant retreats broke morale."[42] In other places, the situation was quite the reverse. The journalist Kwee Thiam Tjing was recruited into the Surabaya, and later Malang, Stadtswacht, a mixed-race Home Guard in which he soon became a sergeant. In his memoir *Indonesia Dalem Api dan Bara*, Kwee writes that the first people to start looting and fleeing were actually Dutch military personnel, which shocked everyone. Later, the Eurasians joined in the looting. In the end, there were only Indonesians and Chinese left at their posts.[43]

At 2:50 p.m. on 9 March, Ter Poorten surrendered. Australian, American and British commanders were obliged to surrender as well. Dutch prestige in the Indies had suffered a blow from which it would never fully recover.* The Japanese had anticipated in December 1941 that it might take them twenty to sixty days to capture Java. In the event, they gained control of the island in just nine days, for the loss of 255 dead. By comparison, more than 3,500 Japanese officers and men had been killed in the Malayan campaign. The Sixteenth Army took 82,600 prisoners of war on Java, including about 10,600 British soldiers, 4,900 Australians and nearly 900 Americans; it captured 85,000 rifles and machine-guns and 89 million rounds of ammunition.[44] Many of these weapons, along with

---

* The one part of the Netherlands East Indies which the Japanese did not capture was the swamp and mangrove region around Merauke, in the southeastern corner of Dutch West New Guinea.

captured Japanese arms, would fall into Indonesian hands within seven weeks of the Proclamation of Independence in August 1945, an inestimable boon to the nationalist movement.

IV

Due to the looming threat of war, Soeharto had moved rapidly up the secondary KNIL promotion ladder, which ran from private to sergeant major. He had gone from unemployed civilian to sergeant 2nd class in just twenty-one months, achieving in less than two years what many older and more seasoned KNIL sergeants had taken seven or eight years to achieve. At the time of the Dutch surrender Soeharto was twenty years old. He had never been stationed in the Outer Islands. He had never commanded more than sixteen or seventeen men, and then only for seven days. He had never fired a shot at an enemy soldier. He had, however, acquired a great deal of valuable military instruction, having spent seventeen of his twenty-one months in the army at KNIL training centres and only four months on attachment to field units. This was to serve him well in the years to come, compensating for his educational shortcomings and for the fact that he left Malang before there was a chance to participate in battalion-level exercises. When Indonesia established an army in 1945, very few of its mid-level officers had as much formal military training as Soeharto. Many years later Soeharto was to draw attention to his rapid rise to sergeant, pointing out that others had taken much longer to achieve what he had achieved.[45] He implied that his success was due to his unusual aptitude. This was disingenuous. Soeharto was a man of considerable ability, but his rise to sergeant stemmed not so much from natural aptitude as from the desperate situation in which the Dutch found themselves in 1940–42.

Soeharto was never destined for high rank in the Dutch colonial army. Had there been no Pacific War and no alteration to the colonial status quo, he might have reached the rank of sergeant 1st class, sergeant-major or warrant officer before he qualified for an army pension after twenty-five years of service, always assuming that he was able to get his Dutch language skills up to the necessary standard. This in itself would have been a significant achievement: sergeant was a position of high status for a *pribumi* of modest background; as a sergeant Soeharto would have been able to send his children to good primary and junior high schools, perhaps even to one of the prestigious AMS senior high schools and then to the military academy. At a pinch, he might have jumped across to the other promotion ladder, which ran from lieutenant to general, and made it to captain, had the Dutch found themselves short of officers and had he been able to qualify in his spare time for a high school diploma. That, too, would have seen him due for retirement in 1965. As it happened, fate was to intervene in the most decisive manner. By 1965 Soeharto would be a major general, not simply a sergeant major or captain, poised not only for a swift ascent to full general but shortly to gain the Indonesian presidency, which he was to hold for thirty years.

For the moment, however, his prospects looked grim. He was a sergeant in a colonial army that had suffered a humiliating defeat. In three months, the official British history of the war in the Far East was to note, the Japanese had conquered Malaya and the Netherlands East Indies and had gained possession of all the resources of that rich southern area for which they had gone to war.[46] The Japanese had little time for those Indonesians who had fought on the Dutch side. They distrusted especially those who had served under the Dutch as officers or NCOs. At Cisarua, Soeharto had some reason to expect that he might soon find himself inside a prisoner of war camp. That was not to be. Before long, the Japanese would offer him even more opportunities in life.

9

A policeman for the Japanese

In the days after the Dutch surrender, Soeharto stayed on in Cisarua, a soldier in a defeated army, waiting to see what would happen next. As a sergeant in the KNIL, he assumed, not unreasonably, that he would become a prisoner of war of the Japanese.[1] For a time nothing happened. Soeharto whiled away the hours playing cards, making, or so he later claimed, a handsome profit in the process. "I had only a guilder in my pocket, but as I played—and won—it soon grew to fifty."[2] Deciding eventually that he had no wish to be incarcerated in a POW camp with his Dutch and Indonesian military comrades, Soeharto made his way to Cimahi, on the western outskirts of Bandung, accompanied by Amat Sudono, his closest friend in the KNIL. Here, they "bought some ordinary clothes" and discarded their distinctive green KNIL uniforms. Here, too, Soeharto encountered the Japanese army for the first time. "I was taking a break outside a civilian's house," he recalled. "Japanese soldiers had driven out the Dutchmen who had controlled us for centuries. They looked full of confidence and their countenances were truly frightening."[3]

A person of pedantic or churlish disposition might be inclined to note that the Dutch had not, in fact, controlled most of the East Indies for centuries. They may have been in the Spice Islands since the 1600s and in Java for a very long time. But in 1942 they had only had full control over Bali, for example, for thirty-four years. That same critic might note that the Dutch had only been able to control Indonesians because they had always been able to find men like Soeharto—men who were willing to take the King or Queen's shilling to keep other Indonesians in their place. A more serious charge might be that Soeharto was now a deserter. Was that the case? The evidence strongly suggests that he was not a deserter. Nor, it would appear, could that be said of aspirant officers (*cadetten*) such as A.H. Nasution and T.B. Simatupang, who had recently attended the Royal Military Academy in Bandung and who would go on to play a central role in the post-war Indonesian National Army. They were not officers yet and had not taken the officer's oath (*officierseed*) to the Dutch Queen. It was a different matter in the case of those somewhat older Indonesian officers who had graduated several years earlier from the Military Academy in the Netherlands.[4] An exception could only be made, on technical grounds, for those of them who may have been attached to units in the surroundings of Bandung. These distinctions, overly fine and fussy perhaps in a time of war and subsequent revolution, did not apply to Soeharto. He was not an officer. He had not sworn an oath of loyalty to the Dutch Queen. Even if he had been an officer, he would, by virtue of his presence near Bandung in March 1942, have had a clean state.

In those early weeks of March 1942, Java was in a state of confusion and panic, powerful Japanese forces having landed at either end of the island and converged on Central Java in a swift pincer movement. But the Dutch were nothing if not efficient. The trans-island trains were still running, lending a spurious air of normality in what was a period of extreme anxiety, at least for Europeans. Soeharto and Sudono bought tickets to Yogyakarta, which had fallen to the Japanese on 5 March. On arrival at Tugu station in the centre of Yogyakarta, the two men heard an announcement, ominous in its implications, ordering all servicemen to report to an office in Jetis, a suburb about half a mile to the north. The idea of turning themselves in now had even less appeal, and they continued on to Sleman, a small town about six miles north of Jetis. From there, they slipped away and spent a night in Sudono's house. The next morning Soeharto took a bus to Wonogiri and then travelled on to Wuryantoro, where he was taken in by his aunt and uncle.[5] For the time being, he was relatively safe. But in Wuryantoro he had a relapse of malaria and was, or so he claimed, bedridden for about six months.

II

Although they had been the unchallenged power in Java for more than 110 years and had made many profound changes, the Dutch had put down shallower roots than they liked to imagine. In Yogyakarta, as in other parts of the island, the brown-uniformed Japanese troops were greeted as liberators, at least initially. For the Japanese, this was quite new. When the 48th Division, now fanning out across eastern Java, had marched into Manila two months earlier it had been "greeted with silence by lines of sullen Filipinos."[6] When Lieutenant General Yamashita Tomoyuki's Twenty-fifth Army, now responsible for Sumatra, Malaya and British North Borneo, had entered Singapore it had faced "a sullen, hostile population."[7] In Java it was different. "When we arrived in Java," recalled Tsuchiya Kiso, a Sixteenth Army intelligence officer who would soon play a key role in Soeharto's career, "all the Indonesians welcomed us.... Nowhere else, such as China or Manchuria, did it happen that the natives welcomed the Japanese occupation."[8]

Kaneko Tomokazu, a member of the Sixteenth Army's Propaganda Corps (Sendenhan) and editor of the Japanese occupation newspaper *Unabara (The Ocean)*, made the same point. "I was surprised because we were welcomed," he explained many decades later. "We hadn't expected it. They were so fantastically welcoming."[9] In the words of Selo Soemardjan, who was working at that time in the political affairs section of the Dutch police force in Yogyakarta, "We were very glad that the Dutch were driven away. So we received the Japanese with open arms. We welcomed them because they were liberators—liberators from the colonial Dutch. I saw the Dutch running away, outside the city.... So we did nothing to help the Dutch. Perhaps one or two people who were very close to the Dutch [helped them]. But in general, nobody helped the Dutch. We were even glad that they had run away."[10]

Nor was it just the warmth of the welcome that left an impression on the Japanese. Many of them were surprised to find that the people of Java seemed physically rather similar to Japanese. Imamura believed there was a link between these two factors. The enthusiastic welcome convinced him that the Indonesians and Japanese were "certainly people of the same race and common stock. If not, how was it possible for them to show so much goodwill and cooperation to the Japanese troops!"[11] Nor, some of the better-educated Japanese officers were aware, was this some indolent South Seas backwater, as many had imagined. The Javanese and the Sundanese were sophisticated people, with ancient cultures and elaborate social codes.

The other side of this coin is that the Japanese were shocked by the looting that broke out in the first two weeks of the occupation. Many of them came to the conclusion that the "natives" were, in fact, worse than they had imagined.[12] At the time of the Dutch surrender, General Imamura told Allied interrogators after the war, "the Indonesian masses, like a rising tide, attacked and plundered mercilessly the properties of the Europeans and the Chinese throughout Java."[13] Many of those who resisted were murdered. The Japanese did not take kindly to lawlessness of this kind. Determined that Java be run with maximum efficiency in the interests of the war effort, they sent field units of the Kenpeitai, the notorious Military Police Corps, to restore order, an instruction the Kenpeitai carried out with exemplary brutality, bringing terror to many parts of the island.[14]

Then there was the infrastructure. The Japanese could not help but admire the cities and towns they found in Java. These were well planned and well laid out, with many imposing European buildings.* There were canals and graceful, tree-lined suburban streets. In the European suburbs there were fine villas, many of which had splendid tropical gardens. It was not difficult, they soon discovered, to live comfortably in Java.[15] At the same time, some Japanese officers, familiar with the advanced factories and shipyards of their own country, professed to be surprised, even angry, that the Dutch had done virtually nothing to industrialize their Southeast Asian possession, never mind that the Japanese had no intention of industrializing it themselves but wanted it, just as the Dutch had wanted it, primarily for its resources. It was true, the Japanese agreed, that the Dutch had built excellent ports and railroads, sugar factories and irrigation canals. But that had been done, they were inclined to suggest, even six decades later, when all the extractive excesses of their own rule were so widely known, to plunder the natural resources of Java, not to help the Javanese themselves.

In the event, it did not take long for the warmth of the Indonesian welcome to cool. While the incoming troops seem on the whole to have

---

* Before long, Imamura had moved into the white, neoclassical palace of the Dutch Governor-General on the northwestern corner of Koningsplein, the great park in the centre of the city. He took for his headquarters a stolid colonial edifice on the southwestern corner of the park. This had been the office of the Nederlandsche-Koloniale Petroleum Maatschappij (NKPM), a subsidiary of the American Standard Oil Co. The head of the Military Administration Department (Gunseikan) established himself in the office of the Batavia Petroleum Company (Bataafse Petroleum Maatschappij, BPM) on the northeastern side of the park. The Kenpeitai moved into the Law Faculty building on the western side of the square.

been well disciplined, as even many Dutch accounts attest, in some places the Japanese behaved with the same kind of cruelty they had shown in China, Hong Kong and Singapore—and not just when dealing with an initial breakdown in law and order. In Yogyakarta one morning in mid-1942 the Japanese rounded up a large group of people and forced them to watch a public execution. Indonesian prisoners, guilty of what crime no one knew, were tied to poles with their hands behind their backs. On a shouted command, Japanese soldiers ran forward and killed them with fixed bayonets. Some of those who had been obliged to watch spent the day vomiting.[16] Nor did the situation improve much as the occupation progressed. On the contrary, Japanese soldiers behaved with arrogance and cruelty, leaving many Javanese and Sundanese humiliated and deeply afraid. Selo Soemardjan's father was a low-level official in the palace of the Sultan. One morning, not long after the start of the occupation, he walked to work past Fort Vredeburg, not realizing that he was expected to stop and bow to the Japanese sentries. When he failed to do so, he was punched and knocked to the ground in front of passers-by. For any Javanese, this would have been deeply humiliating. For a retainer of the Sultan, however lowly, it was an unbearable affront; he felt he had been shamed.[17]

During the early months of the occupation the Japanese began to implement policies, devised well in advance, that were to transform profoundly the former Netherlands East Indies. The guiding ideological principle of Japanese rule in the occupied regions of the Southern Area was the construction of the "Greater East Asia Co-Prosperity Sphere."[18] On the face of it, this principle implied equality among the various races and states in Asia, even if it was understood that Japan had cast itself in the role of dominant older brother. In practice, there was to be no equality and no co-prosperity. From the start, Japanese self-interest was paramount. Two weeks before Pearl Harbor, Tokyo had decided that "the supreme purpose of Japan's southward advance was the acquisition of resources in the Southern Area, with the main emphasis on petroleum."[19] Japan hoped to establish a self-sustaining system that would allow it to wage war and "form a new order in Asia centring around Japan." In support of that goal, the Sixteenth Army's propaganda department launched an intensive campaign designed to convince Indonesians that they and the Japanese were brothers-in-arms in the great struggle for this new order.[20] This campaign was soon undermined by the inescapable evidence of

Japanese cruelty and self-interest. But that did not dampen anti-Dutch sentiment among the Indonesians.

The Japanese, it is true, did not propose to treat the Southern Area as they treated Taiwan, which they had annexed in 1895, or Korea, which they had annexed in 1910. In those colonies, old forms of government had been abolished and replaced by administrative systems built on Japanese lines. Nor did they want to repeat the mistakes they had made more recently in Manchuria and China, where brutal and heavy-handed Japanese occupation had alienated the population. In the South, existing administrative structures and staff were to be utilized to the utmost and local culture respected. Nevertheless, the Japanese were determined to impose careful controls on the people of this area. While "native inhabitants" were to be encouraged to trust the Japanese forces, independence movements were "not to be stimulated *prematurely*."[21]

III

For administrative purposes and as a concession to the Imperial Navy, the Japanese had divided the Dutch East Indies into three distinct regions, with so little contact between them that they might as well have been three watertight compartments. Sumatra was placed under the Twenty-fifth Army, after being linked for a time to Malaya. Java came under the Sixteenth Army. Kalimantan (excluding the British North Borneo territories), Sulawesi, Bali, the Lesser Sunda Islands and West New Guinea were under the control of the Imperial Navy.[22] The Navy planned to transform these regions into permanent colonial possessions, like Taiwan and Korea.[23] The army, it has been claimed, wanted to keep at least Sumatra after victory.[24]

The resources after which the Japanese hungered lay mainly in the Outer Islands. But Java was important, too, first as a source of sugar, rice and salt, and later as a source of labour. Moreover, Java had to be defended against an Allied counter-attack, which General MacArthur, by now Supreme Commander of the South West Pacific Area (SWPA) command, was expected to launch from bases in northern Australia. For the economic goals to be met, Java would have to be run with maximum efficiency, the army brooking no opposition. Nor did the Japanese waste any time in making their intentions plain. On 7 March, two days before the Dutch surrender, General Imamura, a former deputy chief of staff of the notorious Kwantung Army, which had run the puppet state of

Manchukuo (Manchuria) as an Imperial Army fiefdom for the best part of a decade, issued Order No. 1.[25] The Army, it declared, was setting up a military administration in the "occupied territories" in order to "ensure the prosperity of the inhabitants, preserve the peace, and hasten the tranquillity and happiness of the people." The commander of the Japanese army would perform the functions of the governor general, but the "present machinery of government" would continue for the time being. That meant, in practice, that while Allied soldiers and Dutch policemen were detained, some 15,000 Dutch officials on Java were to remain at their desks.[26]

Once established, the Japanese moved to reshape the face of Java. Dutch businesses, plantations and mines were taken over. Dutch banks, including the semi-government Javasche Bank, which issued the currency, were liquidated. The Netherlands East Indies guilder, or florin, remained the currency unit, but came to be better known as the rupiah, an Indonesian term. Later, Japanese military scrip (*gunpyo*), a paper currency, would circulate widely, depreciating in value as more and more notes were printed. Commercial banking was taken over by the Yokohama Specie Bank (which became part of what is now MUFG Bank). A press monopoly was awarded to the Asahi Shimbun group. Strict censorship prevailed, in newspapers, broadcasting, and filmmaking. It became an offence, sometimes punished by torture or death, to listen to foreign radio broadcasts. All existing law courts were abolished and replaced by courts run by the Japanese military administration. The name Batavia was changed back to Jakarta. Even the calendar and the system of timekeeping changed, in line with Japanese practice throughout the conquered territories. The Imperial calendar, which starts with the mythical founding of Japan in 660 BC, was introduced, so that 1942 became 2602. Henceforth, the Japanese declared, Java would operate on Tokyo time, which meant that in much of western Indonesia the sun would rise ninety minutes later than usual (at 7:30 a.m., rather than at 6:00 a.m.).

Then there was the issue of communication. The Japanese faced a huge language problem in the East Indies. Almost no Indonesians knew any Japanese in 1942, and only a handful of Japanese knew any Dutch or even Malay, although some had begun studying rudimentary Malay on the ships carrying them south. Imamura banned the use of the Dutch language in schools, law courts, newspapers, letters and telegrams, and in telephone conversations, mainly because the Japanese could not understand it. He did not, as is often supposed, limit or prohibit people's use of the Dutch language in private.[27] The use of Bahasa Indonesia as a language of instruction in all schools was to prove a positive development for the nation that would come into being in August 1945. Many Indonesians, not least those who had attended Dutch-language middle schools and colleges, now became fluent in the language. "Formerly," recalled Lieutenant General Sayidiman Suryohadiprojo, who was fluent in Javanese and Dutch at that time, "most of us could not speak or write the language well enough. I could speak Javanese well but not Bahasa Indonesia."[28]

Japan's swift conquest of Southeast Asia fostered a widespread belief in Army circles that the war was going exceptionally well. But as Mitsuo Nakamura has noted, Japanese officers drew two contrasting conclusions about future policy for the newly-occupied areas. One was to "colonize" these areas, as Western nations had done. The other was to regard the people of the region as capable of eventual political independence and steer them towards it.[29] Imamura was in the latter camp. Be that as it may, Imamura not willing or indeed permitted to make any political concessions to the Indonesian nationalists, at least initially. On the contrary, during the early stages of the occupation, the Japanese curbed the nationalist movement to a greater extent than had the Dutch.[30] All political parties were banned. The Kenpeitai and the Japanese-run civilian police force monitored any activity which might be considered at all political. The military administration banned the flying of the red-and-white Indonesian flag, insisting that the Japanese red-and-white flag be flown across the island. It also banned the playing of *Indonesia Raya* (Great Indonesia), a rousing anthem, popular in nationalist circles—an anthem that Radio Tokyo had pointedly played at the close of its nightly pre-war propaganda broadcasts to Indonesia as part of the "Asia for the Asians" theme.[31]

Although many of the new measures were harsh, Imamura rejected the even harsher measures being urged on him by Tokyo and by the Southern Army in Singapore.[32] Having seen in China that a repressive policy aroused popular resentment and led to failure, and having been surprised by the enthusiastic welcome his troops had received in Java, Imamura decided at his first staff meeting, on 10 March, to adopt a "mild" policy.[33] Priority would be given to economic reconstruction, the re-establishment of normal civilian life using Dutch engineers and executives and Chinese merchants and economic institutions, the reappointment of Indonesian officials, the reopening of Indonesian schools and a strong propaganda

Imperial Japanese Army Command Structure, Southeast Asia, 1942-45

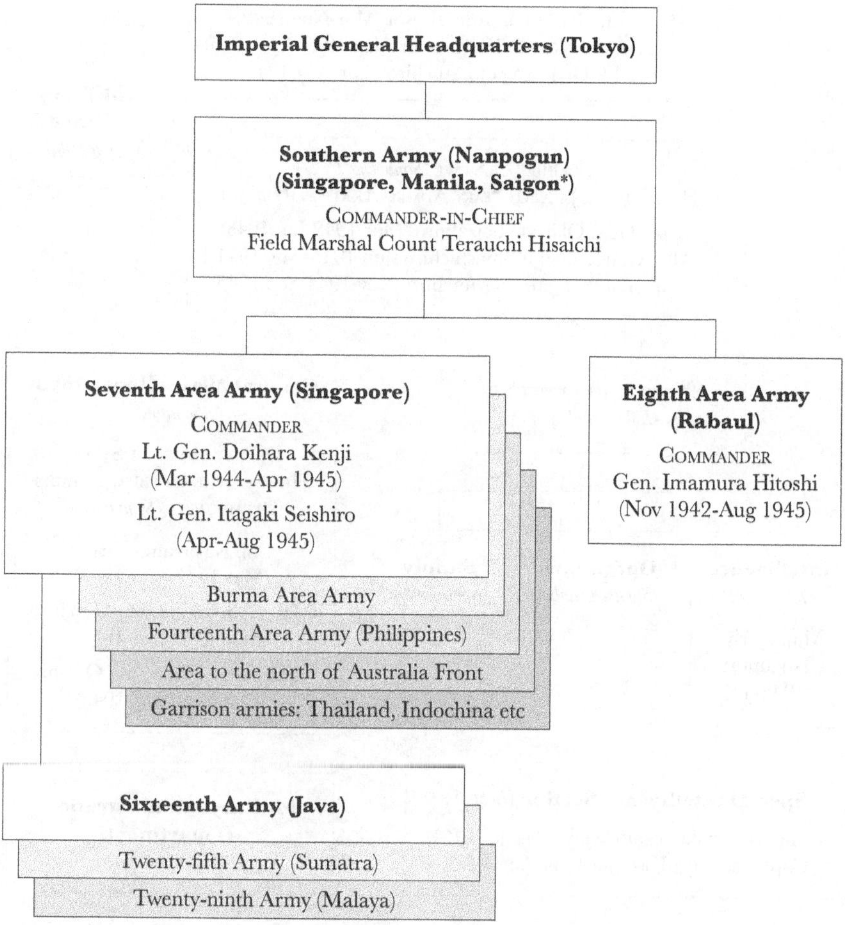

Note: Diacritics have not been used to distinguish long and short vowels.

* Saigon has been renamed Ho Chi Minh City.

Sixteenth Army Command Structure, Java

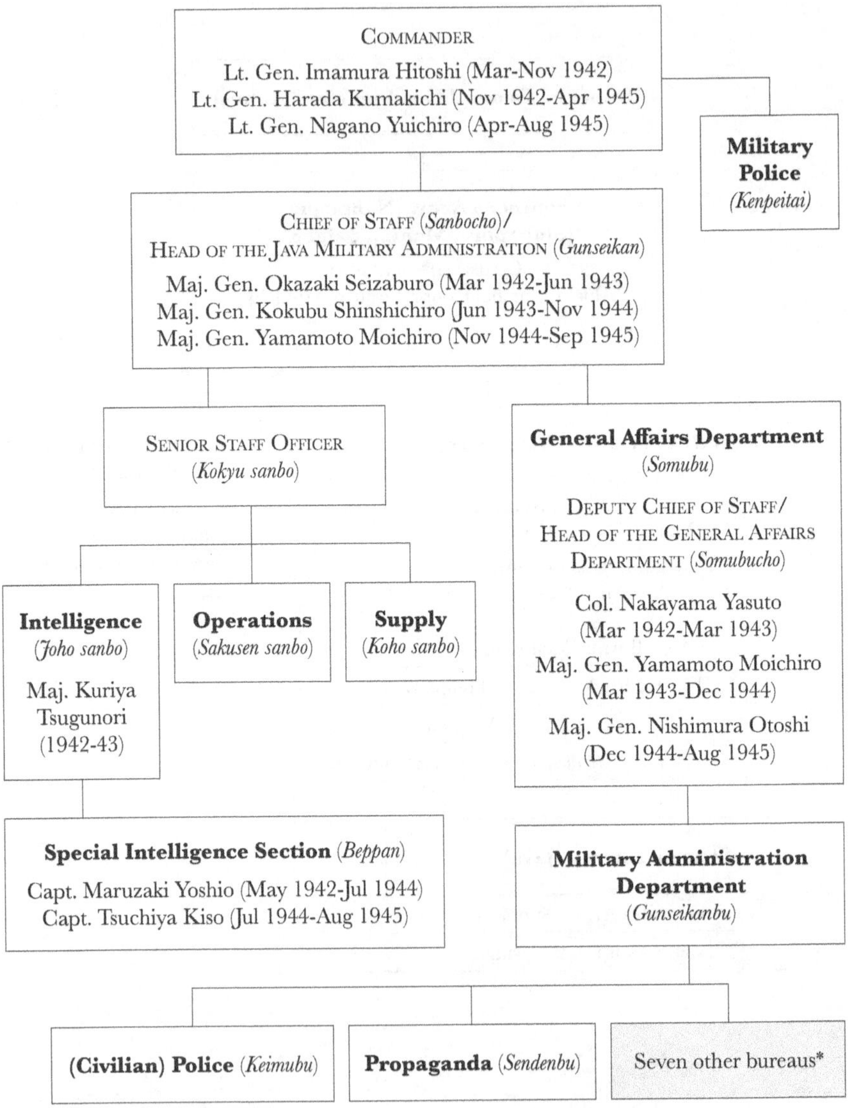

* Cultural Affairs (*Gijutsubu*), Internal Affairs (*Naimubu*), Law (*Shihobu*), Finance (*Zaimubu*), Enemy Property (*Tekisanbu*), Production (*Sangyobu*) and Economic Affairs (*Keizaibu*).

campaign to emphasize friendship and cooperation. In mid-April, barely a month after the Dutch surrender, Imamura came under pressure to modify his "mild" policy. Tokyo felt that the Sixteenth Army should follow the policy in place in Singapore, where the Army was taking a stern line against the Chinese. Imamura, it decreed, need no longer pay much attention to the wishes of the native population; rather, he had to impress on them the power and might of the Japanese. Imamura stood his ground. By June, he had convinced Field Marshal Terauchi Hisaichi, the supreme commander of Japanese forces in the Southern Region, that he was pursuing the correct path. By October, Tokyo was to accept that as well.[34]

In the meantime, Imamura wanted to reach out to the two dominant nationalist leaders, Sukarno and Mohammad Hatta, who, under the Dutch, had endured years of internal exile in far-flung reaches of the archipelago. Believing he could use the two men, and others, to promote support in the community for the Japanese cause, Imamura pushed to have them brought back to Jakarta. Hatta, who was in the West Java hill town of Sukabumi by then, was given a job as an adviser to the Japanese military government—a job he was to hold for about six months, until his advice and criticism became unpalatable, whereupon he was taken up by the Japanese Navy liaison officer in Jakarta. Sukarno was to be brought back from Sumatra, which was outside Imamura's jurisdiction and thus required approval from Terauchi, who needed a lot of persuading that this was wise. As time passed, Indonesians would be allowed to participate in a number of Japanese-sponsored mass organizations—Tiga A Movement, Putera, Jawa Hokokai, Masyumi—set up to mobilize support for the war effort. Putera, which, like the other bodies, had no Dutch precedent, was to give Sukarno and Hatta a highly visible public role. The Japanese would also set up the Seinendan, a para-military Youth Corps.

At the same time, Imamura had to contend with a dramatic reduction in Japanese troop numbers on Java. In March 1942, the Sixteenth Army had been a force of 55,000 men, built around two divisions, with about twenty-two battalions. Some of those troops had been moved on from Java almost immediately. The 5,200-strong Sakaguchi Task Force, which had swept westward through the heartland of Central Java in early March, had been sent, at the end of that month, to rejoin the 56th Division, which was advancing on Burma. At the end of August, the powerful 2nd Division was sent, together with two other units, from West Java to support operations at Guadalcanal, where the Japanese and Americans were locked in a grinding land and sea battle. That would rob Java of another 24,000 front-line troops. On 1 November the 48th Division would be sent from East Java to defend Timor and islands in the Arafura Sea.[35]

Nor was Imamura given suitable replacements. As he noted bitterly at the end of the war, to make up for the units that had been redeployed he was sent "ten battalions of aged soldiers, in all, under thirty thousand men, and with this small military force I had to defend Java."[36] In some ways, the situation seems to have been even worse than that. According to a senior Japanese staff officer, the redeployments left the Sixteenth Army "with a total force of two regiments (consisting of fifteen thousand military men, of whom 8,500 were combat forces, and fifteen thousand Japanese civilians seconded to the army)."[37] Not surprisingly, the Japanese were "acutely aware" of the limitations of their military strength. If they were to concentrate their meagre forces to oppose an Allied landing, they would have no troops in reserve to maintain public order, a prospect that deeply troubled Imamura, who remembered so clearly the outbreak of lawlessness that followed the Dutch surrender. As he said after the war, "I could not but preconceive the occurrence of such similar plunderings and violence when the Japanese army concentrated its forces in the event of an Allied landing on Java."[38]

Fearing an Allied attack from Australia and concerned about public order, Imamura believed he had no option but to intern all the Allied civilian nationals who remained at large.[39] In April 1942 the Japanese had interned about 2,000 Dutch officials. Now, some months later, they began to send (albeit over a twelve-month period) tens of thousands of European men, women, and children, including the 13,000 Dutch officials still at their desks, to civilian camps, where conditions were to prove deplorable and where acts of Japanese brutishness were to be more or less routine. At around the same time, Imamura informed Sukarno that Tokyo had decided to send a large number of Japanese civil servants to administer Java.[40] As the months went by, indirect rule gave way in some areas to a system of direct rule not unlike that prevailing in Taiwan and Korea. Boatloads of Japanese civilian contract employees (*gunzoku*) disembarked, to serve as administrators, policemen, teachers, engineers, judicial officers, interpreters, nurses and clerical workers. The Japanese even brought in errand boys and stable hands.[41] Many of the newcomers had earlier served in Taiwan.[42] For most Japanese, military and civilian alike, life on Java was enviably good. The war may have been raging in Burma, in China and in the South

Pacific. Java was stable, peaceful and, for most Japanese, comfortable. In the Japanese Army at this time a new saying came into vogue: *Biruma jigoku, Jawa tengoku* (Burma is hell, Java is paradise).

In more "normal" colonial circumstances, a system of rule based on Japanese practices on Taiwan might have worked well enough on Java, at least in the short term. Taiwan was ceded to Japan, not invaded, after Japan's brief and hugely successful war against China in Korea. Japanese rulers were authoritarian and paternalistic, but they reformed the school system, modernized agriculture and laid the basis for future Taiwan industrialization. These, however, were anything but normal circumstances. Japan was fighting by far the biggest war in its history against the immensely rich and powerful United States, as well as other enemies, not least in China and in Burma. It needed the resources of the East Indies and it was prepared to go to almost any lengths to obtain them, introducing, as time went on, a system of forced labour and onerous rice levies. As the war progressed, the Japanese were to exploit Java with a singularity and savagery that shocked the Javanese and the Sundanese. This exploitation coincided with a collapse in exports, brought on partly by the loss of traditional markets and partly by the depredations of the US Navy submarine fleet, which was soon sending scores of irreplaceable Japanese merchant ships to the bottom. Before long, Java's entire economy was disrupted. Not surprisingly, whatever honeymoon may have occurred between the Japanese and the Indonesians proved short-lived.

On the surface, wrote Kuroda Hidetoshi, who visited the island in late 1942, Java was indeed "a paradise in the occupied areas," with an abundance of low-priced goods.[43] But it was a paradise built on sand. The symptoms of inflation were already visible. A huge quantity of rice had to be imported from Malaya, where rice fields were being converted to the cultivation of rubber. The supply of clothing was about to run out, with little hope of imports from Japan. Japanese civilians were troublemakers, quick to get intoxicated and quick to quarrel. Japanese soldiers were worse, since they became arrogant. "Thus, the Greater East Asia Co-Prosperity Sphere was turning into a Co-Poverty Sphere and the hearts of the indigenous people were rapidly turning against Japan."[44]

Unlike the Dutch, who had sought to advance their economic interests under a cloak of orderly calm, the Japanese were to pursue a policy of mass mobilization, hoping to energize the population in the interests of the war effort. This was to have major consequences in the years ahead. The Japanese came to see that if they were to galvanize the masses of Java, they would have to use the best-known nationalist leaders.[45] Sutan Sjahrir, a prominent Minangkabau (West Sumatran), chose to remain aloof from the Japanese, whom he despised. But Sukarno and Hatta cooperated with them and were to use their positions skilfully to advance the nationalist cause, making radio broadcasts and addressing mass rallies, thereby building support down to the village level. This development was crucial and helped foster the nationalist impulse the Japanese had always been so eager to contain.

In November 1942, General Imamura, who had pushed so hard for Sukarno's return from Sumatra and who had favoured a "mild" policy, left Java. His new posting was in Rabaul, where he was to take command of the Eighth Area Army, with responsibility for two subordinate Japanese armies, one in the Solomons, the other in New Guinea; both were to suffer major reverses. The new commander-in-chief of the Sixteenth Army was Lieutenant General Harada Kumakichi. Harada, who was to hold that post for most of the Pacific War (November 1942 to April 1945), was an unsavoury officer who had spent many years in China. He had been the military attaché at the Japanese Embassy in China when, on 12 December 1937, during the six-week Rape of Nanking, Japanese naval aircraft attacked and sank the US Navy gunboat *Panay* as she lay at anchor in the Yangtze River, upstream from Nanking (Nanjing). Colonel Hashimoto Kingoro, an aggressive and insubordinate ultranationalist who had masterminded two coup attempts in Japan, had ordered his artillery and a squadron of Japanese Navy bombers temporarily under his command to attack the *Panay* and other neutral foreign vessels, threatening to summarily execute the reluctant Navy squadron commander unless he complied. At a press conference in Shanghai eight days later, Harada, a friend and associate of Hashimoto, sought to put all the blame on the Japanese Navy. Harada told the press he had been to Nanking and had made a personal investigation of the *Panay* incident. He cleared Japanese Army units of any fault. Tokyo later took full responsibility for the attack, but claimed it had been unintentional.

In Shanghai, according to Hallett Abend, a correspondent for the *New York Times*, Harada was known as a drunken, disreputable and mendacious officer who had connections with Shanghai's vice and drug rings "from which the Japanese army profited hugely." Time and again, Abend wrote, Harada called upon the American Consul-General in Shanghai "so drunk that he could scarcely articulate, and actually swayed on his heels when he tried to stand erect."[46] Some of his Japanese subordinates painted a different picture. According to Colonel Miyamoto, who was a senior staff officer at Sixteenth Army headquarters in the latter part of the war, Harada "had a long military career in China and was known as a China specialist [*Shina-ya*]. He had a firm belief that native people's cooperation was indispensable in fighting war."[47]

IV

Soeharto was aware, as he lay bedridden in Wuryantoro, that he could not stay with his relatives once he recovered. That, he felt, would impose "an extra burden to those who were already struggling to make ends meet."[48] Towards the end of 1942 he set out for Yogyakarta, hoping to find employment of some kind. In the event, there was no suitable work in the city for a twenty-one-year-old former KNIL sergeant. At a loose end, but with some money still in hand, he took a typing course in Pathok, a densely-settled district a short distance from the former Dutch governor's palace, by now the official residence of the Japanese governor, Brigadier General Yamanouchi. While here, Soeharto fell ill again. "It was really a trying time, teaching me to be patient, the kind of self-control that I would need later." The typing courses were held in a building opposite the police station. In November 1942, "jobless and at a loss," Soeharto saw an announcement that the Japanese were seeking Indonesian police recruits. "I hesitated for a moment," he recalled, afraid the Japanese would discover he had been in the KNIL. That, he thought, might put paid to any hopes of joining the police. Worse still, it might lead to imprisonment. "Would I be safe in full view of the Japanese? I decided to take the risk and joined."[49] At the police interview, Soeharto said nothing about the KNIL.

Soeharto's claim that he managed to keep the Japanese in the dark about his service in the KNIL would appear, at first sight, to strain credulity. After all, the Japanese followed strict procedures when it came to police recruitment in their colonies and overseas territories, based on the experience they had acquired in Taiwan. To gain admission to the police force, a candidate had to pass a background check, a physical examination, and an academic test.[50] In the normal course of events, Soeharto would have been required to furnish references—his uncle in Wuryantoro would have been one logical referee—and these would have been checked with some care, probably at that time by the Kenpeitai, an organization widely and justifiably feared, even within the Japanese army. But it seems that Soeharto did, indeed, pull off the deception. Many years later, Tsuchiya Kiso, the former Sixteenth Army intelligence officer, was asked whether the Japanese police had known of Soeharto's service in the KNIL. "In the beginning," he replied, "they didn't know."[51]

Having passed this first hurdle, Soeharto was given a medical examination, which, to his relief, failed to detect any trace of malaria. He was then instructed to sit for an entrance test. In Taiwan and Korea, where almost every candidate had a thorough knowledge of Japanese, the exam included questions on Japanese language, composition, history, geography, and arithmetic.[52] In Java, there was little emphasis on Japanese-language skill, at least for the time being, there being so few people who knew much Japanese. Soeharto passed the test and was signed on as a police recruit. He was issued a Japanese-style police uniform and a service cap that featured the Japanese flag. Shortly afterwards, he was sent on what was in all likelihood a rigorous three-month police training course. Here, if the Taiwan model is anything to go by, the recruits' courses would have included lessons in ethics, law, police administration, criminology, sanitation, fire prevention, martial arts and military drill, as well as courses in the Japanese language.[53]

Curiously enough, it is the drilling that Soeharto seemed to remember most vividly. "Before long," he wrote in his autobiography, "I started a three-month training course. It wasn't difficult, as most of the drilling practice consisted of marching, similar to what I'd already experienced during my training for sergeant. I even passed with the highest marks. And because I was rated number one, I was given the job of courier and told to learn Japanese."[54] This, it is worth noting, is at least the third time in nineteen pages that Soeharto tells his readers he ranked at the very top of his class in school or on some course. Nor was it the last such claim he was to make.

In Yogyakarta, Soeharto was to observe firsthand the dramatic changes that were taking place under the Japanese. As Benedict Anderson has noted, the Dutch had ruled in "a calm, businesslike, bourgeois style, buttressing their authority with the myths of white superiority, rationalism, technological prowess, and the historic world mission of

Western civilization."[55] With the defeat of the Dutch, those myths had been dethroned.

> In their place new myths appeared—myths of spiritual power, of the ascendant East, and of self-sacrificing valor. The style of Japanese rule derived not from the utilitarian calculus of tropical capitalism, but from the military and imperial traditions of Japan, and from the violent and radical thought of the Young Officers of the 1930s, not a few of whom served in the Sixteenth Army in Java. It was a profoundly theatrical style, compounded of pageantry, military discipline, public violence, and inexplicable silences.[56]

It could be argued that the Japanese were every bit as utilitarian and calculating as the Dutch when it came to exploiting the resources of Java, although the Japanese were to be let down by their own inefficiency, incompetence and callous disregard of others. Resources were what they wanted, and resources were what they intended to get. Nothing was to stand in the way of that.[57] But Anderson's observation eloquently captures the sense that a new power existed in the land, one which was not only dangerous and unpredictable, but which was shaking loose a society hitherto kept in a state of semi-somnolence by dour European administrators and a complacent native elite. It was a world in which opportunities presented themselves for young men like Soeharto, men who were from modest backgrounds but who were clever and quick to adjust to changing circumstances.

Soeharto may have stumbled by accident on the police job, which he was to hold for the best part of a year, rather than six months, as he later claimed.[58] But as a young man seeking preferment he could hardly have done better had he tried. He had not only moved, almost effortlessly and with only an eight-month break, from the service of one colonial power to that of another; he had landed a job that was to bring him to the attention of senior Japanese police officers in Central Java. They, in turn, would pass him on to important Japanese army officers, putting him back on the fast track to military advancement. Nor could his timing be faulted. In November 1942, the police force on Java was undergoing a thorough makeover.

V

What sort of institution was Soeharto entering when he joined the Japanese-run police force? What kind of powers had the police had in

Dutch times? What new powers had they acquired under the Japanese? What sort of behaviour would Soeharto have been exposed to during his time as a policeman?

Early in the twentieth century the Dutch had moved to centralize control over what had hitherto been a variety of local police forces. At the time of the Japanese invasion, however, the police force remained divided into three separate branches—the Urban Police (Stadspolitie), the Field Police (Veldpolitie), and the political police, or General Investigation Bureau (Algemene Recherche Dienst, ARD).[59] The Field Police and the ARD are of particular interest. Created in response to a general feeling of insecurity among Europeans, the Veldpolitie consisted of mobile units of twenty to sixty men, stationed in eighty-three centres in Java and Madura.[60] It was expected to act as a quick response unit, supervising the roads, combating the theft of cattle and field crops, and arresting important criminals, thereby avoiding any need for recourse to military assistance. It was unlike a typical police force in that it was heavily armed. The ARD was a successor to an earlier body, the Political Intelligence Bureau (Politieke Inlichtingendienst, PID), which, during its brief existence between 1916 and 1919, had monitored the activities of foreigners and local nationalists.[61] Still widely referred to in the 1920s and 1930s as the PID, the ARD was responsible for providing political intelligence to the colonial authorities; in the course of gathering that intelligence it was able to intimidate many who might otherwise have created difficulties for the authorities.[62]

The Sixteenth Army Military Administration, responsible not for a vast colonial possession but only for the "rump" of Java, had decided to abolish the three-branch police system and replace it with a unified police structure, one that was highly centralized and quite separate from the general administration.[63] These structural changes were accompanied by a dramatic shake-up in police personnel. In Dutch times, the police force had been top-heavy with European superintendents and inspectors, with a large number of Indonesian officers serving beneath them. After their lightning conquest of Java, the Japanese had disarmed and interned the Dutch police officers and put the restoration and maintenance of law and order in the hands of front-line army units, operating in conjunction with field units of the Kenpeitai. But, as has been noted, it was Japanese policy to keep most of the Dutch administrative system in place "to avoid provoking the natives by making drastic changes."[64] Indonesian policemen, even high-ranking officers who had been pro-Dutch, were allowed to stay on in their jobs. That meant, however, that for the first few months there were no senior civil police officers.[65]

In October 1942, a new central police department (Keimubu) in the Sixteenth Army Military Administration Headquarters took over the task of civilian policing from the Kenpeitai, although the "latent leadership" of that organization continued and Kenpeitai officers were to intervene often in matters of military administration throughout the Japanese occupation.[66] To fill the places formerly held by Dutchmen, the military authorities brought in a large number of senior Japanese civil police officers, most of them with long experience in Taiwan.[67] These changes were not only to have a profound impact on police practices in Java. They meant that senior Japanese police officers, some of whom Soeharto was to have close contact with for the best part of a year, arrived in Java with fixed ideas about the maintenance of law and order, based on their experiences both in Japan itself and in a tightly-run Japanese colony.

Although Soeharto makes no mention of the fact in his memoirs, he had joined an institution that was deeply unpopular.[68] In the pre-war period the police force had been widely feared and resented on Java, more so than the KNIL, which had tended to keep largely to itself. In the Princely Territory of Yogyakarta, the Dutch maintained a police presence in each of the six regencies (*kabupaten*), usually with two Dutch police officers stationed in an outlying regency capital, with Javanese policemen below them. When Selo Soemardjan was a member of the pre-war police force in Yogyakarta, village people tended to say that *Merdeka* (independence) meant there would no longer be a police force to make their life a misery.

> Because the Dutch police force in the countryside was very much feared. Because they were right there in the peaceful atmosphere of the villages and they have their motorcycles [with their revving engines]. That thing was already frightening. And when they came there must be something wrong. If the Dutch police came at that time there must be something wrong. It must be ... to arrest people. So [the people] were very much afraid. So much so that mothers said to their children, "Behave yourself! If you don't behave, I'll tell the Dutch police!".... So when people said "*Merdeka!*," [they thought] "No police!" They called it Veldpolice [*sic*]. Field Police.[69]

For the pre-war Indonesian nationalists, a still greater problem had come in the guise of the Dutch political police department, which maintained a network of informers and which monitored all significant political meetings, not least in Yogyakarta, a city in which the nationalist flame burned with considerable intensity.[70]

VI

The Japanese-run civilian police force was even more feared than its Dutch-run predecessor, and with good reason. One problem was that the Kenpeitai, which had controlled all police functions for the first seven months, was never completely divested of its powers in civilian policing on Java. In the period that Soeharto spent as a policeman, the Kenpeitai could, and did, intervene at will in civil police matters. As Tsuchiya Kiso put it, "The Kenpeitai in Java, being under the direct supervision of the Sixteenth Army, was always superior to the civil police, which was supervised by the military administration."[71]

Founded by the Meiji government in 1881 to police the army and to monitor growing unrest among those subject to conscription, the Kenpeitai had acquired immense powers, both in Japan itself and in its overseas possessions.[72] In occupied territories, the Kenpeitai "censored the press, monitored suspected subversives, eradicated networks of spies, and maintained an undercover surveillance of post offices, railway stations, hotels, schools, temples, and other public gathering places. For disobedient civilians, it meted out punishments that were swift and harsh."[73] On Java, the military police had three central responsibilities: the maintenance of peace and safety; the prevention of Allied espionage and propaganda; and the suppression of those people, "including natives," who had hostile feelings towards the Japanese.[74] Kenpeitai officers made widespread use of their power to make arrests, to conduct searches, and to confiscate property. They used torture as a matter of course. In nearly 300 cases they resorted to execution without trial, a practice which had the approval of Lieutenant General Harada.

When the Japanese occupied Yogyakarta, the local headquarters of the Dutch police force was in Jalan Bayan Kara. Within that office was the police Special Branch (*bagian politik*), or ARD, which kept detailed dossiers on nationalist politicians and anyone else whose activities were considered potentially inimical to Dutch interests. At a stroke, the Special Branch files fell into the hands of the Kenpeitai.[75] As part of that windfall, the Japanese are said to have taken over, almost intact, the ARD network of informers, which enabled them to roll up the underground Indonesian Communist Party (PKI) very fast.[76] According to Selo Soemardjan, who had, as noted above, been working for the Dutch Special Branch before the war and who was to continue in that office for a year or so under the Japanese, this did not necessarily spell danger for all those the Dutch had been watching given that many of them were willing, at least initially, to work with the Japanese. Nor was that all. The Kenpeitai took offices in the civilian police headquarters, and when they arrested people they took them to Bayan Kara. When they tortured people, however, they did so in secret at another location, apparently in Fort Vredeburg.

To assist it in its work, the Kenpeitai recruited and trained in Jakarta nearly 100 educated young Indonesians. When the training was over, groups of five to ten of these men were attached to each of the main Kenpeitai units on Java. They served as non-commissioned officers (*kenpeiho*) in the Imperial Japanese Army and wore Japanese uniforms and Japanese insignia. In the Kenpeitai office in Malang, for example, there were seven *kenpeiho*. In Yogyakarta, a city with many high schools, the number was said to be greater. Teramoto Masashi, a Kenpeitai sergeant, was in charge of giving additional training to those *kenpeiho* assigned to Solo. "They were," he recalled, "the most capable group of young men!"[77] Many *kenpeiho* were from the middle or lower levels of the *priyayi*. A number were Christians. One prominent ex-*kenpeiho* was Major General Parman Siswondo, who would go on to serve as commander of the Indonesian Military Police Corps (Corps Polisi Militer, CPM) between 1950 and 1953 and head of Indonesian Army intelligence from June 1962 until his death in 1965 at the hands of the September 30th Movement. He was attached to the Yogyakarta Kenpeitai office between 1943 and 1945.

Indonesian *kenpeiho* routinely witnessed Japanese military police torturers at work, given that the Japanese used *kenpeiho* as interpreters during the interrogation and torture of Indonesian prisoners. Nor were the Indonesian assistants simply passive observers of such torture. Many were enthusiastic, and indeed sadistic, participants. Major General Sukotjo Tjokroatmodjo, a former deputy head of the Military Police Corps (1974–78), was attached to an Indonesian military police unit in Probolinggo, East Java, late in 1945, during his cadet training. "I came away full of revulsion at what these ex-*kenpeiho* were doing," he said.[78] Their torturing was "abominable". "They were active [in torturing]! Oh yes! Oh, definitely! Yes!"[79]

Throughout Soeharto's time as a policeman in Yogyakarta, the commander of the local Kenpeitai *buntai* (detachment) was First Lieutenant (later Captain) Sato Heikichi.[80] According to many non-Japanese, Sato was

Military Police Corps (Kenpeitai), Jakarta and Yogyakarta, 1942-45

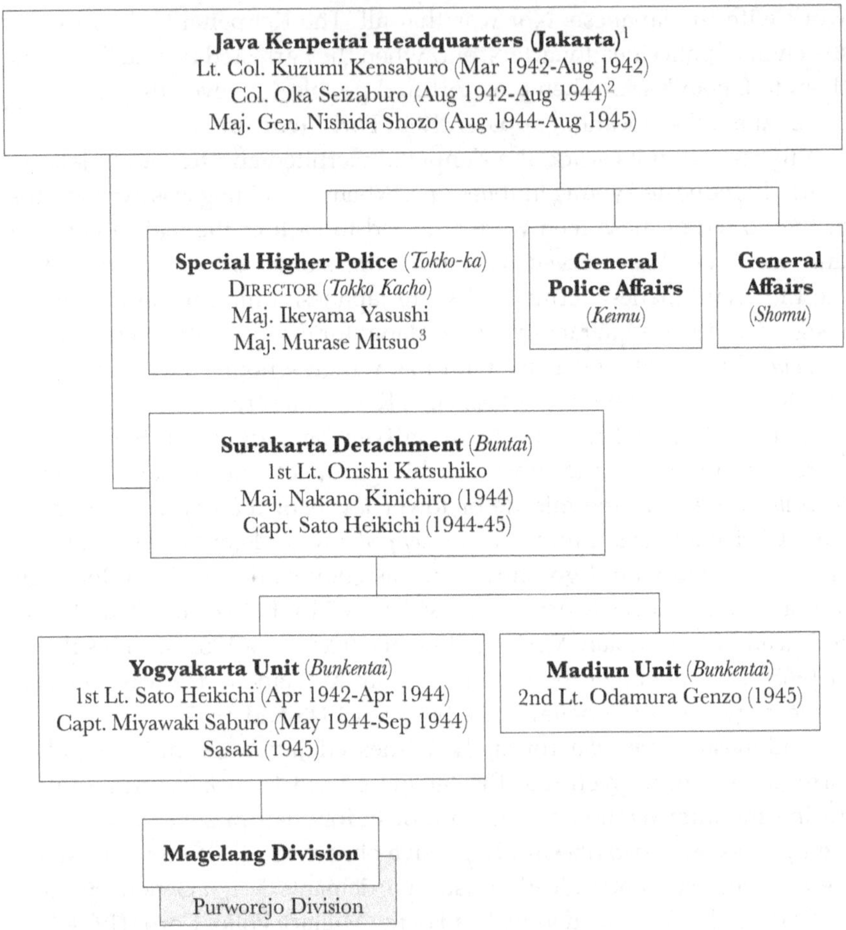

Source: Telephone interview, Nakano Kinichiro, 8 February 1999; interview, Teramoto Masashi, former *kenpei* in Solo, Inba-mura, Chiba Prefecture, 12 February 1999; written communication, former 2nd Lt. Taniguchi Taketsugu, November 1997; "Schema van de Plaatselijke K.P.T. Djokdjakarta, Opgemaakt Naar Gegevens van Kapt. Satoh [Sato], Batavia, 2-2-1947, de Inspecteur van Politie, M. A. Schouten", NANL, 2.10.14, inv. 5192; *Nihon Kenpei Seishi*, Tokyo, 1976, p. 1028; *The Encyclopedia of Indonesia in the Pacific War* and *Sedjarah TNI-AD Kodam VII/Diponegoro, Sirnaning Jakso katon Gapuraning Ratu*, p. 30.

1 The Java Kenpeitai consisted of 30 officers and 492 warrant officers and soldiers. *Nihon Kenpei Seishi*, p. 1028.

2 According to "Schema van de Plaatselijke K.P.T. Djokdjakarta."

3 In 1943, Maj. Gen. Harada gave Maj. Murase Mitsuo permission to execute suspects without trial.

a monster who did not hesitate to torture and kill his opponents. After the Japanese surrender, Sato was brought before a Dutch war-crimes tribunal and charged with "systematic terror" and the "torture of citizens."[81] He was found guilty and hanged in 1948. It is difficult to believe that Soeharto was unaware of Sato's practices, although there was, of course, nothing Soeharto could have done about them. In Yogyakarta, as Selo Soemardjan observed, "everybody was afraid of the Kenpeitai."[82] On one occasion, a subdistrict head was taken in for questioning at the Kenpeitai headquarters in Yogyakarta. "And they were cruel," Selo Soemardjan, one of the man's colleagues, recalled. "That's what he said. They were cruel. And I could believe it because he was terribly afraid. Terribly afraid to think back on the Kenpeitai."[83] On another occasion, a subdistrict head from East Java was taken to Jakarta and accused of spying for the Dutch. From time to time, he was beaten. But that was not the worst of it. For two months he was kept naked and cross-legged on a tiled floor, with his face up against a wall, amid the stench of his own urine and faeces.[84] Brutality of this kind generated intense hatred towards the Japanese forces. According to Tsuchiya Kiso, a former head of the Yogyakarta branch of Beppan, the Sixteenth Army's special intelligence section, and the man who would recruit Soeharto into the Japanese-sponsored volunteer army in 1943, "The reason why the Kenpeitai was feared like a demon [*akuma*] by local people was, I believe, because it abused its powers."[85]

Within the Kenpeitai there was a Special Higher Police (Tokko-ka) section, sometimes known as the "thought control" police. On Java, this body had a daunting list of responsibilities. As well as keeping watch over the local population and their attitude towards the Japanese Military Administration, it sought to learn all it could about the Indonesian Communist Party, the Indonesian independence movement, "subversive movements" within Islamic societies and religious organizations, and potential disturbances to public peace.[86] The Tokko-ka paid particular attention to nationalist leaders such as Sukarno and Hatta. It also sought information on the political sympathies of the traditional rulers of Central Java, censored letters and controlled broadcasting. The best and brightest of the young Indonesian *kenpeiho* were attached to the Tokko-ka.[87]

VII

A second reason why the Japanese-run civilian police force was much feared had to do with its ethos and practices. Established in the late 1800s,

Japan's unified national police system had been likened by its founder, Kawaji Toshiyoshi, to a family "with the government as parents, the people as children, and the police as nursemaid."[88] Not surprisingly, the attitude of civilian police officials towards the people had always been paternalistic. The police were concerned, it is true, about the education and welfare of the people, but they also harboured "feelings of superiority and authority, with the expectation of obedience and submission."[89] Japanese police believed that compliance could be obtained by force, and they had become known very early for their arrogance and condescension towards the public.[90] The Japanese civilian police were equipped with pervasive powers and were not shy about using torture. Nor did the police concern themselves solely with routine law-and-order matters. At the apex of the civilian police structure was the Special Higher Police (Tokubetsu Koto Keisatsu, or Tokko) section, which had functions broadly similar to those enjoyed by the Tokko division within the Kenpeitai.[91] Inspired partly by the police and prison systems in nineteenth-century France but partly, too, by the administrative practices of the British colonial police in East Asia, the Tokko had carved out a place in Japan as the most important and prestigious branch of the police force, with sweeping powers over political organizations, public meetings and newspaper censorship.[92]

Japanese civil police officers had, if anything, become even more arrogant and authoritarian when they found themselves dealing with non-Japanese people. On Taiwan, which was seen in Tokyo as a model for policing in Japanese colonies and occupied territories, the police force was "highly centralized and widely dispersed in the countryside, with awesome authority to manage and to intervene in the life of the Chinese."[93] On Taiwan, recalled Koizumi Saburo, a former police inspector (*keibu*) who had served on the island before his appointment as chief of the Special Higher Police section in Yogyakarta, the police were almighty and did everything.[94]

It was hardly surprising, then, that the Japanese civil police officers who came to Java brought with them not just the paternalistic assumptions that were common among all Japanese police officers, but also the top-down approach of a tightly-run Japanese colony. "We thought sending policemen from Japanese-occupied Taiwan was a good idea because they were experienced in dealing with people from other cultures," said Colonel Miyamoto. "But in hindsight, it would have been better if we had chosen people who were new and fresh. Those policemen from Taiwan were already full of preconceptions about the people under Japan's colonial rule. They had learned to look down on the natives before they were posted to Java. Had they not been from Taiwan, the consequences of Japanese occupation in Java could have been different, could have been better."[95]

The Japanese wasted little time in putting their distinctive—and frequently harsh—stamp on civil police practices in Java. They took over the Dutch colonial police school at Sukabumi and established, in each residency, a permanent course for the training of police personnel.[96] They conducted regular propaganda courses to imbue those already in the service "with the Greater East Asia ideals" and to impress on them the might of Japanese power. "As a result of this propaganda," a post-war Dutch report claimed,

> the police force soon changed in outlook and behaviour. The Japanese system of corporal maltreatment, administered on the spot or at the police station, for the settlement of a minor infraction and thereby sidestepping further legal procedure, was introduced. Maltreatment as a punishment for insignificant offences could be witnessed daily in the streets. The legally powerless position of the population was thereby clearly demonstrated.... Moral standards of the police force were seriously shaken by this training. Examples set by the Kempei in the maltreatment of defenceless suspects were emulated by a certain section of the Indonesian Police Force.[97]

Nor was the civilian police force lacking in resources. As well as its uniformed and plainclothes officers, the Tokko section of the civilian police force had a Special Police Strike Force (Tokubetsu Keisatsutai) with one company in each regency on Java and under the command of the regency police chief.[98] Each company had between 60 and 150 personnel, with more in the major cities. Well-trained and well-equipped, with carbines, machine-guns, and armoured vehicles, these units were designed to respond to any major threat to security, including demonstrations, riots and armed robbery.[99] They also had a combat capacity.[100] Beyond this, senior police officers controlled a 1.3-million-strong Civil Defence Corps (Keibodan), which was in effect an auxiliary police force with a presence in every village and municipality. The Keibodan was designed to counter enemy espionage activities, to serve as an air and coast watch, and to investigate robberies and other crimes.

The Japanese may have abolished the three-branch police system operated by the Dutch, but the abolition was more apparent than real. In the blink of an eye, the powers and responsibilities of those three branches had been replicated, and vastly expanded, in the Japanese-run central police department, especially in its Tokko section, with its sweeping powers of surveillance and its Special Police Strike Force.

In short, Soeharto was entering a world in which discipline was rigid, brutality a fact of life, paternalism taken for granted and police influence all pervasive.

VIII

Not long after he began his career as a policeman, Soeharto was "assigned as assistant [*toban*] to the Japanese police chief" in Yogyakarta,[101] serving, it has been suggested, "almost like a secretary" to him.[102] With obvious pride and probably no exaggeration, Soeharto recalled that his new boss had informed him his "entrance test score and attitude had been rated the best among all applicants."[103] In Yogyakarta at that time there were, in fact, two Japanese civil police "chiefs," operating at different levels. One of them, Lieutenant Colonel Takeoka Kenji, a "mild-mannered" man who had once been a senior official in the Japanese Internal Affairs Ministry, was the head of the police department (*keisatsu bucho*) of the entire Princely Territory of Yogyakarta.[104] As such, he was one of three important officers immediately under General Yamanouchi, a seasoned bureaucrat who had once governed a Japanese prefecture. The other police chief, one of about ten police station commanders (*keisatsu shocho*) under Takeoka, was Superintendent (Keishi) Okamoto Juko, who was responsible for police matters within the city of Yogyakarta itself.[105]

Soeharto provides no details about the office in which he worked. Nor does he name the man for whom he worked. It seems clear, however, that he served as an assistant to Okamoto, an experienced and deeply serious man who, from his headquarters in central Yogyakarta, presided with great watchfulness over the affairs of numerous police substations.[106] A native of Okayama Prefecture in southwest Honshu, Okamoto had come to Java directly from Taiwan, as had so many of his Japanese police colleagues. He was nearly fifty years old, which meant that he was almost two and a half times Soeharto's age, and he seems to have been impressed by his young Javanese assistant, who was polite and clever and quick to learn.[107]

Soeharto would have learned much from his time as an assistant to such a senior police officer. He would have gained an insight into everyday Japanese police practices, which were not only far-reaching but closely supervised, with swift disciplinary action taken against those guilty of conduct "damaging police honor and public confidence in the police."[108] He would have observed the arrogance and almost casual brutality of Japanese police officers, who beat and tortured suspects as a matter of course. "In a job like that," George Orwell wrote about his time as subdivisional police officer of Moulmein, Lower Burma, in the 1920s, "you see the dirty work of Empire at close quarters."[109] At the same time, Soeharto would have learned something about the seamier aspects of local society and come to know a good deal about those who made their living on the wrong side of the law. Nor could he have avoided learning something of the practices of the Kenpeitai, an organization that outdid the civil police when it came to using torture to extract information. He would no doubt have watched with some interest the bureaucratic struggles between the Kenpeitai and the civil police, struggles in which the military police always held the upper hand. By this time, crime rates had generally come down. Serious, violent crimes were rare. However, as economic conditions deteriorated and economic controls were tightened, theft and robbery were becoming more frequent.[110]

In later years, Soeharto appeared to suggest that he had attained the rank of assistant police inspector (*keibuho*) under the Japanese. This claim, which has been accepted and repeated by many writers, is so extraordinary that it raises serious questions about his credibility or memory.[111] *Keibuho* was the fourth rank up the promotional ladder, after policeman (*junsa*), senior policeman (*junsacho*) and police sergeant (*junsabucho*).[112] In Japan, assistant inspector was a rank open only to a police officer with many years' experience or to a young man with a university degree, almost invariably from Tokyo Imperial University.[113] In Java, it was open to an incumbent policeman between the ages of twenty-five and thirty-five with at least secondary education and four years' experience if he was recommended by the resident or the head of a principality; such policemen needed to pass an entrance examination and complete an eighteen-month course at the Java Police School in Sukabumi. Junior middle school graduates between the ages of twenty and twenty-five could also be accepted to the course after passing an examination.[114] *Keibuho* were categorized as middle ranking public servants, with monthly salaries ranging from 70 to 270 guilders for grade one and from 50 to 180 guilders for grade two.[115] In short, *keibuho* was not a rank that would have been lightly awarded to a twenty-one-year-old Javanese who had never even started, let alone finished, junior high school, and who had only limited work experience. It is true that one or two Indonesian policemen did become assistant inspectors under the Japanese, but they were educated men, usually well into their thirties or forties, who had held responsible positions in the Dutch colonial police force. One such man was Assistant Inspector Soedarsono, who would, within three years, become Soeharto's immediate superior in the post-war Indonesian army; he served as a member of the Special Higher Police (Tokko) section in Yogyakarta.[116]

There are strong grounds for believing that Soeharto did not reach the rank of assistant inspector, and his apparent claim that he did has been greeted with disbelief and derision by former Kenpeitai and Japanese civilian police officers who served in Java. According to Taniguchi Taketsugu, the former chief of the Bogor Kenpeitai, it is "almost unthinkable … hard to imagine" that an Indonesian in his early twenties could have achieved such a rank.[117] An identical view is expressed by Teramoto Masashi, the former Military Police sergeant in Solo. "I don't recall any Indonesian in the number-two position in the Yogya police being given the title of *keibuho* in the Japanese sense of the term," he said. "It is unthinkable."[118] Former Inspector Koizumi is almost equally sceptical. As he put it, "I don't think there were very many Indonesian *keibuho* in those days."[119]

Tsuchiya Kiso, the intelligence officer who went on to recruit Soeharto into the volunteer defence force, did not recall what police rank Soeharto held at that time. But he shared the scepticism of his former colleagues. "I think assistant inspector is pretty high up the ladder," Tsuchiya noted. "Even a Japanese has to start off as a policeman before becoming a senior policeman and then assistant inspector. If he really were an assistant inspector, he would have been the youngest. There are few twenty-year-old *keibuho* in the Japanese police force. None! If you are twenty, you can't be anything more than a policeman."[120] All the same, Tsuchiya was unwilling to rule out the possibility that Soeharto may have held such rank. Soeharto, "because he was very capable," had been appointed deputy director (*fukukan*) very quickly, and it was not impossible that he had been given the rank of *keibuho*. Although it was "pretty unlikely" that a man of Soeharto's age was made an assistant inspector, his Japanese superior "had the rank of superintendent, a rank above inspector. So it is possible that [Soeharto] was *keibuho*. I suspect his boss may have wanted his secretary to be not just a policeman, so it is possible he made him *keibuho* and gave him this exceptional promotion."

Police Organization, Jakarta and Yogyakarta 1942-45

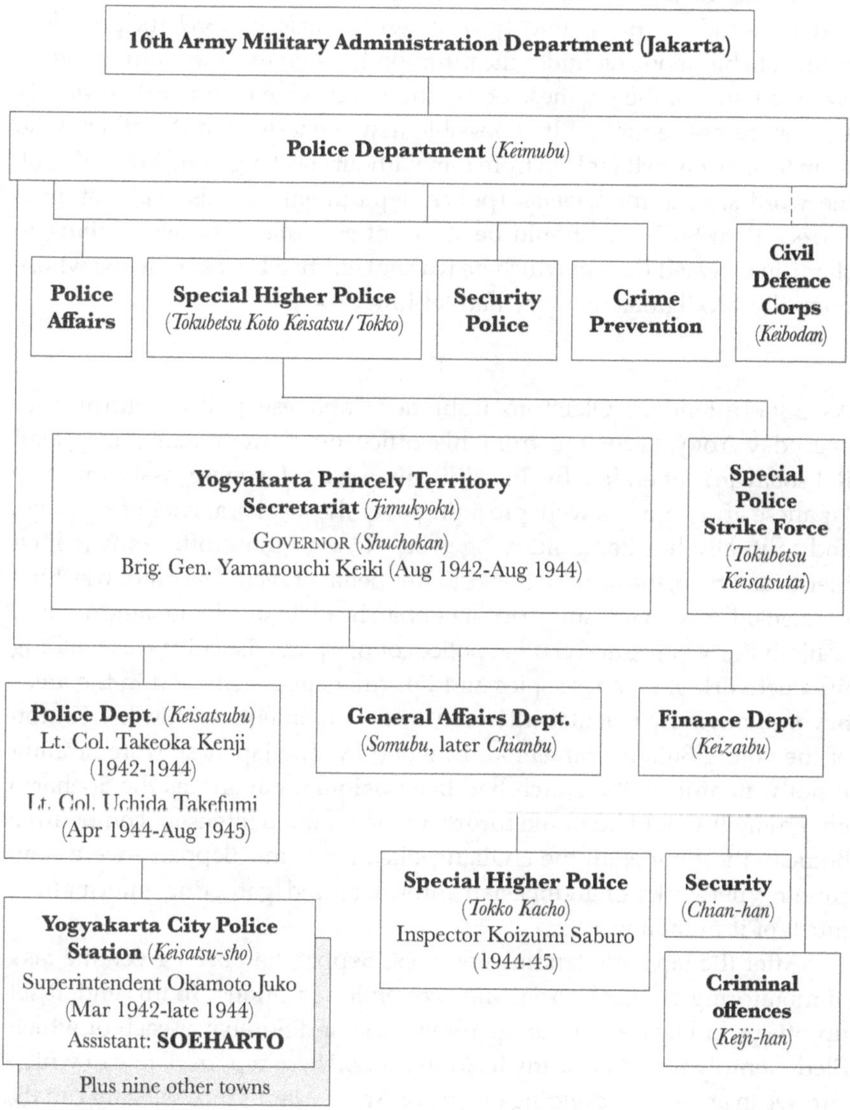

Sources: Interview, Lt. Col. Uchida Takefumi, 12 February 1999; interview, Koizumi Saburo, 13 June 1999; written communication, Taniguchi Taketsugu, November 1997; Waseda Daigaku Okuma Kinen Shakaikagaku Kenkyujo, *Indonesia niokeru nihongunsei no kenkyu*, Tokyo, 1959, pp. 122-123, p. 138, p. 146, pp. 177-178, and M. P. van Bruggen and R. S. Wassing, *Djokja en Solo: Beeld van de Vorstensteden*. Purmerend: Asia Maior, 1998, p. 68.

As it happens, Soeharto's critics may have judged him unfairly on this point. Soeharto may not have intended to claim that he held such a rank under the Japanese. A close reading of the relevant material suggests that a misunderstanding may have arisen, because, by 1969, the president seemed to be labouring under the misapprehension that the word "*keibuho*" was the name of the Japanese occupation police force, rather than simply a Japanese police rank.[121] It is possible that Soeharto, and the others who seem to have taken their lead from him without checking, somehow mistook the word *keibuho* for *keimubu* (police department). If this explanation is correct, then Soeharto should be seen not as a man who was willing to claim an elevated rank to which he was not entitled but as someone whose normally prodigious memory had let him down.

IX

As Superintendent Okamoto tightened Japanese police control over everyday Yogyakarta life from his office on Kantoorlaan (now Jalan Reksobayan), attended by his diligent young Javanese assistant, two Japanese army officers were presiding over the local branches of separate, and mutually hostile, military agencies. One of those officers was First Lieutenant Sato, the head of the local Kenpeitai branch. The other was First Lieutenant Tsuchiya Kiso, the local Beppan head. In much the same manner as his military police and civilian police counterparts, Tsuchiya was building up a network of Javanese spies and informers in the city and in the areas beyond, paying particular attention to developments within the Kraton of the young Sultan, Hamengku Buwono IX. The Japanese were nothing if not watchful, as the Dutch had been before them and as the Soeharto government would be in the future. On Java, three intensely competitive bodies—the Kenpeitai, the civilian police force and Beppan—were now running networks of Indonesian informers and gathering information, much of it mundane.

After the Japanese landings on Java, Beppan had been given the task of monitoring political, social and economic conditions. To this end, it set up offices in Jakarta, Bandung, Yogyakarta and Surabaya, each of which filed monthly reports to army headquarters. These reports, a few of which survive in an archive building on one of Amsterdam's most elegant canals, are written in a telegraphic style that is sometimes irritatingly oblique.[122] But they provide a revealing—and surprisingly frank—picture of conditions in the turbulent world of occupied Java at a time when Soeharto was a member of the Japanese-run police force. In April 1943, a year into the occupation, Beppan had mixed news for Sixteenth Army headquarters. Some developments were positive. "Under the leadership of the Japanese," the Bandung office reported, "progress is noticeable daily, and there is cause for satisfaction in the fact that they [Indonesians] now regard the Dutch rule in NEI as a thing of the past."[123] Sukarno was playing an increasingly important role and had become "head man in control of concentration and movements and more confidence is being placed in him." But there was bad news, too. The "lower classes" were worried about the high cost of living. The drivers of *becaks* (pedicabs) and horse-drawn vehicles were complaining of the difficulty of earning their livelihood now that all Dutch citizens had been interned. Some Muslims were "still not burying their dead with the top pointing to Tokyo and the bottom to Mecca."[124] "Lower-class police officials" were complaining that they would have to be promoted to compensate for recent pay cuts. Corrupt practices were creeping in. Some of the police were "abusing their powers and doing unfair things."

There were problems, too, with the ethnic Chinese. According to Beppan, the Chinese were jealous of the progress made in all ways by the Indonesians and did not like being treated as enemy aliens. "The Indonesians are swaggering about saying they are the spearhead of the Japanese, but [the Chinese are saying] we Chinese are nearer to the Japanese in speech and everything.... They do not like their children to be educated with Indonesian children ..." For their part, the Europeans and Eurasians remained deeply hostile towards the Japanese. Dutch women in the internment camps had been having great difficulty getting food and had been spreading anti-Japanese propaganda. Eurasian women were saying that "when they have no money to buy food they will be forced to sacrifice their chastity." Many Eurasians were insulting the Japanese flag. "It is regretted," Beppan reported sombrely, "that a Japanese flag was found being used in the W.C. of a Eurasian house [that was] searched.... The practice of calling Japanese 'monkeys' has sprung up lately." Eurasians were saying that there was "no need to hoist the Japanese flag as the Japanese Occupation of Java will not last forever and they will be defeated ..." With no reliable information in the strictly censored newspapers, rumours gained a life of their own, many of them conveying a sense that the Japanese war effort was in trouble. Beppan noted these rumours carefully: there was an acute shortage of materials in Japan; the defeat of the Japanese army was imminent; the British and Americans would certainly attack; the German army had been defeated [presumably at Stalingrad, in February]; the Japanese army has been "defeated" in Burma.[125]

On 29 April 1943, Soeharto would have joined Japanese and Indonesian police officers in celebrations marking the forty-second birthday of Emperor Hirohito. But the event does not seem to have greatly moved those living in the cities and towns of Java, at least in West Java. "The customary celebrations of the Emperor's birthday were carried out, and were everywhere on a reduced scale, the only people showing any great enthusiasm being villagers," the Bandung office noted. The report added, almost in passing, what is probably one of the earliest surviving references to the wartime practice of enforced prostitution (sexual slavery) carried out by both the Imperial Army and the Imperial Navy, under which more than 100,000 "comfort women" were sent to officially approved brothels across Asia. "April 29: Emperor's Birthday. Great congratulation ceremony. Meeting to urge complete destruction of England and America. Show put on by native women, comforts [*sic*] girls of the Army, Hospital and Army comforts girls."[126]

Fourteen months after the Dutch surrender, life on Java was harsh and getting harsher. Those foolish enough to complain could be picked up, either by the Kenpeitai or the civilian police. They could be beaten or tortured. Some were killed. Not surprisingly, resentment deepened. "From day to day there was a growing restlessness among the people," recalled Lieutenant General T.B. Simatupang, a former KNIL junior officer who spent much of the Japanese occupation as an employee of the Customs Department in Bandung.[127] This restlessness gave rise to the emergence of groups which did not have any strict organization or clear goals, but which often had contact with one another. "Practically all these groups had the same sense of nationalism, democracy and social justice, as did the movement for Indonesian independence. Slowly, this vague awareness of nationalism, democracy and social justice was combined with a militant factor. Everybody at schools, in offices and in villages was ordered to practise marching and fighting using sharpened bamboo sticks. The Japanese slapped the people here and there. Thus, a militant spirit began to take root among the people, especially among the younger generation." This process, Simatupang wrote, came to a head with the creation of a Japanese-sponsored defence force on Java.

Soeharto was deeply embedded in the police force at this time, perhaps by now having no choice in the matter. But his life would soon take a sudden—and decisive—new turn. Worried that they had too few troops on Java, the Japanese had begun to toy with the idea of setting up an armed volunteer force. This would consist entirely of Indonesians but with a handful of Japanese assigned to each 500-man battalion to help with training and logistics.

When the time came Soeharto would apply for selection as an officer cadet.

TOP LEFT: Field Marshal Terauchi Hisaichi, whose Southern Army swept across Southeast Asia in 1941-42.

TOP RIGHT: General Imamura Hitoshi. A veteran of Japan's long war in China, he put 55,000 combat-hardened troops ashore on Java, overwhelming Allied forces. (*Public domain/Australian War Memorial*)

ABOVE: On 19 February 1942, ten days before their landing on Java, the Japanese sent nearly 250 fighters and bombers to attack Darwin in northern Australia. One aim was to isolate Allied forces in Java and "prevent another Dunkirk." In this view from a Japanese plane, two ships burn furiously. (*Senshi Sosho 26*)

TOP: *Banzai!* Japanese troops celebrate their landing at Merak, West Java, on 1 March 1942.

MIDDLE: Japanese haul a truck ashore at Kragan, East Java. (*Kaneko Tomokazu archive*)

BOTTOM: Lt. Gen. Hein ter Poorten, the Dutch Commander-in-Chief, surrenders to the Japanese at Kalijati, West Java, 9 March 1942.

ABOVE: Japanese troops enter Jakarta in March 1942. In many parts of the Netherlands East Indies, the Japanese were welcomed as liberators, at least initially. Elsewhere in Southeast Asia they were received by sullen or silent crowds. (*Spaarnestad SFA 001003164*)

RIGHT: Japanese sentry guards a partly damaged oil storage depot at Tarakan in East Kalimantan. (*Senshi Sosho 26*)

ABOVE: Sukarno and Hatta greet the Japanese Prime Minister, Lt. Gen. Tojo Hideki, on his arrival in Jakarta in mid-1943. (*Djawa Baroe*)

LEFT: Former First Lt. Tsuchiya Kiso, right, who recruited Soeharto for the 37,500-man Java Volunteer Defence Force (Peta) in 1943, seen here in 1972 with his wartime colleague, former First Lt. Yanagawa Motoshige, who settled in Jakarta after the war. (*Tsuchiya Kiso archive*)

ABOVE: Yanagawa (seated) interviews an Indonesian at the Peta training centre in Bogor, October 1943. Lt. Gen. Harada Kumakichi, the Java commander, stands to Yanagawa's right. Capt. Maruzaki Yoshio is far right. "General Harada loved Peta... and trusted it, too." Some Japanese did not trust it. *(Pradjoerit)*

BELOW: Peta officer cadets at bayonet drill. The Japanese gave the Indonesians intensive small-unit training. This proved invaluable during the 1945-49 independence war against the Dutch. (*Djawa Baroe*)

ABOVE: Peta officer cadets present arms. "Training took place even in heavy rain. Weapons and clothes got soaked. Our lips turned purple. We could not stop trembling. My army sword got rusted through." (*Djawa Baroe*)

ABOVE: "I was still young, just a Japanese-trained officer, you see. You know how Japanese training is.... I hit him. I punished him.... I hit him black and blue." Bashed by the Japanese, some Peta officers became bashers themselves. One who readily admitted as much was Gen. Soemitro, an able, self-confident officer widely seen in the early 1970s as the second most powerful man in Indonesia, after Soeharto. (*Dudi Sudibyo*)

ABOVE: President Soeharto shares a joke with Vice President Adam Malik and Gen. Surono Reksodimedjo in 1982. While serving as Army Chief of Staff, Surono, a *karate-do* enthusiast, struck a captain who swerved in front of his staff car. Soeharto himself could be tough on his men. (*Joe Manguno*).

TOP: Maj. Gen. Moersjid: "We caught our first glimpse of the possibility that Indonesia would some day be independent." (*David Jenkins*)

MIDDLE: Lt. Gen. Kemal Idris, who trained under Yanagawa for five months, seen here in Jakarta in 1969. "He was very rough. But I liked him." (*David Jenkins*)

BOTTOM: Prof. K. P. H. Haryasudirja, a Yogyakarta prince who commanded one of Soeharto's battalions in 1949. In his view, Japan's creation of a volunteer defence force marked, if not the beginning of any nationalist feelings on Soeharto's part, then at least a new way of looking at the world. (*David Jenkins*)

ABOVE: In 1959, Col. Soeharto, left, commander of the Central Java military region, shakes hands with his deputy, Lt. Col. Pranoto Reksosamodra, whom he had befriended on a 1943 Peta course. Pranoto replaced Soeharto months later after reporting him for smuggling. On coming to power, Soeharto jailed Pranoto for 15 years, alleging he was left-wing. There was no trial. (*Catatan Jenderal Pranoto Reksosamodra/Public domain*)

RIGHT: Former Kenpeitai sergeant Teramoto Masashi, saw Soeharto in Solo. "I wasn't particularly impressed with him. I was astounded ... to learn that he had become President." (*Yamaoka Yasuko*).

FAR RIGHT: Kaneko Tomokazu, a civilian propagandist in wartime Java, met Soeharto during his 1968 visit to Tokyo. "He was extremely happy to come to Japan after all those experiences as a Peta officer and so on." (*David Jenkins*)

LEFT: Sukarno leads Indonesian dignitaries in a rousing cry of "*Banzai!*" at the former Dutch Governor General's palace in Jakarta in 1944. Sukarno would hold sway at the palace himself between 1945-65. (*Spaarnestad SFA 002022132*)

BELOW: Dutch propaganda leaflet shows dead and gravely undernourished Indonesian auxiliary soldiers (*heiho*) or forced labourers (*romusha*) in West New Guinea late in the war. Some had been bayoneted by the Japanese, others killed in Allied bombing raids. On Numfoor, an island off the north coast of West New Guinea, starving Japanese troops resorted to cannibalism. (*John Scott archive*)

Beriboe2 kawan saudara sebangsa jang tertipoe djadi Heiho atau Romusha soedah diangkat ketempat2 jang djaoeh oentoek kerdja boeat si Djepang. Banjaklah orang telah dikoeboer, djaoeh dari tanah air.

Adalah jang ikoet tenggelam dalam kapal2 Djepang; ada djoega jang mati oleh bom selagi kerdja dilapang2 penerbangan tempat2 kapal dibangoenkan d.l.l. jang digoenakan oleh Djepang: lain lagi mati karena sakit, sebab obat2 doktor tak diberikan oleh si Kate.

Gambar2 ini mempertoendjoekkan bagaimana sisa dari kawan2 saudara dianiajanja. Kebanjakannja mati karena lapar, sebab si Djepang tida memberi tjoekoep makanan pada mereka itoe. Lain2nja lagi, mati dibajonet oleh si Kate.

Hampir semoea jang masih hidoep, kedapat lemah sekali karena lapar dan sakit, sehingga ketika tentara Serikat datang boeat menolong, mereka tida koeat berdiri lagi.

ABOVE LEFT: Col. Miyamoto Shizuo at his Tokyo home in 1999. As the 16th Army staff officer for supply, he sent Indonesian forced labourers to the notorious Thai-Burma "death railway" and other projects. Later, as operations officer, he armed, but came to distrust, the Indonesian volunteer army. (*David Jenkins*)

ABOVE RIGHT: "I shipped them to their deaths. Yes, yes, yes, yes, I am the one." In a photograph taken near Bogor in 1944, Sukarno exhorts Indonesian *romusha* to work harder. (*Spaarnestad SFA 001021676*)

BELOW: A line of *romusha*, pressed into debilitating servitude by the Japanese, carry earth for a project on the Brantas River in East Java. Tens of thousands of *romusha* died. (*Djawa Baroe*)

ABOVE: Officers of the 16th Army gather for a group portrait on the steps of the palace in Jakarta in late 1944. Maj. Gen. Yamamoto was both 16th Army Chief of Staff under Lt. Gen. Harada and Head of the Military Administration on Java. Capt. Maruzaki presided over the birth of Peta, the forerunner of the Indonesian Army. Lieut. Tsuchiya recruited the first 230 officer cadets from Central Java and went on to establish and train three 500-man Peta battalions on Bali. *(Tsuchiya Kiso archive)*

ABOVE: The Japanese Military Administration on Java issued its own stamps. (*Ken Ward archive*)

RIGHT: As well as setting up Peta, the 16th Army sent a handful of Indonesians to Japan for higher military training. One of them was Gen. Yoga Sugama, who attended the Imperial Military Academy outside Tokyo. A blunt, flamboyant, high-living intelligence officer, Yoga would become a key pillar of Soeharto's New Order government. (*Sinar Harapan*)

ABOVE: Lt. Gen. Harada at a 1943 lunch with Sukarno, right, and his wife, Fatmawati. Harada had been active in pre-war Shanghai, where he was remembered as a "drunken, disreputable and mendacious officer." He was hanged in Singapore in 1947 for war crimes committed in Java. (*Boekoe peringatan*)

ABOVE: Fifty-five Indonesian soldiers who revolted against the Japanese at Blitar in February 1945 were brought before a Japanese military court in Jakarta in June that year. All were convicted. At least five were beheaded. The Japanese sent Soeharto, a trusted company commander, to retrain the rump of the Peta Blitar battalion. (*Ipphos*) INSET: Suprijadi, who led the Blitar revolt. "A strange person, very suggestible."

ABOVE: Members of the Yogyakarta Kenpeitai detachment. Widely feared enforcers of Japanese rule, the Kenpeitai executed 300 people in Java and intervened at will in civilian police affairs. Soeharto, who served in both the police force and Peta, claimed the Kenpeitai suspected him of disloyalty. *NIOD 161765*)

ABOVE: Rear Adm. Maeda Tadashi, seated, left, the Japanese Navy liaison officer in Jakarta, receives an Indonesian guest at his home. In the early hours of 17 August 1945, Maeda allowed Sukarno and Hatta to use his house to draft a Proclamation of Independence. (*Public domain*)

RIGHT: Adm. Maeda's house, the residence of British ambassadors for many years, is now a museum. (*David Jenkins*)

ABOVE: At 10am on 17 August 1945 Sukarno proclaims Indonesian independence. The 16th Army, which had strongly opposed such a move only eight hours earlier, did not intervene. (*Frans Mendur, Ipphos*)

ABOVE: President Soeharto and the author, Rawamangun golf course, Jakarta, 1970. Soeharto played golf several times a week. At weekends, he liked to relax at his cattle ranch in the hills behind Bogor. (*Burt Glinn*)

10

An armed force conjured out of nothing

The Japanese had had much to celebrate in the days after the Sixteenth Army landed in Java in March 1942. The island at the heart of the Dutch East Indies had fallen into their hands after a land campaign lasting a little more than a week. Elsewhere, the forces of the Imperial Army and the Imperial Navy were carrying all before them, from the Andaman Islands in the Bay of Bengal to the Solomon Islands in the South Pacific. But success in war is often fleeting, and by mid-1942 the war was starting to go badly for Japan. An almost unbroken string of Japanese military triumphs had come to an abrupt halt at the Battle of Midway in early June, almost six months to the day after the opening strike against Pearl Harbor and only three months after the Japanese landings in Java. At Midway, the Imperial Navy lost four of its largest aircraft carriers in one day; the US Navy lost only one. It was a blow from which the Japanese would never recover.

As 1942 wore on, the Japanese Southern Army, which had primary responsibility for Burma, Malaya, Sumatra, Java, British North Borneo and the Philippines, and which maintained garrison armies in French Indochina and Thailand, found itself increasingly cut off from the Japanese home islands as a result of US submarine attacks on Japanese merchant shipping. As a result, Java assumed even greater importance as a supply base, for food, raw materials and manpower.[1] But as the Japanese were well aware, Java was itself vulnerable. During the six months he spent on Java, General Imamura was, as we have seen, "keenly expecting" an Allied attack on Java from bases in Australia. And as he knew only too well, his "ten battalions of aged soldiers" would be quite insufficient in the event of any such attack.[2] Those concerns remained after Imamura was transferred to Rabaul.

One solution to the manpower problem was to create an indigenous army of some kind, using either conscripts or volunteers, as the Japanese had done when they founded the Indian National Army and the Burma Independence Army at the end of 1941.[3] But the Japanese were not sure that Indonesians were physically or temperamentally suited to military service. In an attempt to resolve the matter, they turned, in November 1942, to Beppan, the special intelligence section of the Sixteenth Army. It was a move with far-reaching consequences, not least for Soeharto, who at that time had just been accepted into the Japanese-run police force in Yogyakarta.

II

The work of Beppan has gone largely unrecorded, but this agency was to have a lasting impact on Indonesia's military and political life. In less than two years, Beppan was to recruit and train a 37,500-strong Java Volunteer Defence Force, the basis of the future Indonesian National Army. It was to recruit and train a small but potent Special Guerrilla Force (Yugekitai), the embryo of the Indonesian Army intelligence service and, in East Java at least, of the TNI's powerful Military Police Corps.[4] Beppan was also to recruit and train 500 young Indonesian Muslims as leaders of the Barisan Hizbullah (Army of God), a paramilitary force designed to harness Islamic support behind the Japanese at the time of an expected Allied invasion of Java.[5] Some Hizbullah members, along with other devout Muslims, would play a role in the bitter post-war drive to make Indonesia an Islamic state.

Beppan came out of a distinctly unsavoury tradition. Before and during World War II, Japanese army intelligence and covert action work was conducted by three separate bodies: the conventional tactical and combat intelligence G2 units; the Kenpeitai for counter-intelligence and security functions; and a great many Tokumukikan, or special task agencies, for clandestine operations (*boryaku*).[6] The latter were responsible for softening up and penetrating target national groups, supporting and training puppet national armies, preparing propaganda material and spinning intelligence-gathering webs designed to help the conventional forces maintain the subjugation of occupied areas. Brutal in their methods, especially in China and Manchuria, Tokumukikan were hated and feared almost as much as the Kenpeitai.[7] The Tokumukikan tended to obtain the best-trained personnel, both military and civilian, drawing especially on recent graduates of an elite army training facility for intelligence gathering, subversion and covert operations which had been provisionally established in July 1938 in the Kundan district in Tokyo, not far from the Yasukuni Shrine. Known initially by the innocuous-sounding name Training Centre for Rear Duties Personnel, the school moved the following year to the Nakano Ward in the northwest of Tokyo, after which it was known as the Nakano Gakko (Nakano School).

The Nakano Gakko was established under the supervision of Section 8 of the Second Department (Intelligence) of the Army General Staff. According to Lieutenant General Fujiwara Iwaichi, who lectured on psychological warfare at the intelligence school before the war, who went on to play a key role in the formation of the Indian National Army and who helped foment a revolt in Aceh in February 1942, the Nakano Gakko was set up because the Japanese, unlike the British, did not station people in an area for much of their careers, so that they became well versed in its affairs.[8] Rather, they moved military attaches and others about after a few years' posting to allow them to rise in the bureaucracy. The Nakano Gakko was designed to provide "country experts" who would be expected to stay in one place more or less permanently, not just in Southeast Asia but also in countries such as Australia and Brazil. Fujiwara cautioned, however, that one should not over-rate the Nakano School: it offered only a one-year course and had not been established long when the Pacific War began.

On the eve of the Pacific War, the army had sent about 1,000 intelligence agents, many of them Nakano Gakko graduates, to Southeast Asia under cover as consular officials, shipping agents, bankers, journalists, migrants, students and businessmen.[9] Other Nakano School graduates, including some who had been posted for a time in Japanese-occupied Taiwan, arrived in Southeast Asia later with the invading Japanese forces. While on Taiwan, a group of young Nakano Gakko graduates in the Tokumukikan had found themselves working in a remodelled warehouse, there being no room for them in the overflowing General Staff office of Army Headquarters. They decided to call themselves Beppan, a word derived from *betsu*, meaning "separate" or "different", and *han*, meaning "group" or "section".[10] They continued to use this name when they were in Java, mainly to avoid the negative connotations of the term Tokumukikan, and before long it became the practice throughout the so-called Southern areas (Nanpo) for army intelligence agencies consisting mainly of Nakano School graduates to be called Beppan. On Java, at least, Beppan seems to have largely eschewed the sort of practices that had given the Tokumukikan such a bad name.

Beppan was a body with high-level connections in the Japanese army. The "big boss" of the organization was Major General Kokubu Shinshichiro, the chief of staff of the Sixteenth Army.[11] He had been "directly appointed" to this position by Japan's wartime prime minister, Lieutenant General Tojo Hideki, who was also War Minister, a clear sign that Tojo considered Java crucial.[12] There was "a strong trust relationship" between the two generals, forged in the days when Kokubu had been a battalion commander in a regiment commanded by Tojo.[13] Those connections seem to have served the agency well. Although initially a very small organization, with only two dozen officers and men on Java, Beppan had an unusual degree of autonomy.[14] This won it no friends in the Kenpeitai, an organization used to getting its own way and not well disposed to those it saw as rivals. According to a seasoned Kenpeitai junior officer, Beppan was a powerful and influential body, "the only organization among the Japanese forces which could override [the] all-feared Kenpeitai."[15] Beppan, he added, had powers of arrest and authority to search and confiscate property. That claim is disputed by former Beppan officers. Unlike the Kenpeitai, they say, Beppan did not have any official powers of arrest nor did it have the authority to conduct searches and confiscate property. In Japanese-occupied Java, however, those constraints meant little. Beppan officers felt free to act as and how they saw fit. "No one complained," said Tsuchiya Kiso, a former Beppan chief, somewhat disingenuously, "when Beppan used those powers if necessary," adding the qualification that the agency probably resorted to these practices no more than ten times during the three-and-a-half year occupation.[16]

General Kokubu was too busy, of course, to direct Beppan's activities on a day-to-day basis. Nor did Major Kuriya Tsugunori, the staff officer in charge of intelligence for the Sixteenth Army, have time to provide more than general oversight of Beppan.[17] That meant, in practice, that Beppan was run by Captain Maruzaki Yoshio, an officer with some very fixed views about the revolutionary potential of Indonesian youth.[18] One of eighteen students to graduate from the Nakano School's first class in

Sixteenth Army Special Intelligence Section (Beppan)

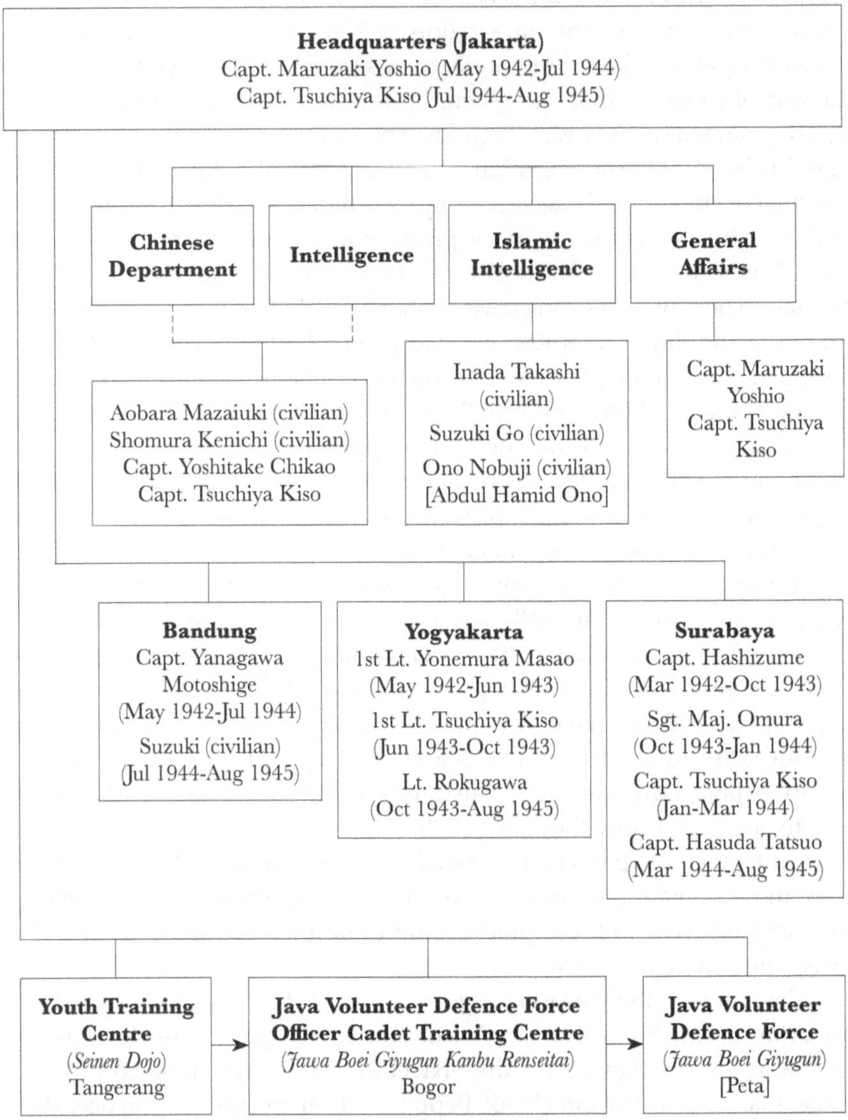

Source: Interview, Tsuchiya Kiso, Asahigaoka, Mishima, 2 February 1999; Tsuchiya Kiso, written communication, 29 May 2002; Interrogation, Captain Tsuchiya Kiso, Glodok Jail, SEATIC Intelligence Bulletin, no. 228, January 1946, WO203/6306. TNA/PRO; Tsuchiya Kiso, Interrogation 3-8 March 1947, NIOD coll. 400, no. 771, and Interrogation, Capt. Yanagawa, 14 December 1945, Javint 3132/2, SEATIC Det., 23 Ind Div., 15 Jan 46. NANL, 2.10.14, inv. 5190.

August 1939, Maruzaki had been posted to the intelligence section of the Army General Staff.[19] Maruzaki was seen by his Japanese colleagues as a broad-minded and tolerant officer, but he was also tough, with a streak of zealotry in his make-up. In early 1941, as war loomed in the Pacific, he had been planted in the Japanese consulate in Surabaya to study Indonesian society.[20] While there, he came to the view that if Japan wanted the assistance of the Indonesians "in the coming struggle against the Westerners, the Indonesians should first be endowed with a fighting spirit, a spirit based on self-confidence as Asians who are not inferior in any way to Westerners."[21] It would be difficult, he felt, to raise the spirit of older Indonesians, but he was confident that younger people could easily be imbued with the necessary fighting spirit.[22] As the head of Beppan, Maruzaki was given the opportunity to imbue young men with precisely that spirit.

In late 1942, Beppan was still monitoring political, social and economic conditions on the island in an attempt to provide headquarters with "a good grasp of the sentiment among the Javanese."[23] But Beppan was no mere sponge, passively absorbing non-military information that might be of interest to army headquarters. Beppan officers were graduates of the Nakano Gakko. They had been recruited in many cases from top pre-war Japanese universities, such as Tokyo Imperial University, the two private universities Keio and Waseda, as well as other centres of higher education, including Takushoku University, which was strongly supported by the military. They had come through a rigorous course of study, where the curriculum included not only intelligence, strategy and propaganda but also languages, philosophy, history, current affairs, martial arts, counter intelligence and the various facets of covert action.[24] They had been instructed in methods thought to be advantageous in winning over "native people" to the Japanese side (*senbu*) and had been taught how to train local recruits (*minzoku shido*). They had mastered techniques relating to the development of spiritual strength (*seishin-ryoku*). They had been shown how to achieve their goals in occupied territories.[25]

In November 1942 Major Kuriya gave Beppan a new and important assignment, one that would eventually eclipse its intelligence-gathering functions. As Yanagawa Motoshige, a Beppan officer who was to have a profound impact on the lives of many future Indonesian army officers, and indeed on the Indonesian National Army, later put it, "we began to study the education of Indonesian youth."[26] This statement, translated into English in a post-war interrogation document, is bland, even opaque, but the import is dramatically clear. Some Japanese officers had begun to toy with the idea that Indonesians could be trained to serve in a separate military formation, not just as auxiliary soldiers (*heiho*) in Japanese army units. The idea, as a senior Indonesian general later put it, was to do a test on some "laboratory mice," to see whether "Indonesian *pemuda* [youth] were physically and mentally strong enough to undergo military training."[27] Initially, it has been suggested, the Japanese had it in mind to produce a squad of strong and determined army intelligence operatives. These men might, as Kuriya saw it, be infiltrated into Australia ahead of a possible Japanese invasion.[28] If that was part of the plan—and there are some grounds for believing it was little more than a "selling point" aimed at higher authority—it did not take long for Beppan to broaden the focus of the programme. After discussions with his colleagues, Maruzaki decided to take this opportunity to test the "overall military capabilities" of young Indonesians, without forgetting the intelligence-gathering aspect of his assignment.[29]

The officer chosen to run the trial programme was First Lieutenant (later Captain) Yanagawa. A graduate of Takushoku University in Tokyo, Yanagawa had done his basic training in the Imperial Japanese Army Air Force before being tapped for intelligence duties.[30] Yanagawa was about five feet four inches tall; he was, as the Japanese say, *chuniku chuzei*, a person of medium height and build. Some of his army colleagues thought him quite ordinary to look at. However, he appears in a post-war photograph with a shock of thick black hair, bushy eyebrows, a slightly quizzical expression and wearing a bow-tie. A man of high intelligence, exacting standards and iron will, Yanagawa made a powerful impression on everyone he met, both Japanese and Indonesian. "He was a very strong-willed, confident man," said Tsuchiya, one of his Beppan contemporaries. "We could plainly say stubborn, someone who didn't listen to others. But, at the same time, he couldn't accept things he considered wrong, like bribery and injustice. He believed in righteousness. He was very sharp."[31]

In the opinion of Kaneko Tomokazu, a civilian journalist who had befriended Yanagawa before the war and who sailed with him to Java on the troopship *Sakura Maru*, Yanagawa's character could be summed up in the Japanese expression *take o watta yona*; this phrase, rich in connotations of admiration and respect, is commonly used to describe a strong and manly individual. Yanagawa was, said Kaneko, straightforward, open-hearted, frank in disposition, someone who did not pay attention to trifling matters.[32] Taniguchi Taketsugu, who headed the thirty-five-man Kenpeitai detachment in Bogor and thus had the responsibility to "watch quietly" all Japanese army personnel within his area, including Beppan officers, remembers Yanagawa as a man of bravery and fortitude, someone who invariably made quick and correct decisions.[33] Nor was Yanagawa lacking in flamboyance. In Bogor, said Taniguchi, he took to riding about on a "wonderfully big thoroughbred horse, pure white. I often saw him on that horse. It was unheard of."

Yanagawa is spoken of with equal awe by some of Indonesia's most senior first-generation military leaders. "He was a very tough man," said Lieutenant General Kemal Idris, who trained under Yanagawa for five months. "He was very rough. But I liked him. He was not only rough towards Indonesians but towards Japanese themselves."[34] According to Lieutenant General Purbo Suwondo, Yanagawa was not really flamboyant at all, the splendid horse notwithstanding. "He was a typical Prussian-style Japanese officer. He was an intelligence officer, not the flamboyant type."[35] No one, said Purbo, ever forgot Yanagawa.

> Everyone remembers him. If he inspects us, he will inspect our eyes, to see if you are sleepy, have no energy, are not vital. Because, according to their philosophy, the eyes are the mirror of the soul, whereas in Javanese culture you must not look into the eyes of an older person. In the old days, we were brought up that way. Here we learned to look directly into someone's eyes, with vigour! Not with "fish eyes." Fish never sleep. "*Mata ikan,*" [fish eyes] Yanagawa would say. "You are a damned fish eyes!".... The eyes were very important. One by one he would look into your eyes.[36]

According to another officer, Major General Moersjid, Yanagawa was not only a man of immense presence, with clear leadership qualities; he had almost mystical powers as well. When Yanagawa was the commander of the officer cadet school in Bogor, he made it his practice to inspect the morning parade mounted on his horse. Although there might be several hundred men lined up before him, Yanagawa claimed that he could tell if even one man blinked. To Moersjid, it was uncanny. "We started thinking, 'How could it be possible that one man, at a distance of, let's say, one hundred metres, could observe one man blinking? That must be supernatural!' But it did happen! He could see that!"[37]

Yanagawa considered himself a man with something that amounted almost to a sacred mission, or so he liked to claim after the war. One of his army intelligence colleagues, Major Fujiwara Iwaichi, had, as noted above, played a key role in setting up the Indian National Army. Another, Colonel Suzuki Keiji, had been instrumental in establishing the Burma Independence Army. Yanagawa believed that it was his destiny to build a similar institution on Java. Each of these three men, it has been claimed, "was imbued with a romantic and idealistic self-image of his own and Japan's role in fostering Indian, Burmese or Javanese independence."[38] Each, it has been further claimed, was struck by the parallel between his own mission and that of Lawrence of Arabia, the British archaeologist and intelligence officer who, while assigned to the Arab Bureau during World War I, led often bickering Arab guerrilla forces against the Ottoman Empire and later pushed for an independent Arab state. It is possible that Yanagawa did indeed see himself in this light. At the army intelligence school which would become known later as the Nakano Gakko, he had been trained to work in the Arab world. He was slated to go to the Middle East, where he would pose as a merchant while undertaking military intelligence activities. He had learned about Lawrence, he said many years later, at the Nakano Gakko.[39] Tsuchiya, however, has cast doubt on the notion that Lawrence's example influenced Yanagawa in his dealings on Java. Yanagawa, he says, did not draw any parallel between himself and Lawrence until well after the war.[40] Whatever the truth of the matter, "Through the imaginative negotiations and promptings of these men, three revolutionary armies were spawned."[41]

Yanagawa, Tsuchiya and another Beppan officer spent December 1942 searching for an appropriate training centre (*asrama*) and suitable Indonesian recruits.[42] By 10 January 1943, they had both. Working in great secrecy, they set up a Youth Training Centre (Seinen Dojo) at Tangerang, just west of Jakarta, and brought together about fifty young Indonesians, most of them in their late teens, for a five-month training programme.[43] The Beppan officers had high hopes for the course and devised a programme that placed extraordinary emphasis on spiritual values and physical fitness, themes that had been so central to their own training in Japan. Cadets were worked hard, with an exhausting round of study and physical activity. They studied the Japanese language, the history of the Netherlands East Indies, world affairs, tactics, communications, espionage, counter-intelligence, propaganda, conspiracy, shooting, reconnaissance, liaison and camouflage. They were subjected to constant drill and devoted many hours to gymnastics, swimming, *sumo* and *kendo*, a martial art which had its origins in *samurai* sword-fighting. They were taught Japanese martial songs.[44] Nothing was said about independence. "As the question of Indonesian independence was not yet settled," Yanagawa noted after the war, "we tried only to inspire cooperation, coexistence and co-prosperity among the peoples of East Asia."[45] The pace was relentless, the pressure intense. The students began to falter. For a time, even Yanagawa wondered whether it had been such a good idea after all. "At the beginning it seemed rather impossible to get any results without keeping a constant watch," he said.[46] "But later the men began to understand our spirit of enthusiasm and worked with a will."

One of those who observed the changes in the Indonesian cadets was Kaneko Tomokazu from the Sixteenth Army Propaganda Corps. "I had many trips to the Tangerang Seinen Dojo," Kaneko recalled. "Because I was in charge of newspapers, Mr. Yanagawa wanted me to go there to see how young Indonesian people were trained and became strong. Whenever I went there, Yanagawa took part in the *sumo* himself with the young Indonesian trainees to show how strong they had become. And I could clearly see the difference after two or three months' training."[47] According to Kusnowibowo, one of the Indonesians who trained at Tangerang, Yanagawa was not only strict and tough, but also keen to ensure that the cadets developed a sense of pride. When, eventually, he let them leave the camp, he encouraged them to travel (without paying) first-class on the train, "saying they shouldn't think it was for foreigners or the rich; it was their country, and they were its hope so deserved the best."[48] Yanagawa "defended his boys strongly if they were hassled by the Japanese, and looked after their interests, so they got great confidence in him." He was perceived as sincere. Those who were trained by him "had a particular pride; indeed, one could say they were *sombong* [arrogant] about it."[49]

By May 1943, when the members of the first intake completed their course, the Japanese were well pleased. The test, Tsuchiya recalled four years later, was a "great success."[50] According to Yoshitake Chikao, another Nakano graduate, "This training, due to the fervour of the instructors and the native youths, gradually produced successful results, which … developed incidentally to become the very foundation of the organization of the militia force, born from the fervent desire of the natives."[51] The Indonesian recruits were also pleased. A second intake of young men entered the training centre in June, graduating in October. On 10 June, as the new recruits began their training, General Kokubu, the officer with close links to Prime Minister Tojo, took up his appointment as chief of staff of the Sixteenth Army and "big boss" of Beppan.

At around the same time, Lieutenant General Inada Masazumi, the new deputy chief of staff of Field Marshal Terauchi Hisaichi's Southern Army, made an inspection tour of Java, Sumatra and Borneo.[52] Concerned about inadequate Japanese troop numbers and knowing that no reinforcements would be forthcoming, he recommended that both Lieutenant General Harada, the Japanese commander on Java, and his opposite number in Sumatra, train a core of local troops to supplement Japanese forces. Harada was already strongly in favour of such a course. Tojo, who happened to be travelling in Southeast Asia, was also in favour. Tokyo shared Inada's concern about Japanese troop numbers (although even some of Inada's own officers are said to have worried that it might be dangerous to arm indigenous forces).[53] Tokyo also felt it needed to mollify Indonesian nationalist leaders. The Indonesians had been bitterly disappointed when, in January 1943, Tojo announced that Burma and the Philippines would be granted "independence" within the year, with no such pledge for Indonesia.[54] Tojo, it is true, had later sent an order that steps be taken to investigate the possibility of granting Indonesia independence.[55] This order was duly passed on to Java, where Harada ordered Major General Yamamoto Moichiro, the chief of the General Affairs Department of the Military Administration in Java, to take charge of the matter. He created an Investigation Organization (Shimon Kikan) in May–June 1943, but nothing much was to happen for more than a year.

In August 1943, the Southern Army issued an order to the armies in Sumatra and Java "approving the establishment of native armies."[56] Implementation of the decision was left to the local commanders. Harada, who had been impressed by the success of the Tangerang experiment, wasted no time in complying with this instruction. He and his staff sought, however, to create the impression that they were responding to local demands. On 7 September, in a "spontaneous" gesture timed and stage-managed by Beppan, Gatot Mangkupradja, who had been a close associate of Sukarno in the pre-war Indonesian National Party, wrote a petition, in his own blood, urging Harada to establish a volunteer force for the defence of the fatherland.[57] The letter was given extensive coverage in the newspapers, and people came to believe that this force was an

Indonesian patriotic initiative. (Beppan had sought to persuade the young Sultan of Yogyakarta to play this role, but without success.[58]) Yanagawa, who had been working on the propaganda film *Goshu e no yobigoe* ("Calling Australia"), was ordered in mid-September to "put out propaganda aiming to rouse enthusiasm for the defence of Java by a Volunteer Defence Force."[59] During this time, he and his Beppan colleagues wrestled with three main questions. What motto should be adopted? What attitude was to be taken on the question of independence? What was the best way to harness Islamic sentiments?[60] As the Japanese policy on independence had not been settled, Yanagawa decided that recruits should be drawn from a religious, rather than a nationalist, background.

On 3 October 1943, Harada announced the formation of a volunteer defence force on Java "based on the spirit of the common defence of ... Greater East Asia and in response to the intense desire of the fifty million Indonesians for homeland defence."[61] The force would be subject to the direction of the supreme commander, with units assigned for local defence against America, Britain and the Netherlands. Candidate officers would not have to have any particular educational qualifications, but they would need to be of "firm ideology and of vigorous will" and be of strong physique. Training would be based on the spirit of sharing a common fate with the Japanese forces. Those who joined were "to devote their souls, flesh and blood to the ideology of Japan and the Greater East Asia" region.[62]

At the same time, the Japanese pushed ahead with a programme, started in May, to train a large number of *heiho*, Indonesian auxiliary soldiers who would be attached to Japanese units on Java. These men, who tended to come from a fairly modest social and educational background, were issued Japanese army rifles and bayonets and "treated on the same level as Japanese soldiers."[63] According to a Japanese document written after the surrender and captured by the Allies, the Sixteenth Army attached more importance to the training of the *heiho* than it did to the training of the Peta. "*Heiho*," the author of this assessment recorded, "attained a higher standard than the Volunteer Army in fighting technique."[64] Lacking sufficient troops of its own, the Sixteenth Army established temporary anti-aircraft, tank, artillery and trench mortar units using *heiho* and Japanese personnel.

As noted earlier, the Dutch had been wary about having too many Indonesian officers and NCOs in the KNIL, mindful of Governor General Willem Rooseboom's 1903 dictum that in an independence movement native officers would be the obvious leaders of the rebels. Forty years after that warning, the Japanese, short of manpower, short of time, seemingly heedless of the possible long-term consequences, and having at hand an agency like Beppan, which was always ready to think imaginatively, threw caution to the winds. This Japanese policy, which would involve training a large number of Indonesian officers and men on Java and Bali and distributing 19,000 weapons among them (with another 7,000 weapons allocated to the Indonesian police force), was to work well enough in the short term. In the long term, as any Rooseboomist might have foreseen, it was to cause the Japanese and others untold grief, while making an inestimable contribution to the Indonesian independence movement. There was every reason to fear that the men the Japanese recruited, having no deep-seated loyalty to the Japanese, might be tempted to turn on those who had armed them, as indeed was to prove the case in due course. Nor were the Japanese unaware of that danger in their locally trained armies. For example, there had for some time been simmering discontent in the Burma Independence Army, later the Burma National Army. This was to erupt in widespread revolt on 8 March 1945, only three weeks after the revolt of the Blitar battalion in East Java.[65]

The Japanese were to create a number of new institutions during their three-and-a-half-year occupation of Java, many of them significant. But none was to have as great an impact as the Java Volunteer Defence Force, or Peta. Conjured out of nothing, virtually overnight, and manned almost entirely by Indonesians, it burst into life as a force of no fewer than thirty-three battalions, each consisting of about 522 officers and men.[66] It was to grow in less than two years into an organization of sixty-nine battalions, or about 37,500 men, on Java and Bali.[67] On Sumatra, the Twenty-fifth Army set up its own 20,000-strong volunteer force, but with 150-man companies as the largest fighting units. Soeharto appears to have had a shaky recall of the structure of the Giyugun on Sumatra. "How many *daidans* [battalions] were there on Sumatra?" he asked a group of ex-Peta colleagues in 1987.[68]

The Japanese did not envisage, at least initially, that the Peta would be in any way an independent force, although they were to move, late in the war, to put it on the path to greater autonomy. Unlike the Indian National Army and the Burma Independence Army in Japanese-occupied Burma, Peta was structured for decentralized activities.[69] Peta would have no higher command, no general staff and no unit larger than a battalion. Instead, it would come under the direct control of the Sixteenth Army, which would deal with the battalions on an individual basis through local Japanese garrisons. Contact between the various Peta battalions, even those in the same residency, would be discouraged.

According to one Sixteenth Army document, Peta was not intended as a front-line force. "The duties of the … PETA were … mainly … those of air-watch along the coast, guarding of important objects and cooperation in the building of fortifications." Peta units were "not to participate in the actions of war." During "actual warfare," they were to remain at the rear, where they would be engaged in guard duty.[70] According to another Sixteenth Army study, written after the Japanese surrender and captured by the Allies, the operational intention of the Japanese Army in the early stage of the war was to fight a defensive battle on the south coast of Java, focusing on eastern Java. Later, following General MacArthur's advances in New Guinea, that strategy had been replaced by one which called for a defensive battle to be fought on the north coast of Java, again centring on eastern Java. Finally, the aim had been to fight to the death in West Java.[71] Peta battalions had been deployed in accordance with these plans. Initially, Peta units had been required to defend the provinces in which they were situated. Later, as their training progressed, they were allowed to act outside their home province.

Looking back nearly thirty years later, Colonel Miyamoto wrote that the aim was to "defend the fatherland and Islam" against reoccupation by the Dutch and to train support troops for the Japanese. But he also stressed another consideration. Harada, "whose administration was influenced by his experience in China," felt that "order among the natives should be maintained by the native military so that the Japanese army could be held in reserve as a core force."[72]

In short, this was, at best, an embryo army. It was to be, nevertheless, a wholly Indonesian force, save for the two or three Japanese officers and four or five Japanese NCOs who would be attached to each battalion, mainly for administrative, liaison and training purposes.[73] The battalion commanders (*daidancho*), company commanders (*chudancho*) and platoon commanders (*shodancho*) would all be Indonesians, mostly Javanese or Sundanese, as would the soldiers.

By early October 1943, Maruzaki had taken over the dormitory of the former KNIL 19th Battalion in Bogor and set it up as the Java Volunteer Defence Force Officer Cadet Training Centre (Jawa Boei Giyugun Kanbu Renseitai). He had also assembled his core staff. What he needed now was

856 young, and not so young, Indonesians who could serve as the backbone of the Peta—33 battalion commanders, 127 company commanders and 696 platoon commanders.[74] These men were to be drawn from various parts of West, Central and East Java and sent back to recruit others to serve in a local force in their home regions, and nowhere else. The assumption was that the trainees had good local knowledge and social ties and would be well placed to fight in that region if the Allies landed. It was envisaged that each Indonesian battalion commander would recruit some 500 men to serve as NCOs and soldiers in his locally raised battalion.

Because Beppan was such a small organization, quite unable to scour Java on its own, Maruzaki asked officials in the Japanese military administration to recommend officer cadet recruits. He consulted Japanese and Indonesians in the provincial bureaucracy. He consulted Kenpeitai officers and regional Japanese police chiefs. He sought advice from Beppan's resident experts on Indonesian Islam, one of whom was a Japanese interpreter named Ono Nobuji (often referred to as Ono Nobuharu), who had lived in Java since 1928, embracing Islam and changing his name to Abdul Hamid Ono.[75] He consulted the Beppan chiefs in Bandung, Yogyakarta and Surabaya. He consulted the Tangerang graduates. At the end of this process, Maruzaki had a long list of names. He now arranged for three of his subordinates to conduct the interviews at which the future Indonesian officers would be chosen. In Central Java that task fell to Lieutenant Tsuchiya, the director of Beppan's Yogyakarta office. Until this time, Tsuchiya had spent his days gathering intelligence, not least about developments within the Kraton, and supervising the Beppan offices in Semarang, Solo and Madiun. Now, in early October 1943, he began a recruiting drive that was to bring in a crop of young officer cadets, a number of whom were to rise to high office in the future Indonesian National Army.

One of them was Soeharto.[76]

11

"The whole island was ablaze with enthusiasm"

On Friday, 8 October 1943, on the advice of his Japanese superior, Superintendent Okamoto, Soeharto presented himself at a temporary army recruitment centre in Yogyakarta.[1] Wearing a *kain* (sarong), white shirt and sandals, rather than his police uniform, he joined about four hundred other young men who gathered in the grounds of an elementary school in the heart of the city.[2] The Sixteenth Army had decided to form a Java Volunteer Defence Force—which was to be known in Japanese as the Jawa Boei Giyugun, or Giyugun for short, and which the Indonesians would come to know as the Fatherland Volunteer Defence Force (Tentara Sukarela Pembela Tanah Air, or Peta)—to augment its own overstretched units. It was now looking for officer cadets. Soeharto may have been "advised" to be at the recruitment centre that day. But this, the evidence suggests, was an opportunity he welcomed. He had just the sort of capabilities the Japanese were looking for and recruitment into Peta would allow him to move on from police duties, which were presumably less to his liking than army life. Soeharto had set his heart on joining the volunteer defence force.

Some of the young, and not so young, Javanese men waiting to be interviewed that day had impressive credentials. They came from a middle- or upper-*priyayi* background and had attended Dutch high schools, some of them quite prestigious. These applicants were relatively healthy, well-fed and well-dressed. They included schoolteachers, policemen, public servants and high school students. Others who waited patiently in the sun were less well qualified for the positions on offer. Most were barefoot. Many were in poor health (the most common medical complaints were skin diseases and TB). Many had only the most rudimentary education. Inside the hall, where they were called in one at a time, a twenty-six-year-old Japanese intelligence officer, First Lieutenant Tsuchiya Kiso, the director (*shibucho*) of Beppan's Yogyakarta branch, sat at a table choosing officer cadets for the new force. Tsuchiya was responsible for recruiting battalion commanders, company commanders and platoon commanders.

In the weeks before this, Tsuchiya, continuing a process begun by Maruzaki, had asked several organizations in Yogyakarta to recommend suitable candidates. He had contacted the provincial government office, which passed his request on to the Seinendan (Youth Corps), the Keibodan (civil defence organization) and schools. He had contacted the Military Police force, the civilian police force and a number of army defence companies (*rikugun-boeitai*). He had sought the views of his colleagues in Beppan.[3] "We used two channels to reach potential *daidanchos*—provincial governors and Beppan's Islamic Guidance Section," he recalled. "We asked provincial governors to recommend people from religious and neighbourhood groups, as well as people from government offices, whom they thought had strong leadership qualities.... Beppan's Islamic section gave us names, too." This effort had yielded a crop of names. Some of those waiting in the courtyard bore letters of recommendation from Japanese or Indonesian officials. But there were many men who came forward of their own volition, fired by a sense that this was a defining moment in the nationalist struggle. As Tsuchiya put it, "The whole island of Java was ablaze with enthusiasm after the Japanese military commander announced that the Peta was being organized and everybody, the young and the old, was so willing to defend the country that a lot of people came to apply without much effort on our part."[4] The men Tsuchiya chose in Yogyakarta that day, and in nine other cities and towns over the next week and a half, would form the core of what was to become in time the powerful Diponegoro Division of Central Java. A number of them, including Soeharto, were to play a key role in the post-war Indonesian National Army (Tentara Nasional Indonesia, TNI).

II

Tsuchiya, who combined intelligence, drive and a good sense of humour with a readiness to engage with other races, other societies, other cultures, a readiness that was not always evident in the Imperial Japanese Army, was to have an impact on the future Indonesian officer corps perhaps second only to that of Yanagawa. A graduate of a technical school in Shizuoka, a medium-size city ninety miles southwest of Tokyo, he had worked for twelve to eighteen months in a Japanese factory that made military binoculars before joining the Army Air Force. He spent a year as a cadet at an Army Air Force school and stayed on for six months as an instructor. In 1938 he was sent to join the first main entering class at the army intelligence school, which would become known the following year as the Nakano Gakko Intelligence School. While there, he met Yanagawa, Yonemura Masao and Yoshitake Chikao, who, like Tsuchiya, would all play an important role in Java. Yonemura was to recruit the first crop of Indonesian officer cadets from East Java. From 1944 he would be associated with the Nami Kikan, which gathered maritime defence intelligence. From December 1944 Yoshitake would be responsible for training the Beppan-sponsored Overseas Chinese Defence Corps (Kakyo Boei-tai). Following his graduation in 1939, Tsuchiya was commissioned as a second lieutenant and assigned to intelligence duties at the War Office in Tokyo. In December that year, he was transferred to military headquarters in Taiwan, where he made a study of the Netherlands East Indies and French Indochina and began to teach himself Malay. Recalled to Tokyo in October 1941, he was assigned to Sixteenth Army headquarters, where he conducted further research on the East Indies. He landed in West Java in March 1942 with a branch force of the invading army and went on to spend about three months in the special intelligence office (*bunshitsu*) of the 2nd Division in Bandung. From there he was posted to Jakarta, where he joined Beppan. In June 1943, he took over as the director of Beppan's Yogyakarta branch from Yonemura, who had also been transferred from Taiwan to Java.[5]

For ten days in mid-October 1943, Tsuchiya conducted a whistle-stop tour of Central Java and parts of East Java, interviewing applicants for the volunteer defence force. Travelling by car and accompanied by an Indies-born Japanese civilian interpreter and a Japanese army medical officer, he visited all ten towns on his list, setting up his mobile recruitment centre in schools and community centres. At each location, Japanese and Indonesian officials had publicized the recruitment programme and attended to the necessary paperwork. But it was Tsuchiya who conducted the interviews and made the selections, sitting at a table, with the interpreter on his left and the doctor on his right. Although it had not been planned that way, the selection of potential Indonesian officer cadets was rushed and rudimentary, even slapdash at times.[6] But the decisions made by Tsuchiya and his Beppan colleagues in East and West Java were to have a profound impact on the shape of the future Indonesian National Army.[7]

In Central Java there were many hopeful applicants, perhaps two thousand in all, and no time for niceties. Tsuchiya did not invite applicants to sit down because it took up too much time. "It was quite rushed," he said. "When I look back, it was a rush."[8] In Yogyakarta, he got through all four hundred applicants in one day. A large number went away disappointed. "There were some to whom I said, 'Leave!' and the guys were so reluctant to leave and said, 'Please recruit me!' There were many of those. But there was a limit to the number we could recruit. It was a hard job to screen out those applicants." Working from early morning until dusk, Tsuchiya had been quick to establish a routine. "I did not give ranking to applicants," he said. "They were simply placed in two categories—either pass or fail. There was no written test. They were asked only two or three oral questions and, if accepted, proceeded to the physical examination. I selected those who were cheerful, pleasant and seemingly smart."[9] When it came to choosing potential company commanders, Tsuchiya tended to favour young men who looked physically strong and who had worked as schoolteachers or served with the police force, the civil defence organization or one of the many youth groups.[10] "As for platoon commanders, I selected vigorous, enthusiastic young men whose attitude was firm and who spoke clearly."[11] How long, Tsuchiya was asked many years later, had each interview lasted: would an applicant have had perhaps ten minutes before the board? "Shorter than that," he replied, his face creasing into a broad smile. "Some, ten seconds! The minute I saw someone I could tell if he was suitable. Usually I spent one or two minutes on those I thought had potential."[12]

One of those deemed to have potential was Soeharto.

"We borrowed the site of an elementary school for the examinations," Tsuchiya recalled, "and it is there that I first met Soeharto. Since many years have passed, I don't have too vivid a memory of Soeharto at that time. But we met each recruit face to face—individual interviews were conducted—and I can say that his manner was so crisp and clear. The words he chose when responding to my questions were very clear-cut and easy to understand. There was nothing I could grade as a minus."[13] Like so many others over the years, Tsuchiya was struck by Soeharto's composure. "He was calm. He looked confident. No appearance of being intimidated." Asked how he would rate Soeharto among the 230 men he selected for the platoon commanders course, Tsuchiya replied, "He belonged to the top class!" That was due in large part to the fact that his education, however incomplete, was infinitely better than that of so many of the others who were seeking admission.

> You must realize that the educational level of Indonesian youngsters in those days was very low. They had very little education. Anybody who had had some years of schooling found it easy to be prominent. Even those who had had only a few years in elementary school could be conspicuous. There weren't many who had a junior-high-school education, and so to have graduated from a high school was something you could be really proud of. Those people with even a little education stood out among those who had only a smattering of education.[14]

Yanagawa, who was conducting interviews in West Java, found the same thing. As he said later, "Quality, both in physique and education, was rather lower than we had expected, and it was very difficult to find suitable people."[15]

Soeharto had been advised by Superintendent Okamoto to apply for selection in the volunteer army. But why was Okamoto willing to dispense with the services of a young Javanese assistant whose contribution he valued? Did he feel under pressure from the army? To some extent he probably did. It was possible, Tsuchiya thought, that he felt pressure "from within himself" to cooperate with the commander's proclamation and with Beppan. But "if he was under any pressure at all, I suspect it could have come from Soeharto himself, with his strong wish to enter the volunteer army."[16] Whatever the explanation, this, it has been plausibly suggested by K.P.H. Haryasudirja, the aristocrat and engineer who was to serve under Soeharto both as a battalion commander and a cabinet minister, was a decisive moment in the future president's life, one which marked, if not the beginning of any nationalist feelings on his part, then at least a new way of looking at the world.[17] Soeharto had seen the Dutch defeated; he now sensed, as did many others, that the tide might be starting to run Indonesia's way, that the volunteer defence force offered the tantalizing promise of a still greater role for Indonesians, even if that role was as yet undefined. Speaking in 2000, by which time he had fallen out with Soeharto and become highly critical of him, Haryasudirja said, "I think he started to commit to another way of thinking when the Peta was created." Others who would go on to serve with Soeharto in the Indonesian Army speak of a similar change in outlook among Peta cadets, while being equally inclined to reject the idea that Soeharto had any nationalist feelings at this stage.

In giving the green light to the formation of the new defence force, the Sixteenth Army had ruled that no former members of the KNIL were to be recruited.[18] The loyalties of such men, it was thought, might be suspect. Aware of the ruling, Soeharto took care to make no mention of his service in the KNIL, just as he had in the police interview nearly a year earlier. He was to remain "watchful" for some time thereafter, "hoping the Japanese would never discover this and arrest me."[19] As it happened, Tsuchiya knew that Soeharto had served in the Dutch colonial army and chose to ignore the fact.[20] "The policy … was that we should not admit anyone who had worked in the former Dutch army, regardless of position. However, those who had worked in the Dutch army were from the elite, and they had good brains as well as physical strength. So I thought it would be a pity if we didn't admit them. And I happened to see Soeharto in Yogyakarta. Soeharto was a former Dutch army non-commissioned officer.… It was against the military policy, but I thought it would be a shame not to hire a capable person like this so I decided to admit him."[21]

As Tsuchiya saw it, Soeharto's attributes outweighed any drawbacks that might have been associated with his prior service in the KNIL. "It was my belief the internal order from military headquarters was a bad one," he said. "Because I was aware that all Indonesians had feelings against the Dutch. And the fact that a person had once been in the Dutch army wouldn't prove that he would cooperate with Holland and fight against the Japanese regime. So I myself thought this order very strange."[22] Having made his decision, Tsuchiya passed Soeharto over to the doctor. Soeharto was asked to strip down to his underpants—he was presumably no longer wearing his KNIL-issue underpants—for a brief examination. He had no skin disease, TB, or any other obvious problem and was pronounced medically fit.

In later years, Soeharto was to claim that he was one of only two applicants selected in Yogyakarta out of about 500 who turned up.[23] This is demonstrably untrue. It is true that only a small number of applicants were deemed suitable, but Tsuchiya recruited at least twenty or thirty men in Yogyakarta that day.[24] And the list of those who joined the same 230-strong training company as Soeharto includes the names of at least three men who were to become close associates of the future President and serve with him during the war and the Revolution: Soedjono, K.R.M.T. Soemyarsono and Pranoto Reksosamodra. Soeharto must have known that his statement about being one of only two men selected in Yogyakarta was false when he made it.

As soon as he had met his recruitment quota, Tsuchiya wound up his Beppan job in Yogyakarta and left for Bogor, where he was to accept the successful candidates from Central Java. He had only one or two days before the entrance ceremony was held, on 20 October.[25] At Bogor, the recruits were to be divided into five groups: a Special Company for the thirty-four (sic) men who were to be trained as battalion commanders (*daidancho*), a 1st Company for the 127 company commanders (*chudancho*), and three companies for the platoon commanders (*shodancho*). Tsuchiya took command of the 4th Company, which was to train the 230 platoon commanders from Central Java, including Soeharto.[26]

The 854 Indonesians who joined the first intake at the Bogor officer training centre—and the 1,300 others who were to follow them in 1944—were, by the very nature of things, overwhelmingly Javanese and Sundanese. This helps explain why, after 1945, the Indonesian Army would have so many Javanese and Sundanese officers, a sore point among some people, both military and civilian, in the Outer Islands. Another part of the explanation for the Java-centric nature of the future Indonesian army is that the Republic was restricted to the Javanese and Sundanese areas, plus Sumatra, during the revolution.* The officer cadets came from three distinct age cohorts and, indeed, three layers in society. Those selected for

* Interestingly, the three brightest stars at Tangerang had been non-Javanese—Zulkifli Lubis (Batak), Daan Mogot (Menadonese), and Kemal Idris (Minangkabau). Equally interesting is the fact that the three most prominent members of the pre-war Royal (Dutch) Military Academy (KMA) in Bandung had been non-Javanese. T.B. Simatupang, who became chief of staff of the armed forces, was a Batak. So, too, was A.H. Nasution, a future army chief of staff. Another KMA cadet, Alex Kawilarang, perhaps the most widely respected field officer in post-war Indonesia, was Menadonese. It is also true that most, if not all, of these six officers had spent at least some of their senior high school years on Java. Three of the six were Christians.

training as battalion commanders were prominent local figures who were thought by the Japanese to have "influence among and authority over the youth."[27] They were district chiefs (*wedana*), Islamic teachers (*kiyai*), schoolteachers and leaders of various social organizations.[28] About 30 or 40 per cent of them had a strong Islamic background.[29] Although their professional military skills would never be up to standard (the Japanese had decided to give the battalion commanders only six weeks' training, which was half the planned time set aside for the instruction of the platoon commanders), their social position and charisma were what counted. Their task was to ensure that the local Peta unit had the all-out support of the community. "The wisdom of this recruitment policy," a retired Indonesian general observed, "became evident during the war against the Dutch: our troops easily got the support of the population."[30]

Battalion commanders were, on average, nearly twenty years older than platoon commanders, most of whom were recruited directly from school and still in their teens. As such, the battalion commanders were more experienced, more politically astute and more wary of the Japanese, if not at times openly hostile to them, than were the younger men. The company commanders, who formed a middle layer between these two groups, were generally about ten to fourteen years older than the platoon commanders. Some were well-educated men who had been teachers in pre-war Dutch-language high schools, but there were also Muslim religious teachers, members of the indigenous administrative corps (*pangréh praja*) and prominent local figures.[31]

Commenting on those he met at the Bogor officer cadet training centre, Lieutenant General G.P.H. Djatikusumo offered a slightly different perspective, one which was mentioned in passing in the Preface but which is worth quoting here in greater detail, even if it overemphasizes some aspects and omits others. The Japanese, Djatikusumo said, had taken the Peta battalion commanders from the Muhammadiyah and the nobility. The company commanders had been young men from various national youth groups. The platoon commanders "were just boys from the streets." "That was the anatomy of the Peta. And that became the nuclei of the TNI. So I say to everybody who would care to listen, 'If you would like to understand this power structure now you cannot afford not to study the anatomy of the Peta.'"[32] Peta battalion commanders were not solely from the Muhammadiyah and the nobility, of course. Nor were the company commanders solely from national youth groups or the platoon commanders solely "boys from the streets." But there is more than a kernel of truth in these remarks.

The officer cadets who joined the Peta were motivated by a range of considerations.[33] Almost all of the battalion and company commanders had been "persuaded" to enlist in the volunteer force during informal meetings with Japanese officials.[34] Many of the company commanders seem to have had no interest at all in a military career but joined because of the pressure that had been brought to bear or because they were convinced that it was necessary for Indonesians to obtain military skills. Although the Japanese were careful to make no promises about independence, "most Indonesians had a feeling that somehow Indonesian independence would soon come, in whatever form."[35] When that time arrived, an army would be one of the prerequisites for the new nation.

"Why did one join Peta?" asked Major General Moersjid, who signed up in 1944. "It was an Indonesian army. We wanted to defend ourselves against the Dutch should they return." Looking back on his career, Moersjid said "it is my time as a Peta officer which stays with me, as a period of promise and budding possibilities. We learned more than elementary military science and basic combat techniques. We also caught our first glimpse of the possibility that Indonesia would some day be independent."[36] While that is true, some of the cadets were driven by careerist considerations. They reasoned that their involvement in the volunteer defence force would open up avenues for social advancement "where other fields of endeavour had for them reached a dead end." Others were simply happy to have a uniform and a good income.

Whatever their motivation, most of the cadet officers joined up willingly, albeit "with various degrees of fervour." Some were convinced that their country's well-being was closely linked to the fortunes of Japan in the Pacific War. Others believed that Peta would serve as "one large training camp to produce military cadres for independent Indonesia."[37] In later years, a number of those who went through the officer-cadet programme said they had been influenced by the 800-year-old Joyoboyo prophesy. According to a version of the prophesy current during the Japanese occupation, "the Javanese would be ruled by white men for three centuries and by yellow dwarfs for the life time of a maize plant, prior to the achievement of a golden age."[38] On balance, an Indonesian academic tactfully concluded, "Most Peta officers were motivated by patriotism, although the element of careerism was not altogether absent."[39]

In a wry and insightful memoir, Lieutenant General Soegih Arto, who went on to serve as attorney general under Soeharto, recalled that he had worked for a time as a high school Japanese-language teacher.

It did not take him long, however, to leave his teaching job, which had a monthly salary of Rp50, and join the Peta, with offered a salary of Rp60. "In the army," he wrote, "everything was taken care of, such as food, clothing, a place to sleep, everything."[40] The Rp60 was net income. As a teacher, he had had to pay Rp15 for board and about Rp5 in instalments on his bicycle. Besides that, he had to be properly dressed, complete with a tie, at a time when clothing was becoming difficult to get.

> What were my motives in joining the Peta? Certainly not for patriotic reasons. Firstly, I liked uniforms, and secondly, I got a better salary. Some of my friends boasted that they joined for patriotic reasons, which was pure nonsense. I definitely was not going to fight for these Japanese—they were like the Dutch, that is, colonial masters. So I decided to join as an administrative officer. You got to wear the same uniform, you had a *samurai* sword hanging at your side, and I was sure that the girls would not know the difference between a fighting officer and an administrative officer who sat behind a desk.

When he finished his training, Soegih Arto was promoted to lieutenant third grade because of his proficiency in Japanese. His salary was Rp100. "No family to take care of, no costs for board and lodging or clothing. What else did I need? I was in paradise. I was very popular with the high school girls in Bandung. I discovered that girls liked uniforms without bothering what was inside them. I looked rather smart in my Peta uniform, which more or less looked like the Japanese army uniforms, though we did not smell as bad as they did. It was a very good time. No war, not even news about the war, because we had no way of getting information. No newspapers or radio. It was a good time for me."

What of Soeharto? What drove him? In the later stages of the war, when the harshness and brutality of Japanese rule was becoming impossible to ignore, Soeharto seems to have become increasingly nationalistic, although he was careful to disguise any anti-Japanese sentiments he may have felt and was to go on serving until the bitter end, trusted by his superiors and rewarded with important assignments. In 1943 it was a very different matter. The evidence suggests that Soeharto joined the Peta for three distinct reasons, none of them associated with nationalism. First, Superintendant Okamoto had encouraged him to apply and Soeharto would have known the Japanese would not look kindly on any refusal. Second, he himself was only too keen to get back into a structured military environment, an environment he had found much to his liking in Dutch times, however hard the training. Finally, his careerist instincts, always well developed, would have told him that Peta was a promising institution, one in which he could put his KNIL training and experience to good effect. According to Nugroho Notosusanto, an Indonesian historian and honorary brigadier general in the TNI, those who were ordered by their superiors to join the Peta, "felt no particular ardour for their new status, but they did not dislike it either. Among them we could find people who would do their best to perform any job entrusted to them, and some of them were to continue their military career after the independence of Indonesia was achieved, reaching top positions in the Indonesian Armed Forces."[41]

Nugroho, who was something of a careerist himself, may not have been thinking of Soeharto when he wrote these words, but the cap does seem to fit, at least to some extent. In later years, however, Soeharto was to place all the emphasis on nationalism, while suggesting, oddly, that Japanese Army officers had done much to instil that nationalism into Peta members, something those instructors had been specifically instructed not to do. "Without the fighting spirit and patriotism that was hammered into us in the Peta," he told a Japanese journalist in 1998, "I don't think we would have been able to drive the Dutch away when they came back to recolonise us. I am grateful to the Japanese army in that sense. However, my gut feeling is that their real purpose in occupying Indonesia was not the 'Liberation of Asia' but something they did in their own interests. The reason why we cooperated with them was to gain our independence."[42]

III

Bogor stands, green and damp, at the foot of Mt Salak (7,185 feet), forty miles south of central Jakarta. Behind the town, which is 860 feet above sea level and often pleasantly cool, a narrow road begins its tortuous climb up through the tea plantations and on across the mountainous backbone of Java towards the upland city of Bandung. In 1745, a Dutch Governor General, Baron G.W. van Imhoff, had built a retreat in Bogor, which he renamed Buitenzorg ("Without a Care"), to escape the chronic malaria and other diseases of Batavia, and had made sketches for a splendid official residence, modelled on Blenheim Palace in England. The building that eventually appeared, remodelled and rebuilt many times, painted a dazzling white and looking nothing like Blenheim, became in time the primary residence of the governors-general. It was set down amid ninety-five acres of lushness and greenery, with sweeping lawns supporting a large herd of spotted deer, imported from Holland. Alongside it was the world famous Botanical Gardens, which had been founded in 1817 by Caspar Georg Carl Reinwardt, a German-born botanist in the employ of the Dutch.

Soeharto arrived in Bogor on Tuesday, 19 October, having travelled from Yogyakarta on a Japanese army truck in the company of other prospective platoon commanders.[43] If he had any misgivings as he entered the former KNIL compound, which stood, with its imposing new Japanese gateway, a short distance to the north of the palace and the adjacent small town, they are likely to have been fleeting. He and his fellow cadets from Central Java were greeted warmly by Tsuchiya, an officer who radiated authority, energy and enthusiasm. Although he was only eight or nine years older than most of his charges, Tsuchiya appears to have had a paternal concern for their education and well-being.

In an interview more than half a century later, Tsuchiya claimed that during this period he had believed in the goal of Indonesian independence, even if he and his colleagues were not permitted to talk of such matters for the time being. "We felt we Japanese should go there and work for their freedom. It was with this wish and this high hope that we departed Japan. Long before Peta was founded, there was, very deep in our hearts, the hope that some day soon Japan would help Indonesia become free."[44] Whatever the truth of that assertion, Soeharto was not entering an unfamiliar world. He already knew a good deal about army life from his time in the KNIL, and he knew a good deal about the Japanese from his time in the police force. Moreover, he was to be billeted with more than 200 other young men from Central Java, cocooned in a Javanese world, just as he had been when he served as a corporal in an ethnic Javanese KNIL infantry company in East Java.

At the same time, Soeharto may have felt that he had little in common with many of those undertaking the *shodancho* course. For one thing, there was the significant age difference separating the cohorts. At the broad base of the officer cadet pyramid, the accent was on youth. As many as 80 per cent of the prospective platoon commanders were either schoolboys, recruited directly from junior high school, or young men not long out of school.[45] The other 20 per cent were, for the most part, low-level government employees, most of them in their late teens or early twenties. Soeharto, who was twenty-two, was five years older than most of those in his intake. He was also a great deal more experienced than most of them, having worked for the Volkskredietbank, having risen up through the KNIL to the rank of sergeant, and having served for nearly a year as a policeman under the Japanese.

Socially and educationally, it was another matter. Among the 2,088 cadets who were to be pushed through the three *shodancho* and *chudancho* courses at Bogor in 1943–44 were eleven young Javanese princes or other members of the nobility, ten of them from the courts of Solo and one from Yogyakarta.[46] Nor were these aristocrats swimming alone in a sea of commoners. As many as 70 or 80 per cent of the *shodancho* cadets came from the ranks of the *priyayi*, albeit in many cases the lower tiers of that social category.[47] "Most of us were from a *priyayi* background," recalled Lieutenant General Purbo Suwondo, an East Javanese officer whose father had been a school inspector in the Dutch education system. "Certain background, certain values, certain philosophies, certain standards of living."[48] Soeharto was, of course, from a non-*priyayi* background, although he had lived for some years with his uncle, a government official in Wuryantoro. This made him something of an outsider.

In pre-war Java, elevated social status had tended to go hand-in-hand with better-than-average education, which served only to deepen the divide between Soeharto and many of his fellow cadets, especially those who had been selected as future company and battalion commanders.[49] As many as 10 per cent of those in Soeharto's intake had attended one of the prestigious Dutch-language senior high schools, or the Japanese occupation equivalent; they were not only fluent in Dutch, but had acquired the European social graces that were essential if one were to rise in pre-war colonial society.[50] Some had gone on, after completing secondary school, to study at the medical faculty, the training school for native civil servants, the agricultural college or one of the teacher training schools. Of those in Soeharto's intake, 80 per cent had spent three (sometimes four) years in a Dutch-language junior high school or its Japanese equivalent. As a result, they had enjoyed an education that had a good deal in common with that of students who had attended Dutch-language senior high schools, save for the fact that their Dutch was not quite as fluent and their schooling had ended by the time they were sixteen, before they could go on to senior high. The remaining 10 per cent came from a much less exalted educational background. Some, like Soeharto, had attended a *schakelschool*. Others had attended vocational schools. A small percentage had come from a *pesantren*, or rural Islamic boarding school.[51] In some of the training companies at Bogor, almost everyone was from an urban, middle-class, Dutch-speaking background. "In my *kutai* [section] of thirty East Java cadets," said Purbo Suwondo, "there was only one who was from a *pesantren*. The rest were at least junior high students. In my one-hundred-man company, I think there were only one or two cadets who came from a *pesantren*.... Maybe 95 per cent had attended a MULO junior high school."[52]

In short, there was a significant educational, as well as a social, cleavage within the ranks of the *shodancho* cadets at Bogor. Ninety per cent of the young men in Soeharto's intake were at home in the Dutch language, at ease in the modern world, and had spent at least three years in junior high school, which put them in the category of the relatively well-educated in 1943. A minority had come from a world in which Javanese families spoke Dutch at home and read Dutch books, newspapers and magazines as a matter of course. They had attended schools in which most of the students were Dutch or Eurasian. The others, while speaking Javanese or Sundanese at home, had had more than ten years' education in schools where the language of instruction was Dutch.

In their school days, these young men had behaved in many ways like young Dutch or Eurasian boys. They had known, almost by heart, the works of Karl May, the best-selling German author who specialized in adventure books about the Wild West, populating his stories with characters such as Winnetou, a fictional Apache chief, and his faithful sidekick, Old Shatterhand, a German émigré who was an outstanding sharpshooter.[53] They had read books about Dik Trom, a corpulent Dutch schoolboy. They were familiar with Pietje Bell, another fictional Dutch schoolboy. They had pored over the Flash Gordon stories in the Dutch magazine *D'Orient*. They had read about Dutch national heroes such as Michiel de Ruyter and Piet Hein, two seventeenth-century admirals, and had committed to memory the school songs dedicated to those men and designed to inculcate the values of Dutch nationalism and Dutch patriotism in students. Those cadets who had reached senior high school by the time the Japanese arrived had, of course, been exposed to a richer intellectual diet. They had read more widely and more deeply. The more serious among them had some familiarity with modern and classical European literature, with philosophy, with international relations, European imperialism, the crisis of capitalism, the rise of fascism and Nazism, and with Marxist thinking.[54]

Soeharto was one of about twenty young men, in a training company of 230, who did not come from a Dutch-language background. He may have had a fleeting acquaintance with things Dutch while attending the *schakelschool*, but it was not his milieu. "He was from another world," observed Major General Moersjid, with the merest sniff of condescension. "I'm not sure whether he had read the books by Karl May about Winnetou. Maybe he knew more than I do about *wayang* [Javanese shadow plays]."[55]

It would be wrong, however, to make too much of these social and educational differences. During the Japanese occupation and in the early post-war years, the distinction between officers who came from a *priyayi* and Dutch-language stream and those such as Soeharto, who came from a more modest background, was of little or no consequence. It would only become important in the 1950s, when attempts were made to transform a large and unwieldy revolutionary army and a range of paramilitary units into a modern professional army. At that time, Soeharto would find himself struggling to keep up with his better-educated colleagues and rivals, only achieving by dint of hard work and after-hours study some of the educational advantages they had so effortlessly acquired. By the late 1950s, Soeharto would find himself bumping up against both a glass, and a class, ceiling in the TNI. Thanks to a combination of application, aptitude and great good luck, he was to become one of the very few officers of his generation—perhaps the only one—to make it to a senior TNI staff position in Jakarta despite having had such a limited education. But it was a close call.

If the prospective Indonesian platoon commanders came from a broad cross-section of Javanese society, albeit weighted heavily towards the educated urban middle-class elite, their Japanese officers and instructors came from a similarly diverse social and skills background. Most of the more senior officers—and they weren't really very senior at all—were Beppan men who had graduated from the Army Intelligence School. They had no expertise whatsoever when it came to training recruits in basic infantry skills. As Tsuchiya readily acknowledged, "We were absolute amateurs. We had not had much military training ourselves before we had to take on the task of training a large number of Indonesian army recruits.... It was like laymen training laymen."[56] The Japanese were, however, brimming with enthusiasm and optimism. And they had recruited two other categories of men to look after the technical training.

Some members of the Japanese training staff at Bogor were recent graduates of the Reserve Officers Academy (Yobishikan Gakko), highly motivated and eager to pass on what they themselves had absorbed during their eight-month training course. Others were combat-hardened Imperial Army non-commissioned officers, many of whom bore the scars of recent fighting in China and on the Malay Peninsula.[57] As Purbo Suwondo remembered, "My company commander, for instance, was a China veteran.... He had lost two of his fingers, so if he salutes back, it's only three fingers.... I think he [had been] wounded two or three times."[58] In Soeharto's 230-man training company, there were twenty-eight Japanese apart from Tsuchiya—four officers, eight NCOs and sixteen of other ranks—as well as four interpreters and a few Indonesian graduates of the Tangerang Youth Training Centre. "What we did," Tsuchiya explained, "was to let the sergeants and corporals take charge of the actual military training while we, the company commanders, concentrated more on enhancing moral and emotional strength. We put the emphasis on nurturing nationalism and agitating them so that they would want to fight together with the Japanese military for the independence of Indonesia."[59]

12

"Don't make them too strong!"

The Japanese entertained high hopes for the Peta, and General Harada travelled to Bogor to preside over the opening ceremony, which was held on Wednesday, 20 October 1943.[1] This did not proceed quite as expected. The young men who were to be trained to lead an Indonesian volunteer force had been drawn up on the parade ground in the early hours of the morning, and as the general took his place on the reviewing stand they looked quite impressive. Their uniforms, which were modelled on those of the Japanese army but made from surplus KNIL cloth, consisted of a green tunic and jodhpurs and a brown leather belt. The prospective battalion commanders had high black boots. The others wore black shoes and black leather leggings.[2] Some wore a Dutch ceremonial sword. All of this gave the Indonesians a superficial resemblance to Japanese officer cadets. It soon proved to be illusory. As Harada began his opening remarks, one of the Indonesian officer cadets fainted. He was followed by another and then another. Before long, cadets were falling like ninepins, even though it was barely 8:00 a.m. and the sun was still low in the sky. The Japanese looked on in dismay. "Everyone stood there in line," Tsuchiya said, "and the commander-in-chief addressed them for about forty minutes. But he was only five minutes into his speech when officer cadets began to fall down, one after another. The commander-in-chief was so disappointed. Later he said to us, 'Can this really be successful with such weak soldiers?' Of course, we were all disappointed."[3] The recruits had succumbed to what the Japanese called *nisshabyo* (sunstroke). "It's more than fainting," said Tsuchiya. "They were hardly alive. They were barely breathing." Tsuchiya and his fellow officers wondered themselves if the Javanese and Sundanese cadets would be able to endure the severe training the Japanese had in store for them. "It was astonishing to us. We were surprised how weak they were. They weren't expected to do anything except stand."[4]

Despite the unpromising start, the Beppan officers were determined to make a success of the training programme. They knew they had too little time to give the cadets all the necessary technical skills. They knew, too, that there were not enough textbooks to go around.[5] None of this fazed them. Fired with enthusiasm themselves, they sought to instil a similar enthusiasm into their Indonesian charges. At Bogor, there was an unrelenting emphasis on the importance of nurturing spiritual strength *(seishin-ryoku)* and enhancing self-awareness and enthusiasm.[6] *Seishin* was fundamental to Japanese army doctrine, which continued to stress the primacy of spiritual factors—loyalty, faith in victory, aggressiveness and fighting spirit—over material ones in warfare.[7] The doctrine had been greatly emphasized in the training of intelligence officers at the Nakano Gakko.[8] The army's successes against superior forces in the Sino-Japanese war (1894–95) and the Russo-Japanese War (1904–5) "gave its leaders confidence that their unique Japanese fighting spirit would ensure victory even against nominally stronger enemies."[9]

As it happened, this was to prove a costly delusion for the Japanese, who misread the lessons of the Russo-Japanese War and who, alone among the great powers, had never experienced at first-hand the destructive firepower of the modern weapons used on the European fronts in World War I.[10] As Edward Drea has shown, Japan waged the Russo-Japanese War by relying heavily on German doctrine, which stressed that firepower secured victory in infantry combat. However, a 1906 Japanese commission, overlooking the evidence that only a handful of bayonet attacks had succeeded, concluded that the bayonet charge was the decisive element. This Japanese "preference for cold steel" reflected repeated frustration over a lack of artillery support during the war with Russia.[11] Put another way, Japanese army logistical and technical shortcomings in 1904–5—a shortage of shells, too many unexploded rounds, inappropriate guns—and a failure to learn the lessons of modern warfare came to distort

Japanese—and eventually Indonesian—military doctrine. That said, the belief in voluntarism, the idea that a highly motivated force can overcome a better equipped enemy, would prove of critical importance in Indonesia. It came to underpin and reinforce the Indonesian concept of *semangat*, or revolutionary ardour, which was to be such an important energizing force in the post-war struggle for independence.

The Japanese knew, of course, that they would be able to get more out of their charges if they could tell them they would be fighting for an independent Indonesia. But for now, the word "independence" was taboo. "The educational goals would have been attained more quickly if we could have openly hoisted the slogan of Indonesian independence," one Japanese historian has written. "But the policy of Imperial Headquarters was that Java was to be secured as a supply base, so any agitation in favour of independence was strictly prohibited."[12] In these circumstances, the Japanese company commanders could only imply that Indonesia deserved to be independent, which they did by hammering away in their morning lectures about the iniquities of Dutch colonialism.

Yanagawa, who was responsible for training the first intake of West Java platoon commanders, the men who would become the all-important battalion commanders of the post-war Siliwangi Division, had his own way of instilling in the recruits the necessary offensive spirit, which the Japanese called *kanto seishin* and the Indonesians *semangat menyerang*. A devotee of *sumo*, he devised a modified form of the sport that stressed the importance of boldness and aggression. In normal *sumo* bouts there is a good deal of unhurried circling and manoeuvring. A wrestler who forces his opponent out of a circular ring, or who makes him touch the ground with anything other than the soles of his feet, is declared the winner, even if his opponent has managed to enter the winner's side of the ring. In the Yanagawa version, which left a deep imprint on the memory of many men who were to rise to prominence in the post-war Indonesian army, a circle was drawn in the sand with a line running across the middle. Wrestlers were taught to fly at one another as soon as they heard the command, "Start!" [*Kakare!*] The man who entered his opponent's territory was declared the winner. "If possible," said one former cadet, "you should meet your enemy on his ground, in his half of the circle ... You had to be faster than your enemy. Even if you ... succeed in throwing him down, that's not important. It's being faster. *Semangat* was emphasized, the warrior spirit."[13] This emphasis on spiritual factors and aggressiveness was entirely in keeping with Japanese army doctrine, which stressed the importance of taking the offence at all times.

As Tsuchiya put it, "Yanagawa had liked having his trainees doing *sumo* back in Tangerang. He loved *sumo*. It was his firm belief that *sumo* was the best sport to nurture the fighting spirit."[14] Those who emerged from the ring with badly grazed skin were taught to rub wet salt into the wound, a painful procedure, but one that aided the healing process. Soeharto and his fellow officer cadets from Central Java were not taught *sumo* in their company, but many of them took part in the *sumo* bouts organized by Yanagawa for the West Java cadets, some of whom found the traditional white *mawashi* (sumo wrestler's loincloth) embarrassingly brief and wore shorts underneath. Soeharto seems to have thrown himself into these contests, although he may not have enjoyed them as much as others did. "We also did *sumo*," he said. "A contestant was not permitted to stop until he won five bouts. I had a hard time since I was thin."[15] As well as the *sumo* wrestling, there was *juken jitsu*, or bayonet drills, the cadets wearing Japanese face masks and using wooden rifles, and *kendo*.

At Bogor, as had been the case at Tangerang, the Indonesian officer cadets were quick to pick up the importance of spiritual training. Indonesia, two former Beppan officers said, was "like a white paper; you could write anything on it."[16] In training sessions, Japanese instructors emphasized the importance of personal commitment. Japanese soldiers were expected to die for their country and Indonesian *pemudas* must be ready to do the same for theirs; a commitment of personal honour.

The Japanese had planned to give Soeharto and the other platoon commanders three months' intensive training at Bogor, but this was cut back to two months "due to the worsening situation of the war."[17] It was impossible, they knew, to turn out well-rounded junior officers in that time, so they concentrated on instilling fighting spirit, on teaching basic infantry skills and on building up the physical strength of the cadets. The emphasis was placed on infantry training, night fighting and static defence. Cadets were not given lessons on guerrilla warfare. At the time, the Japanese still thought they could fight an "authentic war." The idea of guerrilla training would only come later, when the Japanese began to realize they were losing the war.[18] Training was kept simple. Although

90 per cent of the cadets had attended junior high school, and some had gone a good deal further than that, there were others who had had very little education. "There were so many tiers," said Tsuchiya. "That is why we set the level of the training to the level of the lowest peasants."[19]

For Soeharto, the day began at 7:30 a.m. (6:00 a.m. in the "old" Dutch-era timekeeping system), when a Japanese bugler sounded reveille. On this signal, the cadets, bare from the waist up, made their way at the double to the training field for roll call. While waiting for other members of the company to assemble, they engaged in the Japanese practice of *kanpu-masatsu*, or body-rubbing, using a small dry towel and bellowing the words "*yoisho, yoisho!*" (Hi-ho!") under the direction of the cadet class leader. The Japanese believe this practice not only warms the body but also promotes good health. Roll call was followed by the flag-raising ceremony, an event invested with immense solemnity. As the Japanese flag inched its way up the flagpole, Soeharto and the others turned and bowed deeply from the waist in the direction of the Imperial Palace in Tokyo.[20] After that came gymnastics, which was followed, on most days, by a four-kilometre jog through the streets of Bogor, with squads of young men doing a lap of the palace and the botanical gardens. Sometimes, according to two officer cadets who went on to become generals in the post-war Indonesian Army, Yanagawa would follow the runners on his horse and simply trample on those who lagged behind.[21] The run ended with the cadets swarming up a steep hill from the river in a simulated bayonet charge (*totsugeki*), the air echoing with shouts of "*waaa…a!*," a cry designed to instil fear into the heart of any enemy. The slowest ten members of each group would be penalized with an additional 200 metre charge. All of this made a lasting impression on Soeharto. "'*Kakero! Kakero!* [Run! Run!]' I can still clearly remember our instructors' shout in the morning running session," he told a Japanese journalist more than fifty years later. "Even today, the language I use when I talk about those days is Japanese."[22]

After breakfast, the members of the 4th Company broke up into four sections for a ninety-minute classroom lesson, either on spiritual strength or military science. Along with his fellow cadets, Soeharto was instructed in the code of conduct that had been set down in the 1882 Imperial Rescript to Soldiers and Sailors. This code identified five cardinal virtues—loyalty, propriety, valour, righteousness and simplicity—that should guide the behaviour of servicemen, and it made the observation of these virtues a sacred obligation to the Emperor as supreme commander. "Keep well in mind," the Rescript said, "that your duty outweighs death itself as much as a mountain outweighs a feather." In Japan, these ideas had been reinforced in the 1930s when militarists and ultra-nationalists began laying stress on the *Yamato-damashii*, the spiritual qualities supposedly unique to the Japanese people. By the start of the Pacific War, *Yamato-damashii* was equated with unquestioning loyalty to Emperor and nation.

For all that, the Japanese appear to have drawn a clear distinction between their own servicemen and the Indonesian candidate officers. Although the Bogor cadets were required to bow towards the Imperial Palace each morning, there seems to have been no requirement that they take an oath of loyalty to the Emperor. According to Tsuchiya, "They didn't take a pledge of loyalty to the Emperor nor to Japan on arrival at the Peta course. The Emperor's retainers ought to be Japanese military men, whereas the Peta recruits were Indonesian. They joined for the sake of Java's defence. So if I remember correctly, we didn't make them recite an oath of loyalty to the Emperor in our daily routine activities. We did a lot of recitation of the Imperial Rescript, it is true. But those five items were something, I believed, essential not only to a soldier but to any human being."[23]

Oath of loyalty or not, Soeharto was to feel a surge of pride and satisfaction when, on a wintry Tokyo day in late March 1968, he met the Emperor on something like an equal footing, Soeharto as Head of State and head of government, the Emperor, stripped of his divinity and divested of all his powers, by now only a ceremonial Head of State.* "I wore Javanese clothing and I met the Emperor of Japan!" he told an Indonesian political adviser on his return.[24] "Oh yes, I met him! That is the Emperor that we

* If Soeharto and Hirohito were on an equal footing, at least in terms of protocol, there were nonetheless certain differences in their position. Hirohito had been Emperor for forty-two years. He had sat at the apex of a powerful industrialized nation that had conquered and dominated much of Asia in the years to 1945. He had earlier been revered as a god. Soeharto had been head of state of a poor Southeast Asian country for less than forty-two hours when the two men first met. He had come to Tokyo with his hand extended, seeking aid.

had to bow to.... And it was so cold. I forgot to wear socks. I had only sandals." "Oh," recalled the adviser, "he was very happy."[25] Soeharto may have been very happy but it is not clear when, on this visit, the President may have worn Javanese dress. A photo shows Hirohito welcoming Soeharto at Tokyo International Airport at the beginning of a five-day visit to Japan. Both men are wearing dark Western suits. A subsequent formal photo, apparently taken at the palace, shows the President and the Emperor standing solemnly to attention with Ibu Tien Soeharto between them. The two men are dressed in dark grey or black Western suits, conservative ties and black shoes; Ibu Tien is wearing *sarong kebaya* and shoes.

Tsuchiya, who had recruited and trained Soeharto between October and December 1943, was to see him again during this visit. "I met Soeharto," he recalled, "right after he became President, when he visited Tokyo to meet Prime Minister Sato [Eisaku] to report that he had become President." Queried about his use of the word "report", Tsuchiya said, "Report is a nicer word. He came to borrow money."[26] After a brief pause, he rephrased this. "No. As you pointed out, he didn't come to report to a senior but to greet the Prime Minister and ask for help." Asked for his impressions of Soeharto at that time, Tsuchiya replied, "He was still young and very confident. A very well-rounded person. Always smiling. And he didn't forget me. He came up to me and said, 'This is my teacher!' He talked to people about how hard the training was. And I got the impression he was a warm-hearted person."[27] After this meeting, Tsuchiya was bombarded with offers from Japanese company representatives "thinking he had an in and wanting to get him to act as their agent; but he refused."[28]

Kaneko Tomokazu, who had been a civilian member of the Sixteenth Army Propaganda Corps (Sendenhan) during the war, met Soeharto for the first time during this visit. "He was so happy to be President—something he had never dreamed of or expected," Kaneko recalled.[29] "Happiness showed in his whole countenance. The welcoming party took place in the Imperial Hotel. We were able to tell that he was extremely happy to come to Japan after all those experiences as a Peta officer and so on. And he seemed to be pretty modest." At the time of the visit, the Indonesian ambassador in Tokyo was Lieutenant General Rukmito Hendraningrat, who had been a classmate of Soeharto in the No. 4 *chutai* (company) training session. The defence attaché was Brigadier General R.M. Jono Hatmodjo, who was from the No. 2 *chutai*. Jono Hatmodjo, one of seven members of the Mangkunegaran court who joined the Peta, was, as we have seen, a relative of Ibu Tien Soeharto and, at that time, on good terms with her.

The morning lecture in Bogor was followed by instruction in one or more of the standard field exercises set out in the Japanese army infantry textbook (*Hohei soten*).[30] The afternoon was given over to further exercises in the field, the focus being on small-unit tactics, especially those involving offensive action against an enemy. During these sessions, Soeharto learned how to attack and overrun a defensive position. He learned how to face an enemy with his bare hands. He mastered Japanese army bayonet techniques. "After lunch," General Purbo Suwondo remembered, "we had to run to the exercise area, which is now the Bogor golf course. It was hot, and we were soaked with sweat. When we came back in the afternoon, our shirts were often white from the salt of dried up perspiration."[31] It was, Purbo thought, "very, very tough training."[32] From time to time, the acting commander of the Bogor centre, Captain Maruzaki, inspected the training grounds, mounted on a large grey horse and receiving oral reports from the company commanders.[33] With his unyielding manner, Maruzaki was seen as a man to be propitiated. No one took him lightly. When he rode into view, the Japanese instructors and Indonesian cadets threw themselves into the training with renewed vigour.

On most occasions, the cadets were required to run back to the barracks through the streets of Bogor, carrying their KNIL-issue rifles. Many found this so exhausting, a Japanese observer noted, "they were almost ready to cry."[34] But the Japanese granted no respite. If an Indonesian cadet failed to run fast enough or fell out, he would find himself mocked by his instructors. "Hey you!" a Japanese corporal would shout. "You said you want to have independence and you can't even do this! How can you become independent if you can't even run five miles?"[35] On other occasions, cadets would march back to camp, singing Japanese and Indonesian songs. One of the favourites was the Japanese military song *Hohei no honryo*, with its famous first line "Banda no sakura" (Cherry blossoms in full bloom). Back at the barracks, there were still more songs, including *Shina no Yoru* (China Nights)—a romantic ballad, popular at the time but now seldom sung because it is considered deeply offensive in China, and *Umi Yukaba*, a melancholy lament about the inevitable death that awaits a soldier or sailor. More than half a century later, many older Indonesians could recall the words of *Umi Yukaba*, which had been taught at school during the Japanese occupation:

Umi yukaba, mizuku kabane
Yama yukaba, kusa musu kabane
Okimi no he ni koso shiname
Kaerimi wa seji.

If I go away to sea,
I shall become a corpse floating in the water;
If I go away to the mountains,
I shall become a corpse from which grass grows;
If it is for the Emperor,
I will not regret my death.

After dinner, cadets were taught how to shout commands in the field, a procedure known as *gorei chosei*. Members of a platoon would gather at one end of a soccer ground. The cadet chosen to command them would stand at the other end, bellowing out orders like a company sergeant major and suffering punishment and humiliation if those orders could not be clearly understood. Afterwards, there might be compulsory practice of Japanese army songs. The two hours to 9:00 p.m. were set aside for study. A bugler sounded lights-out shortly afterwards.

From time to time, the Japanese would organize night training sessions, which began after dinner on Saturday night and continued until sunrise the following day. As Tsuchiya, the commander of Soeharto's training company, noted, "Everybody looked forward to Sunday."[36] During the course, the cadets were taken three or four times to the firing range, where they would each fire about ten rounds. "There," said one former Peta officer, laconically, "we learned that every bullet should kill one person. Japanese efficiency!"[37] As in any army, great emphasis was placed on the care and maintenance of weapons. Here, Soeharto had an advantage over his fellow cadets. The Peta officer cadets were issued with captured KNIL rifles and machine guns, most of which were familiar to Soeharto, who could strip and reassemble them even when blindfolded.

The training at Bogor was not only intense but relentless, just as it had been at Tangerang. Bogor is one of the wettest places on earth, with an annual rainfall of 160 inches. It has been known to have as many as 300 thunderstorms in a single year. The arrival of the late-year monsoon had no impact on the Japanese training programme, however. "Training took place even in heavy rain," Tsuchiya recalled. "Weapons and clothes got soaked. Our lips turned purple. We could not stop trembling. My army sword got rusted through. Trainees had trouble taking care of their wet clothes and weapons on rainy days."[38]

The acting commander of the 1st Company, who was responsible for training the 127 Indonesian company commanders, was known to his charges as a "madman" (*orang gila*) after he forced them out on midnight manoeuvres in clothes still soaking wet from an afternoon thunderstorm. As the semi-official Japanese history of the Peta notes, "He wanted to teach the company commander cadets that war went on regardless of weather. Since everyone was in high spirits, no one came down with a cold."[39] In short, the Japanese squeezed every available minute from the day. "Because our time was limited," Tsuchiya said, "we couldn't afford to see even a day pass without physical training outdoors. Even if spears fell, we were determined to do this outdoor training."[40] The Indonesians found it difficult to meet the exacting standards of the Japanese NCOs who supervised their field training. "As in every military establishment," one Indonesian officer said, "they were never satisfied with your first effort. You had to do it all four or five times. 'You did not shout loud enough!' 'You did not advance fast enough!'"[41]

Punishments were imposed for the slightest infraction. Perhaps the severest form of corporal punishment (*taibatsu*) inflicted on cadets was *seiza*, which involves kneeling on the floor, folding one's legs under one's thighs, while resting the buttocks on the heels.[42] Most Japanese find it difficult to maintain the *seiza* position for more than thirty minutes, even with a cushion under the knees. Cadets at Bogor were forced to do so for an hour or more, sometimes all night. During that time they were expected to remain still and reflect on themselves. Cadets referred to this mockingly as *zazen*, which is a form of religious meditation in Japan, and among them the term *zazen* became virtually synonymous with corporal punishment. At other times, a cadet might be forced to stand at attention for an hour in the midday sun, his rifle held out in front of his body.

To make matters worse, some Japanese officers and NCOs were in the habit of slapping cadets on the face, a common practice in the Japanese army, but one which the Indonesians found deeply humiliating. Nor was it only individuals who were punished in these ways. If one man in a company erred, the entire unit might be made to sit in the *seiza* position for an entire night, watched by three Japanese NCOs, each carrying a two-meter-long bamboo cane. Very few cadets could do this for long, and when, inevitably, someone fell to the ground, an instructor would move in and strike him viciously across the back. The victim would sit up again, only to fall down yet again and be struck yet again. A unit that spent the night in this way was expected to be on the parade ground at 7:30 a.m. the next day, ready for another full day of training. Recalling this kind of treatment, Major General Moersjid said, "Sometimes I didn't get the point. What kind of training is this? We were treated like that! But afterwards we felt it couldn't be different, it had to be done like that."[43]

Purbo Suwondo was another who was to conclude that there might have been some method in the Japanese madness, even in their penchant for collective punishment. "That happened very often," he said. "That makes for a kind of esprit de corps. That fosters a concern for others. If you do something wrong, the whole platoon will be punished."[44] According to General Widodo, who was a member of the second intake of platoon commander cadets from Central Java and whom Soeharto would appoint as Army Chief of Staff in 1978, "it was very hard training," with a heavy emphasis on physical training, the use of weapons and basic platoon tactics. "And almost every day we received a slap—*pukul!* Almost every day!"[45] Others, looking back, thought the punishment was more mental than physical.[46]

Soeharto and the other *shodancho* cadets from Central Java were fortunate to have Tsuchiya as their company commander. Not only was he sympathetic to the Indonesian nationalist cause; he also kept a tight rein on his Japanese army subordinates, especially the NCOs. At Bogor, Tsuchiya chose to live in the barracks with the Indonesian trainees, forgoing the house that had been set aside outside the camp for the commanders of the training companies. And he had given strict instructions that no cadet was to be slapped on the face. What is more, he went out of his way to empathize with his Indonesian officer cadets. As he said later, "When a *seito* [pupil] was ordered by a *kutaicho* [section commander] to stand through an hour-long recess due to a mistake he made, while others lay in the shade of the trees, I would stand next to him until the recess was over. I didn't want the recruits to think Japanese were merciless and cruel."[47]

Soeharto, looking back years later, said the Japanese instructors were "strict-minded military officers, but we felt their sympathy for us."[48] Even so, the treatment was harsh enough for Soeharto to remember it clearly forty-five years later. As he recalled in his memoirs, "Once during an exercise we were forced to drink filthy water from a river behind a Goodyear rubber factory. At another time, we were made to kneel for hours because one of the recruits had thrown his *hancho*'s [squad leader's] cap away."[49] In an account given to a Japanese newspaper, Soeharto said, "Peta training was beyond imagination. We had military drill, theory and spiritual training from 5:30 in the morning until midnight. The training given to the platoon commanders who would command troops at the front line was especially rigorous. When they found one trainee slacking off, they made all of us kneel with our backs straight [*seiza*] until midnight."[50]

II

Some of the Indonesian officers who graduated from the Bogor training centre were to mete out corporal punishment themselves in later years. In early 1945, not long after the revolt of the Peta battalion in Blitar, *shodancho* (later general) Soemitro was waiting for a train at the Malang railway station. A *kenpeiho* corporal told him he should set an example by standing in line for a ticket like everyone else, rather that use his travel pass, which made that unnecessary. "I turned around and hit him," Soemitro recalled, "I punched him hard." Soon afterwards, Soemitro was summoned to the local Kenpeitai headquarters. The commanding officer asked him why he had struck the corporal. Soemitro said he had felt insulted. "I am an officer and he is a noncommissioned officer. He was rude and overstepped the bounds when he reprimanded me in front of the public." The Kenpeitai chief is said to have nodded his head in understanding but warned Soemitro not to lose his temper so easily. Fortunately for Soemitro, his battalion commander was a "close friend" of the Kenpeitai chief.[51]

In the early fifties, when Soemitro was a battalion commander, he learned that his army driver had advised one of the maids in Soemitro's house to leave because she was not being paid enough. Soemitro was furious. "I was still young," he recalled, "just a Japanese-trained officer, you see. You know how Japanese training is…. What is my salary? Very hard to survive, I mean to manage on my salary. So I cannot afford to pay my servants like the other people…. One day this fellow said, 'Why do you work for Pak Mitro? You'd better quit. It's too low, your salary.' Oh no! I hit him. I punished him…. I hit him black and blue. His shirt was completely torn and I gave him my shirt to wear." As the man was walking home, people asked him what had happened. He told them he had got into a fight with some Chinese.[52] On another occasion, Soemitro learned that a sergeant had slept with the wife of one of his men. Soemitro called him in, hit him and demoted him from sergeant to private. Many years later, when Soemitro, by now a general, arrived at his headquarters in Jakarta, a guard failed to salute him correctly. Appalled by this lapse and too impatient to get the sergeant to "knock" the hapless guard, Soemitro vented his anger by punching his ADC.[53] Nor, it seems, was it only servicemen who felt his wrath. On one occasion, Soemitro is said to have hit an Indian businessman in a Jakarta hotel.

General Surono Reksodimedjo, another Japanese-trained officer, was equally quick with his fists. In the early 1970s, when he was Army Chief of Staff, Surono was in the back seat of his staff car when his driver pulled out of the Department of Defence and Security (Hankam) headquarters in Jakarta. A captain came zig-zagging down the road in a utility and cut him off. Incandescent with anger, Surono told the driver, "Catch him!" They caught up with the captain near the National Monument. Surono, a very fit man, passionate about *karate-do*, jumped out and struck him a powerful blow. "He did it there in the street with everyone watching," General Benny Moerdani recalled. "It is not right to behave like that. The four stars on his number plate! We found out about it because the captain came to me. We said, 'Well, you have two weeks to file a report.' In the end he didn't and that way everyone's sympathy was with the captain. Surono made a fool of himself."[54] Major General Gatot Subroto, a tough, outgoing, Rabelaisian officer who had spent time in both the KNIL and the Peta and who went on to serve as Deputy Army Chief of Staff under General A.H. Nasution, was also known to strike subordinates who incurred his wrath.[55] Another former Peta man, Lieutenant General Mohammad Jasin, took a different tack. Angered in the 1970s that Major General Bustanil Arifin had taken liberties with his daughter, he had a junior officer punch him. Some fellow officers thought that was poor form: he should have done it himself.

Soeharto was not above threatening his men at gunpoint and slapping them. During the first Dutch "Police Action" against the Republic in July 1947 about twenty of Soeharto's soldiers fled their position in the hill country southwest of Semarang amid a heavy mortar barrage. Soeharto happened to be in the area on an inspection tour of the front. He drew his pistol and pointed it at the soldiers. He called them cowards and told them to go back. Afraid of him, they hurriedly did so.[56] In September 1950,

Soeharto slapped the military harbour master at Makassar, First Lieutenant Suparman, on the face several times when he refused to allow Soeharto's men to load half a dozen stolen second-hand cars and jeeps onto a ship taking the Garuda Mataram Brigade back to Java following a deployment in South Sulawesi. Most of the vehicles had been made available by a local car dealer, Ban Hok Liong, on a promise, since dishonoured, that they would be paid for.[57]

Most of the cases set out above involve spontaneous, violent discipline within a hierarchy. Why, we may ask, did these officers—and we are speaking here of a future president, a powerful national security chief who might conceivably have succeeded him as president, an army chief of staff and two deputy army chiefs of staff—feel it appropriate and/or permissible to act in this way? Was such behaviour common, and readily condoned, in pre-colonial and/or colonial Indonesia? Or was it due largely or even exclusively to Japanese influence? What does history tell us about violence in Indonesia? Some forty years ago, the historian Robert Cribb has observed, many scholars tended to think of Indonesia as a fairly non-violent place, with just a few perplexing exceptions, one of which was the mass killing of 1965–66. This perception, he suggests, might have been in part the heritage of the Dutch view that the Indonesians—or at least the Javanese—were naturally gentle, but it also reflected the general level of public order under Soeharto.[58] Then, however, came "a fairly sudden scholarly discovery of violence."

This discovery found expression, inter alia, in the 2002 book *Roots of Violence in Indonesia*, a collection of a dozen scholarly essays. In the ringing opening sentence of that work, the co-editors, Freek Colombijn and J. Thomas Lindblad, declare, "Indonesia is a violent country", echoing the Dutch historian Henk Schulte Nordholt's characterization of the Netherlands East Indies as "a state of violence", one which had established its dominance by ruthless military means.[59] Many of the chapters in the 2002 book focus on inter-group violence. Less is known about inter-personal violence, particularly that within hierarchies during the pre-colonial period, although it is interesting to note that Nasution, when asked if Gatot Subroto's propensity for striking subordinates could be ascribed to Japanese influences, said he thought it "more feudal."[60]

We have a good deal of evidence, however, about hierarchical violence during the colonial era. For example, Erwiza Erman has provided a dark and detailed account of how, in the Ombilin coal mines in West

Sumatra, overseers, guards and police officers systematically caned, beat and kicked the many convict and contract labourers who absconded or refused to work. Harsh treatment continued there under the Japanese. In the rich plantation belt of North Sumatra, Indo-European plantation overseers subjected uncooperative labourers recruited in China, Java and other islands in the NEI to a range of sometimes severe punishments—incarcerating them without food and water; having them run the gauntlet; having them dragged behind a horse with their hands bound; driving slivers of bamboo under their fingernails; having finely ground pepper rubbed onto female sexual organs and having Chinese coolies clubbed to death—under "a draconian rationale" that this was the only way to instill obedience.[61]

If some pre-war civilian overseers and colonial policemen had no compunction about brutalizing workers, at a cost of countless deaths and ruined lives, the KNIL, ruthless as it was against those who took up arms against the Dutch colonial state, seems to have treated its own more humanely. Schulte Nordholt believes that the practice of military superiors punishing subordinates by striking them is very likely a Japanese/Peta legacy. "The form matters here," he observes. "The humiliating slapping in the face was Japanese and featured, as far as I know, never in the pre-colonial repertoire of patron-client relationships. Nor was it common practice in the KNIL."[62]

As Cribb sees it, the violent disciplinary practices of TNI officers are most comparable to the violence of NCOs against new recruits, the violence of overseers against labourers, the violence of teachers against pupils (in the old days) and the violence of warders and guards against prisoners. "In all these cases," he argues, "the characteristic is that the person with higher authority is indulged to get angry and violent in response to minor insubordinations and is never (or almost never) held to account, with the overall effect of upholding the hierarchy." Cribb does not claim that there was no specific Japanese element in the mix. But nor does he single out the Japanese for particular attention. The reason why the habits of men such as Soeharto, Soemitro and Surono became so salient, he believes, was that they became much more important politically than they would have been in a normal, stable society and because they were never forced to unlearn the habits of their youth. That is true. But the fact remains that former Peta officers did learn these techniques from the Japanese and some of them did become important politically. And although many Japanese-trained officers would turn on the Japanese in 1945, they nevertheless went on to perpetuate a form of Japanese behaviour they themselves had once abhorred.

As mentioned earlier, Beppan officers, trained to leverage Japanese power in a more sophisticated way than their mainstream army colleagues, largely abjured the harsher punishments that had made the Japanese Army so hated and feared in much of Asia. Beppan had some remarkable successes in Indonesia, not least the creation of an embryo Indonesian Army. But there was a limit to what a handful of Beppan captains and lieutenants could achieve. The Japanese Army, familiar as it was with blunter and more brutal methods, had limited time for these niceties; and, in any case, most of the Beppan officers were soon given new responsibilities away from Bogor. Before long, there were more and more newly-arrived Japanese NCOs in Java, a significant number of whom were assigned to the Bogor training centre and to Peta units in the field. These men, who had grown up in an environment in which disdain, if not contempt, for the people of the "backward" societies of the southern region was deeply ingrained; who had no understanding of, or sympathy for, Indonesian aspirations or cultural norms, and who had, like all other Japanese recruits, been beaten constantly in their first year in the army in the name of instilling discipline, were only too ready to beat and humiliate those Indonesians over whom they now held dominion.

In view of all this, it is difficult to escape the conclusion that harsh, humiliating and systematic disciplinary measures, a core feature Japanese military life, did indeed have a lasting impact in Indonesia. The Japanese introduced a new and virulent culture of violence, one that encompassed significantly larger sections of society than did colonial violence. In the colonial era, Indonesian elites and members of the middle class did not have to fear being beaten up; they did during the Japanese period.[63] An unnerving fear of swift and unpredictable violence was a feature of everyday life in occupied Indonesia, both in those areas in the west that were ruled by the Japanese Army and those in the east that came under the Japanese Navy. This fear was felt in both the civilian and the military domain. That had long-term consequences. In the twenty-two months to August 1945, a crop of young Indonesian Peta officers came to believe that it was appropriate and permissible to punch and slap subordinates. At the same time, scores of young, educated Indonesians from a lower- or middle-*priyayi* background, were exposed, in the Kenpeitai, to the sickening

Japanese torture of suspects—practices they would go on to practice themselves in the post-war Indonesian Military Police Corps. Suddenly, it was not just foreigners, and the callous indigenous hard-men who had always been willing to ply their trade in the unlit, unregulated backblocks of the colonial state, who were abusing Indonesians. Now, Indonesia's future leaders, many of them educated members of the middle class, freed at last from any fear of random Japanese violence, were behaving that way too, slapping, punching and sometimes torturing their fellow Indonesians, including their military subordinates.

III

Throughout the course, the Japanese stressed the importance of showing respect towards superiors and attending to the welfare of subordinates. "We had water bottles made from coconuts," one officer remembered. "When you took a break you would first offer your water bottle to the instructor. We also learned the techniques of leadership. You have to think of your subordinates, your *anak buah*. Your concern is for your subordinates. It's called *buka no shoaku*."[64] Soeharto, who had of course been made aware of such considerations in the KNIL, took all this very much to heart. In later years, he was to be known for the exceptional attention he paid to the welfare of his men. Indeed, the efforts he made to advance those interests were to lead him into dubious fund-raising and business deals, which were to be a hallmark of his years both as a senior officer and as President, and which, when taken to excess, would do so much to undermine his legitimacy as President.

The Japanese went to some pains to feed their officer cadets well. Breakfast might include Japanese *miso* soup, made from bean paste, accompanied by white rice, sometimes mixed with corn, sometimes with soy beans.[65] A typical dinner consisted of beef or fish, rice, tomatoes, green vegetables, peanuts and other items. Still, there never seemed to be enough food, and some cadets risked beatings by seeking more outside the camp. Once, during a night exercise involving both *chudancho* and *shodancho* cadets, G.P.H. Djatikusumo, a prince of the royal court of Solo, son of the popular and corpulent Pakubuwono X, and K.R.M.T. Soemyarsono, a member of the Pakualaman, the minor court in Yogyakarta, stopped to collect sweet potatoes from a village garden—two well-educated young Javanese aristocrats scrabbling about at night in a West Java potato patch, a metaphor for a world in transition.

On another occasion, in 1944, Soemitro, who went on to become a four-star general and who was seen in the early seventies as a possible successor to President Soeharto, got out of his bunk at night and left camp through a hedge, seeking food, even though that was strictly prohibited. According to Morimoto Takeshi, who was Soemitro's platoon commander at Bogor, Yanagawa saw a cadet coming back to camp but was unable to catch him.[66] Back in his dormitory, Soemitro swapped his tell-tale muddy shoes for those of Sukaryadi, with whom he shared a mosquito net. When Yanagawa discovered the shoes he interrogated Sukaryadi, who refused to say anything. Furious, Yanagawa slapped him repeatedly. As Soemitro told the story, he and two other cadets from East Java, Sukaryadi and Ponidi, went out that night. Sukaryadi was caught by the Japanese and beaten. The Japanese knew that he had gone out with two fellow cadets. But despite the punishment he refused to divulge the names of his companions, who had no intention of turning themselves in. Soemitro and Ponidi were deeply grateful.[67] Soemitro made no reference to exchanging his dirty shoes.

As time passed, the Indonesians gained in strength. Even those who had fainted during the entrance ceremony "learned to endure the severe training and to give a fierce look back at their instructors when in the beginning they failed in focusing their loosely opened eyes."[68] "After a week or ten days," said Tsuchiya, "we noticed a change in their eyes. They had a sharper look in their eyes. That was obvious."[69] The Japanese noted, too, that the Indonesian cadets were growing darker after long hours out in the sun.

Most of the cadets were Muslims, and the Japanese had, of course, gone out of their way to recruit a number of prominent Islamic figures as future battalion and company commanders. Beppan was anxious not to offend any religious sensibilities, if at all possible. Care was taken to ensure that all food was *halal* (permitted). But there were limits to the concessions that Beppan felt it could make. This was wartime, and the Peta was a special force being trained for defence purposes.[70] "I'm sorry," said Tsuchiya. "We had to ignore Islam. In Islam there is a provision that says that, in a time of emergency, followers do not have to abide by the regulations.... So we made use of that. So Friday wasn't a day off, and we didn't let them do their prayers every day. There could be some people who made regular daily prayers behind our backs, but we didn't set up a regular time for prayers."[71] According to Tsuchiya, the Japanese did not encounter any difficulties on this front. On the contrary, those *daidanchos* who were from a strongly Islamic background "persuaded the lower ones not to demand their religious observances." According to Morimoto, Japanese officers had come to an agreement with Indonesian religious leaders, who conceded that they did not have to pay special consideration to religious practices. Although no time was set aside for mosque attendance on Friday, Morimoto said, cadets were free to pray before reveille and after lights-out if they chose.[72]

On Friday afternoons, the cadets were expected to rest in the camp. Family members could visit if they lived nearby, but cadets were not permitted to leave the training centre at any time, except when they were under instruction or on the closely supervised morning run. For Soeharto, one of the treats at Bogor was the *daifuku-mochi*, a Japanese confection made of sweet bean paste and available in the canteen. For others, an even greater treat was the cigarette ration. The Japanese provided each cadet with two or three packs of Western-style cigarettes each week, a rare treat in wartime Java. These could be either be smoked or exchanged with visitors for fruit and snacks.

Soeharto made several important friends among the *shodancho* cadets at Bogor, all of them within his sixty-man training section, one-third of which consisted of recruits from the Princely Territory of Yogyakarta. His closest friend was Soedjono, the son of a *pegawai negeri* (official) of the Pakualaman.[73] A solidly built young man, bespectacled and always neatly turned out, Soedjono was seen by colleagues as "a good fellow", a man of principle who was later to display considerable gifts as a military commander. In the years after 1945, when Indonesia was fighting for its independence against the returning Dutch, Soedjono was not only Soeharto's closest friend but one of his two most competent and dependable battalion commanders. Soedjono is of interest for two reasons. First, he had not completed elementary school. That meant that he had even less formal education than Soeharto. Of the sixteen men who were to serve as battalion commanders under Soeharto between 1945 and 1950, all but Soedjono were better educated than their commanding officer, sometimes by a long chalk.[74] Second, Soedjono was a Roman Catholic. During his early years as an army officer, and later as President, Soeharto was to depend, to a marked degree, on officers from a Christian background. Of those sixteen battalion commanders in the late 1940s, no fewer than five were Catholics.[75] There was, however, no political or religious significance in this fact, as there would be in later years, when Soeharto seemed to go out of his way to appoint Christian officers to senior positions, conscious, no doubt, that they could pose no threat to his position. Rather, the disproportionate number of Christians was a reflection of both the high educational standards in Christian schools and the broad social, political and religious backing for the revolutionary movement.

Another cadet whom Soeharto befriended at Bogor was Pranoto Reksosamodra. Pranoto was from Purworejo, an area in which the Communist Party was to gain many supporters; indeed, his uncle, it has been claimed, was to emerge as a prominent local Communist.[76] In Yogyakarta, Pranoto had attended Muhammadiyah junior and senior high schools established on the Dutch pattern and with a "Western" orientation. He had gone on to a Teacher's Training School (HIK), where he studied to be a teacher in the Dutch-language Muhammadiyah system.[77] Intelligent and reserved, Pranoto was seen by his colleagues as a good Javanese: very humble, very honest, interested in *wayang* and in mysticism and, perhaps because of that, one of them thought, a bit inclined to the left in later years.[78] Yet another colleague from this time was Soemyarsono, the quietly spoken aristocrat from the Pakualaman. He had attended the same Muhammadiyah junior high school as Pranoto, and, though two years younger than Pranoto, was as close to him as Soeharto was to Soedjono. In 1945, Soemyarsono was to set up his own battalion in Yogyakarta, alongside Soeharto. A year later, after Soeharto was promoted to regimental commander, Soemyarsono served under him as a battalion commander. Later, in December 1947, he was one of a small group of people invited to Soeharto's wedding.

Two of these friendships, it is worth noting, would come under strain during the 1945–49 Revolution, when these men were serving under Soeharto as battalion commanders. A third would descend into bitterness and acrimony in 1959. Initially, it is true, Soeharto enjoyed a close personal rapport with his post-war battalion commanders. As time passed, however, the relationship would become more "feudal", as was often the case in Central Java. Soedjono was to remain Soeharto's closest friend in the period to 1948. But according to one of their mutual friends, he came in time to fear Soeharto.[79] In 1948, Soeharto would relieve Soemyarsono of his battalion on the grounds that he was insufficiently decisive. In 1959, Soeharto and Pranoto were to fall out irrevocably when the latter reported Soeharto, who was by then military commander in Central Java, to army headquarters over freewheeling business and trading deals, which Pranoto, who personified the puritanical ethos of most Central Javanese officers, found deeply offensive; Soeharto never forgave this "betrayal." He refused to accept President Sukarno's appointment of Pranoto as acting army commander in October 1965, and when he came to power, he lost no time in finding reasons to jail his former friend.

Curiously, Soeharto makes no mention of these men in his autobiography, referring only to other "friends" from his time at Bogor. One is a man named Supio. "We were assigned to the same barracks and became close friends," he wrote of Supio, while nevertheless relegating him to a subservient position in the Soeharto narrative. "After an exercise, he would wash both his and my clothes while I cleaned our guns. He would also wait in line in the canteen to buy us *mochi* [sweet, glutinous rice].... There was never enough, so you had to line up fast to get any."[80] The other friend is a man whom Soeharto refers to as "Pranoto Wijono." This is odd. There was no one of that name involved in the *shodancho* course at Bogor. The only Pranoto at Bogor was Pranoto Reksosamodra.[81] This suggests either that Soeharto's exceptionally good memory and almost obsessive attention to detail failed him when he came to dictate his memoirs, or that he was, once more, rewriting the historical record, unable, perhaps, to acknowledge that he had once been friends with Pranoto Reksosamodra, a man he had come to detest.

Among the others in his platoon were Bardosono, a young man of a mystic bent who was to hold key positions in Soeharto's New Order government, and Maryono, who went on to serve as a company commander in Soeharto's Battalion X in Yogyakarta in 1945.[82] In 1965, while serving as Assistant III (Personnel) in the Diponegoro (Central Java) military region, Colonel Maryono sided fatally with the September 30th Movement; he and his fellow Central Java plotters were hunted down and killed by troops operating on Soeharto's orders.

Another *shodancho* cadet from Central Java was Amad Jani (later Achmad Yani), who would be killed in the failed 1965 "coup". The son of a Javanese chauffeur who had, on the recommendation of his Dutch employer, taken his young family from rural Central Java to work for a Dutch general in Jakarta, Yani had grown up under the wing of several Dutch families and attended a series of Dutch-language schools, culminating in the prestigious Christelijke AMS-B senior high school on Oranje Boulevard (now Jl. Diponegoro) in Jakarta. He joined the KNIL, where he served in the Military Topography Service and rose to sergeant.[83] Yet another cadet from Central Java was Sarwo Edhie Wibowo, who became a close friend of Yani's at Bogor.[84] In 1965, Sarwo Edhie was commander of the Army Para-commando Regiment (Resimen Para Komando Angkatan Darat, RPKAD), which would lead a brutal crackdown on alleged Communists in Central Java and Bali, and track down Maryono and his colleagues. Others on the course were Surono Reksodimedjo, the future Army chief of staff, and Munadi, whom Soeharto would later appoint as governor of Central Java.

The list of *shodancho* cadets from West Java included Amir Machmud, a blunt and unsophisticated officer who would do Soeharto's bidding for fourteen years (1969–82) as Indonesia's all-important interior minister. Umar Wirahadikusumah, who was to serve as vice president under Soeharto (1983–88), was also attached to the West Java company, presumably as a trainer, given that he had graduated from the Tangerang course. The East Java Training Company included Mohammad Jasin, who, in the 1970s, after a time as deputy army chief of staff, would risk everything by daring to accuse Soeharto of greed and hypocrisy. Some of these men were to rise to high office by dint of their own ability. Others were to win preferment because Soeharto made it a practice to intervene in the promotions system. Throughout his career, Soeharto was to value personal connections more highly than competence. He would reach back across the decades to bring forward men whom he knew and trusted and who could be counted on to implement his wishes.

As well as those in his immediate circle, Soeharto was thrown together with a number of instructors and officer cadets who were to play key roles in the post-war Indonesian National Army. One of them was Zulkifli Lubis, an intense, austere and strong-willed, albeit somewhat reserved, young man whom Beppan officers considered the brightest Indonesian they ever recruited.[85] Lubis was one of ten children of a Mandailing Batak schoolteacher who had gone on to become a government official. He was born in Aceh, where his mother, who was also a Mandailing Batak, had herself been born, and he attended primary school and junior high school there. The family, Lubis once said, considered itself more Acehnese than Mandailing. His education was in Dutch, which he spoke fluently with a distinctive lisp. He understood the Mandailing Batak dialect but could not speak it. In 1940 Lubis moved to Yogyakarta, enrolling in the AMS-B senior high school, where the emphasis was on physics and mathematics. He was in the second year when the Japanese came.[86]

Zulkifli Lubis was deeply religious, with a mystical streak in his make-up. Selected as a member of the first intake at the Tangerang training centre, he learned Japanese very quickly and displayed a natural flair for intelligence work, propaganda and clandestine operations. At Tangerang, he never said anything if he was angry but would quietly obey the command he had been given.[87] But if Lubis did not make trouble, he was much stronger in his private criticism of the Japanese than his fellow students. Lubis was never slapped by the Japanese, although everyone else was, at one time or another, as a result of which some of his less gifted fellow cadets labelled him a Japanese lackey (*antek jepang*).[88] Rated number one at Tangerang, both in class work and outdoor military training, Lubis was sent to the Peta training school at Bogor as an assistant instructor (*shido-gakusei*) in Soeharto's training company, which means that Soeharto would have been in contact with him on a daily basis. Lubis was nineteen when the Bogor course began, two and a half years younger than Soeharto. Tsuchiya, responsible for training the Central Java company, found Lubis "plain and simple, quiet, sober, restrained, modest, low-keyed" and quite the most impressive of all the Indonesians who underwent officer training during the occupation.[89] In the 1950s, Lubis would be the stormy petrel of Indonesian military politics, enveloped in an air of mystery and intrigue, serving for a time as acting army chief of staff and allegedly behind an unsuccessful coup.

Another assistant instructor in Soeharto's company was Daan Mogot, who had been the runner-up at Tangerang, behind Lubis. As Tsuchiya saw it, Daan Mogot was "more Japanese than an ordinary Japanese officer" and "willing to do anything."[90] Kemal Idris, an outgoing West Sumatran who had attended the pre-war HBS high school in Yogyakarta and who was to serve as the Chief of Staff of Kostrad, the Army Strategic Reserve Command, immediately after the 1965 coup attempt, was another who transferred from Tangerang to Bogor.

To his fellow cadets at Bogor, Soeharto seemed uncommonly taciturn. Asked to recall his first impressions of Soeharto, Soemyarsono could do no better than anyone else. "He was polite," he said. "But he did not speak too much." He was "low-profile."[91] The Japanese also found Soeharto quiet, but were much impressed by his abilities. Tsuchiya, who observed him closely during his two months in the training company, felt that he was one of the best and brightest of the officer cadets at Bogor. He was not as gifted as Zulkifli Lubis. Nor was he as good as Daan Mogot. But he was one of the stars of the 4th Company. As Tsuchiya put it, Soeharto "did an outstanding job in both classroom work and in military training outdoors. He was always able to do a model demonstration when we asked him to do so. Let's suppose there's an 'enemy' out there with a gun. In training, he was able to give a good example and run to the enemy and kill him."[92]

For one or two of the cadets, the relentless combat training was tiresome, and they undertook it reluctantly. Soeharto treated it with the utmost seriousness, charging headlong at imaginary enemies with rifle and bayonet, shouting in the approved manner, abandoning all normal reserve. The Japanese instructors watched all this admiringly. "You have to be really serious in showing a good example," Tsuchiya explained. "If the example is done poorly, the others can't learn." In these exercises, Soeharto would show exactly how an attack was to be carried out, crawling forward towards the enemy for about 150 yards, then charging the last fifty yards, screaming as he went, disposing of the enemy in hand-to-hand fighting with the bayonet. At the end of the course, Tsuchiya ranked his Indonesian cadets in order of ability, from one down to 230, although no cadet was told where he had finished. "I can't remember where Soeharto was," Tsuchiya said. "Maybe he was within the top ten. But he was never number one. Lubis was easily number one. And number two was Daan Mogot .... They rose to the top through ability .... They became almost like Japanese military officers."[93] A retired Indonesian army historian who graduated from the Bogor course was a little less generous in his assessment. "Pak Harto," he said, somewhat dismissively, "was not that outstanding."[94]

In late November 1943, as the Peta officer cadets were nearing the end of their training at Bogor, the Japanese flew Sukarno and Hatta to Tokyo. They were taken to see Emperor Hirohito, who awarded them decorations, and had discussions with Tojo. By now, Burma and the Philippines had been given their "independence." Sukarno and Hatta pressed Tojo once again to accept Indonesia as a single political entity, not three separate territories, and grant it independence. Once again, Tojo refused. They also sought permission to fly the red-and-white nationalist flag and play *Indonesia Raya*. Tojo showed some willingness to consider the second request. He warned, however, that he would have to confer with his officials in Java. Those officials shot the idea down.

On Thursday, 2 December 1943, when Soeharto's intake had less than three weeks of training to complete, Field Marshal Terauchi Hisaichi, the sixty-five-year-old Supreme Commander of Japanese forces in the Southern Region, visited the Bogor centre, resplendent in khaki pith helmet, full uniform and spurred riding boots. He was accompanied by an aide-de-camp to Emperor Hirohito, by General Harada and by the commanders of all the Japanese battalions deployed on Java. As he strode from his car to the ceremonial Japanese gate, Terauchi unexpectedly approached an Indonesian sentry who was presenting arms. "*Erai-ka*?", he asked in the Osaka dialect. "How's that?" Unable to grasp his meaning, the sentry simply blinked. "*Kutabireru-ka?*", Terauchi asked. "Is it tiring?" This time, he received a stunningly loud reply. "*Kutabiremasen!*" ["It's not tiring!"] Taken aback, Terauchi said to Harada, "Oh, he's answered in Japanese!" The Java commander did not miss the opportunity to tease his superior. "Sir," he said, "he can only understand standard Japanese." Both officers were laughing at this as they entered the camp.[95]

Before the visit, Yanagawa had told the 246 future platoon commanders in his company, "Pretend the general is a Dutchman, your enemy! Glare at him!," an instruction that was obeyed to the letter, as the future officers of the West Java Siliwangi Division fixed the visitor with an "angry stare." When Terauchi had finished his inspection, he turned to Harada and said, only half-jokingly, "Don't make them too strong! The Japanese may have to suffer later."[96] It was a concern that would in time prove real enough. Interestingly, the officers of the Japanese high command took no chances during Terauchi's visit to Bogor. No Indonesian officer cadet was allowed near the high-ranking visitors, who were guarded by *kenpei* and other Japanese soldiers.

The next day, Sukarno and Hatta called on Harada and Major General Kokubu in Jakarta. Kokubu, who is said to have feared uncontrollable nationalist sentiment if the people of Java were allowed their own flag and anthem, rebuked the Indonesian leaders. "You seem to have received very warm treatment in Japan," he told them, "so that you were spoiled and asked for more than your due. But if the central government of Japan is a grandfather, the military on the spot is a father. A grandfather blindly indulges and spoils his grandchild, but the father is responsible for his child's education; he gives stricter discipline for the good of the child's future."[97] This was the authentic voice of Japanese Army paternalism.

Japan was, as had always been envisaged, the dominant member of the Asian "family"; now, it appeared, it was not just the older brother but father and grandfather as well.

Wednesday, 8 December, was the second anniversary of the beginning of what the Japanese called the "Greater East Asia War," which had begun with the surprise attack on Pearl Harbor. The Indonesian battalion commanders had by now completed their course and were commissioned during a ceremony in Gambir Square (now Merdeka Square), in the heart of Jakarta, during which each man was presented with a Japanese-style ceremonial sword. General Harada took the salute as around 800 members of the first Peta intake marched past the reviewing stand and out into the streets of Jakarta, led by the band of the Japanese Sixteenth Army. "It was," one Japanese wrote, "a good opportunity to show the newly established Java Volunteer Defence Force to the Indonesian public."[98] Two days later, the new battalion commanders left for their home regions, where they were to recruit and train 500-man battalions.

The appointment ceremony for the company and platoon commanders was held on the lawns of the Bogor Palace on 20 December, with Harada once more taking the salute. Zulkifli Lubis made a "pledge of acceptance" on behalf of the Indonesian company and platoon commanders.[99] When the ceremonies were over, Harada held two separate parties, one for the Japanese officers inside the palace, another for the Indonesian officers, who gathered on the lawns at the front of the palace.[100] For Soeharto and his fellow trainees, it was a day of triumph and pride. The next day, Soeharto left to join his battalion. As a *shodancho*, he wore on each collar three gold stripes on a field of blue, the Peta badges of rank having been modelled on the Japanese ones.[101] After a course that had lasted barely two months—Soeharto was to claim in his memoirs that his *shodancho* training had taken four months, which was the length of a more intensive course that would be given only to recruits in the second intake—Soeharto was an officer in the first Indonesian defence force. By now, he had good Japanese connections. "That first *giyugun* generation was something special," Masui Tadashi, a senior Japanese diplomat, said many years later. "They were extra bright and they were the ones who formed the closest relationship with their Japanese mentors."[102] But Soeharto, Masui added, was not seen as a really major figure by the Japanese until he became *panglima* (commander) of the West New Guinea operation in the early 1960s.

The Japanese had been ambitious in the extreme to imagine that they could create an Indonesian self-defence force from scratch in just a few months, not least when the raw material seemed at first to be so unpromising. But they succeeded. Officers who were to play a central role in the Indonesian army for the first thirty years of independence came away from Bogor with three key attributes: fitness, fighting spirit and a familiarity with small-unit infantry tactics. All this, of course, was of immediate benefit to the Japanese. But it was to stand the Peta officers in good stead during the post-war clashes with the Dutch colonial authorities. The intensity of this training, the emphasis on spiritual strength and physical toughness, had had a profound impact on the cadets, especially those who had gone straight from school to the platoon commanders course. As Major General Moersjid observed, "We were at the age of being like wax, you know. You can make whatever you want from that material. Because you are receptive to anything."[103] But that did not mean, he added, that the Indonesian officer cadets were simply stooges of the Japanese. "Some people [have said], 'You were cooperating with the Japanese.' You can say that. We can also say something else. No, we were not cooperating, we were just seeing what we could do for our own nation."

Alwin Nurdin, who would later become a major in West Java's renowned Siliwangi Division, was one of those whose life was totally changed by his experience in the Peta. Born into a privileged middle-class West Sumatran family, he had grown up in Aceh, where his father was a government official, and had gone on to attend the HBS in Medan. At school, he had felt no animosity towards the Dutch. "But still," he said, "the Japanese time came, and it was an inspiration for us."[104] While the arrival of the Japanese may have been the downfall of the Dutch, "for us it was a chance in a million. We had to grab [our] independence. When the Japanese came, we were just Dutch [*sic*] schoolboys. [When they left we were highly motivated army officers]."

Despite the hardships and humiliations of the Bogor course, not one man had dropped out. On the contrary, the young Indonesian officers had developed an intense pride in their training and their capabilities. They felt they were members of a highly favoured elite. They were fired with enthusiasm. As one Japanese officer noted, they were "very ardent, except for a few, and their abilities could not be neglected."[105] Soeharto was no less enthusiastic than his colleagues. Soon, he knew, he would take command of a forty-four-man infantry platoon, one that would have to be established from the ground up. It was going to be an enormous challenge, but it was a challenge he was confident he could meet.

For their part, senior Japanese staff officers were "especially enthusiastic" about the volunteer force, no one more so than General Harada, who was to remain a supporter of Peta throughout his time on Java.[106] In the words of Colonel Miyamoto, "General Harada loved Peta, and I could see he couldn't help smiling when he talked about it. He was always willing to review the Peta .... He was very keen on Peta, and trusted it, too."[107] According to a Japanese staff assessment written immediately after the war, "the Japanese army had great expectations [for] these troops. The Japanese C-in-C and all ranks, mindful of the Army's intention, favoured them heartily."[108] That was not entirely true. Some Japanese officers were to become deeply sceptical about the volunteer force. Although Peta was a decentralized set of units, with no higher command structure, these officers saw potential danger to themselves in an armed Indonesian defence force. Their reservations echoed the sort of concerns that had been expressed by Governor General Rooseboom in 1903. One of the sceptics was Miyamoto. He was not sure it was wise to put "total trust" in the Indonesian force.[109] He feared it might one day turn on its mentor.

13

"Soeharto was a cautious man"

On his return to Central Java, Soeharto was assigned to the Peta battalion being established at Wates, seventeen miles southwest of Yogyakarta. Still fearing an Allied attack from Australia, the Japanese had drawn up operational plans to fight a defensive battle on the south coast of Java, concentrating the bulk of their forces on East Java but with other units guarding the southern coast of Central and West Java.[1] Under these plans, Indonesian battalions would defend the beaches most susceptible to amphibious assault while Japanese troops were held in reserve, ready to launch an immediate counterattack. It was, of course, a strategy of desperation. No one doubted for a moment that the Japanese excelled in the art of beach defence. Imperial Army engineers were skilled in the construction of bunkers, dugouts and blockhouses, all of them mutually supporting and extremely well camouflaged. It is also true that the south coast of Java is notoriously forbidding, with dangerous seas and very few beaches. But the Japanese could not hope to defend every beach on the south coast. Nor could one or two 500-man Peta battalions stem a full-scale Allied landing, which, the Japanese estimated, would consist of as many as ten divisions.[2] At best, a defending battalion could cover a beach frontage of 900 to 2,000 yards. That meant that Peta units would be very thinly distributed. It also meant that frontline Peta battalions would be subjected to a devastating naval bombardment before any Allied landing. Japanese reserve units, as hopelessly outnumbered as the Dutch had been when they faced the Japanese in 1942, would be pounded from the air and sea as they sought to join the battle. To make matters worse, this strategy created political problems. It did not take long for Indonesian leaders to conclude, erroneously, that the Japanese had decided to let local troops do the fighting and dying while the Japanese remained safely out of sight. "Sukarno," Morimoto Takeshi recalled, "hated the idea of using Indonesians as a shield for the Japanese."[3]

As these plans were put into operation Soeharto was posted to Glagah, a hamlet on the Indian Ocean, nine miles west of Wates. Glagah stands on a narrow strip of low-lying ground between the Menoreh Hills and the ocean, a few miles south of the east-west highway. It is a forlorn and decrepit little town, set deep among coconut palms and banana trees. To the north are rice fields, to the south, uncultivated land that gives way to grass-covered dunes. These extend for several hundred yards, to the uninviting coastline of the Indian Ocean, the domain of Ratu Loro Kidul, the Goddess of the South Sea, a spirit much feared in Javanese mythology. As he approached the town, Soeharto would have caught the smell of salt-laden air and heard the muffled roar of the surf. Beyond the dunes, the waves roll in relentlessly, dark and powerful, crashing onto the beach and tossing plumes of spray into the air, creating an almost permanent curtain of haze over the beach.

The Japanese had chosen their defensive position here well, as might be expected, and it is likely that work was already underway on the construction of the necessary fortifications. These would have been designed with great care. In most places, Japanese strong points were earth emplacements, reinforced with timber, particularly palm logs or teak, and sometimes with corrugated iron.[4] The roofs of these structures were made of several layers of logs, covered with dirt and rocks and planted with fast-growing vegetation for camouflage. From narrow firing slits, anti-tank guns and medium machine guns were sited to fire on landing craft as they beached, ready to cut down assault troops as they struggled through rows of barbed-wire obstacles, some of them below water level. Field guns deployed well behind the coastal strip were positioned to bring fire to bear on the beaches, supported by light and heavy mortars, which, the Japanese had found, often proved to be even more deadly.

If the Glagah defences were already under construction, Soeharto may have seen for the first time the way the Japanese treated their Javanese *romusha* (labourers), men and women, most of them poor peasants, who had been mobilized into a vast and terrible slave army, working under appalling conditions on defence and infrastructure projects. The Sixteenth Army had begun drafting forced labourers in October 1943, the month Soeharto joined the first Peta intake at Bogor, and in the twenty-two months that were to follow, hundreds of thousands—possibly many millions—of Javanese were pressed into service at one time or another.[5] Some were put to work on a hopelessly ambitious scheme to double rice production in three years. Others were sent to build fortifications and airfields and other defence projects. Still others were packed off to West Java and West Sumatra, where they were sent down into the mines. Tens of thousands more were sent as far away as Thailand and Burma to work on the notorious Death Railway.

Wherever they served, the *romusha* were treated brutally by their Japanese or Indonesian overseers, who fed them meagrely, beat them savagely and worked them to the point of exhaustion. Tens of thousands died, from pneumonia, tuberculosis, malaria, dysentery and yaws. Many thousands more seem simply to have been worked to death. In time, the ill-treatment of the *romusha* would do more than anything else to generate anti-Japanese resentment among the young men of the Peta.[6] It also left many civilians with feelings of contempt for the lower-level Javanese and Sundanese officials charged with bringing in the required number of *romusha,* and it sullied the image of political leaders such as Sukarno, who reluctantly endorsed the scheme.

The last week of 1943 and the early months of 1944 were a time of intense activity for Soeharto. An Indonesian volunteer defence force was being created from scratch. It had to be manned and trained and supplied. The commander of the 1st Battalion (Wates), Sunjoyo Purbokusumo, had gone on ahead to recruit the 500 young men who were to serve as soldiers in his new battalion, drawing on his contacts in the local community.[7] He and his fellow battalion commanders seem to have had no difficulty in finding volunteers. As one historian has noted, "the lure of a uniform, a steady diet, pay or adventure attracted many young aspirants."[8] Nor were entry standards especially high for the foot soldiers. There was no minimum standard of education, no requirement that a recruit have any knowledge of Japanese or even that he be able to produce a letter of recommendation from someone in the bureaucracy. All that he needed was a strong physique and the necessary fighting spirit. Many recruits were peasant boys, "apolitical, with little or no schooling."[9] Others came from humble backgrounds in the cities and towns of Java. In the years ahead, these recruits were to be the dependable foot soldiers not only of Peta but also of the post-war Indonesian Army. And they were to prove remarkably sturdy and steadfast, even in times of great adversity, when some of their better-educated superiors were to fall into despair at the apparent hopelessness of the anti-Dutch struggle.[10]

For Soeharto, as for the other Indonesian officers, the establishment of Peta would have brought an exhilarating sense of purpose. It was an honour to be part of a volunteer defence force of 16,500 armed men. It was a challenge to be asked to train a forty-four-man infantry platoon (*shodan*), to pass on the skills learned at Bogor (and before that, of course, in the Dutch colonial army), to instil in the recruits something of the fighting spirit that had formed such a central part of the Japanese indoctrination. For the recruits, too, this was a deeply satisfying time. These men were equally proud to be part of an all-Indonesian armed force, kitted out in the distinctive dark green Peta uniform, which set them apart as members of a new and important institution in local society, issued with rifles taken from KNIL armouries and trained to handle heavy machine guns and mortars. As the rainy season dragged on in early 1944, turning the ground to oozing red mud, these men were drilled and trained intensively by their platoon commanders and company commanders, just as the latter had been by the Japanese. Enormous emphasis was placed on the development of physical stamina and *semangat*, just as it had been at Bogor. In the Peta, *semangat* "came to mean an almost reckless kind of physical courage, defiant of bodily injury and even death."[11]

In Wates and Glagah, Soeharto was given command of the 1st Platoon, one of three such units in the 1st Company of the 1st Battalion. He now found himself working alongside several Peta officers whose lives were to be closely interwoven with his in the years ahead. One of them was his company commander, Sunarwibowo. A well-educated a man in his early thirties, Sunarwibowo had been a senior-school teacher under the Dutch, when teacher standards had been high. Identified by the Japanese as a potential leader, he had been recruited by Tsuchiya Kiso and sent to the *chudancho* course at Bogor, as had a number of other high-school teachers. Sunarwibowo would be Soeharto's regimental commander when, in Yogyakarta in October 1945, Soeharto set up his first battalion. Another man Soeharto served with on the Indian Ocean beach at Glagah was Bardosono, a platoon commander who had been a student at the AMS-B senior high school at the time of the Dutch surrender. The third platoon commander was Hadjid Soedibjo, who was to serve in 1945 as one of Soeharto's fellow battalion commanders under Sunarwibowo. Two of Soeharto's friends from Bogor—Pranoto Reksosamodra and Soedjono—were serving nearby, having been given command of platoons in the 2nd Company.[12]

Each Peta battalion came under the wing of a Japanese battalion—in places, one Japanese battalion might have responsibility for seven or eight Peta battalions—and in each Peta battalion there were three or four Japanese officers and up to five NCOs responsible for such matters as logistics and training. But the Peta battalion commanders were proud of their "independence" and sensitive to slights, be they real or imagined. That meant that the Japanese officers attached to these units needed to act with considerable tact. As the months wore on, strains were to develop between some Japanese battalions and their Indonesian "brother" units.

II

Soeharto spent an exceptionally short time in a Peta fighting unit. On 10 May 1944, less than five months after he had graduated as a platoon commander, he found himself back at the Officer Cadet Training Centre in Bogor.[13] With the war going from bad to worse, the Japanese had decided to create another twenty-two Peta battalions, in addition to the thirty-three already in place, to bolster their defences along the south coast. That meant they needed another twenty-two battalion commanders, another eighty-eight company commanders, and about 350 platoon commanders.[14] Soeharto, having made a good impression as a platoon commander, had been chosen for training as a company commander, which would put him in charge of three platoons, or 132 men. One of those who joined him on the company commanders' course was Pranoto.[15]

Bogor in mid-1944 was a changed place, a noisy military town with many bars and brothels, all of them well patronized by Japanese soldiers and civilians. At the training centre, which was now under the command of Yanagawa, there was the same high-minded emphasis on Japan's wartime goals, the same commitment to the idea of building an Indonesian defence force that would fight alongside the Japanese army. But the Indonesian officer cadets were all too aware of the ugly realities of Japanese occupation, and fissures were opening up between the Japanese and the Indonesians. To some extent, too, fissures were opening up in the Japanese ranks. When Soeharto was first in Bogor, for the platoon commanders' course, the training centre had been run by Beppan. Now, with Peta growing by leaps and bounds, the Japanese had established in Jakarta a Planning Department for the Guidance of the Java Volunteer Defence Force (Giyugun Shidobu). This body, which took its orders from the Sixteenth Army headquarters and which was intended "as a sort of proto-general staff" for Peta, carried out much of the work formerly done by Beppan.[16] It was the Planning Department, not Beppan, which now ran the training centre.[17]

These changes coincided with a gradual deterioration in the ideals that had attended the creation of the Peta. Members of the instruction staff that had been assembled for the new Peta levy came mostly from Japan. They had no knowledge of the local languages or customs.[18] To make matters worse, about 100 Japanese officer cadets had arrived directly from Japan and been assigned to Peta battalions across Java without proper orientation.[19] A number of the new arrivals were overbearing and brutal. In theory, corporal punishment was prohibited in the Peta. But, according to Morimoto Takeshi, who served both a section commander and mortar instructor at Bogor, some Japanese resorted to slapping Indonesians on the face almost daily.[20] As it happens, Morimoto appears to have been well-qualified to make that observation. Lieutenant General Purbo Suwondo, recalling his time as an officer cadet at Bogor, said that Second Lieutenant Morimoto's company was notorious for its "daily slapping practices."[21]

The restructuring notwithstanding, Beppan officers continued to play an important role in Peta training. Yanagawa, recently back from a two-month visit to Japan, threw himself into his role as commanding officer at the training centre, which included a four-man Carrier Pigeon Research Unit.[22] He was still as demanding and determined as ever. But his new responsibilities, some of his Beppan colleagues felt, had given him an inflated sense of his own importance. As noted earlier, he had taken to riding around Bogor on a large grey horse, as his predecessor, Captain Maruzaki, had done.[23] In the months ahead, he was to have a running battle with Lieutenant Colonel Masugi Kazuo, the new Sixteenth Army intelligence chief.[24] He was also to become caught up in an increasingly bitter dispute between young Japanese officers at the training centre and Japanese working in the local Japanese civilian administration.

By the time Soeharto attended the company commanders' course, there was a palpable antagonism between the Japanese members of Yanagawa's training company and members of the Military Administration Department, which was headed by the Chief of Staff of the Sixteenth Army. Young Japanese officers at the Peta training centre were complaining among themselves about what they saw as the comfortable lifestyle of those working in the administration. These officers, they said, routinely took afternoon naps and "played around with Eurasian women." For their part, those in the administration objected to the behaviour of off-duty officers and NCOs from the Peta training company. These men, according to the administrators, filled the Bogor restaurants and the local Japan Club every night, drinking to excess and hiring prostitutes. Administrators were angered, in particular, by Probationary Officer Takagi Nobuhiro, a notorious drunkard and troublemaker who was always getting into fights. He often drew his sword and threatened Japanese civilians and administrators. Even when he was sober, Takagi was inclined to commandeer the main street to give his recruits combat training, and become enraged if a car sought to pass.

In a post-war memoir that was seen by some as boastful and perhaps not entirely accurate, Yanagawa said that, one day in June 1944, when he himself was absent, the Sixteenth Army Chief of Staff, General Kokubu, having heard the complaints of the administration staff, descended on the Peta training centre. He rebuked the centre's Japanese staff severely and ordered that no one was to leave camp. Infuriated that Kokubu had apparently accepted at face value the administrators' one-sided story, Yanagawa is said to have expressed the view privately to some of his colleagues that the chief of staff should be killed. Fearing the worst, Captain Maruzaki, the head of Beppan, made a violent and somewhat theatrical attempt to defuse the situation. Unsheathing his military sword, he sliced off the little finger of his left hand in the presence of Yanagawa, Tsuchiya and Yoshitake. "You may want Kokubu's head," he told his subordinate, "but I will give you my finger instead. Give up such an idea."[25]

Soeharto spent three months on the company commanders' course, from 10 May to 10 August. This was a month longer than the term of the first such course in 1943, and it gave him a solid grounding in the subjects he studied.[26] Parallel courses were run for the new batch of *shodancho* cadets, who were given four months' training, and those attending the *daidancho* course, who were given two months. One of those in the battalion commanders' course while Soeharto was at Bogor for the second time was Sudirman, an ascetic twenty-eight-year-old Islamic schoolteacher who, eighteen months later, would be elected Supreme

Commander of the Indonesian National Army. Sudirman was to become a legendary figure in Indonesian history: a man who, though shockingly wasted from tuberculosis in his later years, was seen to embody some of the most admirable qualities of the independence struggle, above all a selfless, unswerving dedication to duty. There is no reason to believe that Sudirman and Soeharto met at this time, and indeed it is highly unlikely that they did. Men in the three training tiers were largely kept apart from one another.

Once again, Soeharto made an indelible impression on his Japanese army instructors. Decades later, they could recall with ease his coolness, his composure, his competence. According to former Second Lieutenant Nakamoto Yoshiyuki, who was the head of his training section, "Soeharto was a cautious man and never showed off his talent. He was a steady man who never lost his temper."[27] According to Morimoto, Soeharto "was remembered by all his instructors as a very capable man." Soeharto, he said, was "modest but very sharp" and, although capable, never took advantage of other people to make himself look good.[28]

On Thursday, 10 August 1944, at the end of the course, a formal graduation ceremony was held in Jakarta. A photograph taken at what had once been the Dutch governor general's palace shows the inauguration ceremony for new Peta battalions. Indonesian officers stand in neat rows, rigidly at attention, feet slightly splayed. The ban on the red-and-white national flag remains in force, but each man carries a Peta flag, which, with its green field, its distinctive red sun, and sixteen red beams radiating in all directions, and its white crescent moon and star, was an overripe and overdesigned amalgam of Imperial Japanese Army and Islamic symbols.[29] A Japanese flag, with its blood-red circle on a field of white, hangs at the front of the hall. As Soeharto and his fellow company commanders were sworn in, each was presented with a Japanese-style ceremonial sword. "It was not a genuine Japanese sword, and the length was less than [that of] the swords worn by Japanese officers," an Indonesian historian was to remark dryly. "Yet it was received with a certain measure of pride."[30]

By the time he left Bogor for the second time, Soeharto had spent a total of thirty-one months in military service: twenty-one of them with the Dutch, ten with the Japanese. Remarkably, he had spent twenty-two (and, by one count, almost twenty-four) of those thirty-one months in training centres, receiving instruction from experienced Dutch and Japanese army instructors, to say nothing of his three-month police training course.[31] This training, when combined with his determination, his initiative, his natural aptitude, his capacity to organize and his willingness to take charge, was to give him a distinct advantage, not only during the Japanese occupation, when he was to be singled out for preferment and given at least two important and sensitive assignments, but during the post-war struggle against the returning Dutch.

In 1945, when the revolutionary struggle began, Soeharto had more than five times as much military training as the average Peta platoon commander or company commander and eleven times as much as those officers who had attended only the first Japanese-run platoon commanders' course or who had been on the parallel company commanders' course. This was a striking difference.[32] He had between ten and fourteen times as much formal military training as the Peta battalion commanders, including Sudirman, whose subsequent importance to the independence movement stemmed not from his professional military qualifications, which were slight, but from his spiritual qualities, which led him to be seen as the almost mystical embodiment of revolutionary struggle. As well as all that training, Soeharto had gained practical experience during his attachment to a KNIL infantry battalion. If he lagged a long way behind most Peta officers when it came to secondary education and social position, he was streets ahead of all but a handful of them when it came to professional military training.

There were limits, of course, to what Soeharto and the other Peta officers were taught. As we have seen, the Japanese gave the cadets a brief but excellent introduction to small-unit tactics, especially at the platoon and company level. This was to prove invaluable during the 1945–49 struggle for independence against the Dutch, which was all that mattered in the short run. But it meant that many of the officers who were to form the backbone of the Indonesian National Army (TNI) for the best part of three decades had, for the time being, no higher military education and were capable of mounting nothing more than battalion-size operations, if that. That limitation was to play into the hands of officers such as A.H. Nasution, T.B. Simatupang, Alex Kawilarang, Hidajat Martaatmadja and Didi Kartasasmita, who had attended either the pre-war Royal Military Academy (KMA) in Breda in the Netherlands or the substitute KMA established in Bandung after the German invasion of Holland in 1940. Not surprisingly, these officers were considered more suitable for senior staff and command positions in the early years of the TNI.

III

In July 1944, while Soeharto was on the company commander's course, the Americans captured Numfoor, a small, almost circular island off the northwest coast of New Guinea. The 2,000 Japanese defenders had been on short rations and put up little resistance. Some, however, withdrew to the interior. In early August, starving Japanese resorted to cannibalism. Advancing US troops came across Japanese, Taiwanese and American bodies from which portions of flesh had been cut.[33] During the war, the Japanese had sent some 3,000 Javanese men, women and children to Numfoor, where they were put to work building roads and airfields almost entirely by hand. Only 400 of them remained alive at the end of August 1944.

In the meantime, US Marines had captured Saipan, an island in the Western Pacific Ocean only 1,200 miles from Tokyo. The fall of Saipan and the first B-29 raid against the Japanese home islands led to the collapse of Tojo's government. Tojo was replaced as prime minister by Koiso Kuniaki, a retired general who had served as Chief of Staff of the Kwantung Army. In September, US forces seized Morotai, an island in the East Indies 500 miles northwest of Biak. MacArthur saw the island as a jumping-off point for the Philippines, a further 300 miles away.

Observing this remorseless American advance, Sixteenth Army planning officers concluded, correctly, that MacArthur would now seek to move on Java from the north, rather than from the south or east. Increasingly alarmed at the inadequacies of their defences on Java, the Japanese pushed ahead with yet another expansion of Peta, which, they had decided, needed a further eleven battalions to strengthen defences on the north coast of Java. The third and final intake of Peta officers was in no way special. Like the Dutch on the eve of the Pacific War, the Japanese were desperate for Indonesian officers and NCOs and could not afford to be too choosy about whom they took. "As this was the third batch of trainees," Yanagawa noted, "the quality was very inferior to the previous ones."[34] Moreover, the Japanese had cut their training courses to the bone, just as the Dutch had done. The third Bogor course ran for barely a month; the cadets were rushed through at a pace that left the Japanese training staff "a bit bewildered."[35]

By late 1944 Peta had sixty-six battalions on Java and another three on Bali, with more than 37,500 men in all. This made the Java defences look a little more respectable, at least on paper, but it created a new problem. As Colonel Miyamoto, soon to become the Sixteenth Army staff officer for operations, wrote in his memoirs, "This was twice as large as the entire Sixteenth Army, and four times the actual combat strength of the army."[36] The Japanese had equipped Peta with 18,700 rifles, nearly 700 heavy machine guns, nearly 200 light machine guns, nearly 100 trench mortars and 20 artillery pieces. Although Indonesian officers were not aware of the fact, they now had in their control two-fifths of the arms on Java, while the Japanese held three-fifths.[37]

Beppan, which had set up and trained the Indonesian volunteer force, was still as enthusiastic as ever about Peta. So, too, was General Harada. But Miyamoto, a latecomer to Java, had misgivings. As he wrote many years later, "when I first saw the Peta, I thought I couldn't place total trust in it ... to me it seemed dangerous to allow Indonesians to carry weapons when more than ten thousand Japanese nationals were living in various parts of the island. I thought the Indonesians in Peta would soon learn of our wartime reverses and that we should be ready to change our policy in regard to the force."[38] Despite these reservations, Miyamoto decided not to push for changes "since no other staff officers seemed to share my concerns." Captain Tsuchiya Kiso, who had done so much to train and build Peta, both on Java and Bali, had reservations of a different kind. "After Japan lost in Burma, Guadalcanal and Saipan," he said, "we were aware that the Japanese military itself was no match for the Allies. How could the Japanese military (Nihongun) count on the Giyugun [Peta] when we lost confidence in ourselves as the military?"[39]

With their military fortunes in dramatic decline and their need for local support now greater than ever, the Japanese changed their tune on the question of Indonesian independence.[40] On 7 September 1944, Prime Minister Koiso promised that independence would be granted "in the future" or "someday" (*Indonesia shorai dokuritsu*), with the word *shorai* translated into Indonesian as *di kemudian hari*.[41] The Koiso statement was hedged with caveats. The timing of independence was not to be discussed. Nor were there to be any "formal activities" for independence. But Tokyo was signalling that it was willing to promote political participation in the Indies, prepared to encourage "enthusiasm for independence" and ready to conduct propaganda in favour of independence. It would allow Indonesians to fly the red-and-white flag, to play and sing *Indonesia Raya* and to use the term "Indonesia."[42] In a top-secret document, the head of the Military Administration on Java, Major General Yamamoto, told key army officers "we must approach the natives with affectionate feelings although we must instruct and guide them sternly like parents or older brothers or sisters.... Although the insatiability which springs from the Indonesian character may sometimes provoke our resentment we must not regard them with hostility, but guide them, sternly showing the established policy."[43]

Although stopping well short of Indonesian demands, the Koiso statement was seen in Java as further evidence that Indonesia would soon be free. In the wake of the announcement, the Sixteenth Army believed it had "clear authority to make the Giyugun [Peta] and *heiho* the foundation of a future national army of Indonesia."[44] As a result, those responsible for Peta were ordered to begin "a gradual conversion of infantry to other arms."[45] According to a document captured at the end of the war, Japanese officers now began to organize Peta MT (motor transport) battalions, Peta "tank battalions" and Peta engineering battalions.[46] According to a Sixteenth Army study, the Japanese had "a plan under consideration" to organize an "Indonesian National Army" after the granting of independence.[47]

On the face of it, the Japanese were preparing to make Peta more like a conventional army. But references to new Peta tank and artillery units need to be treated with circumspection. Although the Japanese are said to have eventually turned over 20 armoured cars, 20 artillery pieces, and 330 trucks to the Peta, a former head of Beppan has claimed that he never heard the expression "Peta MT."[48] Nor is there any reference to such a unit in the detailed and semi-official Japanese history of the Peta. There is certainly no reason to believe that the Japanese gave serious thought to handing over any tanks. Indeed, as Beppan officers saw it, some senior officers at Sixteenth Army headquarters were using the talk of "a gradual conversion of infantry to other arms" as a device to reduce the number of Peta fighting battalions, which they viewed as a potential threat.

The nuances of the Koiso statement were lost on many of the Indonesians who were being rushed through the third and final training courses at Bogor. "In response to this announcement," Yanagawa told Allied interrogators, "we began, in training the Giyugun, to inculcate the idea that the Giyugun was the army for Indonesian independence. As a result of these lessons, however, those cadets who were not well-educated misunderstood and supposed that independence had already been granted, which caused us considerable difficulties in the training."[49]

In November 1944, as fears of an Allied landing grew, Sixteenth Army headquarters ordered Yanagawa to create a Special Guerrilla Force (Yugekitai) to gather intelligence and conduct guerrilla operations behind the lines in the event of an Allied attack.[50] As it happened, the Yugekitai was to play little or no role in the war, given the lateness of the hour. But it was much better trained than Peta and it was to be a progenitor of the post-war Indonesian intelligence service and, in some ways, the Military Police. Based at a new headquarters in Bandung, Yanagawa established the force using forty-one Japanese and about 160 of the best second-intake Indonesian platoon commanders, who, in addition to their four-month *shodancho* training, were given four months' instruction in intelligence-gathering and guerrilla warfare.[51] The members of this team were to train 610 young Indonesians as *shodancho* and send them back to their home areas in East, West and Central Java, where each was expected to recruit and train an additional five guerrilla fighters.[52] "Our plan," Tsuchiya explained many years later, "was to hold out as long as possible, fighting a guerrilla war together with the Japanese Army once it moved back up [into the mountains] after being beaten by the Allies down in front."[53] Those plans came to naught. The first course finished in July 1945, only weeks before the Japanese surrender. For all that, former Yugekitai officers would go on to hold some of the most senior positions in the Indonesian army and state intelligence services.

IV

As Japan's fortunes fell, those of Soeharto rose. For the second time in four years, he was reaping the benefits that came from joining the armed forces of an alien monarch in the northern hemisphere. What is more, important new appointments were about to come his way, giving him some early experience as a staff officer. In late 1944 the Japanese continued to look on Peta as a potentially valuable reserve force. But it was an administrative burden for the Sixteenth Army, which was preoccupied with its efforts to meet an expected Allied invasion.[54]

In an attempt to address this problem, the Japanese decided to overhaul the organization of the volunteer army. On 20 December 1944, they set up three separate "regional headquarters" (Chikutai Shireibu) for the Peta, in East, Central and West Java.[55] These offices, which were to receive their orders from the Planning Department or directly from Sixteenth Army headquarters, were not really headquarters (*shireibu*) in the accepted sense of the term; they were to have no command responsibility. Rather, they would take care of the administrative, logistical, training, financial and medical needs of the Peta battalions.[56] Nevertheless, they were important. Each would be headed by a Japanese colonel or lieutenant colonel, and each would have a staff of about fifty officers and men, about forty of them Japanese who had worked either in the Peta regional offices or in the Peta sections of the various Japanese battalions, the rest of them trusted Indonesian "apprentices" from the Peta.[57] Each "headquarters" would take care of the eighteen to twenty-five Peta battalions stationed in its region.[58]

The Japanese saw this as another step towards the creation of a more independent Indonesian defence force. In the words of Miyamoto, the intention was that the Indonesians "would soon run all three Chikutai Shireibu by themselves."[59] Nor was that all. Despite his misgivings about the volunteer army, Miyamoto planned, or so he claimed in later years, to bring Peta battalions together in regiments and brigades, so that the Indonesian force "would be able to grow to be their national military."[60] This meant, presumably, that Indonesian officers were to be trained for higher staff and command positions.

For the Japanese, there were two things to be said for the new regional headquarters. First, they could be presented to the Indonesians as evidence that Japan envisaged that a separate Peta Headquarters (Giyugun Shireibu) would be set up at some stage, taking Indonesia another step closer to an independent defence force. Second, these regional headquarters would allow the Sixteenth Army to "slim down" to fighting strength ahead of what was expected to be a climactic battle for Java, leaving the Peta free to proceed in its own way.[61] That strategy, which may seem remarkable in view of all the expectations invested in Peta, reflected the thinking of Miyamoto. A China veteran who had arrived in Java in April 1944, more than two years after the key Beppan officers, Miyamoto had no familiarity with the Peta and no sympathy with the Indonesian youth movement. On the contrary, he distrusted the armed Indonesian units that the Japanese had created and was ill-at-ease with the rising anti-Japanese sentiment on Java. In the words of Tsuchiya, who had done so much to build the Peta, both on Java and Bali, "He believed that Indonesians had no war potential.... He always tried to make a strategy using mainly the Japanese army and excluding the Peta. He was an executive [*kanbu*] who was anti-Peta."[62] Miyamoto, according to Tsuchiya, did not trust Peta and wanted it to fight separately. As we shall see, Miyamoto did not take issue with that assessment. He came to believe, he said, that Peta members "should choose their own way [*jibun no michi*]" when the war went into a decisive phase.

With much riding on this new administrative structure, the Japanese went to some lengths to select capable Indonesian staff officers, calling on some of Peta's best battalion and company commanders. One of those officers was Soeharto, who had continued to make a positive impression on his Japanese superiors. After completing the company commanders' course at Bogor, which gave him a rank equivalent to captain, Soeharto was sent to the office of the Central Java Chikutai Shireibu in Solo, where he was placed in charge of training.[63] There were, of course, Japanese officers above Soeharto in the Solo office. But the appointment was a clear sign of the regard in which he was held by his Sixteenth Army superiors. "Looking at this," said Morimoto Takeshi, the author of the definitive Japanese history of the Peta, "you can be sure Soeharto was trusted by the Japanese."[64] Tsuchiya, who had recruited and trained Soeharto, but who had lost track of him after that, felt the same way. "The Chikutai Shireibu was an organization that oversaw all the battalions in that region," he noted. "So if Soeharto was assigned to the Chikutai Shireibu, it must have been a really important position."[65] According to Colonel Soepardio, the former Peta platoon commander who went on to become deputy head of the Indonesian Armed Forces' Military History Division, "the most important Indonesian Peta officer was Soeharto."[66] Soeharto, he claimed, "was supposed [in time] to be the regional commander for Central Java."

As the senior Javanese training officer at regional headquarters in Solo, Soeharto would, in theory, have been in regular communication with about twenty Peta battalions. He would have had contact with a wide range of Peta officers and had a good sense of conditions in Java at a time of mounting hardship and privation, when most Peta officers were confined to their own districts, with little or no opportunity for travel and little or no contact with other Peta battalions. Owing to the exigencies of war, however, Soeharto seems to have held this position for no more than seven or eight weeks, hardly enough time for him to have made many new contacts with Peta battalions.

For the most part, Japanese officers and NCOs formed a favourable impression of Soeharto, but this was not always the case. Some were sceptical. One such man was Sergeant Teramoto Masashi, who was attached to the Kenpeitai office in Solo, where it was his job was to keep a close eye both on Peta units and on the young Mangkunegoro VIII and other members of the minor court in that city. Looking back fifty-five years later, Teramoto, a short and stout man of eighty-two, recalled, "I saw *Shodancho* [sic] Soeharto a few times when he was in the Chikutai Shireibu office in Solo when I visited a Peta unit where my old friend Captain Goto Tetsuo was an instructor. I wasn't particularly impressed with him. He was rather inconspicuous. He seemed restless and inconsequential and didn't look brilliant. That is why I was astounded in later years to learn that he had become President."[67] At the same time, Teramoto acknowledged that his colleagues had found something to admire in Soeharto. Asked if he thought the Kenpeitai had "cleared" Soeharto before his admission to the Peta, he replied, "I don't think so. Few of us paid particular attention to him; he seemed reliable."

After a short stay in Solo, Soeharto was transferred to the Jaga Monyet camp in Jakarta to train students from technical schools "for the Engineering Corps." It was the first time he lived in the future capital. One of those he trained was platoon commander Singgih, whom he had earlier encountered at Bogor and who, on 16 August 1945, was one of the young men who would kidnap Sukarno and Hatta in an attempt to force the pace of the proclamation of independence. When the Jakarta assignment was over, Soeharto returned to the Chikutai Shireibu, which had in the meantime moved from Solo to Madiun. Here, for the first time in his military career, he lived not in the barracks but in a house provided by the Japanese, another sign of the growing regard in which he was held by them. Although there is no suggestion that Soeharto followed such a course, some Peta officers billeted in houses away from the barracks lived with women. According to the Japanese historian Sato Shigeru, some Peta officers "even married these women during their term of service. At some places the local communities set up brothels for the Peta."[68]

Throughout this time, the Japanese continued to beat the propaganda drum, with strident denunciations of the emperor's enemies. Late in 1944, the army commander had issued instructions concerning the ideals of the volunteer forces. The Peta, he said, should "aim at the independence and preservation of the people and religion" and "march forward toward the annihilation of the enemies, Americans, British and Dutch."[69] Increasingly, however, statements of that kind fell on deaf ears. By now, many Peta officers combined a deepening hostility towards the Japanese with an increasingly virulent nationalism. At one level, there was resentment over small personal humiliations. Peta officers had been led to believe that they were members of an elite corps that would play a vital role in the achievement of Indonesian independence; but they found themselves treated in many cases like second-class citizens, obliged to salute Japanese NCOs and to accept without complaint the "arrogant and humiliating" attitude of Japanese NCOs and soldiers.[70] To make matters worse, the food allowance of the Peta "conspicuously declined" from the middle of 1944, aggravating the dissatisfaction of some Peta members.[71]

At a more serious level, Peta officers were embittered over the suffering that had been visited on Java during the occupation. For the Japanese, Java was a major supply centre for the armies in the "Southern areas," which were now all but cut off from the Japanese home islands as a result of the relentless US Navy submarine campaign. For the Indonesians, Java had become an island of immense hardship. In 1944 the rice crop failed in many parts of Java, and Japanese rice requisitions hit especially hard. On top of that, the economy suffered from huge inflation as the Japanese printed money as fast as they could. As was to happen again in the 1960s, inflation eroded the buying power of official salaries, spawning racketeering and corruption. Java was chronically short of food, medicine, textiles, bicycle tyres and kerosene. In many places, Indonesian families were reduced to one meal a day.

As the textile shortages worsened, some people had nothing to wear. In June 1944, according to a Japanese report, the clothing shortage was so acute that children could not go to school, women could not leave their homes and men could not visit the mosque. In Madura, "government employees were seen working in their offices wearing shorts made of old gunny sacks and nothing else." Later in the same year, farmers "were seen here and there working stark naked in the fields."[72] In some places, people went about wearing sarongs made from odoriferous rubber sheeting. In Purworejo they wove a kind of "cloth" from the fibre of the *waru* tree or went about in clothing made from jute bags. One senior official in Yogyakarta had a single shirt and a single pair of trousers, both made from jute sacks. When he sent his houseboy out, he lent him his clothes and stayed inside, naked.

Sukarno, still obliged to make pro-Japan propaganda broadcasts but using them perhaps to give Indonesians a sly update on Japanese reverses, said in a speech on 16 August 1944, that final victory would belong to the Japanese, "who have helped us and asked us to cooperate for the general well-being of Asia. Thus, right and justice are on the side of Japan.... Comrades [sic], should the Japanese be defeated, we shall not be disheartened and discontinue our struggle—even should we be destroyed—to protect our dear Fatherland [sic], Indonesia." He went on,

> Comrades, when the Allies bombed Surabaya they also dropped pamphlets from their planes. In these pamphlets it was written that when the Allies arrive they will share sufficient food, clothes, etc., with the Indonesians. Comrades, these statements are lies. For 350 years the Allies [sic] occupied our land without giving food or clothes to the people.... If they arrive here, they will be able to give us sufficient food and clothing, but these are no longer needed, comrades.[73]

With their problems mounting, the Japanese recruited more and more *romusha*, topping up their army of civilian slave labourers as men and women succumbed to disease, malnutrition, overwork and ill-treatment. Many *romusha* continued to toil on defence projects alongside Peta units, their suffering plainly visible. Recalling the hardships of those times, Selo Soemardjan said, "rice was taken away, cattle were taken away, young people were taken away. So the whole economic life was disrupted."[74] Families thought only of survival. "People hated the Japanese," said Kemal Idris, who had been one of Beppan's more promising trainees at Tangerang. "They were not the people we thought they were. They were worse than the Dutch. They were very harsh. They took all the food—rice and all these things—for their own purposes."[75] As conditions deteriorated, there was open peasant resistance to Japanese rice levies.

The first uprising was at Singaparna in western Tasikmalaya, West Java, on 25 February 1944.[76] It was led by a local Islamic leader, K.H. Zainal Mustafa, who was embittered over the conscription of *romusha* and the forced delivery of rice. Four Japanese military policemen were sent to Singaparna, where, in the middle of a prayer meeting, they urged Mustafa to cooperate. Angered by this intrusion, Mustafa and his followers captured and killed two of the Japanese. The Japanese returned in force the next day; during a fight eighty-six Indonesians and three Japanese military policemen were killed. Nearly 800 villagers were detained, including Mustafa and his three wives. Mustafa and twenty-two others were tried and executed. A still larger rebellion took place in Indramayu, one of the major rice-producing areas on the north coast of West Java, between April and August 1944. Once again, the Japanese dealt harshly with the protests. Hundreds were killed, and many more died of malnutrition.[77]

Looking back years later, Soeharto said that he was as much affected by this suffering as anyone else. "My feelings towards the Japanese army were gradually changing," he told a Japanese journalist. "Most of us had welcomed them as our Asian big brothers, who, we thought, would help us attain independence. But we were beginning to find the conduct of many Japanese soldiers unbearable. Food was taken by force from the villagers, and hundreds of thousands of people who were transferred to the battlefields in Burma as *romusha* never returned to their homeland."[78]

Allied prisoners of war and internees were also suffering greatly. Wing Commander Alan Groom, an Australian who had joined Britain's Royal Air Force, spent the war years as a POW in Java. In late January 1945, Groom was included in a party of about 300 political prisoners sent to Ambarawa in Central Java. Within moments of their arrival, he wrote later, the beating had begun.

> The guards using canes, sticks, fists and feet to impress upon us that we were special prisoners, a selected party for special treatment. I was the only Britisher in a party of Dutch, Indo-European, Chinese and Indonesian prisoners and one of the guards came to me after we were locked up and warned me to do just as ordered and keep quiet as they could all beat us to death and need fear no inquiry. A short time later we saw a native thrashed, kicked and beaten for hours so that he died some 10 hours later. He had stolen a pair of spectacles.[79]

At around the same time, the Kenpeitai interrogated three Royal Australian Air Force NCOs whose aircraft had crashed near Makassar in mid-January. Although Beppan seems to have had no involvement with POWs since Yanagawa made his propaganda film *Calling Australia* in 1943, a Kenpeitai subaltern told Allied interrogators that members of Beppan witnessed the interrogations "as they were collecting and investigating conditions in Australia for future use."[80] One can only wonder why Beppan would have still been interested in conditions in Australia when the Japanese position remained under such dire threat in eastern Indonesia.

V

At Sixteenth Army headquarters Colonel Miyamoto felt a growing sense of disquiet about the size and firepower of the Indonesian volunteer army. What would happen, he continued to wonder, if Peta units were to rebel or desert in response to the worsening Japanese military position? Had the Japanese, in seeking to boost their defences against an external enemy, created a potentially serious internal threat to their position on Java? Could the Indonesians be trusted? "With regard to their fidelity towards the Japanese army," an unnamed Sixteenth Army officer wrote (and this may well have been Miyamoto himself), "we could not help entertaining a slight feeling of apprehension arising from our superficial study of them, but we regarded them as a grateful race appreciative of our endeavours to promote their welfare."[81]

In February 1945 the worst Japanese fears materialized when the Peta battalion in Blitar, a town in East Java, revolted.[82] The leader of the revolt was a militant twenty-one-year-old platoon commander named Suprijadi. The son of a government official, Suprijadi was seen by his friends as a solitary and slightly eccentric young man.[83] While still a schoolboy, he had made a point of swimming alone in the notoriously dangerous waters of the south coast wearing a green bathing suit, even though legend has it that anyone dressed in green will offend the Goddess of the Southern Sea and be drowned.[84] After finishing junior high, he attended the Secondary Training School for Native Officials (Middelbare Opleidingsschool voor Inlandsche Ambtenaren, MOSVIA) in Magelang.[85] Although angry with the Japanese for disrupting his career, Suprijadi joined the initial Beppan military training course at Tangerang. During that course, his close friend Zulkifli Lubis once remarked, Suprijadi kept his thoughts to himself. "But by the time we were at Bogor, he often said, 'We can't trust the Japanese!' "[86] That distrust had grown deeper over the next two years, not least because the Japanese had evidently beaten his younger half-brother, Haryono, who subsequently died.[87] One of Suprijadi's motives, it has been claimed, was revenge. By early 1945, it appears, Suprijadi had his heart set on immediate independence, to be achieved by revolution.[88] In the opinion of a Japanese army investigator, Suprijadi was "a strange person, very suggestible but with strong powers of leadership."[89] Suprijadi had likened himself to both Prince Diponegoro, the leader of the 1825–30 rebellion against the Dutch, and to a mystic who was Diponegoro's spiritual adviser.

In the early hours of 14 February, backed by most of the officers in the battalion, two of them his seniors, Suprijadi led some 360 men out of the barracks in an emotionally charged but ineptly planned rebellion.[90] The Indonesian volunteer troops attacked both the "telephone bureau" and the Sakura Hotel, where Japanese officers were billeted. According to a book produced by Kenpeitai veterans, they killed the telephone bureau director and two female employees of the hotel, while injuring several others.[91] Indonesians have claimed, perhaps implausibly, that the Peta soldiers directed mortar fire at the hotel in the initial attack. According to the same sources, the attackers followed up with bursts of machine-gun fire aimed at houses occupied by the Japanese "supervising officers" and at the local Kenpeitai headquarters, killing four Japanese civilians and seven ethnic Chinese who were thought to be pro-Japanese.[92] The attackers then left Blitar, with three columns heading north and one south. Despite months of talk and preparation on the Indonesian side, during which attempts were made to enlist the support of other Peta battalions, the revolt collapsed. The Japanese dealt with it swiftly and effectively, rushing troops to the area while seeking to negotiate a settlement with the rebel leaders.

Colonel Miyamoto, the staff officer in charge of operations, was put in charge of clearing up the Blitar Affair. He was keen to go to Blitar to investigate. But fearing this might be the start of an Indonesia-wide, anti-Japanese, pro-Allied revolt, with other Peta battalions following suit, he decided he could not leave Jakarta.[93] Instead, he sent the head of intelligence, Lieutenant Colonel Masugi Kazuo. Masugi was to recommend that the leaders of the revolt be court-martialled.[94] Captain Yanagawa, who had done so much to establish the Indonesian Volunteer Defence Force and who had recently set up the Indonesian Special Guerrilla Unit, was also sent to Blitar. He was joined by a three-man party from the East Java Yugekitai, headed by twenty-year-old Yugeki *shodancho* Bambang Supeno.[95] The decision to send even a few members of the Special Guerrilla Unit to Blitar in the wake of the mutiny spawned a rumour in Peta circles that the Yugekitai was a kind of "Kenpeitai" within the Volunteer Defence Force. Nor was this the only problem. The East Java unit of the Yugekitai Task Force was so "influenced by the Blitar riot [*sic*] and we had to give other education to these Giyugun."[96]

Unable to locate Suprijadi, who seemed to have vanished, Supeno sought to persuade Muradi, another leader of the revolt, to bring the main

Sixteenth Army Order of Battle, 1945

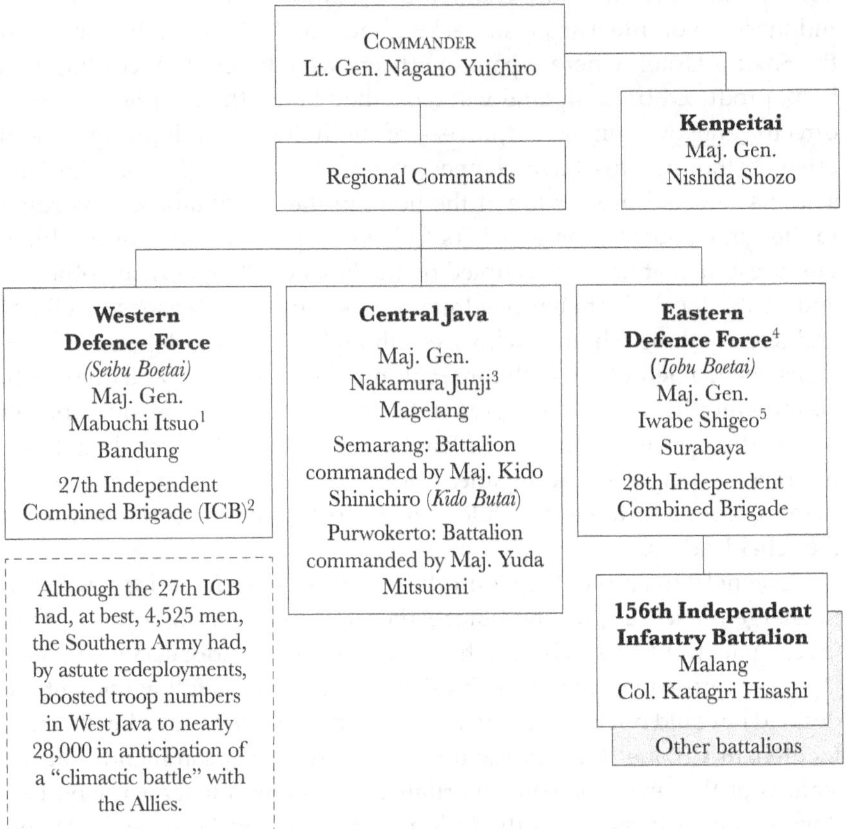

---

1 Mabuchi was responsible for West Java including Cheribon and Preanger. See "Japanese Report of the state of affairs in Java. For the Commander-in-Chief of the Allied Forces in Java," Jakarta, September 27, 1945, p. 4. NANL, 2.10.14, inv. 5203.

2 According to the Japanese, the 27th ICB had a strength of 3,712 men. For details of Japanese troop strengths on Java in the period March-August 1945, see *Senshi Sosho. Nanseihomen Rikugun sakusen: Marei Ranin no boei*, No. 92, pp. 306, 350, 395, 473-474. According to a British count, in October 1945 the 27th ICB had 4,525 men. Total Japanese strength in West Java in October 1945, the British study shows, was just under 28,000 men, of whom 6,285 were Army Air Force and 5,000 Navy. Appendix H, War Diary, 37 Ind Inf Bde Int Summary 2, 25 October 1945, p. 3. TNA/PRO WO 172/7104.

3 Nakamura was responsible for Semarang, Kedu, Yogyakarta, Pekalongan and Banyumas. According to the official Japanese war history, Nakamura had only 781 men in mid-1945, not enough for even one battalion. According to the British summary, there were some 2,800 Japanese troops in Central Java in October 1945.

4 The Eastern Defence Force had a strength of 3,364 men.

5 Iwabe was responsible for Surabaya, Malang, Besuki, Bojonegoro, Pati, Kediri, Madiun, Solo and Madura.

body of the battalion back to Blitar. The negotiations remained deadlocked until Colonel Katagiri Hisashi, the commander of the 156th Independent Infantry Battalion in Malang, handed his ceremonial sword to Muradi as an act of good faith, pledging that he would honour his commitments, one of which was an assurance that no one would be court-martialled.[97] The units returned to Blitar on 17 February. Suprijadi did not return with them. It is now believed he had been captured and killed on the first day of the revolt by troops under the command of Katagiri.[98] Afterwards, Miyamoto reprimanded Yanagawa on the grounds that the training of the volunteer force was at fault. "In reality, however, I was not angry at Yanagawa," he claimed many years later, "because I was beginning to regard the Giyugun as a purely political creation aimed at winning the hearts and minds of the people, rather than as a military force to be used at a time of decisive action. Had I regarded the Giyugun as a military force, I would have had to assume responsibility for the rebellion, Captain Yanagawa would have been expelled from Java, and the Giyugun would have been completely reorganised."[99]

What caused the revolt, apart from any personal grievances held by Suprijadi? One key factor was resentment at the economic misery that had been visited on the island under the Japanese and the suffering of the civilian population, especially the *romusha*.[100] A second had to do with the daily humiliations of military servitude under the Japanese, not least the slappings, which were such an affront to Javanese. But there were particular local factors as well. By early 1945 Japanese soldiers in Blitar were widely disliked on account of their arrogance and insensitivity. Discipline was lax. Some Japanese officers seem to have spent much of their time forcing their attentions on local women. The behaviour of Japanese civilians seconded to the army was no better. According to Miyamoto, there was resentment in Blitar over "the licentious and luxurious lifestyle of the Japanese," who were heedless of the hardships of the local people. There was anger, too, over the Japanese attitude towards the issue of independence.[101] "As Blitar is located away from the centre," Captain Yamazaki Hajime, the officer in charge of the supervision of the Peta, noted in a report to headquarters, "there was not adequate supervision of the Giyugun there, and the Japanese trainers [as well as] civilians seconded to the military and ordinary civilians had been leading a dissolute life."[102] Resentment, which had been simmering for months, is said to have come to a head when a wealthy Japanese raped the fiancée of a Peta officer.[103]

In an outburst of fury, the (always unidentified) Indonesian officer killed a Japanese instructor and fanned "dissatisfaction among the people over the Japanese attitude towards the independence issue, in order to gain wider support for his actions."[104]

Why did Surachmad, the Peta battalion commander in Blitar, not join the revolt? Why, with one or two smaller exceptions, did other Peta units not revolt?[105] The main reason seems to have been that it was clear by now that Japan would lose the war. Why provoke the Japanese when the outcome was in sight, especially as Prime Minister Koiso had promised, five months earlier, that independence would be granted in the future. "In my *daidan* in Ponorogo," fifty miles west of Blitar, said Major General Soetarto Sigit, "we never spoke about fighting the Japanese."[106] Soetarto was one of the few in his battalion who knew a little English and he was able to converse with the Japanese in that language. "So, on the grapevine, I knew the Japanese were losing. The *daidancho* was a Dutch-educated doctor and he got all this information.... We knew they were retreating. We had a different view from Suprijadi. I think Suprijadi was emotionally motivated but not politically motivated. We had Sukarno and Hatta and we trusted them. And Sukarno said that when the Pacific War is over we will have *merdeka* [freedom, independence.]"

At Blitar, an entire Peta battalion had taken part in an armed uprising, the first time an Indonesian unit had turned on its mentors. Alarmed by this development and fearing that the unrest could spread, the Japanese disarmed the battalion and arrested no fewer than fifty-five officers and men, ignoring the promises of clemency that are said to have been given by Katagiri. Among the detainees were two of the four company commanders, eight of the twelve platoon commanders (the number would have been nine had Suprijadi been produced), and thirty-three of the forty-eight *bundanchos* (squad leaders, or NCOs). These men were sent to Jakarta to face a court martial. All were convicted. Six (by some accounts five) were sentenced to death. They were beheaded on the beach at Ancol, near Jakarta. All of the executed men, it has been claimed, had killed Japanese during the revolt.[107] Three men were sentenced to life imprisonment, and the others to various periods of imprisonment.

The remaining officers and men of the battalion were taken to a remote village in the Brebeg district south of Nganjuk.[108] Brebeg is on the lower slopes of Mt Wilis (8,404 ft) in an area known mainly for its pine forests and its poisonous black-widow spiders. According to Morimoto

Takeshi, who had trained Peta recruits at Bogor and who would go on to write the definitive Japanese-language history of the volunteer army, "After the rebellion, the Japanese army removed the battalion from Blitar to somewhere remote so they would not influence others. It was almost like imprisonment! No weapons! As punishment, they took away all the weapons. Instead, they were given wooden guns."[109] In the wake of the revolt Miyamoto shelved his earlier plans to organize Peta regiments and brigades; these, he had envisaged, would be able to grow eventually into an Indonesian national army. He also shelved a plan to put the three Peta regional headquarters entirely in Indonesian hands.[110]

In a report written immediately after the Japanese surrender, a Sixteenth Army officer reflected on what he thought had gone wrong as far as the volunteer army was concerned. In training the Indonesians, he wrote, the Japanese should always have kept in mind "that they are of a different race from us. But their resemblance to the Japanese in ideas and colour of skin led us unconsciously to adopt Japanese training methods in their training. We tended to concentrate on the outward aspects of training to the detriment of fundamentals. Our instructors were not always suitable." Misconceptions of this kind had not been apparent at first. But as Japan's military fortunes had gone into decline and as its exactions had increased, a unit of the volunteer army had rebelled at Blitar. This had shown that the training policy for the Indonesians was wrong. In the wake of the revolt, the emphasis had been changed to "mental education (especially advocating 'fight and die together with the Japanese Army' and 'devolution for the sake of racial happiness') instead of fighting technique." The new policy had also failed "due to the fact that NCO instructors were lacking in powers of leadership towards another race, whereas their technical instruction left nothing to be desired."[111] Towards the end of his report, the author seemed to acknowledge, finally, that it was not just the form of instruction or the approach taken by the instructors that was wrong. The Japanese, he wrote, had come to realize that the Indonesians "would not be content with a situation of dependence on the Japanese Army but aimed at achieving their complete independence." It is difficult to argue with that assessment.

There can be no doubt that Suprijadi, an emotional and impulsive, not to say reckless, young man, had paid a high price for his actions, as had many of those who followed him. But his actions, though seemingly futile, had not been in vain. The Blitar revolt alarmed the Japanese. It helped convince them, belatedly, that the Indonesians would settle for nothing less than complete independence, an argument Japanese Army and Navy leaders were to make with some conviction to senior British officers in September 1945.

At Blitar the Japanese had received an unwelcome shock. For Soeharto, the abortive revolt was to provide yet another opportunity.

14

"Why did they choose Soeharto?"

In writing about this period Soeharto is at pains to stress his mounting anti-Japanese feeling. All his experience in the Peta, he wrote in his memoir, had convinced him "that in no way could we condone the brutal treatment meted out by some of the Japanese officers. I felt a growing desire to fight back."[1] In the aftermath of the Blitar incident, he adds, the Japanese decided to purge the Peta officer corps not just in Blitar but in various other places as well. "I had a feeling that I was one of those who would be ousted, but a number of Japanese officers who respected me saved me from expulsion."[2] Some years later, Soeharto gave this story a further polish. The Kenpeitai, he said, "began watching me closely because they knew I was beginning to feel critical about them."[3] Even if these fears were well founded, which seems unlikely, it is notable that Kenpeitai "suspicion" is not referred to until 1945.

Soeharto may have felt some concern about his position at that time. But the Japanese confined their wrath to those who had played a key role in the Blitar revolt, and it is difficult to avoid the impression that Soeharto is attempting here to embellish his nationalist credentials. If indeed he felt a growing desire to fight back, he had an odd way of showing it. Everything suggests that he was quite willing to go on cooperating with the Japanese. Nor, it seems, did the Japanese entertain any serious doubts about Soeharto's loyalty at the time of the Blitar uprising. On the contrary, he was the one man, out of 250 Peta company commanders on Java, to whom they turned in their hour of need. Immediately after the revolt, Soeharto was sent to Brebeg to train junior Peta members as squad leaders or NCOs (*bundancho*), to replace those arrested by the Japanese.[4] Given the state of Japanese paranoia about the loyalty of the volunteer army, there could hardly have been a more sensitive assignment at that time or stronger evidence of the faith that Soeharto's superiors had in him.

Japanese officers who served in Java reject out of hand Soeharto's claim that he fell under suspicion at this time. "In his memoirs, he claimed that he was considered a dangerous person by the Japanese army," said Morimoto Takeshi, author of the most comprehensive book on the Peta. "But that was not true …. I think Mr Soeharto concocted a story that the Japanese army didn't like him and considered him a dangerous person. He wanted to give the impression he was a person who always fought against the Japanese."[5] As Morimoto saw it, Soeharto's claims were "laughable, strange." The Japanese, he said, had never had any reason to doubt Soeharto's loyalty. They would not have sent him to Jakarta in late 1944 to train students from the technical schools had they not trusted him implicitly. Nor would they have sent him to help retrain the remnants of the Blitar battalion after the February 1945 revolt. "Do you believe that the Japanese Army would give responsibility to someone they considered dangerous? The Japanese Army selected Soeharto to become the head of this training group for *heiki bundancho* [ordnance squad leaders], so we obviously trusted him." Morimoto was equally unimpressed by Soeharto's claim that the Kenpeitai was paying him particular attention. "Soeharto said he was closely watched by the *kenpei* because he was saying things against the Japanese Army. But everyone, including myself, was watched by the *kenpei*. So he wasn't the only one."[6] In an interview, Morimoto spoke, unbidden, of Soeharto's "forgeries" and "fairy tales."

Morimoto was not alone in claiming that the Japanese had reason to believe they could rely on Soeharto at this time. According to Tsuchiya, Soeharto had always done everything the Japanese had asked of him and more. Soeharto had been an "outstanding" platoon commander and had been sent back to Bogor to train as a company commander. He had moved up "the elite ladder of the Peta organization" and been chosen to "clear up" the Blitar rebellion. "This shows, I think, that he was trusted by the Japanese military."[7] Asked why the Japanese chose Soeharto for such a highly sensitive assignment, Tsuchiya replied, "Since I wasn't closely working with Soeharto at that time, I can only guess it was because he was considered capable by Japanese military officers to do this rather difficult task of grasping the Blitar battalion as a whole and bringing it under control."

Some Indonesians who served with Soeharto in the Peta are equally puzzled by the claim that he fell under Japanese suspicion after the Blitar revolt. "Speaking of the suspicious attitudes of the Japanese," said Colonel Soepardio, the retired military historian, "even [prominent future leaders such as] Sudirman and Achmad Yani and Sarwo Edhie were suspected by Japanese intelligence. They were suspected by the Kenpeitai and the higher command. They used all sorts of channels for information."[8] But that, said Soepardio, made it even more difficult to understand why Soeharto would have been given such a sensitive assignment. As he put it, "we … don't understand why! But those were the facts! He was assigned there." It may simply have been that Soeharto was the most qualified man for the job. "He had been a sergeant in the KNIL and promoted from *shodancho* to *chudancho*. He may be classified as an outstanding [officer.] Maybe. [But we ask ourselves] 'Why did they choose Soeharto to do that job?'"[9] The only conclusion that could be drawn, he felt, was that the Japanese had decided they could trust Soeharto.

Soeharto's NCO in Brebeg was Imam Munandar, a *shodancho* who had been born in Blitar.[10] Imam Munandar was to prove a blunt and brutally direct Soeharto subordinate in later years. In 1966, when he was the military district commander in Surabaya, his commanding officer, Major General (later General) Soemitro, observed that it was strange that, while many low-level supporters of the Communist Party had been killed, many PKI cadres were in jail. "In that case," Imam Munandar replied, "let's just release the ones we have in jail and kill them."[11]

Soeharto did not achieve much at Brebeg, where he remained for about five months, from March until mid-August 1945. The atmosphere in the camp seems to have been one of distrust and disillusionment, of languor and half-hearted training. "The battalion was under what we call confinement," recalled former Staff Sergeant Murakami Kiyota, who was in charge of training non-commissioned officers at Brebeg. "It was the size of four middle-sized companies and had about 400 men. They were not serious about training any more…. There were a few houses in the area, one of which was used by the instructors and another as a brothel. Several prostitutes lived there. I was wondering if this was the way things should be, but soon enough the war ended. Then the corps was dispersed."[12]

On 15 February 1945, while he was preoccupied with his Special Guerrilla Force duties, Yanagawa had been ordered to help establish yet another para-military body: Hizbullah. Soon afterwards, twenty young Yugekitai *shodancho* from residencies across Java, all of them "very enthusiastic" Muslims, were sent as instructors to a former camp for Australian POWs in Cibarusa, about twenty-two miles southeast of Jakarta. Eventually, 500 Hizbullah trainees, devout Muslims aged between seventeen and twenty, would be trained here.[13] Major General Yamamoto officially opened the camp on 18 February, a sure sign that the formation of an Islamic unit commanded support at the highest levels. The training of those in the Islamic Youth Corps (Kaikyo Seinen Teishintai)—or "Islamite Youth Forwarder Unit," as it was rather awkwardly described in a subsequent Allied report—was conducted by the Department of Religious Affairs of the Military Administration with help from the Yugekitai. Although the 500 young men were given three months' military instruction, they were not equipped with arms, these being in such short supply. Instead, they trained with bamboo spears and wooden rifles.[14] Yanagawa told Allied interrogators that "owing to the indifference of the Indonesian staff and the quarrels among the different sects of Islam" this effort "remained nominal." Later on, there had been differences between the Japanese-sponsored Committee for the Preparation of Indonesian Independence (Panitia Persiapan Kemerdekaan Indonesia, PPKI) and Muslim staff at the training centre. As a result, the Military Administration lost enthusiasm for the undertaking. "So no good effect," Yanagawa concluded, perhaps prematurely, "came out of this endeavour."[15]

II

In late 1944 and early 1945, as Soeharto shuttled between Solo, Jakarta, Madiun and Brebeg, Japan's military position grew increasingly untenable. By early March 1945, MacArthur's forces had recaptured Manila after heavy fighting. Meanwhile, US Army Air Force B-29 Superfortress bombers were taking the war to the Japanese home islands, with devastating consequences. On 9–10 March, General Curtis LeMay's XXIst Bomber Command staged its first incendiary attack on Tokyo, a city of 4.3 million people. Roaring in from the east at low altitude, 325 Superfortresses dropped almost half a million incendiary cylinders of jellied petroleum on the capital, targeting the vulnerable wood and paper Japanese houses.[16] Almost sixteen square miles of the city were burnt out and 267,000 buildings destroyed. At least 80,000, and perhaps 100,000, people died; more than a million others fled. In the months ahead, the B-29s were to return night after night, triggering firestorms in as many as fifty cities.[17] On the volcanic island of Iwo Jima, 760 miles south of Tokyo, all but a handful of the 21,000 Japanese defenders were killed in fighting which dragged on for six bitter weeks, until the end of March. At Okinawa, 350 miles southwest of Japan, 65,000 Japanese soldiers and perhaps 100,000 non-combatants would be killed in the twelve weeks to 21 June.[18] Nearly 7,000 US Marines had died at Iwo Jima. Another 12,000 Americans would be killed at Okinawa, with 36,000 others wounded.[19]

As the officers of the Sixteenth Army planning staff saw it, a "decisive battle" on Java would only come after Singapore, Banjarmasin and Makassar had fallen to the Allies. These officers were well aware, of course, that an attack on Java, which they now expected to be launched "from the direction of Sumatra," would be unstoppable. There could be no hope of holding off an Allied force with a handful of understrength Japanese battalions, backed up by untested Peta units scattered across the island. As Colonel Miyamoto wrote after the war, "The enemy was expected to attack Java with at least ten divisions equipped with tanks and other sophisticated weapons and under a complete air cover."[20]

In late 1944, Japanese Army and Navy commanders on Java had formulated a new strategy: the Army would concentrate its main forces in West Java and fight a last-ditch battle on the Bandung, or Preanger, plateau, just as the Dutch had planned to do three years earlier. The focus of these efforts would be a fortified defence complex around Mt Malabar (7,687 ft), fifteen miles south of Bandung.[21] In the event of an invasion, most of the Japanese on Java, military and civilian alike, were to withdraw to this position. Here, they would prepare to withstand a long-term, but predictably hopeless, siege. This time, there would be no surrender. The Japanese would be ordered to fight to the death, as their comrades were to do at Iwo Jima and at Okinawa. Senior Japanese Peta instructors were told of this change in strategy at a meeting in Jakarta on 13 February 1945, six days before US Marines went ashore at Iwo Jima. In April, the Japanese held a "council of war" and endorsed the new plan of operations. In the months thereafter, the Japanese began stockpiling massive quantities of food, weapons and ammunition in the highlands of West Java. According to a former Japanese Army officer cadet (supply), big naval guns from battleships were transported to the Malabar area.[22] By the time of the Japanese surrender the defences would be about 80 per cent complete.

At the same time, the Japanese planned to bring their smaller forces in eastern Java together in a hill redoubt at Kampung Pujon, to the west of Malang.[23] They, too, would fight to the death. The only Japanese soldiers who would stay behind were those attached to Peta battalions across Java; they would remain with, and fight alongside, their Indonesian units. In the meantime, the Japanese envisaged, somewhat grandiloquently, that the coast of Java would become "a nest of bases" for "special attack" (*kamikaze*) forces; these would seek out the approaching enemy on sea, land and in the air. For the Allies, it is clear, any landing on Java would have been costly, at least in the final phase. Like the Dutch before them, the Japanese would all but abandon central Java. Japanese forces there would be used to guard the roads as some units from the east were shunted through to west, after which the central Java units would themselves pull back to the west.[24] Miyamoto had a fall-back plan, however. This involved sending Japanese forces in the west to the east "to destroy the enemy if he attacked East Java from Tarakan."[25] That was prudent. In early 1945 MacArthur was considering just such a landing in eastern Java. As he saw it, the Australian 1st Corps, including the 6th and 7th Divisions, would attack Surabaya on 1 July. MacArthur would later tell Washington that he might have to use one or two American divisions "if found necessary" in Java.[26] In the event, his planned Java landings were vetoed in Washington.

How many troops did the Japanese have to defend Java? In early 1945 the Sixteenth Army consisted of 15,000 men, of whom only 8,500 were combat forces, and 15,000 Japanese civilians in military employment (*gunzoku*).[27] The combat troops were in two Independent Combined Brigades (ICB's), one stationed in western Java, the other in eastern Java.[28] In June 1945 Miyamoto requested the transfer of the 25,000-man 48th Division, which was in Timor, to Java. The request was approved in large part: 20,000 men arrived in Java: the other 5,000 were sent to Singapore.[29] As a result, the Japanese Army had 50,000 men in Java. There were, as well, 10,000 Japanese Army Air Force personnel and 20,000 men from the Navy. That made a grand total of 80,000. In some ways, it is true, that figure is misleadingly high. For one thing, perhaps only 20,000 of the

Sixteenth Army Senior Staff Officers and Special Units, 1945

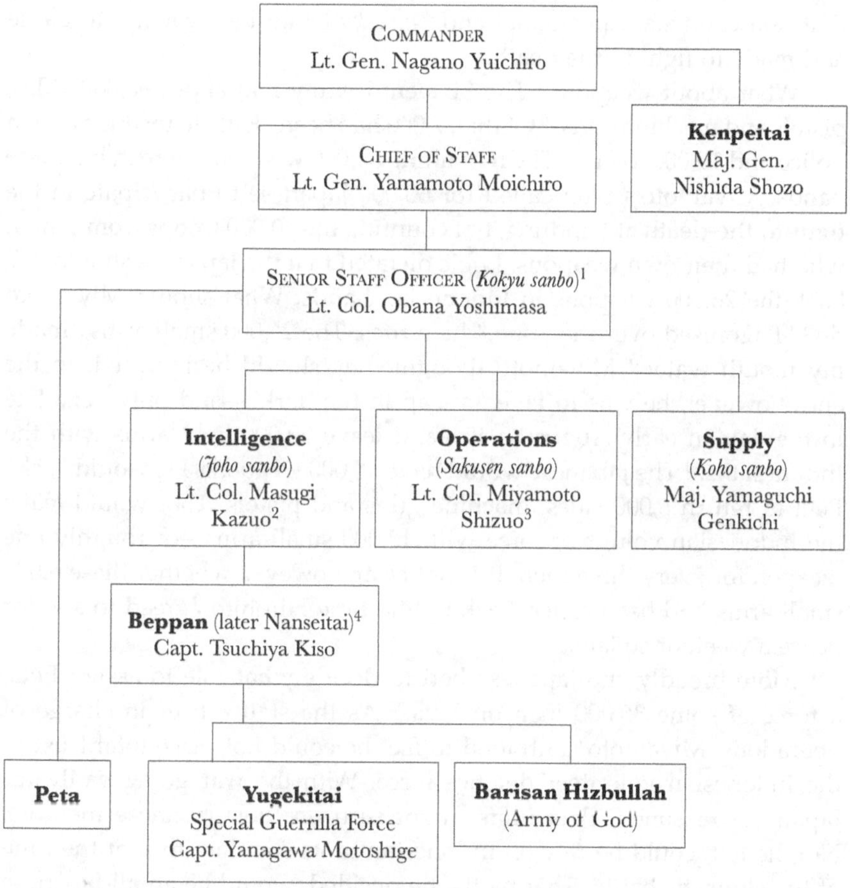

1 Concurrently responsible for the 37,500-strong Java Volunteer Defence Force.

2 Masugi was transferred to Malaya in mid-1945 and spent more time with the Southern Army, after which Colonel Obana took on these additional duties, even though he, Obana, was often ill. This meant that there were in effect only three key staff officers: Obana, Miyamoto and Major Yamaguchi Genkichi. Interview, Colonel Miyamoto Shizuo, Suginami-ku, Tokyo, 25 May 1999, and "Statement by Capt. YANAGAWA, dated 14 Dec 1945," p. 20, Part III, p. 3 , NANL, 2.10.14, inv. 5190.

3 Colonel Miyamoto arrived in Java in April 1944 as the staff officer in charge of supply (*Koho sanbo*). By 1945 he was the staff officer for operations (*Sakusen sanbo*). As Obana was often ill, Miyamoto served, in effect, as the key planning officer of the Sixteenth Army.

4 Beppan was renamed Nanseitai in April 1945. Until then, Beppan had been concerned solely with intelligence matters. After April it had an active defence role as well. Interrogation, Captain Tsuchiya Kiso, Glodok Jail, SEATIC Intelligence Bulletin, no. 228, January 1946, WO203/6306, TNA/PRO, and Tsuchiya Kiso statement, 3-8 March 1947.

50,000 army personnel were combat troops. For another, the Air Force and Navy personnel were not trained for ground operations. In other ways, that did not matter. The Japanese had shown at Iwo Jima and Okinawa that non-combatant personnel and *gunzoku* could be thrown into battle and made to fight to the death.

What about weapons? The Sixteenth Army had about 60,000 rifles, pistols and machine guns.[30] Of that, 7,000 had been "lent" to the Indonesian police and 19,000 to Peta. The remaining 34,000 weapons were in Japanese hands. Miyamoto's plan called for 60,000 Japanese to participate in the fight-to-the-death at Bandung, not counting the 20,000 troops from Timor, who had their own weapons. Logic dictated that the Japanese should call back the 26,000 weapons in Indonesian hands. What should Miyamoto do? "I agonised over the issue," he writes. The 26,000 small arms "made my mouth water." Miyamoto thought they should be returned. In the end, however, he was to take "a leap in the dark"—and only very late in the day, in early August 1945—and leave 20,000 light arms with the Indonesians.[31] The Japanese would have 40,000 weapons. He would "ask" Peta to return 6,000 rifles, machine guns and pistols. That would leave the Indonesian volunteer force with 13,000 small arms—or roughly one weapon for every three men. It is not clear, however, whether these 6,000 small arms had been called back by the time Hirohito agreed to sue for peace a week or so later.

More broadly, the Japanese had to decide what role to assign Peta, a force of some 36,000 men on Java.[32] As the staff officer in charge of operations, Miyamoto continued to feel he could not place total trust in the Indonesian volunteer defence force. With the war going badly for Japan, he reasoned, Peta units might turn on their Japanese mentors. Nor, he felt, could he rely on Indonesian units standing firm at the time of the climactic battle. That battle, he decided, would be an all-Japanese affair. Peta could go its own way. Nor would he involve the 25,000 *heiho*, Indonesian soldiers serving in Japanese rear guard units.

If the Japanese Army ground forces were preparing for a bloody showdown on Java, then so too were Army Air Force and the Naval Air Force units. Between them, the Allies believed, these services had 435 aircraft on Java, although it was accepted that that estimate might have been too high.[33] About 100 of these aircraft were in the Jakarta area and a further 60 at Bandung. The rest were well dispersed across the island. At Maguwo airfield in Yogyakarta, the Imperial Japanese Navy's

31st Air Division was busy training suicide pilots. This unit had about eighty, two-seater Yokosuka training biplanes with fabric-covered wings. Though small and light, these aircraft could carry two external sixty-six pound bombs or 10 twenty-two pound bombs. Lieutenant (later Vice Admiral) Uekusa Nobushige, who was twenty-five in late 1945, was the chief instructor of the 31st Navy Air Division. In response to a "request" from his commanding officer, Uekusa came up with the idea of selecting eighty aircrew and forty training planes and forming an air attack corps (*kogekitai*).[34] *Tokubetsu kogekitai* (Special Attack Force) was a Japanese euphemism for *kamikaze* squad. Flying at night from airbases across Java, Japanese planes—fighters, bombers, trainers—would attack Allied troopships up to 100 miles offshore. In April 1945 the Yogyakarta air attack corps began special *kogekitai* training.

Despite all these endeavours the Japanese position was hopeless. And that hopelessness was well known in Indonesia. As the months passed, the calls for independence grew increasingly strident. The popular view now, Rear Admiral Maeda recalled, was that Japan "was useless and powerless."[35] That is true. Washington was preparing, albeit with great reluctance given the anticipated costs, for a final assault on the Japanese home islands. Moscow, though officially neutral vis-à-vis Japan, was preparing to unleash its armies against Japanese forces in Manchuria. In the overall scheme of things, it is true, Indonesia was a sideshow. Even so, planners in Tokyo were obliged to give it a good deal of attention.

III

In New Mexico on 16 July, the United States successfully tested an atomic bomb, a fearsome new weapon it intended to use against Japan. In Tokyo the following day, quite unaware of this development, the Supreme War Council met to consider ways of bolstering the Japanese military position in Malaya and Indonesia in the face of an expected Allied attack there.[36] Members of the council recognized the need to placate the Indonesians lest they withhold labour and logistic support from the Sixteenth Army at this critical juncture and were confident that any new government in Jakarta would be amenable to continuing Japanese direction on defence and foreign policy. This being so, they settled on September as the probable date for Indonesian independence, at least in Java, and asked regional commanders to recommend dates for their respective areas. At the same time, Tokyo ordered that the Committee for the Preparation of Indonesian

Independence be set up immediately in Java.[37] This committee was to make final arrangements for the transfer of power from the Japanese to the Indonesians and thus pave the way for a new state. It would consist entirely of Indonesians hand-picked by the Japanese.

On 25 July the commander of the US Army' Strategic Air Force in the Pacific was ordered to drop two atomic bombs on Japan. The next day, American, British and (in absentia) Chinese leaders issued what became known as the Potsdam Declaration. This called for the unconditional surrender of all Japanese armed forces. The alternative for Japan was "prompt and utter destruction." The Japanese Government, increasingly interested in some kind of negotiated end to the war but unable to accept the phrase "unconditional surrender" or any diminution in the powers of the Emperor, did not respond.

On 7 August, the day after the United States dropped a single atomic bomb on Hiroshima, killing 80,000 people instantly (another 50,000 to 60,000 would die from radiation and injuries over the following months), Japan's Southern Army announced that the Preparatory Committee would be established immediately in Java: the proclamation of independence would be approved as soon as the committee had made the necessary arrangements.[38] On 9 August, the United States dropped a single bomb on Nagasaki, killing 70,000 people. On the same day, a million Soviet troops stormed into Manchuria, putting the Japanese to flight. In Vietnam on 11–12 August, Field Marshal Terauchi told Sukarno and Hatta the Japanese Government "had agreed to grant independence to Indonesia" as soon as possible.

At midday on 15 August 1945, while Soeharto was retraining the disarmed and dispirited soldiers from the Peta battalion in Blitar, Emperor Hirohito announced in a radio broadcast that Japan had formally accepted the terms of the Potsdam Declaration—while taking care not to use the word "surrender", let alone "unconditional surrender". At his headquarters in Jakarta, the new commander of the Sixteenth Army, Lieutenant General Nagano Yuichiro, and his senior officers listened to the broadcast in disbelief. "All of us," General Yamamoto recalled, "stood upright solemnly unable to utter a single word .... Commander Nagano left the room totteringly with a grave and sorrowful look."[39] For Major General Nishimura Otoshi, the head of the General Affairs Department of the Java Military Administration, the broadcast came "like a thunderbolt from a clear sky."[40]

That evening, radical *pemuda* leaders urged Sukarno and Hatta to make a declaration of independence as soon as possible and to do it outside the Japanese-sponsored Preparatory Committee. The two leaders refused. A few hours later, the *pemuda* kidnapped Sukarno and Hatta and drove them to Rengasdengklok, a small town thirty-five miles east of Jakarta, hoping they would now do as they were bidden. Anxious to avert a bloody *pemuda*-instigated confrontation with the Japanese and not a little angered by their kidnappers' rashness and presumption, they again refused. The *pemuda* gave ground. Sukarno and Hatta were taken back to Jakarta. During a testy meeting at General Nishimura's house in the early hours of 17 August, the two Indonesian leaders called in effect on the Japanese Army to look the other way while they proclaimed independence. Nishimura told them that was out of the question; Japan could not possibly allow it. But in circumstances which have never been adequately explained, the Japanese did allow it, with Admiral Maeda playing a vital role as "cut-out", allowing Sukarno and Hatta to prepare a final draft of the Proclamation at his house.

At a ceremony in front of his Jakarta villa at 10:00 a.m. on 17 August, Sukarno delivered a short speech and then read out the Proclamation of Independence. After this announcement, so brief but so pivotal, the Peta company commander in Jakarta, Latief Hendraningrat, raised the red-and-white national flag. Those present joined in singing *Indonesia Raya*. Two days later, Nagano issued a four-point order: support for the Indonesian independence movement was to cease immediately; the Japanese military administration was to remain in power until the arrival of Allied troops; law and order was to be maintained; and the status quo at the time of the surrender was to be maintained. Now, it was clear to all, there would be no further help from the Japanese, a development greeted "with great annoyance and resentment."[41] Before long, the Japanese would be fighting to contain an islandwide outburst of revolutionary fury, in which more than a thousand Japanese soldiers and civilians—not to mention tens of thousands of Indonesians, Europeans and Eurasians, as well as 600 British and Indian soldiers—would be killed in 1945–46, with casualties mounting still further as Dutch forces were fed into the conflict.

Although the Sixteenth Army had decided to disarm and demobilize the Peta, the Japanese had legitimate grounds for concern. What if Peta units refused to hand in their weapons? What if they rioted? As it happened, the Peta weapons were reclaimed without incident on 19 August, thanks to careful planning—and a certain amount of duplicity—on the part of the Japanese. Some Peta battalions were told that, in view of the critical situation, they were about to be given Japanese weapons in place of the Dutch ones they had been using.[42] After they turned their weapons in at the armoury, the Indonesian soldiers were assembled on the parade ground. As they listened to lengthy speeches, soldiers from local Japanese battalions stood guard around their compounds, in some cases training their machine guns on the Indonesians. Other Japanese placed the weapons on waiting trucks, which promptly drove away.

Looking back years later, Soeharto said that on 18 August (*sic*), after he had conducted a training exercise at Brebeg, "we were dismissed and ordered to surrender our arms, and even our vehicles were seized by the Japanese."[43] Morimoto, the author of the definitive Japanese-language history of the Peta, disputes the claim. The idea, he said, is "unthinkable." The Blitar battalion had been disarmed months earlier; it had no "real" weapons, only wooden rifles, without bayonets. "It couldn't happen!" That is true. Soeharto and one or two others may have had weapons while stationed at Mt Wilis. The men of the Blitar battalion did not. Of all the sixty-six Peta battalions on Java, this was the one the Japanese now had least reason to fear.

Like every other Peta member, Soeharto was paid six months' salary in advance and given an allowance of clothing and food, including rice, salt and sugar, after which he was left to make his way home. His first thought was to return to Kemusu, the village of his birth. But he was to stop on the way in Yogyakarta, where, before long, he would be swept up in the revolution. The Java Volunteer Defence Force had ended not with a bang, not even with a whimper. The events of 19 August must have been deeply puzzling to Soeharto. He had no idea that the Japanese had surrendered. Nor did he have any idea that Sukarno had proclaimed Indonesia's independence. All he knew was that, some time after the unit had surrendered its few weapons, a party of Japanese army officers turned up mysteriously at Mt Wilis to announce that the Peta had been disbanded. A day or so later, it appears, the Indonesians were told about the Japanese surrender and the decision to disband the Peta. They were not told about the proclamation of independence. The Indonesian *heiho* serving in the Japanese army were paid off soon afterwards.

With that, there were only three land forces on Java with arms. One was the Sixteenth Army, which had 34,000 (and perhaps by now 40,000) weapons of its own, plus the 19,000 (or possibly 13,000) former Peta weapons now in storage, and which had been joined by 20,000 soldiers from field units in Timor and Maluku, who were also well-armed. A second was the 24,000-strong Indonesian police force, which had 7,000 light arms, and which appears to have remained under Japanese control in several places for a number of weeks after the surrender.[44] Finally, there was the small but well-trained Indonesian guerrilla force (Yugekitai). In the weeks after the surrender Japanese special intelligence officers secretly transferred at least 275 modern small arms to former members of this force.[45]

In early 1942 people on Java had largely accepted, and had long since accommodated themselves to, Dutch rule, however much they may have disliked it. Now, three-and-a-half years later, a growing number had no wish to see the Dutch return to power. An old world had been turned on its head. There were many reasons for this, but they all came back to the fact that the mystique of Dutch power had been irrevocably shattered. In March 1942, Indonesians had seen the Dutch on Java surrender to an Asian power after a land campaign lasting only eight days. They had then looked on as the Japanese went out of their way to humiliate and mistreat Europeans. During the Japanese occupation, many Indonesians had moved up the bureaucratic ladder to occupy places once largely reserved for Europeans. Others had been trained in armed bodies or been mobilized in Japanese-created youth groups. All had been subjected to unremitting Japanese propaganda, which was virulently anti-American, anti-British and anti-Dutch. Japanese promises of independence had whetted the Indonesian desire for self-rule. Japanese abuses had sharpened Indonesian anger and a determination to go it alone.

Now, the Indonesians found themselves in a political vacuum, with the Japanese defeated and the Dutch yet to return. Indonesian leaders, both political and military, were more than willing to fill the void. The Dutch, meanwhile, laboured under the delusion that nothing had really changed in the East Indies. The Dutch in the Netherlands had endured five years of German occupation, during which there had been virtually no news from Java. The Dutch on Java, languishing in POW and civilian internment camps, were almost equally ignorant about events that were taking place beyond the barbed wire. Nor did Dutch commanders in Australia know very much more; each time they had sent agents to Java, the Javanese had betrayed them to the Japanese, which should itself have told them something.

IV

The people of Java had suffered dreadful privations during the Japanese occupation. Soeharto, blessed by luck and a born survivor, had had rather a good war. He had served in two armies, first on one side, then on the other. He had been well fed, well dressed and well paid. And although he was yet to fire a shot in anger, his career was coming along nicely. The Dutch had pushed him through their pre-war NCO training programmes as they prepared to face a Japanese onslaught. The Japanese had pushed him through their wartime officer training programmes as they prepared to face an Allied onslaught. Now, with the Japanese beginning to withdraw, dejected and apprehensive, to their camps and cantonments, and the Dutch yet to return, Soeharto was poised to play his part in the struggle that would secure Indonesia's independence.

In August 1945, Soeharto had a lot to be thankful for. During his twenty-two months in the Peta, he had gained a great deal of invaluable experience. He had been sent on an abbreviated but rigorous platoon commander's course under experienced Japanese NCOs, many of them veterans of the war in China. He had created and trained a forty-four-man platoon and led it for four months. He had qualified as the leader of a 132-man company, with a rank equivalent to captain. He had served in a series of important training and administrative positions. It had, in short, been a time of rare and unexpected opportunity, allowing him to build on all he had learned in the KNIL. In August 1945, at the age of twenty-four, Soeharto had more military training by far, and more military experience, than perhaps 98 per cent of his fellow Peta officers, the men who would form the backbone of a new Indonesian army.

For the moment, it is true, Soeharto was just another ex-Peta officer, one of about 2,150 such men demobilized and disarmed by the Japanese.[46] His prospects did not seem especially bright. In the small world of the Indonesian elite, Soeharto was very much an outsider, socially and educationally. He was unknown outside the Peta—and not especially well known within the Peta, given the Japanese practice of allowing minimal lateral contact among Indonesian volunteer units. Nor, as yet, did he have any connections with the nationalist movement. Indeed, he would have been regarded with scepticism by some of the established nationalist leaders, partly on account of his service in the Dutch colonial army, partly on account of his uncritical support for what a number of them saw as

Japanese fascism. Times were changing, however. The tantalizing dream of Indonesian independence had taken hold in the popular imagination, especially among the young. In the months that lay ahead, support for independence was to sweep across Java like an irresistible tide. Soeharto would be swept along with it. The Japanese may have trusted Soeharto until the bitter end. But he, like so many others, was ready in August 1945 to abandon them and hitch his fortunes to those of the nationalist movement. In the fluid and dangerous world of post-surrender Java, Soeharto held some important cards: he had ability, training, experience, judgement and determination, as well as courage and a wide range of contacts among young men from Yogyakarta who had been trained to fight. As one of his Indonesian colleagues put it, "The Peta made him."[47]

The Indonesian National Revolution (1945–49) was about to begin. During that revolution, which would see the Republican Government fighting successively against the Japanese, the British and the returning Dutch, Soeharto was to prove his worth as a military commander. In doing so, he would more than make up for his modest social origins and educational attainments; he would set himself up for what was to become, against all the odds, an extraordinary ascent to the top of the military ladder and, from there, to the presidency.

Glossary and Abbreviations

In the following listing, Indonesian and English terms are given without any explanatory tag to indicate the language in question.[1] In the case of words, phrases and abbreviations from other languages or from Islamic belief, an explanatory tag has been added. It goes without saying that many Javanese terms have found their way into the Indonesian language; in those cases, no tag is added. The following designators are used:

D	Dutch	Jp	Japanese
Isl	Islamic	Jv	Javanese

abangan	Those who, while nominally Muslim, follow a syncretic Javanese religion in which elements of animism, Hinduism or Buddhism co-exist or predominate
ABRI	Angkatan Bersenjata Republik Indonesia; Armed Forces of the Republic of Indonesia
adat	custom, tradition, customary law
adik, dik	younger brother
agama	religion
agama Jawa	Javanese religion, also known as *kepercayaan* or, more commonly, *kebatinan*; a varying mix of Hindu, Buddhist, Islamic and animist elements
alarmpositie (D)	defensive circle formed by KNIL patrol when under attack by an indigenous enemy. Known also as *sikap awas*

Allah	God
Allahu Akbar (Isl)	God is Great
aliran	[social] stream or current
alon-alon asal kelakon (Jv)	slow but sure
AMS (D)	Algemeene Middelbare School; General Intermediate School; Dutch-medium senior high school
anak buah	younger associate, follower
anak haram	illegitimate child
anak kolong	army child, someone born in the barracks
anak mas	favoured child, pupil, follower
ANRI	Arsip Nasional Republik Indonesia; National Archives of the Republic of Indonesia
ARA (D)	Algemeen Rijksarchief; General State Archives
ARD (D)	Algemene Recherche Dienst; General Investigation Bureau
asrama, ashrama	dormitory; live-in training centre
Astana Giri Bangun	Soeharto family mausoleum in Central Java
bahasa	language
Bahasa Indonesia	Indonesian language
Bakin	Badan Koordinasi Intelijen Negara; State Intelligence Coordination Board
bapak	father, patron, leader, form of address to an older man
barisan	front, paramilitary corps
Barisan Hizbullah	Army of God; paramilitary force designed to harness Islamic support behind the Japanese
Beppan (Jp)	Special intelligence section of the Japanese Sixteenth Army
binta (Jp)	slap a person on the face; box a person's ears
boryaku (Jp)	clandestine operations
BPM (D)	Bataafse Petroleum Maatschappij; Batavia Petroleum Company.
Budi Utomo	Noble Endeavour; society which sought to

	promote the study of Javanese culture and achieve improved access to Western education
Buitengewesten (D)	Outer Islands
bundan (Jp)	military squad
bundancho (Jp)	Peta squad leader, or NCO
bupati	regent, head of a *kabupaten*
Butir-Butir Budaya Jawa	*Seeds of Javanese Culture;* a compendium of Javanese moral guidance
camat	subdistrict head
Chian-bu (Jp)	Public Security Section of the Military Administration Department
Chikutai Shireibu (Jp)	regional "headquarters" for Peta units
chudan, chudancho (Jp)	company, company commander
chui (Jp)	first lieutenant
Cina	derogatory term for China, Chinese
Comintern	Communist International; a body established by the Russians in March 1919 after the Boshevik Revolution to foster, and closely monitor, communist revolutions
controleur (D)	a lower level Dutch official
CORO (D)	Corps Opleiding Reserve-Officieren; Reserve Officers Training Corps
CPM	Corps Polisi Militer; Military Police Corps
daerah	territory
Daerah Istimewa Yogyakarta	Special Territory of Yogyakarta
daidan, daidancho (Jp)	battalion, battalion commander
Darul Islam	Abode of Islam; movement which sought to create an Islamic state in Indonesia
Defensiegrondslagen (D)	Defence Foundations; Dutch policy paper
desa	village
desascholen	local village schools, also known as people's schools (*volksscholen*)
domin (Jp)	the natives
Drs. (D)	*Doctorandus;* equivalent of an MA, not, as is widely supposed, a PhD

DSD	Defence Signals Directorate; now the Australian Signals Directorate, ASD.
dukuh (dhukuh)	hamlet
dukun	shaman, spiritual healer
dukun bayi	midwife
EIPW	*The Encyclopedia of Indonesia in the Pacific War*
ELS (D)	Europese Lagere School; European Lower School. Colonial-era elementary school where students were given seven years schooling with Dutch as the medium of instruction
f, fl.	Dutch florins/guilders
G-30-S	*Gerakan 30 September*; September 30th Movement; Indonesian Government term for the failed 1965 "coup" attempt
gamelan (Jv)	Javanese gong-and-chime orchestra
garnizoenbataljons (D)	garrison "battalions"
GHS (D)	Geneeskundige Hogeschool; pre-war medical faculty in Batavia (Jakarta)
genjumin (Jp)	native; discriminatory Japanese word for *pribumi*, akin to the Dutch *inlander*
giyu (Jp)	volunteer army, militia
Giyugun (Jp)	Volunteer Force. Abbreviation of Jawa Boei Giyugun (Java Volunteer Defence Force), the Japanese name for Peta
Giyugun Gakari (Jp)	section in charge of the Peta in a Japanese battalion
Giyugun Shidobu (Jp)	Planning Department for the Guidance of the Java Volunteer Defence Force
Giyugun Shireibu (Jp)	Peta headquarters envisaged by the Japanese
Giyugun Shitsu (Jp)	Regional office of the Giyugun Shidobu
GPH (Jv)	Gusti Pangeran Haryo; high aristocratic title
guna-guna	black magic
gunpyo (Jp)	Japanese military scrip
Gunseibu (Jp)	Military Administration Department
Gunseikan (Jp)	Military Administrator

Gunseikanbu (Jp)	Military Administrator's Department
gunzoku (Jp)	Japanese civilian in military employment
haj (Isl)	pilgrimage to Mecca
haji (Isl)	Muslim who has made the pilgrimage to Mecca
halal (Isl)	allowed, permitted
halus, alus	refined, pure, equisite
Hamengku Buwono (Jv)	"Protector of the World"; part of the full name of the Sultan of Yogyakarta
hancho (Jp)	squad leader
harta (Jv)	money, wealth, property
HBS (D)	Hogere Burger School; Higher Civil School; Dutch-medium high school which prepared students for higher education
heiho (Jp)	Indonesian auxiliary soldier attached to Japanese Army unit
heiki bundancho (Jp)	ordnance squad leader
HIK (D)	Hollandsch-Inlandsche Kweekschool; Teacher's Training College for Natives; school providing a six-year course of training for HIS teachers
HIS (D)	Hollandsch-Inlandsche School; Dutch-Native School; Dutch-medium primary school
Hizbul Wathon	Boy Scout movement of Muhammadiyah
Hizbullah	Army of God; Japanese-trained Muslim paramilitary group
HKS (D)	Hogere Krijgsschool; Dutch Higher War College
ibu, bu	mother; also a form of address for an older woman or one of high standing
ICATS	Indonesian Current Affairs Translation Service
ICMI	Ikatan Cendekiawan Muslim se-Indonesia; All-Indonesia Union of Muslim Intellectuals.
IGHQ	Imperial General Headquarters; the Japanese high command unit which linked the Army and Navy general staffs
Ika Daigaku (Jp)	Medical Faculty in Jakarta during the Japanese occupation

ilmu klenik	dubious magical practices, charlatanism
IJN	Imperial Japanese Navy
Indo	Indo-European, Eurasian
Indonesia Raya	"Great Indonesia"; national anthem
inheems (D)	roughly equivalent to "native"
inlander (D)	native; Indonesians saw the term as offensive
Insya Allah (Isl)	God willing
IPPHOS	Indonesia Press Photo Service
ISDV	Indische Sociaal-Democratische Vereeniging; Indies Social Democratic Association
jalan, jl.	street
Jawa-gun (Jp)	[Japanese] Java Army
Jawa Boei Giyugun (Jp)	Java Volunteer Defence Force; Japanese name for Peta; (Giyugun, for short)
Jawa Boei Giyugun Kanbu Renseitai (Jp)	Java Volunteer Defence Force Officer Cadet Training Centre
Jawa Boei Giyugun Tokusetsu Yugekitai I Go Kinmutai (Jp)	Special Guerrilla Force No. I Task Force
Jawa Hokokai (Jp)	Java Service Association. Central political control organization set up by the Japanese
Jawa no kai (Jp)	Java Society
Jemaah Islamiyah	Islamic Community; a terrorist organization
joho kyoku (Jp)	Third Bureau of the Japanese Naval General Staff
junsa (Jp)	policeman
junsabucho (Jp)	police sergeant
junsacho (Jp)	senior policeman
kabupaten	regency, administrative district
Kaigun (Jp)	[Imperial Japanese] Navy
Kaigun Bukanfu (Jp)	[Wartime Japanese] Navy Liaison Office [in Jakarta]
Kaigun Minseifu (Jp)	Navy Civil Government
Kaikyo Seinen Teishintai (Jp)	Islamic Youth Volunteer Corps; Japanese-

	sponsored militia unit known in Indonesia as Hizbullah.
kain	cloth, material, *sarong*
kampung	village, or neighbourhood for poorer urban workers
kanto seishin (Jp)	offensive spirit
kasar	uncivilized, coarse, rude
kebatinan	Javanese spiritualism, religion, mysticism; also known as *kepercayaan*
Keibodan (Jp)	Japanese-sponsored civil defence Vigilance Corps
keibu (Jp)	police inspector
keibuho (Jp)	assistant police inspector
Keimu (Jp)	Police Affairs Division within the Kenpeitai
Keimubu (Jp)	Central police department in the Sixteenth Army Military Administration Headquarters
keisatsu bucho (Jp)	police department
keisatsu shocho (Jp)	police station commander
keisatsukan (Jp)	policeman
keishi (Jp)	police superintendent
kejawen	Javanese, Javaneseness, Javanist; a term used for nominal or non-practising Muslims or *kebatinan* adherents, who see themselves as having an authentic Javanese identity
kelompok	groups or categories
kenpei (Jp)	member of the Kenpeitai
kenpeiho (Jp)	non-commissioned officer in the Kenpeitai
Kenpeitai (Jp)	Japanese Military Police Corps
kepercayaan	Javanese mystical beliefs
keras	hard, strong, firm
K.H.	Kiayi Haji; title or reference to a respected scholar or Islamic teacher who has made the pilgrimage to Mecca
KIM (D)	Koninklijk Instituut voor de Marine; Royal Naval Institute

KITLV (D)	Koninklijk Instuut voor Taal-, Land- en Volkenkunde; Royal Institute for Linguistics, Geography and Ethnography
kiyai, kyai, kiai	Respectful term of address for Islamic teachers and for revered objects full of supernatural or spiritual power
KL (D)	Koninklijke Landmacht; Royal [Netherlands] Army
klewang	sabre or machete with a broad, curved blade
KM (D)	Koninklijke Marine; Royal [Netherlands] Navy
KMA (D)	Koninklijke Militaire Academie; Royal [Netherlands] Military Academy
KNIL (D)	Koninklijk Nederlands-Indisch Leger; Royal Netherlands Indies Army
KNIL-ML (D)	KNIL-Militaire Luchtvaartafdeling. Colonial army air wing; de facto air force
kokutai (Jp)	Japan's ostensibly unique "national structure"
Korps Maréchaussée (D)	KNIL counter-guerrilla and commando force; known in Indonesian as *marsosé*
KPH (Jv)	Kanjeng Pangeran Haryo; high aristocratic title
KPM (D)	Koninklijke Paketvaart Maatschappij; Royal Mail Steam Packet Company.
kraton (Jv)	palace, especially of a Javanese Sultan or Susuhunan
K.R.A.Y.	Kanjeng Ratu Ayu; title of a female member of the aristocracy
K.R.M.H. (Jv)	Kanjeng Raden Mas Haryo; form of address for high-ranking noble
K.R.M.T. (Jv)	Kanjeng Raden Mas Tumenggung; Javanese nobility title; one level down from prince
kromo (Jv)	respectful high Javanese sublanguage used to and among social superiors
K.R.T. (Jv)	Kanjeng Raden Tumenggung; regent
Kwantung Army	Japanese force which ran the puppet state of Manchukuo (Manchuria)
langgar (Isl)	prayer house

latihan jiwa	spiritual training
LHCMA	Liddell Hart Centre for Military Archives, King's College London
lurah	village head, neighbourhood head, boss (coll.)
Mahabharata	Hindu epic
malu	shame, ashamed, embarrassed, shy
Mandala Command	Command for the Liberation of West New Guinea
Mangadeg Foundation	body set up at instigation of the Soeharto family
Mangkunegaran	subsidiary royal court in Solo
Maréchaussée (D)	*see* Korps Maréchaussée
mas	sir, brother; term used to address or refer to male of similar age; Javanese title below *raden*
Masyumi	Majelis Syuro Muslimin Indonesia; Consultative Council of Indonesian Muslims; in 1945, transformed itself into a political party
mbah (Jv)	1. In a family relationship: grandmother or grandfather; 2. term of address to a senior (in age)
mbak (Jv)	1. In a family relationship: older sister; 2. term of address to a younger woman who is older than the speaker; 3. in contemporary usage, term of address to a younger woman working in a shop, hotel, bank, office, etc.
mbok (Jv)	*ngoko* for "mother"; form of address for an older Javanese woman of modest origin
ménak	Sundanese upper *priyayi*
merdeka	free, independent
MOSVIA (D)	Middelbare Opleidingsschool voor Inlandsche Ambtenaren; Secondary Training School for Native Officials.
MPR	Majelis Permusyawaratan Rakyat; People's Deliberative Assembly
Muhammadiyah	"Followers of Muhammad"; Muslim educational and social welfare association that seeks a purified Islam stripped of local accretions

MULO (D)	Meer Uitgebreid Lager Onderwijs; More Extensive Lower Education, i.e., Lower Secondary School
NA, NANL (D)	Nationaal Archief. National Archives of the Netherlands
NAA	National Archives of Australia
Nahdlatul Ulama	Council of Islamic Scholars
Nakano Gakko (Jp)	Army intelligence school in Tokyo
Nami Kikan (Jp)	Wave Agency
Nanpo (Jp)	the south, southern region
Nanpogun (Jp)	Southern Army
Nan'yo (Jp)	the South Seas
Ndalem Kalitan (Jv)	name of a palace in Solo
NEI	Netherlands East Indies
ngéngér (Jv)	a form of adoption where one lives with relatives and does chores in return for room and board
ngoko (Jv)	low Javanese; speech level used among friends and family or when speaking to those of lower social status
NIAS (D)	Nederlandsch-Indische Artsen School; Netherlands Indies Medical School in pre-war Surabaya
Nihongun (Jp)	Japanese military
NIOD-IC (D)	Nederlands Instituut voor Oorlogs-, Holocaust- en Genocidestudies – Indische Collectie; NIOD Institute for War, Holocaust and Genocide Studies – Indies Collection
ojo kagetan, ojo gumunan, ojo gugupan (Jv)	don't be easily surprised, but remain calm; don't be overwhelmed by anything; don't act haphazardly
ojo dumeh (Jv)	be aware of yourself, who you are
Oost-Indische leger	East Indies Army; pre-1933 name for the KNIL
orang ngéngér	someone reared by better-off relatives
Pak	abbreviation of *bapak* (father); can be used as a form of address to an older man or as a title conveying respect

Paku Alam	the head of the minor royal court in Yogyakarta
Pakualaman	the minor court in Yogyakarta
pamong praja	"Guardians of the Realm"; the indigenous administrative corps
Pancasila	Five principles (belief in God, just and civilized humanitarianism, Indonesian unity, popular sovereignty and social justice) advocated by Sukarno and later adopted as the state "ideology" or doctrine
pangeran	prince
panglima besar	supreme commander
pangréh pradja (Jv)	"Rulers of the Realm"; indigenous administrative corps on Java dating from pre-colonial times; known after 1946 as *pamong praja* ("Guardians of the Realm")
Partai Komunis Indonesia	*see* PKI
Partai Nasional Indonesia	*see* PNI
pegawai negeri	official
pejuang	freedom fighter, warrior
Pembela Tanah Air	*see* Peta
pemuda	youth; young activist; freedom fighter
peranakan	Chinese born in Indonesia, often with some Indonesian ancestry, who has adopted local ways
pergerakan	Movement, the Movement; anti-Dutch political activity
perjuangan	struggle, fight
pesantren	rural Islamic boarding school
Peta	Tentara Sukarela Pembela Tanah Air; Fatherland Volunteer Defence Force; Indonesian name for the Japanese-created Java Volunteer Defence Force (Jawa Boei Giyugun, or simply Giyugun)
PID (D)	Politieke Inlichtingendienst; Political Intelligence Bureau
PKI	Perserikatan Kommunist di India; Communist

	Association in the Indies. Forerunner of the Indonesian Communist Party
PKI	Partai Komunis Indonesia; Indonesian Communist Party
PNI	Partai Nasional Indonesia; Indonesian National Party
PPKI	Panitia Persiapan Kemerdekaan Indonesia; Committee for the Preparation of Indonesian Independence; known in Japanese as the Dokuritsu Junbi Iinkai
pribumi	indigenous
priyayi	The term referred originally to junior members, in age and rank, of the Javanese royalty and high aristocracy. By the late nineteenth century it had come to mean the salaried officialdom of Java
PRO	Public Record Office of the National Archives, London
PS	Partai Sosialis; Socialist Party
Pusat Rohani Islam (Pusrohis)	Indonesian Army's Islamic Spiritual Centre
Qur'an	Koran; the holy scripture of Islam
r.	reigned
Raden (R.) (Jv)	a low nobility title
Raden Bagus (Jv)	a low nobility title
rakyat	people, the masses
Ramayana	Hindu epic from which many Indonesian literary and other themes are drawn
Ratu Loro Kidul (Jv)	Goddess of the South Sea
regu	squad
Ridlo [*Ridho, Réla*] *Allah* (Jv)	"with God's blessing"
rikugun-boeitai (Jp)	army defence companies
Rikugun-sho (Jp)	Ministry of the Army
R.M. (Jv)	Raden Mas; title of minor Javanese nobility higher than Raden

R.M.T. (Jv)	Raden Mas Tumenggung; Javanese title given to a *bupati* (regent)
romo (Jv)	high Javanese term for *bapak*, or father; used in Bahasa Indonesia as a form of address for Roman Catholic priest
romu (Jp)	labour, work
romusha (Jp)	unskilled labourer; in Indonesia the word quickly came to be associated with forced labour
R.P. (Jv)	Raden Panji; title of the lower Javanese nobility
Rp	rupiah
RPKAD	Resimen Para Komando Angkatan Darat; Army Para-commando Regiment
rust en orde (D)	peace and order
sabar	patient, calm
sakusen sanbo (Jp)	staff officer for operations
samadi	meditation
santri	pious or orthodox Muslim
Sarekat Islam	Islamic Union; first mass political movement in Indonesia
Saréngat Islam (Jv)	term for *syariah* (or *syariat*) *Islam* (Islamic law)
schakelschool (D)	link school
seibu boetai (Jp)	western defence [zone]; in this context, western Java
Seinendan (Jp)	Japanese-run para-military Youth Corps
Seinen Dojo (Jp)	Youth [Military] Training Centre at Tangerang
seishin-ryoku (Jp)	spiritual strength
seito (Jp)	pupil
seiza (Jp)	kneeling on the floor, with one's legs under one's thighs
sekolah rakyat	elementary school
selir	concubine
semangat	spirit, revolutionary ardour
semangat menyerang	offensive spirit

Sendenhan (Jp)	[Sixteenth Army] Propaganda Corps; known later in the war as the Sendenbu
Sendenbu (Jp)	Propaganda Department of the Japanese Military Administration on Java
shidokan (Jp)	supervisor
Shimon Kikan (Jp)	Investigation Organization
shireibu (Jp)	headquarters
shodan, shodancho (Jp)	platoon, platoon commander
Shomu (Jp)	general affairs division within the Kenpeitai
silsilah	genealogy, family tree
slametan	ritual communal meal to observe major occasions such as birth, death and marriage; ceremony at which benign spirits are invoked and harmful spirits propitiated
SMP	Sekolah Menengah Pertama; Lower Middle School
SMT	Sekolah Menengah Tinggi. Higher Middle School
sociëteit (D)	Dutch club; the social heart of the prewar Dutch community in the larger NEI towns
soe (Jv)	good, much
Somubu (Jp)	General Affairs Department [of the Sixteenth Army's Military Administration on Java]
Somubucho (Jp)	Head of the General Affairs Department
Stadspolitie (D)	Urban Police
Sunan (Jv)	ruler of Surakarta
Susuhunan (Jv)	title of the ruler of Surakarta
SWPA	South West Pacific Area (Command)
Syahadat (Shahadat) (Isl)	the Islamic confession of faith
Syariah (Syariat, Shari'a) Islam	Islamic law; in Javanese, *Sarëngat Islam*
Taman Guru (Jv)	school educating Taman Siswa teachers
Taman Siswa (Jv)	Garden of Pupils; pre-war nationalist school system
Taman Madya (Jv)	Taman Siswa senior high school

tangsi	barracks
tentara	army
Tentara Keamanan Rakyat	*see* TKR
Tentara Nasional Indonesia	*see* TNI
THS (D)	Technische Hogeschool; pre-war Technical Faculty in Bandung
TKR	Tentara Keamanan Rakyat; People's Security Army
TNI	Tentara Nasional Indonesia; Indonesian National Army
tobu boeitai (Jp)	eastern defence [zone], that is, eastern Java
Tokko (Jp)	Special Higher Police
Tokko-ka (Jp)	Special Higher Police section of the Kenpeitai
Tokubetsu Koto Keisatsu, or Tokko (Jp)	Special Higher Police at the apex of the civilian police structure
Tokubetsu Keisatsutai (Jp)	Special Police Strike Force within the Tokko section of the Japanese-run civilian police force
Tokubetsu kogekitai (Jp)	Special Attack Force. Japanese euphemism for *kamikazi* squad
Tokumukikan (Jp)	special task agency
totok	full-blooded, newcomer; usually referring to a Dutchman or ethnic Chinese
Tumenggung (Jv)	title of high-ranking royal official
tut wuri handayani (Jv)	leading from behind
ulama (Isl)	Islamic scholar, Muslim religious teacher or leader
ulu-ulu (Jv)	hamlet irrigation official
USETUPS	US Embassy Translation Unit Press Summary
vakscholen (D)	low-level vocational schools
Veldpolitie (D)	Field Police
VOC (D)	Vereenigde Oost-Indische Compagnie; Dutch East India Company
Vorstenlanden (D)	Dutch name for the four Central Javanese

	principalities, two of them in Surakarta and two in Yogyakarta
VPTL (D)	Voorschrift voor de Uitoefening van de Politiek-Politionele Taak van het Leger; Regulations for Exercising the Political and Police Task of the Army
volksscholen (D)	people's schools, also known as *desascholen*
Wali Sanga (Isl)	the semi-legendary nine apostles of Islam in Java
wayang	shadow play
wedana (Jv)	district chief
wong cilik (Jv)	lit. "little people", the common people
Yamato-damashii (Jp)	spiritual qualities supposedly unique to the Japanese people
yayasan	foundation
Yobishikan Gakko (Jp)	Reserve Officers Academy
yugeki (Jp)	member of the Yugekitai
Yugekitai (Jp)	Japanese-created Indonesian Special Guerrilla Force on Java
zazen (Jp)	a form of religious meditation

Notes

A Note on Military Organization

1. Marc Lohnstein, *Royal Netherlands East Indies Army* 1936–42 (Oxford: Osprey, 2018), p. 8.
2. J.J. Nortier, P. Kuijt and P.M.H. Groen, *De Japanse aanval op Java, Maart 1942* (Amsterdam: De Bataafsche Leeuw, 1994), p. 305.
3. Lionel Wigmore, *Australia in the War of 1939–1945, Series One, Army, Volume IV, The Japanese Thrust* (Canberra: Australian War Memorial, 1957), p. 445.

Preface

1. In his speech, Soeharto said he wanted to pass on the facts "as far as we know them" concerning the situation "which we have all been experiencing and witnessing together" in connection with the September 30th Movement. For an English-language translation of the speech, which ran to some 6,000 words, see "Speech by Major-General Suharto on October 15, 1965, to Central and Regional Leaders of the National Front", in The Editors, "Selected Documents Relating to the September 30th Movement and Its Epilogue", *Indonesia*, Vol. 1 (April 1966), Cornell Modern Indonesia Project, at pp. 160–78. On the National Front, see Harold Crouch, *The Army and Politics in Indonesia*, rev. ed. (Ithaca: Cornell University Press, 1988), p. 34. Sukarno had at one stage privately told the American ambassador he saw the National Front as a vehicle through which he could create a one-party state. The parties successfully opposed the idea, however, and the front became a propaganda agency for the government, increasingly influenced by Communists. Howard Palfrey Jones, *Indonesia: The Possible Dream*, 4th ed. (Singapore: Gunung Agung, 1980), p. 245.
2. Interviews, Professor K.P.H. Haryasudirja Sasraningrat, Jakarta, 31 January 2000, 13 May 2000, and 22 January 2001, on which this account draws. Recalling this incident thirty-five years later, Haryasudirja thought that Soeharto had

addressed the National Front on the evening of 4 October. That is most unlikely. Harry Tjan Silalahi, the then secretary of the anti-Communist Front Pancasila, was one of a small group of conservative civilian leaders who called on Soeharto on 7 October 1965, and who was to attend a number of meetings chaired by him in the months that followed. He argues convincingly that it would have been too soon for Soeharto to have addressed the National Front on 4 October; the situation had not yet stabilized. Harry Tjan Silalahi, personal communication, 15 January 2020.

In his speech, Soeharto asked National Front members for their forgiveness for any lack of polish or coherence in his analysis. He was, he said, no expert at public speaking. He added, "I think we have a friend here who knows me, Mr Haryo Sudirdjo, who is also from Jogja. [He knows that] I am someone who very rarely makes public statements." Soeharto is not recorded as saying anything more than that in regard to Haryasudirja. Can we believe Haryasudirja's claim that Soeharto went further and told front members that if they had any questions about him they should ask Haryasudirja? Tjan, who was, like Haryasudirja, a Roman Catholic from Yogyakarta, albeit from a very different background, and who would go on to co-found a think-tank closely aligned with two of Soeharto's key "political" and "financial" generals, was to become sharply critical of Haryasudirja in later years. But he found it entirely plausible that Soeharto did indeed make such a suggestion.

Haryasudirja was a leader of a small group of anti-Communist Catholic intellectuals in the National Front. K.P.H. is an abbreviation of Kanjeng Pangeran Haryo, a high-ranking noble title, equivalent to prince. Haryo, with an *o*, was the spelling he himself used for his title; he preferred Haryasudirja, with an *a*, when spelling his name.

3. Haryasudirja's grandmother was a great granddaughter of Prince Diponegoro, who led the Java War (1825–30) against the Dutch. Haryasudirja's grandfather on his mother's side (the husband of this grandmother) was the son of Paku Alam III, ruler of the minor court in Yogyakarta. Paku Alam I was installed in 1812 by Sir Thomas Stamford Raffles, when the latter was Lieutenant-Governor of Java. Haryasudirja was a nephew of Paku Alam VIII and an uncle of Paku Alam IX, over whose installation he presided.
4. In March 1966 Soeharto would appoint Haryasudirja, who had studied engineering in London, Minister for Estates (Plantations) in his first cabinet (1966–67). That did not stop him dismissing Haryasudirja and the Minister for Oil and Mining, Slamet Bratanata, in October 1967. It was widely believed that the two men were sacked because they were *not* corrupt. They controlled the two most lucrative ministries in cabinet but were unwilling to allow funds to be siphoned off to support dubious "off-budget" government spending.

   Haryasudirja had no contact with Soeharto or Ibu Tien in the three years after his dismissal from the cabinet. But in 1970 the First Lady asked him to become a key adviser to the couple as they embarked on their plan to build a controversial Taman Mini "Indonesia Indah" (Beautiful Indonesia-in-Miniature) theme park on the outskirts of Jakarta. Haryasudirja accepted and held that position between 1970 and 1975. He went on to serve as rector of Trisakti University, one of the largest private universities in Jakarta, between 1980 and 1988. In the late nineties, he was chairman of the Paguyuban Wehrkreis III Yogyakarta, an association of veterans who had fought under Soeharto's command in the Yogyakarta military region in 1948–49. Interviews, Haryasudirja, Jakarta, 31 January, 9 February, 5 May and 13 May 2000, and 22 January and 12 February 2001. See also P.K. Haryasudirja Sasraningrat, "Kenangan Penuh Syukur Ulang Tahun, 'Commendatore di San Gregorio Magno' Prof. Dr. Ir. KPH, P.K. Haryasudirja Sasraningrat", 20 October 2000, and J. Pamudji Suptandar, et al., *Prof. Dr. Ir. P.K. Haryasudirja: Tokoh Pejuang Kemerdekaan, Pembangunan dan Pendidikan* (Jakarta: Universitas Trisakti, 2005).

5. *Soeharto, Pikiran, Ucapan, dan Tindakan Saya: Otobiografi, Seperti Dipaparkan kepada G. Dwipayana dan Ramadhan K.H.*, henceforth Soeharto, *Pikiran* (Jakarta: Citra Lamtoro Gung Persada, 1989), pp. 90–91. In this book, Soeharto claims that the exchange took place when Sukarno visited Semarang for celebrations marking the first ten years of the Central Java military command (Tentara & Teritorium IV/Diponegoro), which would have made it October 1960. That is plainly wrong. Soeharto was dismissed as the military commander in Central Java in October 1959. In 1982, Soeharto had told a delegation of pro-government youth leaders that he discussed this matter with Sukarno in Semarang in 1956. See Ken Ward, "Soeharto's Javanese Pancasila", in *Soeharto's New Order and its Legacy: Essays in Honour of Harold Crouch*, edited by Edward Aspinall and Greg Fealy (Canberra: Griffin Press, 2010), p. 30. Once again, the suggested date looks wrong. Ward believes that if this conversation took place at all, it is more likely to have been in 1957, after the establishment that year of the Fourth Territory Development Foundation. While the exchange does appear to have come after the birth of the foundation, a more likely date is October 1958, when the President attended a celebration to mark the eighth anniversary of T&T IV, the eight-year cycle (*windu*) being of particular significance in the Javanese calendar. Soeharto's 1982 account of the alleged conversation surfaced later in what was claimed to be a secret recording of his words. In his 1988 book *Pak Harto: Pandangan dan Harapannya*, the then Youth and Sports Minister Abdul Gafur wrote that Soeharto asked visiting President Sukarno after the 1955 general election whether the PKI's success at the polls did not endanger Pancasila, the state ideology or doctrine, which includes "belief in God". Sukarno is said to have replied that the PKI was a fact and that he would change it to become "PKI Indonesia" or "PKI Pancasila". Soeharto reportedly asked, "Is it possible?", *Indonesia News Service*, no. 81, 9 March 1988, p. 3, citing *Jawa Pos* and *Kompas*.

6. This would not, it is true, be politics as usual. In the words of the American political scientist Douglas Kammen, it would be "the politics of blatant falsehoods, of hatred, of mass mobilization and of violence". Douglas Kammen, personal communication. Few would argue with Kammen's assessment. That said, there had been no shortage of falsehood, hatred and mass mobilization in the run-up to 30 September. For months, if not years, political pressures had been building. Communists and non-Communists had been circling one another with deadly intent, preparing for a showdown, mobilizing ceaselessly, both in towns and villages. What was new and significant was the sheer scale of the violence.
7. This saying comes with a subsidiary clause (*kebat keliwat-liwat*) which usually goes unquoted but which Soeharto never failed to mention and which warns in effect that if you rush into something you may overstep and fail.
8. Telephone interview, Colonel George Benson, 27 June 1992.
9. In early 1966, Colonel H.N. "Ventje" Sumual was serving time in a Jakarta jail for his central role in the PRRI-Permesta regional rebellion of the late 1950s. In jail with him were some of the political leaders of that rebellion: Syafruddin Prawiranegara, who had been prime minister of the emergency government of the Republic on Sumatra in the late 1940s; Mohammad Natsir, a modernist Muslim leader and former Prime Minister, and Mohamad Roem, another Muslim modernist and one who had earlier held a string of important cabinet positions. Sumual knew Soeharto well; like Haryasudirja he had fought under him in Central Java during the latter part of the 1945–49 Revolution. The politicians did not know him. "Who is this Soeharto?" they asked Sumual. Interview, Colonel Ventje Sumual, Jakarta, 20 September 1996. It may be more accurate to say that the jailed politicians knew very little about Soeharto.
10. US Central Intelligence Agency, Directorate of Intelligence, *Intelligence Report: Indonesia – 1965: The Coup That Backfired* (Washington, DC: 1968), p. 71.
11. Confidential Source One, 22 June 2019.
12. Annual World Bank Report on Indonesia, 1998, p. 1.
13. Subroto, "Recollections of My Career", *Bulletin of Indonesian Economic Studies* 34, no. 2 (August 1998), p. 92.
14. What he did create was Kopkamtib, a repressive *military* command.
15. The other economies were Japan, the "four tigers" (South Korea, Taiwan, Hong Kong and Singapore), plus Malaysia and Thailand. For details, see "The East Asian Miracle: Economic Growth and Public Policy" (New York: Oxford University Press, 1993), p. 1. The World Bank used this term about Indonesia until the Asian Financial Crisis. What is striking about this report is that it makes almost no mention of China, except for a passing reference to the fact that China was growing rapidly.
16. Terence Hull, personal communication, 16 April 2015 and 31 July 2019.

17. Sukarno announced Indonesia out of the UN when Malaysia became a temporary member of the Security Council; Soeharto sent Indonesian diplomats back to the world body late in 1966.
18. Paul Preston, *Franco: A Biography* (London: Fontana Press, 1995), p. xviii.
19. Ruth McVey, written communication, 18 March 2017.
20. For a critique of "culture", and its "compelling promise to explain nearly everything", see Daniel S. Lev, "Conceptual Filters and Obfuscation in the Study of Indonesian Politics", revision of a lecture for the Herb Feith Foundation, November 2002.
21. Harold Crouch, personal communication.
22. For his comments on the ways in which Soeharto differed from Napoleon and Bismarck, I am indebted to Dan Lev. Personal communication.
23. David Halberstam, *The Best and the Brightest* (Greenwich, Connecticut: Fawcett, 1973), p. 528.
24. Robert W. Hefner, "Islam, State, and Civil Society: ICMI and the Struggle for the Indonesian Middle Class", *Indonesia* no. 56 (October 1993), p. 1, fn. 2.
25. Strictly speaking, the "nation" was never asked for its views on the matter. Arguments for an Islamic state were rejected when a team of Japanese-appointed delegates drafted the 1945 Constitution on the grounds that this would discriminate against non-Muslim minorities. A compromise that would have required Muslims to follow Islamic law was written into a preamble to the constitution. But this was dropped a day after the Proclamation of Independence when Hatta and several other leaders were advised that Christians in eastern Indonesia felt this implied a form of discrimination against minorities.
26. For an eloquent and persuasive explanation of how this was done, see Daniel S. Lev, "Memory, Knowledge and Reform", in *Beginning to Remember the Past in the Indonesian Present*, edited by Mary S. Zurbuchen (Singapore: Singapore University Press, 2005), pp. 195–208. For a fuller treatment of this subject, see Lev, *The Transition to Guided Democracy: Indonesian Politics 1957–1959* (Ithaca: Cornell Modern Indonesia Project, 1966.)
27. Transparency International, a Berlin-based anti-corruption NGO, branded Soeharto one of the world's most corrupt leaders, allegedly misappropriating between US$15–32 billion during his thirty-two-year presidency. But this figure appeared to include a number of government bookkeeping transfers and concessions which, however dubious, did not necessarily result in funds flowing into Soeharto family bank accounts.
28. Hugh Trevor-Roper, *The Crisis of the Seventeenth Century: Religion, The Reformation, and Social Change* (Indianapolis: Liberty Fund, 2001), pp. 228–29; originally published by Harper & Row (New York: 1967). During and after the 1945–49 National Revolution, it is true, many of the political, social and

religious issues that had divided nationalist leaders in the pre-war period would resurface, and this generation would become increasingly disunited, promoting a range of visions for the future. Even so, the spirit of '45 remained of central importance, not least to officers of the Indonesian Army.

29. Paul Preston, *Franco*, p. xx.
30. David Jenkins, *Suharto and His Generals: Indonesian Military Politics 1975–1983* (Ithaca: Cornell University, Cornell Modern Indonesia Project, Monograph Series, Publication No. 64, 1984).
31. "After Marcos, Now for the Soeharto Billions", *Sydney Morning Herald*, 10 April 1986.
32. Their ranks include two other former presidents of Indonesia, two former vice presidents, a former prime minister, a former deputy prime minister, cabinet ministers, retired Japanese Army officers who selected and trained the young Soeharto, retired British and Dutch officers who fought in Central Java in 1945–49, senior Indonesian Army, Navy, Air Force and Police officers, as well as economists, student leaders, newspaper editors, Islamic leaders, Javanese mystics, intelligence chiefs, academics, think-tank directors, business people, novelists, political prisoners, diplomats, a former head of the presidential security detail, a former head of palace protocol and even the odd film star.
33. "In Memoriam: R. Darsono, Pioneer of Independence, Dies", *Sinar Harapan*, 20 January 1976, *Current Affairs Translation*, published by *Antara*, January 1976 Bulletin, p. 77. According to the *Sinar Harapan* report, Darsono had been told the government was willing to allow him to be buried in a heroes cemetery but chose instead to be buried elsewhere. An infantry colonel acted as inspector of ceremonies at the funeral. It was only in 1950, on the intervention of Vice President Mohammad Hatta, whom he had met in Hamburg in 1921, that Darsono had been able to return to Indonesia, where he was given a position in the Foreign Ministry.
34. Arthur M. Schlesinger, Jr., *The Age of Roosevelt, Volume I: The Crisis of the Old Order, 1919–1933* (Boston: Mariner, 1985), p. xi.
35. Interview, Lieutenant General G.P.H. Djatikusumo, Jakarta, 9 March 1981.

1. "The Sultan came to me and asked about that family tree"

1. Soeharto, *My Thoughts, Words, and Deeds: An Autobiography as Told to G. Dwipayana and Ramadhan K.H.*, edited by Mutiah Lestiono (Jakarta: Citra Lamtoro Gung Persada, 1989), p. 6.

   This book, first published in Indonesian as *Soeharto: Pikiran, Ucapan dan Tindakan Saya*, has an interesting history. Colonel (later Brigadier General) Gufrani Dwipayana, a long-time aide to Soeharto, asked Ramadhan, who had produced a number of biographies of prominent Indonesians, to write about Soeharto. Ramadhan said he was not able to do that but indicated that if Soeharto were to tell his story himself, he would compose it. In the two years it took him to write the book, he met Soeharto only twice, once at the President's home in Jalan Cendana and once at his ranch, Tapos, in the hills behind Bogor. Once a week, Ramadhan submitted questions to Dwipa, and, every Friday, received recorded answers and a transcript. He then submitted follow-up questions. Ramadhan confessed once that he found it difficult to convey much of an impression of Soeharto, who was quiet and whose manner of speaking was flat and devoid of emotion. He was unable, he said, to draw out Soeharto's feelings. This was in contrast with the rapport he had established with Lieutenant General Ali Sadikin, the former governor of Jakarta, and General Soemitro, the former head of the Command for the Restoration of Security and Order (Kopkamtib). See Kumala Dewi, "Saya Kira Angker", *Info Buku, Gatra,* No. 23 Tahun III, 26 April 1997.

2. The hamlet (*dusun*) was one of a number of such clusters in the village (*desa*) of Argomulyo.
3. This description of a typical peasant house in Central Java is based on Koentjaraningrat, "Tjelapar: A Village in South Central Java", in Koentjaraningrat, ed., *Villages in Indonesia* (Ithaca: Cornell University Press, 1967), p. 248.
4. A photograph from the late 1960s shows a quite substantial dwelling, erected on a high, brick-enclosed base, with a tiled roof and *gedek*-panel walls; there are several large unglazed windows. As a substantial figure in the village, Soeharto's father would have had a good house, but perhaps not as good a house as this. The original dwelling, upgraded when his father was appointed *ulu-ulu,* is likely to have been improved still further over Soeharto's lifetime. Whenever anyone in a village got some windfall money it was used to upgrade the house. The first thing people did was put in a cement floor. This involves building a brick surround, filling it with earth and finishing it with a two-inch cement layer, which becomes quite shiny after years of being swept. As it happens, Soeharto may have spent only forty or so days in this house, although it is possible that he lived here again from the age of about fourteen to eighteen. For the photograph, see Roeder, *The Smiling General*, photo insert section after p. 148.

   Soeharto told the *Nihon Keizai Shimbun* that his house had a thatched roof. See Soeharto, "Watashi no Rirekisho (My Personal History)", *Nihon Keizai Shimbun*, 3 January 1998. In the dying months of the New Order, the *Nihon Keizai Shimbun* carried an exclusive first-person account of Soeharto's life story in thirty segments, publishing one instalment each day from 1 to 31 January 1998, with the exception of 2 January. The account, which was given to the paper's staff correspondent, Komaki Toshihisa (or Toshikazu), appears to be based fairly loosely on the Soeharto autobiography. Though containing some new insights, it repeats many of the mistakes and distortions of Soeharto's book.

5. As Benedict Anderson has noted, "the old stable coordinates of the world had been unmoored by locomotive, clock, and print-capitalism." See Benedict R. O'G. Anderson, "Language, Fantasy, Revolution: Java 1900–1950", in *Making Indonesia: Essays on Modern Indonesia in Honor of George McT. Kahin*, edited by Daniel S. Lev and Ruth McVey (Ithaca: Southeast Asia Program, Cornell University, 1996), p. 38.
6. "In those days," Soeharto recalled, "there was no such thing as resident registration and so the date of my birth derives only from what [my great-aunt] told me." Soeharto, "Watashi no Rirekisho", *Nihon Keizai Shimbun*, 3 January 1998. Writing in 1967, Koentjaraningrat noted that village people rarely knew their age. See *Villages in Indonesia*, p. 249.
7. See O.G. Roeder, *The Smiling General: President Soeharto of Indonesia* (Jakarta: Gunung Agung, 1969), p. 78. In this semi-authorized biography, Roeder speaks of Kartoredjo, not Kertoredjo, or, as that name is spelled in this book, Kertorejo. This is not uncommon: people often say *kerto* instead or *karto*, as in the case of Kertanegara and Kartanegara. Roeder's book veers frequently into hagiography.
8. See O.G. Roeder, *Anak Desa: Biografi Presiden Soeharto* (Jakarta: Masagung, 1990), p. 130. This book was first published in 1976. That account tallies with the one given in Suryohadi, ed., *Silsilah Presiden Soeharto Anak Petani: Bahan dan Foto-Foto dari HUMAS SEKNEG Jakarta* (Surabaya: Penerbit 'Grip', 1974), p. 42. In the 1974 account, Kertorejo does not simply separate from his first wife; he divorces her.
9. He chose as his new name Notokariyo.
10. For details, see Soeharto, *Pikiran*, pp. 568–69.
11. For an excellent introduction to the micro-ecology of irrigated rice, see Clifford Geertz, *Agricultural Involution: The Processes of Ecological Change in Indonesia* (Berkeley: University of California Press, 1963), pp. 28–37, especially p. 31, on which this description is based.
12. The figure of 96 per cent is taken from M.P. van Bruggen and R.S. Wassing, *Djokja en Solo, Beeld van de Vorstensteden* (Purmerend: Asia Maior, 1998), p. 53.
13. Roeder, *The Smiling General*, p. 78.
14. I am indebted to Joan Hardjono, Anne Booth and Bob Elson for a number of observations about the sort of life Soeharto's father would have led.
15. For an account of this system, see Koentjaraningrat, "Tjelapar", in *Villages in Indonesia*, p. 273.
16. Anne Booth, written communication, 27 July 2019.
17. Geertz, *Agricultural Involution*, pp. 97–98, with the plot size figures in fn. 21.
18. Anne Booth, 27 July 2019.
19. Joan Hardjono, personal communication.

20. In 1998, recalling his life in Kemusu, Soeharto said, "Most of what we could see there on earth was green, like rice paddies and sugar cane fields." *Nihon Keizai Shimbun*, 3 January 1998.
21. In 1920, more than a third of the land in a broad crescent to the north, west and south of Yogyakarta was in sugar production. Geertz, *Agricultural Involution*, p. 73. Under the 1870 Agrarian Law, a ban on the sale of freehold land to non-natives was strengthened. However, Western companies were now allowed to acquire long-term leases over land. Robert Cribb, *Historical Dictionary of Indonesia* (Metuchen, NJ: Scarecrow Press, 1992), p. 6. These leases were often acquired with the collusion of the village head.
22. See Retnowati Abdulgani-Knapp, *Soeharto: The Life and Legacy of Indonesia's Second President* (Singapore: Marshall Cavendish International (Asia), 2007), pp. 19–20. Although hagiographic, the book contains some interesting details.
23. The claim that Sukirah was sixteen is given in Abdulgani-Knapp, *Soeharto*, p. 19.
24. Writing in 1985, sixty-five years after the marriage of Soeharto's parents, the Indonesian anthropologist Koentjaraningrat made the point that, even then, village girls tended to marry between the ages of twelve and fifteen. See Koentjaraningrat, *Javanese Culture* (Singapore: Oxford University Press, paperback ed., 1989), p. 120.
25. Roeder, *The Smiling General*, p. 79. That error arose, Soeharto later explained, helpfully but mysteriously, because "Fatimah is the name of the younger sister of my mother." R.E. Elson, *Soeharto: A Political Biography* (Cambridge: Cambridge University Press, 2001), p. 4, and "*Penjelasan Presiden Soeharto tentang silsilah keturunan beliau di depan pers bertempat di Binagraha tanggal 28 October 1974, jam 11.30–1315 WIB*", p. 22, in Suryohadi, ed., *Silsilah Presiden Soeharto Anak Petani*, p. 21.
26. *AB*, 17 February 1975, *Indonesian Current Affairs Translation Service* (henceforth ICATS), February 1975. Sukirah died of stomach cancer in 1946 and was buried in a family plot close to her father and grandfather. The cemetery, which is beside the road leading to Kemusu, was later upgraded by Soeharto. Kertosudiro died of malaria in 1951 and was buried in a simple family grave compound behind his house in Kemusu Kidul (South Kemusu), about one kilometre from the grave of his former wife. Departemen Penerangan, *Keterangan Presiden Soeharto tentang silsilah keluarga dalam pertemuan dengan pers dalam dan luar negeri bertempat di kamar kerja Presiden R.I. di Bina Graha, pada hari Senin, tanggal 28 Oktober 1974*, p. 15; Elson, footnotes to draft of Chapter 1, citing "*Penjelasan Presiden Soeharto*", p. 33, and "Kata Pendahuluan: Uraian Bapak Probosutedjo", in Suryohadi, ed., *Silsilah Presiden Soeharto Anak Petani*, p. 7, and Abdulgani-Knapp, *Soeharto*, pp. 305 and 319. *AB*, an abbreviation

of *Angkatan Bersenjata* [Armed Forces], was a newspaper published by the Department of Defence and Security.

27. Abdulgani-Knapp, *Soeharto*, p. 305.
28. For an excellent account of the *slametan* cycles, see Clifford Geertz, *The Religion of Java* (New York: The Free Press, 1960), pp. 30–85, on which this section draws.
29. See Geertz, *The Religion of Java*, p. 39.
30. Ibid., p. 40.
31. Ibid., p. 47.
32. Soeharto, *My Thoughts*, p. 5. For more on Sukirah, see Abdulgani-Knapp, *Soeharto*, p. 305.
33. Gavin W. Jones, *Marriage and Divorce in Islamic South-East Asia* (Kuala Lumpur: Oxford University Press, 1994), p. 187.
34. "*Penjelasan Presiden Soeharto*", p. 22.
35. See "Kata Pendahuluan: Uraian Bapak Probosutedjo", in Suryohadi, ed., *Silsilah Presiden Soeharto Anak Petani*. As Probosutedjo was born nine years after Soeharto it is not clear how valuable his confirmation could have been.
36. These details are from Roeder, *Anak Desa*, 1976, p. 133. The translation is by Angus McIntyre in *The Indonesian Presidency: The Shift from Personal toward Constitutional Rule* (London: Rowman & Littlefield, 2005), p. 111.
37. See Soeharto, *Pikiran*, p. 6, and the English-language edition of that book, Soeharto, *My Thoughts, Words and Deeds: An Autobiography*, p. 5, which make it clear that Mbah Kromo was a younger sister of Soeharto's paternal grandfather and thus his great-aunt. Confusingly, the official English-language autobiography goes on to describe Mbah Kromo, incorrectly, as Soeharto's grandmother. See *My Thoughts*, pp. 5 and 7. See also the Soeharto family tree on p. 568 of Soeharto, *Pikiran*.
38. For an account of these events and a clarification of the family relationships, see *Keterangan Presiden Soeharto tentang silsilah keluarga* and Soeharto, *Pikiran*, p. 6; McIntyre, *The Indonesian Presidency*, p. 110; and "Soeharto Outlines His Family Tree", *Merdeka*, 28 October 1974, *Indonesian Current Affairs Translation Service*, October 1974 bulletin, p. 726. Soeharto said at a press conference in 1974 that he was "not yet forty days old" when his mother and father were divorced. See *Keterangan Presiden Soeharto*, p. 11.
39. Suryohadi, *Silsilah Presiden Soeharto Anak Petani*, p. 40. Sukirah remarried at the age of nineteen and went on to have another seven children. One of them, Probosutedjo, became a wealthy businessman in New Order Indonesia. Another son, Suwito, was for many years the *lurah* (village chief) in Kemusu. For details, see Alberthiene Endah, *Memoar Romantika Probosutedjo: Saya dan Mas Harto* (Jakarta: Gramedia, 2010), pp. 47–49.
40. Interview, K.P.H. Haryasudirja, Jakarta, 12 February 2001. Haryasudirja

was adamant on this point. So too was his friend Major General Sukotjo Tjokroatmodjo, a former deputy head of the Military Police. As will be seen, in 1974 Sukotjo was ordered to investigate a magazine claim that Soeharto was illegitimate. Sukotjo interview, 3 August 2000.

41. One of those who claimed to believe this was Haryasudirja, who was, as noted earlier, a prince of the Pakualaman. Another, according to Haryasudirja, was his friend Sultan Hamengku Buwono IX. Interviews, Haryasudirja, Jakarta, 31 January 2000, and 12 February 2001. Haryasudirja had personal experience of this practice. When a former Paku Alam made a servant girl pregnant, he passed her on to Haryasudirja and his wife.
42. According to Islamic teaching, the birth of an illegitimate child (*anak haram* or *anak jadah*) is deeply shameful.
43. J.D. Legge, *Sukarno: A Political Biography* (Middlesex, England: Pelican, 1973). p. 25.
44. Elson, *Suharto*, p. 4.
45. Soeharto, *My Thoughts*, p. 8. Soeharto does not say what this working relationship was. Nor does he say how it came about. According to one controversial, and hotly disputed, account, Notosudiro was a descendant, five generations removed, of a prince who was a son of Sultan Hamengku Buwono V by his first concubine. See "Disekitar 'Silsilah POP' itu," *Tempo*, 9 November 1974, p. 47, and Angus McIntyre, "Soeharto's Composure: Considering the Biographical and Autobiographical Accounts" (Clayton, Victoria: Monash Asia Institute, 1996), p. 8. According to Elson, who bases himself on Anon., "Disekitar 'Silsilah POP itu", Notosudiro had taken for his wife a woman descended, by a distance of five generations, from the princely son of Hamengku Buwono V by his first concubine. See Elson, *Suharto*, p. 4.
46. This account is taken from Soeharto, *My Thoughts*, pp. 8–9, but I have modified parts of it to give a better sense of the words in Soeharto, *Pikiran*, pp. 10–11.
47. See Supomo Surjohudojo, "Growing Up in a Javanese Village: Personal Reminiscences", Centre of Southeast Asian Studies, Working Paper No. 20, Monash University, 1980.
48. Raden Rio Padmodipuro was known subsequently as R.L. Prawirowiyono. *Anak Desa*, p. 139. Haryasudirja wrote the name as "Rd. Rio Parwodipuro, Adjutan HB VIII" on his copy of a letter sent to him by the author on 26 January 2001.
49. Raden Rio was a *raden* by birth (the title can also be given as a reward) and had a connection with the Yogyakarta court, but he was five or six grades down the royal ladder. Rio is also a rank.
50. Interview, Haryasudirja, Jakarta, 12 January 2001.
51. Haryasudirja interview. According to the story, Sukirah caught Raden Rio's eye because she had a voluptuous figure. This is questionable: at that time,

very few poor Javanese women were well enough fed to have sizable breasts; what is more, the *kemben* flattens the breasts and completely conceals them.

52. Hamish McDonald refers to rumours that Soeharto was either "a lost or unacknowledged son" of the eighth Sultan of Yogyakarta or a grandson of "a distinguished officer in the sultan's private army." See McDonald, *Suharto's Indonesia*, p. 9. Michael Vatikiotis mentions rumours that the ninth Sultan once confirmed that Soeharto was of royal descent. See Michael R.J. Vatikiotis, *Indonesian Politics Under Soeharto: Order, Development and Pressure for Change* (London and New York: Routledge, 1993), p. 10. Elson records that he heard similar rumours. Elson, *Suharto*, p. 3.
53. Throughout that five-year period, Haryasudirja claimed, Soeharto either dealt with the Sultan through an intermediary or went to some lengths to ensure that the State Secretary, Lieutenant General Sudharmono, was present if he and the Sultan met face to face.
54. The conversation, conducted in a mixture of Indonesian and high Javanese, is said to have gone as follows:

    Sultan: *Har, pernah lihat ayahnya Harto?*
    Haryasudirja: *Oh, belum!*
    Sultan: *Ini lo! Bapaknya penyongsong waktu Rama seda.*

    There is one small cloud hanging over this story. Although Haryasudirja claimed to recall the exact words used by the Sultan, he gave conflicting evidence about the date on which those remarks were made. On one occasion he said that this conversation took place some time in 1966 or 1967 when he, Haryasudirja, was a minister in Soeharto's cabinet. Interview, Haryasudirja, 31 January 2000. On another occasion he said that the Sultan made these remarks in the late 1970s after he had stood down as Vice President. Haryasudirja, interview, Jakarta, 12 February 2001.

    By the time of Hamengku Buwono VIII's death, Padmodipuro is said to have moved up a grade, from Raden Rio to Kanjeng Raden Tumenggung, or Regent. If Raden Rio was Soeharto's father it would follow that the former was born no later than the very early years of the twentieth century. It has not been possible to establish whether this was in fact the case. Haryasudirja conceded that it was possible Raden Rio was born after that time.
55. Interview, Haryasudirja, Jakarta, 31 January 2000.
56. Interview, Haryasudirja, 5 May 2000. It might be asked why, if Soeharto felt himself to be part-royal, he would publicly deny it. What Haryasudirja was getting at, or imagined, was that Soeharto felt this way privately and derived some confidence or satisfaction or inner strength from that belief.

    Sumiskum, a diplomat who went on to serve as Deputy Speaker of Parliament, told a similar story. Soeharto, he assured Elson, "was the son of a courtly servant entrusted with wielding the yellow parasol above the head of Sultan Hamengku Buwono VIII." Elson, *Suharto*, p. 316, fn. 9, citing a 12 July 1997 interview with Sumiskum. It may or may not be relevant that Sumiskum, like Haryasudirja, had turned against Soeharto by the time he made these comments.

57. Jono had served as Indonesian defence attaché in Beijing in the mid-sixties and as counsellor at the Indonesian Embassy in Tokyo (1967–68 and 1971–75).
58. In an interview, Jono Hatmodjo said that in pre-revolutionary times it had been difficult for a woman from a noble family to marry a commoner. He knew this well from his own experience; his father had refused to allow his daughter, Jono's sister, to marry a commoner. After the Revolution, his father had changed his mind and the marriage had gone ahead. Interview, Jono Hatmodjo, Jakarta, 2 February 2000. Did it follow that Soeharto, who married in 1947, would have had no such problem? Not at all, Jono Hatmodjo answered. Siti Hartinah could not have married Soeharto had he been a commoner. "If he was not royal," Jono declared, grandly and a little pompously, "he could not marry my niece." Interview, Brigadier General Jono Hatmodjo, Jakarta, 6 May 1999. In the earlier interview, Jono had made it clear that Hartinah's family would have needed to know everything about Soeharto's family background. They would not have been at all pleased to learn that Soeharto's father was a lowly village irrigation official, and the fact that Soeharto was a lieutenant-colonel would not have been enough to change their mind. What persuaded them, he claimed, was the fact that Soeharto was the secret son of an aristocrat. This claim, which carried more than a trace of snobbish disdain for the commoner, is not persuasive. Besides, it is not at all certain that Hartinah's family would have known anything in 1947 about Soeharto's alleged royal connections.
59. Interview, Mohamad Roem, Jakarta, 24 June 1979.
60. "Soeharto Outlines His Family Tree", *Merdeka*, 28 October 1974.
61. "When the Sultan resigned," Mochtar Lubis, a prominent newspaper editor and author, recalled some years later, "I asked [him] why. 'He [Soeharto] never consulted me on anything while I was Vice President.'" Interview, Mochtar Lubis, Jakarta, 29 February 1984. The Sultan had earlier told General A.H. Nasution, a former Army Chief of Staff and Defence Minister, the same thing. "He said he was Vice President," Nasution recalled, "but was not used as Vice President. For protocol! And secondly he would like to see the civilian counterparts of the government with more authority. He's the man for the civilians. But Soeharto is dictating." Interview, General Nasution, Jakarta, 11 March 1982.

    The Sultan may have had still another reason for stepping down. Shortly after the 1974 Malari riots the Vice President agreed to receive members of a Bandung student group who were coming to Jakarta to protest against some new government policy. He thought it only sensible to give them a hearing.

On the day of the visit, the Sultan found that his personal security detail had been changed and the meeting cancelled. Learning from the mass media that he was "ill", the Sultan made a point of driving around town to show that he was, in fact, perfectly well. As John Bresnan, a former head of the Ford Foundation in Jakarta, wrote, "If Suharto could treat his own vice-president—the legendary Sultan of Yogyakarta, no less—in this heavy-handed fashion, what chance was there for freedom or justice for the ordinary citizen?" John Bresnan, *At Home Abroad: A Memoir of the Ford Foundation in Indonesia 1953–1973* (Jakarta and Singapore: Equinox, 2006), pp. 196–97.

62. See Anon., "Isu Soeharto Cina, Siapa Bapaknya?", wysiwyg://47/http:www.geocities.com/CapitolHill/4120/soeharto.html, accessed September 4, 2008, and Elson, *Soeharto*, p. 4. Mashuri is said to have made these observations in an interview with a magazine published by the Jawa Pos group. The date of publication is not given.
63. Confidential Source One, 1 February 2016, and 7 February 2017. Although Soeharto had apparently been angry with Mashuri over the claim that he was of Chinese descent, this source said, he had chosen not to make an issue of it; the two men went back a long way.
64. Interview, Haryasudirja, Jakarta, 4 August 2000.
65. Interview, Haryasudirja, Jakarta, 31 January 2000.
66. Interview, Sabam Siagian, Sydney, 25 September 2006. The banknotes were printed in Australia, when Siagian was serving there as ambassador in the early 1990s.
67. See R. Soedjana Tirtakoesoema, "The anniversary of the accession of His Highness the Sultan of Yogyakarta (Tingalan Panjenengan)," in *The Kraton: Selected Essays on Javanese Courts*, edited by Stuart Robson (Leiden: KITLV Press, 2003), p. 143.
68. See John Elliott Monfries, "A Prince in a Republic: The Political Life of Sultan Hamengku Buwono IX of Jogjakarta" (PhD dissertation, The Australian National University, 2005), p. 35, citing a fourteen-page unpublished memoir *Yogyase Roddels* (Yogya Gossip) by Dr Rudolf Frederick Westerkamp, who was the private physician first of Hamengku Buwono VIII and then of Hamengku Buwono IX between 1939 and 1942. Dr Westerkamp wrote the memoir for his family in about 1983. The claim that the seventh Sultan was senile is made on p. 4.
69. See Bruggen and Wassing, *Djokja en Solo*, p. 35, and Robson, *The Kraton*, pp. 145–46. By one account, the eighth sultan had only forty-four children. See https://id.wikipedia.org/wiki/Hamengkubuwana VIII (accessed 25 April 2019).
70. Interview, Onghokham, Jakarta, 11 May 1999.
71. Interview, Selo Soemardjan, Jakarta, 7 August 2000.

72. *POP* was an abbreviation of *Peragaan, Olah Raga, Perfilman*.
73. *AB*, 17 February 1975, in ICATS, February 1975, p. 135, and *Tempo*, 9 November 1974, pp. 45–46. This summary of the relevant part of the *POP* article is drawn from McIntyre, *The Indonesian Presidency*, p. 108.
74. *Anak Desa*, pp. 139–40. According to the *POP* article, the President was the nephew of B.P.H. Hadinegoro, a prince of the Yogyakarta court. Hadinegoro was a younger brother of the eighth Sultan and an uncle of Hamengku Buwono IX.
75. Harold Crouch, "The Anniversary of a Riot Celebrated in Jakarta by a New Political Trial", *National Times*, 17 February 1975.
76. To a critic, Moertopo could thus be seen as both a Savary and an unsavoury character. The quoted observation, by Pierre Lanfrey, is cited in Pieter Geyl, *Napoleon: For and Against* (Harmondsworth, England: Peregrine, 1965), p. 99. One of Moertopo's former civilian advisers has confirmed that Moertopo knew in advance about the contents of the *POP* article. Confidential Source One, Jakarta, 17 April 1998.
77. During two days of unrest, gangs set fire to Japanese and other cars, wrecked the showrooms of the company which imported Toyotas and burned and looted the large Senen shopping complex. It was widely believed that the rioting was instigated by Moertopo's agents in an attempt to discredit Moertopo's chief rival, General Soemitro, the head of the Command for the Restoration of Security and Order (Kopkamtib). The riots embarrassed Soeharto, who was hosting a visit by Japanese Prime Minister Tanaka Kakuei. Soeharto forced Soemitro to retire and dissolved Aspri.
78. McDonald, *Soeharto's Indonesia*, p. 198. A subordinate of Lieutenant Colonel Slamet Riyadi in Solo during the 1945–49 Revolution, Soegianto had gone on to become the first intelligence officer of the Army para-commando Regiment (Resimen Para Komando Angkatan Darat, RPKAD) and was senior at that time to 2nd Lieutenant (later General) Benny Moerdani, an up-and-coming special forces officer who would become one of the most powerful figures in Soeharto's New Order government. All three men were Roman Catholics. Drummed out of the RPKAD—but not cashiered—following an abortive 1956 coup attempt and not subsequently promoted, Soegianto was taken up, or "rescued", in 1966 by Moertopo, a man of the shadows who liked to surround himself with men who had a similar background and who shared similar characteristics. Personal communication, Harry Tjan Silalahi, 8 December 2015, and interview, Lieutenant Colonel Aloysius Soegianto, Jakarta, 3 September 1997.
79. Confidential Source One, 15 November 2018. The two Solonese principalities, the Sunanate and the Mangkunegaran, were formally abolished in 1946 after they failed to adequately support the Republic. Following the death

of Mangkunegoro VIII in 1987, however, President Soeharto and Ibu Tien would give their blessing to the view that the late ruler's heir should assume the position as head of the Mangkunegaran royal family in the interests of preserving the court culture. *Kompas*, 28 September 1987, *INS*, No. 39, 14 October 1987, p. 3.

80. Confidential Source One.
81. Interview, Major General Sukotjo Tjokroatmodjo, Jakarta, 3 August 2000.
82. Confidential Source One, 17 April 1998.
83. Confidential Source One, 24 September 2008.
84. Also present were the Attorney General, Major General Ali Said, the Minister of Information, Mashuri, and the head of the State Intelligence Coordination Board (Bakin), General Yoga Sugama.
85. *Merdeka*, 28 October 1974.
86. In a subsequent court case, the journalist who wrote the *POP* magazine piece, Lisa Sulistio, said she was no longer convinced of the truth of her article.
87. *AB*, 17 February 1975, ICATS, February 1975, p. 135.
88. To back up his case, Probosutedjo introduced four villagers from Kemusu, all of whom had been flown to Jakarta that morning, a clear indication of the seriousness with which the "revelations" were viewed and of the extraordinarily rapid response of those who sought to counter them. One of the four was a man named Prawirosudarmadi, who was described, correctly, as a younger brother of Sukirah.
89. He referred, inter alia, to Mbah Rono, a villager of his father's generation who was now eighty, and Mbak Idris, who used to nurse him when he was small. One of those "authentic witnesses" who had come to Bina Graha was Prawirosudarmadi, who was now described not as a younger brother of Sukirah but as the pensioned head of the technical school at Sentolo and a man "who was acquainted with the Head of State's mother from the time she was pregnant until the baby Soeharto was born." See Soeharto, *My Thoughts*, p. 5, and "Soeharto Outlines His Family Tree", *Merdeka*, 28 October 1974, in *Indonesian Current Affairs Translation Service*, October 1974 bulletin, pp. 725–26.
90. "*Penjelasan Presiden Soeharto*", and "Soeharto outlines his family tree. People may not act arbitrarily with the mask of 'Opsus'", *Merdeka*, 28 October 1974, ICATS, October 1974.
91. Soeharto, *My Thoughts*, p. 6.
92. "Soeharto outlines his family tree", *Merdeka*, 28 October 1974.
93. Confidential communications.
94. Soegianto and another of Moertopo's military operatives, Lieutenant Colonel (later Brigadier General) Irawan ("Kacang" ["Peanut"]) Soekarno, would be associated with the so-called "Balibo Declaration", a 30 November 1975 appeal from anti-Communist East Timorese leaders to President Soeharto,

seeking integration with Indonesia. In an interview twenty-two years later, Soegianto claimed that the "*konseptor*" of the Balibo Declaration was Jose Martins, leader of the small KOTA party in East Timor. Martins, he said, typed the "declaration" up on a portable typewriter with a Portuguese keyboard when he and Soegianto and Soekarno were staying at the Hotel Penida in Bali. Martins may have typed the final document under the watchful eye of Soegianto. But he was not the *konseptor*. The evidence suggests that the Balibo Declaration was drafted not in Balibo nor even in Bali but in Jakarta by one of Moertopo's senior civilian advisers. Soegianto, who had earlier liaised with anti-Communist East Timorese leaders inside East Timor, had simply carried the draft document from Jakarta to Bali and was to take it on, presumably to Indonesian West Timor, to which the signatories had by then fled, to be signed by them with varying degrees of enthusiasm. There are echoes here of the spurious, but seemingly spontaneous, 1943 "petition" which Gatot Mangkupradja, who had been a close associate of Sukarno, wrote in his own blood urging the Japanese Occupation authorities to create an Indonesian volunteer defence force. That affair had been stage-managed by Japanese intelligence officers. Interview, Lieutenant Colonel Soegianto, Jakarta, 3 September 1997, and Confidential Source One. See also Jill Jollife, *East Timor: Nationalism and Colonialism* (St Lucia, Queensland: University of Queensland Press, 1978) , p. 150.

95. By one account, Ibu Tien's father was the second son of RMT Haryokusumo, who was the second son of KPA Suryodiningrat, who was in turn the fourth son of Mangkunegoro III (r. 1835–1853). Ibu Tien's mother was herself a distant descendant of Mangkunegoro III. See Arwan Tuti Artha, *Bu Tien: Wangsit Keprabon Soeharto* (Yogyakarta: Galangpress, 2007), p. 51.
96. Arifin Surya Nugraha, *Keluarga Cendana* (Yogyakarta: Bio Pustaka, 2008), p. 35. Arifin does not give an explanation for what looks to have been an early retirement.
97. Interview, Haryasudirja, Jakarta, 31 January 2000, and Confidential Source One, 15 January 2008, and 15 November 2018.
98. Confidential Source One, 15 January 2008.
99. Interview, Brigadier General Jono Hatmodjo, Jakarta, 2 February 2000, and personal communication, Lieutenant General Sayidiman Suryohadiprojo, 2 April 2016. Jono Hatmodjo was not always the most reliable witness—he seldom came across a conspiracy theory that did not enchant and bedazzle him—and some of his claims need to be treated with care. But there is no reason to doubt that he and Ibu Tien had once been close or that he and the Mangkunegaran royal family were dismayed at the eventual outcome of this affair. Sayidiman was a friend of Jonosewojo.
100. All but one of the subsequent Mangkunegaran rulers are buried at the Astana

Girilayu complex, an elegant but suitably sombre European-style building some distance northeast of the Astana Mangadeg.

101. Interview, Jono Hatmodjo, 2 February 2000.
102. A second reason for the estrangement, Jono claimed, was that one of Ibu Tien's sons, whom he did not name, wanted to marry the daughter of Jono's elder brother, but nothing came of this. According to another source, Ibu Tien sought to arrange marriages between some of her children and court aristocrats, but was unsuccessful, a sign, allegedly, that the courts did not regard her as in any sense aristocratic or royal. Benedict Anderson, written communication, September 2008. There was, it is true, a precedent for that kind of marriage. Sudjiwo Kusumo (G.P.H. Jiwokusumo), who succeeded his father and became Mangkunegoro IX, had married Sukmawati Sukarno, a daughter of the former president. The marriage was unhappy, however, and the couple divorced in 1984, after seven years. *Kompas*, 11 October 1987, in *INS*, No. 43, 28 October 1987, p. 3.
103. If Ibu Tien was displeased with some of her Mangkunegaran relatives, Soeharto does not seem to have taken any steps to "punish" them. Jonosewojo stayed on as national chairman of a number of sporting bodies, including those associated with lawn tennis, basketball and bodybuilding. Soeharto appointed Jono Hatmodjo Deputy IV at the State Intelligence Coordinating Board (1975–80), after which Jono took up a senior position in the Foreign Ministry (1980–81).
104. Confidential Source One, 15 January 2008.
105. *Indonesia News Service*, No. 35, 30 September 1987, p. 3, citing a "protected source". On 3 September 1987, the day Mangkunegoro VIII died, the chairman of the DPR [Parliament] Commission IX, told reporters "the bestowal of traditional titles such as was done by the Mangkunegaran in Solo was best regulated by the government since some considered this to constitute feudalism. Others saw it as the right of the Mangkunegaran." *Kompas*, 4 September 1987, in *INS*, No. 32, 19 September 1987, p. 3.
106. The ceremony was held twenty-five days before the first general election of the New Order period, although there may have been no connection between the two events.
107. For an account of this event, from which this chronicle is taken, see John Pemberton, *On the Subject of "Java"* (Ithaca and London: Cornell University Press, 1994), pp. 164–66.
108. Ibid., p. 165.
109. Ibid.
110. See L.R. Baskoro et al., *Suharto: Farewell to the King* (Jakarta: Tempo, 2013).
111. James T. Siegel, *Solo in the New Order: Language and Hierarchy in an Indonesian City* (Princeton, New Jersey: Princeton University Press, 1986), pp. 281–82 and 331.

When Mangkunegoro VIII died in 1987, he was buried in the Mangkunegaran burial complex Astana Girilayu. *Jawa Pos*, 5 September 1987, in *Indonesia News Service*, No. 33, 1987. For further details of the Soeharto mausoleum, see "'Astana Giri Bangun' cemetery costs Rp437.8m, not Rp4 billion", Antara News Bulletin, Jakarta, 20 November 1977, and "Kaskopkamtib investigates Yayasan Mangadeg", Antara, 24 November 1977.

112. Abdulgani-Knapp, *Soeharto*, p. 326.
113. Confidential Source One, 15 January 2008.
114. Abdulgani-Knapp, *Soeharto*, p. 324.
115. Writing about his schooldays in Wuryantoro in the early thirties, Soeharto notes that the district chief (*wedana*) was Raden Mas Soemoharjomo. Raden Mas is a title of the Javanese nobility, higher than Raden. Soemoharjomo was later awarded the more elevated nobility title Kanjeng Raden Mas Tumenggung, KRMT, which is one level down from prince. In some later narratives Soemoharjomo is even referred to as Kanjeng Pangeran. *Pangeran* is a high royal title, meaning prince. Soemoharjomo was never a prince of the Mangkunegaran house. But it is possible, some believe, that the title *pangeran* was given to him as a "souvenir" to honour his service in generating financial support for the household. If so, this would appear to be the first case in which the *pangeran* title was conferred. See Soeharto, *Pikiran*, p. 13, and Abdul Gafur, *Siti Hartinah Soeharto: Ibu Utama Indonesia* (Jakarta: Citra Lamtoro Gung Persada, 1992), p. 122.
116. Confidential Source One, 7 February 2017.
117. Ibid.
118. Pemberton, *On the Subject of "Java"*, p. 166. Pemberton does not discuss the Ndalem Kalitan.
119. For an excellent account of this affair, see Margot Cohen, "A Royal Mess", *Far Eastern Economic Review*, 1 April 1993.
120. Interview, Haryasudirja, Jakarta, 31 January 2000, and 5 May 2000.
121. Confidential Source One, 15 January 2008.
122. Interview, Haryasudirja, 31 January 2000.
123. Krishna Sen, *Indonesian Cinema: Framing the New Order* (London and New Jersey: Zed Books, 1994), pp. 100–1.
124. See Wibisono Singgih, ed., *Museum Purna Bhakti Pertiwi* (Jakarta: Yayasan Purna Bhakti Pertiwi, 1983), p. 28.
125. Ibid., p. 22.
126. I am grateful to Merle Ricklefs for his observations about the non-existent sultanate of Kediri.
127. Soeharto, "Watashi no Rirekisho", *Nihon Keizai Shimbun*, 3 January 1998.
128. That story, with its implicit criticism of Sukirah, appeared in the first edition of *The Smiling General*, in 1969. It was deleted when a revised, Indonesian-language

version of the book, *Anak Desa: Biografi Presiden Soeharto*, appeared in 1976. See Roeder, *The Smiling General*, p. 81. As we have seen, in 1969 Roeder was under the misapprehension that Mbah Kromo was Soeharto's grandmother.

129. John Bowlby, *Attachment and Loss, Volume I: Attachment* (London: Pimlico, Random House, 1998), p. 223.
130. Ibid., p. xiii.
131. Ibid., pp. xiii–xiv.
132. Soeharto, *Pikiran*, p. 8, and *My Thoughts*, p. 7.
133. Ibid.
134. John Monfries, *A Prince in a Republic: The Life of Sultan Hamengku Buwono IX of Yogyakarta* (Singapore: Institute of Southeast Asian Studies, 2015), pp. 291–92.

2. "The cork on which the Netherlands floats"

1. Interview, Haryasudirja, Jakarta, 5 May 2000.
2. Robert Cribb and Colin Brown, *Modern Indonesia: A History Since 1945* (London and New York: Longman, 1995), p. 2.
3. J.D. Legge, *Indonesia*, 2nd ed. (Sydney: Prentice-Hall, 1977), p. 5.
4. Keith W. Taylor, "The Early Kingdoms", in *The Cambridge History of Southeast Asia, Volume I: From Early Times to c. 1800*, edited by Nicholas Tarling (Cambridge: Cambridge University Press, 1992), p. 173.
5. See Kenneth Hall, "Economic History of Early Southeast Asia", in *The Cambridge History of Southeast Asia, Vol. I*, p. 215.
6. Clifford Geertz, *The Religion of Java* (New York: The Free Press, 1969), pp. 231–32.
7. See M.C. Ricklefs, *A History of Modern Indonesia Since c. 1200*, 4th ed. (Stanford: Stanford University Press, 2008), pp. 6 and 15–16. This book provides a balanced, authoritative and highly readable account of Indonesian history over the past 800 years. Chapter 1 (pp. 3–16) gives a valuable short account of the coming of Islam.
8. See Barbara Watson Andaya and Yoneo Ishii, "Religious Developments in Southeast Asia, c1500–1800", in *The Cambridge History of Southeast Asia, Vol. I*, p. 517.
9. Ibid., p. 523.
10. Ricklefs, *A History of Modern Indonesia*, 4th ed., p. 16.
11. See Barbara Sillars Harvey, *Tradition, Islam, and Rebellion: South Sulawesi 1950–1965* (PhD dissertation, Cornell University, 1974), pp. 36–37.
12. Ricklefs, *A History of Modern Indonesia*, 4th ed., p. 43.
13. Robert Cribb, *Historical Dictionary of Indonesia* (Metuchen, NJ: Scarecrow Press, 1992), p. 130.
14. Ricklefs, *A History of Modern Indonesia*, 4th ed., p. 142.
15. The Cultivation System was not introduced in the four princely territories of Central Java, of which Yogyakarta was one. But large private plantations

developed there. Cribb, *Historical Dictionary*, p. 487. This resulted in exploitation of a similar kind, not least in sugar production.

16. Ricklefs, *A History of Modern Indonesia*, 4th ed., pp. 148–49.
17. Cornelis Fasseur, *The Politics of Colonial Exploitation: Java, the Dutch, and the Cultivation System*, translated from the Dutch by R.E. Elson and Ary Kraal, edited by R.E. Elson (Ithaca: Cornell University Southeast Asia Program, 1992), p. 57.
18. Ricklefs, *A History of Modern Indonesia*, 4th ed., p. 149.
19. I am indebted to Benedict Anderson for his comments on this process.
20. Ricklefs, *A History of Modern Indonesia*, 4th ed., p. 157.
21. For an excellent short summary, on which this paragraph draws, see Cribb, *Historical Dictionary*, pp. 79–83. See also the admirable paper by James Rush, "Placing the Chinese in Java on the Eve of the Twentieth Century", in *Indonesia: The Role of the Indonesian Chinese in Shaping Modern Indonesian Life* (Ithaca: Cornell Southeast Asia Program, 1991).
22. Cribb, *Historical Dictionary*, p. 3. See also H.L. Zwitzer and C.A. Heshusius, *Het Koninklijk Nederlands-Indisch Leger 1830–1950* [The Royal Netherlands Indies Army, 1830–1950] ('s-Gravenhage: Staatsuitgeverij, 1977), p. 25, which gives a figure of 70,000. Soeharto's ten-year war and repression in Aceh is said to have cost about 15,000 lives. Ricklefs, *A History of Modern Indonesia*, 4th ed., p. 408.
23. Interview, Colonel C.A. Heshusius, The Hague, 23 April 2001. See also Zwitzer and Heshusius, *Het Koninklijk Nederlands-Indisch Leger 1830–1950*, p. 25.
24. Cribb, *Historical Dictionary*, p. 40.
25. Ricklefs, *A History of Modern Indonesia*, 4th ed., p. 178.
26. Anthony J.S. Reid, *The Indonesian National Revolution, 1945–1950* (Hawthorn, Melbourne: Longman, 1974), p. 1. Sometimes, it is true, these power relations varied. Eduard Douwes Dekker (Multatuli), a European official who was Assistant Resident of Lebak, Banten, in the 1850s, was dismissed after he clashed with the Regent (*bupati*).
27. Ricklefs, *A History of Modern Indonesia*, 4th ed., p. 179.
28. Ibid., p. 185.
29. Cribb, *Historical Dictionary*, p. 145.

3. "They regard Holland as a very weak power"

1. The population figures are taken from van Bruggen and Wassing, *Djokja en Solo, Beeld van de Vorstensteden*, p. 41.
2. Another half squadron was kept in Solo for the Sunan.
3. For an account of how the people of Yogyakarta saw the Sultan, see Selosoemardjan, *Social Change in Jogjakarta*, p. 20.
4. Personal communication, Harry Tjan Silalahi, 7 January 2016. Tjan, who

was born in Yogyakarta in 1934, was known, when he was young, as Tjan Tjoen Hok. He is from a *peranakan* family which has been in Java for nine generations.

5. Soeharto, "Watasahi no Rirekisho", *Nihon Keizai Shimbun*, 3 January 1998.
6. Ricklefs, *A History*, 4th ed., p. 188.
7. Minute by Frank Ashton-Gwatkin, 7 March 1921. The National Archives of the UK: Public Record Office (hereafter TNA: PRO) FO 371/6696 [F902/902/23], cited in Nicholas Tarling, *Britain, Southeast Asia and the Onset of the Pacific War* (Cambridge: Cambridge University Press, 1996), p. 22.
8. Minute by Frank Ashton-Gwatkin, 7 March 1921.
9. See Stuart R. Schram, *The Political Thought of Mao Tse-tung* (Harmondsworth: Pelican Books, 1969), p. 37.
10. Ibid., pp. 38–40.
11. For accounts of the situation in China and Vietnam, see ibid.; Alexander V. Pantsov and Stephen I. Levine, *Mao: The Real Story* (New York: Simon & Schuster, 2012); Edgar Snow, *Red Star Over China* (New York: Grove Press, 1961), p. 153; and William J. Duiker, *Ho Chi Minh* (Crows Nest, NSW: Allen & Unwin, 2000), p. 64.
12. Expelled from the East Indies in late 1919, Sneevliet returned to the Netherlands. By June 1920 he was in Moscow, where he became well acquainted with Lenin and Trotsky. Impressed by his experience as a labour organizer, the Comintern leaders appointed him their representative in China. He arrived there on 3 June 1921, using the pseudonym Maring. Ruth T. McVey, *The Rise of Indonesian Communism* (Ithaca: Cornell University Press, 1965), pp. 34 and 368, and Pantsov and Levine, *Mao: The Real Story*, pp. 100 and 102.
13. McVey, *The Rise of Indonesian Communism*, p. 353.
14. See Judith M. Brown, *Modern India: The Origins of an Asian Democracy* (Oxford: Oxford University Press, 1985), p. 217, and Jawaharlal Nehru, *Toward Freedom: The Autobiography of Jawaharlal Nehru* (Boston: Beacon Press, 1963), pp. 69–70.
15. Cribb, *Historical Dictionary*, pp. 66–67.
16. See Ricklefs, *A History*, 4th ed., pp. 200–1, on which this section is based.
17. Bernhard Dahm, *Sukarno and the Struggle for Indonesian Independence* (Ithaca and London: Cornell University Press, 1969), pp. 12–16.
18. Ricklefs, *A History*, 4th ed., p. 205.
19. McVey, *The Rise of Indonesian Communism*, p. 113. The Volksraad did not actually meet until 1918.
20. There is a consensus among historians and some demographers that the 1800 Dutch estimate and the 1815 Raffles census, which put the figure at 4.6 million, are undercounts by a factor of 50 per cent or more. Personal communication, Terence Hull, 8 May 2020. Geertz, writing in 1963, thought there were probably

about seven million people on Java in 1800. *Agricultural Involution*, p. 69. For a discussion on the matter, see Graeme Hugo, Terence H. Hull, Valerie J. Hull and Gavin W. Jones, *The Demographic Dimension in Indonesian Development* (Singapore: Oxford University Press, 1987), pp. 32–34, where the figure of seven to ten million is given.

21. Hugo, et al., *The Demographic Dimension*, p. 39, and Terence Hull, personal comunication, 10 May 2020.
22. N. Keyfitz, "Indonesian population and the European industrial revolution", *Asian Survey* 10 (1965), p. 505, cited in G.J. Missen, *Viewpoint on Indonesia: A Geographical Study* (Melbourne: Nelson, 1972), p. 186.
23. See Anne Booth and Konta Damanik, "Central Java and Yogyakarta: Malthus Overcome?", in *Unity and Diversity: Regional Economic Development in Indonesia Since 1970*, edited by Hal Hill (Singapore, Oxford, New York: Oxford University Press, 1989), p. 285.
24. Booth and Damanik, *Unity and Diversity*, pp. 285–86.
25. See John Ingleson, *In Search of Justice: Workers and Unions in Colonial Java, 1908–1926*. (Singapore: Oxford University Press, 1986), p. 32.
26. *Neratja*, 23 April 1921, in *Overzicht van de Inlandsche en Maleisch-Chineesche Pers* [Survey of the Native and Malay-Chinese Press], IPO 17 (1921), p. 157, quoted in Ingleson, *In Search of Justice*, p. 32.
27. Ingleson, *In Search of Justice*, p. 148.
28. McVey, *The Rise of Indonesian Communism*, p. 109.
29. Ingleson, *In Search of Justice*, p. 149.
30. Ibid., p. 255.
31. Soeharto, "Watashi no Rirekisho", *Nihon Keizai Shimbun*, Part 2, 3 January 1998.
32. Ibid.
33. Interview, Sabam Siagian, 14 March 1986.
34. Soeharto, *My Thoughts*, pp. 7–8, on which this and the following two paragraphs draw.
35. See Roeder, *The Smiling General*, p. 82.
36. See "Watashi no Rirekisho", *Nihon Keizai Shimbun*, 4 January 1998. According to Elson, Soeharto's schooling began at "an unusually early age". See Elson, *Suharto*, p. 2.
37. The *Merdeka* report of the President's 1974 press conference says Soeharto began school "in the village of Buluan [sic], Pedes." *Merdeka*, 29 October 1974.
38. For an admirable outline of the late colonial education system, see Merle Ricklefs, *A History of Modern Indonesia*, 4th ed., pp. 189–93, on which this paragraph is based.
39. By the thirties, there were some 9,600 of them "and, of Indonesian children

between the ages of six and nine, over 40 per cent attended a school of some sort at some time, most of them at government village schools and many of them more or less unwillingly." Ricklefs, *A History*, 4th ed., p. 192.

40. Roeder, *The Smiling General*, p. 83.
41. In 1974, responding to the claims made in *POP* magazine, the President said that his father took him away in 1929, when he was about eight. See *Penjelasan Presiden Soeharto tentang silsilah*, p. 26. Other accounts suggest that he was almost ten at the time and in second year. In 1998, Soeharto told a Japanese journalist he left "a little before I turned ten". *Nihon Keizai Shimbun*, 4 January 1998. According to Probosutedjo, Soeharto left in 1931, when he was about ten. See "Kata Pendahuluan: Uraian Bapak Probosutedjo", p. 6. Probosutedjo may be right about that, but his testimony suffers from the fact that he was born in May 1930, and can have had no recollection of the event.
42. Roeder, *Anak Desa*, p. 137.
43. "Watashi no Rirekisho", *Nihon Keizai Shimbun*, 4 January 1998.
44. Soeharto, *My Thoughts*, p. 9.
45. See "Suharto's Regard for Foster Mother", *New Straits Times*, 30 October 1974. Soeharto is said to have reminisced about his childhood to a close friend after attending the funeral of his father's younger sister, Ibu Bei Prawirowihardjo, or Bu Bei as she was widely known, in 1971.
46. Soeharto, *My Thoughts*, p. 9, and *Keterangan*, pp. 13–14.
47. It was claimed later in a semi-authorized biography that the Prawirowihardjo family was living at that time in Solo. See O.G. Roeder, *The Smiling General*, p. 83. Soeharto is quoted as saying the same thing in the *Nihon Keizai Shimbun*, on 4 January 1998. As Elson notes, the story is repeated in Anon, *Soeharto, President of the Republic of Indonesia* (Jakarta?: Department of Information, Republic of Indonesia, 1988?), p. 2. See Elson, draft of Chapter 1, fn 45, p. 7.
48. Roeder, *The Smiling General*, p. 83.
49. Sometimes, too, children from poor families are sent to live with non-relatives. Some prominent Indonesian army officers underwent such an experience. One was the 1945–49 Commander-in-Chief, General Sudirman. Another was the 1962–65 army intelligence chief, Major General Parman Siswondo. Sometimes, in the colonial period, the adoptive parents were Dutch. Alimin Prawirodirdjo, who was chairman of the Indonesian Communist Party in the late 1940s, was born into a poor family; he became, at the age of nine, the foster son of a Dutch official and attended good schools in Jakarta.
50. Koentjaraningrat, *Javanese Culture*, p. 260.
51. *Anak Desa*, p. 137, and *Keterangan Presiden Soeharto tentang silsilah keluarga*, p. 14.

52. A former Indonesian politician supported the claim that Soeharto was exploited while living with foster families. Confidential Source One: 7 September 1998. Soeharto makes no mention of any specific ill treatment in his memoirs.
53. Soeharto, *My Thoughts*, p. 10.
54. Roeder, *The Smiling General*, p. 83.
55. Ibid.
56. Ibid., p. 84.
57. *Keterangan Presiden Soeharto tentang silsilah keluarga*, p. 14.

4. "An invisible motivating force"

1. See John Pemberton's marvellously droll account in *On the Subject of "Java"*, pp. 112–13.
2. Ibid., p. 122.
3. Marc Perlman, *Java* (Singapore: Periplus Editions, 1991), p. 239.
4. For a description of this event, see Pemberton, *On the Subject of "Java"*, p. 165.
5. See Roeder, *The Smiling General*, pp. 85–86, and "Watashi no Rirekisho", *Nihon Keizai Shimbun*, Part 3, 4 January 1998. Roeder goes on to say that Soeharto did not stay long in Solo: later that year, he writes, the Prawirowihardjos moved to Wuryantoro.
6. *Keterangan Presiden Soeharto tentang silsilah keluarga*, p. 14. In a subsequent Indonesian-language edition of his biography, Roeder made the necessary changes: father and son had gone straight on from Solo to Wonogiri by bus and had continued from there to Wuryantoro by taxi. Roeder, *Anak Desa*, pp. 144–61.
7. Suryohadi, "Penjelasan Presiden Soeharto", p. 29. Soeharto told the *Nihon Keizai Shimbun* his uncle was "a civil servant working in the agricultural bureau". For an (anonymous) account of the kindness of Soeharto's aunt, see *New Straits Times*, 30 October 1974. See also "The Night Suharto Buried His Mother", *Sun-Herald*, 9 January 1972, p. 49. In a magazine profile of the businessman Sudwikatmono, Ibu Prawirowihardjo's name is given as Sukatinah. See "Raja Bisnis dari Wuryantoro", *Forum Keadilan*, no. 20, tahun VI, 12 Januari 1998, p. 37. In the *Forum* version, Soeharto was seven when he went to live with his aunt and uncle.
8. Roeder, *The Smiling General*, p. 86.
9. Soeharto, *My Thoughts*, p. 9. The account of Bu Bei's character is taken from the *New Straits Times*, 30 October 1974.
10. See *New Straits Times*, 30 October 1974.
11. "The Night Suharto Buried His Mother", *Sun-Herald*, 9 January 1972.
12. McDonald, *Suharto's Indonesia*, pp. 11–12, on which the following sentences draw.

13. Soeharto, *My Thoughts*, p. 9.
14. Roeder, *The Smiling General*, p. 86.
15. Abdul Gafur, *Siti Hartinah Soeharto: Ibu Utama Indonesia*, p. 119.
16. At the time of her death, Hartinah's mother's was described as Kanjeng Raden Ayu Siti Hatmanti Soemoharjomo. She was buried in the family Mangadeg Mausoleum. *Indonesia News Service*, citing *Jawa Pos*, 1 May 1988, referred to her as "Ibu Sumoharyono". But in its 31 July 1988 report on her death, *INS*, citing three newspapers, gives the spelling as Soemoharyomo—i.e., a half-modern spelling. Hatmohudojo is sometimes given as Atmohandoyo.
17. The story is told by Roeder, who interviewed the teacher. *The Smiling General*, p. 87.
18. Roeder, *The Smiling General*, p. 87.
19. Soeharto, *My Thoughts*, p. 10.
20. Ibid., pp. 9–10.
21. "Watashi no Rirekisho", *Nihon Keizai Shimbun*, 4 January 1998.
22. This section draws on interviews with Indonesians who came through the pre-war education system and on a number of written sources. For further details, see Merle Ricklefs, *A History of Modern Indonesia*, 4th ed., pp. 189–93; Amry Vandenbosch, *The Dutch East Indies: Its Government, Problems, and Politics* (Berkeley: University of California Press, 1944), pp. 198–222; J.D. Legge, *Intellectuals and Nationalism in Indonesia: A Study of the Following Recruited by Sutan Sjahrir in Occupation Jakarta*, Monograph Series, Publication No. 68 (Ithaca, NY: Cornell Modern Indonesia Project, 1988), pp. 73–77; and Cribb, *Historical Dictionary of Indonesia*, pp. 140–44.
23. There were nine government-run HBS schools, two of them in Jakarta (Koning Willem III and Prins Hendrik School) and one each in Medan, Bandung, Semarang, Yogyakarta, Surabaya, Malang and Makassar. As well, there were three privately-run HBS schools, two in Jakarta (Christelijke HBS and Carpentier Alting Stichting [Carpentier Alting Foundation], or CAS) and one in Bandung (Christelijk Lyceum). Only one or two cities had a *lyceum*, which consisted of a HBS part and a gymnasium part. The lyceum provided six years of study, including the study of Latin and Greek.
24. Cribb, *Historical Dictionary*, p. 141. Most of the HBS teachers were university graduates.
25. Sukarno went on to study engineering at the Bandung Institute of Technology. Mohammad Hatta, after graduating from the Prins Hendrik School, studied economics at the University of Rotterdam.
26. A number of Indonesian National Army (Tentara Nasional Indonesia, TNI) officers—including R. Didi Kartasasmita, R. Hidajat Martaatmadja, Muhammad Rachmat Kartakusumah, G.P.H. Djatikusumo, Alex Kawilarang and Eri Sudewo—had graduated from the HBS system before the Japanese

Occupation. A number of other future officers were in that school system when the Japanese shut it down in 1942. They included Kemal Idris, Daan Jahja, Sentot Iskandardinata, Ashari Danudirdjo, Alwin Nurdin, Purbo Suwondo, H.R. Dharsono, Satari, Sayidiman Suryohadiprojo, Achmad Wiranatakusumah, Muskita, M.T. Harjono, Oetojo Oetomo, Maulwi Saelan and Koesno Oetomo.

27. Written communication, Lieutenant General Purbo Suwondo, 20 May 2002. Purbo attended the pre-war HBS in Malang. HBS graduates were generally eighteen when they left school.
28. In some cases, as many half the HIS graduates were sent to the Voor-Klas.
29. There were two separate streams in the AMS system. At the sole AMS-A, a government-run school in Yogyakarta, where the language of instruction was Dutch, the curriculum was organized around two sub-streams: AMS-A I, which focused on Eastern culture and languages, and AMS-A II, focusing on Western culture and languages. The languages taught at AMS-A I were Javanese, Kawi Javanese (classical Javanese, akin to Latin in Europe), Malay, Dutch, French, English and German, as well as all the usual subjects. At the AMS-A II students took Latin, Dutch, French, English and German, as well as the usual range of subjects.

At the AMS-B, where the language of instruction was also Dutch and where English, German and French were compulsory as well, the focus was on physics and mathematics. AMS graduates were twenty at least if they had attended a MULO Voor-Klas. In addition to the one government-run AMS-A school, there were five government-run AMS-B schools, in Jakarta, Semarang, Yogyakarta, Surabaya and Malang. There were, as well, two privately-operated AMS-B schools, the Christelijke AMS in Jakarta and the Taman Madya of the Taman Siswa in Yogyakarta. The Dutch government did not recognize most private schools, especially those of non-Dutch organizations such as the Taman Siswa and Muhummadiyah. If, for example, a Taman Madya graduate wanted to enter the Law School in Jakarta he had to pass the final examination at either the AMS-A or AMS-B.

Students who graduated from a Teacher's Training College for Natives (Hollandsch-Inlandsche Kweekschool, HIK), a six-year high school course for prospective teachers, were likewise obliged to pass this exam if they wanted to go on to higher education. The Christelijke HBS and the Christelijke AMS-B in Jakarta (which both Lieutenant General Simatupang and Lieutenant General Achmad Yani attended) and the Christelijk Lyceum in Bandung were the only private schools with government recognition, meaning that their final exams were equal to those of the government-run HBS and AMS schools.

As well as the AMS and the HIK schools, there were a number of senior high schools for vocational education: the Senior Technical High School

(Middelbare Technische School, MTS,), apparently in Bandung, the Senior Forestry High School (Middelbare Bosbouw School) in Madiun, the Senior Agriculture High School (Middelbare Landbouw School) in Bogor and two Secondary Training Schools for Native Civil Servants (Middelbare Opleiding School voor Inlandsche Ambtenaren, MOSVIA), one in Bandung, the other in Magelang. MOSVIA educated MULO graduates for the civil administration (Pangreh Pradja). There was as well the Nederlandsch-Indische Artsen School (NIAS, Netherlands Indies Medical School) in Surabaya, which offered MULO graduates a nine-year education as medical officers. Though well trained, NIAS graduates did not have the same status as those who had passed through the Geneeskundige Hoge School (Medical Faculty) in Jakarta.

At the beginning on the Japanese Occupation all Dutch schools were closed. The Japanese set up the Sekolah Rakyat system to provide elementary education for children aged 6–14 years, including those who had formerly attended one of the four types of Dutch elementary school: the ELS, HIS and HCS, where the language of instruction was Dutch, and the Tweede Inlandsche School, a second-rank school which used the vernacular language. The Japanese established Lower Secondary Schools (Sekolah Menengah Pertama, SMP) for all former students of the Dutch MULO and for grades 1–3 of the HBS and Upper Secondary Schools (Sekolah Menengah Tinggi, SMT) for students of the AMS-A, AMS-B and HBS grades 4–5.

30. Among the officers who had attended an AMS school were T.B. Simatupang, Achmad Yani, Zulkifli Lubis, Siswondo Parman, Bambang Sugeng, Suwarto, Tjakradipura, Sastra Prawira, Kharis Suhud, Soetarto Sigit, Abimanyu, Solichin GP, Suprapto, Abdul Kadir, R.H. Askari, K.R.M.H. Soerjosoemarno, R.M. Soerjosoerarso, Soetojo Siswomihardjo, Sahirdjan, Yoga Sugama, Latief Hendraningrat, Setiadi, Achmad Tirtosudiro and Edi Sukardi.

Four HBS or AMS graduates who were to hold prominent leadership positions in the post-war Indonesian National Army had, on completing their secondary education, been accepted by the pre-war Royal Military Academy (Koninklijke Militaire Academie, KMA) at Breda in the Netherlands: R. Didi Kartasasmita, R. Hidajat Martaatmadja, Soerjosoerarso and R.S. Suryadarma. A number of other men who had come up through the HBS or the AMS system and who were also to hold prominent leadership positions in the TNI had been accepted as pre-war officer cadets in the East Indies. Djatikusumo attended the Reserve Officers Training Corps (Corps Opleiding Reserve-Officieren, or CORO) in Bandung. Others, including Simatupang, A.H. Nasution, H.M. Rachmat Kartakusumah, Askari, Kawilarang, A.J. Mokoginta, R.O. Alibasjah Satari, Soerjosoemarno, Suprapto, Suryo and Abdul Kadir, attended a substitute KMA set up in Bandung after the fall of Holland. Mokoginta and Satari were in the second (1941) intake at the KMA Bandung. Nasution, a graduate of a Teacher's Training College (HIK), had been obliged to pass the final AMS-B exam before entering the KMA Bandung.

31. Legge, *Intellectuals and Nationalism in Indonesia*, p. 74.
32. Ricklefs, *A History*, 4th ed., pp. 192–93.
33. Ibid., p. 192, and Amry Vandenbosch, *The Dutch East Indies*, p. 203.
34. Vandenbosch, *The Dutch East Indies*, p. 214.
35. Although Soeharto does not say in his autobiography when he began at the *schakelschool*, 1934 appears to be the most likely date. Abdul Gafur says that Soeharto started *schakelschool* in 1931, which means he would have been only ten at the time. See Abdul Gafur, *Siti Hartinah*, p. 119. That would mean that he had begun at the *volksscholen* at six. This appears to be wrong. What is more, if Soeharto started at the *schakelschool* in 1931, he would have completed the five-year course in 1936, not 1939, as was the case.
36. At the *schakelschool*, according to Colonel Soepardio, who retired in 1980 as Deputy Head of the Armed Forces of the Republic of Indonesia (Angkatan Bersenjata Republik Indonesia, ABRI) Military History Division and who had himself attended such a school, "Pak Harto came up through the Dutch language stream basically." Colonel Soepardio, written communication, 21 May 2002. That would appear to overstate the case.
37. Interview, Dr B.J. Habibie, Paris, 28 June 2001.
38. Interview, Slamet Bratanata, Jakarta, 13 March 1982. Bratanata was appointed Minister for Mining and Energy in 1966 but Soeharto dismissed him the following year. Bratanata had sought to ensure that Pertamina, the state-owned oil company, which came under his ministry, transfer taxes collected from Caltex directly to the government. The head of Pertamina, Brigadier General Ibnu Sutowo, an all-but-autonomous oil czar, was widely believed to be transferring large sums to an army slush fund. Bratanata later became an outspoken critic of Soeharto.
39. Interview, Major General Achmad Sukendro, Jakarta, 15 March 1982. Sukendro had no particular reason to like Soeharto, who had jailed him for eight months in 1967. But he could not help admire the way in which Soeharto had gathered so much power in his own hands. "The 'king-makers' at Hankam [Department of Defence and Security] do not exist," he said. "The king is the maker!"
40. Roeder, *The Smiling General*, p. 87. Roeder says they rode on borrowed bicycles.
41. Soeharto had evidently turned ten when he was in Wuryantoro, in grade three of primary school. He had spent his eleventh year in Kemusu, presumably repeating year three, there being only three grades in the village schools. He had come back to primary school in Wuryantoro after he left Kemusu but it can only have been for a very short time, perhaps a month or two.

42. See "President denies having amassed riches", *Antara*, 27 January 1978.
43. "Watashi no Rirekisho", *Nihon Keizai Shimbun*, 4 January 1998.
44. Soeharto, *My Thoughts*, p. 12.
45. "Watashi no Rirekisho", 4 January 1998.
46. See Elson, *Suharto*, p. 7. The quotation is cited in Toriq Hadad, "Mengayunkan langkah keenam", *Tempo*, 13 March 1993, p. 16.
47. See Mashuri's comment in Anon., "Isu Soeharto Cina, Siapa Bapaknya?".
48. Interview, Haryasudirja, Jakarta, 4 August 2000.
49. Ibid.
50. Ibid.
51. Nono Makarim, personal communication, Sydney, 27 June 1989.
52. Interview, Dr B.J. Habibie, Paris, 28 June 2001.
53. The quotations in this paragraph are drawn from interviews in Jakarta with Confidential Source One, on 17 April 1998, 7 September 1998, and 8 August 2000.
54. See McIntyre, *The Indonesian Presidency*, p. 104. This kind of analysis is not without its critics. Benedict Anderson, for example, did not accept what he saw as McIntyre's unquestioning borrowing of Western psychology theory for Indonesians. Personal communication.
55. McIntyre, *The Indonesian Presidency*, pp. 113–15.
56. Elson, *Suharto*, p. 8.
57. McIntyre argues that Soeharto's disrupted childhood may have made him unusually receptive to these behaviour patterns. Personal communication, 9 February 2007, and McIntyre, *The Indonesian Presidency*, p. 114.

5. "What kind of Islam is this?"

1. When Geertz speaks of Java, he means "East and Central Java"; the Sundanese people of West Java have a quite distinct culture.
2. Koentjaraningrat, *Javanese Culture*, pp. 324–25.
3. M.C. Ricklefs, *Islamisation and Its Opponents in Java: A Political, Social, Cultural and Religious History, c. 1930 to the Present* (Singapore: NUS Press, 2012), p. 56 and p. 269, on which these sentences draw.
4. Benedict O'Gorman Anderson, "Perspective and Method in American Research on Indonesia (1973)", in *Interpreting Indonesian Politics: Thirteen Contributions to the Debate*, edited by Benedict Anderson and Audrey Kahin (Ithaca: Southeast Asia Program, Cornell University, 1992), at pp. 78–79, and Anderson, personal communication, 1 September 2012. For a valuable analysis of the origins of *santri-abangan* differences, and tensions, see M.C. Ricklefs, *Polarising Javanese Society: Islamic and other visions c. 1830–1930* (Singapore: NUS Press, 2007).
5. As Robert Hefner notes, Marshall G.S. Hodgson gave voice to such concerns

in 1974. See Robert W. Hefner, "Islam, State, and Civil Society: ICMI and the Struggle for the Indonesian Middle Class", *Indonesia* no. 56 (October 1993), p. 1.

6. Ricklefs, *Islamisation and Its Opponents in Java*, pp. 85 and 461.

   Writing in 1999, the Australian political scientist Lance Castles noted that there had been a huge swing to Islamic parties since 1955. Three factors, he suggested, were involved. One was demographic. Family planning had caught on earlier among the Javanese, so that they had declined as a proportion of the population—and they had been the stronghold of the non-Islamic vote. Second, there had been an Islamic revival. Finally, the total elimination of the PKI and its affiliated organizations from village Java had possibly left survivors susceptible to the blandishments of the invigorated rural-based Nahdlatul Ulama (NU). See Lance Castles, "Is the *aliran* pattern in Indonesian voting in decline?", typescript, Yogyakarta, 9 March 1999, pp. 3–4.
7. For details, see Soeharto, *Pikiran*, p. 13.
8. The words in quotation marks are those of Benedict Anderson, personal communication.
9. The front brought together leaders from all the main political parties except the PKI and the Ali Sastroamidjojo wing of the Indonesian National Party (Partai Nasional Indonesia, PNI).
10. Tjan was deputizing for the chairman of the front, Subchan Z.E., who was in Semarang.
11. Interviews, Harry Tjan Silalahi, Jakarta, 7 and 8 June 2002, and Sydney, 7 April 2008. Members of the delegation had sought the meeting to raise concerns about Soeharto's decision to ban KAMI, the anti-Communist student action front. Among the generals present were Alamsjah Ratu Perwiranegara, Maraden Panggabean and Basuki Rachmat. For a slightly different account of this meeting, see J.B. Soedarmanta, *Tengara Orde Baru: Kisah Harry Tjan Silalahi* (Jakarta: Gunung Agung, 2004), pp. 173–74
12. Harry Tjan Silalahi, personal communication, 29 July 2019.
13. Brian May, *The Indonesian Tragedy* (Singapore: Graham Brash, 1978), p. 239. Before long, however, Soeharto's people would promote a rival PNI leader.
14. Roeder, *The Smiling General*, p. 85.
15. Soeharto, *Pikiran*, p. 13.
16. For details, see Geertz, *The Religion of Java*, pp. 51–53, on which the following passage is based.
17. Geertz, *The Religion of Java*, pp. 51–52.
18. Ibid., pp. 52–53 and pp. 240–41. As Geertz notes, *iklas* conveys a sense of "detachment from the contingencies of the external world so as not to be disturbed when things go awry in it or if something unexpected occurs. Geertz's account of the way a mother steps over her son three times was

drawn from his observations in Pare, near Kediri, in East Java. It is not clear how widespread this practice was.

19. Benedict Anderson, personal communication, on which the following sentences are based.
20. Soeharto, *Pikiran*, p. 15.
21. Soeharto, *My Thoughts*, p. 12.
22. Ibid.
23. Koentjaraningrat, *Javanese Culture*, p. 398.
24. Geertz, *The Religion of Java*, pp. 310–11.
25. Ibid., p. 326.
26. I am indebted to Mohammad Said Reksohadiprodjo, Susilo Harjoprakoso and Major General Sudjono Humardani for my understanding of some of the matters discussed in this and the following paragraphs. Interviews, Mohammad Said, Jakarta, 8 March 1978; Susilo Harjoprakoso, Jakarta, March 1978, and Major General Sudjono Humardani, Jakarta, 12 March 1978. As Sudjono saw it, there are four elements—water, air, fire and earth—and one draws from them additional powers which one can use to do good. It is necessary to do this continuously to develop one's harmony with God. You do this not only for yourself and your community but also for your country.
27. Interview, Mohammad Said Reksohadiprodjo, Jakarta, 8 March 1978.
28. Interview Sudjono Humardani, 12 March 1978.
29. Geertz, *The Religion of Java*, p. 96.
30. In his memoirs, Soeharto makes no mention of the fact that he lived with Daryatmo, saying only that he sometimes went alone to his home. But the claim is made quite explicitly in Roeder, *The Smiling General*, p. 89, and there is no reason to disbelieve it, given that Soeharto was Roeder's primary source when he wrote that book. Another source is adamant that Soeharto lived as *orang ngéngér* with Daryatmo. Confidential communication, Jakarta, 7 September 1998.
31. I am indebted to Angus McIntyre for his observations on this point and for his insights, reflected in the following sentences of this paragraph, into the way in which Daryatmo was to influence Soeharto's life. Personal communications, 9 and 14 February 2007.
32. "Watashi no Rirekisho", *Nihon Keizai Shimbun*, Pt 4, 5 January 1998. It is not clear whether "creed" means the Islamic Confession of Faith. It is possible that something was lost in the translation from Indonesian to Japanese and then to English. The Japanese journalist uses the words *shoto chugakko* (elementary junior high). The reference is clearly to the *schakelschool*. As has been noted, *schakelschool* was not junior high school but a prelude to it.
33. Soeharto, *My Thoughts*, p. 13.
34. Ibid., p. 12.
35. Interview, Romo Daryatmo, Wonogiri, 1969.

36. "Isu Soeharto Cina, Siapa Bapaknya?", wysiwyg://47/http:www.geocities.com/CapitolHill/4120/soeharto.html (accessed 4 September 2008).
37. Soeharto, *My Thoughts*, p. 13.
38. Koentjaraningrat, *Javanese Culture*, p. 425.
39. See Soeharto, *Pikiran*, pp. 441–42. This translation is from McIntyre, "Soeharto's Composure: Considering the Biographical and Autobiographical Accounts", p. 17, and the official English-language version of the autobiography, p. 379, with minor modifications.
40. Confidential Source Seven.
41. Personal communication, Sabam Siagian, 28 January 1989.
42. Interview, General Benny Moerdani, Jakarta, 18 September 1998.
43. Interview, Mohammad Natsir, Jakarta, 8 March 1978. Natsir, who was sixty-nine in early 1978, was born in West Sumatra. Educated at the pre-war AMS-A II senior high school in Bandung, he served as Minister of Information in 1946–47 and 1948–49 and as Prime Minister in 1950–51. In 1967 he founded, and became general chairman of, the Dewan Dakwah Islamiyah Indonesia (Indonesian Islamic Propagation Council) which sought to promote the further Islamization of Indonesian society. He was also vice president of the World Islamic Congress. The Dewan Dakwah received significant sums of money from Saudi Arabia, something that continues to this day. Surprisingly perhaps, Soeharto did not see any danger in that.
44. Roeslan's title was Ketua Tim Penasihat Presiden mengenai Pelaksanaan Pedoman Penghayatan dan Pengamalan Pancasila (P7).
45. Interview, Roeslan Abdulgani, Jakarta, 26 March 1982. It might be argued that Sukarno was naïve in believing that the deeply divergent interests and aspirations of Indonesian Communists and Muslims, differences which had surfaced as early as the 1920s, could be kept in check indefinitely. There had been stark evidence of those distinctions when Communists and Muslims clashed during the bitter Madiun Affair of 1948, with the Hatta Government and the central army leaders lining up against the Communists. The differences between Communists and Muslims were to come to the fore again, with far greater bloodletting, following the attempted "coup" of 1965. Whether that was at heart an internal army affair, as some historians argue, or something rather more complex, there can be no doubt that army officers, angry and determined men led by Soeharto, encouraged the mass slaughter on Java, Bali and elsewhere. That should not, however, blind us to the deeply entrenched religious and class hatreds that underlay the extreme violence of that time. Many of the Muslims, Hindus and Christians who participated in the killing appear to have done so quite willingly.
46. Interview, Slamet Bratanata, 25 March 1982. Frans Seda related the story, Bratanata said, at the home of the Australian ambassador.
47. Interview, Soedjatmoko, Jakarta, 8 August 1978. I drew on this interview in

Suharto and His Generals, albeit without identifying Soedjatmoko, who wished at that time to remain out of the limelight. But as these observations go to the heart of Soeharto's attitude towards Islam, or at least political Islam, in the late seventies, I think they bear repeating here. I have corrected one or two minor errors in the interview transcript.

48. Soedjatmoko interview, 8 August 1978.
49. Written communication, General Nasution, 1978.
50. Ken Ward, "Soeharto's Javanese Pancasila", in *Soeharto's New Order and Its Legacy*, edited by Edward Aspinall and Greg Fealy (Canberra: ANU E Press, 2010), pp. 27–37.
51. More prosaically, it might be argued that Pancasila was not so very different from the generalized principles enunciated by other political leaders, including Sun Yat-sen, the Chinese revolutionary who, in 1898, had proclaimed his Three Principles (nationalism, democracy and socialism).
52. See, for example, Hefner, "Islam, State and Civil Society", p. 32, fn. 83. An article on the president's pilgrimage in *Tempo*, 6 July 1991, Hefner notes, made the point that the president received part of his education in Muhammadiyah schools and read the Arabic script. *Tempo* may have over-egged that argument. As far as one can tell, Soeharto attended only one Muslim-run school, the Muhammadiyah *schakelschool* in Yogyakarta. Nor is it clear how much of the Arabic script he would have learnt, or remembered, from his school days, or what bearing that might have had on his thinking about Islam. As we have seen, the evidence suggests that Islamic principles and doctrines impinged only marginally on his attachment to Javanese beliefs. It is possible that Soeharto studied Arabic in the late 1980s and early 1990s; but, once again, we are entitled to wonder what, if any, impact that had on his thinking.
53. Born in 1936, Kosim Nurseha did not participate in the 1945–49 Revolution but subsequently joined the Indonesian National Army. The Soeharto family is said to have become especially close to Professor Mohammad Quraish Shihab, rector of the tertiary-level State Islamic Religious Institute (Institut Agama Islam Negeri, IAIN) in Jakarta, following the funeral of Ibu Tien. Quraish Shihab served as Minister for Religion during the final two months of Soeharto's presidency.
54. Ward, "Soeharto's Javanese Pancasila", p. 36.
55. General Nasution, commenting on Soeharto's use of *bismillah* in speeches, thought this might have been a reflection of Habibie's influence. Interview, Nasution, Jakarta, 15 July 1995.
56. Confidential Source One.
57. Moerdani interview, 17 September, 1997.
58. Ricklefs, *Islamisation and Its Opponents in Java*, p. 197. For Sultan Agung, see also Ricklefs, *A History of Modern Indonesia Since c. 1200*, 4th ed. (Stanford: Stanford University Press, 2008), p. 37.

59. Ricklefs, *Islamisation and Its Opponents in Java*, pp. 7 and 121.
60. Ibid., p. 121.
61. Greg Fealy, quoting a Muslim intellectual who was close to the Habibie family. Personal communication. Traditionalist Muslims, such as those in the NU, will have the *imam* whisper instructions into the ear of the deceased regarding what they should say on Judgment Day. Muhammadiyah people do not do this. As Fealy notes, some members of Muhammadiyah claimed Soeharto as one of their own, "although it is by no means clear, of course, that he saw things this way," because he had spent some time at a Muhammadiyah school and because he appointed many Muhammadiyah people, but not NU people, to key positions. That is true. Soeharto *was* closer to Muhammadiyah leaders and members than he was to those from NU. That may also be due to the fact that Muhammadiyah is centred on Yogyakarta, while NU has much of its core strength in East Java. There are clear differences in the mentality of the Yogyanese and the East Javanese. In Yogyakarta, and indeed in Indonesia more broadly, the East Javanese are seen as blunt, open-minded and, in certain districts, somewhat *kasar* (unrefined). For an account of Javanese customs relating to death, see Geertz, *The Religion of Java*, pp. 68–72, and Koentjaraningrat, *Javanese Culture*, pp. 361–65.
62. Confidential Source 14, 11 December 2019.
63. Interview, General Benny Moerdani, Jakarta, 17 September 1997. Moerdani had attended some, if not all, of these ceremonies, at the Soeharto house in Jalan Cendana in Jakarta and at a family retreat, presumably the Ndalem Kalitan palace, in Solo. In Fealy's view, Moerdani's remarks about the funeral might be seen by some as typical Catholic stereotyping of Muslim practices. As he puts it, "Yes, he's correct that there's no *slametan* in Saudi Arabia but that's hardly the benchmark for Indonesian Islam, and especially at that time. NU people do often use *slametan*, or a somewhat Arabized version of it. Muhammadiyah people don't." Greg Fealy, personal communication.
64. Written communication, Lieutenant General Sayidiman Suryohadiprojo, 6 December 2018. Sayidiman, who was born in 1927, had been a student at the pre-war HBS high school in Semarang, where the language of instruction was Dutch and the teaching standards high. When the Japanese closed all Dutch schools he enrolled in the Taman Madya senior high school in Yogyakarta. Taman Madya was run by the Taman Siswa, the nationalist school system founded by Ki Hadjar Dewantoro. Dewantoro was concerned about Javanese identity and held views on Islam that would have been anathema "to the more puritanical of Islamic reformers". Ricklefs, *Islamisation and Its Opponents*, p. 49. Taman Siswa's *kebatinan* background, Ruth McVey notes, marked it as on the *abangan* side of Java's great cultural cleavage. Ruth T. McVey, "Taman Siswa and the Indonesian National Awakening", *Indonesia*, No. 4 (October 1967), p. 131. Although Sayidiman was much influenced by

his education at the Taman Madya, he would later become a member of ICMI.

6. "Soeharto is a closed book"

1. Soeharto was not overly particular in his categorization. In the text of his *Pikiran*, he refers to three "don'ts" and includes *ojo dumeh*, the odd aphorism out, as the third in the listing. In an appendix, he includes all four "don'ts", with *ojo gugupan* tacked on at the end. For details see Soeharto, *Pikiran*, p. 13 and pp. 570–71, and Soeharto, *My Thoughts*, p. 11 and p. 488.
2. Soeharto, *Pikiran*, p. 11.
3. *Pikiran*, p. 570, and *My Thoughts*, p. 488.
4. Nono Anwar Makarim, personal communication, Sydney, 27 June 1989. A second message of the speech, said Makarim, was that there had been a constitutional transfer of power in 1966; there had been no coup d'etat.
5. The phrase is "*Digdaya tanpa aji, menang tanpa ngasoraké.*" See Soeharto, *Pikiran*, p. 578.
6. At the same time, his management style was often surprisingly hands-off. Once he had determined the course, Soeharto left its implementation to his subordinates, often giving them no clear instructions about how a goal was to be achieved, leaving them to fathom his intentions, not always an easy task.
7. Harold Crouch, *The Army and Politics in Indonesia*, rev. ed. (Ithaca: Cornell University Press, 1988), p. 272. Yet another aphorism that commended itself to Soeharto was *mikul dhuwur mendhem jero*, which literally means "to lift up high and to bury deep". This, as he was fond of pointing out, encapsulated the attitude one should adopt towards one's parents or ancestors. "We must not defame them in any way," Soeharto explained. Should they have erred or made mistakes, there was no need to bring those faults or shortcomings into the open. Rather, those faults should buried deep while those who had observed them should do their best not to make similar mistakes. Soeharto, *Pikiran*, p. 576. As well as all this, Soeharto said he liked to remember "the teachings of our ancestors: respect for God, teacher, government and parents". He realized, he says, in a homily that sits uneasily alongside some of his other, more direct remarks, "how much I loved my parents and how much I was loved by them, my foster parents, my brothers and sisters, both the children of my own parents as well as those of my stepfather". The translation is from Soeharto, *My Thoughts*, p. 11.
8. Personal communication, Sabam Siagian, 28 January 1989.
9. See J.B. Soedarmanta, *Tengara Orde Baru: Kisah Harry Tjan Silalahi*, p. 190. Djatikusumo was a son of Pakubuwono X by one of his forty secondary wives.
10. Confidential Source Ten.

11. Geertz, *The Religion of Java*, p. 29.
12. For details, see ibid., pp. 227–48, on which the following section is substantially based.
13. Ibid., p. 232.
14. Ibid., p. 231.
15. Ibid., pp. 239–40.
16. As noted earlier, *iklas* involves making oneself as impervious as possible to the inevitable disruptions and dislocations of everyday life, achieving a certain inner serenity, calmness, tranquillity and imperturbability. See Geertz, *The Religion of Java*, pp. 240–41. I am indebted also to Ben Anderson for his insights into these Javanese values.
17. Ibid., p. 241.
18. Selo Soemardjan, *Business and Culture in Indonesia*, Australia-Indonesia Business Co-Operation Committee, Confederation of Australian Industry, Canberra, 1986, p. 10.
19. Personal communication, Roeslan Abdulgani.
20. Ward, "Soeharto's Javanese Pancasila", pp. 28–29.
21. Elson, *Suharto*, p. 5.
22. See "Soldier, Farmer, Philosopher", *Asiaweek*, 4 May 1986.
23. Interview, Jusuf Wanandi, Canberra, 7 April 1993. In 1967 Wanandi joined the staff of Major General Ali Moertopo, a member of Soeharto's personal staff (Spri), which was widely seen as a powerful "kitchen cabinet".
24. See "President's Sharp Comment", *Merdeka*, 18 May 1978. US Embassy Translation Unit Press Summary (henceforth USETUPS), No. 49/1985. *Ngécap* is not as strong as *bohong* (lying).
25. *Asiaweek*, 4 May 1986.
26. See "View from the Tri-S Coral", *Time*, 10 May 1976.
27. See *Jakarta Post*, *Sinar Harapan* and *Terbit*, 12 March 1985. USETUPS.
28. Personal communication, Richard Woolcott.
29. Personal communication, Sabam Siagian.
30. Ibid., 28 January 1989.
31. Soeharto, *My Thoughts*, p. 13.
32. *Abangan* families preferred to send their children to government-run schools, but that opportunity was not always available. If a place could not be found in a government school few *abangan* parents were opposed to sending a child to a privately-run Muslim or Christian school.
33. Soeharto, *My Thoughts*, p. 13.
34. The suggestion that he attended a MULO school is in Elson, *Suharto*, p. 6, citing *Kompas*, 23 March 1973, and in Ricklefs, *Islamisation and Its Opponents in Java*, p. 118. *Kompas* erred in claiming that Soeharto had two years at a MULO school. Soeharto makes it plain he did not go beyond the Muhammadiyah

schakelschool, which he completed in 1939. See Soeharto, *Pikiran*, p. 16. If Soeharto had attended a MULO school, even for two years, he would have been able to speak Dutch quite well, which was not the case.

35. Elson, *Suharto*, p. 7.
36. Taman Madya was the senior high school run by the Taman Siswa.
37. Interviews, Haryasudirja, Jakarta, 9 February 2000, and 13 May 2000.
38. Soeharto, *My Thoughts*, p. 13.
39. See "President Denies Having Amassed Riches", *Antara*, 27 January 1978.
40. Confidential Source One, Jakarta, 7 September 1998.
41. Soeharto, *Pikiran*, p. 16.
42. This is now Bank Rakyat Indonesia.
43. "Watashi no Rirekisho", *Nihon Keizai Shimbun*, 5 January 1998.
44. In 1998 Soeharto told a Japanese journalist he left the bank due to a minor "*shippai*". *Shippai* is a Japanese word which can be translated as a mistake, a failure, a blunder or a goof. *Nihon Keizai Shimbun*, 5 January 1998.
45. Soeharto, *Pikiran*, p. 17.
46. Dr B.J. Habibie, who was to meet Soeharto in 1950 and remain close for the best part of half a century, was asked once to name some of Soeharto's friends. After thinking it over for some time he tentatively suggested the names of several senior army officers, none of whom would have seen himself as a friend of the former President or have been seen as such by anyone else. Interview, Dr B.J. Habibie, Paris, 28 June 2001. Nor could anyone else name many or any friends, save for the odd *cukong* (Chinese businessman), which was itself revealing.
47. Confidential Source One, Jakarta, 7 September 1998. This source acknowledged that the rumours, though persistent, had never been confirmed. As it happens, the *mantri polisi* was the future father-in-law of a future Attorney General, Sukarton.
48. Interview, Soebadio Sastrosatomo, Jakarta, 5 September 1998.
49. Personal communication, Colonel Carel Heshusius.
50. For good accounts of Sukarno's life prior to the Japanese occupation of the East Indies, see *Sukarno: An Autobiography, As Told to Cindy Adams* (Hong Kong: Gunung Agung, 1966), pp. 17–155; Legge, *Sukarno: A Political Biography*, pp. 16–148, and Dahm, *Sukarno and the Struggle for Indonesian Independence*, pp. 23–208.
51. Legge, *Sukarno*, p. 17.
52. Mohammad Hatta, Indonesia's first Vice President, made the disclosure about Sukarno's mercy plea during a reunion of pioneers in 1968. See *Antara* in English, 13.42 GMT, 16 February 1968.
53. Sabam Siagian, personal communication.
54. Interview, Selo Soemardjan, Jakarta, 3 September 1998.
55. R.H. Bruce Lockhart, *Return to Malaya* (London: Putnam, 1938), pp. 275–76

and 324–27. During his time in Moscow, Lockhart had been implicated in a plot to assassinate Lenin.

56. Herbert Feith, basing himself on Sjahrir, who cites no source, has De Jonge saying, "we have ruled here for 300 years with the whip and the club and we shall still be doing it in another 300 years." Herbert Feith, *The Decline of Constitutional Democracy in Indonesia* (Ithaca: Cornell University Press, 1962), p. 5, and Soetan Sjahrir, *Out of Exile*, translated by Charles Wolf, Jr. (New York: John Day, 1949), p. 112.
57. A.J.S. Reid, "The Revolution in Regional Perspective", in *The Indonesian Revolution*, Conference papers, Utrecht, 17–20 June 1986, Utrechtse Historische Cahiers jaargang 7 (1986) nr. 2/3, p. 186.
58. Soeharto, *My Thoughts*, p. 13.
59. *Nihon Keizai Shimbun*, 5 January 1998.
60. Ibid.
61. Written communication. Lieutenant General Sayidiman.
62. It is not true that an official sign expressly equating Chinese and dogs ever stood at the park. That said, signs erected between 1903 and 1928 did make an indirect association. The 1917 sign read: "1. The gardens are reserved for the Foreign Community.... 4. Dogs and bicycles are not admitted." For details, see Robert A. Bickers and Jeffrey N. Wasserstrom, "Shanghai's 'Dogs and Chinese Not Admitted' Sign: Legend, History and Contemporary Symbol", *The China Quarterly*, 1995, pp. 444–66.
63. Lieutenant General Sayidiman Suryohadiprodjo, written communication, May 2019, and Colonel Heshusius, The Hague, 22 August 2000.
64. I am indebted to Henk Schulte Nordholt for making this point.
65. Roeder, *The Smiling General*, p. 93.
66. Ibid.
67. Soeharto, *My Thoughts*, p. 16.
68. *Nihon Keizai Shimbun*, 5 January 1998.
69. I am grateful to Angus McIntyre for his comments on this section and have drawn significantly on his thinking, not least about the notion of compensation. McIntyre, personal communications, 9 and 14 February 2007.

7. "I was suited to the disciplined life of the military"

1. On Queen Wilhelmina's decision to go to the United Kingdom, see Herman Theodore Bussemaker, "Paradise in Peril: Western Colonial Power and Japanese Expansion in South-East Asia, 1905–1941", Part I (PhD dissertation, University of Amsterdam, 2001), p. 303.
2. See record of conversation between the British Foreign Secretary, Lord Halifax, and the Dutch Minister, E. Michiels van Verduynen, 29 July 1940, FO 371/24717 [F3687/2739/61], cited in Tarling, *Britain, Southeast Asia and the Onset of the Pacific War*, pp. 144–45. As it turned out, the Dutch would never have been

prepared to resist the Japanese alone. Written communication, Dr P.M.H. Groen, 3 June 2019.

3. Tarling, *Britain, Southeast Asia and the Onset of the Pacific War*, p. 146, and Bussemaker, "Paradise in Peril", p. 317.
4. Tarling, *Britain, Southeast Asia and the Onset of the Pacific War*, p. 147.
5. Cited in J.J. Nortier, P. Kuijt and P.M.H. Groen, *De Japanse aanval op Java, Maart 1942* [The Japanese Attack on Java in March 1942] (Amsterdam: De Bataafsche Leeuw, 1994), p. 28.
6. "Watashi no Rirekisho", *Nihon Keizai Shimbun*, 5 January 1998.
7. Soeharto, *My Thoughts*, p. 16.
8. *Nihon Keizai Shimbun*, 5 January 1998.
9. This phrase, which seems so apposite, is taken from Peter Ackroyd's masterly study of Charles Dickens. *Dickens* (London: Vintage Books, 2002), p. 5.
10. From the time of its formation in 1830 until 1933 this force was known simply as the East Indies Army (Oost-Indische leger). At that time, it assumed the name KNIL. See Zwitzer and Heshusius, *Het Koninklijk Nederlands-Indisch Leger 1830–1950*, p. 10. At the end of 1948 the word "Indonesisch" was substituted for the word "Indisch".
11. Historians believe that perhaps 250,000 Javanese died during the Java War, with the Dutch side losing the lives of 8,000 European and 7,000 indigenous soldiers. About 100,000 Acehnese (and 12,000 men from the Dutch side) lost their lives in operations during the Aceh War. According to Dutch sources, 58,000 Acehnese were killed during the last fifteen years of the Aceh War (1899–1914). Cribb, *Historical Dictionary*, p. 226, Ricklefs, *A History of Modern Indonesia*, 4th ed., p. 142, and written communication, Dr Petra Groen, 3 June 2019.
12. Interview, Major General Sukotjo Tjokroatmodjo, Jakarta, 3 August 2000.
13. Geographical Section of the Naval Intelligence Division, Naval Staff, Admiralty, *A Manual of Netherlands India (Dutch East Indies)* (London: HM Stationary Office, nd [c. 1919]), p. 128.
14. For an excellent overview, on which this account draws, see C. [Cornelis] Fasseur, "Cornerstone and Stumbling Block: Racial Classification and the Late Colonial State in Indonesia", in *The Late Colonial State in Indonesia: Political and Economic Foundations of the Netherlands Indies 1880–1942*, edited by Robert Cribb (Leiden: KITLV Press, 1994), pp. 31–56; and Iris Heidebrink, "The Eurasian Community during the Japanese Occupation, 1942–1945", in *EIPW*, pp. 334–41. I am indebted as well to Robert Cribb and Henk Schulte Nordholt for their observations on this subject.
15. Cribb, *Historical Dictionary*, pp. 198–99 and pp. 392–93.
16. Ian Buruma, *The Missionary and the Libertine: Love and War in East and West* (London: Faber, 2002), p. 72.
17. Colonel Heshusius, personal communication.

18. In 1938, when the population of the East Indies was approaching seventy million, the KNIL was a force of 35,400 men. At the top of the pyramid was an officer corps of 1,066 men, about half of them "true Dutch", the others Eurasian. At the next level down were 8,200 non-commissioned officers. Most of the sergeant-majors were Dutch or Eurasian. But about half the sergeants were Indonesian, as were about 85 per cent of the corporals. At the base of the pyramid were 26,150 enlisted men, most of them Indonesian but with about 1,500 Europeans and Eurasians. Written communication, Colonel Heshusius, 18 April 2001.
19. Written communication, Dr Petra Groen, 3–5 June 2019, citing the *Koloniaal Verslag*, a report on the situation in the Dutch colonies which was sent to the Dutch Parliament annually from 1848 to 1939. From 1930 onwards this report was known as the *Indisch Verslag*. The annual recruitment figures are to be found in Annexes B, C or D of the *Koloniaal Verslagen*.
20. Interview, Colonel Heshusius, The Hague, 22 August 2000, and written communication, Colonel J.J. Nortier, 5 March 1996.
21. See Hanneke Ming, "Barracks-Concubinage in the Indies, 1887–1920", *Indonesia* 35 (April 1983), p. 65, and J.A. de Moor, *Generaal Spoor: Triomf en tragiek van een legercommandant* (Amsterdam: Boom, 2011), p. 53.
22. Zwitzer and Heshusius, *Het Koninklijk Nederlands-Indisch Leger 1830–1950*, p. 11. I have used here the translation in Ming, "Barracks-Concubinage in the Indies", p. 66.
23. Ming, "Barracks-Concubinage in the Indies", p. 66.
24. Not that this made much difference. The *Koloniale Verslagen* reported year after year that it was impossible to recruit enough Eurasian soldiers.
25. Ben Anderson, personal communication.
26. Written communication. Colonel J.J. Nortier, 5 March 1996.
27. In 1998 Soeharto claimed that until the immediate pre-war period the Dutch had "recruited soldiers *mainly* from the eastern islands, such as Ambon, where the people were Christians who felt close to the Dutch. But as it became necessary to meet the Japanese advance to the southern areas they changed their recruitment policy and hired Muslim Javanese as well." [Italics added]. Soeharto, "Watashi no Rirekisho", *Nihon Keizai Shimbun*, 5 January 1998. Soeharto may not have been guilty of bad faith when he made that observation. But his comments betray, at the very least, a certain disregard for the truth and a pervasive ignorance, characteristics which seemed to exist side-by-side with an excellent memory and, when it suited him, fastidious attention to detail. The belief that the KNIL was made up largely of Menadonese and Ambonese finds expression in numerous Western academic studies. For example, Benda writes that the KNIL "had been predominantly recruited from among Christian Indonesians." See Harry J. Benda, *The Crescent and the Rising Sun: Indonesian Islam Under the Japanese Occupation 1942–1945* (KITLV,

Dordrecht: Foris Publications Holland/USA, 1983 [original: The Hague: W. van Hoeve, 1958]), p. 254, fn 48. Benedict Anderson has argued that Soeharto was following the established national line when he made these observations. That line was influenced, he believes, by the fact that *after* the revolution broke out, most Javanese ex-KNIL disappeared or entered the TNI, while many Menadonese and Ambonese stayed with the KNIL, so that probably the ratios of Easterners and Javanese changed completely from 1940 to 1946. Personal communication.

28. See J.J. Nortier, *De Japanse aanval op Nederlands-Indie* [The Japanese Attack on the Netherlands Indies] (Rotterdam: Ad. Donker, 1988), p. 10. The other main groups were the Menadonese (15 per cent), the Ambonese (12 per cent), the Sundanese (5 per cent) and the Timorese (4 per cent). The Dutch drew no distinction between those from East and Central Java. In 1905, the colonial army and navy had consisted of 15,866 European officers and men and 26,276 Indonesians, most of whom were in the army. Of these, 68 per cent were Javanese. Ricklefs, *A History of Modern Indonesia*, 4th ed., p. 179.
29. Zwitzer and Heshusius, *Het Koninklijk Nederlands-Indisch Leger 1830–1950*, p. 10. The other main ethnic groups at that time were the Sundanese (1,800) and the Timorese (1,100). There were 400 others, including Madurese, Buginese, Acehnese and Malays.
30. Roeslan Abdulgani, 9 September 1998.
31. The 1940 population estimate for the Dutch East Indies was 70.4 million, with Java accounting for 48.4 million of that. Widjojo Nitisastro, *Population Trends in Indonesia* (Ithaca: Cornell University Press, 1970), pp. 116–17.
32. Nortier, Kuijt and Groen, *De Japanse aanval op Java, Maart 1942*, pp. 255–56. Some Indonesian and Western writers have failed to pay sufficient attention to this striking post-1936 bifurcation within the KNIL. Writing in 1956, the then Indonesian Army Chief of Staff, Major General A.H. Nasution, who had joined the KNIL in 1940, claimed that, "The KNIL army was simply a police army, comparable to our present [Police] Mobile Brigade and State Police. Its assignment was to suppress 'the enemy within the country', its organization was smaller than our present Mobile Brigade and it had only a few more men than the [East Indies] Police. Thanks to the efficient policies of the colonizers, these two small police organizations, the [East Indies] Police and the KNIL, were able to maintain internal security in the widespread archipelago." Nasution, *Tentara Nasional Indonesia*, vol. I [The Indonesian National Army, vol. I] (Jakarta: Jajasan Pustaka Militer, 1956), JPRS translation, p. 50.
33. The KNIL was entirely separate from the Dutch Army, or Koninklijke Landmacht. As previously mentioned, the Commander-in-Chief of the KNIL

came under the Governor General of the Netherlands East Indies, who was generally a civilian but sometimes a retired general. The Commander-in-Chief of the East Indies squadron of the Dutch Navy (Koninklijke Marine) reported administratively to the Minister of Defence but was placed at the operational disposal of the Governor General, who reported to the Minister of Colonies. Bussemaker, "Paradise in Peril", p. 328.

34. The Java-based field battalions were supported by seven squadrons of cavalry, by artillery units, some of them mechanized, some of them dependent on pack horses, and by twenty-four light tanks, the nucleus of a planned armoured corps. Six of the garrison battalions were on Java, the remaining twelve in the Outer Islands. Interview, Colonel C.A. Heshusius, The Hague, 23 April 2001, and written communication, Petra Groen, 5 July 2019.

    In 1890, when conventional military tactics were found wanting in Aceh, the Dutch had established a Korps Maréchaussée. The corps had considerable success in counter guerrilla and commando operations. Maréchaussée battalions, each consisting of two companies, were later set up on Java to deal with such things as banditry; the theft of plantation rubber and sugar cane, a common problem in East Java, and arson attacks on sugar plantations carried out by villagers unhappy at being forced to plant so much of their land under sugar cane. These units were known informally as the "*asfalt* [ashphalt] Maréchaussée" because they were deployed by road. Interview, Colonel C.A. Heshusius, The Hague, 23 April 2001, Zwitzer and Heshusius, *Het Koninklijk Nederlands-Indisch Leger, 1830–1950*, p. 102, and Cribb, *Historical Dictionary*, pp. 285–86.

35. Petra Groen, written communication, 5 July 2019, citing "HQ KNIL. The Netherlands East Indies Army," prepared at the office of the US Army Liaison Officer and the Netherlands Indies War Office, Bandoeng, Java, 1940–1941. NIMH.

36. These two forts were almost self-contained towns, sheltering behind ramparts up to six yards thick, sprawling over many acres, home to more than 250 officers and men, with administration and accommodation blocks, armouries, storerooms, kitchens, garages and blacksmiths forges, many of the buildings with steeply-pitched North Sea roofs, everything kept neat and freshly whitewashed.

37. It has been suggested that the police had only a limited presence in the Outer Islands and that responsibility for meeting serious challenges to public order rested with the army. Interview, Colonel C.A. Heshusius, The Hague, 23 April 2001. That may have been the case in the early years of the twentieth century. In 1905, the colonial police force had only 2,235 men in the Outer Islands. See Eric Tagliacozzo, *Secret Trades: Porous Borders: Smuggling and States Along a Southeast Asian Frontier, 1865–1915* (New Haven and London: Yale University

Press, 2005), p. 66. Twenty-five years later, however, police numbers outside Java had more than quadrupled. In 1930, the Veldpolitie (Field Police) had 4,654 men in the Outer Islands while the Algemene Politie (General Police) had 5,063 men, of whom 183 were European. Written communication, Dr Petra Groen, 3–5 June 2019, citing the *Koloniale Verslagen.* In the 1930s the colonial police force reached a maximum strength of 54,000 men, some 52,000 of whom were Indonesian. By that time, it was well established that it was the police force which had to deal with civil unrest in the first instance. The army only assisted the police when the latter could not handle the situation, as happened, for example, during the PKI uprisings of 1926–27. For a comprehensive study of the police in the Netherlands East Indies, see Marieke Bloembergen, *De geschiedenis van de politie in Nederlands-Indië: Uit zorg en angst* (Amsterdam: Boom; Leiden: KITLV Uitgeverij, 2009), published in Indonesian as *Polisi Zaman Hindia Belanda: Dari Kepedulian dan Ketakutan* (Jakarta, Kompas and KITLV-Jakarta, 2011). The figure of 54,000 is from the *Indisch Verslag II* 1933. See *Polisi Zaman Hindia Belanda,* p. xxxi. Bloembergen argues that the Veldpolitie had extensive experience in riot control.

38. Written communication, Colonel J.J. Nortier, 5 March 1996. For further information on these matters, see Nortier, Kuijt and Groen, *De Japanse aanval op Java, Maart 1942*; Zwitzer and Heshusius, *Het Koninklijk Nederlands-Indisch Leger 1830–1950,* and B. Bouman, *Van Driekleur tot Rood-Wit: De Indonesische officieren uit het KNIL, 1900–1950,* [From Tricolour to Red and White: The Indonesian KNIL Officers, 1900–1950] ('s-Gravenhage: Sectie Militaire Geschiedenis, 1995).
39. Each *brigade* was commanded by a European, a Eurasian or an Indonesian sergeant first class. In Aceh, many of these nineteen-man patrols were conducted by the Korps Maréchaussée. In 1927 there were some 560 KNIL *brigades* in the Outer Islands, of which 168 were in Aceh. Of these 168, 108 were infantry *brigades* and 60 Maréchaussée *brigades*. Zwitzer and Heshusius, *Het Koninklijk Nederlands-Indisch Leger, 1830–1950,* p. 102. In many armies, a brigade is a much larger force, made up of several regiments.
40. Interview, Colonel Alex Kawilarang, Jakarta, 31 August 1998. By the time the Japanese did attack Sumatra, in February 1942, Palembang was defended by six infantry companies (equivalent to one-and-a-half battalions), one machine-gun company and a section of artillery. Needless to say, that was no deterrent to the Japanese, who had launched the Pacific War to secure, above all, the oil at Palembang. They assigned a full division and some 300 aircraft to Operation L, the seizure of Bangka Island and Palembang. For details of the Japanese attack, see Willem Remmelink, ed. and trans., *The Invasion of the Dutch East Indies* [a translation of Volume 3 of the 102-volume Japanese War History Series, *Ran-In Koryaku Sakusen* (Tokyo: Asagumo Shimbunsha, 1967)] (Leiden: Leiden University Press, 2015), p. 265.

41. These troops were based, for the most part, at large garrisons on Java.
42. Soeharto, *My Thoughts*, p. 16.
43. He would also have received, as part of the standard issue for new recruits, a sleeping mat, a blanket, a leather belt, singlets, underpants, socks, puttees, a bamboo hat, a cap, a bivouac balaclava, a spoon and fork, a bowl, a pocket knife, a water bottle, a gas mask and a collapsible spade.
44. Written communication, Colonel Heshusius, 17 October 1999. The material in this section draws on information provided by Colonel Heshusius.
45. Marc Lohnstein, *Royal Netherlands East Indies Army 1936–42* (Oxford: Osprey, 2018), p. 20.
46. Interview, Colonel Heshusius, The Hague, 23 April 2001. The same point is made in Nortier, Kuijt and Groen, *De Japanse aanval op Java*, pp. 255–66.
47. Written communication, Colonel Heshusius, 18 April 2001.
48. Written communication, Colonel Heshusius, 22 August 2000.
49. In earlier times, some recruits appear to have had their first (homosexual) sexual experience in the barracks. In the early 1890s, well over half the recruits at Gombong "were guilty of practicing unnatural vice." The army leadership "felt that this kind of situation fully demonstrated the value of concubinage". Ming, "Barracks-Concubinage in the Indies", p. 69.
50. Edward J. Drea, *Japan's Imperial Army: Its Rise and Fall, 1853–1945* (Lawrence, Kansas: University Press of Kansas, 2009), p. 210.
51. Yanagawa Motoshige in an interview with Ruth McVey, Jakarta, 13 November 1980.
52. Drea, *Japan's Imperial Army*, p. 211.
53. Arthur J. Marden, *Old Friends, New Enemies: The Royal Navy and the Imperial Japanese Navy, Strategic Illusions, 1936–1941* (Oxford: Clarendon Press, 1981), p. 88.
54. Imperial Navy position paper, "Study of Policy toward French Indochina", 1 August 1940, cited in Henry P. Frei, *Japan's Southward Advance and Australia: From the Sixteenth Century to World War II* (Melbourne: Melbourne University Press, 1991), p. 147.
55. Stephen Howarth, *Morning Glory: The Story of the Imperial Japanese Navy* (London: Arrow Books, 1985), p. 254.
56. For details, see Bussemaker, "Paradise in Peril", pp. 326–72. According to another source, the Dutch had only three light cruisers, six destroyers and eleven submarines. See John Prados, *Combined Fleet Decoded: The Secret History of American Intelligence and the Japanese Navy in World War II* (New York: Random House, 1995), p. 249.
57. I am indebted here to Benedict Anderson and, in this paragraph, draw extensively on his exposition. Personal communication.
58. See Tarling, *Britain, Southeast Asia*, p. 146.

59. Ibid., p. 151. The United States, seeing the Dutch equivocate, was reluctant to sell them the military equipment they so sorely needed. Bussemaker, "Paradise in Peril", pp. 125–26. On 7 December 1941, after the attack on Pearl Harbor, the Netherlands declared war on Japan.
60. Written communication, Colonel J.J. Nortier, 5 March 1996.
61. In 1940 the *kwetsbare punten* were Tarakan, Balikpapan, Palembang and Ambon.
62. For details of the *Defensiegrondslagen*, see Nortier, Kuijt and Groen, *De Japanse aanval op Java*, pp. 19–22, and Bussemaker, "Paradise in Peril", pp. 351–52 and 381–82.
63. G.H. Bousquet, "The International Position of Netherlands India", *Pacific Affairs* XII, no. 4 (December 1939), p. 389. In the pre-war period, the Dutch relied on the semi-official de Javasche Bank (Bank of Java) to maintain the official rate of exchange between the Netherlands East Indies guilder and the Netherlands guilder.
64. Colonel Nortier, personal communication.
65. H.W. Ponder, *Java Pageant: Impressions from the 1930s* (Singapore: Oxford University Press, 1988), pp. 279–80. Originally published as *Java Pageant* by Seeley Service & Co. Ltd, London, 1934.
66. Much of the Wehrmacht, it is true, was pulled by horse at this time. But the Germans had also invested heavily in tanks and armoured cars.
67. It was the task of the cavalry to conduct reconnaissance and secure important road junctions.
68. In 1940, these battalions moved across the hills and rice fields of Java with their 75mm guns broken down into eight component parts, each of which was carried on a pack horse. A battalion on the move consisted of about 800 men, 157 large Australian packhorses, 411 Indonesian ponies, 34 bicycles, 14 horse-drawn cooking and water wagons and 89 other horse-drawn carts. (See Zwitzer and Heshusius, *Het Koninklijk Nederlands-Indisch Leger*, p. 120.) This enabled the mountain artillery battalions to go almost anywhere. But it meant they would be no match for the Japanese, who were to land on Java with trucks, light tanks and motorized artillery, allowing them to move at great speed.
69. For details, see Bussemaker, "Paradise in Peril", p. 401.
70. The KNIL Chief of Staff, Major General Hein ter Poorten, a 220-lb officer who had been born in Surabaya, was not only an artilleryman but also an airman. He had won an international balloon race in Germany and had learned to fly an aircraft in 1911. "Het is Zoover", *Time*, 26 January 1942.
71. The KNIL had capitulated by the time the first of these aircraft could be delivered.
72. Bussemaker, "Paradise in Peril", p. 394. According to another account, the KNIL-ML was equipped with 83 Glenn Martins, 71 Brewster Buffaloes and

70 other aircraft, including fighters, reconnaissance planes and trainers. See John Douglas, "The Dutch Air Forces in the Pacific War", www.pacificwrecks.com/douglas/articles/neiaf.html (accessed 29 January 2011).

73. When the Japanese attacked the Philippines on 8 December 1941, General Douglas MacArthur had the strongest American air forces outside the United States, with 277 planes, including 35 Boeing B-17 heavy bombers and about 100 modern fighters. He lost almost half of his best aircraft on the first day. See Ronald H. Spector, *Eagle Against the Sun: The American War with Japan* (London: Penguin, 1987), pp. 107–8.
74. Ibid., p. 108.
75. See Gerard J. Casius, "Brewster Buffaloes for the Militaire Luchtvaart KNIL", www.warbirdsforum.com/casius.htm (accessed 29 January 2011).
76. Bussemaker, "Paradise in Peril", pp. 385–86. Each brigade would include ninety light and medium tanks, a squadron of scout cars, two battalions of motorized infantry as well as mechanized field artillery, mechanized anti-tank guns and mechanized anti-aircraft artillery. The word brigade is used here in its more conventional sense.
77. The KNIL was thus dependent mainly on its 24 Vickers Carden tanks. At around the same time, the Netherlands East Indies agreed to buy a consignment of second-hand Italian weapons captured by the British in North Africa. Once again, very few of the weapons arrived in time and they were allocated to the home guard.
78. Bouman, *Van Driekleur*, p. 446.
79. Interview, Lieutenant General G.P.H. Djatikusumo, Jakarta, 9 March 1981. Djatikusumo's older brother was the second Indonesian cadet admitted to Breda. In 1936 Djatikusumo was himself offered a place on the course. He declined the invitation, saying he could not swear an oath to the Dutch queen. In 1939 the Dutch increased the number of Indonesian cadets at Breda, too late to have any impact.
80. Bouman, *Van Driekleur*, p. 448.
81. The first reserve officers training in the Indies had begun in 1936 at the First Depot Battalion in Bandung. In 1938 this became CORO. In 1940, Djatikusumo joined the CORO. The Dutch also established a Royal Naval Institute (Koninklijk Instituut voor de Marine, KIM) in Surabaya in August 1940 after the German occupation of the Netherlands.
82. This percentage is not especially high. Part of the problem may have been that young, educated Indonesians found the idea of service in the KNIL politically distasteful. Another problem was that the entry bar was set quite high; cadets were supposed to have a HBS education.
83. In the 1870s the Dutch Army discarded its early attachment to French military science in favour of emerging Prussian doctrines, which had been showcased so

successfully in the 1870–71 Franco-Prussian war. These doctrines stressed that victory depended not simply on advanced weaponry: the decisive feature was élan and fighting spirit. The Dutch Higher War College (Hogere Krijgsschool, HKS) was designed on the Prussian model; and in this institution, as well as in the Royal Netherlands Military Academy at Breda (and, after 1940, at a new KMA in Bandung), officers and military cadets got a thorough grounding in German military theory. The reading list was heavy with German texts, including Carl von Clausewitz's *Vom Kriege (On War)* and Hans Delbrück's *Geschichte der Kriegskunst im Rahmen der politischen Geschichte* [*History of Warfare in the Framework of Political History*], *Volume IV: The Modern Era*. In the Netherlands and in the Indies, as in Germany itself, officers were very much interested during the inter-war years in theories about the mechanization and motorization of the army. As noted above, until 1935 no attempt was made to mechanize the KNIL, there being no money for this. The Japanese Army, which made a similar switch from French to German thinking between 1879 and 1885, would in due course place great emphasis on élan and fighting spirit during the instruction of Indonesian officer cadets in Bogor. For an excellent account of the German impact on Japanese military thinking, see Edward J. Drea, *Japan's Imperial Army: Its Rise and Fall, 1853–1945* (Lawrence, Kansas: University Press of Kansas, 2009), pp. 58–59.

84. Magelang could no longer cope with the demands imposed on it and a new cadre school for candidate corporals had to be set up in Yogyakarta.
85. *Nihon Keizai Shimbun*, 5 January 1998.
86. Written communication, Colonel Heshusius, 17 October 1999.
87. Soeharto said that he undertook not only his basic training but also his two NCO courses at Gombong. See, for example, Roeder, *The Smiling General*, p. 93, and Soeharto, *Pikiran*, p. 20. See also Soeharto's curriculum vitae in Harsja W. Bachtiar, *Siapa Dia? Perwira Tinggi Tentara National Indonesia, Angkatan Darat* (Jakarta: Djambatan, 1988), pp. 341–42. Reference is made in this entry to the "Sekolah Kader Militer, Gombong, 2 Desember 1940".
88. Written communication, Colonel Heshusius, 18 April 2001.
89. Magelang was the headquarters of the KNIL 2nd Division, which was not a division at all in the usual military sense, meaning a force of perhaps 12,000 to 15,000 men, but simply a headquarters responsible for the various KNIL forces in Central Java. It was also a regimental headquarters, the base of two infantry battalions and a heavy weapons company as well as the cadre school and a first-class army hospital, complete with medical specialists and dentists.
90. Soeharto, *Pikiran*, p. 20.
91. See *Soeharto: Mijn Gedachten, Woorden en Daden* (Franeker: Van Wijnen, 1991), p. 26. The Dutch version says: "*Ik slaagde als de beste, en moest vervolgens*

praktijkervaring opdoen als ondercommandant van een peloton van het Dertiende Bataljon te Tampel (sic), nabij Malang." In this case, there has been a careless translation of the units below company level. In the pre-war KNIL infantry, one did not speak of a *peloton* but used the word *sectie*. Before the war, a KNIL infantry battalion, which was commanded by a major or lieutenant colonel, always a Dutchman or Eurasian, consisted of three (sometimes four) 180-man rifle companies and one weapons company, with each of the rifle companies headed by a captain or older first-lieutenant. Each rifle company consisted of a command group (*compagniesstaf*) and three 50-man *secties* (platoons). *Secties* were subdivided into three *brigades* (sections), each of fifteen men. Each *brigade* was headed by a sergeant, assisted by two corporals, and a command group. Personal communication, Colonel J.J. (Joop) Nortier, 30 August 1994. In a normal infantry company, two platoons were commanded by a first or second lieutenant, almost without exception a Dutchman or Eurasian, the third by a senior NCO, usually a Dutchman or Eurasian.

92. Tarling, *Britain, Southeast Asia and the Onset of the Pacific War*, pp. 161–79.
93. Frei, *Japan's Southward Advance*, p. 149. Rear Admiral Maeda Tadashi told Allied interrogators that in September 1941 his brother had been head of the European section of the Third Bureau, not the bureau as a whole. "Interrogation of Rear Admiral Maeda Tadashi at Changi Gaol, Singapore Island, between 31st May and 14th June 1946." Nederlands Instituut voor Oorlogs-, Holocaust- en Genocidestudies – Indische Collectie [NIOD Institute for War, Holocaust and Genocide Studies, Indies Collection] (henceforth NIOD), coll. 400, no. 718 and no. 314. Later, it appears, Maeda Minoru did head the bureau.
94. The Japanese presented their formal demand on 22 July. Tarling, *Britain, Southeast Asia and the Onset of the Pacific War*, p. 332.
95. Ibid., p. 331.
96. John Keegan, ed., *The Times Atlas of the Second World War* (Times Books, 1989), p. 67.

8. A reassuringly familiar world

1. Infantry Battalion 502 was to behave with great brutality in Dili after Soeharto gave the order for an invasion of Portuguese East Timor in 1975.
2. Interview, Major General Sukotjo Tjokroatmodjo, Jakarta, 3 August 2000.
3. Written communication. Colonel J.J. Nortier, 30 August 1994.
4. In the heavy weapons companies, which were equipped with mortars and machine guns, the races were always mixed, experience having shown that it was not practicable to maintain ethnically "pure" units. A similar disregard for ethnicity was to be found in the nineteen-man fixed patrolling brigades in the Outer Islands. Here, too, the races were mixed, although not to any formula. Under the sergeant, who would be European, Eurasian or Indonesian,

there might be eight or nine Javanese, four Ambonese, four Menadonese and perhaps one Sundanese, Timorese or Batak.

5. Battalion commanders, who were always European, liked to have one European rifle company, it being thought that Europeans were better trained and more reliable. But they never said no to a Menadonese or Ambonese company and they considered the Javanese were good soldiers and found them easy to manage. If two of the three rifle companies were Javanese, as was sometimes the case, care was taken to ensure that the other was Menadonese, Ambonese or Sundanese. I have not been able to obtain data for 1941. But in 1935, the ethnic identity of the forty-seven rifle companies in the sixteen KNIL infantry battalions was as follows: Javanese 15, Menadonese 10, European 9, Ambonese 6, Timorese 3, Sundanese 2 and "mixed" 2. Personal communication, Colonel Heshusius, 22 August 2000. That would indicate that in 1935 Javanese accounted for about one-third of the manpower in the KNIL rifle companies. As noted earlier, in 1929 Javanese are said to have accounted for 40 per cent of overall KNIL manpower. By 1937, it appears, they accounted for just over 50 per cent. This may stem from the fact that the recruitment of Javanese soldiers varied, depending on how many men of the preferred ethnic groups (Ambonese, Menadonese and Timorese) could be recruited. I am indebted to Petra Groen for making this point. It is also possible that Javanese were present in larger numbers in the heavy weapons companies and elsewhere.
6. Interview, Colonel Heshusius, The Hague, 23 April 2001.
7. Married Indonesian NCOs from sergeant 2nd class upwards had their own small army houses, most of them inside the barracks but some just outside the barbed wire outer fence. Married European and Eurasian personnel, no matter what their rank, lived in army houses outside the compound. Unmarried Europeans and Eurasians were housed inside the barracks, the sergeants in private rooms, the corporals in a small room at the end of the shared dormitory of the European and Eurasian privates.
8. Soeharto, *My Thoughts*, p. 17.
9. Dutch officers were supposed to speak elementary Malay (*pasar maleis*).
10. It has been suggested that another possible explanation for the salary differentials is that Javanese were living in their own region and had access to their kinfolk. Ambonese and Menadonese were living far from home and unlikely to get any easy help. Benedict Anderson, personal communication. That may only be true up to a point. During the twentieth century, Moluccan and Menadonese quarters grew up around KNIL garrisons on Java: soldiers from those regions could get help from there. Javanese often had no wider family support during their long postings in the Outer Islands.
11. Dutch army records indicate that there was a Captain K.J.J. Drijber serving in 1941. He was born in 1897, which would mean that he was in his mid-forties

in 1941. However there was also a First Lieutenant F. Drijber; he was born in 1906 and might have been a captain in 1941. Written communication, Dr Petra M.H. Groen, Military History Section, Royal Netherlands Army, The Hague, 27 October 1994, and Colonel J.J. Nortier, 30 August 1994.

12. The "Hyneman" referred to by Soeharto may have been Sub-Lieutenant J.D. Heineman, who was born in 1903, or Sub-Lieutenant C.G. Heineman, who was born in 1904. Both were serving in 1941. Sub-Lieutenant (Onderluitenant) was the highest rank an NCO could reach before the war. Jansen is one of the commonest names in Holland. The Dutch have no record of an NCO by the name of Janssen or Jantzen. Here, too, I am grateful to Dr Groen for her help. As noted earlier, the term platoon was not used in the KNIL.
13. The responsibilities of a sergeant were considerably greater than those of a corporal. A corporal might have charge of a group of six men. A sergeant was responsible for a section (squad), or one-third of a fifty-man *sectie* (platoon). If he happened to be the most senior of the three sergeants in the platoon he had to be ready at all times to take command of the platoon if the second lieutenant was killed or wounded. In the Outer Islands, an Indonesian sergeant 1st class might find himself in command of a standard patrolling brigade of nineteen men, operating away from base for perhaps three weeks at a time, alone and self-supporting. He was the man in charge when the brigade was given riot-control duties, responsible for maintaining law and order while inflicting the absolute minimum number of deaths or casualties.
14. *Voorschrift voor de Uitoefening van de Politiek-Politioneele Taak van het Leger* (VPTL) (Batavia: Departement van Oorlog, 1928).
15. For details, see Jaap de Moor, "Colonial Warfare: Theory and Practice. The Dutch Experience in Indonesia, 1816–1949", *Journal of the Japan-Netherlands Institute* II (1990): 98–114.
16. A sergeant 2nd class could get by without much written Dutch; all he needed was some understanding of spoken Dutch. But a man could not advance to sergeant 1st class or go on to attend the nine-month sergeant-majors course until he was reasonably fluent in Dutch and able to make simple written reports in Dutch. Indonesians of this rank were mostly Menadonese and Ambonese, who had benefited from the higher educational standards in their home regions.
17. John Toland, *The Rising Sun: The Decline and Fall of the Japanese Empire, 1936–1945* (New York: Bantam, 1986), p. 288.
18. For a valuable (and weighty) account of the Japanese landings in the Netherlands East Indies, see War History Office, National Defense College of Japan, *Senshi Sosho 3. Ran-In Koryaku Sakusen* [War History Series, Volume 3. *The Invasion of the Dutch East Indies*] (Tokyo: Asagumo Shimbunsha, 1967). This volume is now available in English. See Willem Remmelink, editor and

translator, *The Invasion of the Dutch East Indies* (Leiden: Leiden University Press, 2015).

19. Remmelink, *The Invasion of the Dutch East Indies*, p. 225.
20. Affidavit of Sgt. Maj. J.M.J. Muller, RNIA, prosecution document No. 5951, Exhibit No. 1685, The International Military Tribunal for the Far East, Tokyo, 23 December 1946.
21. Nicholas Tarling, *A Sudden Rampage: The Japanese Occupation of Southeast Asia, 1941–1945* (London: Hurst, 2001), p. 93, citing J. Th. Lindblad, *Between Dayak and Dutch* (Dordrecht: Foris, 1988), p. 115. See also John W. Dower, *War Without Mercy: Race and Power in the Pacific War* (New York: Pantheon Books, 1986), p. 44.
22. See Nortier, Kuijt and Groen, *De Japanse aanval op Java*, p. 305, P.C. Boer, *The Loss of Java: The final battles for the possession of Java fought by Allied air, naval and land forces in the period of 18 February – 7 March 1942* (Singapore: NUS Press, 2011), pp. xxvi–xxvii, and Nortier, *De Japanse aanval op Nederlands-Indië*.
23. According to an official British history, there were four infantry regiments, each of three battalions. See S. Woodburn Kirby et al., *The War Against Japan, Volume I, The Loss of Singapore, History of the Second World War, United Kingdom Military Series* (London: HM Stationary Office, 1957), p. 432.
24. Lionel Wigmore, *Australia in the War of 1939–1945, Series One: Army, Volume IV, The Japanese Thrust* (Canberra: Australian War Memorial, 1957), p. 495.
25. Woodburn Kirby, *The Loss of Singapore*, p. 432.
26. After the fall of Singapore, General Sir Archibald Wavell, the British Commander-in-Chief of the American-British-Dutch-Australian (ABDA) Command, told the Chiefs of Staff that the loss of Java, though a severe blow, would not be fatal, but that Australia and Burma were vital. The Australian 7th Division, which was on its way to Java, should be diverted to Burma. Curtin refused to allow Australian forces to be sent to Burma. For details, see Nicholas Tarling, *A Sudden Rampage*, p. 97. For a good account of the Australian Government's position, see John Edwards, *John Curtins's War*, Vol. I (Australia: Penguin Viking, 2017), pp. 416–19.
27. Wigmore, *Australia in the War of 1939–1945*, p. 495.
28. Boer, *The Loss of Java*, p. xxvi.
29. Indeed, the Japanese would threaten to bomb Bandung when, on 8–9 March, the Dutch argued over legal niceties during the surrender negotiations.
30. *Senshi Sosho 3. Ran-In Koryaku Sakusen*, pp. 570–71.
31. By 1942, it is true, KNIL numbers had swollen to 122,600, made up of 45,800 Europeans and 76,800 Indonesians. But the KNIL was never in any position to resist a sustained attack. Included in the total were 19,000 Indonesians serving as part of a Dad's Army on plantations and 4,700 elderly soldiers

who had been recalled to duty. Also included were 8,500 Dutchmen serving as part of the Home Guard. Written communication, Colonel C.A. Heshusius, 17 October 1999.

32. *Senshi Sosho 3. Ran-In Koryaku Sakusen*, pp. 76 and 570–71. See also Woodburn Kirby, *The Loss of Singapore*, p. 443.
33. Yuki Tanaka, *Japan's Comfort Women: Sexual Slavery and Prostitution During World War II and the US Occupation* (London: Routledge, 2002), pp. 61–62, citing The International Military Tribunal for the Far East (Tokyo: 1946), transcripts, pp. 13,639–642. For Tsuchihashi's movements, see *The Invasion of the Dutch East Indies*, pp. 554–55.
34. Soeharto, *My Thoughts*, p. 17. In 1998 Soeharto was quoted as claiming that he "was transferred to Army Headquarters in Bandung." *Nihon Keizai Shimbun*, 5 January 1998.
35. See Boer, *The Loss of Java*, pp. 472–73. See also Nortier, Kuijt and Groen, *De Japanse aanval op Java Maart 1942*, p. 152.
36. Boer, *The Loss of Java*, p. 479.
37. Lieutenant General Joannes Benedictus van Heutsz, who served as governor of Aceh (1898–1904) and Governor-General (1904–1909), had himself been a *foerier* for three years.
38. Interview, Colonel Heshusius, The Hague, 22 August 2000.
39. For the hopelessness of the American position in the Philippines, see Spector, *Eagle Against the Sun*, pp. 137–38, on which this sentence is based.
40. Bussemaker, "Paradise in Peril", p. 426.
41. Ibid.
42. Written communication, Colonel J.J. Nortier, 5 March 1996.
43. Tjamboek Berdoeri [Kwee Thiam Tjing], *Indonesia Dalem Api dan Bara* [Indonesia Aflame and on the Coals] (Jakarta: Elkasa, 2004). First published 1947.
44. Remmelink, *The Invasion of the Dutch East Indies*, pp. 567–69.
45. Soeharto, "Watashi no Rirekisho", *Nihon Keizai Shimbun*, 5 January 1998.
46. Woodburn Kirby, *The Loss of Singapore*, p. 449.

9. A policeman for the Japanese

1. Soeharto, *My Thoughts, Words, and Deeds*, p. 17.
2. Ibid.
3. Soeharto, "Watashi no rirekisho", part 5, *Nihon Keizai Shimbun*, 6 January 1998.
4. Indonesians who had been KNIL officers in 1942 and who went on to fight for independence in 1945 were to argue that General Ter Poorten's 8 and 9 March statements absolved them of any further loyalty to the Dutch Queen. However, Lieutenant General S.H. Spoor, the post-war commander-in-chief of Dutch forces in the East Indies/Indonesia, would take the view that only the Queen could discharge these men from their oath of loyalty and that they

were, formally speaking, deserters. See Memorandum from Lieutenant General S.H. Spoor to the Lieutenant Governor-General, 21 February 1946, Nationaal Archief, Den Haag, Algemene Secretarie van de Nederlands-Indische Regering en de daarbij gedeponeerde Archieven, 1942–1950, archiefinventaris 2.10.14, inventarisnummer 2601, hereafter abbreviated NANL 2.10.14, inv. 2601. This was an important point in Dutch military eyes. As the Dutch saw it, Indonesian officers remained bound by their oaths of allegiance.

5. Soeharto, *My Thoughts*, pp. 17–18.
6. Toland, *The Rising Sun*, p. 296.
7. Christopher Bayly and Tim Harper, *Forgotten Armies: The Fall of British Asia, 1941–1945* (Cambridge, Massachusetts: The Belknap Press of Harvard University Press, 2006), p. 210.
8. Interview, Tsuchiya Kiso, Mishima, Shizuoka Prefecture, 2 February 1999.
9. Interview, Kaneko Tomokazu, Tokyo, 3 February 1999. Kaneko had worked before the war as a writer for the Japanese Army magazine *Rikugun Gaho* (*Army Illustrated*). He was one of many Japanese civilian writers, poets, painters and cartoonists—the Japanese term was *bunkajin*, meaning "person of culture"—attached to the Sixteenth Army Propaganda Corps under Lieutenant Colonel Machida Keiji, who headed that department until November 1942. In August 1942, the Propaganda Corps was incorporated into the Military Administration (Gunseikanbu) and changed its name to Propaganda Department (Sendenbu).
10. Interviews, Selo Soemardjan, Jakarta, 2 September 1997, and 3 September 1998. In his CV, Selo Soemardjan indicated, without elaboration, that he was an official in the Sultanate/Government of the Special Territory of Yogyakarta between 1935 and 1949 (Pegawai Kesultanan/Pemerintah Daerah Istimewa Yogyakarta 1935–1949). In Yogyakarta in the pre-war period, there were, in fact, two different sets of offices, those of the Sultan and those of the Dutch. The police force came under the Dutch, with Dutch police officers at the apex of the pyramid and Indonesians below them. Selo was one of those Indonesians. When the Japanese occupied Yogyakarta, he was working in the political section, or what one might call the Special Branch, of the Yogyakarta police force, which kept a strict watch on the nationalist movement. "I had to learn the trade," he explained half a century later. His office was in Jalan Bayan Kara in Reksobayan. In the first of these interviews, Selo gave the impression that he was appointed as a subdistrict head (*camat*) in Kulon Progo not long after the Japanese arrived. Pressed on the point, he conceded that this appointment had actually come in 1943. This would suggest that he stayed on in the special branch for perhaps a year, if not longer, under the Japanese. He said he was surprised to learn, only then, in the late 1990s, that Soeharto had worked for a time in the Japanese-run police force. Although his

surprise is itself surprising, it is likely that Selo had taken up his appointment as a *camat* by the time Soeharto joined the police force. For a fuller than usual account of Selo Soemardjan's CV, see P.J. Suwarno, *Hamengku Buwono IX dan Sistem Birokrasi Pemerintahan Yogyakarta, 1942–1974: Sebuah Tinjuan Historis* (Yogyakarta: Kanisius, 1994), pp. 444–45. According to this account, Selo worked in the criminal section and then the political section of the Yogyakarta police force between 1940 and 1942 (sic).

11. *Imamura Hitoshi Taisho Kaikoroku* [Memoirs of General Imamura Hitoshi] (Tokyo: Jiyu Ajai-sha, 1960), 4 vols., vol. II, p. 148, cited in Mitsuo Nakamura, "General Imamura and the Early Period of Japanese Occupation", *Indonesia*, vol. 10, p. 10.
12. I am grateful to Bill Frederick for making this point. As he notes, even some of the *bunkajin* attached to the Propaganda Corps, although predisposed to think well of the indigenes, felt they had to adjust their opinions.
13. "Interrogation of General Imamura Hitoshi, Supplement", undated, Algemene Secretarie van de Nederlands-Indische Regering en de daarbij gedeponeerde Archieven, 1942–1950. Entry Code: 2.10.14, inv. 5284A, NANL, The Hague, pp. 53–55 (p. 1 of Allied translation).
14. For details of Kenpeitai responsibilities at the time of the Dutch surrender, see Zenkoku Kenyukai Rengokai Hensan Iinkai [Editorial Committee of the National Federation of Kenpeitai Veterans' Associations], *Nihon Kenpei Seishi* [The Authoritative History of the Japanese Kenpeitai] (Tokyo: Kenbunshoin, 1976), p. 1026.
15. Interviews with Colonel Miyamoto Shizuo, Tokyo, Kaneko Tomokazu, Tokyo, Morimoto Takeshi, Tokorozawa, Saitama Prefecture, and Tsuchiya Kiso, Asahigaoka, Mishima-shi, Shizuoka Prefecture, 2 February 1999.
16. Interview, Selo Soemardjan, 2 September 1997.
17. Ibid.
18. See Kishi Koichi and Nishijima Shigetada, eds., *Indonesia ni Okeru Nihon Gunsei no Kenkyu* [Research on the Japanese Military Administration in Indonesia] (Tokyo: Waseda University, Okuma Memorial Social Sciences Research Institute, Kinokuniya Shoten, 1959). An English translation of this pioneering work, *Japanese Military Administration in Indonesia*, was produced in 1963 by the Joint Publications Research Service (JPRS) of the US Department of Commerce. The material in this section is derived from the JPRS version, 3rd printing, February 1968, pp. 103–15.
19. *Japanese Military Administration in Indonesia*, pp. 114–15.
20. Ricklefs, *A History of Modern Indonesia Since c. 1200*, 4th ed., p. 238.
21. *Japanese Military Administration in Indonesia*, p. 107. The word "prematurely" is underlined in this document.
22. The eastern islands came under the Commander-in-Chief of the 2nd Southern

Expeditionary Fleet, who had his headquarters at Surabaya. Day-to-day affairs were in the hands of the Naval Civil Administration Office (Minseifu) headquartered in Makassar. Because the area under naval administration was generally poor and underdeveloped, the Japanese there were heavily dependent on Java for food, transport and labour. An Imperial Japanese Navy liaison office (Bukanfu) was set up in Jakarta in August 1942 under Rear Admiral Maeda Tadashi. For details of the Japanese liaison office and Japanese administration in the Navy regions, see "Interrogation of Rear Admiral Maeda Tadashi at Changi Gaol, Singapore Island, between 31st May and 14th June 1946."

23. Navy officers were working on the basis of a March 1942 order from the Ministry of the Navy that the occupation of areas under Navy administration "shall be directed toward their *permanent retention* under Japanese control." See Ooi Keat Gin, "Of 'Permanent Possession': Territories under the Imperial Japanese Navy", in *The Encyclopedia of Indonesia in the Pacific War*, edited by Peter Post, William H. Frederick, Iris Heidebrink and Shigeru Sato (henceforth *EIPW*) (Leiden: Brill, 2010), pp. 71–73. Italics added.

    The Imperial Japanese Navy's unrealistic conceit that it could gain permanent possession of key Outer Island territories was fatally compromised, as were Tokyo's wider war aims, when the US Navy inflicted a crippling defeat on the Japanese at the Battle of Midway in June 1942. The defeat came only three months after Japan had brought the Netherlands East Indies under its control.

24. Miyoshi Shunkichiro, "Jawa senryo gunsei kaikoroku" [Memoirs of the military administration of Java], 15 pts., *Kokusai Mondai* (April 1965 – January 1967), p. 66, cited in Theodore Friend, *The Blue-Eyed Enemy: Japan Against the West in Java and Luzon, 1942–1945* (Princeton, NJ: Princeton University Press, 1988), p. 106.

25. A translation of "Order No. 1 – Operation of Military Administration," can be found in JAVINT 3131/4, SEATIC Det. HQ 23 Ind Div, 1 Feb 46, NANL, 2.10.14, inv. 5185. This was the first public notice issued by the Japanese in Java. It had been prepared and printed in Taiwan and was posted up everywhere behind the advancing troops. Although Imamura had served in the Kwantung Army, he had a broader background than most other army officers. In 1918, he had been posted to London as a military attaché. A decade later, he served as a military attaché in British India. See "Hitoshi Imamura," Wikipedia (accessed April 15, 2009). Before World War II, few Japanese army officers visited Britain or the United States. See Spector, *Eagle Against the Sun*, p. 38. Imamura's chief of staff, Major General (later Lieutenant General) Okazaki Seizaburo, who doubled as the head of Military Administration, had worked in both London and Geneva and had commanded a garrison regiment in China in 1937–39. He was considered a liberal in army terms. See *EIPW*, p. 568.

26. Shigeru Sato, *War, Nationalism and Peasants: Java Under the Japanese Occupation 1942–1945* (Sydney: Allen & Unwin, 1994), pp. 22–24.
27. See Imamura, "Supplement", p. 2.
28. Written communication, Lieutenant General Sayidiman, 25 January 2020.
29. Mitsuo Nakamura, "General Imamura", p. 22.
30. Robert Cribb, *Historical Dictionary of Indonesia*, p. 221, from which this paragraph is in part drawn.
31. Ahmad Subardjo Djayadisurya, "An inside story of the Proclamation of Indonesian Independence, August 17, 1945", Part 4, *The Djakarta Times*, 4 July 1970.
32. Nakamura, "General Imamura", pp. 11–13, on which this paragraph is largely based.
33. *Imamura Hitoshi Taisho Kaikoroku*, pp. 146–47, cited in Nakamura, "General Imamura", pp. 10–12.
34. Nakamura, "General Imamura", pp. 13–19.
35. *Senshi Sosho 92. Nanseihomen Rikugun sakusen: Marei Ranin no boei* [War History Series, Volume 92. *Army Operations in the Southern Theatre: The Defense of Malaya and the Dutch East Indies*] (Tokyo: Asagumo Shimbunsha, 1976), p. 48.
36. Imamura, "Supplement", p. 2 (translation).
37. Miyamoto Shizuo, "Jawa shusen shori-ki" [An Account of the Cessation of Hostilities in Java], in *The Japanese Experience in Indonesia: Selected Memoirs of 1942–1945*, edited by Anthony Reid and Oki Akira, Monographs in International Studies, Southeast Asia Series, No. 72 (Athens, Ohio: Ohio University, 1986), p. 220. A more literal translation of *Jawa shusen shori-ki* is "An Account of the Management of the End of the War in Java".
38. Imamura, "Supplement", p. 2 (translation). Although self-serving in some respects, Imamura's statement captures well the Japanese dilemma.
39. Imamura, "Supplement", pp. 1–2. Imamura was "keenly expecting" that Java would be the chief target for an attack by US and Australian forces. He was concerned that Europeans would work in concert with any Allied force that landed in Java and that, at the time of such an attack, Indonesians would once again turn on Europeans.
40. The aim, he said, was to coordinate the administration and the military in the expectation of defence operations. See Nakamura, "General Imamura", p. 20. See also *Japanese Military Administration in Indonesia*, p. 109, which makes the point that the Japanese officials were needed owing to a shortage of trained Indonesian officials and the difficulty of employing Dutch and Eurasians.
41. Colonel Miyamoto Shizuo in an interview conducted by Yamaoka Yasuko on behalf of the author, 8 April 1999.
42. Although a number of Japanese interviewees spoke of their earlier service in

Taiwan, in no case did anyone refer to prior service in Korea, where Japanese rule was infinitely harsher than it was in Taiwan.

43. Kuroda Hidetoshi, *Gunsei* [Military Government] (Tokyo: Gakufu-shoin, 1952), pp. 82–83, 219, cited in Nakamura, "General Imamura", pp. 25–26.
44. Ibid.
45. Ricklefs, *A History of Modern Indonesia Since c. 1200*, 4th ed., p. 239.
46. For a good account of these events, see Hallett Abend, *My Life in China 1926–1941* (New York, NY: Harcourt Brace and Company, 1943), pp. 268–75.
47. "Miyamoto Shizuo no hanashi", pp. 195–217.
48. Soeharto, *My Thoughts*, p. 18.
49. See Soeharto, "*Watashi no Rirekisho*"; and Soeharto, *My Thoughts*, p. 18.
50. See Ching-chih Chen, "Police and Community Control Systems in the Empire", in *The Japanese Colonial Empire, 1895–1945*, edited by Ramon H. Myers and Mark R. Peattie (Princeton, NJ: Princeton University Press, 1984), p. 236.
51. Interview, Tsuchiya Kiso, 2 February 1999. Although the Japanese put great store by efficiency, both in Japan and in occupied territories such as Taiwan and Korea, the recruitment process used in Java shows anything but efficiency on the part of the Japanese, who were operating under wartime conditions and struggling with language problems.
52. Chen, "Police and Community Control Systems", p. 236.
53. Ibid., p. 237.
54. Soeharto, *Pikiran*, p. 22.
55. Benedict R. O'G. Anderson, *Java in a Time of Revolution: Occupation and Resistance, 1944–46* (Ithaca: Cornell University Press, 1972). Republished by Equinox Publishing, Jakarta and Singapore, 2006. This citation is from the Equinox edition, p. 31.
56. Ibid.
57. When asked in 1960 why the Japanese did not grant Islamic groups many of their demands, Abikusno Tjokrosujoso, an Islamic political leader, replied that the occupation government "was primarily interested in keeping things calm and manageable"; they were interested in the continuing production of war material. Daniel S. Lev, *Islamic Courts in Indonesia: A Study in the Political Bases of Legal Institutions* (Berkeley: University of California Press, 1972), p. 34.
58. In his memoirs, Soeharto claims that he enlisted in the volunteer army "soon after" he joined the police force. This is demonstrably untrue. According to a semi-authorized biography, Soeharto joined the police force on 1 November 1942. He remained in the police force until at least 8 October 1943, or very nearly a year. For details, see Soeharto, *My Thoughts*, p. 19, and Roeder, *The Smiling General*, p. 193.
59. Cribb, *Historical Dictionary*, pp. 375–76; Takashi Shiraishi, "A New Regime of

Order: The Origin of Modern Surveillance Politics in Indonesia", in *Southeast Asia over Three Generations: Essays Presented to Benedict R. O'G. Anderson*, edited by James T. Siegel and Audrey R. Kahin (Ithaca: Cornell University Southeast Asia Program Publications, 2003), pp. 47–74; and M. Oudang, *Perkembangan Kepolisian di Indonesia* (Jakarta: Mahabarata, 1952), pp. 15–17. Oudang, a Pembantu Komisaris Besar Polisi (Assistant Commissioner of Police) in 1952, married a sister of Madame Soeharto.

60. See Elsbeth Locher-Scholten, "State Violence and the Police in Colonial Indonesia Circa 1920: Exploration of a Theme", in *Roots of Violence in Indonesia: Contemporary Violence in Historical Perspective*, edited by Freek Colombijn and J. Thomas Lindblad (Leiden: KITLV Press, 2002), pp. 93–94; and Sidney Jones, Ronny Lihawa, Santiago Villaveces-Izquierdo and Ignatius Priambodo, "Reforming the Indonesian Police Mobile Brigade (BRIMOB)", Partnership for Governance Reform in Indonesia, 16 February 2004, p. 6, www.kemitraan.or.id. (accessed 2 October 2008).
61. Harry A. Poeze, "Political Intelligence in the Netherlands Indies", in *The Late Colonial State in Indonesia: Political and Economic Foundations of the Netherlands Indies, 1880–1942*, edited by Robert Cribb (Leiden: KITLV Press, 1994), pp. 230–31.
62. Takashi Shiraishi, "A New Regime of Order", p. 71.
63. *Japanese Military Administration in Indonesia*, pp. 138 and 177–78. For further details about the Japanese-run police force during the Occupation, see Oudang, *Perkembangan Kepolisian di Indonesia*, pp. 32–47.
64. *Japanese Military Administration in Indonesia*, pp. 122–23, 177. See also *Nihon Kenpei Seishi*, p. 1026.
65. Ibid.
66. *Japanese Military Administration in Indonesia*, p. 178. In October 1944, the Keimubu changed its name to Chianbu. According to another source the change was made in November 1944. See Hata Ikuhiko, ed., *Nanpo gunsei no kiko, kanbu gunsei-kan ichiran* [Japanese Military Administration of Southeast Asia 1941–45 Organization and Personnel] (Tokyo: Nanpogun Gunsei-shi Kenkyu Forum, 1998). According to the *Java Yearbook*, the Keimubu was created within the Military Administrator's Office (Gunseikanbu) in September 1942. On 1 November that year, police affairs were officially transferred from the Kenpeitai to the police. See *Jawa Nenkan* (*Java Yearbook*) (Jakarta: Jawa Shimbunsha, 1944), reprinted by Bibrio (Tokyo) in 1973, pp. 129–32. I am indebted to Bob Elson for passing on Sato Shigeru's partial summary of the entry in *Jawa Nenkan*.
67. It should be noted, however, that the Kenpeitai recruited heavily among Koreans and that some of the most sadistic Kenpei were Koreans.
68. Interview, Selo Soemardjan, Jakarta, 2 September 1997. According to a Japanese

naval source, Dutch officials and police authorities had been "dreaded ... and greatly abhorred by the Indonesians-at-large as the direct perpetrator [*sic*] of exploitations." See "Appreciation of Political Developments by Kaigun (Japanese Navy)", NIOD coll. 400, no. 581. This typed, five-page document, which is unsigned and undated, appears to have been written by Rear Admiral Maeda Tadashi, the head of the Japanese Navy liaison office in Jakarta. A handwritten entry at the top of the first page says, "*bp 26/9/1945 opgesteld door Maeda*" ["bp 26 September 1945, drawn up by Maeda"]. Professor Elson has questioned the claim that the Dutch police were deeply unpopular. Personal communication.

69. Interview, Selo Soemardjan, Jakarta, 2 September 1997.
70. Yogyakarta was the home of two important Indies-wide institutions: the Taman Siswa school system and the Muhammadiyah, the modernist Islamic social and educational organization.
71. Written communication, Tsuchiya Kiso, 29 May 2002. According to a post-war study, "the police strongly tended to be subservient to the Military Police." *Japanese Military Administration in Indonesia*, p. 180. Even within the army, the Kenpeitai cast a long shadow.
72. See Theodore Friend, "Hellcraft, Nostalgia, and Terror: Thoughts on Memoirs of the Kenpeitai in Wartime Indonesia", in *The Kenpeitai in Java and Sumatra (Selections from Nihon Kenpei Seishi),* translated by Barbara G. Shimer and Guy Hobbs (Ithaca: Cornell Modern Indonesia Project, Publication No. 65, 1986), p. 12; and Theodore Friend, *The Blue-Eyed Enemy: Japan Against the West in Java and Luzon, 1942–1945* (Princeton: Princeton University Press, 1988), p. 186.
73. Friend, "Hellcraft", p. 13.
74. Interview, Taniguchi Taketsugu, Tokyo, 1 February 1999. Taniguchi was a former chief of the Bogor Kenpeitai.
75. Interview, Selo Soemardjan, Jakarta, 2 September 1997.
76. Personal communication, Benedict Anderson.
77. Teramoto Masashi in an interview conducted by Yamaoka Yasuko on behalf of the author, Inba-mura, Chiba Prefecture, 12 February 1999.
78. Major General Sukotjo Tjokroatmodjo, personal communication, 18 August 2009. Sukotjo said that although the actions of former Kenpeiho NCOs had been abominable, "as soon as they became officers, they behaved themselves." On the other hand, non-commissioned CPM officers and soldiers had continued to torture people until "around '62-'63." The practice stopped at that time, Sukotjo claimed, due to the impact of new courses at the CPM training centre in Cimahi. Sukotjo interview, Jakarta, 23 February 2011. Sukotjo spent eight years (1956–64) at Cimahi, initially as an instructor, later as deputy commander.

79. For claims that *kenpeiho* in Blitar beat detainees, especially alleged Communists, as a matter of course, see Soeryana, "Blitar: The Changing of the Guard", translated and annotated by David Bourchier, in *Local Opposition and Underground Resistance to the Japanese in Java, 1942–1945*, edited by Anton Lucas, Monash University Papers on Southeast Asia, No. 13 (Clayton, Victoria: Centre of Southeast Asian Studies, 1986), pp. 283–87.

Significantly, the Indonesians who served in the Kenpeitai did not form a post-war association of former *kenpeiho*. This was due to an abiding repugnance in Indonesian society over the behaviour of the Japanese Military Police Corps. There were no such inhibitions among men who had served in the Japanese-sponsored volunteer defence force (Peta) and various other mass bodies set up by the Japanese. On the contrary, they were proud of their association with these institutions.

80. Sato, who was born in Miyagi Prefecture, north of Tokyo, in 1897, was one of the oldest detachment heads in the Kenpeitai. A man with a square face and a solitary manner, he had worked his way up from the rank of private but appears to have led a life that was irredeemably gloomy. According to Taniguchi Taketsugu, a former teacher who headed the Military Police detachment in Bogor (and who was afterwards sentenced to fifteen years in jail on war-crimes charges), Sato was an honest and affable officer who did not drink and who could often be found sitting cross-legged, "like people do when they meditate." Interview, Taniguchi Taketsugu, Tokyo, 1 February 1999. Taniguchi provided additional information about Sato on 5 September 2003. To Taniguchi, "he looked like a Buddha." But there was something about Sato that set him apart from his colleagues. "He was a little different—in a negative way, if I may say so—from the *buntaicho* [detachment commander] pattern. He was conservative and deeply serious."

Sato took up his appointment in April 1942, shortly after the Japanese landings on Java, and remained in the post for more than two years, at which time he was transferred to Solo. The Kenpeitai unit in Yogyakarta, which controlled subunits in Purworejo and Magelang, had a complement of thirty-three to thirty-five Japanese. Interview, former Major Nakano Kinichiro, 8 February 1999; interview Taniguchi Taketsugu, 5 September 2003, and written communication, Captain Kawano Teruaki, Military History Department, National Institute for Defense Studies, Tokyo, 21 February 1997, based on a conversation with Taniguchi Taketsugu. See also "Schema van de Plaatselijke K.P.T. [Kenpeitai] Djokdjakarta", NANL, 2.10.14, inv. 5192. Additional information about Sato's military career and trial was provided by Rolf Utermöhlen of NIOD. Written communication, 14 July 1997. NIOD staff have been unable to locate Sato's file. No fewer than 199 of the 538 Kenpei stationed in Java at the end of the war were convicted at the subsequent war-crimes trials in Jakarta. Forty received the death sentence. Only fifty-eight non-Kenpei soldiers were convicted from a pool of 20,000 regular army soldiers. See *The Kenpeitai in Java and Sumatra,* translators' preface, p. 17.

81. The charges related to the treatment Sato meted out to the Dutch governor of Yogyakarta, Lucien Adam, to members of the Roman Catholic clergy and to employees of the Gondang Lipuro sugar mill, as well as to his ruthlessness in investigating the wrecking of the railway in Tugu. In Surabaya, it was said, Sato did nothing to curb the excesses of his subordinates. Written communication, Rolf Utermöhlen, NIOD, 14 July 1997. For more on Adam's career, see Robson, *The Kraton*, p. 372.
82. Interview, Selo Soemardjan, Jakarta, 2 September 1997.
83. Ibid.
84. Ibid.
85. Written communication, Tsuchiya Kiso, 29 May 2002.
86. See "Interrogation of Lieutenant Onishi Kyutaro, Glodok Jail, Batavia, May 17, 1946", NANL, 2.10.14, inv. 5280. Theodore Friend notes that the "Japanese army in general and the Kenpeitai in particular tended to replicate Dutch fears about communism and Islam. They distrusted them both as blind faiths, fanatical and unpredictable" (Friend, *The Blue-Eyed Enemy*, p. 206, citing *Nihon Kenpei Seishi*, p. 1038). For most of his presidency, it might be added, Soeharto was to harbour an identical fear of communism on the left and political Islam on the right, which allowed him to claim, conveniently but somewhat implausibly, that he was a man of the political centre. Above all, the Kenpeitai had "supreme responsibility for army discipline." See Friend, *The Blue-Eyed Enemy*, pp. 186–87.
87. Interview, Teramoto Masashi, 12 February 1999.
88. Elise K. Tipton, *The Japanese Police State: The Tokko in Interwar Japan* (Honolulu: University of Hawai'i Press, 1990), p. 47.
89. Ibid., p. 48.
90. Ibid., pp. 48–49.
91. This elite unit had the mission of protecting the *kokutai*, Japan's ostensibly unique "national structure," through "the proper guidance of thought." Tipton, *The Japanese Police State*, p. 153. During the 1930s, the Tokko had dealt ruthlessly with left-wing and labour groups, while fighting a rearguard and increasingly unequal battle with the Kenpeitai, which was interfering more and more in civil police matters. Nor was Java spared the attentions of the Japanese political police. A Tokko division was set up in Jakarta, with a branch in Yogyakarta.

    The Kenpeitai had three divisions, namely, Tokko, Keimu (police affairs), and Shomu (general affairs.) Organizationally, the Kenpeitai belonged to the

Ministry of the Army (Rikugun-sho), while the police reported to the Minister of Internal Affairs (Naimu-sho). According to a former Kenpeitai officer who served in Java, in Japan the main task of the Kenpeitai's Tokko section was the control (*torishimari*) of spies (*choja*) and cabals (*inbodan*) from outside Japan. The Tokko section of the civil police, on the other hand, concentrated on identifying communists. However, in overseas territories such as Java, he said, the two groups had more or less the same function. Nevertheless, the Kenpeitai chief was higher than the police chief and could give orders to the latter. Taniguchi Taketsugu in a telephone interview with Yamaoka Yasuko on behalf of the author, 13 May 2003.

92. It has been argued that the Tokko drew its inspiration from Joseph Fouché, the former terrorist and intriguer who founded Napoleon's political police. See Tipton, *The Japanese Police State*, p. 45, citing Brian Chapman, *Police State* (New York: Praeger, 1970), pp. 27–29. However, as Umemori Naoyuki has shown, the Meiji government sent officials not only to European countries but also to British colonial East Asia and Southeast Asia (Hong Kong, Shanghai and Singapore) to research their police and prison systems. The institutions and practices of the Metropolitan Police Office were influenced by the practices of the British colonial police in several important aspects. See Umemori Naoyuki, "Modernization through Colonial Mediations: The Establishment of the Police and Prison System in Meiji Japan" (PhD dissertation, The University of Chicago, 2002), pp. 13–14.
93. Chen, "Police and Community Control Systems", p. 218.
94. Koizumi Saburo, 13 June 1999, in an interview conducted by Yamaoka Yasuko on behalf of the author.
95. Miyamoto Shizuo, 8 April 1999.
96. "The Japanese Occupation of the Netherlands Indies, prepared statement of K.A. de Weerd, Attorney-at-Law, Major RNIA, International Prosecution Section, Netherlands Division", November 1946. TNA: PRO WO 325/111, 75491, p. 39. Major Klaas de Weerd, who had practised law in East Java, Bali, Southeast Borneo [Kalimantan], and North Sumatra between 1929 and 1941, was a reserve officer in the KNIL. He spent the war as a POW in West Java.
97. "The Japanese Occupation of the Netherlands Indies, prepared statement of K.A. de Weerd", p. 39.
98. The strike force was set up in April 1944. For details, see Situs Brimob Polri, 0.1 Sejarah Brimob, http://brimobpolri.wordpress.com/sejarah-brimob/ (accessed 2 October 2008); M. Oudang, *Perkembangan Kepolisian di Indonesia*, pp. 46–47; and Jones et al., "Reforming the Indonesian Police Mobile Brigade (BRIMOB)", p. 6. The details in the main text about the Tokubetsu Keisatsutai arsenal and duties are from the Brimob Polri site.

A number of Indonesians who had earlier served in the KNIL joined either the regular civilian police force or the Tokubetsu Keisatsutai. One of them was R.M. Soerjosoerarso, an aristocrat from the Mangkunegaran court who had attended the Royal Military Academy (KMA) at Breda in the Netherlands and who would retire as a major general. In 1943–45 he was the deputy police chief in the Residency of Kedu, in Central Java. Another was A.J. Mokoginta, who had attended the KMA in Bandung and who retired as a lieutenant general.

99. The heavily armed mobile units of the Japanese-era Special Higher Police became, after the proclamation of independence in 1945, the Indonesian Special Police (Pasukan Polisi Istimewa), evolving, in 1946, into the Police Mobile Brigade (MOBRIG, later BRIMOB). To this day, BRIMOB is used primarily for military-type operations. It is not known whether the Polisi Istimewa and its successors inherited the unique and all-embracing powers of the Tokko section of the Japanese civilian police force or just those of its well-equipped mobile strike force. It has been suggested that today's BRIMOB is in some ways the direct heir of the NEI Veldpolitie; see Jones et al., "Reforming the Indonesian Police Mobile Brigade (BRIMOB)", p. 6. That is only partly true. While it is quite likely that the Dutch-era Field Police was, institutionally, a forebear of BRIMOB, in terms of police practices, the Japanese lineage appears to be of greater significance. The pre-war Field Police force was indeed well armed; but it was set up to deal with criminal activity. The Tokubetsu Keisatsutai was given combat training and, during the Revolution, Special Police units performed as well as normal army infantry units. In practice, BRIMOB traces its descent from the powerful and repressive Japanese-era Special Police Strike Force in much the same way that the Indonesian Army's Military Police Corps (CPM) traces its lineage back in some ways to both the Yugekitai, the Japanese-sponsored Special Guerrilla Force, and to the Kenpeitai.
100. Lieutenant General Purbo Suwondo, personal communication, 22 April 2009.
101. Soeharto, "Watashi no Rirekisho".
102. Interview, Tsuchiya Kiso, 2 February 1999. There must have been at least one Japanese secretary as well. As noted earlier, Tsuchiya was the senior Beppan officer in Yogyakarta at that time.
103. Soeharto, "Watashi no Rirekisho". As we have seen, Soeharto also mentioned this in his autobiography.
104. Lieutenant Colonel Uchida Takefumi, 12 February 1999, and 5 September 2003. A former judge of the Yokaichiba District Court in Chiba Prefecture, Uchida was the head of the police department in the Yogyakarta Princely Territory from April 1944 until the end of the war, having succeeded Takeoka Kenji. Uchida was not aware in 1999 that Soeharto had once worked as a policeman in Yogyakarta. Nor did Takeoka, whom Uchida met for the first time at post-war gatherings of the Jawa no kai (Java Society), ever mention

Soeharto's name. Former civilian police officers, most of whom had served in Taiwan, were given military rank before they took up their new positions in the civilian police force in Java. The interviews with Colonel Uchida were conducted by Yamaoka Yasuko on behalf of the author. I am indebted to Yasuko for her help in establishing the police chain of command in Yogyakarta at this time.

105. Other major police stations were in towns such as Wates and Wonosari.
106. According to Tsuchiya, "Soeharto was a policeman [*keisatsukan*] working under the Japanese police station commander [*keisatsu shocho*]."
107. The details of Okamoto's career come from the 12 February 1999, interview with Uchida Takefumi.
108. Chen, "Police and Community Control Systems", p. 238.
109. George Orwell, "Shooting an Elephant", in *The Collected Essays, Journalism and Letters of George Orwell*, Vol. I, *An Age Like This, 1920–1940* (Harmondsworth, England: Penguin, 1970), p. 266.
110. *Jawa Nenkan*, pp. 129–32.
111. Elson writes that Soeharto carried out his police duties "apparently at the rank of *keibuho*." Elson, *Suharto*, p. 9.
112. Strictly speaking, there were eight police ranks after July 1943: *keishi* (superintendent), *keibu* (inspector), *keibuho* (assistant inspector) (grade one and two), *junsabucho* (sergeant) and *junsa* (policeman) (grade one, two and three). *Jawa Nenkan*, pp. 129–32. According to Taniguchi Taketsugu, the civilian police ranks were as follows: *keishisokan* (superintendent general), *keishikan* (superintent supervisor), *keishicho* (chief superintendent), *keishisei* (senior superintendent), *keishi* (superintendent), *keibu* (police inspector), *keibuho* (assistant police inspector), *junsabucho* (police sergeant), *junsacho* (senior policeman) and *junsa* (policeman). The *keishisokan* position only ever existed in Tokyo. Written communication, Taniguchi Taketsugu, November 1997. This footnote draws also on a written communication from Kawano Teruaki, 21 February 1997. In the Netherlands Indies there had been some twenty police ranks.
113. Tipton, *The Japanese Police State*, pp. 98–100.
114. *Jawa Nenkan*, pp. 129–32.
115. These rates were set out in regulations issued on 1 July 1943. See *Genchi Min Shokuin Jinji Jimu Teiyo*, pp. 3–14.
116. Koizumi Saburo interview, 13 June 1999. During his time as chief of the Special Higher Police section in Yogyakarta, Koizumi worked closely with Soedarsono. Soeharto would be ordered to arrest Soedarsono at the time of the 3 July Affair in 1946. In some ways, it is true, Soedarsono was an exception to the rule when it came to education; he had attended only a Dutch medium primary school (HIS) set up for children of the indigenous elite. Another

man, who went even further, was a Javanese officer who, it is said, was also named Soeharto. According to a former Japanese chief of police in the Princely Territory of Yogyakarta, there was "a very capable Indonesian police officer everyone called Soeharto *Keibu* (Inspector Soeharto), who worked in the Yogya police station." However, this was "definitely not the same Soeharto who later became the president, for he was at that time already thirty-seven to forty years old." Interview, Lieutenant Colonel Uchida Takefumi, 12 February 1999.

117. Interview, Taniguchi Taketsugu, Tokyo, 1 February 1999.
118. Interview, Teramoto Masashi, 12 February 1999.
119. Interview, Koizumi Saburo, 13 June 1999.
120. Interview, Tsuchiya Kiso, 2 February 1999.
121. There is evidence for this view in Roeder, *The Smiling General*. Roeder says (p. 96) that Soeharto enlisted as a volunteer "in the Japanese-sponsored police force, KEIBUHO." An official curriculum vitae published during Soeharto's presidency said that in 1942 Soeharto joined the "police (*Keibuho*) in Yogyakarta." See *Almanak "Antara," 78/79, Edisi Ke-III, 1978/1979* (Jakarta: Antara, nd.), p. 79. In his 1988 autobiography, Soeharto wrote that he saw an announcement that "*Keibuho*, the police" wanted new recruits (see Soeharto, *My Thoughts*, p. 18. On p. 22 of the Indonesian-language version, *Pikiran, Ucapan, dan Tindakan Saya*, Soeharto writes "*bahwa Keibuho, Polisi, menerima anggota baru*"). See also Hasja W. Bachtiar, *Siapa Dia?*, p. 341.
122. The documents are housed in the NIOD archive on Herengracht. Copies of some of these documents are also held at the Nationaal Archief in The Hague.
123. "Staff Beppan Isum for April. 30 April, 1943. Bandung branch of Beppan", JAVINT 3117/14, SEATIC Det. 23 Ind. Div., 28 Nov. 1945. NANL, 2.10.14, inv. 5197, p. 1.
124. Ibid., p. 2. The Japanese do not appear to have widely pushed these burial instructions, which would have produced a furore wherever they were introduced. Muslim dead should be buried with their faces towards Mecca.
125. "Staff Beppan Isum", April 1943.
126. Ibid. Japanese Army military brothels, or "comfort stations", were supervised by the Kenpeitai.
127. T.B. Simatupang, *The Fallacy of a Myth: Tracing the Experimental Significance of an Army Officer Belonging to the Generation of Liberator for the Future of Indonesia* (Translated and Introduced by Peter Suwarno) (Jakarta: Pustaka Sinar Harapan, 1996), p. 96. I have made one or two very minor changes to the wording given.

10. An armed force conjured out of nothing

1. Miyamoto, "Jawa shusen shori-ki", in *The Japanese Experience*, p. 220."
2. Interrogation of General Imamura Hitoshi, "Supplement", p. 1.
3. About half of the 45,000 British Indian troops who had surrendered in Singapore volunteered to join the INA within two months of its formation.

4. Created at the end of 1944, the Yugekitai was an undercover force designed to gather intelligence and conduct guerrilla operations behind the lines in the event of an Allied landing on Java. Six hundred recruits enrolled in January 1945 and a further 600 in July.
5. A Barisan Hizbullah training camp was officially opened in West Java on 18 February 1945. For details about Hizbullah, see "Statement by Capt. YANAGAWA, dated 14 Dec 1945", Javint 3132/2, SEATIC Det., GSI, 23 Ind Div., 15 Jan 45," NANL, 2.10.14, inv. 5190. The twenty-one-page Yanagawa "Statement," which contains invaluable details about the establishment and training of Peta, the Yugekitai and Hizbullah, is in three parts: Part I (8 pp.), Part II (9 pp.), and Part III (4 pp.). A three-page attachment gives an account of Yanagawa's actions after the Japanese surrender. Page 1 of Part II of the "Statement" is missing from the file held at the Nationaal Archief. However, Part II of the "Statement" can be found in the NIOD Indische Collectie. See "Translation of statement by Capt Yanagawa Munenari [sic], dated 14 Dec 45. (Continued)." NIOD coll. 400, no. 601B. In the "Statement", the translator has erred in rendering Yanagawa's given name as "Munenari", a common mistake. It should be Yanagawa Motoshige. The same error appears in Joyce C. Lebra, *Japanese-Trained Armies in Southeast Asia: Independence and Volunteer Forces in World War II* (Singapore: Heinemann, 1977); and in Mitsuo Nakamura, "General Imamura and the Early Period of Japanese Occupation", pp. 1–26. Masashi Nishihara, *The Japanese and Sukarno's Indonesia: Tokyo-Jakarta Relations, 1951–1966* (Honolulu: University Press of Hawaii, 1976), refers throughout to Yanagawa Tomoshige, although this may be a typographical error.
6. "Intelligence in the New Japan", CIA website, www.cia.gov/library/center-for-the-study-of-intelligence/kent-csi/docs/v07i3a01p_0005.htm, pp. 5–6, on which this and the following two sentences are based (accessed 20 September 2007). *Tokumu* means "special task". *Kikan* is "organization" or "system".
7. Written communication, Tsuchiya Kiso, 29 May 2002.
8. Lieutenant General Fujiwara Iwaichi, interviewed by Ruth McVey, Kyoto, 16 October 1980, McVey Archive, and Tsuchiya Kiso, in an interview with the present writer, 2 February 1999. I am indebted to Ruth McVey for permission to copy and cite her interviews with Fujiwara, Yanagawa Motoshige, Tsuchiya Kiso, Togashi Tomoshige and Yoshitake Chikao, among many others. The characters used in Japanese names can sometimes be read in more than one way. When Yanagawa, who had worked closely with Togashi during the early part of the occupation, referred to him a number of times in his 14 December 1945, "statement", Allied interrogators took the name down as Togashi Takeomi. Taketomi is another possibility. For details see Togashi interview with Ruth McVey, October 1980, and "Statement by Capt. YANAGAWA, dated 14 Dec 1945", Javint 3132/2, SEATIC Det., GSI, 23 Ind Div., 15 Jan 46." NANL, 2.10.14, inv. 5190, p. 2.

9. See, for example, Lebra, *Japanese-Trained Armies in Southeast Asia*, p. 6.
10. Written communication, Tsuchiya Kiso, 20 August 2002. The transformation from *han* to *pan* is explained by phonetics.
11. Written communication, Tsuchiya Kiso, 29 May 2002. Kokubu was chief of staff from May (some sources say June) 1943 to November 1944.
12. Colonel Miyamoto Shizuo, in a reply to written questions from the author, 25 May 1999. See also "Miyamoto Shizuo no hanashi" [Miyamoto Shizuo's Story], the last four chapters of Ara Kenichi, *Jakaruta yoakemae: Indonesia dokuritsu ni kaketa hitotachi* [Jakarta before the Dawn: Those Who Staked All on Indonesian Independence] (Tokyo: Keiso Shobo, 1994), pp. 195–217. In compiling this book, Ara interviewed four people, including Miyamoto, Kaneko Tomokazu and Zulkifli Lubis. He presented their stories in a first-person narrative style.
13. Kokubu later served under Tojo in the War Ministry.
14. "Written Statement of Kempeitai [*sic*] Capt. Yoshitake", Item 2047, Southeast Asia Translation and Interrogation Center (SEATIC) Intelligence Bulletin, No. 225, 4 January 1946, TNA/PRO WO 203/6303. The claim that Yoshitake was a member of the Kenpeitai is a glaring error; he was a member of Beppan. See also "Captain YOSHITAKE, The Beppan of the General Staff", Kantoor voor Japansche Zaken, Batavia, undated. NANL, 2.10.14, inv. 5300, p. 4. By the end of the war, Beppan appears to have had a staff of about 300 people.
15. Interrogation of Lieutenant Onishi Kyutaro, Glodok Prison, Batavia, 18 May 1946. NANL, 2.10.14, inv. 5280. Onishi, who was stationed in Java throughout the Japanese occupation, joined the Imperial Army as a private in 1919, transferring to the Kenpeitai two years later. In 1933, he was attached to the feared Kwantung Army Kenpeitai in Manchuria and reached the rank of warrant officer four years later. Between 1943 and 1945, he was attached to the Tokko (Special Higher Police) division of the Java Kenpeitai Headquarters in Jakarta. In the words of Captain Yoshitake, "Sometimes the Kempeitai misunderstood Special Section as if it was an organization to keep a check on Kempeitai. At times there was very bad feeling between the two organizations." "Written Statement of Kempeitai Capt. Yoshitake", pp. 12–13.
16. Written communication, Tsuchiya Kiso, 20 August 2002. Tsuchiya was the head of Beppan during the final stages of the war.
17. Kokubu may have been the "big boss" of Beppan, but Major Kuriya actually directed it. Although his name is usually given as Kuriya Tsugunori, Tsuchiya said that he and his colleagues in Beppan called him Jisuke. Written communication, Tsuchiya Kiso, 29 May 2002. Kuriya had served in Jakarta as a military attaché. Tsuchiya Kiso, in an interview with Ruth McVey, October 1980. See also Stephen C. Mercado, *The Shadow Warriors of Nakano: A History of the Imperial Japanese Army's Elite Intelligence School* (Washington, DC: Brassey's, 2002), p. 36.

18. The name is sometimes given as Marusaki.
19. Letter from Lt. Gen. Fujiwara Iwaichi to Col. Hugh Toye, 6 May 1982, pp. 2 and 6, McVey Archive, and Mercado, *The Shadow Warriors of Nakano*, p. 35.
20. Supported by a government-run company set up to finance intelligence operations, Maruzaki took lessons in Indonesian and Dutch and, as one writer put it, "generally had quite a good time," at least until December 1941, when he and other Japanese officials were interned by the Dutch following the attack on Pearl Harbor. Nugroho Notosusanto, *Tentara Peta Pada Jaman Pendudukan Jepang di Indonesia* [The Peta Army during the Japanese Occupation of Indonesia] (Jakarta: Gramedia, 1979), p. 59.
21. Ibid.
22. Ibid.
23. Tsuchiya Kiso, written communication, 29 May 2002. Beppan's task, another officer observed, was to "collect and properly arrange ... information on the movements of each race and the voice of the general population in the island." See Yoshitake "Statement", p. 4. To this end, Beppan's offices in Jakarta, Bandung, Yogyakarta and Surabaya compiled monthly reports for Sixteenth Army headquarters.
24. Tsuchiya Kiso, 29 May 2002. See also "Nakano agents and the Japanese forces in New Guinea, 1942–1945", www.thefreelibrary.com/Nakano+agents+and +the+Japanese+ forces+in+New+Guinea,+1942–1945–012316110 (accessed 21 September 2007); and www.thefreelibrary. com/Nakano+agents+and+the+Japanese+forces+in+New+Guinea%2c+1942–1945.-a0123162110 (accessed 4 August 2009).
25. Interview, Tsuchiya Kiso, 2 February 1999, and Tsuchiya Kiso, written communication, 29 May 2002.
26. Yanagawa "Statement", Pt I, p. 3.
27. Interview, Lieutenant General Purbo Suwondo, 15 September 1998.
28. Nugroho Notosusanto, "The Peta Army During the Japanese Occupation of Indonesia" (PhD dissertation, Universitas Indonesia, 1977), p. 97. Kuriya "thought that Indonesians would be less conspicuous than Japanese in Australia", especially as many Indonesians were in Australia with the Dutch. The aim was to assess the possibility of training Indonesians as "excellent suppliers of infm," to create "good observers along Jap[anese] army lines." Yanagawa "Statement", Pt I, p. 3.
29. Nugroho, "The Peta Army During the Japanese Occupation", pp. 97–98.
30. Yanagawa Motoshige in an interview with Ruth McVey, Jakarta, 13 November 1980.
31. Interview, Tsuchiya Kiso, Mishima, 2 February 1999.
32. Interview, Kaneko Tomokazu, Tokyo, 3 February 1999.
33. Interview, Taniguchi Taketsugu, Tokyo, 1 February 1999.
34. Interview, Lieutenant General Kemal Idris, Jakarta, 1 September 1998.

35. Interview, Lieutenant General Purbo Suwondo, Jakarta, 13 February 2000.
36. Interview, Purbo Suwondo, Jakarta, 1 September 1998.
37. Interview, Major General Moersjid, Jakarta, 29 April 1999. Ruth McVey, who interviewed Yanagawa in 1980, found him "an impressive old man, probably was a very impressive character for *pemudas* in the war." Ruth McVey's notes of an interview with Yanagawa, Jakarta, 13 November 1980. McVey Archive.
38. Lebra, *Japanese-Trained Armies in Southeast Asia*, pp. 7–8.
39. Yanagawa, 13 November 1980. For more details, see Yanagawa Motoshige, *Rikugun chohoin Yanagawa Chui* [Army Intelligence Officer First Lieutenant Yanagawa] (Tokyo: Sankei Shimbun, 1967). Yanagawa lived in Indonesia after the war.
40. "I never heard him say a word about Lawrence of Arabia," said Tsuchiya, who was one of Yanagawa's key army associates during the Japanese occupation of Java. "Nor can one find any such references in his book *Rikugun chohoin Yanagawa Chui*. However, when I met him in Jakarta in about 1970, I gained the impression that he was isolated from the Japanese community in Indonesia, which may have led him to a state of mind much like that of Lawrence of Arabia." Written communication, Tsuchiya Kiso, 29 May 2002. There are, in fact, two references to Lawrence of Arabia in Yanagawa's book. In one instance, he refers to Colonel Suzuki as the "Lawrence of Burma." In the other, he says, in effect, that the people of Indonesia should all become like Lawrence in order to win independence. This hardly proves that Yanagawa saw himself playing such a role in the early 1940s, but the possibility should not be discounted.
41. Lebra, *Japanese-Trained Armies in Southeast Asia*, p. 8.
42. Yanagawa is generally given the credit for establishing the *asrama*. Tsuchiya and Yoshitake believe this was not solely Yanagawa's achievement, but Maruzaki's too. Yanagawa, they feel, claims too much credit. Yanagawa was, however, the head of the *asrama*. Tsuchiya and Yoshitake in an interview with Ruth McVey, Osaka, October 1980.
43. Among those in the first intake were R.M. Jonosewojo Handayaningrat, Suprapto Sukawati, Zulkifli Lubis, Daan Mogot, Kemal Idris, R. Hidajat Martaatmadja, Sroehardojo, Dr Sutjipto and Suprijadi, who was to lead a revolt against the Japanese in 1945. Sroehardojo was to serve later as a battalion commander under Soeharto. Among those in the second intake were R. Umar Wirahadikusumah, who would serve as Vice President (1983–88) under Soeharto, R. Achmad Kosasih, Kusnowibowo and Rukmito Hendraningrat. Morimoto, *Jawa boei giyugun-shi*, p. 52. According to Yanagawa, the recruits were mostly from Jakarta; about ten were from Surabaya, half a dozen from Central Java, and several from Bandung. Yanagawa "Statement", Part I, p. 4. According to Togashi, Beppan asked each *kabupaten* (regency) on Java to send

three or four people, who should be devout Muslims (*tegas Islam*). Togashi interview with Ruth McVey, October 1980.

44. Nugroho, "The Peta Army During the Japanese Occupation", p. 98.
45. Yanagawa "Statement", Part I, p. 3. In his book, Yanagawa writes that he took a warning from the case of Colonel Suzuki in Burma, who, "when he tried to redeem his promise to the BIA of independence, lost his position as head of the Minami Kikan." Yanagawa, *Rikugun chohoin Yanagawa Chui*, p. 112, cited in Lebra, *Japanese-Trained Armies in Southeast Asia*, p. 100. Yanagawa told Ruth McVey the same thing. When Suzuki had pushed for Burmese independence, he was "sent to Siberia," so Yanagawa decided he would keep his mouth shut and concentrate on training Indonesians to be ready for independence. Yanagawa in an interview with Ruth McVey, Jakarta, 13 November 1980.
46. Yanagawa "Statement", Pt I, p. 4.
47. Interview, Kaneko Tomokazu, Tokyo, 3 February 1999.
48. Kusnowibowo in an interview with Ruth McVey, Jakarta, 20 November 1980. Kusnowibowo served later as a senior officer in Bakin, the State Intelligence Coordinating Board. See also Yanagawa Motoshige, Jakarta, 13 November 1980.
49. Kusnowibowo, 20 November 1980.
50. "Statement" of Captain Tsuchiya Kiso, 3–8 March 1947, p. 3.
51. Yoshitake, "The Beppan of the General Staff", p. 3.
52. Lebra, *Japanese-Trained Armies in Southeast Asia*, p. 11, based on an interview with Inada.
53. Kanahele, "The Japanese Occupation of Indonesia," p. 119.
54. On 1 August 1943, Burma was declared officially independent. For details, see Robert H. Taylor, *General Ne Win: A Political Biography* (Singapore: Institute of Southeast Asian Studies, 2015), p. 56.
55. "Interrogation of Gunzoku Saito Shizuo on the Independence Movement in Java", Changi Jail, Singapore, 4 5 June 1946. NIOD coll. 400, no. 338, p. 1. Saito seems to have erred when he told Allied interrogators that this order was passed down via Lieutenant General Itagaki Seishiro, the commander of the Seventh Area Army in Singapore. Itagaki did not take up that command until April 1945.
56. Miyamoto, "Jawa shusen shori-ki", p. 221.
57. Interview, Tsuchiya Kiso, 2 February 1999. See also Anderson, *Java in a Time of Revolution*, pp. 32, 420; Lebra, *Japanese-Trained Armies in Southeast Asia*, pp. 99–100; and Gatot Mangkupradja, "The Peta and My Relations with the Japanese", translated by Harumi Wanasita Evans and Ruth McVey, *Indonesia* 5 (April 1968): 105–34. Tsuchiya said that although Gatot's petition was a Beppan initiative, it gave expression to a widely held aspiration. Afterwards, "the whole of Indonesia flared up with hope that Japan would do something,

and many petitions came in from many islands, some written in blood." These were spontaneous, and "even when we said, 'We don't need any more petitions!' they kept pouring in."

58. Tsuchiya revealed this in a 1972 interview with Joyce Lebra. See Lebra, *Japanese-Trained Armies in Southeast Asia*, p. 99, n. 65.
59. The film was made by the Korean director Ho Yong (aka Hinatsu Eitaro and Hu Yung) under the direction of Major Kuriya and Captain Maruzaki. Wilfully misleading, it showed Australian prisoners of war living in "exemplary conditions". It was designed to "soften the Australian public for the anticipated Japanese invasion." For details see Yanagawa "Statement", 14 December 1945, Pt I, pp. 1 and 4; *The Encyclopedia of Indonesia in the Pacific War*, p. 509, and National Film and Sound Archives, Canberra, http://trove.nla.gov.au/work/34948415. For a description of this film and of the techniques used to produce it, see L. de Jong, *The Collapse of a Colonial Society: The Dutch in Indonesia during the Second World War* (Leiden: KITLV Press, 2002), p. 299.
60. Yanagawa "Statement", p. 5.
61. Kishi Koichi et al., eds., *Japanese Military Administration in Indonesia* (JPRS), p. 194.
62. Ibid., pp. 195–96.
63. "Explanations Regarding All Kinds of Armed Bodies", a document drawn up by the headquarters of the Sixteenth Army. NIOD coll. 400, no. 792. According to this document, in August 1945 there were nearly 25,000 *heiho* in the region of Java, 2,500 in the region of Timor and around 15,000 distributed in other parts of the eastern region, in Sumatra and in mainland Southeast Asia. These figures refer only to *heiho* under the command of the Sixteenth Army. Kaori Maekawa believes there may have been twice as many *heiho* as there were members of Peta, meaning more than 70,000 in all. See Kaori Maekawa, "The *Heiho* during the Japanese Occupation of Indonesia", in *Asian Labor in the Wartime Japanese Empire*, edited by Paul H. Kratoska (Singapore: Singapore University Press, 2006), p. 191. Although trained to fight, the *heiho* were used mainly as guards, drivers and labourers.
64. "Supplementary explanation of armed parties in Java under Japanese mil. adm.", in "Document taken from 16 Army HQ", NEFIS Document 2618, 14 November 1946, p. 4. NIOD coll. 400, no. 601A.
65. For details, see Lebra, *Japanese-Trained Armies in Southeast Asia*, p. 163.
66. A Japanese battalion normally comprised one thousand men, but the Sixteenth Army thought it would be hard to control 1,000-man Peta battalions and made them half that size instead. Interview, Colonel Miyamoto Shizuo, Tokyo, 4 February 1999.
67. There were sixty-six battalions on Java, with a total of 35,853 men, and three battalions on Bali, with 1,626 men. "Explanations Regarding All Kinds of

Armed Bodies", pp. 2–3. Nugroho says each battalion had about 535 members. Nugroho, "The Peta Army During the Japanese Occupation", p. 147.

Although Bali was administered by the Imperial Navy, it had insufficient men to defend the island against Allied attack. In 1944, Tokyo would order the Sixteenth Army to take charge of Bali's defence. When Captain Tsuchiya Kiso left for Bali to recruit and train three Balinese Peta battalions, he took with him seven young Indonesians who had performed exceptionally well on either the Seinen Dojo or the Bogor courses. The group included Zulkifli Lubis, Daan Mogot, Kemal Idris, Kusnowibowo and Sabirin Mochtar. Tsuchiya put Lubis in charge of the *daidancho* and *chudancho* cadets, while Mogot was responsible for training *shodancho*. Tsuchiya Kiso, written communication, 29 May 2002. The Japanese sent Kemal Idris to train the Peta battalion at Negara, while Daan Mogot was given responsibility for the unit at Tabanan and Zulkifli Lubis the one at Klungkung. Rosihan Anwar, Ramadhan, K.H., Ray Rizal and Din Madjid, *Kemal Idris: Bertarung Dalam Revolusi* (Jakarta: Sinar Harapan, 1996), p. 46. See also Dr R. Koestedjo, "Pengalaman-pengalaman sebagai dokter Peta di Bali", in Purbo S. Suwondo, ed., *Peta: Tentara Sukarela Pembela Tanah Air Di Jawa dan Sumatera 1942–1945* (Jakarta: Sinar Harapan, 1996), p. 117. The date in the title of this book is misleading; Peta was not established until 1943. For a valuable account of the Japanese occupation of Bali, see Geoffrey Robinson, *The Dark Side of Paradise: Political Violence in Bali* (Ithaca, New York: Cornell University Press, 1995), pp. 70–94. In later years, Kemal Idris would remember his time in Bali as "a golden period", when, in his off-duty hours, he made many Balinese friends. Sabam Siagian private communication, 19 November 2012.

68. "Dialog Presiden dengan mantan anggota Peta dan Giyu-gun", in *Peta: Tentara Sukarela Pembela Tanah Air Di Jawa dan Sumatera 1942–1945*, edited by Purbo Suwondo, p. 223.

69. After the war, Colonel Miyamoto asked General Kokubu whether he or other senior officers had had any concerns at all about Peta. Kokubu replied that he had had no such worries in the beginning because when Peta was first established the tide of war was going in Japan's favour. "But," wrote Miyamoto, "considering a case of the worst coming to the worst, they didn't put Peta under Sukarno's control but kept it in the hands of the Japanese staff officer in charge of operations [*sakusen sanbo*]." See "Miyamoto Shizuo no hanashi", pp. 195–217. Needless to say, this did not stop Sukarno claiming later that, "The [Japanese] High Command requested Sukarno's help in attracting the proper candidates for officers .... I looked for young men whom I could control .... I singlehandedly proposed the future colonels and generals of our Republican Army back in the fall of 1943." *Sukarno: An Autobiography, As Told to Cindy Adams* (Hong Kong: Gunung Agung, 1966), pp. 186–87.

70. "Explanations Regarding All Kinds of Armed Bodies", p. 3.
71. "Supplementary explanation of armed parties in Java under Japanese mil. adm.", p. 5.
72. Miyamoto Shizuo, "Jawa shusen shori-ki", in *The Japanese Experience*, p. 221.
73. Yanagawa "Statement", Pt I, p. 7. According to Miyamoto, about five Japanese were attached to each battalion "as trainers." See Miyamoto Shizuo, "Jawa shusen shori-ki", p. 222. According to Nugroho Notosusanto, each *daidancho* had a *shidokan* (supervisor), usually a captain or first lieutenant, who advised him how to run his battalion. The *shidokan* was assisted by several subordinate officers, who advised the *chudanchos* and the *shodanchos*. There were also Japanese noncommissioned officers who helped supervise the sections. Nugroho Notosusanto, "The Peta Army in Indonesia 1943–1945", in *Japan in Asia*, edited by William H. Newell (Singapore: Singapore University Press, 1981), p. 40.
74. Yanagawa "Statement", Pt I, p. 6. The figures vary somewhat. Morimoto says there were 33 *daidanchos*, about 140 *chudanchos*, and approximately 600 *shodanchos*, 200 each from East, West and Central Java. Morimoto Takeshi, *Jawa boei giyugun-shi*, pp. 86–87. Yanagawa gave a figure of 34 *daidanchos*. An Indonesian *daidancho* was the equivalent, on paper, of a Japanese Army *daitaicho*, who carried the rank of major. A *chudancho* was the equivalent of a *chutaicho*, who was a captain. A *shodancho* was the equivalent of a *shotaicho*, who was usually a second lieutenant. However, the ranks of major, captain and second lieutenant were not awarded in the Peta.
75. For details, see *EIPW*, p. 568.
76. Among the others recruited in Central Java, either in this or in the two subsequent Peta intakes, were Sudirman, the future *panglima besar* (supreme commander) of the Indonesian National Army; five future army chiefs of staff (G.P.H. Djatikusumo, Bambang Sugeng, Achmad Yani, Widodo and Surono), as well as Gatot Subroto, a future deputy army chief of staff; Sarwo Edhie, a future commander of the elite red beret unit, and Sarbini, a future commander of the East Java (Brawijaya) and Central Java (Diponegoro) military regions and a cabinet minister between 1964 and 1971. It does not follow, however, that Tsuchiya recruited all these officers. For one thing, he was responsible only for the first intake from Central Java; some of these men were in later intakes. For another, Banyumas, though part of Central Java, appears to have fallen within Yanagawa's West Java recruitment pool. Tsuchiya was unable to recall visiting Banyumas; he thought that that region, known for producing many good soldiers, may have been part of Yanagawa's zone. According to Kusnowibowo, it was. Yanagawa's 3rd Company, as Kusnowibowo remembered it, consisted of people from the second intake at Tangerang and from Jakarta, Banten and Banyumas. Kusnowibowo in an interview

with Ruth McVey, Jakarta, 20 November 1980. On the other hand, Brigadier General Soemyarsono thought that young men from "Solo, Banyumas, Yogya" were in Tsuchiya's training company, of which he was himself a member. K.R.M.T. Soemyarsono, telephone interview, 5 April 2001.

11. "The whole island was ablaze with enthusiasm"

1. Soeharto makes it clear that he was "advised" by his police superior to apply to join the defence force. Soeharto, "Watashi no rirekisho," Part 5, *Nihon Keizai Shimbun*, 6 January 1998.
2. That, at least, is what Tsuchiya Kiso, the Japanese army officer who recruited Soeharto that day, remembered him wearing. Soeharto, he felt certain, was not wearing his police uniform (Tsuchiya Kiso, personal communication). How reliable was Tsuchiya's memory, both on minor matters such as this and on matters of substance? In a series of interviews, and in subsequent correspondence, Tsuchiya came across as an intelligent, objective and honest man, proud in an understated way of the role that he and his Beppan colleagues had played in forging an Indonesian volunteer defence force, but with no wish to overstate the case or downplay negative aspects of the Japanese occupation or, indeed, his wartime disagreements with fellow Japanese officers. His memory proved to be excellent on matters of substance that are easily cross-checked. After the war, Tsuchiya was arrested by the Allies and interrogated at length. The detailed account he provided in 1999, when he was eighty-two, and over the next five years, is remarkably consistent with the account he gave Allied interrogators in 1945–47. It is in accordance, too, with the picture that emerges both from Morimoto Takeshi, *Jawa boei giyugun-shi* [History of the Java Volunteer Defence Force] (Tokyo: Ryukeishosha, 1992), the 783–page semi-official Japanese history of the volunteer force, and with the memories of a significant number of Indonesian officers who served in that corps. At the same time, Tsuchiya readily acknowledged in 1999 that he could not recall a great deal about Soeharto from 1943. He told Ruth McVey in 1980 that he really couldn't remember Soeharto. Ruth McVey, notes from interview with Tsuchiya Kiso, Osaka, October 1980. McVey archive. His 1980 claim appears to overstate the case somewhat, given the substantial evidence to the contrary.
3. Tsuchiya Kiso, written communication, 6 May 2003.
4. Ibid.
5. The Yogyakarta branch had one officer, one sergeant-major and three interpreters. Interviews, Tsuchiya Kiso, 2 February 1999 and March 2001; Tsuchiya Kiso, written communication 29 May 2002; "Interrogation of Captain Tsuchiya Kiso at Glodok Jail," Southeast Asia Translation and Interrogation Center, Intelligence Bulletin No. 228, 25 January 1946, p. 26, TNA:PRO WO

203/6306; and "VERKLARING. Afgelegd door: Kapitein TSUCHIYA Kiso (verbonden aan de Staf van de BEPPAN-NANSEITAI) gedurende verhoor afgenomen in de TJIPINANG-gevangenis te Meester-Cornelis (3-8 Maart 1947)." NIOD-IC, no. 006524–006535.

6. "Selection was to be made after strict screening of a large number of volunteers," a Japanese officer noted immediately after the war. "But as a matter of fact, urgency led to indiscriminate selection." "Document taken from 16 Army HQ," NEFIS Document 2618, 14 November 1946, NIOD IC No. 006501-006506, p. 3.
7. Using Yogyakarta as his base, Tsuchiya made day trips to most of the towns on his list but stayed overnight at one or two of the more distant locations, such as Pati and Bojonegoro. During his recruitment drive, he interviewed candidates in Yogyakarta, Magelang, Semarang, Solo, Madiun, Pati, Mojokerto, Bojonegoro, and, according to Morimoto Takeshi, Banyumas. As noted above, Banyumas does not appear to have been in the Central Java catchment area. If Yanagawa was in fact recruiting at Banyumas, which is well inside Central Java, then Tsuchiya was operating well inside East Java when he recruited at Bojonegoro. Equally, if Tsuchiya is referring in his list to the Mojokerto some thirty miles southwest of Surabaya, his travels would have taken him surprisingly deep inside East Java. Tsuchiya Kiso, written communication, 6 May 2003, and Morimoto, *Jawa boei giyugun-shi*, p. 84.
8. Interview, Tsuchiya Kiso, 2 February 1999.
9. Candidates of interest were asked to give their age, address and educational background, and to answer one or two other questions. They were also required to provide information about family members. Tsuchiya Kiso, written communication, 6 May 2003 and 16–17 September 2003.
10. The main consideration of the Japanese was that the candidates be reasonably literate; in 1943, illiteracy was widespread in Java. Officers had to be able to read and understand instructions, write reports, keep records and so on. Benedict Anderson, personal communication, 26 February 2009.
11. Tsuchiya Kiso, written communication, 6 May 2003.
12. Interview, Tsuchiya Kiso, 2 February 1999.
13. Ibid.
14. Ibid.
15. Yanagawa "Statement," Part I, p. 5.
16. Tsuchiya Kiso, written communication, 6 May 2003.
17. Interview, K.P.H. Haryasudirja, Jakarta, 9 February 2000.
18. Morimoto, *Jawa boei giyugun-shi*, p. 83.
19. Soeharto, *My Thoughts*, p. 19.
20. In his memoir in the *Nihon Keizai Shimbun*, Tsuchiya noted, "Soeharto said he hid the fact that he had once belonged to the Dutch army in order to be

admitted to the Peta. But we knew he had been there." Interview, Tsuchiya Kiso, 2 February 1999.

21. Interview, Tsuchiya Kiso, 2 February 1999. Lieutenant Colonel Miyamoto Shizuo, who was one of four staff officers responsible to the chief of staff of the Sixteenth Army, echoed those sentiments. Although he did not meet Soeharto at that time—"[Soeharto] was way, way down" in the hierarchy—he heard from his fellow officers before the end of the war that "Soeharto was so capable that he should be recruited even though he had been with the Dutch army." Interview, Colonel Miyamoto Shizuo, Tokyo, 4 February 1999. According to Taniguchi Taketsugu, the former Kenpeitai chief in Bogor, Soeharto's service in the KNIL was not something Soeharto needed to hide. "The Sixteenth Army," he said, "didn't take it as a big issue." Interview, Taniguchi Taketsugu, Tokyo, 1 February 1999. Six decades later, Tsuchiya was unaware that another of the men whom he, or possibly Yanagawa, recruited, Achmad Yani, had, like Soeharto, been a sergeant in the KNIL.
22. Interview, Tsuchiya Kiso, 2 February 1999.
23. Soeharto, "Watashi no Rirekisho".
24. Tsuchiya Kiso in a telephone conversation with Yamaoka Yasuko, 15 September 2003.
25. See Morimoto, *Jawa boei giyugun-shi*, p. 85. Yanagawa says the course opened on 22 October. See Yanagawa "Statement", Pt I, p. 5.
26. For the details, see Yanagawa "Statement", Pt I, p. 7. Morimoto gives slightly different, rounded figures. Morimoto, *Jawa boei giyugun-shi*, pp. 86–87. The 2nd Company, commanded by First Lieutenant Rokugawa Masami, had 220 cadets from East Java. Yanagawa was the commander of the 3rd Company, which had 246 cadets from West Java. The three *shodancho* training companies consisted of four sections (*kutai*), each with about fifty-five to sixty men. On paper, the commanding officer at Bogor was Colonel Uchino Uichi. But he was busy with other duties at Sixteenth Army Headquarters and the man who actually ran the centre and who personally trained the future Indonesian battalion and company commanders was the deputy commander, Captain Maruzaki. See Yanagawa "Statement", 14 December 1945, Pt 1, p. 6. Morimoto writes that First Lieutenant Ito Seiji was in charge of training the battalion commanders. According to Yanagawa, the East Java cadets were supervised by First Lieutenant Mutsukawa Masayoshi.
27. Anderson, *Java in a Time of Revolution*, pp. 20–21.
28. Written communication, Lieutenant General Purbo Suwondo, 1 March 2009.
29. This estimate was given by Purbo Suwondo, who has written extensively about the Peta. Personal communication, 8 July 2009. A well-regarded post-war Japanese study claimed that the volunteer force was centred around Muslim youth and oriented towards the exclusion of Dutch-educated youth and that

this was in distinct contrast to the way in which Dutch forces under the old regime were organized mainly among "Christianized Indonesians" such as Ambonese, Menadonese and Bataks. See *Japanese Military Administration in Indonesia*, a translation of *Indonesia ni Okeru Nihon Gunsei no Kenkyu*, p. 195. That observation is misleading. For one thing, as noted earlier the KNIL counted a greater number of non-Christian Javanese than is widely acknowledged. For another, the Japanese were not seeking to exclude Dutch-educated youth from the Peta, only those Indonesians who had received officer training under the Dutch, a proviso that at least one key Japanese recruiter was willing to ignore from the start. Finally, there never were many Bataks in the KNIL.

Harry Benda, working from incomplete data and admitting that his conclusions are tentative, appears to overstate the Islamic dimension. Discussing the Peta, he writes that, "Muslims played an outstanding role from the very beginning." The Indonesian officer corps, he adds, "contained a great number of *kiyai*. As far as can be ascertained, the new Indonesian military elite in effect drew its main strength from Muslim leaders and from members of the aristocracy." Muslims "soon occupied an important, and perhaps even a predominant, place" in the Peta officer corps. Benda, *The Crescent and the Rising Sun*, pp. 138–40.

While it is true that there were a number of devout Muslim battalion commanders in the Peta—including such men as Kasman Singodimedjo (a lawyer and former head of the Muhammadiyah in Jakarta) (Jakarta Daidan); Sudirman (a Cilacap schoolteacher who would be elected in 1945 as the supreme commander of the Indonesian Army) (Kroya Daidan); Iskandar Idris (Pekalongan Daidan); Mohammad Saleh (Yogyakarta Daidan); Moeljadi Djojomartono (Solo Daidan); Abdul Kadir (Gombong Daidan); Arudji Kartawinata (Cimahi Daidan), and Imam Sudjai'i (Malang Daidan)—the Islamic factor should not be exaggerated. It was in areas such as Banten, West Java, East Java and Madura, which tend to have a stronger association with Islam, that the Japanese were inclined to recruit Islamic teachers and Islamic social and political leaders as battalion commanders. An identification with Islam does not seem to have been disproportionately strong, at least in Central Java, among the *chudanchos*, and still less so among the *shodanchos*, who would go on to play such a significant role in the future national army.

30. Written communication, Major General Soetarto Sigit, 5 August 2000. As one Japanese document put it, the aim was to recruit "local influential persons with an intense racial spirit." See "Document taken from 16 Army HQ", p. 3. The word "racial" should perhaps have been translated as "nationalist". The central role of the *daidancho* "was to give moral leadership and exercise political supervision over their subordinates."
31. Interview, Colonel Soepardio, Bogor, 10 September 1998.

32. Interview, Lieutenant General Djatikusumo, Jakarta, 9 March 1981.
33. Nugroho Notosusanto, "The Peta Army During the Japanese Occupation", pp. 125–29, on which this section is based.
34. Ibid., p. 125. It seems unlikely that most of them were persuaded by members of Beppan, as Nugroho claims. According to Nugroho, those with a Muslim background were approached by Abdul Hamid Ono, the so-called Islamic expert in Beppan. Those with a non-Islamic background were approached by Yanagawa and his colleagues.
35. Ibid., p. 126.
36. Moersjid, "Pembawa Kenangan", in *Representing the Japanese Occupation of Indonesia: Personal Testimonies and Public Images in Indonesia, Japan, and the Netherlands*, edited by Remco Raben (Zwolle and Amsterdam: Waanders Publishers and Netherlands Institute for War Documentation, 1999), pp. 87–88. Moersjid, who had attended a Muhammadiyah elementary school, was sixteen and in the middle of his third year at a MULO junior high school when the Japanese came. In late 1942 he was selected to attend an officers course in Japan but his family objected. Instead, he joined the second Peta intake in Bogor. Interview, Major General Moersjid, Jakarta, 26 April 1999.
37. Nugroho, "The Peta Army", p. 128.
38. Cribb, *Historical Dictionary of Indonesia*, p. 228.
39. Nugroho, "The Peta Army", p. 128. Nugroho went on to become the head of the Indonesian Army history department. He was later appointed rector of the University of Indonesia and then Minister of Education under Soeharto.
40. Soegih Arto, *Indonesia & I* (Singapore: Times Books International, 1994), pp. 92–93.
41. Nugroho, "The Peta Army", p. 127.
42. Soeharto, "Watashi no Rirekisho."
43. Morimoto, *Jawa boei giyugun-shi*, p. 84.
44. Interview, Tsuchiya Kiso, 2 February 1999.
45. Interview, Lieutenant General Purbo Suwondo, 31 July 2002.
46. Princelings and other young aristocrats of the two royal courts of Solo were well represented in the Peta officer corps, with no fewer than ten signing up. The two royal courts of Yogyakarta were represented hardly at all, and what representation there was came from the Pakualaman.

    Four members of the Sunanate of Surakarta (Solo) joined—or, in one case, nearly joined—the Peta. They were G.P.H. Poerbonagoro, a Breda graduate and former KNIL officer who was to have joined a *daidancho* course, only to withdraw; G.P.H. Djatikusumo, a former cadet at the KNIL Reserve Officers Training Corps (CORO) in Bandung who became a *chudancho*; R.M. Subroto Kusmardjo, who became a Yugeki *shodancho*; and R.M. Sukandar Tjokronegoro, a *chudancho* who became a senior officer at TNI headquarters in Yogya. As we have seen, Djatikusumo had been offered a place at the Royal Military Academy in Breda. He had turned it down because, as an officer in the Dutch army, he would have had to swear an oath of loyalty to the Dutch Queen "and that is too difficult." Interview, Lieutenant General Djatikusumo, Jakarta, 9 March 1981.

Sukandar had been expelled from the HBS senior high school in Malang after a clash with a Dutch teacher who is said to have hated *pribumis*; he finished senior high school in Jakarta. Later, he took a ship to Japan, where he studied economics. When the war broke out, he joined a Japanese army officers' school and graduated as a first lieutenant (*chui*). He landed at Kragen, East Java, with the Japanese invasion force. When the Peta was established, he was transferred to that body as a *chudancho* and was posted to Bogor, where he served as a staff officer. He was later assigned to the Yugekitai in Malang, where he played an active role in forming the Untung Suropati Division. He became deputy chief of staff of the TNI under Lieutenant General Oerip Soemohardjo. He died, as did Oerip, in 1948.

Seven members of the Mangkunegaran joined the Peta. They were: the future Mangkunegoro VIII, K.P.H. Hamidjojo Saroso, who became a *chudancho*; his younger brother, K.P.H. Hamidjojo Santoso, who became a *shodancho*; and five grandsons of Mangkunegoro VI—R.M. Jonosewojo Handayaningrat ("Piet") (*shodancho*), R.M. Jono Hatmodjo ("Molly") (*shodancho*), R.M. Ronokusumo (Yugeki *shodancho* and later *chudancho*), R.M. Ronopuspito (Yugeki *shodancho*), and R.M. Ronopradopo (Yugeki *shodancho*). Written communication, Lieutenant General Purbo Suwondo, 20 May 2002, and *Siapa Dia?*, p. 155. I am not aware of any members of the Yogyakarta Kraton who became Peta officers. As far as I know, only one member of the Pakualaman, K.R.M.T. Soemyarsono, joined the Peta. Reflecting on this phenomenon, Djatikusumo said that one group of cadets had come from the *bangsawan* (nobility). "What is *bangsawan*? The bluebloods! The Tjakraningrats from Madura. Mangkunegoro, with his younger brother. And us. Not from Yogya! Very strange!" Asked why this was so, he replied, "I don't know!" Interview, Lieutenant General Djatikusumo, Jakarta, 9 March 1981.

47. By this time, it has been noted, the word *priyayi* was being used in such a loose manner that even a postal clerk could describe himself as low *priyayi*, allowing him to bask in the glow of a term still tinged with connotations of aristocracy. In the 1940s, there was not much of a nobility left on Java. Many of these *priyayi* were simply children of officials, "quite petty bourgeois but with typical aristocratic pretensions." Benedict Anderson, personal communication.
48. Interview, Lieutenant General Purbo Suwondo, Jakarta, 1 September 1998. Purbo's suggestion that 70 to 80 per cent of the *shodancho* cadets were from a

priyayi background fits broadly with the findings of a 1977 study. In a sample of 124 ex-Peta officers, Nugroho Notosusanto found that fifty-nine out of eighty-four of the *shodanchos* were from a *priyayi* background. However, thirty-eight of them were from the low *priyayi*, a category that included men whose fathers were train conductors, pawnshop keepers, and NCOs; nineteen were from the "middle" *priyayi* and two from the "grand" *priyayi*. There was one member of the nobility, and twenty-four commoners. See Nugroho, "The Peta Army During the Japanese Occupation", p. 122. According to Major General Moersjid, more than half the Peta platoon commanders were the sons of government officials. Interview, General Moersjid, Jakarta, 8 May 2000. Moersjid was a member of the second *shodancho* intake in 1944, together with Widodo, who later became Army Chief of Staff; Supardjo Rustam, who became Interior Minister; and Daryatmo, who became Speaker of the People's Deliberative Assembly (Majelis Permusyawaratan Rakyat, MPR). Some *shodancho* cadets were the sons of aristocrats and entitled to call themselves Raden Mas. Some others were the grandsons of aristocrats and in a position to call themselves Raden. Most chose not to use these titles as a gesture to the new spirit of egalitarianism that came with the revolution.

49. The correlation between social status and education was not automatic, of course. A man such as Djatikusumo, a son of Pakubuwono X of Solo, might have received a sound Dutch education, in Java and in the Netherlands. But many Kraton princelings had little education.
50. As noted earlier, the Dutch-run high schools were the HBS and the AMS. Under the Japanese, these schools were replaced by the Sekolah Menengah Tinggi (Higher Middle School), in which the language of instruction was Indonesian. Below that was the Sekolah Menengah Pertama (Lower Middle School), which replaced the MULO junior high schools.
51. A non-Western education was by no means an impediment to a successful post-war military career. Muchlas Rowi, a *pesantren* student who trained as a company commander, became a successful battalion commander in the post-war Untung Suropati Division in Malang. In the early 1950s he took private Dutch-language classes in the afternoons and evenings so that he would be able to attend lectures given by officers of the Dutch Military Mission. Muchlas Rowi retired as a major general.
52. Interviews, Lieutenant General Purbo Suwondo, 31 July 2002, and 8 July 2009. Almost all of the cadets had some knowledge of the Japanese language, the high-school students having studied it for two hours a day for the previous eighteen months.
53. Some of the Indonesians liked to say in later years that they had identified not with the white men in the books, as their Dutch school friends are said to have done, but with the Native American chief, a man "oppressed" by Europeans.

As it happens, the Germans themselves identified with Winnetou, who was seen by his creator as a "truly noble man." "Winnetou," the magazine *Der Spiegel* noted in 2006, "is the quintessential German national hero, a paragon of virtue, a nature freak, a romantic, a pacifist at heart, but in a world at war he is the best warrior, alert, strong, sure." See Michael Kimmelman, "In Germany, Wild for Winnetou", *New York Times*, 12 September 2007, www.nytimes.com/2007/09/12/arts/design/12karl.html (accessed 17 July 2009).

54. This sketch of the intellectual horizons of those who had reached senior high school and university is drawn from J.D. Legge, *Intellectuals and Nationalism in Indonesia: A Study of the Following Recruited by Sutan Sjahrir in Occupation Jakarta*, Monograph Series, Publication No. 68 (Ithaca: Cornell Modern Indonesia Project, 1988), pp. 76–77. Legge is writing about the young intellectuals associated with Sjahrir, a privileged, unique and well-educated group. But his study gives a sense of an intellectual environment that would not have been foreign to some Peta cadets, particularly those at the *chudancho* level.
55. Interview, Major General Moersjid, Jakarta, 8 May 2000. Moersjid, it is true, had some reason to dislike Soeharto. When Soeharto came to power, Moersjid was arrested and jailed for more than three years, with no charges ever filed. At the time, his only "crime" appeared to be his unswerving loyalty to President Sukarno. Moersjid and Soeharto had clashed on at least two occasions in the early 1960s, however. In 1961, when Moersjid was the Assistant for Operations and Soeharto the Commander of the Army General Reserve Corps (Caduad), Moersjid blocked Soeharto's attempts to have the battalions that had been earmarked for Caduad duties in the event of an emergency put under his immediate command. In 1962, when Soeharto, who was head of the Mandala command for the liberation of West New Guinea, sought to bypass both Moersjid, who was by then Deputy Chief of Staff of the Army for Operations, and Major General Soeprapto, the Deputy for Administration, Moersjid brought him into line.
56. Interview, Tsuchiya Kiso, 27 August 2001.
57. Ibid., and Morimoto, *Jawa boei giyugun-shi*, p. 89.
58. Interview, Purbo Suwondo, 14 April 1998.
59. Interview, Tsuchiya Kiso, 27 August 2001.

12. "Don't make them too strong!"

1. Morimoto, *Jawa boei giyugun-shi*, p. 85.
2. Nugroho, "The Peta Army During the Japanese Occupation", pp. 171–72.
3. Interview, Tsuchiya Kiso, 2 February 1999.
4. Ibid. See also Morimoto, *Jawa boei giyugun-shi*, p. 88.

5. Captain Yamazaki Hajime, who was later to head the Planning Department for the Guidance of the Java Volunteer Defence Force (Giyugun Shidobu), although formally he was only the number-three man in that organization, has left an example of how difficult it was to translate Japanese military texts into Indonesian: "It took almost a month before we agreed on the translation of such basic terms as *heishi* (soldier). We didn't want to use *soldaat* because it was Dutch, the enemy language. *Kesatria* sounded as archaic as *mononofu* in Japanese. After much discussion, we settled on *prajurit*. But even that didn't seem just right. *Prajurit* sounded a little outdated, like *samurai* in Japanese." Yamazaki Hajime, *Kita-ni minami-ni* [Northward, Southward] (published privately by Yamazaki in Takasaki, Gunma Prefecture, 1977), pp. 80–81.
6. Morimoto, *Jawa boei giyugun-shi*, p. 91.
7. See Spector, *Eagle Against the Sun*, p. 37.
8. Tsuchiya Kiso and Yoshitake Chikao in an interview with Ruth McVey, Osaka, October 1980.
9. Spector, *Eagle Against the Sun*, p. 37.
10. Alvin Coox and Saburo Hayashi, *Kogun: The Japanese Army in the Pacific War* (Quantico, VA: Marine Corps Association, 1959), p. 16; and Leonard A. Humphreys, "Crisis and Reaction: The Japanese Army in the 'Liberal' Twenties", *Armed Forces and Society* 5 (Fall 1978), pp. 173–77, cited in Spector, *Eagle Against the Sun*, p. 37.
11. Drea, *Japan's Imperial Army*, pp. 132–33.
12. Morimoto, *Jawa boei giyugun-shi*, p. 91.
13. Interview, Purbo Suwondo, 1 September 1998.
14. Interview, Tsuchiya Kiso, 2 February 1999.
15. Soeharto, "Watashi no Rirekisho". It is possible Soeharto did not begin *sumo* training until he returned to Bogor some five months later, when Yanagawa was the commanding officer.
16. Tsuchiya Kiso and Yoshitake Chikao, October 1980, on which this paragraph draws.
17. Morimoto, *Jawa boei giyugun-shi*, p. 89.
18. Interview, Tsuchiya Kiso, 2 February 1999.
19. Ibid.
20. Morimoto, *Jawa boei giyugun-shi*, p. 105.
21. Colonel (later Brigadier General) Francis Xavier Sardjono and Colonel (later Brigadier General) Brotohamidjojo in an interview with Benedict Anderson, Jakarta, 4 February 1964. Anderson made a note that Sardjono and Brotohamidjojo spoke of Yanagawa with "a good deal of fear and respect." Sardjono would prove to be Soeharto's best battalion commander during the 1945–49 Revolution.

22. Soeharto, "Watashi no Rirekisho".
23. Written communication, Tsuchiya Kiso, 15 February 1999.
24. Confidential Source One, November 15, 2004.
25. Soeharto, who set out on his first official trip abroad at 7:30 a.m. on the day after he had been sworn in as full president, went directly from the airport to the Imperial Palace, where he was received in audience by the Emperor. In what seems an odd omission, the published presidential diary makes no reference to any meetings with Hirohito. It does mention that on his next stopover, in Cambodia, Soeharto met Prince Sihanouk, who had stood down as King to become head of the government but who later resumed the role of Head of State. See G. Dwipayana and Nazaruddin Sjamsuddin, Team [sic] Dokumentasi Presiden RI, *Jejak Langkah Pak Harto, 28 Maret 1968–23 Maret 1973* (Jakarta: Citra Lamtoro Gung Persada, 1991), pp. 5–9.
26. Interview, Tsuchiya Kiso, February 2, 1999.
27. Before his visit to Japan, Soeharto had asked to meet Tsuchiya "to thank him for the service he gave during the war." *Japan Times*, May 26, 1968, quoting a Kyodo report. Tsuchiya, who was then fifty, said he remembered Soeharto as an alert man full of vigour.

    On a subsequent visit to Japan, in 1975, Soeharto was to meet five former second lieutenants—Kobayashi Yasuo, Urawa Shizuo, Fukuoka Masao, Nakamoto Yoshiyuki and Morimoto Takeshi—who had been instructors at Bogor in 1943–44. In the event, the Japanese Foreign Ministry invited only the first two men to a meeting with Soeharto at the Imperial Hotel. Fukuoka, "a very modest man" who had accompanied his former comrades to the hotel, waited in the next room when they went in to see the President. Hearing that he was there, Soeharto invited him to join them. Interview, Morimoto Takeshi, Tokorozawa, Saitama Prefecture, February 1, 1999, and *Mainichi Daily News*, July 9, 1975.
28. Tsuchiya Kiso and Yoshitake Chikao in an interview with Ruth McVey, October 1980. At the time of Soeharto's visit, Tsuchiya was working for the Nissan Motor Company.
29. Interview, Kaneko Tomokazu, Tokyo, 3 February 1999.
30. Morimoto, *Jawa boei giyugun-shi*, p. 90.
31. Interview, Purbo Suwondo, 1 September 1998.
32. Interview, Purbo Suwondo, 10 September 1998.
33. Morimoto, *Jawa boei giyugun-shi*, p. 90.
34. Ibid.
35. Interview, Purbo Suwondo, 4 April 1998.
36. Written communication, Tsuchiya Kiso, 21 January 1999.
37. Interview, Purbo Suwondo, 1 September 1998.
38. Written communication, Tsuchiya Kiso, 21 January 1999.

39. Morimoto, *Jawa boei giyugun-shi*, p. 91.
40. Interview, Tsuchiya Kiso, 2 February 1999.
41. Interview, Purbo Suwondo, 1 September 1998.
42. Morimoto, *Jawa boei giyugun-shi*, p. 119.
43. Interview, Major General Moersjid, Jakarta, 29 April 1999.
44. Interview, Purbo Suwondo, Jakarta, 1 September 1998. Purbo made the point, however, that his company commander, First Lieutenant Shindo Kazuma, a veteran of the war in China, did not slap his charges. Written communication, 1 March 2009.
45. Interview, General Widodo, Jakarta, 17 November 1981. Widodo was in the second intake at Bogor.
46. Interview, Moersjid, 8 May 2000.
47. Written communication, Tsuchiya Kiso, 21 January 1999.
48. Soeharto, "Watashi no Rirekisho".
49. Soeharto, *My Thoughts*, p. 20.
50. Soeharto, "Watashi no Rirekisho".
51. Ramadhan, K.H., *Soemitro: Dari Pangdam Mulawarman Sampai Pangkopkamtib* (Jakarta: Sinar Harapan, 1994), p. 35.
52. Interview, General Soemitro, Jakarta, 18 July 1981. Although Soemitro made an explicit link between his behaviour and his Japanese training, he was always ready to acknowledge that he had got into a lot of fights at school. Speaking once about General Benny Moerdani, Soemitro described him admiringly as "a fighting animal."
53. Interview, General A.H. Nasution, Jakarta, 7 July 1980.
54. Personal communication, General Benny Moerdani, Yogyakarta, 3 July 1980. In an interview four days later, General Nasution confirmed that Surono was inclined to hit people from time to time.
55. Interview, General Nasution, Jakarta, 2 March 1981.
56. Interview, Brigadier General K.R.M.T. Soemyarsono Prawirodiningrat, Jakarta, 2 February 2000.
57. Interviews, Colonel Alex Kawilarang, Jakarta, 25 July 1995 and 31 August 1998. Kawilarang, who was Soeharto's commanding officer, had gone to the docks to farewell the brigade. Seeing Soeharto strike Suparman, he shouted out to him to stop.
58. Robert Cribb, written communication, 1 June and 3 June 2020.
59. Freek Colombijn and J. Thomas Lindblad, eds., *Roots of Violence in Indonesia: Contemporary Violence in Historical Perspective* (Leiden: KITLV Press; and Singapore: Institute of Southeast Asian Studies, 2002), p. 1. For a valuable historical overview, see Schulte Nordholt, "A Genealogy of Violence", in *Roots of Violence*, pp. 33–61.
60. Interview, Nasution, Jakarta, 2 March 1981.

61. See Erwiza Erman, "Generalized Violence: A Case Study of the Ombilin Coal Mines, 1892–1996", in *Roots of Violence*, pp. 105–31, and Budi Agustono, "Violence on North Sumatra's Plantations", in *Roots of Violence*, pp. 133–41. It might be argued that Ombilin should not be cited as an example. It was an extreme. As Cribb notes, the hierarchical distance between guards and prisoners was much greater than that between overseers and labourers, which was in turn greater than that between NCOs and recruits. It is not clear whether the punishments on the North Sumatran estates were customary or whether they were one-off.
62. Henk Schulte Nordholt, written communication, 28 May 2020.
63. I am indebted to Robert Cribb for making this point.
64. Interview, Purbo Suwondo, 1 September 1998. *Buka* means subordinate. *Shoaku* means "to be in control of."
65. Interview, Tsuchiya Kiso, 12 June 2003.
66. Interview Morimoto Takeshi, Tokyo, 1 February 1999.
67. General Soemitro, personal communication. See also Ramadhan, K.H., *Soemitro: Dari Pangdam Mulawarman Sampai Pangkopkamtib*, p. 35.
68. Morimoto, Jawa boei giyugun-shi, p. 89.
69. Interview, Tsuchiya Kiso, 2 February 1999.
70. Morimoto, *Jawa boei giyugun-shi*, p. 92.
71. Interview, Tsuchiya Kiso, 2 February 1999.
72. Morimoto, *Jawa boei giyugun-shi*, p. 92.
73. Interview, Soemyarsono, Jakarta, 24 April 2000. This Soedjono is not to be confused with Sudjono Humardani, a Central Java financial affairs officer whom Soeharto came to know in the mid-1950s.
74. Two of the sixteen had reached technical college, two had reached teacher's college, and another two had reached senior high school.
75. Aristocratic families did not become Catholics, with a few rare exceptions. But two of Soeharto's five Catholic battalion commanders were from the court of the Pakualaman.
76. Interview, Dayino, Jakarta, 3 February 2000.
77. For details, see Imelda Bachtiar, ed., *Catatan Jenderal Pranoto Reksosamodra: Dari RTM Boedi Oetomo Sampai Nirbaya* (Jakarta: Kompas, 2014), p. 34. Before World War II, the Muhammadiyah worked hard to modernize Indonesian education.
78. Interview, Lieutenant General Sayidiman Suryohadiprojo, Jakarta, 8 January 2013.
79. Interview, Haryasudirja, 31 January 2000.
80. Soeharto, *My Thoughts*, p. 19.
81. Soeharto's claim has puzzled former Peta colleagues. Soemyarsono, who was in the same *shodancho* training platoon as Soeharto and Pranoto Reksosamodra, was adamant that there was only one Pranoto in that platoon: Pranoto

Reksosamodra. Interview, Soemyarsono, 23 February 2001. That claim is supported by Colonel Soepardio, the former deputy head of the Military History Division of the Indonesian Armed Forces. Written communication, Colonel Soepardio, 21 May 2002. Pranoto makes it clear in his memoirs that he was on the same *shodancho* course as Soeharto and that he went on to serve, as did Soeharto, as a platoon commander in the 1st Battalion in Wates. Later, he was on the same *chudancho* course as Soeharto. See Pranoto Reksosamodra, *Memoar Mayor Jenderal Raden Pranoto Reksosamodra* (Yogyakarta: Syarikat, 2002), pp. 58–59, and Bachtiar, ed., *Catatan Jenderal Pranoto Reksosamodra*, pp. 38–39.

82. In the 1960s and 1970s, Bardosono, by then a brigadier general, was given important positions both at Bina Graha, the presidential office block in Jakarta, and at the powerful Command for the Restoration of Security and Order (Kopkamtib), while doubling as the general chairman of the All-Indonesia Soccer Association. Bardosono's appointment to the latter job was to bring him national attention. Bardosono had been "handpicked by Soeharto [and] was also a practising mystic." See Hamish McDonald, *Suharto's Indonesia* (Melbourne: Fontana Books, 1980), p. 239. In 1977, during a soccer scandal in which Indonesian team managers allegedly paid bribes to opposing players during a preliminary World Cup regional tournament in Singapore, Bardosono returned to Jakarta "flourishing a Buddha statuette, which he claimed had been placed by the Thai team behind the Indonesian goal to exert a powerful attractive force on the ball."
83. Although Yani attended high school in West Java, he was from Banyumas in southwestern Central Java. As noted earlier, Banyumas appears to have come within the "catchment area" of Captain Yanagawa, who was responsible for recruiting and training officer cadets from West Java.
84. If, as seems likely, Yani was in Yanagawa's training company, then Sarwo Edhie may have been in that company too.
85. Interview Tsuchiya Kiso, 2 February 1999. Tsuchiya and Yoshitake made the same point in an interview with Ruth McVey in October 1980.
86. For details, see Muchsin Lubis, "Zulkifli Lubis, Komandan Intelijen Pertama di Indonesia", *Tempo*, 29 July 1989, reproduced in *M.E.M.O.A.R: Senarai Kiprah Sejarah, Diangkat dari Majalah TEMPO Buku Kedua* (Jakarta: Grafiti, 1993), pp. 37–42.
87. Tsuchiya Kiso in an interview with Ruth McVey, Osaka, October 1980.
88. Zulkifli Lubis in an interview with Ruth McVey, Jakarta, 11 November 1980.
89. Interview, Tsuchiya Kiso, 2 February 1999.
90. Ibid.
91. Interview, Soemyarsono, 2 February 2000.
92. Tsuchiya Kiso, 2 February 1999.
93. Ibid.

94. Written communication, Colonel Soepardio, 21 May 2002.
95. Morimoto, *Jawa boei giyugun-shi*, p. 94.
96. Ibid.
97. Ken'ichi Goto, *Tensions of Empire: Japan and Southeast Asia in the Colonial & Postcolonial World* (Athens, Ohio: Ohio University Press, 2003), p. 74. For a slightly different translation, see Ken'ichi Goto, "Indonesia during the Japanese Occupation", *EIPW*, pp. 40–41, and p. 532.
98. Morimoto, *Jawa boei giyugun-shi*, p. 95.
99. Tsuchiya interview, 2 February 1999.
100. Morimoto, *Jawa boei giyugun-shi*, p. 95.
101. Pamoe Rahardjo, ed., *Tentara Peta (Pembela Tanah Air): Mengawal Proklamasi 17 Agustus 1945 Mulai dari Rengasdengklok*, 2nd ed. (Jakarta: Peta Press, 1993), p. 71, and Purbo Suwono, personal communication, 24 July 2009. Nugroho says the *shodanchos* had two gold stripes on a field of blue. See Nugroho, "The Peta Army During the Japanese Occupation", p. 172.
102. Masui Tadashi in an interview with Ruth McVey, 26 June 1980. McVey Archives. In June 1980 Masui was counsellor at the Japanese Embassy in London.
103. Interview, Major General Moersjid, Jakarta, 8 May 2000.
104. Interview, Alwin Nurdin, Jakarta, 14 April 1998.
105. "Document taken from 16 Army HQ", p. 4. Some recruits, it is true, had found the training and the punishment impossibly hard, and had applied for a discharge. However, they were "talked into staying by strong persuasion." The Japanese reminded them of "the situation of their motherland" and of the heavy future responsibility of the younger generation. Morimoto, *Jawa boei giyugun-shi*, p. 89.
106. Harada was the commanding officer of the Sixteenth Army until April 1945. After the war, he was brought before an Australian war-crimes tribunal for his role in the summary execution of three Royal Australian Air Force flight sergeants at Tanjung Priok in February 1945. He was found guilty and hanged in 1947.
107. "Miyamoto Shizuo no hanashi", pp. 205–6.
108. "Supplementary explanation of armed parties in Java under Japanese mil. adm. (Condensed translation)," from "Document taken from 16 Army HQ", p. 2. "C-in-C" refers to "commander in chief."
109. "Miyamoto Shizuo no hanashi", p. 206. According to Tsuchiya, Miyamoto "did not understand Peta and totally distrusted it." Tsuchiya Kiso, written communication, 29 May 2002.

13. "Soeharto was a cautious man"

1. If General MacArthur's forces in Australia were to seize Timor, the Japanese reasoned, it would take "only one night" for them to reach Java. In view of

that, the Sixteenth Army had to be ready with sufficient force to defend the coastal regions of East Java. Looking back, Colonel Miyamoto said he should have realized, on his arrival in Java in April 1944, that there would be no counter-attack from Australia. Only in about March 1945, as the Americans moved on Okinawa, 350 miles southwest of Japan, did he and his fellow planners finally realize there would be no attack on Java from Australia. See Miyamoto, "Miyamoto Shizuo no hanashi", pp. 195–217.

2. Miyamoto, "Jawa shusen shori-ki", in *The Japanese Experience*, p. 230.
3. Interview, Morimoto Takeshi, 1 February 1999.
4. Japanese Beach Defences in South East Asia, Directorate of Combined Operations, Headquarters India Command, New Delhi, 11 April 1945, TNA: PRO WO 203/3671 58604. In early 1944, it is true, Japanese beach defences were not as elaborate as those recommended in the August 1944 "Essentials of Island Defence."
5. It has generally been thought that 200,000 to 500,000 *romusha* were put to work on military construction sites outside their own areas. See, for example, Anderson, *Java in a Time of Revolution*, p. 13; and Cribb, *Historical Dictionary*, p. 408. However, Sato Shigeru has argued that historians have tended to underestimate the magnitude of *romusha* recruitment because they have focused primarily on those who were sent overseas. Sato argues that the mobilization programme involved "many millions" of people. See Shigeru Sato, *War, Nationalism, and Peasants*, pp. 154–200.
6. See, for example, Nugroho Notosusanto, *The Revolt Against the Japanese of a Peta Battalion in Blitar, February 14, 1945* (Jakarta: Centre for Armed Forces History, Department of Defence and Security, 1974). This theme is emphasized in a diorama at the Peta Museum in the grounds of the former Peta training depot in Bogor.
7. Morimoto Takeshi, *Jawa boei giyugun-shi*, p. 397, and *Memoar Mayor Jenderal Raden Pranoto Reksosamodra*, p. 61. Pranoto, who was stationed for a time in Wates, said that after the Proclamation he became the secretary of former *daidancho* Sunjoyo Purbokusumo.
8. Kanahele, "The Japanese Occupation of Indonesia", p. 125.
9. Ibid.
10. Personal communication, Major General Sukotjo Tjokroatmodjo, Jakarta.
11. Kanahele, "The Japanese Occupation of Indonesia", p. 125.
12. Raden Sutomo, who was in charge of the battalion's financial affairs, was made chief of supply at the Defence Ministry in May 1946, with the rank of major general. Selo Adji, the commander of the 3rd Company, later became a regimental commander in Yogyakarta.
13. Yanagawa "Statement", Pt II, p. 4.
14. Ibid., pp. 3–4, and Morimoto, *Jawa boei giyugun-shi*, pp. 98 and 124. The figures

and dates given in these two accounts vary. Yanagawa told Allied interrogators there were 20 battalion commander cadets, 81 company commander cadets and 780 platoon commander cadets. The new intake of *shodancho* cadets, he said, began their training on 10 April, with the *chudancho* cadets starting on 10 May and the *daidancho* cadets on 10 June. All three training courses finished on 10 August. Morimoto writes that the company commanders course began on 1 April and ended on 10 August. If Morimoto is correct, Soeharto would have spent more than four months on the company commanders course, not three months. This would be in keeping with Soeharto's claim that the course lasted four months.

15. See *Memoar Mayor Jenderal Raden Pranoto Reksosamodra*, p. 59, and Bachtiar, ed., *Catatan Jenderal Pranoto Reksosamodra*, p. 38.
16. Tsuchiya Kiso and Yoshitake Chikao interview with Ruth McVey, Osaka, October 1980.
17. As part of the overhaul, the Training Centre (Renseitai) had been renamed the Education Corps (Kyoiku-tai).
18. Yanagawa "Statement", Pt II, p. 2.
19. Morimoto, *Jawa boei giyugun-shi*, pp. 102–3.
20. Ibid.
21. Written communication, Lieutenant General Purbo Suwondo, 9 March 2009.
22. According to one account, Yanagawa had taken back "photographic negatives plus research materials and reports." While in Japan, he made a vain attempt to find thirty Japanese "for secret-service work in Beppan in connection with Chinese affairs." Yanagawa "Statement", Pt II, p. 1. What Yanagawa actually took back, it seems clear, was his propaganda film "Calling Australia." Tsuchiya Kiso, written communication, 29 May 2002.
23. Interview, Tsuchiya Kiso, 2 February 1999. Yanagawa was promoted to captain on 1 December 1944. See Yanagawa "Statement", Pt II, p. 1. This promotion, said Tsuchiya, "led him to mistakenly believe that he was also number one among the Japanese living in Bogor. He became arrogant." Tsuchiya seems to have erred on the timing of Yanagawa's promotion, however. It came through the day *after* he completed his stint as the commanding officer at the Bogor centre—so any perceived arrogance cannot be attributed to that promotion.
24. See Yanagawa "Statement", Pt II, pp. 8–9. These differences centred mainly on the army's treatment of the ethnic Chinese community.
25. For details, see Yanagawa Motoshige, *Rikugun chohoin Yanagawa Chui*, pp. 146–56. In November 1944, it was decided that Maruzaki should return to Japan "owing to his illness." With his departure, Tsuchiya took over as the head of Beppan. The trouble-making Takagi was shunted off to the Peta battalion in Bojonegoro, East Java. See Yanagawa "Statement", Pt II, pp. 3 and 8. Maruzaki's illness cannot have been too serious. Back in Japan, he

was promoted to major and went to work in the Izumi (Spring) Unit, which was "to wage campaigns of assassination and terror against the Allied troops and Japanese collaborators." He was later transferred to Korea. Mercado, *The Shadow Warriors of Nakano*, pp. 127 and 160.

26. See Yanagawa "Statement", Pt I, p. 5, and Pt II, p. 4.
27. Morimoto, *Jawa boei giyugun-shi*, p. 127.
28. Morimoto interview, 1 February 1999. In his book, Morimoto says "it is assumed" that Soeharto attended the third company commanders' course, in September 1944. The assumption is incorrect. Indonesian colleagues insist he was a member of the second intake.
29. The Peta flag was designed on the basis that it should not resemble the Indonesian flag, should look similar to the Japanese military flag and should incorporate the Islamic crescent and star. Tsuchiya Kiso, personal communication. Benda has suggested that the aim was to express "the desired identification of Japan's war with a Holy War for the defence of Indonesian Islam against the Christian, imperialist West." See Benda, *The Crescent and the Rising Sun*, p. 141. Retired Peta officers claim that an Indonesian, Moetakat Hoerip, suggested a flag with twenty rays, reflecting the essence of Javanese philosophy and religion and a large star. What the Japanese produced was a flag with sixteen rays and a small star. Colonel Miyamoto is said to have confirmed that the sixteen rays represented the Japanese Sixteenth Army. See Purbo Suwondo, ed., *Peta: Tentara Sukarela Pembela Tanah Air Di Jawa dan Sumatera 1942–1945*, p. 223.
30. Nugroho, "The Peta Army During the Japanese Occupation", p. 134.
31. He had spent seventeen of his twenty-one months in the KNIL in training establishments and only four months on attachment to a battalion. He had spent five of his first ten months in the Peta in training establishments.
32. The disparities were somewhat less, of course, in the case of those platoon commanders who, like Soeharto, had also been selected for a company commanders' course, and in the case of those men who had begun their military training in 1944, when the courses were longer. But even here, Soeharto was a long way ahead; he still had more than four times as much training as the platoon or company commanders who had attended either a longer course or two separate courses.
33. Robert Ross Smith, *United States Army in World War II, The War in the Pacific: The Approach to the Philippines* (Washington, D.C.: Office of the Chief of Military History, Department of the Army, 1953), pp. 421–22.
34. Yanagawa "Statement", Pt II, p. 6.
35. Morimoto, *Jawa boei giyugun-shi*, p. 126. The course began on 21 August and wound up on 20 September. Yanagawa suggests it ran for about six weeks. See Yanagawa "Statement", Pt II, p. 5.

36. Miyamoto, "Jawa shusen shori-ki", in *The Japanese Experience*, p. 223. Colonel Miyamoto, it will be recalled, had arrived in Java in April 1944. At that time, he was staff officer in charge of supply (*koho sanbo*), with responsibility, inter alia, for distributing arms and munitions to the Peta battalions. By 1945 he had been promoted to staff officer for operations (*sakusen sanbo*), under Colonel Obana Yoshimasa, the senior staff officer (*kokyu sanbo*). As Obana was often ill, Miyamoto served, in effect, as the key planning officer of the Sixteenth Army. Miyamoto Shizuo, reply given in response to written questions from the author, 25 May 1999.
37. Miyamoto, "Jawa shusen shori-ki", in *The Japanese Experience*, p. 224.
38. Miyamoto, "Miyamoto Shizuo no hanashi", pp. 195–217.
39. Tsuchiya Kiso, in a telephone conversation with Yamaoka Yasuko on 19 June 1999, responding to questions submitted by the author.
40. For an account of Japanese thinking, see "Report of Interrogation of Tadashi Maeda, Rear-admiral, in Struiswijk jail near Batavia, on the 1st and 10th August 1946."
41. A week or so earlier, at the end of August, Tokyo had advised the Sixteenth Army that this declaration was to be made. See Item 1 of Javint 3134/3 of 4 March 1946. "Taken from Capt Nakamura Hiroshi. Table of stages in the realisation of the plan for an Indonesian Independence Movement, Item 1 of a file, dated 12 Dec 45, on 'Record of Progress of the Independence Movement', prepared by 16 Army Mil Adm." NIOD coll. 400, no. 594.
42. See Nishijima Shigetada, "The Independence Proclamation in Jakarta", in *Shogen: Indoneshia Dokuritsu Kakumei—Aru Kakumeika no Hansho* [Testimony: Indonesian Independence and Revolution—A Half Life History of a Revolutionary] (Tokyo: Shin Jimbutsu Orai-sha, 1975), pp. 186–221, in *The Japanese Experience in Indonesia*, pp. 303–4. See also Major General Nishimura, 10 April 1947, reply to questionnaire of A.P.M. Audretsch, Office of the Attorney General, Netherlands East Indies. NIOD coll. 400, no. 722, p. 9.
43. "Notification regarding the Measures Ensuing from the Proclamation of Admission of the Independence of the East Indies", 7 September 1944, NIOD no. 005913-14, cited in Friend, *The Blue-Eyed Enemy*, p. 108. It has not been possible to ascertain the new NIOD file number.
44. Miyamoto, "Jawa shusen shori-ki", in *The Japanese Experience*, p. 225. As noted earlier, the *heiho* were rear echelon troops (*koho butai*).
45. "Supplementary explanation of armed parties in Java under Japanese mil. adm.", in "Document taken from 16 Army HQ", p. 4. There is nothing to indicate who wrote this study. However, the sentiments expressed, not least the scepticism about the wisdom of relying on the Peta, suggest that the author could well have been Miyamoto.
46. "Document taken from 16 Army HQ", p. 4.

47. See "Explanations Regarding all Kinds of Armed Bodies", p. 5.
48. Written communication, Tsuchiya Kiso, 29 May 2002. In a similar vein, Purbo Suwondo said he and his fellow Peta officers in Malang did not hear anything about future motor transport, artillery or armoured units. Written communication, Lieutenant General Purbo Suwondo, 9 March 2009.
49. Yanagawa "Statement", Pt II, p. 6.
50. The full name of the organization, which, Yanagawa later said, "doesn't make sense deliberately," was Jawa Boei Giyugun Tokusetsu Yugekitai I Go Kinmutai (Special Guerrilla Force No. I Task Force). Interview, Morimoto Takeshi, 1 February 1999. The Yugekitai had no organic relation to the Peta but was established by and controlled by Beppan officers. Until the Allies landed, it was to concentrate on intelligence work. Personal communication, Purbo Suwondo, 5 March 2009. For further details about the Yugekitai, see "The Organization of the 'I GO' Task Force", Yanagawa "Statement", Pt III, pp. 1–4. See also Hasuda Tatsuo in an interview with Ruth McVey, Tokyo, 23 October 1980. McVey Archive.
51. Yanagawa "Statement", Pt II, p. 2, and interview, Purbo Suwondo, 1 September 1998. Yugekitai training was totally different from Peta training and in many ways more difficult. Yugeki were given automatic rifles and other arms and were trained especially for night action. They were taught not only how to use but also how to repair all kinds of weapons, and how to live on their own and make decisions individually rather than as a unit. They were trained in clandestine operations (*boryaku*) and in collecting information from *kampung* residents. Members of the force wore dark blue civilian clothing (the clothing was supposed to be black, but there was no black dye) and were allowed to grow their hair long, which helped them blend in with the population. (Yanagawa had a major fight about that with more senior officers before he got permission, "pointing out that it was unrealistic to require people who were going to melt into the countryside to crop their hair in the Japanese military fashion.") Because it was crucial to keep the Yugekitai a secret so that the Allies would not roll it up right away, its existence was not known to other units. Tsuchiya Kiso and Yoshitake Chikao in an interview with Ruth McVey, Osaka, October 1980, and Yanagawa interview with McVey, Jakarta, 13 November 1980. See also Yanagawa "Statement", Pt III, p. 3. Yanagawa, who took the most talented Indonesian officers who had trained in Tangerang and Bogor to act as instructors, ranked the Yugekitai as the best of the Japanese-trained Indonesian units. The West Java headquarters was in Lembang. The headquarters for Central Java was in Salatiga and the one for East Java in Malang. Some graduates of the third *shodancho* course were also recruited into the Yugekitai. According to Yanagawa, the Yugeki officers "were generally people of the education and status of schoolteachers."

52. There were 49 *shodancho* from West Java, and they went on to train 230 other young men from their home region. The figures for Central Java were about 52 and 180 and for East Java about 57 and 200. Yanagawa "Statement", Pt III, pp. 1–2. The Yugekitai officers were graduates of the Tangerang *asrama* or the Peta training courses in Bogor; those who were not, did not become more than NCO's. Tsuchiya Kiso in an interview with Ruth McVey, October 1980.
53. Interview, Tsuchiya Kiso, 19 June 1999.
54. The Japanese had their Planning Department for the Guidance of the Java Volunteer Defence Force (Giyugun Shidobu) in Jakarta. They also had two regional offices (Giyugun Shitsu) to take care of matters concerning the volunteer army, one attached to the Japanese forces in the eastern half of Java (Tobu boeitai), the other attached to the forces in the western part of the island (Seibu boeitai). But the growing size of the Peta was creating difficulties for the staff at the regional offices. It was also creating difficulties for the sections (Giyugun Gakari) in charge of the Peta in each of the various Japanese battalions. The fact that there were sixty-six Peta battalions on Java and only eight Japanese ones suggests that a typical Japanese battalion may have been responsible for about eight Peta battalions.
55. Morimoto, *Jawa boei giyugun-shi*, p. 232. Duties that had been covered by the Giyugun Shitsu and by the battalions' Giyugun Gakari were expanded, solidified and transferred to the Chikutai Shireibu.
56. Each Chikutai Shireibu consisted of six departments—general affairs, education, intelligence, weapons, finance and medical. Morimoto, *Jawa boei giyugun-shi*, p. 231. As such, they were responsible for the bookkeeping, distribution of food and weapons, training programme, and the relationship between the Japanese instructors attached to each battalion and the senior Indonesian officers in those battalions. Interview, Morimoto Takeshi, 1 February 1999.
57. Interview, Miyamoto Shizuo, Tokyo, 20 February 1999. For further details, see "Document taken from 16 Army HQ", p. 3.
58. On 17 May 1945, a fourth Chikutai Shireibu was created. With this, the number of battalions that each Shireibu was responsible for was reduced to between eleven and twenty-two.
59. Miyamoto interview, 20 February 1999.
60. Miyamoto, "Miyamoto Shizuo no hanashi", p. 206.
61. Morimoto, *Jawa boei giyugun-shi*, p. 231.
62. Written communication, Tsuchiya Kiso, 29 May 2002.
63. Interview, Morimoto, 1 February 1999. See also Soeharto, *My Thoughts*, p. 20.
64. Interview, Morimoto, 1 February 1999.
65. Interview, Tsuchiya Kiso, Mishima, 2 February 1999.
66. Interview, Colonel Soepardio, Jakarta, 10 September 1998.

67. Teramoto Masashi in an interview conducted by Yamaoka Yasuko on behalf of the author, Inba-mura, Chiba Prefecture, 12 February 1999. See also Morimoto, *Jawa boei giyugun-shi*, p. 234. Soeharto was, of course, a *chudancho*, not a *shodancho*, by this time. Responding to Teramoto's claim that he was astounded by Soeharto's rise to the presidency, Lieutenant General Purbo Suwondo not only hurried to the latter's defence but gave expression to a lingering resentment towards a certain kind of Japanese. The observation, he said, was a typically "arrogant and uncivilised statement of a low-class Japanese NCO vis-à-vis a better educated and higher-class Peta officer, still considered as a *genjumin* [native; a discriminatory Japanese word, like the Dutch *inlander*, for *pribumis*].... I think ... Pak Harto as president was much better than Prime Minister ... Tojo during the war." Purbo Suwondo, written communication, 9 March 2009.
68. Shigeru Sato, "The Peta", *EIPW*, p. 140.
69. *Jawa Shimbun*, 9 October 1944, quoted in *Japanese Military Administration in Indonesia* (JPRS), p. 196.
70. Lebra, *Japanese-Trained Armies in Southeast Asia*, p. 148, and Nugroho, "The Peta Army During the Japanese Occupation", p. 174. Junior officers were answerable only to their battalion commanders, and those battalion commanders, jealous of their rights and privileges, were sometimes unwilling to take much direction from Japanese liaison officers.
71. Nugroho Notosusanto, *The Peta Army During the Japanese Occupation of Indonesia* (Tokyo: Waseda University Press, 1979), p. 151, cited in Sato, *War, Nationalism and Peasants*, p. 262. It might be more accurate to say that in many areas the food allowance declined. There seem to have been no food-related problems, for example, for those serving in the Yugekitai in Malang, which was considered a prosperous area.
72. Sato, *War, Nationalism and Peasants*, p. 76.
73. Speech in Jakarta, 16 August 1944. See "Ir. Soekarno", a two-page typewritten document containing edited extracts from Sukarno's wartime speeches and broadcasts, p. 1. Dutch Government Information Service. NANL, 2.10.14, inv. 5509.
74. Interview, Selo Soemardjan, Jakarta, 2 September 1997.
75. Interview, Lieutenant General Kemal Idris, Jakarta, 8 September 1997.
76. For details, see *EIPW*, pp. 590–91, from which this account is taken.
77. Sato, *War, Nationalism and Peasants*, pp. 144–48.
78. Soeharto, "Watashi no Rirekisho".
79. Alan Groom, "Brief report on Life in Ambarawa Prison", Papers of Wg Cdr Thomas Stuart Tull, CBE, DSO, OBE (1914–1982). Tull Papers, 2/1, 1945 Sep 25–30. Liddell Hart Centre for Military Archives, King's College London.

80. "Statement written by [2nd Lt.] Shiroguchi, Kempei", 2 November 1945. NANL, 2.10.14, inv. 5291.
81. "Supplementary explanation of armed parties in Java under Japanese mil. adm. (Condensed translation)", in "Document taken from 16 Army HQ", p. 2.
82. For an account of the revolt and its aftermath, see Nugroho Notosusanto, *Tentara Peta Pada Jaman Pendudukan Jepang di Indonesia* (Jakarta: Gramedia, 1979); Nugroho Notosusanto, *The Revolt Against the Japanese of a Peta Battalion in Blitar, February 14, 1945* (Jakarta: Centre for Armed Forces History, Department of Defence and Security, 1974); Joyce C. Lebra, *Japanese-Trained Armies in Southeast Asia*, pp. 147–53; and Aiko Shiraishi, "The Anti-Japanese Revolt of the Peta Army in Blitar", *Southeast Asian Studies* 13, no. 4 (1976): 535–58.
83. Interview, Major General Sukotjo Tjokroatmodjo, Jakarta, 28 May 2009. Sukotjo's wife, Sri Koestijah Nunek Sukotjo, had been a good friend of Suprijadi before the war. Personal communication, Sri Koestijah, Jakarta, 18 August 2009, and Lieutenant General Purbo Suwondo, Jakarta, 8 March 2009. After the Blitar revolt, the Kenpeitai called in Koestijah's two sisters and threatened them in an attempt to extract information.
84. Personal communication, Sri Koestijah, 18 August 2009.
85. Interview, Sukotjo Tjokroatmodjo, 12 May 2009. According to another source, Suprijadi attended the MOSVIA in Jakarta. Interview, Colonel Soepardio, Bogor, 10 September 1998. Sukotjo appears to be a more reliable source on this point.
86. See "Zulkifli Lubis, Komandan Intelijen Pertama Indonesia", *Tempo*, 29 July 1989, pp. 54–55.
87. The claim that the Japanese killed Suprijadi's brother was made by Major General Sukotjo, Jakarta, 11 January 2013. A graduate of a Japanese-run Senior Seamanship School (Sekolah Pelayaran Tinggi, SPT), Haryono is said to have been beaten for insubordination while serving on a Japanese ship. Sukotjo said he was told of these matters by one of Suprijadi's younger half-brothers.
88. Lebra, *Japanese-Trained Armies*, p. 150.
89. See report by Captain Yamazaki Hajime, quoted in Miyamoto, "Jawa shusen shori-ki", p. 227.
90. One of the few officers not to join the revolt was the battalion commander, Surachmad, who had been the *wedana* (district chief) in Blitar under the Dutch. It has been claimed that Surachmad warned the Japanese military *shidokan* (supervising officer) that Suprijadi and his associates were planning to rebel. For details of that allegation, see Soeryana, "Blitar: The Changing of the Guard", in *Local Opposition and Underground Resistance to the Japanese in Java 1942–1945*, p. 307, and translator's footnote, pp. 320–21. See also Jacques Leclerc, "Afterword: The Masked Hero", in *Local Opposition and*

Underground Resistance, pp. 328–30. Former Peta officers confirm that Surachmad remained a *daidancho* until the end of the war, which might seem odd in the circumstances. But they reject the charge that Surachmad betrayed his own men by alerting the Japanese to the plot. The uprising, they argue, came as a surprise to the Japanese. They also reject the claim that Surachmad escaped punishment. They say that he was, in fact, beaten by the Japanese. Personal communication, Lieutenant General Purbo Suwondo, 8 August 2012, and Major General Soetarto Sigit, Jakarta, 14 January 2013. After the Proclamation, Surachmad became a TNI regimental commander in Kediri. It was a company from one of Surachmad's battalions that captured and shot the revolutionary leader Tan Malaka in 1949. For further details about the Blitar affair, see Soedianto Sastroatmodjo and Aboelkahar, *TKR Divisi VII Untung Suropati Malang-Besuki 1945–1948* (Malang: UM Press, 2000), pp. 42–48. According to Soeryana, whose name is sometimes given as "Soerjono", Surachmad had been a member of the pre-war Dutch political police.

91. *The Kenpeitai in Java and Sumatra* (Selections from *The Authentic History of the Kenpeitai* [Nihon Kenpei Seishi] by the National Federation of Kenpeitai Veterans' Associations [Zenkoku Kenyukai Rengokai Hensan Iinkai], translated by Barbara Gifford Shimer and Guy Hobbs (Ithaca: Cornell Modern Indonesia Project, Publication no. 65, Cornell University, 1986), p. 43.
92. See *Peta: Tentara Sukarela Pembela Tanah Air Di Jawa dan Sumatera 1942–1945*, p. 169, and Shiraishi, "The Anti-Japanese Revolt", p. 535.
93. Interview, Colonel Miyamoto, 4 February 1999.
94. Ibid.
95. This was the first and last operating order given to the Yugekitai.
96. "The Organization of 'I GO' Task Force", Yanagawa "Statement", Pt III, p. 3.
97. That, at least, is how the Indonesians tell the story. See Nugroho Notosusanto, *The Revolt Against the Japanese of a Peta Battalion in Blitar*, pp. 22–23.
98. Yanagawa told Allied interrogators after the war that the Japanese units sent to Blitar "failed to arrest the leader." According to Sukotjo, the Japanese admitted later that they captured and killed Suprijadi on the first day of the revolt. Yanagawa "Statement", 14 December 1945, Pt III, p. 3, and Sukotjo interview, Jakarta, June 29, 2010.
99. Miyamoto Shizuo, *Jawa shusen shori-ki*, p. 21. Translation by Yamaoka Yasuko. In *The Japanese Experience in Indonesia: Selected Memoirs of 1942–1945*, the translator has made a small but crucial mistake, failing to pick up "*haragamae ga dekihajimete ita*" in line 9 of p. 21 of the Miyamoto book. As a result, the phrase is translated there as "I *regarded* the Giyugun…."
100. See, for example, Nugroho Notosusanto, "The Peta Army During the Japanese

Occupation", p. 178; and Nugroho, *The Revolt Against the Japanese of a Peta Battalion in Blitar*, p. 13.

101. Miyamoto, *Jawa shusen shori-ki*, pp. 12–44, in *The Japanese Experience*, p. 227.
102. Ibid., p. 227.
103. The rape was mentioned by Yanagawa in a 1962 interview with Nugroho Notosusanto. See Nugroho, "The Peta Army During the Japanese Ocupation", p. 187. According to Colonel Miyamoto, Yanagawa subsequently reported that the Japanese man "had robbed a Giyugun officer of his girlfriend." See Miyamoto, *Jawa shusen shori-ki*, pp. 12–44, in *The Japanese Experience*, pp. 227–28.
104. This account is based on a report made by Captain Yanagawa. See Miyamoto, *Jawa shusen shori-ki*, in *The Japanese Experience in Indonesia*, pp. 227–28.
105. In April 1945, several sergeants in a Peta company at Gumilir, three miles north of Cilacap, attacked and killed a Japanese corporal. No Peta officers took part and the company commander, Toeloes Soebroto, who was away at the time, was spared. The Japanese asked Sudirman, the Peta battalion commander in Banyumas, to go to Gumilir, to help deal with the problem. Interview, Brigadier General Abimanyu, Jakarta, 7 March 1982. Abimanyu was a company commander in a nearby battalion.

    In mid-1945, the 1st Company of the 4th Battalion, which was guarding three hydroelectric plants in the area of Pangalengan, a mountain resort town to the south of Bandung, rebelled against two Japanese instructors attached to the company. Two platoons then made what is described as an abortive attempt to defect to the mountains. Subsequently, the Indonesian company sergeant-major struck a Japanese officer-instructor. Some time later, the Japanese officer slapped the company medic, "taking the already tense and emotional situation to its climax". Acting on orders from their company sergeant major, two Indonesians soldiers killed a certain Sergeant Hara and attempted to kill a Second Lieutenant Yamamoto. Yamamoto managed to escape by motorcycle. Retribution was swift and thorough. The Japanese beheaded an Indonesian officer, two NCOs and two soldiers. Others were tortured by the Kenpeitai. See Tim Perumus, "Peristiwa Pemberontakan Peta di Cileunca Pangalengan, Bandung Selatan, Jawa Barat", in *Peta: Tentara Sukarela Pembela Tanah Air Di Jawa dan Sumatera 1942–1945*, pp. 175–91, and Purbo S. Suwondo, "The genesis of the Indonesian National Army and some political implications". Paper prepared for a seminar at the Institute of Netherlands History and The Royal Society of Historians of the Netherlands at The Hague, 27–29 March 1996, p. 21. See also *Japanese Military Administration in Indonesia*, p. 205.
106. Interview, Major General Soetarto Sigit, Jakarta, 14 January 2013. Even so, this was to prove a tense and difficult time for Soetarto. Suprijadi's father was

married to a younger sister of Soetarto's mother. Suspecting that Soetarto was involved in the Blitar affair, the Kenpeitai in Ponorogo came to interrogate him. Soetarto was lucky: there were three Japanese officers stationed with his battalion; they liked him and spoke up for him.

107. Miyamoto, *Jawa shusen shori-ki*, pp. 12–44, in *The Japanese Experience*, p. 229.
108. Morimoto, *Jawa boei giyugun-shi*, p. 595. Brebeg may be a different spelling of Berbeg, a town about five miles south of Nganjuk.
109. Interview, Morimoto Takeshi, Tokyo, 1 February 1999.
110. Interview, Colonel Miyamoto, 20 February 1999. See also "Miyamoto no hanashi", pp. 195–217.
111. "Supplementary explanation of armed parties in Java", pp. 3–4.

14. "Why did they choose Soeharto?"

1. Soeharto, *My Thoughts*, p. 21.
2. Ibid.
3. Soeharto, "Watashi no Rirekisho".
4. According to Morimoto, Soeharto was put in charge of retraining the Second Company of the Blitar battalion. Interview, Morimoto Takeshi, 1 February 1999.
5. Interview, Morimoto, 1 February 1999.
6. Ibid.
7. Interview, Tsuchiya Kiso, 2 February 1999.
8. Interview Colonel Soepardio, Jakarta, 10 September 1998.
9. Ibid.
10. Colonel Soepardio, Jakarta, 10 September 1998, and Bachtiar, *Siapa Dia?*, pp. 214–15.
11. Ramadhan K.H., *Soemitro: Former Commander of Indonesian Security Apparatus* (Jakarta: Sinar Harapan, 1996), p. 113. During the New Order period, Imam Munandar rose to major general. He served as governor of Riau between 1980 and 1990.
12. Morimoto, *Jawa boei giyugun-shi*, p. 595.
13. Yanagawa "Statement", Pt III, p. 3.
14. *Japanese Military Administration in Indonesia*, p. 201.
15. Ibid. Yanagawa himself never seemed to work up much enthusiasm for Hizbullah. "I was rather busy with my own work in Bandung," he told Allied interrogators, "so I used to go to this training camp every other week."
16. Paul Ham, *Hiroshima Nagasaki* (Sydney: HarperCollins, 2011), pp. 57–61.
17. Spector, *Eagle Against the Sun*, pp. 504–5.
18. Drea, *Japan's Imperial Army*, p. 248, citing Japanese sources. Herbert Bix, the author of a major study of Emperor Hirohito, writes that an estimated 94,000 to 120,000 Japanese soldiers and 150,000 to 170,000 non-combatants were killed

at Okinawa. See Herbert P. Bix, *Hirohito and the Making of Modern Japan* (New York: HarperCollins, 2000), p. 485.

19. David McCullough, *Truman* (New York: Touchstone, 1992), p. 395.
20. Miyamoto, "Jawa shusen shori-ki", in *The Japanese Experience*, p. 230.
21. Shigeru Sato, "The Peta", *EIPW*, pp. 132–46, at p. 139.
22. Oba Sadao, "My Recollections of Indonesia, 1944–1947", paper presented at a symposium on Indonesia at the London School of Economics, 12 January 1979, p. 5.
23. Translation of interrogation of Vice (*sic*) Admiral Maeda Tadashi, Batavia, 9 November 1946, NIOD coll. 400, no. 718, and Shigeru Sato, "The Peta", *EIPW*, pp. 132–46, at p. 139. See also undated "translation of the Report of Maeda" that was made in reply to two questions put to him by Allied interrogators. NIOD coll. 400, no. 336. The two Maeda documents provide ample confirmation that the Japanese intended to fight in East Java as well as West Java, a development that has sometimes been ignored or glossed over. Maeda's rank is given incorrectly in the first of these documents: as noted earlier, he was a rear admiral.
24. Miyamoto, "Jawa shusen shori-ki", in *The Japanese Experience*, p. 230.
25. Ibid., pp. 230–31.
26. David Horner, *High Command: Australia's Struggle for an Independent War Strategy, 1939–1945*, 2nd ed. (St Leonards, New South Wales: Allen & Unwin, 1992), p. 395.
27. Miyamoto, "Jawa shusen shori-ki," in *The Japanese Experience*, p. 220; and "Miyamoto Shizuo no hanashi", pp. 195–217.
28. "Miyamoto Shizuo no hanashi", pp. 195–217; and Miyamoto, "Jawa shusen shori-ki", in *The Japanese Experience*, p. 231, from which much of the material in this and the following paragraph is drawn.
29. "Miyamoto Shizuo no hanashi", pp. 195–217.
30. The Japanese also had a factory that could produce 175 tons of gunpowder a month and 50,000 hand grenades. Miyamoto, "Jawa shusen shori-ki", in *The Japanese Experience*, pp. 231–32.
31. "Miyamoto Shizuo no hanashi", pp. 195–217.
32. There were another three Peta battalions on Bali.
33. See "Force Plan No. 3. 'Occupation of Java'. Joint Planning Staff, Headquarters, Supreme Allied Commander South East Asia, 5 September 1945". WO 203/5470. TNA: PRO.
34. Preface written by Vice Admiral Uekusa Nobushige in the book *Dai Sanjuichi Kaigun Kokutai no Ayumi* [The History of the 31st Naval Air Division] (Tokyo: San-ichi Kukai, Bunkyo-ku, 1960), p. 15.
35. Maeda interrogation, 31 May – 14 June 1946, p. 7.
36. The Supreme War Council, which had held its first meeting on 19 August

1944, brought together the service chiefs of staff, the Prime Minister and the War Minister. Drea, *Japan's Imperial Army*, pp. 240–41.

37. "To: Chiefs of Staff 2nd Southern Expeditionary Fleet and 10th Area Fleet. Information Resident Naval Officer Batavia [Rear Admiral Maeda]. From: Bureau of Military Affairs." 172127 July 1945. This signal was intercepted and read by code-breakers at the joint US Navy-Royal Australian Navy Fleet Radio Unit Melbourne (FRUMEL). For details, see "translated messages from FRUMEL records dealing with the genesis of Indonesian 'independence'" in "Translated [Imperial Japanese Navy] messages from FRUMEL records." Commonwealth Record Series B5555, Defence Signals Directorate, Translations of Cypher Messages, 1945–1946, National Archives of Australia, Victorian Archives Centre [hereafter: CRS B5555, DSD, TCM, 1945–1946, NAA, VAC], File No. 6, p. 6. This file is stamped "Top Secret". Others are stamped "Top Secret ULTRA." The Sixteenth Army received the same order from Tokyo, by way of Saigon and Singapore. The army was just about to "start" such a committee when Japan surrendered. See "Interrogation of Maj. Gen. Nishimura Otoshi", 31 May–6 June 1946, p. 4, and Nishimura, 10 April 1947, reply to questionnaire. From mid-1941, information gleaned from decrypts of high-grade Japanese Navy and Army codes, and from other sources, was given the codename "ULTRA".
38. The Southern Area Army had announced the planned formation of this committee four days earlier, on 3 August. See "Independence for the East Indies", 3 August 1945, message from Chief of Staff, 2nd Expeditionary Fleet, CRS B5555, DSD, TCM, 1945–46, NAA, VAC, File No. 6, p. 6(a).
39. Yamamoto Moichiro, "Watashi-no Indonesia: Dai Juroku Gun Jidai-no Kaiso" [My Indonesia: A Memoir on the Period of My Service in the Sixteenth Army] (Tokyo: Nihon-Indonesia Kyokai, 1979), p. 77, cited in Goto Ken'ichi, "Caught in the Middle: Japanese Attitudes toward Indonesian Independence in 1945", *Journal of Southeast Asian Studies* 27, no. 1 (1996): 37–48.
40. Major General Nishimura, 10 April 1947, reply to questionnaire, p. 15.
41. Nishimura interrogation, 31 May – 6 June 1946.
42. For a good account of the process, on which this section is based, see Nugroho, "The Peta Army During the Japanese Occupation", pp. 197–98.
43. Soeharto, *Pikiran*, p. 26; and Soeharto, "Watashi no Rirekisho", *Nihon Keizai Shimbun*, 1998.
44. Han Bing Siong, "The Indonesian Need of Arms after the Proclamation of Independence", *Bijdragen tot de Taal-, Land- en Volkenkunde* 157, no. 4 (2001), p. 807, fn. 16.
45. Hasuda Tatsuo in an interview with Ruth McVey, Tokyo, 23 October 1980, and Kusnowibowo in an interview with Ruth McVey, Jakarta, 20 November 1980.

46. The number of Peta officers is derived from figures given in the Yanagawa "Statement", Pt I, pp. 6–7; Pt II, pp. 3–6, and 8; Pt III, pp. 1–2.
47. Interview, Lieutenant General Purbo Suwondo, Jakarta, 14 April 1998.

Glossary and Abbreviations

1. In compiling the Glossary I have drawn on innumerable sources. But I am particularly indebted to formulations in Ben Anderson's *Java in a Time of Revolution* (1972), to Robert Cribb for his constantly helpful *Historical Dictionary of Indonesia* (1992), which he and Audrey Kahin subsequently updated, to William Frederick for his *Visions and Heat* (1988), to Niels Mulder, *Individual and Society in Java: A Cultural Analysis* (1989), to Peter Post and his fellow editors of *The Encyclopedia of Indonesia in the Pacific War* (2010) and to Merle Ricklefs for his painstaking dissection of many words and phrases, pertaining especially to Islam and to Javanese mystical beliefs, in *Islamisation and Its Opponents in Java* (2012). Like so many others, I have found the *Kamus Indonesia Inggris* by John M. Echols and Hassan Shadily indispensable.

Acknowledgements

In the course of writing this book I have incurred many debts. My paramount debt is to all those men and women, particularly in Indonesia, the Netherlands and Japan, who gave up their time to be interviewed, not only about former President Soeharto but also about developments in the Dutch East Indies during the late colonial period and the ensuing Japanese occupation. Many of the interviews, but by no means all, were with retired Indonesian army officers, men who were able to speak at length about Indonesian military politics in general and Soeharto in particular. To them and to all the others who agreed to be interviewed, so many of whom have since died, I wish to record my gratitude.

In Indonesia, I am particularly grateful to President Soeharto himself for granting me an interview soon after my arrival in Jakarta in 1969, and to his two immediate successors, President B.J. Habibie and President Abdurrahman Wahid, both of whom shed important light on Soeharto's early years and on his attitudes towards Islam. I wish to record as well my thanks to Siti Hartinah Soeharto, whom I also interviewed in 1969. Gen. A.H. Nasution, whom I met at around the same time, gave me, in long and revealing interviews over the next quarter of a century, an extraordinarily detailed account of modern Indonesian history and politics, as seen from a military perspective, as did Lt. Gen. T.B. Simatupang. Lt. Gen. Sayidiman Suryohadiprojo, who remains as alert and well informed as ever at ninety-two, has answered my many queries with inexhaustible patience and generosity. I count myself most fortunate to have been in close contact for the best part of twenty years with two retired Military Police officers, Maj. Gen. Sukotjo Tjokroatmodjo and Lt. Gen. Purbo Suwondo, whose help was greatly appreciated. I am grateful also to R. Darsono Notosudirdjo, Lt. Gen. G.P.H. Djatikusumo, K.P.H. Haryasudirja Sasraningrat, Brig. Gen. R.M. Jono Hatmodjo, Lt. Gen. Kemal Idris, Maj. Gen. Moersjid, Gen. Soemitro, Brig. Gen. K.R.M.T. Soemyarsono Prawirodiningrat, Maj. Gen. Soetarto Sigit, Maj. Gen. Achmad Sukendro and Col. Soepardio. Three members of the Center for Strategic and International Studies in Jakarta—Jusuf Wanandi (Liem Bian Kie), Harry Tjan Silalahi and Clara Joewono—have been exceptionally generous with their help for more than four decades.

At the same time, I am grateful for the friendship and help of many remarkable Indonesian journalists and editors, men and women with encyclopedic knowledge of their nation's history, politics, business, cultural, artistic, religious and social life, as well as an awareness of so much that goes on behind the curtain of everyday life. Among those to whom I owe particular debts, incurred over decades, are Rosihan Anwar, Fikri Jufri, Aristides Katoppo, Mochtar Lubis, Nono Anwar Makarim, Goenawan Mohamad and Sabam Siagian, all of whom had their newspapers or magazines shut down at one time or another, either by Sukarno or Soeharto. I am especially indebted to Sabam. A convivial companion and engaging raconteur, he encouraged me to push ahead with this project and provided invaluable support: insights, introductions, anecdotes and recollections, along with relevant books, articles, archive documents and photographs. I would also like to thank the editors of *Kompas* who, at Sabam's behest, kindly gave me access to hundreds of rare and precious photos from the Ipphos photo archive. Yuli Ismartono, a former foreign correspondent and senior editor at *Tempo*, has helped in innumerable ways. She and John McBeth were generous hosts in Jakarta.

Many other people in Indonesia have given up their time to talk to me or write to me about Soeharto and the world in which he lived and operated. Others have sent me books, papers and photographs. I am grateful to all of them and wish that I had the space to thank them more adequately than in the following list: Roeslan Abdulgani, Brig. Gen. Abimanyu, Brig. Gen. Mohamad Abdulkadir Besar, Toeti Adhitama, Ali (Alex) Alatas, Brig. Gen. Atwar Nurhadi, Joop Avé, Slamet Bratanata, Ali Budiardjo, Romo Daryatmo, Gen. Daryatmo, Dayino, Ny. Umi Dayino, Sumitro Djojohadikusumo, Joan Hardjono, Susilo Harjoprakoso, Brig. Gen. A.S. Hassan, Gen. Hoegeng Iman Santoso, Maj. Gen. Amir Joedowinarno, Gen. Mohammad Jusuf, Col. Alex Kawilarang,

Vice President Adam Malik, Col. Marsoedi, Gen. L.B. (Benny) Moerdani, Lt. Gen. A.J. Mokoginta, Col. Muktio, Mohammad Munawar, Maj. Gen. Amir Murtono, Maj. Gen. Eddie Marzuki Nalapraya, Mohammad Natsir, Brig. Gen. (Titular) R.P. Nugroho Notosusanto, Alwin Nurdin, Onghokham, Pramoedya Ananta Toer, Brig. Gen. Agoes Prasmono, Pamoe Rahardjo, Mohammad Said Reksohadiprodjo, Mohamad Roem, Mohammad Sadli, Salim Said, Subadio Sastrosatomo, Brig. Gen. F.X. Sardjono, Selo Soemardjan, Semaun, Col. Soedianto Sastroatmodjo, Otje Soedioto, Soedjatmoko, Stephanus Soedjono, Col. Aloysius Soegianto, Maj. Gen. Soenarso, Gen. Soepardjo Roestam, Brig. Gen. Imam Soepomo, Lt. Gen. Himawan Soetanto, Maj. Gen. R. Sudjono Humardani, Adm. Sudomo, Gen. Yoga Sugama, Lt. Gen. Kharis Suhud, Maj. Gen. Chandra Sukotjo, Sri Koestijah Nunek Sukotjo, Col. H.N. ("Ventje") Sumual, Lt. Gen. R. Sutopo Juwono, Lt. Gen. Ibnu Sutowo, Lt. Gen. Tjokropranolo, Rear Adm. Kunto Wibisono, Gen. R. Widodo and Clive Williams.

Yenny Wahid (or, more formally, Zannuba Ariffah Chafsoh), who worked in the *Sydney Morning Herald* Jakarta bureau until one day her father became President and needed her at the palace, brightened up all our lives and was continually helpful, as was Karuni Rompies. David and Gill Kersey kindly invited me to stay with them in Jakarta when I began my research for a book-length study of Indonesian military politics all those years ago.

For assistance during research in Japan I am indebted especially to Tsuchiya Kiso, the former Imperial Japanese Army special intelligence officer who recruited Soeharto into the Java Volunteer Defence Force, and to Col. Miyamoto Shizuo, who was a senior staff officer in Jakarta in 1944–45. I am most grateful also to Mr S. Chang, who located Mr Tsuchiya and put me in touch with him. (I asked Mr Chang once what the "S" stood for, to which he replied, enigmatically, "Secret!") I am much indebted as well to Fusayama Takao, Kadota Masami, Kaneko Tomokazu, Koizumi Saburo, Morimoto Takeshi, Nakano Kinichiro, Okazaki Masami, Taniguchi Taketsugu, Teramoto Masashi, Lt. Col. Uchida Takefumi, Vice Adm. Ueda Kazuo and Vice Adm. Uekusa Nobushige. In Tokyo I was greatly assisted by Professor Kawano Teruaki at the Center for Military History of the National Institute for Defense Studies (NIDS). He and his staff kindly translated dozens of pages from volumes in the 102-volume *Senshi Sosho* (War History Series) and answered my many questions about Japanese operations in Java. Kanno Naoki, the Head of Military Archives at the

CMH, generously granted me permission to use a number of rare archival photographs. I owe an especially heavy *on* to my friend Yamaoka Yasuko, who tracked down so many retired Imperial Army and Navy officers and NCOs who had served in Java, who interpreted so expertly during the many interviews she arranged when I visited Japan in early 1999 and who kept in close touch with these and other veterans in the years thereafter, putting to them my innumerable follow-up questions.

In the Netherlands, I wish to record my gratitude to Col. C.A. (Carel) Heshusius, who contributed greatly to my understanding of the structure, ethos, training, tactics, operating procedures and belated modernization of the pre-war KNIL. I benefitted also from innumerable discussions with my friend Brig. Gen. Ben Bouman, who, on his retirement from the army, wrote a PhD dissertation on the Indonesian officers who attended the pre-war Royal Military Academies in Breda and Bandung. Col. J.J. (Joop) Nortier, an ex-KNIL officer who wrote a valuable book about the Japanese invasion of the East Indies and co-authored another, provided insights into the costs and consequences of the KNIL's far-reaching makeover in the late 1930s and kindly invited me to stay for a lunch of Indonesian noodles when I called on him at his home in Harderwijk. I am indebted also to Jan Bakker and Col. K.C. Hernaus. Rolf Utermöhlen sent me the new citation numbers for more than two dozen files in the NIOD Indies collection.

In Australia, I would like to thank a number of Dutch civilians who endured dreadful privation and cruelty in Japanese internment camps on Java, in particular Ank van Vliet-Berg, Betty Berghuis, Margriet van Dalen, and Joke and Dave Bromet. Shirley Fenton Huie, who wrote a book about the women who had suffered so greatly in those camps, put me in touch with many of those she had interviewed. I am grateful also to Mayu Kanamori, Sawane Sakiko and Soemarsono, who had been a prominent youth leader in Surabaya in 1945 and who went on to play an important role in the 1948 Madiun Affair.

Needless to say, I am indebted as well to whole concourses of Asian and Western diplomats and military attachés who have served in Jakarta over the past half-century. It would be impossible to name them all and some would prefer to remain anonymous. I thank them all most warmly for their insights and their hospitality. I have also benefitted immeasurably from discussions over many years with fellow foreign correspondents.

At the same time, I am profoundly grateful to many academic specialists on Indonesia. They have been a constant source of wisdom, guidance and inspiration. The greatest of my debts is to Benedict Anderson of Cornell University. Ben read each chapter with exceptional care and patience, correcting errors, suggesting new lines of enquiry and drawing my attention to works I was unaware of. Throughout this process, which spanned the best part of a decade, he offered unflagging support and encouragement. As well, he sent me copies of the typed notes of interviews he had conducted with a number of Indonesian army officers and civilians, mostly in the early 1960s. Many of these notes begin with a pen portrait of the interviewee: each one brings the subject succinctly and splendidly alive, noting particular strengths, inconsistencies and eccentricities and, on occasion, puncturing pretension. I greatly miss Ben's company and his emails, which were full of warmth, wisdom, insights, integrity and good humour.

I also wish to express special thanks to Ruth McVey, who co-authored with Ben the "Cornell Paper" on the convulsive events of 1965 and whose magisterial book *The Rise of Indonesian Communism* remains unsurpassed. It was delightful to spend time at Ruth's home in the Italian countryside, discussing Indonesia over late afternoon gin-and-tonics and visiting nearby hilltowns, and a privilege to examine documents in her extensive archive. Ruth very kindly allowed me to make photocopies of the notes of interviews she conducted with dozens of people in Indonesia, Japan and the United States. (Like Ben, Ruth often includes an astute character sketch of the interviewee.) She also read several draft chapters, making incisive comments on my typescript, comments which helped steer me away from error. I am grateful as well to another Cornell-trained political scientist, Dan Lev, a scholar of great warmth, charm and erudition, for his close and perceptive reading of many draft chapters. I recall with fondness the discussions we had when Dan and Arlene invited me to stay with them in Seattle in late 2005, although I was distressed to learn on arrival that Dan was battling a grave illness.

Like so many others, I am indebted to George McTurnan Kahin, who, in 1948–49, conducted fieldwork for what has become a classic work of political science, *Nationalism and Revolution in Indonesia*, and who went on to build the Cornell Modern Indonesia Project, which has had such an extraordinary impact on Indonesian studies. He, too, was wonderfully helpful and encouraging over many years. I would like to thank Audrey Kahin, who so expertly edited my monograph *Suharto and His Generals* and who sent me copies of interviews George conducted in Indonesia in the late 1940s. At the Cornell University Southeast Asia Program journal *Indonesia* I have accumulated many other debts, to Fred Conner, Deborah Homsher and Sarah Grossman. I must also express my thanks to William H. Frederick of Ohio University for his unstinting help and guidance on developments during the Japanese occupation.

In Australia I owe an immeasurable debt to Jamie Mackie, who, when he and Alwynne (Onnie) were staying with Ann and me in Menteng in 1970, suggested that I look more closely at what seemed at times the opaque and all but impenetrable world of Indonesian military politics, and who was endlessly helpful with his time and sound advice in the decades thereafter. The assistance of Herb Feith, whom I met in Jakarta at the same time, is also greatly appreciated. I also wish to record my thanks to Ken Ward, who has been reading chapters, critiquing arguments and pouncing on stylistic shortcomings over a long period. I owe a great debt as well to Bob Elson, who, with characteristic generosity, guided me when I was making my first forays into the Dutch archives and who later sent me the two large boxes of material he had gathered while researching his 2001 book *Suharto: A Political Biography*. Robert Cribb has been unfailingly generous in providing help on matters of history and orthography. Peter McCawley, who invited me to stay in Jakarta, read each of the chapters and made many valuable comments. Harold Crouch was a source of expert advice on Indonesian military politics. David Bourchier, Greg Fealy, Hal Hill, Terence Hull, John Legge, Angus McIntyre, Chris Manning, John Monfries, George Quinn, David Reeve, Tony Reid, Merle Ricklefs and "Jon" Soemarjono offered helpful advice on a range of specialist matters. Onnie Mackie has been a constant source of wise counsel, good humour and sound editorial advice. I wish to thank Mandy van den Elshout from the Australian Society of Authors for her expert legal advice. Philip Bowring suggested a small but important change in the Preface.

Petra M.H. Groen, senior researcher at the Netherlands Institute of Military History, has, over many years, kindly provided answers to queries about both the Dutch colonial and metropolitan armies. Three other Dutch scholars—Harry Poeze, Willem Remmelink and Henk Schulte Nordholt—provided invaluable assistance on political and military developments in Java and Sumatra before and during the Japanese occupation. Liesanne Bouman, Linawati Sidarto and Erin Vencken helped with translations. In London, Anne Booth offered timely advice on agricultural practices in

Java in the 1920s. In Japan, Goto Ken'ichi most thoughtfully went back into seldom examined archives to answer questions about the Japanese command structure in West Sumatra. In Singapore I wish to record my particular thanks to Douglas Kammen, a Cornell-trained scholar who writes so perceptively about Indonesia and who has been a source of invaluable advice on many fronts. I also wish to thank Leo Suryadinata for his generous assistance.

Ben Anderson, Bob Elson, Peter McCawley, Jamie Mackie, Onnie Mackie, Justine Scott, Ken Ward and two anonymous reviewers read all, or in one case almost all, of the typescript. This book has benefitted greatly from their constructive criticism. At the same time, I wish to record my gratitude to those who read and commented on one or more chapters, or portions thereof, and whose advice is also deeply appreciated: Roger Bayliss, Francesca Beddie, Paul Bernadou, Ben Bouman, Robert Cribb, Harold Crouch, Greg Fealy, Stephen Grenville, Petra Groen, Joan Hardjono, Carel Heshusius, Terence Hull, Douglas Kammen, John Legge, Dan Lev, Angus McIntyre, Ruth McVey, Tony Patrick, Harry Poeze, Andrew Richards, Merle Ricklefs, Peter Rodgers, Sayidiman Suryohadiprojo, Henk Schulte Nordholt, Sabam Siagian, Harry Tjan Silalahi, Sukotjo Tjokroatmodjo, Purbo Suwondo, Brian Toohey and Christine Wilson. Yamaoka Yasuko read the chapters on the Japanese occupation and offered many invaluable comments.

Interview material has been augmented by extensive archival research. In the Netherlands I have debts extending over twenty-five years to the staff at what was, when I began, the Algemeen Rijksarchief in The Hague and what is now the Nationaal Archief (NA) in that city; at the former Centraal Archievendepot of the Ministerie van Defensie in Rijswijk, which has since transferred its collections to the Nationaal Archief; the Sectie Militaire Geschiedenis of the Koninklijke Landmacht, which in 2005 became part of a new Nederlands Instituut voor Militaire Historie (NIMH) in The Hague; the Ministerie van Buitenlandse Zaken in The Hague, which has now transferred its collection of Indonesia-related documents from the 1940s to the NA, and the former Rijksinstituut voor Oorlogs Documentatie (RIOD) in Amsterdam, which has since evolved into the Nederlands Instituut voor Oorlogs-, Holocaust- en Genocidestudies (NIOD).

In the United Kingdom I am indebted to the staff at the National Archives of the UK/Public Record Office, Kew; the Imperial War Museum,

London, and the Liddell Hart Centre for Military Archives—King's College London. I am especially grateful to the Trustees of the Liddell Hart Centre for permision to publish an extract from a report by Wg Cdr Alan Groom, RAF, which is located in the Papers of Wg Cdr Thomas Stuart Tull, RAF. At the National Archives of Australia annex in Melbourne I was most fortunate, while researching an earlier book on Imperial Japanese Navy submarine operations, to come upon Top Secret ULTRA decrypts of Japanese Navy signal traffic relating to the "management" of the Indonesian independence movement in 1945. Other debts of gratitude are to the staff at the Menzies and Chifley libraries at the Australian National University; the National Library of Australia; the School of Oriental and African Studies Library, University of London; the NIOD Library in Amsterdam; the Erasmus Huis Library in Jakarta; the CSIS Library in Jakarta and the Perpustakaan ABRI at the Museum Waspada Purbawisesa, in the grounds of Dewi Sukarno's former house in Jakarta.

Sections of this book draw on previously published material. One or two short passages in Chapter 8 are from my review of the book *The Invasion of the Dutch East Indies* which was published in the Cornell University journal *Indonesia 102* (October 2016). An earlier version of Chapters 9–14 appeared in my essay "Soeharto and the Japanese Occupation" in *Indonesia 88* (October 2009). These chapters have been revised; they also contain new material. One or two paragraphs elsewhere in the book draw on my essay "President Soeharto" in *Mental Maps in the Era of Détente and the End of the Cold War 1968–91*, edited by Steven Casey and Jonathan Wright (Basingstoke: Palgrave Macmillan, 2015). I thank the publishers of *Indonesia* and the editors of the 2015 book for permission to reprint that material here.

At ISEAS – Yusof Ishak Institute, I wish to thank especially Ng Kok Kiong, Head, Publishing and Managing Editor, who commissioned this book, and Senior Editor Rahilah Yusuf. They have steered *Young Soeharto* towards publication with great care and patience. My family have had to live with my work on this project for many years and I thank especially my son Tim, who has been endlessly supportive, and his wife Hannah and their children Ollie and Millie; my partner Justine Scott, for her love and practical advice, for waving her graphic designer wand over the cover and the photo insert sections, for drawing the maps, the charts and the Soeharto family tree, and for the fortitude with which she has borne my absorption in Indonesian history; and, finally, our daughter Charlotte, a delightful companion who has always managed to spirit me away for one adventure or another in the fresh air when I have spent too long in the office. I would also like to record my thanks to John Scott, who has an unrivalled capacity for unearthing rare books and documents across almost any discipline. Unless otherwise stated, all interviews were conducted by the author.

This book has had a long—some would say too long—gestation period. Indeed, it has sometimes seemed that it was taking me more time to write Soeharto's life than it took him to live it. One consequence of this seeming lack of urgency is that I have had time to conduct more interviews, examine more documents, read more books and reflect more deeply than would otherwise have been the case. One obvious drawback is that many of those who contributed so greatly to this volume and who might have enjoyed reading it have since died. In the course of writing the book, I have weighed carefully all the advice I have received. However, I have not always taken that advice, if only because in one or two cases those who read the manuscript were irreconcilably opposed in their opinions. It goes without saying that I bear sole responsibility for any errors or omissions that remain.

Bibliography

UNPUBLISHED SOURCES

ARCHIVAL SOURCES

NETHERLANDS

Nationaal Archief (NA), den Haag (The National Archives of the Netherlands, NANL, The Hague)

Algemene Secretarie van de Nederlands-Indische Regering en de daarbij gedeponeerde Archieven, 1942–1950. Entry Code: 2.10.14

"Staff Beppan Isum for April. 30 April, 1943. Bandung branch of Beppan", JAVINT 3117/14, SEATIC Det. 23 Ind. Div., 28 November 1945. NANL, 2.10.14, inv. 5197.

Translation of Beppan "Isum" for March 1943 compiled by Bandung branch of 16 Army Staff Beppan. NANL, 2.10.14, inv. 5197.

"Ir. Soekarno". Two-page typewritten document containing edited extracts from Sukarno's wartime speeches and broadcasts. Dutch Government Information Service. NANL, 2.10.14, inv. 5509.

"Japanese report of the state of affairs in Java. For the Commander-in-Chief of the Allied Forces in Java". Batavia, September 27, 1945. NANL, 2.10.14, inv. 5203. 8 pages plus one-page annex. According to this English-language typescript, the document was signed by a major general acting for the "Supreme Commander of [the] Japanese Army in Java". The officer in question was almost certainly Major General Yamamoto Moichiro.

"Statement written by [2nd Lt.] Shiroguchi, Kempei", 2 November 1945. NANL, 2.10.14, inv. 5291.

"Statement by Capt. YANAGAWA, dated 14 Dec 1945", Javint 3132/2, SEATIC Det., GSI, 23 Ind Div., 15 January 46. NANL, 2.10.14, inv. 5190.

"Order No. 1 – Operation of Military Administration", JAVINT 3131/4, SEATIC Det. HQ 23 Ind Div, 1 February 46. NANL, 2.10.14, inv. 5185.

Memorandum from Lieutenant General S.H. Spoor to the Lieutenant Governor-General, 21 February 1946. NANL, 2.10.14. inv. 2662.

"Schema van de Plaatselijke K.P.T. [Kenpeitai] Djokdjakarta". NANL, 2.10.14, inv. 5192.

"Interrogation of Lieutenant Onishi Kyutaro, Glodok Jail, Batavia, 17 May 1946". NANL, 2.10.14, inv. 5280.

Interrogation of Lieutenant Onishi Kyutaro, Glodok Prison, Batavia, 18 May 1946. NANL, 2.10.14, inv. 5280.

"Interrogation of General Imamura Hitoshi, Supplement", undated. NANL, 2.10.14, inv. 5284A.

"Captain YOSHITAKE, The Beppan of the General Staff", Kantoor voor Japansche Zaken, Batavia, undated. NANL, 2.10.14, inv. 5300.

Archief van de Netherlands Forces Intelligence Service/Centrale Militaire Inlichtingendienst (NEFIS/CMI), 1942–1949:

"TAN MALAKKA alias IBRAHIM BIN RASAD, ONG SUNG LI alias SOETAN IBRAHIM", Anschrift Van: Letter No. 30. Dated 12 January 1946. To: D.L. Page. From: G.K. Dulling, "Communist Activities in the N.E.I.", NEFIS/CMI, 1942–1949, inv. 1621.

"Mohammed [sic] Hatta", NEFIS/CMI inv. 1621.

Netherlands Forces Intelligence Service/Centrale Militaire Inlichtingendienst NEFIS/CMI 1942–1949. inv. 2781 Abdoerachman Sajadin Panotogomo Senopati Ingalogo Hamenkoe Boewono IX.

"Sultan of Djokjakarta", Netherlands Indies Government Information Service (NIGIS) [WW II Radio] Monitoring reports, Reports No. 446, 729, 864, 882, 994, 1218, 1271 and 1355. NEFIS/CMI 1942–1949. inv. 2781.

"Sultan van Djokjakarta – Zeer Geheim". Netherlands Forces Intelligence Service/ Centrale Militaire Inlichtingendienst NEFIS/CMI, 1942–1949. Inv. Nr. 2781.

"Zoelkifli Loebis", NEFIS/CMI 2744, inv. 0036.

"T.B. Simatoepang, Kolonel", File no. 0081, NEFIS/CMI inv. 2772.

"Points of Talks. Date: 16 August 45, begins at 12 o'clock night. At: The mess of General Nishimura." "Taken from the documents of Capt Nakamura Hiroshi". 4 March 1946. NEFIS/CMI, 1942–49, transferred from Ministerie van Buitenlandse Zaken, inv. 2016.

Nederlands Instituut voor Oorlogs-, Holocaust- en Genocidestudies – Indische Collectie, Amsterdam (NIOD Institute for War, Holocaust and Genocide Studies, Indies Collection, NIOD-IC, Amsterdam)*

"The start of the national movement and the natives reactions", translation of document B 29 taken from Prapatan Gambir 64, formerly Beppan GHQ, 24 March 1943, prepared by the Bandung branch of 16th Army Beppan. Java Int 3117, SEATIC Det., 4 Int. Unit, 23 Ind. Div., 14 December 1945. NIOD coll. 400, no. 581.

"Appreciation of Political Developments by Kaigun (Japanese Navy)". NIOD coll. 400, no. 581.

"Interrogation of Shimizu Hitoshi, 27th November, 1945", and "Report on further interrogation of Shimizu Hitoshi, 2nd December 1945", with explanatory notes by a Dutch intelligence officer. Signed by Colonel S.H. Spoor, Director NEFIS. NIOD coll. 400, no. 601B.

"Lt. Kol. Nomura Tetsu". Kantoor voor Japanse Zaken, Batavia. Undated. NIOD coll. 400, no. 772.

"Explanations Regarding All Kinds of Armed Bodies", a document drawn up by the headquarters of the Sixteenth Army. NIOD coll. 400, no. 792.

"Translation of statement by Capt. Yanagawa Munenari [sic], dated 14 Dec 45. (Continued)". NIOD coll. 400, no. 601B. This is Part II of "Statement by Capt. YANAGAWA, dated 14 Dec 1945", Javint 3132/2, SEATIC Det., GSI, 23 Ind Div., 15 January 45, held by the Nationaal Archief as 2.10.14, inv. 5190.

"Record of the progress of the independence movement". Gunseikanbu. Recollections of Nakatani Yoshio, 21 February 1946. NIOD coll. 400, no. 788.

"Supplementary explanation of armed parties in Java under Japanese mil. adm.", in "Document taken from 16 Army HQ", NEFIS Document 2618, 14 November 1946. NIOD coll. 400, no. 601A.

"VERKLARING. Afgelegd door: Kapitein TSUCHIYA Kiso (verbonden aan de Staf van de BEPPAN-NANSEITAI) gedurende verhoor afgenomen in de TJIPINANG-gevangenis te Meester-Cornelis (3–8 Maart 1947)". NIOD coll. 400, no. 771.

*Much of the research in the NIOD Indies Collection was conducted in 1999–2001 when that archive employed a six-figure file numbering system. However, research there continued intermittently until 2017, by which time most NIOD files had been digitized and renumbered using an entirely different four-digit system. In this book the new file numbers are given, except in rare cases where it has not been possible to identify a document consulted under the six-digit system.

Item 1 of Javint 3134/3 of 4 March 46. "Taken from Capt Nakamura Hiroshi. Table of stages in the realisation of the plan for an Indonesian Independence Movement, Item 1 of a file dated 12 Dec 45, on 'Record of Progress of the Independence Movement', prepared by 16 Army Mil Adm." NIOD coll. 400, no. 594.

"Points of Talks" concerning a meeting at the mess of General Nishimura beginning at midnight on 16–17 August taken from the documents of Captain Nakamura Hiroshi. NIOD coll. 400, no. 4736.

"Interrogation of Maj. Gen. Nishimura Otoshi on the Indonesian Independence Movement", Changi Gaol, Singapore, 31 May – 6 June 1946. NIOD coll. 400, no. 339, also at coll. 400, no. 8251.

Major General Nishimura, 10 April 1947, reply to questionaire of Mr. A.P.M. Audretsch, Office of the Attorney General, Netherlands East Indies. 15 pp. NIOD coll. 400, no. 722 and no. 774.

Major General Nishimura, answers to additional questions from Mr. A.P.M. Audretsch, 15 April 1947. 4 pp. NIOD coll. 400, no. 722.

Major General Nishimura Ototsugu (sic), answers to 22 April 1947, questions from Mr. A.P.M. Audretsch, 25 April 1947. 6 pp. NIOD coll. 400, no. 774 (formerly 059334). A different, and fuller, translation of this exchange, setting out both the questions and the answers, is to be found in what was formerly NIOD-IC 059333. 14 pp.

"Interrogation of Rear Admiral Maeda Tadashi at Changi Gaol, Singapore Island, between 31st May and 14th June 1946". NIOD coll. 400, no. 718 and no. 334.

"Report of Interrogation of Tadashi Maeda, Rear-admiral, in Struiswijk jail near Batavia, on the 1st and 10th August 1946". NIOD coll. 400, no. 718 and no. 335.

"Record of Evidence". Interrogation of Tadashi Maeda, Batavia, 26 August 1946. NIOD coll. 400, no. 718.

Undated "translation of the Report of Maeda" made in reply to two questions put to him by Allied interrogators. NIOD coll. 400, no. 336.

Translation of interrogation of Vice (sic) Admiral Maeda Tadashi, Batavia, 9 November 1946. NIOD coll. 400, no. 718.

"Interrogatie Rapport" Maeda Tadasi (sic), NEFIS, Batavia, 16 April 1946. NIOD coll. 400, no. 718.

Statement "To: Mr Audretsch, attached to the Attorney-General of the Netherlands East Indies. Submitted by Rear-Admiral Maeda (16 April 1947)". Translated by Nishijima Shigetada. NIOD coll. 400, no. 779.

"Statement of Yamamoto Moichiro on Indonesian Independence Movement during Japan's occupation". 13 pp. Undated. NIOD coll. 400, no. 1443.

"Meeting on board HMS Cumberland, 21st September 1945". An account of a report made by Major General Yamamoto, with attached "Statement of Ch. O. van der Plas, Batavia", 2 September 1946. NIOD coll. 400, no. 757.

Major General Yamamoto, "An Individual Opinion Which May Interest the Allied Powers With Regard to the Future Management of Indonesia", plus covering letter addressed to Rear Admiral W.R. Patterson, Batavia, 23 September 1945. NIOD coll. 400, no. 750.

Letter from Major General Yamamoto to Major General D.C. Hawthorn, Commander of the 23rd Division, Batavia, 3 October 1945. NIOD-IC no. 007337.

"Interview" between Major General Yamamoto and Captain D.J. Joyce and Captain Salter, Bandung, 7 March 1946. NIOD coll. 400, no. 714.

Afschrift, Pro Justinia No. 1/1948. 24313/R. Roodnr.: 336. "De Temporaire Krijgsraad te Batavia". Sato Heikichi death sentence. NIOD coll. 400, no. 5723.

"Interrogation of Gunzoku Saito Shizuo on the Independence Movement in Java", Changi Jail, Singapore, 4–5 June 1946. NIOD coll. 400, no. 338.

"Sworn deposition by Maeda Minoru", undated. Tokyo Trial. NIOD coll. 402, no. 5936.

UNITED KINGDOM

The National Archives of the UK/Public Record Office (TNA: PRO), Kew

War Office

WO 203/3671 58604. Japanese Beach Defences in South East Asia, Directorate of Combined Operations, Headquarters India Command, New Delhi, 11 April 1945.

WO 203/4573. 58552. "Report by General Yamamoto, Chief of Staff, Sixteenth Japanese Army", undated, in "Report by Lieutenant General Christison. Situation in NEI, 4 Oct 45", sent by Christison to Mountbatten.

WO 203/5294. "N.I.C.A. Japanese sponsored militant organizations in the Netherlands Indies".

WO 203/5470. "Force Plan No. 3. 'Occupation of Java'. Joint Planning Staff, Headquarters, Supreme Allied Commander South East Asia, 5 September 1945".

WO 203/6303. "Written Statement of Kempeitai [*sic*] Capt. Yoshitake", Item 2047, Southeast Asia Translation and Interrogation Center (SEATIC), Intelligence Bulletin, No. 225, 4 January 1946.

WO 203/6306. "Interrogation of Captain Tsuchiya Kiso at Glodok Jail", Southeast Asia Translation and Interrogation Center, Intelligence Bulletin No. 228, 25 January 1946.

WO 203/6418. 58696. Supplementary report by Lt. Col. L. van der Post for Brigadier Nicholson, 10 November 1945.

WO 325/111. 75491. "The Japanese Occupation of the Netherlands Indies, prepared statement of K.A. de Weerd, Attorney-at-Law, Major RNIA, International Prosecution Section, Netherlands Division", November 1946.

Liddell Hart Centre for Military Archives, King's College London

Alan Groom, "Brief report on Life in Ambarawa Prison". Papers of Wg Cdr Thomas Stuart Tull, CBE, DSO, OBE (1914–1982), 2/1. 25–30 September 1945.

AUSTRALIA

National Archives of Australia (NAA), Canberra

"Indonesian Biographies – General List, 1957", Series A 1838/280, Item 3004/5/1.

"Who's Who in Indonesia", External Affairs. Series: A1838/280. Item: 3004/5/1.

National Archives of Australia (NAA), Victorian Archives Centre (VAC), North Melbourne

"Top Secret-ULTRA. Translated [Imperial Japanese Navy] messages from FRUMEL [Fleet Radio Unit, Melbourne] records." Commonwealth Record Series B5555, Defence Signals Directorate, Translations of Cypher Messages, 1945–1946, File Nos. 1–14, and Parts B, K and M 6.

"To: Chiefs of Staff 2nd Southern Expeditionary Fleet and 10th Area Fleet. Information Resident Naval Officer Batavia. From: Bureau of Military Affairs." 172127 July 1945. Top Secret "translated messages from FRUMEL records dealing with the genesis of Indonesian 'independence'", CRS B5555, DSD, TCM, 1945–1946, File No. 6.

"Independence for the East Indies", 3 August 1945, message from Chief of Staff, 2nd Expeditionary Fleet, FRUMEL, CRS B5555, DSD, TCM, 1945–1946, File No. 6.

PUBLISHED SOURCES

OFFICIAL HISTORIES AND SEMI-OFFICIAL PUBLICATIONS

AUSTRALIA

Long, Gavin. *Australia in the War of 1939–1945, Series One, Army, Volume VII, The Final Campaigns.* Canberra: Australian War Memorial, 1963.

Odgers, George. *Australia in the War of 1939–1945, Series Three, Air, Volume II, Air War Against Japan, 1943–45.* Canberra: Australian War Memorial, 1957.

Wigmore, Lionel, *Australia in the War of 1939–1945, Series One, Army, Volume IV, The Japanese Thrust.* Canberra: Australian War Memorial, 1957.

INDONESIA

Anhar, Ratnawati. "Pahlawan Nasional: Supriyadi". Jakarta: Departemen Pendidikan dan Kebudayaan, 1977.

Anon. *"Penjelasan Presiden Soeharto tentang silsilah keturunan beliau di depan pers bertempat di Binagraha tanggal 28 October 1974, jam 11.30-1315 WIB"*. In *Silsilah Presiden Soeharto anak petani: bahan dan foto-foto dari HUMAS SEKNEG Jakarta,* edited by Suryohadi

Dwipayana, G., and Nazaruddin Sjamsuddin, Team (sic) Dokumentasi Presiden RI.

Jejak Langkah Pak Harto, 28 Maret 1968–23 Maret 1973. Jakarta: Citra Lamtoro Gung Persada, 1991.

Keterangan Presiden Soeharto tentang silsilah keluarga dalam pertemuan dengan pers dalam dan luar negeri bertempat di kamar kerja Presiden R.I. di Bina Graha, pada hari Senin, tanggal 28 Oktober 1974. Jakarta: Departemen Penerangan.

Pramono, ed. *Biografi Pahlawan Nasional Dari Lingkungan ABRI*. Jakarta: Angkatan Bersenjata Republik Indonesia, 1988.

Sedjarah Militer Kodam VII/Diponegoro, *Sedjarah TNI-AD Kodam VII/Diponegoro: Sirnaning Jakso katon Gapuraning Ratu*. Semarang: Jajasan Penerbit Diponegoro, 1968.

Soetrisno. "Biografi Pahlawan Revolusi Letnan Jenderal Anumerta Siswondo Parman". Jakarta: Departemen Pendidikan dan Kebudayaan, 1979/1980.

Suprapto, ed., *Soeharto: Jenderal Besar dari Kemusuk* (Bandung: Dinas Sejarah Angkatan Darat, 2010).

Suryohadi, ed. *Silsilah Presiden Soeharto Anak Petani: Bahan dan Foto-Foto dari HUMAS SEKNEG Jakarta*. Surabaya: Penerbit "Grip", 1974.

JAPAN

War History Office of the National Defense College of Japan [now the Center for Military History of the National Institute for Defense Studies]. *Senshi Sosho 3. Ran-In Koryaku Sakusen* [War History Series, Volume 3. *The Invasion of the Dutch East Indies*]. Tokyo: Asagumo Shimbunsha, 1967.

War History Office of the National Defense College of Japan. *Senshi Sosho 5. Biruma Koryaku Sakusen* [War History Series, Volume 5. *The Invasion of Burma*. Tokyo: Asagumo Shimbunsha, 1967.

War History Office of the National Defense College of Japan. *Senshi Sosho 26. Ran-In Bengaru-wan Homen Kaigun Shinko Sakusen* [War History Series, Volume 26. *The Operations of the Navy in the Dutch East Indies and the Bay of Bengal*]. Tokyo: Asagumo Shimbunsha, Tokyo, 1969.

War History Office of the National Defense College of Japan. *Senshi Sosho 92. Nanseihomen Rikugun sakusen: Marei Ranin no Boei* [War History Series, Volume 92. *Army Operations in the Southern Theatre: The Defense of Malaya and the Dutch East Indies*]. Tokyo: Asagumo Shimbunsha, 1976.

THE NETHERLANDS

Anon. *Voorschrift voor de Uitoefening van de Politiek-Politioneele Taak van het Leger* [VPTL, "Regulations for Exercising the Political and Police Task of the Army]. Batavia: Departement van Oorlog, 1928.

UNITED KINGDOM

Donnison, F.S.V. *British Military Administration in the Far East 1943–46*. History of the Second World War, United Kingdom Military Series. London: HM Stationary Office, 1956.

General Staff, H.M. Naval Base Singapore. *Japanese Forces: Typical Photographs (Supplement to Japanese Army: Notes on Chacteristics, Organisation, Training etc., September 1940)*. Singapore: Government Printer, 1941.

Geographical Section of the Naval Intelligence Division, Naval Staff, Admiralty. *A Manual of Netherlands India (Dutch East Indies)*. London: HM Stationary Office, n.d. [c. 1919].

Woodburn Kirby, S. et al. *The War Against Japan, Volume I, The Loss of Singapore, History of the Second World War, United Kingdom Military Series*. London: HM Stationary Office, 1957.

———. *The War Against Japan, Volume III, The Decisive Battles, History of the Second World War, United Kingdom Military Series*. London: HM Stationary Office, 1961.

———. *The War Against Japan, Volume V, The Surrender of Japan, History of the Second World War, United Kingdom Military Series* (London: HM Stationary Office, 1969).

UNITED STATES

Joint Publications Research Service (JPRS). *Japanese Military Administration in Indonesia*. Washington, DC: US Department of Commerce, 1963. A translation of *Indonesia ni Okeru Nihon Gunsei no Kenkyu*. Tokyo: Waseda University, Okuma Memorial Social Sciences Research Institute, Kinokuniya Shoten, 1959.

Joint Publications Research Service (JPRS), A.H. Nasution. *The Indonesian National Army*, Vol. I. A translation of *Tentara Nasional Indonesia*, Djilid I. Jakarta: Jajasan Pustaka Militer, 1956. Washington, DC: US Department of Commerce, n.d.

Morison, Samuel Eliot. *History of United States Naval Operations in World War II, Vol. VIII, New Guinea and the Marianas, March 1944–August 1944*. Boston: Little, Brown and Company, 1989.

Smith, Robert Ross. *United States Army in World War II, The War in the Pacific: The Approach to the Philippines*. Washington, DC: Office of the Chief of Military History, Department of the Army, 1953.

US Ministry of Army. *Nippon rikugun binran* [Handbook on Japanese Military Forces, War Department Technical Manual TM-E 30-480, War Department, October 1944]. Tokyo: Kojinsha, 1998.

BOOKS

Abdulgani-Knapp, Retnowati. *Soeharto: The Life and Legacy of Indonesia's Second President*. Singapore: Marshall Cavendish International (Asia), 2007.

Abdul Halim, Soejitno Hardjosoediro, Anwar and Sugeng Wibowo, eds., Markas

Besar Legiun Veteran RI. *Bunga Rampai Perjuangan dan Pengorbanan*, vol. VI. Jakarta: Jaya Abadi, 1997.

Abend, Hallett. *My Life in China 1926–1941*. New York: Harcourt Brace and Company, 1943.

———. *Pacific Charter*. London: John Lane The Bodley Head, 1943..

Abu Hanifah. *Tales of a Revolution: A Leader of the Indonesian Revolution Looks Back*. Sydney: Angus and Robertson, 1972.

Ahn, Yonson, *Whose Comfort?: Body, Sexuality and Identities of Korean 'Comfort Women' and Japanese Soldiers during WWII*. Singapore: World Scientific Publishing, 2020.

Alisjahbana, S. Takdir. *Indonesia: Social and Cultural Revolution*. Kuala Lumpur: Oxford University Press, 1966. First published in 1961 under the title *Indonesia in the Modern World*; translated from the Indonesian by Benedict R. Anderson.

Almanak "Antara," 78/79, Edisi Ke-III, 1978/1979. Jakarta: Antara, n.d.

Anderson, Benedict R. O'G. *Some Aspects of Indonesian Politics Under the Japanese Occupation, 1944–1945*. Cornell Modern Indonesia Project, Interim Report Series. Ithaca, NY: Cornell University, 1961. Republished by Equinox Publishing, Singapore, 2009.

———. *Mythology and the Tolerance of the Javanese*. Ithaca, NY: Southeast Asia Program, Cornell University, 1965.

———. *Java in a Time of Revolution: Occupation and Resistance, 1944–46*. Ithaca, NY: Cornell University Press, 1972. Republished by Equinox Publishing, Jakarta and Singapore, 2006.

———. *Imagined Communities: Reflections on the Origin and Spread of Nationalism*. London: Verso, 1983.

———. *Language and Power: Exploring Political Cultures in Indonesia*. Ithaca and London: Cornell University Press, 1990.

———. *A Life Beyond Boundaries*. London: Verso, 2016. Originally published in Japanese by NTT Publishing Co., Ltd, 2009.

———, and Audrey Kahin, eds. *Interpreting Indonesian Politics: Thirteen Contributions to the Debate*. Ithaca, NY: Southeast Asia Program, Cornell University, 1992.

Anon. *An Official Guide to Eastern Asia, Vol. V, East Indies*. Tokyo: The Imperial Government Railways of Japan, 1917.

———. *Regeerings Almanak Voor Nederlandsch-Indië, 1942*. Batavia: Landsdrukkerij, n.d.

———. *Butir-Butir Budaya Jawa: Hanggayuh Kasampurnaning Hurip Berbudi Bawaleksana Ngudi Sejatining Becik* [Seeds of Javanese Culture: Striving for the Perfection of a Life that is Generous and Set Upon the Right Path, Striving for the Essence of the Good]. Privately published by Hardiyanti Rukmana (Tutut Soeharto), 1987.

———. *Statistical Pocket Book of Indonesia, 1941*. Batavia: Central Bureau of Statistics, 1941.

———. *Kennis van het V.P.T.L.: Een kwestie van leven of dood!* N.p.: n.p., n.d.
———. *The Kenpeitai in Java and Sumatra* (Selections from *The Authentic History of the Kenpeitai* [Nihon Kenpei Seishi] by the National Federation of Kenpeitai Veterans' Associations [Zenkoku Kenyukai Rengokai Hensan Iinkai], translated by Barbara Gifford Shimer and Guy Hobbs. Ithaca, NY: Cornell Modern Indonesia Project, Publication no. 65, Cornell University, 1986.
———. *Gedenkschrift Koninklijk Nederlands-Indisch Leger, 1830–1950.* Dordrecht: Stichting Herdenking Koninklijk Nederlandsch-Indisch Leger, 1990.
———. *M.E.M.O.A.R: senarai kiprah sejarah, Diangkat dari Majalah TEMPO Buku Kedua.* Jakarta: Grafiti, 1993.
———. *M.E.M.O.A.R: senarai kiprah sejarah, Diangkat dari Majalah Tempo, Buku Ketiga.* Jakarta: Grafiti, 1993.
———. *80 Tahun Dr. H. Roeslan Abdulgani, 24 Nopember 1994.* Jakarta: Forum Komunikasi Alumni GMNI, Jawa Timur, 1994.
———. *Album 97 Pahlawan Nasional Dan Sejarah Perjuangannya.* Jakarta: Bahtera Jaya, 1996.
Anwar, H. Rosihan. *Kisah-Kisah Jakarta Setelah Proklamasi.* Jakarta: Pustaka Jaya, 1977.
———. *Sejarah Kecil "Petite Histoire" Indonesia,* vols. 1–4. Jakarta: Kompas, 2009–2010.
———. *Sutan Sjahrir: Demokrat Sejati, Pejuang Kemanusiaan, True Democrat, Fighter for Humanity, 1909–1966.* Jakarta: KITLV Press and Kompas, 2010.
———. *Sejarah Kecil (Petite Histoire) Indonesia, Jilid 5, Sang Pelopor: Tokoh-Tokoh Sepanjang Perjalanan Bangsa.* Jakarta, Kompas, 2012.
———. *Sejarah Kecil (Petite Histoire) Indonesia, Jilid 6, Sang Pelopor: Anak Bangsa Dalam Pusaran Sejarah.* Jakarta, Kompas, 2012.
———, K.H. Ramadhan, Ray Rizal and Din Madjid. *Kemal Idris: Bertarung Dalam Revolusi.* Jakarta: Sinar Harapan, 1996.
Ara Kenichi. *Jakaruta yoakemae: Indonesia dokuritsu ni kaketa hitotachi* [Jakarta before the Dawn: Those Who Staked All on Indonesian Independence]. Tokyo: Keiso Shobo, 1994.
Arief, Sritua, ed. *Who's Who In Indonesian Military.* N.p.: Sritua Arief Associates, 1977.
Arif Zulkifli and Bagja Hidayat, eds. *Aidit: Dua Wajah Dipa Nusantara, Seri Buku Tempo: Orang Kiri Indonesia.* Jakarta: Kepustakaan Populer Gramedia bekerjasama dengan Majalah *Tempo*, 2010.
Arif Zulkifli and Wahyu Dhyatmika, eds. *Soedirman: Seorang Panglima, Serorang Martir, Seri Buku Tempo: Tokoh Militer.* Jakarta: Kepustakaan Populer Gramedia bekerjasama dengan Majalah *Tempo*, 2012.
Arifin Surya Nugraha. *Keluarga Cendana.* Yogyakarta: Bio Pustaka, 2008.
Arwan Tuti Artha. *Bu Tien: Wangsit Keprabon Soeharto.* Yogyakarta: Galangpress, 2007.

Aspinall, Edward, and Greg Fealy, eds. *Soeharto's New Order and its Legacy: Essays in Honour of Harold Crouch*. Canberra: Griffin Press, 2010.

Bachtiar, Harsja W. *Siapa Dia?: Perwira Tinggi Tentara Nasional Indonesia Angkatan Darat (TNI-AD)*. Jakarta: Djambatan, 1988.

Bachtiar, Imelda, ed. *Catatan Jenderal Pranoto Reksosamodra: Dari RTM Boedi Oetomo Sampai Nirbaya*. Jakarta: Kompas, 2014.

Bayly, Christopher, and Tim Harper. *Forgotten Armies: The Fall of British Asia, 1941–1945*. Cambridge, Massachusetts: Belknap Press of Harvard University Press, 2006.

Benda, Harry J. *The Crescent and the Rising Sun: Indonesian Islam Under the Japanese Occupation 1942–1945*. Dordrecht: KITLV; Holland/USA: Foris Publications, 1983 [original: The Hague: W. van Hoeve, 1958].

Benda, Harry J., and Ruth T. McVey, eds. *The Communist Uprisings of 1926–1927 in Indonesia: Key Documents*. Ithaca, NY: Cornell Modern Indonesia Project Translation Series, 1960.

Bix, Herbert P. *Hirohito and the Making of Modern Japan*. New York: HarperCollins, 2000.

Blair, Jr., Clay. *Silent Victory: The U.S. Submarine War Against Japan*. New York: Bantam, 1976.

Bloembergen, Marieke. *Polisi Zaman Hindia Belanda: Dari Kepedulian dan Ketakutan*. Jakarta, Kompas and KITLV-Jakarta, 2011. Originally published as *De geschiedenis van de politie in Nederlands-Indië: Uit zorg en angst*. Amsterdam: Boom; Leiden: KITLV Uitgeverij, 2009.

Boediardjo. *Siapa Sudi Saya Dongengi*. Jakarta: Pustaka Sinar Harapan, 1996.

Boer, P.C. *The Loss of Java: The final battles for the possession of Java fought by Allied air, naval and land forces in the period of 18 February–7 March 1942*. Singapore: NUS Press, 2011.

Booth, Anne. *The Indonesian Economy in the Nineteenth and Twentieth Centuries: A History of Missed Opportunities*. London: Macmillan, 1998.

———, W.J.O'Malley and Anna Weidemann, eds. *Indonesian Economic History in the Dutch Colonial Era*. New Haven, Connecticut: Monograph Series 35/Yale University Southeast Asia Studies, 1990.

Bouman, B. *Van Driekleur tot Rood-Wit: De Indonesische officieren uit het KNIL, 1900–1950* [From Tricolour to Red and White: The Indonesian KNIL officers, 1900–1950]. 's-Gravenhage: Sectie Militaire Geschiedenis, 1995.

Bourchier, David. *Illiberal Democracy in Indonesia: The Ideology of the Family State*. Abington, Oxon: Routledge, 2015.

———, and Vedi R. Hadiz, eds. *Indonesian Politics and Society: A Reader*. London: RoutledgeCurzon, 2003.

Bowlby, John. *Attachment and Loss, Volume I: Attachment*. London: Pimlico, Random House, 1998.

Brabander, W.H., J.M. Koster. H.W. Neidig and J.R.J. Rugebregt, eds. *Officiersopleidingen van het Koninklyk Nederlands-Indisch Leger in Nederlands Indie, 1936–1950*. Aerdenhout: Vereniging Officieren Ex-K.M.A. Bandoeng, Ex-K.I.M. Soerabaja en Ex-Res. Officieren Bandoeng, 1990.

Bresnan, John. *At Home Abroad: A Memoir of the Ford Foundation in Indonesia 1953–1973*. Jakarta and Singapore: Equinox, 2006.

Brommer, B., E. Budihardjo, A.B. Montens, S. Setiadi, A. Sidharta, A. Siswanto, Soewarno and Th. Stevens. *Semarang: Beeld van een stad*. Purmerend: Asia Maior, 1995.

Brown, Judith M. *Modern India: The Origins of an Asian Democracy*. Oxford: Oxford University Press, 1985.

Bruggen, M.P. van, and R S. Wassing. *Djokja en Solo: Beeld van de Vorstensteden*. Purmerend: Asia Maior, 1998.

Brugmans, I.J., ed., H.J. de Graaf, A.H. Joustra and A.G. Vromans. *Nederlandsch-Indië onder Japanse bezetting: Gegevens en documenten over de jaren 1942–1945, Stichting Indië in de Tweede Wereldoorlog*. Franeker: T. Wever, 1960.

Budiman, Arief, ed. *State and Civil Society in Indonesia*. Clayton, Victoria: Monash Papers on Southeast Asia, No. 22, Centre of Southeast Asian Studies, Monash University, 1990.

Burleigh, Michael. *The Third Reich: A New History*. London: Pan Books, 2001.

Buruma, Ian. *The Missionary and the Libertine: Love and War in East and West*. London: Faber, 2002.

Chandler, David P., and M.C. Ricklefs, eds. *Nineteenth and Twentieth Century Indonesia: Essays in honour of Professor J.D. Legge*. Clayton, Melbourne: Centre of Southeast Asian Studies, Monash University, 1986.

Chauvel, Richard. *Nationalists, Soldiers and Separatists: The Ambonese Islands from Colonialism to Revolt, 1880–1950*. Leiden: KITLV Press, 1990.

Coffey, Thomas M. *Imperial Tragedy: Japan in World War II, The First Days and the Last*. New York: World Publishing, 1970.

Collier, Basil. *The War in the Far East, 1941–1945: A Military History*. London: Heinemann, 1969.

Colombijn, Freek, and J. Thomas Lindblad, eds. *Roots of Violence in Indonesia: Contemporary Violence in Historical Perspective*. Leiden: KITLV Press, 2002, and Singapore: Institute of Southeast Asian Studies, 2002.

Cribb, Robert. *Gangsters and Revolutionaries: The Jakarta People's Militia and the Indonesian Revolution 1945–1949*. North Sydney: Allen & Unwin, 1991. Published in North America by University of Hawaii Press. Reprinted by Equinox, Jakarta and Kuala Lumpur, 2009.

———. *Historical Dictionary of Indonesia*. Metuchen, NJ: Scarecrow Press, 1992.

———, ed. *The Late Colonial State in Indonesia: Political and Economic Foundations of the Netherlands Indies, 1880–1942*. Leiden: KITLV Press, 1994.

———. *Historical Atlas of Indonesia*. Honolulu: University of Hawai'i Press, 2000.

———, and Colin Brown. *Modern Indonesia: A History since 1945*. London and New York: Longman, 1995.

Crouch, Harold. *The Army and Politics in Indonesia*. Rev. ed. Ithaca, NY: Cornell University Press, 1988.

Dahm, Bernhard. *Sukarno and the Struggle for Indonesian Independence*. Ithaca and London: Cornell University Press, 1969.

———. *The History of Indonesia in the Twentieth Century*. New York: Praeger, 1971.

Daves, Joseph H., *The Indonesian Army from Revolusi to Reformasi. Volume I: The Struggle for Independence and the Sukarno Era*. n.p.: n.p., 2013.

Dennis, Peter, Jeffrey Grey, Ewan Morris, Robin Prior with Jean Bou. *The Oxford Companion to Australian Military History*, 2nd ed. South Melbourne: Oxford, 2008.

Diessen, J.R. van, ed., *Soerabaja 1900–1950: Havens, Marine, Stadsbeeld* [Soerabaja 1900–1950: Port, Navy, Townscape]. Zierikzee, Netherlands: Asia Maior, 2004.

Dinas Sejarah Militer Kodam VII/Diponegoro. *Sejarah Rumpun Diponegoro dan Pengabdiannya*. Semarang: Dinas Sejarah Militer Kodam VII/Diponegoro kerja sama dengan CV Borobudur Megah, 1977.

Djudjuk Juyoto S.T., Lazuardi Adi Sage, and S. Budhi Raharjo. *Gemuruh Kemusuk: Profile Desa Perjuangan*. Jakarta: Tifa Proyeksi Utama, 1991.

Dower, John W. *War Without Mercy: Race and Power in the Pacific War*. New York: Pantheon Books, 1986.

Drea, Edward J. *MacArthur's ULTRA: Codebreaking and the War against Japan, 1942–1945*. Lawrence, Kansas: University Press of Kansas, 1992.

———. *In the Service of the Emperor: Essays on the Imperial Japanese Army*. Lincoln, NA: University of Nebraska Press, 1998.

———. *Japan's Imperial Army: Its Rise and Fall, 1853–1945*. Lawrence, Kansas: University Press of Kansas, 2009.

Drooglever, P.J., M.J.B. Schouten and Mona Lohanda. *Guide to the Archives on Relations between the Netherlands and Indonesia 1945–1963*. The Hague: Institute of Netherlands History, 1999.

Dulm, J. van, W.J. Krijgsveld, H.J. Legemaate, H.A.M. Liesker and G. Weijers. *Geillustreerde Atlas van der Japanse Kampen in Nederlands-Indie 1942–1945*. Purmerend: Asia Maior, 2000.

Dwipayana, G., and Nazaruddin Sjamsuddin, eds. *Jejak Langkah Pak Harto, 28 Maret 1968 – 23 Maret 1973*. Jakarta: Citra Lamtoro Gung Persada, 1991.

——— and Nazaruddin Sjamsuddin, eds. *Diantara Para Sahabat: Pak Harto 70 Tahun*. Jakarta: Citra Lamtoro Gung Persada, 1991.

——— and Nazaruddin Sjamsuddin, eds. *Among Friends: Pak Harto at 70*. Jakarta: Citra Lamtoro Gung Persada, 1993.

Echols, John M. *Preliminary Checklist of Indonesian Imprints During the Japanese Period (March 1942 – August 1945)*. Cornell Modern Indonesia Project, Bibliography Series. Ithaca, NY: Cornell University, 1963.

——— and Hassan Shadily. *Kamus Indonesia Inggris*, 3rd ed. Jakarta: Gramedia, 1998.

Edwards, John. *John Curtin's War*, Vol. I. Australia: Penguin Viking, 2017.

Elson, R.E. *Suharto: A Political Biography*. Cambridge: Cambridge University Press, 2001.

Endah, Alberthiene. *Memoar Romantika Probosutedjo: Saya dan Mas Harto*. Jakarta: Gramedia, 2010.

Endo, Masako. *Singaporu no Yunionjakku*. Tokyo: Shueisha, 1996.

Fasseur, Cornelis. *The Politics of Colonial Exploitation: Java, the Dutch, and the Cultivation System*. Translated from the Dutch by R.E. Elson and Ary Kraal. Edited by R.E. Elson. Ithaca, NY: Cornell University Southeast Asia Program, 1992.

Fenton Huie, Shirley. *The Forgotten Ones: Women and Children Under Nippon*. Pymble, New South Wales: Angus&Robertson, 1992.

Frederick, William H. *Visions and Heat: The Making of the Indonesian Revolution*. Athens, Ohio: Ohio University Press, 1989.

Frei, Henry P. *Japan's Southward Advance and Australia: From the Sixteenth Century to World War II*. Carlton, Victoria: Melbourne University Press, 1991.

Frey, Marc, Ronald W. Pruessen and Tan Tai Yong, eds. *The Transformation of Southeast Asia: International Perspectives on Decolonization*. Singapore: Singapore University Press, 2004.

Friend, Theodore. *The Blue-Eyed Enemy: Japan Against the West in Java and Luzon, 1942–1945*. Princeton, NJ: Princeton University Press, 1988.

———. *Indonesian Destinies*. Cambridge, Mass.: Belknap Press, 2003.

Fujiwara Iwaichi. *F-Kikan: Japanese Army Intelligence Operations in S.E. Asia*. Hong Kong: Heinemann, 1983.

Fusayama Takao. *A Japanese Memoir of Sumatra 1945–1946: Love and Hatred in the Liberation War*. Ithaca, NY: Cornell Modern Indonesia Project, Monograph Series (Publication no. 71), 1993.

Gafur, Abdul. *Siti Hartinah Soeharto: Ibu Utama Indonesia*. Jakarta: Citra Lamtoro Gung Persada, 1992.

Gardner, Paul F. *Shared Hopes, Separate Fears: Fifty Years of US-Indonesian Relations*. Boulder, Colorado, and Oxford, UK: Westview Press, 1997.

Geertz, Clifford. *Agricultural Involution: The Processes of Ecological Change in Indonesia*. Berkeley: University of California Press, 1963.

———. *The Religion of Java*. New York: The Free Press, 1969.

Geyl, Pieter. *Napoleon: For and Against*. Harmondsworth, England: Peregrine, 1965.

Giebels, Lambert. *Soekarno Nederlandsch onderdaan: Een biografie 1901–1950*. Amsterdam: Bert Bakker, 1999.

Goldsworthy, David, ed. *Facing North: A Century of Australian Engagement with Asia, Vol. I: 1901 to the 1970s*. Carlton, Victoria: Department of Foreign Affairs and Trade and Melbourne University Press, 2001.

Goor, J. van, ed. *The Indonesian Revolution,* Conference Papers, Utrecht, 17–20 June 1986, Utrechtse Historische Cahiers, uitgegeven vanwege het Instituut voor Geschiedenis der Rijksuniversiteit te Utrecht, jaargang 7 (1986) nr. 2/3.

Goto Ken'ichi. *"Returning to Asia": Japan-Indonesia Relations, 1930s–1942*. Tokyo: Ryukei Shyosha, 1997.

———. *Tensions of Empire: Japan and Southeast Asia in the Colonial and Postcolonial World*. Athens, Ohio: Ohio University Press, 2003.

Groen, P.M.H., and E. Touwen-Bouwsma. *Nederlands-Indie 1942: Illusie en ontgoocheling*. The Hague: SDU Uitgevers, 1992.

Groot, L.F. de. *Berechting Japanse oorlogsmisdadigers in Nederlands-Indië 1946–1949*. 's-Hertogenbosch: Art & Research, 1990.

Hadi, Kuncoro, dkk. *Kronik '65: Catanan Hari Per Hari Peristiwa G30S Sebelum Hingga Setelahnya (1963–1971)*. Yogyakarta: Pressindo, 2017.

Halim, Abdul, Soejitno Hardjosoediro, Anwar and Sugeng Wibowo, eds., Markas Besar Legiun Veteran RI. *Bunga Rampai Perjuangan dan Pengorbanan*, vol. VI. Jakarta: Jaya Abadi, 1997.

Ham, Paul. *Hiroshima Nagasaki*. Sydney: HarperCollins, 2011.

Hanafi, A.M. *Menteng 31, Markas Pemuda Revolusioner Angkatan 45: Membangun Jembatan Dua Angkatan*. Jakarta: Sinar Harapan, 1996.

Hardjono, Joan. *Indonesia: Land and People*. Jakarta: Gunung Agung, 1971.

Hata Ikuhiko, ed. *Nanpo gunsei no kiko, kanbu gunsei-kan ichiran*. Tokyo: Nanpogun Gunsei-shi Kenkyu Forum, 1998.

Hatta, Mohammad. *Portrait of a Patriot: Selected Writings*. The Hague: Mouton, 1972.

———. *Memoir*. Jakarta: Tintamas, 1979.

Hayashida Yukio. *Dari Hati Ke Hati*. Tokyo: Kokumin Shimbunsha, 1999.

Hering, Bob. *Soekarno: Founding Father of Indonesia, 1901–1945*. Leiden: KITLV Press, 2002.

Heshusius, C.A. *Soldaten van de Kompenie KNIL, 1830–1950: Een Fotodocumentaire over het Dagelijks Leven van het Koloniale Leger in Nederlands-Indie*. Houten: De Haan/Unieboek, 1986.

Holt, Claire, ed., with the assistance of Benedict R. O'G Anderson and James Siegel. *Culture and Politics in Indonesia*. Ithaca and London: Cornell University Press, 1972.

Horner, David. *High Command: Australia's Struggle for an Independent War Strategy, 1939–1945*. 2nd ed. St Leonards, New South Wales: Allen & Unwin, 1992.

Howarth, Stephen. *Morning Glory: The Story of the Imperial Japanese Navy*. London: Arrow Books, 1985.

Hugo, Graeme J., Terrence H. Hull, Valerie J. Hull and Gavin W. Jones. *The Demographic Dimension in Indonesian Development*. Singapore: Oxford University Press, 1987.

Imamura Hitoshi. *Imamura Hitoshi Taisho Kaikoroku*, vol. II. Tokyo: Jiyu Ajai-sha, 1960.

Ingleson, John. *In Search of Justice: Workers and Unions in Colonial Java, 1908–1926*. Singapore: Oxford University Press, 1986.

Isnaeni, Hendri F. *17-8-45: Fakta-Drama-Misteri*. 2nd ed. Jakarta: Change, 2015.

———, ed. *Seputar Proklamasi Kemerdekaan: Kesaksian, Penyiaran dan Keterlibatan Jepang*. Jakarta: Kompas, 2015.

Jackson, Karl D. *Traditional Authority, Islam, and Rebellion: A Study of Indonesian Political Behaviour*. Berkeley: University of California Press, 1980.

Jasin, H. Moehammad (with Ridwan Jasin Zachrie and B. Cavara Wiwanto, eds.). *Memoar Jasin Sang Polisi Pejuang: Meluruskan Sejarah Kelahiran Polisi Indonesia*. Jakarta: Gramedia, 2010.

Jawa Nenkan (Java Yearbook). Jakarta: Jawa Shimbunsha, 1944. Reprinted by Bibrio (Tokyo) in 1973.

Jenkins, David. *Suharto and His Generals: Indonesian Military Politics 1975–1983*. Ithaca, NY: Cornell University, Cornell Modern Indonesia Project, Monograph Series, Publication No. 64, 1984.

Jong, L. de. *The Collapse of a Colonial Society: The Dutch in Indonesia during the Second World War*. Leiden: KITLV Press, 2002.

Jones, Gavin W. *Marriage and Divorce in Islamic South-East Asia*. Kuala Lumpur: Oxford University Press, 1994.

Jones, Howard Palfrey. *Indonesia: The Possible Dream*. 4th ed. Singapore: Gunung Agung, 1980.

Junus Jahja. *Catatan Orang Indonesia*. Jakarta: Komunitas Bambu, 2009.

Kadota Masami. *Yoshu*, privately published by the author, Tokyo, 1994.

Kahin, George McT. *Nationalism and Revolution in Indonesia*. Ithaca, NY: Cornell University Press, 1952.

Kartohadikusumo, Setiadi. *Peristiwa Rengasdengklok*. Jakarta: Yayasan Soetardjo, 1995.

Kasenda, Peter. *Komandan Intelijen Pertama Indonesia Zulkifli Lubis: Kolonel Misterius di Balik Pergolakan TNI AD*. Jakarta: Kompas, 2012.

Keegan, John, ed. *The Times Atlas of the Second World War*. Times Books, 1989.

Keeler, Ward. *Javanese: A Cultural Approach*. Athens, Ohio: Ohio University, Monographs in International Studies, Southeast Asia Series, No. 69, 1984.

Kishi Koichi and Nishijima Shigetada, eds. *Indonesia ni okeru Nihon gunsei no kenkyu*. Tokyo: Waseda University, Okuma Memorial Social Sciences Research Institute, Kinokuniya Shoten, 1959.

Klooster, H.A.J. *Bibliography of the Indonesian Revolution: Publications from 1942 to 1994*. Leiden: KITLV Press, 1997.

Koentjaraningrat, ed. *Villages in Indonesia*. Ithaca, NY: Cornell University Press, 1967.

———. *Javanese Culture*. Singapore: Oxford University Press, 1989.

Kok, Rene, Erik Somers, and Louis Zweers. *Koloniale Oorlog 1945–1949: Van Indie naar Indonesie*. Amsterdam: Uitgeverij Carrera, 2009.

Komar, Herry, ed. Majalah Berita Mingguan *Tempo*. *Apa & Siapa: Sejumlah Orang Indonesia 1985–1986*. Jakarta: Grafiti Pers, 1986.

Kotani, Ken. *Japanese Intelligence in World War II*. Botley, Oxford and New York: Osprey, 2009.

Kratoska, Paul H., ed. *Asian Labor in the Wartime Japanese Empire: Unknown Histories*. Armonk, New York, and London, England: M.E. Sharpe, 2005. Also published as Paul H. Kratoska, ed., *Asian Labor in the Wartime Japanese Empire*. Singapore: Singapore University Press, 2006.

———. *The Japanese Occupation of Malaya and Singapore, 1941–1945: A Social and Economic History*, 2nd ed. Singapore: NUS Press, 2018.

Kroef, Justus M. van der. *The Communist Party of Indonesia: Its History, Program and Tactics*. Vancouver: University of British Columbia, 1965.

Kurasawa Aiko, ed. *Jawa Baru Vol. 1–5* [A reprinted edition of *Djawa Baroe*]. Tokyo: Ryukeishosha, 1992.

Kuroda Hidetoshi. *Gunsei*. Tokyo: Gakufu-shoin, 1952.

Kusuma, A.B. *Lahirnya Undang-undang Dasar 1945: Memuat Salinan Dokumen Otentik Badan Oentoek Menyelidiki Oesaha2 Persiapan Kemerdekaan*. Jakarta: Fakultas Hukum Universitas Indonesia, 2004.

Lapian, A.B., ed. *Semangat '45: Dalam Rekaman Gambar IPPHOS*. Jakarta: Sinar Harapan, 1985.

Lapré, S.A. *Nederlands-Indie 1940–1950 in kort bestek*. Veenoord: Zalsman Nieuw-Amsterdam, n.d.

Layton, Edwin T. et al. *"And I Was There": Pearl Harbor and Midway – Breaking the Secrets*. New York: Quill, 1985.

Lebra, Joyce C. *Japanese-Trained Armies in Southeast Asia: Independence and Volunteer Forces in World War II*. Singapore: Heinemann, 1977.

Legge, J.D. *Sukarno: A Political Biography*. London: Allen Lane The Penguin Press, 1972; also published as *Sukarno: A Political Biography*. Middlesex, England: Pelican, 1973.

———. *Indonesia*, 2nd ed. Sydney: Prentice-Hall, 1977.

———. *Intellectuals and Nationalism in Indonesia: A Study of the Following Recruited by Sutan Sjahrir in Occupation Jakarta*. Monograph Series, Publication No. 68. Ithaca, NY: Cornell Modern Indonesia Project, 1988.

Lev, Daniel S. *Islamic Courts in Indonesia: A Study in the Political Bases of Legal Institutions*. Berkeley: University of California Press, 1972.

——— and Ruth McVey, eds. *Making Indonesia: Essays on Modern Indonesia in Honor of George McT. Kahin*. Ithaca, NY: Southeast Asia Program, Cornell University, 1996.

Lockhart, R.H. Bruce. *Return to Malaya*. London: Putnam, 1938.

Logevall, Fredrik. *Embers of War: The Fall of an Empire and The Making of America's Vietnam*. New York: Random House, 2012.

Lohnstein, Marc. *Royal Netherlands East Indies Army 1936–42*. Oxford: Osprey, 2018.

Lucas, Anton. *One Soul One Struggle: Religion and Revolution in Indonesia*. Sydney: Allen & Unwin, 1991.

MacArthur, Douglas,. *Reminiscences*. New York: McGraw-Hill, 1964.

McCullough, David. *Truman*. New York: Touchstone, 1992.

McDonald, Hamish. *Suharto's Indonesia*. Melbourne: Fontana Books, 1980.

McIntyre, Angus. *The Indonesian Presidency: The Shift from Personal toward Constitutional Rule.* Lanham, MD: Rowman & Littlefield, 2005.

McVey Ruth T. *The Rise of Indonesian Communism*. Ithaca, NY: Cornell University Press, 1965.

Malik, Adam. *Mengabdi Republik, Jilid I: Adam Dari Andalas*. Jakarta: Gunung Agung, 1978.

———. *Mengabdi Republik, Jilid II: Angkatan 45*. Jakarta: Gunung Agung, 1978.

———. *In the Service of the Republic*. Singapore: Gunung Agung, 1980.

Mallarangeng, Rizal. *Chairul Basri: Apa Yang Saya Ingat*. Jakarta: Pustaka Sinar Harapan, 2003.

Mark, Ethan. *Japan's Occupation of Java in the Second World War: A Transnational History*. London: Bloomsbury Academic, 2018.

Masao, Yamabe. *Kaigun Rakkasanbutai*. Masushobo, 1956.

Matondang, Victor, ed. *Percakapan Dengan Dr. T.B. Simatupang*, 2nd ed. Jakarta: BPK Gunung Mulia, 1989.

May, Brian. *The Indonesian Tragedy*. Singapore: Graham Brash, 1978.

Mercado, Stephen C. *The Shadow Warriors of Nakano: A History of the Imperial Japanese Army's Elite Intelligence School.* Washington, DC: Brassey's, 2002.

Missen, G.J. *Viewpoint on Indonesia: A Geographical Study*. Melbourne: Nelson, 1972.

Miyamoto Shizuo. *Jawa shusen shori-ki* [An Account of the Cessation of Hostilities in Java]. Tokyo: Jawa Shusenshoriki Kankokai, 1973.

Monfries, John. *A Prince in a Republic: The Life of Sultan Hamengku Buwono IX of Yogyakarta*. Singapore: Institute of Southeast Asian Studies, 2015.

Moor, J.A. de. *Indisch Militair Tijdschrift (1870–1942): A Selective and Annotated Bibliography*. The Hague: Sectie Militaire Geschiedenis van de Landmachtstaf, 1983, and the Centre for The History of European Expansion, Leiden, 1983.

———. *Generaal Spoor: Triomf en tragiek van een legercommandant*. Amsterdam: Boom, 2011.

Morimoto Takeshi. *Jawa boei giyugun-shi* [History of the Java Volunteer Defence Force]. Tokyo: Ryukeishosha, 1992.

Mrázek, Rudolf. *Sjahrir: Politics and Exile in Indonesia*. Studies on Southeast Asia. Ithaca, NY: Southeast Asia Program, Cornell University, 1994.

Mulder, Niels. *Mysticism and Everyday Life in Contemporary Java: Cultural Persistence and Change*. Singapore: Singapore University Press, 1978.

———. *Individual and Society in Java: A Cultural Analysis*. Yogyakarta: Gadjah Mada University Press, 1989.

Myers, Ramon H., and Mark R. Peattie, eds. *The Japanese Colonial Empire, 1895–1945*. Princeton, NJ: Princeton University Press, 1984.

Nagazumi Akira, ed. *Pemberontakan Indonesia di Masa Pendudukan Jepang*. Jakarta: Yayasan Obor Indonesia, 1988.

Nasution, A.H. *Tentara Nasional Indonesia*, djilid I,. Jakarta: Jajasan Pustaka Militer, 1956.

———. *Towards a People's Army*. Jakarta: Delegasi, 1964.

———. *Fundamentals of Guerrilla Warfare*. Facsimile ed. New York: Frederick A. Praeger, 1965.

———. *Sekitar Perang Kemerdekaan Indonesia, Jilid 1: Proklamasi*. Bandung: Disjarah-AD and Angkasa, 1977.

———. *Memenuhi Panggilan Tugas; Jilid 1: Kenangan Masa Muda*. Jakarta: Gunung Agung, 1982.

Nehru, Jawaharlal. *Toward Freedom: The Autobiography of Jawaharlal Nehru*. Boston: Beacon Press, 1963.

Nihon Kenpei seishi. Tokyo: Zenkoku Kenyukai Rengokai Hensan Iinkai, Kenbunshoin, 1976.

Nishihara Masashi. *The Japanese and Sukarno's Indonesia: Tokyo-Jakarta Relations, 1951–1966*. Honolulu: University Press of Hawaii, 1976.

Nishijima Collection, The. *Materials on the Japanese Military Administration in Indonesia*. Institute of Social Sciences. Tokyo: Waseda University, 1973.

Noer, Deliar. *Mohammad Hatta: Hati Nurani Bangsa/Conscience of a Nation, 1902–1980*. Djambatan Perwakilan KITLV, 2002.

Nortier, J.J. *De Japanse aanval op Nederlands-Indië* . Rotterdam: Ad. Donker, 1988.

———, P. Kuijt and P.M.H. Groen. *De Japanse aanval op Java, Maart 1942*. Amsterdam: De Bataafsche Leeuw, 1994.

Nugroho Notosusanto. *Tentara Peta Pada Jaman Pendudukan Jepang di Indonesia*. Jakarta: Gramedia, 1979.

———. *The Peta Army During the Japanese Occupation of Indonesia*. Tokyo: Waseda University Press, 1979.

———. *The National Struggle and the Armed Forces in Indonesia*. Jakarta: Department of Defence and Security, 1980.

Oetama, Jakob, ed. *Warisan (daripada) Soeharto*. Jakarta: Kompas, 2008.

Okazaki Kiyoshi. *Okazaki Seizaburo nikki: Aru Rikugun gunjin no chiisana Showa-shi.* Fujisawa: Shonan Guddo, 1990.

Ong Chit Chung. *Operation Matador: Britain's War Plans against the Japanese 1918–1941.* Singapore: Times Academic Press, 1997.

Oudang, M. *Perkembangan Kepolisian di Indonesia.* Jakarta: Mahabarata, 1952.

Pamudji Suptandar J. et al. *Prof. Dr. Ir. P.K. Haryasudirja: Tokoh Pejuang Kemerdekaan, Pembangunan dan Pendidikan.* Jakarta: Universitas Trisakti, 2005.

Pemberton, John. *On the Subject of "Java".* Ithaca and London: Cornell University Press, 1994.

Penders, C.L.M., ed. *Mohammad Hatta, Indonesian Patriot: Memoirs.* Singapore: Gunung Agung, 1981.

———, and Ulf Sundhaussen. *Abdul Haris Nasution: A Political Biography.* St Lucia [Queensland], London, New York: University of Queensland Press, 1985.

Perlman, Marc. *Java.* Singapore: Periplus Editions, 1991.

Poeze, Harry A. *Tan Malaka: Strijder Voor Indonesië's Vrijheid Levensloop van 1897 tot 1945.* 's-Gravenhage: Martinus Nijhoff, 1976.

———. *Tan Malaka: Pergulatan Menuju Republik, 1925–1945.* Jakarta: Pustaka Utama Grafiti, 1999.

———. *Verguisd en Vergeten: Tan Malaka, de linkse beweging en de Indonesische Revolutie, 1945–1949.* Deel I-III. Leiden: KITLV Uitgeverij, 2007.

Ponder, H.W. *Java Pageant: Impressions from the 1930s.* Singapore: Oxford University Press, 1988. Originally published as *Java Pageant* by Seeley Service & Co. Ltd., London, 1934.

Post, Peter, and Elly Touwen-Bouwsma, eds. *Japan, Indonesia and the War: Myths and Realities.* Leiden: KITLV Press, 1997.

———, William H. Frederick, Iris Heidebrink, and Shigeru Sato, eds. *The Encyclopedia of Indonesia in the Pacific War.* Leiden: Brill, 2010.

Pour, Julius, and Nur Adji, eds. *Sepanjang Hayat Bersama Rakyat: 100 Tahun Sultan Hamengku Buwono IX.* Jakarta: Kompas Media Nusantara, 2012.

Powell, Alan. *War by Stealth: Australians and the Allied Intelligence Bureau 1942–1945.* Carlton South, Victoria: Melbourne University Press, 1996.

Prados, John. *Combined Fleet Decoded: The Secret History of American Intelligence and the Japanese Navy in World War II.* New York: Random House, 1995.

Pranoto Reksosamodra. *Memoar Mayor Jenderal Raden Pranoto Reksosamodra.* Yogyakarta: Syarikat, 2002.

Prawiroatmodjo, Soehoed. *Perlawanan Bersendjata Terhadap Fasisme Djepang.* Jakarta: Merdeka Press, 1953.

Preston, Paul. *Franco: A Biography.* London: Fontana Press, 1995.

Pusat Sejarah ABRI. *Museum ABRI Satriamandala, Buku Panduan.* N.p.: Departemen Pertahanan Keamanan, 1980.

Quinn, George. *Bandit Saints of Java.* Burrough on the Hill, UK: Monsoon Books, 2019.

Raben, Remco, ed. *Representing the Japanese Occupation of Indonesia: Personal Testimonies and Public Images in Indonesia, Japan, and the Netherlands*. Zwolle: Waanders Publishers, and Netherlands Institute for War Documentation, Amsterdam, 1999.

Rahardjo, Pamoe, ed. *Tentara Peta (Pembela Tanah Air): Mengawal Proklamasi 17 Agustus 1945 mulai dari Rengasdengklok*. 2nd ed. Jakarta: Peta Press, 1993.

Ramadhan K.H. *A.E. Kawilarang: Untuk Sang Merah Putih*. Jakarta: Pustaka Sinar Harapan, 1988.

———. *Soemitro: Dari Pangdam Mulawarman Sampai Pangkopkamtib*. Jakarta: Sinar Harapan, 1994.

———. *Soemitro: Former Commander of Indonesian Security Apparatus*. Jakarta: Sinar Harapan, 1996.

Ramage, Douglas E. *Politics in Indonesia: Democracy, Islam and the Ideology of Tolerance*. London: Routledge, 1995.

Reeve, David. *Golkar of Indonesia: An Alternative to the Party System*. Singapore: Oxford University Press, 1985.

Reid, Anthony J.S., *The Indonesian National Revolution, 1945–1950*. Hawthorn, Melbourne: Longman, 1974.

———, and Oki Akira, eds. *The Japanese Experience in Indonesia: Selected Memoirs of 1942–1945*, Monographs in International Studies, Southeast Asia Series, No. 72. Athens, Ohio: Ohio University, 1986.

Remmelink, Willem, ed. and tran. *The Invasion of the Dutch East Indies* (a translation of vol. 3 of the 102-volume Japanese War History Series, *Ran-In Koryaku Sakusen)*. Tokyo: Asagumo Shimbunsha, 1967; Leiden: Leiden University Press, 2015.

———, ed. and tran. *The Operations of the Navy in the Dutch East Indies and the Bay of Bengal* (a translation of War History Series, vol. 26, *Ran-In Bengaru-wan Homen Kaigun Shinko Sakusen*). Tokyo: Asagumo Shimbunsha, 1969; Leiden: Leiden University Press, 2018.

———, ed. and tran., *The Invasion of the South: Army Air Force Operations, and the Invasion of Northern and Central Sumatra* (selected translations from War History Series vol. 34, *Rikugun Koku Sakusen: Nanpo Shinko*. Tokyo: Asagumo Shimbunsha, 1970), with an addendum on the invasion of Northern and Central Sumatra (a translation of Ch 4 from War History Series vol. 5, *Biruma Koryaku Sakusen* [*The Invasion of Burma*]). Tokyo: Asagumo Shimbunsha, 1967; Leiden: Leiden University Press, forthcoming.

Riadi Ngasiran. *Kesabaran Revolusioner Djohan Sjahroezah, Perjuang Kemerdekaan Bawah Tanah*. Jakarta: Kompas, 2015.

Ricklefs, M.C. *Polarising Javanese Society: Islamic and Other Visions (c. 1830–1930)*. Singapore: NUS Press, 2007.

———. *A History of Modern Indonesia since c. 1200*, 4th ed. Stanford: Stanford University Press, 2008.

———. *Islamisation and Its Opponents in Java: A Political, Social, Cultural and Religious History, c. 1930 to the Present*. Singapore: NUS Press, 2012.

Robinson, Geoffrey. *The Dark Side of Paradise: Political Violence in Bali*. Ithaca, NY: Cornell University Press, 1995.

Robson, Stuart, ed. *The Kraton: Selected Essays on Javanese Courts*. Leiden: KITLV Press, 2003.

Roeder, O.G. *The Smiling General: President Soeharto of Indonesia*. Jakarta: Gunung Agung, 1969.

———. *Anak Desa: Biografi Presiden Soeharto*. Jakarta: Masagung, 1990.

Rose, Mavis. *Indonesia Free: A Political Biography of Mohammad Hatta*. Ithaca, NY: Cornell Modern Indonesia Project, 1987.

Ruff-O'Herne, Jan. *Fifty Years of Silence: The Extraordinary Memoir of a War Rape Survivor*. North Sydney: William Heinemann, 2008.

Saleh, R.H.A. *"... Mari Bung, Rebut Kembali!"*. Jakarta: Pustaka Sinar Harapan, 2000.

Sanseido's New Concise Japanese-English Dictionary. Sanseido, 1985.

Sato Shigeru. *War, Nationalism and Peasants: Java Under the Japanese Occupation 1942–1945*. Sydney: Allen & Unwin, 1994.

Sayidiman Suryohadiprojo. *Kepemimpinan ABRI: Dalam Sejarah dan Perjuangannya*. Jakarta: Intermasa, 1996.

———. *Mengabdi Negara Sebagai Prajurit TNI: Sebuah Otobiografi*. Jakarta, Sinar Harapan, 1997.

Schaik, A. van. *Malang: Beeld van een stad*. Purmerend: Asia Maior, 1996.

Schlesinger, Jr., Arthur M. *The Age of Roosevelt, Volume I: The Crisis of the Old Order, 1919–1933*. Boston: Mariner, 1985.

Schram, Stuart. *Mao Tse-tung*. Harmondsworth, Middlesex, England: Penguin, 1967.

———. *The Political Thought of Mao Tse-tung*. Harmondsworth, England: Pelican Books, 1969.

Selosoemardjan. *Social Changes in Jogjakarta*. Ithaca, NY: Cornell University Press, 1962.

Selo Soemardjan and Kennon Breazeale. *Cultural Change in Rural Indonesia: Impact of Village Development*. Surakarta: Sebelas Maret University Press, 1993.

Sen, Krishna. *Indonesian Cinema: Framing the New Order*. London and New Jersey: Zed Books, 1994.

Shiraishi Saya and Shiraishi Takashi, eds. *The Japanese in Colonial Southeast Asia*, vol. III, Translation of Contemporary Japanese Scholarship on Southeast Asia, Southeast Asia Program. Ithaca, NY: Cornell University, 1993.

Siegel, James T. *Solo in the New Order: Language and Hierarchy in an Indonesian City*. Princeton, New Jersey: Princeton University Press, 1986.

———, and Audrey R. Kahin, eds. *Southeast Asia over Three Generations: Essays*

Presented to Benedict R. O'G. Anderson, ed. Ithaca, NY: Cornell University Southeast Asia Program Publications, 2003.

Simatupang, T.B. *Membuktikan Ketidakbenaran Suatu Mitos: Menelusuri Makna Pengalaman Seorang Prajurit Generasi Pembebas Bagi Masa Depan Masyarakat, Bangsa Dan Negara*. Jakarta: Pustaka Sinar Harapan, 1991.

———. *The Fallacy of a Myth: Tracing the Experimental Significance of an Army Officer Belonging to the Generation of Liberator for the Future of Indonesia*, translated and introduced by Peter Suwarno. Jakarta: Pustaka Sinar Harapan, 1996.

Sjahrir, Soetan. *Out of Exile*, translated by Charles Wolf, Jr. New York: John Day, 1949.

———. *Our Struggle*, translated with an Introduction by Benedict R. O'G Anderson. Ithaca, NY: Cornell University Modern Indonesia Project, 1968.

Snow, Edgar. *Red Star Over China*. New York: Grove Press, 1961.

Soedarmanta, J.B. *Tengara Orde Baru: Kisah Harry Tjan Silalahi*. Jakarta: Gunung Agung, 2004.

Soedianto Sastroatmodjo and Aboelkahar. *TKR Divisi VII Untung Suropati Malang-Besuki 1945–1948*. Malang: UM Press, 2000.

Soedirgo, R., Rachmat Padmaredja and Islam Salim, eds. *Kebangkitan Jiwa Keprajuritan Nasional: Yayasan Pembela Tanah Air, Monumen dan Museum Peta Bogor*. N.p.: Yayasan Pembela Tanah Air, 1997.

Soedjatmoko, ed. *An Introduction to Indonesian Historiography*. Ithaca, NY: Cornell University Press, 1965.

Soegih Arto. *Indonesia & I*. Singapore: Times Books International, 1994.

Soeharto, My Thoughts, Words, and Deeds: An Autobiography as told to G. Dwipayana and Ramadhan K.H., ed. Mutiah Lestiono. Jakarta: Citra Lamtoro Gung Persada, 1989.

Soeharto, Pikiran, Ucapan, dan Tindakan Saya: Otobiografi, seperti dipaparkan kepada C. Dwipayana dan Ramadhan K.H.. Jakarta: Citra Lamtoro Gung Persada, 1989.

Soeharto: Mijn gedachten, woorden en daden. Co-auteurs: Ramadhan en Dwipayana. Franeker: Van Wijnen, 1991.

Soemarsono. *Revolusi Agustus: Kesaksian Seorang Pelaku Sejarah*. Sebagaimana dicatat/transkrip dan edit oleh Komisi Tulisan Soemarsono di Europa. n.p.: Hasta Mitra, 2008.

Soewito, Dra. Irna H.N. Hadi et al. *Chairul Saleh, Tokoh Kontroversial*. Jakarta: Mutiara Rakyat, 1993.

Spector, Ronald H. *Eagle Against the Sun: The American War with Japan*. London: Penguin, 1987.

———. *In the Ruins of Empire: The Japanese Surrender and the Battle for Postwar Asia*. New York: Random House, 2007.

Stripp, Alan. *Codebreaker in the Far East*. Oxford: Oxford University Press, 1995.

Subardjo Djoyoadisuryo, Ahmad. *Kesadaran Nasional: Otobiografi*. Jakarta: Gunung Agung, 1978.

Sudirjo, Radik Utoyo, ed. *Album Perang Kemerdekaan 1945–1950*. Jakarta: Penerbit Almanak RI/BP Alda bekerjasama Dewan Harian Nasional Angkatan 45, 1982.

Suhud, Kharis. *Catatan Seorang Prajurit*. Jakarta: Pustaka Sinar Harapan, 2004.

Sukarno: An Autobiography, As Told to Cindy Adams. Hong Kong: Gunung Agung, 1966.

Sukarni, Emalia Iragiliati. *Sukarni dan Actie Rengasdengklok*. Yogyakarta: Ombak, 2013.

Sullivan, John. *Local Government and Community in Java: An Urban Case-study*. Singapore, Oxford, New York: Oxford University Press, 1992.

Sumantri, Iwa Kusuma. *Sedjarah Revolusi Indonesia: Masa Revolusi Bersendjata*, Djilid Kedua. Djakarta: self-published, n.d.

Suripto. *Ibu Tien Soeharto: Ibu Negara Jang Ramah Tamah*. Surabaya: Pantja Pudjibangun, n.d.

Sutherland, Heather. *The Making of a Bureaucratic Elite: The Colonial Transformation of the Javanese Priyayi*. Singapore: Heinemann, 1979.

Suwarno, P.J. *Hamengku Buwono IX dan Sistem Birokrasi Pemerintahan Yogyakarta, 1942–1974: Sebuah Tinjuan Historis*. Yogyakarta: Kanisius, 1994.

Suwondo, Purbo S., ed. *Peta: Tentara Sukarela Pembela Tanah Air Di Jawa dan Sumatera 1942–1945*. Jakarta: Sinar Harapan, 1996.

———. *Kemanunggalan Tentara Sukarela Pembela Tanah Air Dengan Pergerakan Kebangsaan Untuk Indonesia Merdeka dan Badan Keamanan Rakyat Dalam Penyelenggaraan Bela Negara Republik Indonesia*. N.p.: Legiun Veteran, 2009.

———. *Sejarah Keberadaan Tentara Sukarela Pembela Tanah Air Dalam Perjuangan Kemerdekaan Indonesia*. Jakarta: Yayasan Pembela Tanah Air, 2013.

Tagliacozzo, Eric. *Secret Trades, Porous Borders: Smuggling and States Along a Southeast Asian Frontier, 1865–1915*. New Haven and London: Yale University Press, 2005.

Tanaka Yuki. *Japan's Comfort Women: Sexual Slavery and Prostitution During World War II and the US Occupation*. London: Routledge, 2002.

Taniguchi Taketsugu. *Gekido no seiki: Ichi senpan kenpei no kaiso*. Tokyo: Taipin-kai, 1997.

Tarling, Nicholas, ed. *The Cambridge History of Southeast Asia, Vol. I: From Early Times to c. 1800*. Cambridge: Cambridge University Press, 1992.

———, ed. *The Cambridge History of Southeast Asia, Vol. 2: The Nineteenth and Twentieth Centuries*. Cambridge: Cambridge University Press, 1992.

———. *Britain, Southeast Asia and the Onset of the Pacific War*. Cambridge: Cambridge University Press, 1996.

———. *A Sudden Rampage: The Japanese Occupation of Southeast Asia, 1941–1945*. London: Hurst, 2001.

Taylor, A.J.P. *Bismarck: The Man and the Statesman*. London: Penguin, 1995.

Taylor, Robert H. *General Ne Win: A Political Biography*. Singapore: Institute of Southeast Asian Studies, 2015.

Terada Chikao. *Nippon guntai yogo-shu*. Tokyo: Rippushobo, 1992.

———. *Zoku Nippon guntai yogo-shu*. Tokyo: Rippushobo, 1995.

Tipton, Elise K. *The Japanese Police State: The Tokko in Interwar Japan*. Honolulu, HI: University of Hawai'i Press, 1990.

Toland, John. *The Rising Sun: The Decline and Fall of the Japanese Empire, 1936–1945*. New York: Bantam, 1986.

Tolischus, Otto D. *Tokyo Record*. London: Hamish Hamilton, Australian Edition, 1944.

Trevor-Roper, Hugh. *The Crisis of the Seventeenth Century: Religion, The Reformation, and Social Change*. Indianapolis: Liberty Fund, 2001. Originally published by Harper & Row, New York, 1967.

Twang Peck Yang. *The Chinese Business Elite in Indonesia and the Transition to Independence, 1940–1950*. Kuala Lumpur, Oxford, Singapore and New York: Oxford University Press, 1998.

Vandenbosch, Amry. *The Dutch East Indies: Its Government, Problems, and Politics*. Berkeley: University of California Press, 1944.

Vatikiotis, Michael R.J. *Indonesian Politics Under Soeharto: Order, Development and Pressure for Change*. London and New York: Routledge, 1993.

Vreeland, Nena, Peter Just, Kenneth W. Martindale, Philip W. Moeller and Rinn-Sup Shinn. *Area Handbook for Indonesia*. Washington: The American University, 1975.

Wanandi, Jusuf. *Shades of Grey: A Political Memoir of Modern Indonesia 1965-1998*. Singapore: Equinox, 2012.

Wanhar, Wenri. *Jejak Intel Jepang: Kisah Pembelotan Tomegoro Yoshizumi*. Jakarta: Kompas, 2014.

Wardaya, Baskara T. *Mencari Supriyadi: Kesaksian Pembantu Utama Bung Karno*. Yogyakarta: Galangpress, 2008.

Wibisono Singgih, ed. *Museum Purna Bhakti Pertiwi*. Jakarta: Yayasan Purna Bhakti Pertiwi, 1983.

Widjojo Nitisastro. *Population Trends in Indonesia*. Ithaca, NY: Cornell University Press, 1970.

Wild, Colin, and Peter Carey, eds. *Born in Fire: The Indonesian Struggle for Independence: An Anthology*. Athens, Ohio: Ohio University Press, 1988, published by arrangement with BBC Publications.

Willoughby, Charles A., and John Chamberlain. *MacArthur 1941–1951: Victory in the Pacific*. London: William Heinemann, 1956.

Wilson, Sandra, Robert Cribb, Beatrice Trefalt and Dean Aszkielowicz. *Japanese War Criminals: The Politics of Justice After the Second World War*. New York: Columbia University Press, 2017.

Winton, John. *ULTRA in the Pacific: How Breaking Japanese Codes and Cyphers Affected Naval Operations Against Japan, 1941–45*. London: Leo Cooper, 1993.

Yamamoto Moichiro. *Kaisoroku: Gekido no jinsei hachijunen*. Published privately by Yamamoto Mitsuko in Tokyo, 1978.

Yamazaki Hajime. *Kita-ni minami-ni*. Published privately by Yamazaki in Takasaki, Gunma Prefecture, 1977.

Yanagawa Motoshige. *Rikugun chohoin Yanagawa Chui*. Tokyo: Sankei Shimbun, 1967.

Yayasan Pembela Tanah Air. *Bumi Keprajuritan Indonesia: Pusat Pendidikan Perwira Tentara Sukarela Pembela Tanah Air Bogor*. Bogor: nd [c. 1995].

Yunus Yahya. *Catatan Orang Indonesia*. Jakarta: Komunitas Bamboo, 2009.

Zenkoku Kenyukai Rengokai Hensan Iinkai. *Nihon Kenpei Seishi*. Tokyo: Kenbunshoin, 1976.

Ziegler, Philip. *Mountbatten: The Official Biography*. London: Collins, 1985.

———, ed. *Personal Diary of Admiral The Lord Louis Mountbatten, 1943–1946*. London: Collins, 1988.

Zurbuchen, Mary S., ed. *Beginning to Remember: The Past in the Indonesian Present*. Singapore: Singapore University Press in association with University of Washington Press, 2005.

Zwitzer, H.L., and C.A. Heshusius. *Het Koninklijk Nederlands-Indisch Leger 1830–1950*. 's-Gravenhage: Staatsuitgeverij, 1977.

JOURNAL ARTICLES, CHAPTERS IN EDITED COLLECTIONS, BOOKLETS, UNPUBLISHED DOCUMENTS, RESEARCH MEMORANDA

Agustono, Budi. "Violence on North Sumatra's Plantations". In *Roots of Violence in Indonesia: Contemporary Violence in Historical Perspective*, edited by Freek Colombijn and J. Thomas Lindblad. Leiden: KITLV Press, 2002, and Singapore: Institute of Southeast Asian Studies, 2002.

Andaya, Barbara Watson, and Yoneo Ishii. "Religious Developments in Southeast Asia, c1500–1800". In *The Cambridge History of Southeast Asia, Volume I: From Early Times to c. 1800*, edited by Nicholas Tarling. Cambridge: Cambridge University Press, 1992.

Anderson, Benedict R. O'G. "The Idea of Power in Javanese Culture". In *Culture and Politics in Indonesia*, edited by Claire Holt with the assistance of Benedict R. O'G Anderson and James Siegel. Ithaca and London: Cornell University Press, 1972.

———. "Nationalism and the State in Modern Indonesia". Paper contributed to the

Japanese Political Science Association Round Table Conference on National Interest and Political Leadership, Tokyo, 29 March – 1 April 1982.

———. "Perspective and Method in American Research on Indonesia (1973)". In *Interpreting Indonesian Politics: Thirteen Contributions to the Debate*, edited by Benedict Anderson and Audrey Kahin. Ithaca, NY: Southeast Asia Program, Cornell University, 1992.

———. "Language, Fantasy, Revolution: Java 1900–1950". In *Making Indonesia: Essays on Modern Indonesia in Honor of George McT. Kahin*, edited by Daniel S. Lev and Ruth McVey. Ithaca, NY: Southeast Asia Program, Cornell University, 1996.

———. "Indonesian Nationalism Today and in the Future". *New Left Review* 235 (1999).

———. "Exit Suharto: Obituary for a Mediocre Tyrant". *New Left Review* 50 (March–April 2008).

Anon. "Dialog Presiden dengan mantan anggota Peta dan Giyu-gun". In *Peta: Tentara Sukarela Pembela Tanah Air Di Jawa dan Sumatera 1942–1945*, edited by Purbo Suwondo. Jakarta: Sinar Harapan, 1996.

———. "Kenangan Penuh Syukur Ulang Tahun, 'Commendatore di San Gregorio Magno' Prof. Dr. Ir. KPH. P.K. Haryasudirja Sasraningrat". 20 October 2000.

———. "Mengenal Kehidupan Presiden Soeharto, The Life of President Soeharto". *Indonesia Magazine*, no. 14 (1973).

———. *Tentara Peta Sayap Militer Pergerakan Kemerdekaan Nasional*. Jakarta: Yayasan Pembela Tanah Air, 1999.

———. *Tjeritera Orang2 Heiho Jang Ikoet Perang*. n.p.: n.p., n.d.

Arifin S. U., Edy Burhan. "Pemberontakan Tentara Peta di Blitar: Sebuah Kesaksian Sejarah". In *Peta: Tentara Sukarela Pembela Tanah Air Di Jawa dan Sumatera 1942–1945*, edited by Purbo S. Suwondo. Jakarta: Sinar Harapan, 1996.

Bickers, Robert A., and Jeffrey N. Wasserstrom. "Shanghai's 'Dogs and Chinese Not Admitted' Sign: Legend, History and Contemporary Symbol". *The China Quarterly*, 1995.

Booth, Anne, and Konta Damanik. "Central Java and Yogyakarta: Malthus Overcome?". In *Unity and Diversity: Regional Economic Development in Indonesia Since 1970*, edited by Hal Hill. Singapore, Oxford, New York: Oxford University Press, 1989.

Bourchier, David. "Positivism and Romanticism in Indonesian Legal Thought". In *Indonesia: Law and Society*, edited by Timothy Lindsey. Sydney: Federation Press, 1999.

Bousquet, G.H. "The International Position of Netherlands India". *Pacific Affairs* XII, no. 4 (December 1939).

Brenner, Suzanne A. "Competing Hierarchies: Javanese Merchants and the *Priyayi*

Elite in Solo, Central Java". *Indonesia*, no. 52 (October 1991) (Ithaca, NY: Cornell Southeast Asia Program, 1991).

Castles, Lance. "Is the *Aliran* Pattern in Indonesian Voting in Decline?". Yogyakarta, 9 March 1999. Typescript in author's possession.

Chen Ching-chih. "Police and Community Control Systems in the Empire". In *The Japanese Colonial Empire, 1895–1945*, edited by Ramon H. Myers and Mark R. Peattie. Princeton, NJ: Princeton University Press, 1984.

Djatikusumo, GPH, Letjen Purn. "Prajurit Pejuang Dari Kraton Surakarta". In *Bunga Rampai Perjuangan dan Pengorbanan*, vol. VI, edited by Abdul Halim, Soejitno Hardjosoediro, Anwar and Sugeng Wibowo; Markas Besar Legiun Veteran RI. Jakarta: Jaya Abadi, 1997.

Elson, R.E. "Aspects of Peasant Life in Early 19th Century Java". In *Nineteenth and Twentieth Century Indonesia: Essays in honour of Professor J.D. Legge*, edited by David P. Chandler and M.C. Ricklefs. Clayton, Melbourne: Centre of Southeast Asian Studies, Monash University, 1986.

———. "Another Look at the Jakarta Charter Controversy of 1945". *Indonesia* 88 (October 2009).

Erman, Erwiza. "Generalized Violence:: A Case Study of the Ombilin Coal Mines, 1892–1996". In *Roots of Violence in Indonesia: Contemporary Violence in Historical Perspective*, edited by Freek Colombijn and J. Thomas Lindblad. Leiden: KITLV Press, 2002, and Singapore: Institute of Southeast Asian Studies, 2002.

Fasseur, C. [Cornelis]. "Cornerstone and Stumbling Block: Racial Classification and the Late Colonial State in Indonesia". In *The Late Colonial State in Indonesia: Political and Economic Foundations of the Netherlands Indies 1880–1942*, edited by Robert Cribb. Leiden: KITLV Press, 1994.

Frey, Marc. "The Indonesian Revolution and the Fall of the Dutch Empire: Actors, Factors, and Strategies". In *The Transformation of Southeast Asia: International Perspectives on Decolonization*, edited by Marc Frey, Ronald W. Pruessen, and Tan Tai Yong. Singapore: Singapore University Press, 2004.

Friend, Theodore. "Hellcraft, Nostalgia, and Terror: Thoughts on Memoirs of the Kenpeitai in Wartime Indonesia". In *The Kenpeitai in Java and Sumatra (Selections from Nihon Kenpei Seishi)*, translated by Barbara G. Shimer and Guy Hobbs. Ithaca, NY: Cornell Modern Indonesia Project, Publication No. 65, 1986.

Fukami Sumio. "Japanese Source Materials on the Japanese Military Administration in Indonesia". In *The Indonesian Revolution*, edited by J. van Goor. Conference Papers, Utrecht, 17–20 June 1986, Utrechtse Historische Cahiers, uitgegeven vanwege het Instituut voor Geschiedenis der Rijksuniversiteit te Utrecht, jaargang 7 (1986) nr. 2/3.

Gatot Mangkupradja, Raden. "The Peta and My Relations with the Japanese", translated by Harumi Wanasita Evans and Ruth McVey. *Indonesia* 5 (April 1968): 105–34.

Geertz, Clifford. "Afterword: The Politics of Meaning". In *Culture and Politics in Indonesia*, edited by Claire Holt, with the assistance of Benedict R. O'G Anderson and James Siegel. Ithaca and London: Cornell University Press, 1972.

Goto Ken'ichi. "Caught in the Middle: Japanese Attitudes toward Indonesian Independence in 1945". *Journal of Southeast Asian Studies* 27, no. 1 (1996).

Hall, Kenneth, R. "Economic History of Early Southeast Asia". In *The Cambridge History of Southeast Asia, Volume I: From Early Times to c. 1800*, edited by Nicholas Tarling. Cambridge: Cambridge University Press, 1992.

Han Bing Siong. "Sukarno-Hatta Versus the *Pemuda* in the First Months after the Surrender of Japan (August–November 1945)". *Bijdragen tot de Taal-, Land- en Volkenkunde* 156, no. 2 (2000): 233–73.

———. "The Indonesian Need of Arms after the Proclamation of Independence". *Bijdragen tot de Taal-, Land- en Volkenkunde* 157, no. 4 (2001): 799–830.

Harvey, Barbara S. "Diplomacy and Armed Struggle in the Indonesian National Revolution: Choice and Constraint in a Comparative Perspective". In *Making Indonesia: Essays on Modern Indonesia in Honor of George McT. Kahin*, edited by Daniel S. Lev and Ruth McVey. Ithaca, NY: Southeast Asia Program, Cornell University, 1996.

Hefner, Robert W. "Islam, State, and Civil Society: ICMI and the Struggle for the Indonesian Middle Class". *Indonesia* no. 56 (October 1993).

Heidebrink, H. Iris. "The Eurasian Community during the Japanese Occupation, 1942–1945". In *The Encyclopedia of Indonesia in the Pacific War*, edited by Peter Post, William H. Frederick, Iris Heidebrink and Shigeru Sato, eds. Leiden: Brill, 2010.

Heine-Geldern, Robert. "Conceptions of State and Kingship in Southeast Asia". (Revised version of an article published in the *Far Eastern Quarterly*, vol. 2, November 1942). Ithaca, NY: Cornell University Southeast Asia Program, Data Paper No. 18, 1956.

Idris, A. Kemal. "Jenderal yang Memilih Jalan Sendiri". In *M.E.M.O.A.R Senarai Kiprah Sejarah, Diangkat dari Majalah Tempo, Buku Ketiga*. Jakarta: Grafiti, 1993.

Ingleson, John. "Prostitution in Colonial Java". In *Nineteenth and Twentieth Century Indonesia: Essays in honour of Professor J.D. Legge*, edited by David P. Chandler and M.C. Ricklefs. Clayton, Melbourne: Centre of Southeast Asian Studies, Monash University, 1986.

———. "Review of *The Collapse of a Colonial Society: The Dutch in Indonesia during the Second World War*, by L. de Jong. Introduced by Jerouen Kemperman. Leiden: KITLV Press, 2002, 570 pp.". *Indonesia* 80 (October 2005).

Jenkins, David. "Soeharto and the Japanese Occupation". *Indonesia* 88 (October 2009). Cornell Southeast Asia Program.

———. "President Soeharto". In *Mental Maps in the Era of Détente and the End of the Cold War 1968–91*, edited by Steven Casey and Jonathan Wright. Basingstoke, UK: Palgrave Macmillan, 2015.

———. "Review of *The Invasion of the Dutch East Indies*, edited and translated by Willem Remmelink. Compiled by the War History Office of the National Defense College of Japan. Leiden: Leiden University Press, 2015. 640 pp.". *Indonesia* 102 (October 2016).

Kahin, George McT. "Some Recollections and Reflections on the Indonesian Revolution". *Indonesia* 60 (October 1995).

———. "Sukarno's Proclamation of Indonesian Independence". *Indonesia* 69 (April 2000).

Koentjaraningrat. "Tjelapar: A Village in South Central Java". In *Villages in Indonesia*, edited by Koentjaraningrat. Ithaca, NY: Cornell University Press, 1967.

Koestedjo, R. "Pengalaman-pengalaman sebagai dokter Peta di Bali". In *Peta: Tentara Sukarela Pembela Tanah Air Di Jawa dan Sumatera 1942–1945*, edited by Purbo Suwondo. Jakarta: Sinar Harapan, 1996.

Kurasawa Aiko. "Japanese Occupation and Leadership Changes in Javanese Villages". In *The Indonesian Revolution*, edited by J. van Goor. Conference Papers, Utrecht, 17–20 June 1986, Utrechtse Historische Cahiers, uitgegeven vanwege het Instituut voor Geschiedenis der Rijksuniversiteit te Utrecht, jaargang 7 (1986) nr. 2/3.

———. "Propaganda Media on Java Under the Japanese 1942–1945". *Indonesia* 44 (October) 1987. Cornell Southeast Asia Program.

Kusuma, A.B., and R.E. Elson. "A Note on the Sources for the 1945 Constitutional Debates in Indonesia". *Bijdragen tot de Taal- Land- en Volkenkunde* 167, no. 2–3 (2011).

Leclerc, Jacques. "Afterword: The Masked Hero". In *Local Opposition and Underground Resistance to the Japanese in Java, 1942–1945*, edited by Anton Lucas. Monash University Papers on Southeast Asia, No. 13. Clayton, Victoria: Centre of Southeast Asian Studies, 1986.

Lev, Daniel S. "The Political Role of the Army in Indonesia". *Pacific Affairs* 36, no. 4 (Winter 1963–64).

———. "Review of *Van Vollenhoven on Indonesian Adat Law, Selections from Het Adatrecht van Nederlandsch-Indie* (vol. I, 1918; vol. II, 1931), edited by J.F. Holleman, Martinus Nijhoff, The Hague, 1981". *Journal of Legal Pluralism* 22 (1984).

———. "Conceptual Filters and Obfuscation in the Study of Indonesian Politics". Revision of a lecture for the Herb Feith Foundation, November 2002.

———. "Memory, Knowledge and Reform". In *Beginning to Remember the Past in the Indonesian Present*, edited by Mary S. Zurbuchen. Singapore: Singapore University Press, 2005.

Locher-Scholten, Elsbeth. "State Violence and the Police in Colonial Indonesia Circa 1920: Exploration of a Theme". In *Roots of Violence in Indonesia: Contemporary Violence in Historical Perspective*, edited by Freek Colombijn and J. Thomas Lindblad. Leiden: KITLV Press, 2002, and Singapore: Institute of Southeast Asian Studies, 2002.

Lubis, Muchsin. "Zulkifli Lubis, Komandan Intelijen Pertama di Indonesia". *Tempo*, 29 July 1989. Reproduced in *M.E.M.O.A.R: Senarai Kiprah Sejarah, Diangkat dari Majalah TEMPO Buku Kedua*. Jakarta: Grafiti, 1993.

Lucas, Anton, ed. *Local Opposition and Underground Resistance to the Japanese in Java 1942–1945*. Monash University Papers on Southeast Asia, No. 13. Clayton, Victoria: Centre of Southeast Asian Studies, 1986.

Lyon, Margot L. "Mystical Biography: Soeharto and Kejawen in the Political Domain". In *Indonesian Political Biography: In Search of Cross-Cultural Understanding*, edited by Angus McIntyre. Clayton, Victoria: Monash University, Centre of Southeast Asian Studies, 1993.

McIntyre, Angus, ed. *Indonesian Political Biography: In Search of Cross-Cultural Understanding*. Working paper. Clayton, Victoria: Monash University, Centre of Southeast Asian Studies, 1993.

———. *Soeharto's Composure: Considering the Biographical and Autobiographical Accounts*. Working paper. Clayton, Vic.: Monash Asia Institute, 1996.

McVey, Ruth T. "Taman Siswa and the Indonesian National Awakening". *Indonesia*, No. 4 (October 1967).

———. "Teaching Modernity: The PKI as an Educational Institution". *Indonesia*, No. 50 (October 1990).

———. "Building Behemoth". In *Making Indonesia: Essays on Modern Indonesia in Honor of George McT. Kahin*, edited by Daniel S. Lev and Ruth McVey. Ithaca, NY: Southeast Asia Program, Cornell University, 1996.

———. "Nationalism, Revolution, and Organization in Indonesian Communism". In *Making Indonesia: Essays on Modern Indonesia in Honor of George McT. Kahin*, edited by Daniel S. Lev and Ruth McVey. Ithaca, NY: Southeast Asia Program, Cornell University, 1996.

———. "Review of *Verguisd en Vergeten: Tan Malaka, de linkse beweging en de Indonesische Revolutie, 1945–1949* [*Reviled and Forgotten: Tan Malaka, the Leftist Movement, and the Indonesian Revolution, 1945–1949*], by Harry A. Poeze". *Indonesia* 86 (October 2008).

Mackie, Jamie. "Towkays and Tycoons: The Chinese in Indonesian Economic Life in the 1920s and 1980s". In "The Role of the Indonesian Chinese in Shaping Modern Indonesian Life: Proceedings of the symposium held at Cornell University in conjunction with the Southeast Asian Studies Summer Institute, July 13–15, 1990". *Indonesia*, Cornell Southeast Asia Program, 1991.

Maekawa Kaori. "The *Heiho* during the Japanese Occupation of Indonesia". In *Asian*

Labor in the Wartime Japanese Empire, edited by Paul H. Kratoska. Singapore: Singapore University Press, 2006.

Melati, Sintha. "In the Service of the Underground: The Struggle Against the Japanese in Java", translated and annotated by David Bourchier. In *Local Opposition and Underground Resistance to the Japanese in Java 1942-1945*, edited by Anton Lucas. Monash University Papers on Southeast Asia, No. 13. Clayton, Victoria: Monash University Centre of Southeast Asian Studies, 1986.

Ming, Hanneke. "Barracks-Concubinage in the Indies, 1887–1920". *Indonesia*, no. 35 (April 1983): 65–93.

"Miyamoto Shizuo no hanashi" [Miyamoto Shizuo's Story]. In *Jakaruta yoakemae: Indonesia dokuritsu ni kaketa hitotachi* [Jakarta before the Dawn: Those Who Staked All on Indonesian Independence], by Ara Kenichi. Tokyo: Keiso Shobo, 1994.

Moersjid. "Pembawa Kenangan". In *Representing the Japanese Occupation of Indonesia: Personal Testimonies and Public Images in Indonesia, Japan, and the Netherlands*, edited by Remco Raben. Zwolle, Netherlands and Amsterdam: Waanders Publishers and Netherlands Institute for War Documentation, 1999.

Mohamad, Goenawan. "Introduction". In *Apa & Siapa: Sejumlah Orang Indonesia, 1983–1984*. Jakarta: Grafiti Pers, 1984.

Monfries, John. "The Sultan and the Revolution". *Bijdragen tot de Taal-, Land- en Volkenkunde* 164, no. 2/3 (2008).

Moor J.A. de. "Het korps Speciale Troepen: tussen marechausse-formule en politionele actie". In *De politionele acties* [The Police Actions], edited by G. Teitler and P.M.H. Groen. Amsterdam: De Bataafsche Leeuw, 1987.

Mrázek, Rudolf. "Tan Malaka: "Just as Artisans, When Gathered Together". *Indonesia* 53 (April 1992).

Nakamura Mitsuo. "General Imamura and the Early Period of Japanese Occupation". *Indonesia* 10 (October 1970).

Nishijima Shigetada. "The Independence Proclamation in Jakarta". In *Shogen: Indoneshia Dokuritsu Kakumei – Aru Kakumeika no Hansho* [Testimony: Indonesian Independence and Revolution – A Half Life History of a Revolutionary]. Tokyo: Shin Jimbutsu Orai-sha, 1975, a translated extract of which is published in *The Japanese Experience in Indonesia: Selected Memoirs of 1942–1945*, edited by Anthony Reid and Oki Akira. Monographs in International Studies, Southeast Asia Series, No. 72. Athens, OH: Ohio University, 1986.

Nugroho Notosusanto. *The PETA-army in Indonesia 1943–1945*. Jakarta: Centre for Armed Forces History, Department of Defence and Security, 1971.

———. *The Revolt Against the Japanese of a Peta Battalion in Blitar, February 14, 1945*. Jakarta: Centre for Armed Forces History, Department of Defence and Security, 1974.

———. *The Japanese Occupation and Indonesian Independence*. Jakarta: Centre for Armed Forces History, Department of Defence and Security, 1975.

———. "The Peta Army in Indonesia 1943–1945". In *Japan in Asia*, edited by William H. Newell. Singapore: Singapore University Press, 1981.

Oba Sadao. "My Recollections of Indonesia, 1944–1947". Paper presented at a symposium on Indonesia at the London School of Economics, 12 January 1979.

Ooi Keat Gin. "Of 'Permanent Possession': Territories under the Imperial Japanese Navy". In *The Encyclopedia of Indonesia in the Pacific War*, edited by Peter Post, William H. Frederick, Iris Heidebrink and Shigeru Sato. Leiden: Brill, 2010.

Poeze, Harry A. "Political Intelligence in the Netherlands Indies". In *The Late Colonial State in Indonesia: Political and Economic Foundations of the Netherlands Indies, 1880–1942*, edited by Robert Cribb. Leiden: KITLV Press, 1994.

Priyono B. Sumbogo and Bunga Surawidjaja. "Djatikusumo: Prajurit dari Keraton". In *M.E.M.O.A.R Senarai Kiprah Sejarah, Diangkat dari Majalah Tempo, Buku Ketiga*. Jakarta: Grafiti, 1993.

Probosutedjo. "Ungkapan: Heboh Kekayaan Presiden Soeharto dan Hasil Karyanya, Diuraikan Berdasarkan Fakta". Typescript, 42 pp., 1 February 1978.

Quinn, George. "The Javanese Science of Burglary". *Review of Indonesian and Malayan Affairs* 9, no. 1 (Jan–Jun 1975).

Reid, Anthony J.S. "The Revolution in Regional Perspective". In *The Indonesian Revolution*, edited by J. van Goor. Conference Papers, Utrecht, 17–20 June 1986, Utrechtse Historische Cahiers jaargang 7 (1986) nr. 2/3.

———. "Economic and Social Change, c. 1400–1800". In *The Cambridge History of Southeast Asia, Volume I: From Early Times to c. 1800*, edited by Nicholas Tarling. Cambridge: Cambridge University Press, 1992.

———. "Remembering and Forgetting War and Revolution". In *Beginning to Remember: The Past in the Indonesian Present*, edited by Mary S. Zurbuchen. Singapore: Singapore University Press in association with University of Washington Press, 2005.

Rocher, Jean. "Les cadets de Bandung (1940–1945)". *Archipel* 51 (1996).

Rush, James. "Placing the Chinese in Java on the Eve of the Twentieth Century". In "The Role of the Indonesian Chinese in Shaping Modern Indonesian Life", *Indonesia*. Ithaca, NY: Cornell Southeast Asia Program, 1991.

Sato Shigeru. "The Pangreh Praja in Java under Japanese Military Rule". In *Japan, Indonesia and the War: Myths and Realities*, edited by Peter Post and Elly Touwen-Bouwsma. Leiden: KITLV Press, 1997.

———. "The Peta". In *The Encyclopedia of Indonesia in the Pacific War*, edited by Peter Post, William H. Frederick, Iris Heidebrink and Shigeru Sato. Leiden: Brill, 2010.

Schulte Nordholt, Henk. "A Genealogy of Violence". In *Roots of Violence in Indonesia: Contemporary Violence in Historical Perspective*, edited by Freek Colombijn and J. Thomas Lindblad. Leiden: KITLV Press, 2002, and Singapore: Institute of Southeast Asian Studies, 2002.

Shiraishi Aiko. "The Anti-Japanese Revolt of the Peta Army in Blitar". *Southeast Asian Studies* [Kyoto University] 13, no. 4 (1976): 535–58.

Shiraishi Takashi. "A New Regime of Order: The Origin of Modern Surveillance Politics in Indonesia". In *Southeast Asia over Three Generations: Essays Presented to Benedict R. O'G. Anderson*, edited by James T. Siegel and Audrey R. Kahin. Ithaca, NY: Cornell University Southeast Asia Program Publications, 2003.

Siagian, Sabam. "Thoughts Along Jalan Jenderal Soedirman". In *General Sudirman: The Leader Who Finally Destroyed Colonialism in Indonesia*, by Tjokropranolo. Canberra: Australian Defence Studies Centre, 1995.

Siegel, James T. "Review Essay: The Establishment of Revolutionary Violence". *Indonesia* 79 (April 2005).

Soedirgo, R., and Pamoe Rahardjo. *Tentara Peta Sayap Militer Pergerakan Kemerdekaan Nasional*. Jakarta: Yayasan Pembela Tanah Air, 1999.

Soedjana Tirtakoesoema. "The Anniversary of the Accession of His Highness the Sultan of Yogyakarta (Tingalan Panjenengan)". In *The Kraton: Selected Essays on Javanese Courts*, edited by Stuart Robson. Leiden: KITLV Press, 2003.

Soedjono Humardhani, ed. *Suatu Ajaran Tentang Hidup Manusia dan Hubungannya Dengan Tuhan Yang Digali Dari Kedalaman Makna Huruf Jawa*, n.p.: n.p, 1981.

Soemardjan, Selo. *Business and Culture in Indonesia*. Australia-Indonesia Business Co-operation Committee, Confederation of Australian Industry, Canberra, 1986.

———. "In Memoriam: Hamengkubuwono IX, Sultan of Yogyakarta, 1912–1988". *Indonesia*, no. 47 (April 1989). Ithaca, NY: Cornell Southeast Asia Program.

Soeryana. "Blitar: The Changing of the Guard", translated and annotated by David Bourchier. In *Local Opposition and Underground Resistance to the Japanese in Java 1942–1945*, edited by Anton Lucas. Monash University Papers on Southeast Asia, No. 13. Clayton, Victoria: Centre of Southeast Asian Studies, 1986.

Soetarto Sigit. "Some observations on the role of the PETA Daidan in the organisation and preparation of the regional defence". Handwritten document in the possession of the author, 8pp. Jakarta, 5 August 2003.

Stockwell, A.J. "Southeast Asia in War and Peace: The End of European Colonial Empires". In *The Cambridge History of Southeast Asia, Vol. 2: The Nineteenth and Twentieth Centuries*, edited by Nicholas Tarling. Cambridge: Cambridge University Press, 1992.

Subardjo Djoyoadisuryo, Ahmad. "An inside story of the Proclamation of Indonesian Independence, August 17, 1945". *The Djakarta Times*, 1 July – 18 August 1970.

Subroto. "Recollections of My Career". *Bulletin of Indonesian Economic Studies* 34, no. 2 (August 1998).

Supomo. "An Integralistic State". In *Indonesian Political Thinking 1945–1965,* edited by Herb Feith and Lance Castles. Ithaca, NY: Cornell University Press, 1970.

Supomo Surjohudojo. "Growing Up in a Javanese Village: Personal Reminiscences". Clayton, Victoria: Centre of Southeast Asian Studies, Monash University, Working Paper No. 20, 1980.

Suwondo, Purbo S. *Beberapa Aspek dari Gerakan Kebangsaan dan Perjuangan Indonesia Untuk Mencapai Kemerdekaan 1908–1950.* Ujung Pandang: Sarasehan Syukuran Makasar, 1996.

———. "The Genesis of the Indonesian National Army and Some Political Implications". Paper prepared for a seminar at the Institute of Netherlands History and The Royal Society of Historians of the Netherlands, The Hague, 27–29 March 1996.

———. *Tinjauan Historik Sekitar 1942–1945.* Jakarta: n.p., 1998.

———. "HBS di Malang Yang Kukenang: Suatu Renungan Kembali Pengalaman Hidup Sebelum Indonesia Merdeka". Jakarta, 2000.

———. "Some Background Notes on the Establishment of the Peta Army". Letter sent in response to questions submitted by the author, Jakarta, 20 May 2002.

Tas, Salomon. "Souvenirs of Sjahrir". *Indonesia* 8 (October 1969).

Taylor, Keith W. "The Early Kingdoms". In *The Cambridge History of Southeast Asia, Volume I: From Early Times to c. 1800,* edited by Nicholas Tarling. Cambridge: Cambridge University Press, 1992.

Tim Perumus. "Peristiwa Pemberontakan Peta di Cileunca Pangalengan, Bandung Selatan, Jawa Barat". In *Peta: Tentara Sukarela Pembela Tanah Air Di Jawa dan Sumatera 1942–1945,* edited by Purbo Suwondo. Jakarta: Sinar Harapan, 1996.

Touwen-Bouwsma, Elly. "Japanese Minority Policy: The Eurasians on Java and the Dilemma of Ethnic Loyalty". In *Japan, Indonesia and the War: Myths and Realities,* edited by Peter Post and Elly Touwen-Bouwsma. Leiden: KITLV Press, 1997.

Uekusa Nobushige. Preface to *Dai Sanjuichi Kaigun Kokutai no Ayumi* [The History of the 31st Naval Air Division]. Tokyo: San-ichi Kukai, Bunkyo-ku, 1960.

Ward, Ken. "Soeharto's Javanese Pancasila". In *Soeharto's New Order and Its Legacy: Essays in Honour of Harold Crouch,* edited by Edward Aspinall and Greg Fealy. Canberra: Griffin Press, 2010.

Yoshitada Murayama. "The Pattern of Japanese Economic Penetration of the Prewar Netherlands East Indies". In *The Japanese in Colonial Southeast Asia,* vol. III, edited by Saya Shiraishi and Takashi Shiraishi. Translation of Contemporary

Japanese Scholarship on Southeast Asia, Southeast Asia Program. Ithaca, NY: Cornell University, 1993.

DISSERTATIONS

Bourchier, David. "Lineages of Organicist Political Thought in Indonesia". PhD dissertation, Monash University, 1996.

Bussemaker, H. Th. [Herman Theodore]. "Paradise in Peril: Western Colonial Power and Japanese Expansion in South-East Asia, 1905–1941". Parts I and II, PhD dissertation, University of Amsterdam, 2001.

Harvey, Barbara Sillars. "Tradition, Islam, and Rebellion: South Sulawesi 1950–1965". PhD dissertation, Cornell University, 1974.

Kanahele, George S. "The Japanese Occupation of Indonesia: Prelude to Independence". PhD dissertation, Cornell University, 1967.

Larson, George D. "Prelude to Revolution: Palaces and Politics in Surakarta, 1912–1942". PhD dissertation, Northern Illinois University, 1979.

McKemmish, Susan Marilyn. "A Political Biography of General A.H. Nasution". MA dissertation, Monash University, 1976.

Monfries, John Elliott. "A Prince in a Republic: The Political Life of Sultan Hamengku Buwono IX of Jogjakarta". PhD dissertation, The Australian National University, 2005.

Nugroho Notosusanto. "The Peta Army During the Japanese Occupation of Indonesia" [Tentara Peta Pada Jaman Pendudukan Jepang di Indonesia]. PhD dissertation, Universitas Indonesia, 1977.

O'Malley, William Joseph. "Indonesia in the Great Depression: A Study of East Sumatra and Jogjakarta in the 1930's". PhD dissertation, Cornell University, 1977.

Turner, Barry. "Nasution: Total People's Resistance and Organicist Thinking in Indonesia". PhD dissertation, Swinburne University of Technology, Melbourne, 2005.

Umemori Naoyuki. "Modernization through Colonial Mediations: The Establishment of the Police and Prison System in Meiji Japan". PhD dissertation, The University of Chicago, 2002.

ARTICLES

Anon. "Disekitar 'Silsilah POP' itu". *Tempo*, 9 November 1974.

———. "Het is Zoover". *Time*, 26 January 1942.

———. "Soldier, Farmer, Philosopher". *Asiaweek*, 4 May 1986.

———. "View from the Tri-S Coral". *Time*, 10 May 1976.

"'Astana Giri Bangun' Cemetery Costs Rp437.8m, Not Rp4 billion". *Antara News Bulletin*, Jakarta, 20 November 1977.

Crouch, Harold. "The Anniversary of a Riot Celebrated in Jakarta by a New Political Trial". *National Times*, 17 February 1975.

Feith, Herb. "Last-Ditch Stand Politics Revisited". *Jakarta Post*, 8 October 1998.

Frank, Richard B. "Why Truman Dropped the Bomb". *The Weekly Standard*, 8 August 2005.

"Kaskopkamtib Investigates Yayasan Mangadeg". *Antara*, 24 November 1977.

Kumala Dewi. "Saya Kira Angker". *Info Buku, Gatra*, No. 23 Tahun III, 26 April 1997.

Marsoedi. "Saya Sudah Mengingatkan Pak Harto". *Forum Keadilan*, 26 December 1999.

Onghokham. "The Bureaucratic Elite in Indonesia: A Historical Background". *Prisma*, No. 19, December 1980.

"Pamoe Rahardjo: 'Tentara Sekarang Tidak Berani Kudeta'". *Tempo*, 30 January 2000.

"The Night Suharto Buried His Mother". *Sun-Herald*, 9 January 1972.

"Soeharto Outlines His Family Tree". *Merdeka*, 28 October 1974.

"Suharto's Regard for Foster Mother". *New Straits Times*, 30 October 1974.

"President Denies Having Amassed Riches". *Antara*, 27 January 1978.

"Raja Bisnis dari Wuryantoro". *Forum Keadilan*, Nomor 20, Tahun VI, 12 January 1998.

Soeharto, "Watashi no Rirekisho". *Nihon Keizai Shimbun*, 1–31 January 1998.

"Zulkifli Lubis: Komandan Intelijen Pertama Indonesia". *Tempo*, 29 July 1989.

NEWSPAPERS AND PERIODICALS

AB [Angkatan Bersenjata] (Jakarta)
Abadi (Jakarta)
Advertiser (Adelaide)
Algemeen Dagblad (Rotterdam)
Aneta News Bulletin (Jakarta)
Antara (Jakarta)
Argus (Melbourne)
Asahi Shimbun (Tokyo)
Asiaweek (Hongkong)
Berita Yudha (Jakarta)
Canberra Times (Canberra)
Daily Express (London)
De Opmaat (The Netherlands)
DeTAK (Jakarta)
Djakarta Times (Jakarta)
Djawa Baroe (Jakarta)
Editor (Jakarta)

Evening News (Batavia)
Far Eastern Economic Review (Hongkong)
Forum Keadilan (Jakarta)
Harian Rakyat (Jakarta)
Harian Umum AB (Jakarta)
Herald (Melbourne)
Hindustan Times (Madras)
Jakarta Post (Jakarta)
Japan Times (Tokyo)
Jawa Baru (Jakarta)
Jawa Pos (Surabaya)
Jawa Shimbun (Jakarta)
Kalgoolie Miner (Kalgoolie)
Keng Po (Batavia/Jakarta)
Kompas (Jakarta)
Life (New York)
London Gazette (London)
Mainichi Daily News (Tokyo)
Mainichi Shimbun (Tokyo)
Merdeka (Jakarta)
Morning Post (Rockhampton)
National Times (Sydney)
New Straits Times (Kuala Lumpur)
New York Review of Books (New York)
New York Times (New York)
Newsweek (New York)
Nihon Keizai Shimbun (Tokyo)
NRC Handelsblad (Rotterdam)
Sankei Shimbun (Tokyo)
Sin Min (Semarang)
Sinar Harapan (Jakarta)
The Singapore Free Press (Singapore)
Stabelan (Dordrecht)
Straits Times (Singapore)
Suara Merdeka (Semarang)
Sun-Herald (Sydney)
Sydney Morning Herald (Sydney)
Sunday Times (Perth)
Tajuk (Jakarta)
Tempo (Jakarta)
Terbit (Jakarta)

Time (New York)
The Times (London)
Tokoh (Jakarta)
Topik (Jakarta)
Townsville Daily Bulletin (Townsville)
Washington Post (Washington)
Yomiuri Shimbun (Tokyo)

PRESS TRANSLATION SERVICES

Indonesian Current Affairs Translation Service, Jakarta.
Indonesia News Service, Indonesia Publications, Lanham-Seabrook, Maryland, USA.
United States Embassy Press Translation Service, Jakarta

PHOTOGRAPHIC SOURCES

Imperial War Museum, London.
Indonesia Press and Photo Service (Ipphos), Jakarta.
David Jenkins, personal photographic archive.
Kaneko Tomokazu, personal photographic collection.
Nationaal Archief, The Hague.
Nationaal Museum van Wereldculturen, Rotterdam.
Nederlands Instituut voor Militaire Historie, The Hague.
Spaarnestad Photo Agency, The Hague.
Tsuchiya Kiso, personal photographic collection.
War History Office, National Defense College of Japan, Tokyo.

WEBSITES

Ali Budiardjo. "Comments on Salim Said's Paper". Prepared for the International Seminar of the Institute of Netherlands History and the Royal Society of Historians of the Netherlands, 27–29 March 1996, at The Hague (accessed 29 August 2008).

Anon. "Intelligence in the New Japan". CIA website, www.cia.gov/library/center-for-the-study-of-intelligence/kent-csi/docs/v07i3a01p_0005.htm, pp. 5–6 (accessed 20 September 2007).

———. "Isu Soeharto Cina, Siapa Bapaknya?". wysiwyg://47/http:www.geocities.com/CapitolHill/4120/soeharto.html (accessed 4 September 2008).

———. "Nakano Agents and the Japanese Forces in New Guinea, 1942–1945". www.thefreelibrary.com/Nakano+agents+and+the+Japanese+ forces+in+New+Guinea,+1942–1945–012316110 (accessed 21 September 2007); and www.thefreelibrary. com/Nakano+agents+and+the+Japanese+forces+in+New+Guinea%2c+1942–1945.-a0123162110 (accessed 4 August 2009).

Drooglever, P.J. "SEAC in Indonesia: voices from the past?". International

Association of Historians of Asia, Jakarta, 27 August – 1 September 1998. resources.huygens.knaw.nl/indonesischebetrekkingen1945-1969 (accessed 25 February 2015.

Dheera Sujan. "A Black Page in Dutch History". Radio Netherlands Worldwide, 8 December 2010 (accessed 15 June 2013).

Douglas, John. "The Dutch Air Forces in the Pacific War". www.pacificwrecks.com/douglas/articles/neiaf.html (accessed 29 January 2011).

Foo, Cynthia. "Interview with Benedict Anderson". http://www.rochester.edu/in_visible_culture/issue_13_/foo/index.html (accessed 26 January 2011).

"Hitoshi Imamura". Wikipedia (accessed 15 April 2009).

Jones, Sidney, Ronny Lihawa, Santiago Villaveces-Izquierdo and Ignatius Priambodo. "Reforming the Indonesian Police Mobile Brigade (BRIMOB)". Partnership for Governance Reform in Indonesia, 16 February 2004, www.kemitraan.or.id/ (accessed 2 October 2008).

Kimmelman, Michael. "In Germany, Wild for Winnetou". *New York Times*, 12 September 2007. www.nytimes.com/2007/09/12/arts/design/12karl.html (accessed 17 July 2009).

National Film and Sound Archives, Canberra. http://trove.nla.gov.au/work/34948415.

Situs Brimob Polri. 0.1 Sejarah Brimob. http://brimobpolri.wordpress.com/sejarah-brimob/ (accessed 2 October 2008).

"Siar XPOS: Kolonel (Purn) A. Latief: 'Soeharto itu Pendendam' ". Xpos, No. 40/1/3 – Oktober 1998. http://www.minihub.org/siarlist/msg01017.html (accessed 2 June 2008).

Index

Note: Page numbers followed by "n" refer to notes and "fn" refer to footnotes.

I

Q

R

About the Author

David Jenkins, who graduated in Law (1965) and Arts (1967) from Melbourne University, was a foreign correspondent in Southeast Asia for many years. In 1969, after news and feature-writing assignments in India and Southeast Asia, including a second trip to cover the war in Vietnam, he was appointed the staff correspondent in Indonesia for the Herald and Weekly Times group of newspapers across Australia. During this time he covered the 1970 overthrow of Prince Sihanouk and the violent spillover of the Vietnam War into Cambodia.

Awarded a three-month Churchill Fellowship to study the Communist insurgency in Northeast Thailand in 1973, he went on to run the Associated Press (AP) bureau in Vientiane during the final years (1973–75) of the Indochina War and was the correspondent in Laos for the *Far Eastern Economic Review*. He was the *Review's* Indonesia bureau chief (1976–80), Singapore-based ASEAN correspondent (1980–82) and Regional Editor in Hongkong (1982–84).

Appointed Foreign Editor of the *Sydney Morning Herald* in 1985, he spent six months as acting Editor of the *Times on Sunday*, a national broadsheet, after which he became Asia Editor of the *SMH*. In 1991 he was a Senior Research Fellow (Regional Security) at the Strategic and Defence Studies Centre, Australian National University, Canberra. He was a co-winner of a Walkley Award for his contribution to the *Herald's* coverage from Jakarta and East Timor during the violent 1999 referendum on independence.